THE UNOFFICIAL MURDER, SHE WROTE CASEBOOK

THE UNOFFICIAL MURDER, SHE WROTE CASEBOOK

James Robert Parish

KENSINGTON BOOKS
http://www.kensingtonbooks.com

KENSINGTON BOOKS are published by

Kensington Publishing Corp.
850 Third Avenue
New York, NY 10022

This book has not been approved or licensed by any entity involved in creating or producing *Murder, She Wrote.*

ISBN 1-57566-210-8

First Kensington Trade Paperback Printing: September, 1997
10 9 8 7 6 5 4 3 2 1

Printed in the United States of America

Dedicated to

Ms. ANGELA LANSBURY

A Star For <u>All</u> Seasons

Acknowledgments

I wish to thank the following for their generous assistance with this project: Kathy Bartels, Larry Billman, Billy Rose Theatre Collection of the New York Public Library at the Lincoln Center, Tom Bremer, John Cocchi, Audrey DeLisle, Annette D'Agostino, Nancy Dugan, Film Favorites, James Harris, Jani Klain, Steve Klain, Larry Edmund Book Shop (Peter Bateman), Alfred E. Lehman, Alvin H. Marill, Doug McClelland, Jim Meyer, Eric Monder, Museum of Television & Radio (Jonathan Rosenthal), Lucille Pederson, Photofest (Howard Mandelbaum), Michael R. Pitts, Barry Rivadue, Jerry Roberts, David Romas (*Magnum P.I.* Memorabilia), Brenda Scott Royce, Bob Rusk, Margie Schultz, Arleen Schwartz, Les Spindle, Kevin Sweeney, Vincent Terrace, Roi A. Uselton, Jerry Vermilye, Tom Walsh, and Don Wigal.

With special thanks to researcher Steven Lance.

Editorial Consultant for this project: Allan Taylor

Contents

A BRIEF INTRODUCTION

Welcome to the delightfully deadly world of *Murder, She Wrote.* It features a most compassionate, down-to-earth heroine, Mrs. Jessica Beatrice Fletcher. In each sixty-minute episode of this long-running series, Jessica finds herself drawn into a murderous situation. Driven by her insatiable curiosity, she insists on piecing together the clues. In the process, the TV viewer can match wits with the observant Mrs. Fletcher as she sifts out the red herrings and pinpoints the actual killer's identity.

In several ways, Jessica is quite a remarkable individual. In mid-life, this former (substitute) English teacher from small-town New England not only surprises herself by writing a whodunit novel, but, to her amazement, the book becomes a best-seller. Its success leads to her becoming a world-famous mystery author, J.B. Fletcher. Her works are translated into several languages as well as inspiring Broadway plays and Hollywood movies. As such, this whodunit writer has legions of fans in every part of the globe.

Equally amazing about this very friendly person—some regard her as a busybody—is her knack for stumbling upon real-life crimes. As devout *Murder, She Wrote* viewers know, murder and mayhem follow Jessica wherever she happens to be (Cabot Cove, Maine; New York City, etc.). Once caught up in a murder case, she exercises her sharp skills of observation at a crime scene, no matter what the danger or the physical activity involved. As the trail leads her from suspect to suspect, Mrs. Fletcher proves dauntless, enterprising and generally shrewder than the police officers assigned to solve the homicide. Mixing her hunches with astuteness, it isn't long before the amateur detective unmasks the killer's identity.

What do we know about sweet, slightly eccentric Mrs. Fletcher? Her mother came from Kilcleer, Ireland. When Jessica was growing up in New England—she now admits—she had occasionally gone skinny dipping at the lake in back of her family's house. She spent one college year vacation as an apprentice at the Applewood Playhouse. There she first met coworker Frank Fletcher, whom she later married. On another summer break from college, Jessica worked as an intern reporter for a newspaper wire service.

During Jessica's long and happy marriage to Frank Fletcher, their only disappointment was never having been blessed with children. Over the years together, the couple was only separated once. That occurred in the early 1950s when he served in the armed forces during the Korean War. On the other hand, the Fletchers once vacationed in the south of France. Years back, Frank, a real estate broker, was responsible for forming the Cabot Cove Dramatic Society. As would be established in episode #1, when her publisher, Preston Giles, takes a romantic interest in her, Jessica's happy memories of her late husband are so intense that she cannot bring herself to seriously contemplate a new romance. (Besides, it's intimated, it would tie down this self-sufficient woman far too much.)

At the time of Frank's death from natural causes in the early 1980s, Jessica had been teaching high school English for nineteen years. It was not long after that tragedy that she quit her vocation to indulge her creative writing full-time. This activity led to her first novel, *The Corpse Danced at Midnight.* Composed as a lark, Mrs. Fletcher was delighted when this murder mystery became a best-seller. It created a profitable new career for this very unpretentious woman. Despite this spectacular career change, Mrs. Fletcher still found time to garden, cook and to help with local charities. Later, her fame and wealth allowed her to become a part-time resident of New York City and a global traveler. And, of course, no matter where, she is always ready to figure out real-life whodunits. After all, she reasons, they are grist for her professional mill. Besides, she has an international reputation as an amateur crime-solver and she is never one to let her public down.

As episode after episode demonstrates—especially in the show's early seasons—Jessica has an endless supply of relatives. Faithful show watchers know that every time one of her large family pops into Mrs. Fletcher's hectic life, homicide is sure to be not far behind. (Later, it would become her friends and business associates who had to be wary when Jessica came into view.)

Among the kin folk who bring chaos into Mrs. Fletcher's busy life are several nieces: Victoria Brandon Griffin (episodes #3, 48, 123), Pamela Crane (#14), Nita Cochran (#25), Carol Fletcher (#45a, 45b), Tracy Macgill (#30a), and Jill Morton (#85). Then, there is Jessica's well-meaning but bumbling nephew, Grady Fletcher, who has appeared on several occasions (#1, 12, 34, 41, 56, 62, 76, 84, 96, 129, 235). There's also Mrs. Fletcher's many cousins, including Calhoun Fletcher (#43) and Ann Owens and her brother George (#87). Most of all, there's Jessica's look-alike British cousin, Emma Macgill

(#27, 91), a veteran music hall entertainer living in London, as well as Jessica's aunts, Mildred (#43) and Agnes (#25). However, not to be overlooked, is the detective writer's forebear, the (in)famous Eamonn Magill (with the strange surname spelling) who died most unceremoniously in the outback of Australia in 1896.

In the first seasons of *Murder, She Wrote,* Jessica's only home was 698 Candlewood Lane in Cabot Cove, Maine (population 3,560 and a zip code of 03041). In more recent times, she's taken a New York apartment where she lives during the week while teaching criminology at Manhattan University as well as creative writing at inner city high schools. Her Manhattan address is #4B at the Penfield House Apartments at 941 West 61st Street, and her phone number is (212) 124-7199. Two of her favorite new pastimes are volunteer work on behalf of the Museum of Cultural History and the Literary Foundation.

Jessica has several distinctive traits. She is friendly, talkative and willing to help even a near stranger out of a scrape. She is very democratic in her choice of friends, unbiased by the other person's age or ethnic background. She loves to exercise and frequently jogs. Because she refuses to learn to drive a car, whenever she's in the country she relies on her bicycle for transportation. Mrs. Fletcher is a fine cook, as well as an excellent gardener. She rarely drinks, and when she does it is white wine. Typically, her outfit is a pants suit accented by a jewelry pin on her lapel. However, as her book tours and pleasure treks take her around the world, she has favored increasingly a more chic wardrobe and coiffure.

For the record, Jessica is a very prolific novelist, which is remarkable given the amount of time she devotes to travel, charity work *and* solving crimes. She has recently traded in her manual typewriter for a personal computer. (She is a very up-to-date person, intrigued with the latest high tech equipment, including cellular phones and fax machines.) This very cultured lady is also a stickler for detail in her writing. It leads her to personally research a host of subject matters and locales no matter where she must travel to obtain the requisite information. In these expeditions, she often finds herself innocently caught up in murder and mayhem.

J.B. Fletcher's literary output includes *Murder on the Amazon* (mentioned in episode #13), *Lover's Revenge* (#14), *Dirge for a Dead Dachshund* (#23), *The Umbrella Murders* (#28, 207), *The Killer Called Collect* (#29), *Murder at the Digs* (#33), *The Stain on the Stairs* (#64), *The Belgrade Murders* (#67), *Sanitarium of Death* (#68), *Calvin Canterbury's Revenge* (#73), *Murder at the Asylum* (#73), *The Messenger at Midnight* (#162), *Murder Comes to Maine* (#87), *Ashes, Ashes, Fall Down Dead* (#156), *Murder at the Ridge Top* (#177), *The Corpse at Vespers* (#188), *The Triple Crown Murders* (#188, 202), *The Crypt of Death* (#199), *The Uncaught* (#205, 208), *The Dead Must Sing* (#207), *Stone Cold Dead* (#212), *The Launch*

Pad Murder (#222), *Runway to Murder* (#234), *Venomous Valentine* (#248), and *A Case and a Half of Murder* (#261). Her most famous novel—and the one most frequently mentioned on the series—is *The Corpse Danced at Midnight* (#1, 4, 29, 66, 184, 207, 227, etc.). Other books by J.B. are *The Corpse Wasn't There*, and *Yours Truly, Damian Sinclair*. Two of her frequent lead fictional characters are Inspector Dison and Inspector Gelico.

Now, join zesty Jessica Fletcher as her fame and crime-solving reputation lead her into a host of entertaining capers at home and abroad. See if you can determine the killer's identity *before* Mrs. Fletcher in typical fashion announces, "I think I know who the murderer is. Now to prove it!" And prove it, she does, with the actual criminal(s) giving full confession before the final episode fade-out. (To be noted in the later years of the series, the viewer is provided with detailed information as to what happens to various characters in that segment's plot line.)

To allow you the fun of personally figuring out the murderers' identities, the plot synopsis for each episode does *not* reveal the killer's or killers' identity. Likewise, because so many *Murder, She Wrote* installments employ a guest cast of acting veterans and interesting newcomers, the Trivia section for each segment's write-up includes career facts about most of the more familiar faces and some of the new. Please note that when an actor's credits are mentioned, the years of a television series included in parentheses following the show's title refer to the years the performer was a cast regular on that series, *not* to the span of that program's full run on the air. If a series was still in its first run during this writing, the debut year of airing is followed by a dash and blank spaces to designate the still-to-be-determined finale year of the program.

THE HISTORY OF *MURDER, SHE WROTE*

> I think she's so broad-minded in her thinking. She's a hep cat, a smart cookie; she really is. She knows a lot about a lot of things, so whenever they tend to get her a little eccentric in a wrong way, I just take it right out. . . . No matronizing or being a smart-ass.
>
> (Angela Lansbury on Jessica Fletcher of *Murder, She Wrote*)

> In *Murder, She Wrote* I often think of myself as Bugs Bunny: I have to run in and grab the evidence, race out in a cloud of dust and return to say, "That's all, folks."
>
> (Angela Lansbury)

In retrospect, once all the pieces had fallen happily into place, it all seemed so very obvious and natural. However, when *Murder, She Wrote* premiered on Sunday, September 30, 1984, in a two-hour pilot, there were *very few* people who expected the new series to be a hit, let alone to last the season or to eventually play for twelve (!) years with a record nine consecutive seasons as television's #1 drama.

Most knowledgeable individuals in the TV industry were shaking their heads about this new show which was trying to break all the "established" rules. It was a weekly dramatic program that not only featured a female solo lead, but dared to have a decidedly middle-aged actress as its focal figure. This scenario just didn't compute with what the viewing public usually liked—or at least what they had been convinced they preferred by the networks and advertisers.

In the 1950s and early 1960s—during TV's golden age—there had been several mature Hollywood movie actresses who had crossed over from feature films to the "small box" in a weekly dramatic format show. However, these stars (Loretta Young, June Allyson, Barbara Stanwyck, *et al.*) all chose to host a weekly half-hour anthology series, in which they might or might not be the focal figure of that week's particular story line.

In later decades, a few female talents such as Anne Francis *(Honey West)*, Lynda Carter *(Wonder Woman)*, Angie Dickinson *(Police Woman)* and Lindsay Wagner *(The Bionic Woman)* succeeded in getting starring dramatic series onto the network airwaves. However, they were a rare exception, and, noticeably, these newcomers were sexy, younger actresses whose show format veered more to action than to heavy dramatics.

So what prompted the creation of *Murder, She Wrote?*

First of all there was a successful longtime literary tradition that featured women amateur sleuths. For example, there was Agatha Christie's Miss Jane Marple, an elderly inhabitant of a small English village. In such entries as *Murder at the Vicarage* (1930), *What Mrs. McGillicuddy Saw* (1957) and *At Bertram's Hotel* (1965), Miss Marple proved to be wonderfully adroit at solving murders. Other book favorites included Mingon G. Eberhardt (with her character mystery writer Susan Dare solving crimes), Stuart Palmer (featuring spinster New York school teacher Hildegarde Withers), Mary Roberts Rinehart's Miss Pinkerton (about registered nurse Hilda Adams), Phyllis Bentley (British mystery novelist Marian Phipps), and the list goes on. Some of these had translated into popular movie series, especially the 1960s feature films starring Margaret Rutherford as a rather sheepdoggish Miss Jane Marple.

The success of the Rutherford/Marple series persuaded later filmmakers to try to mine the same gold. In particular, the CBS-TV network had a series of made-for-television movies revolving around Agatha Christie characters. One of these, *Agatha Christie's A Caribbean Murder* aired on October 22, 1983. It presented Helen Hayes, the first lady of the American theater, as the latest incarnation of Miss Jane Marple. She did very well as the elderly British villager who is both a busybody and quite worldly-wise about crime.

Among those watching that entertaining whodunit was TV producer-writer Richard Levinson. He was one-half of the writing team of 6′2″ Levinson and 5′7″ William Link. This Mutt and Jeff pair had met first in junior high school in Elkins Park, Pennsylvania (near Philadelphia), in the 1950s. They had been writing ever since, including the time when both were students at the University of Pennsylvania. On campus there, they founded several mini-magazines and authored class musicals. While still at this Ivy League college, they made their first free-lance sale when *Ellery Queen's Mystery Magazine* published their unsolicited short story.

By the late 1950s, the team of Levinson and Link had a staff position in Hollywood at Four Star Studio where they wrote and "doctored" such TV series as *Johnny Ringo* and *Richard Diamond, Private Detective.* Their premier "Created By" project was CBS-TV's *Jericho* (1966–1967), an espionage series set in World War II, written in tandem with then partner, Merwin A. Bloch. By mid-1980s Levinson and Link had been professional writers (and producers) for twenty-five years and had created such above-par TV (police) detective series as *Mannix, Tenafly, Columbo* and *The Adventures of Ellery Queen.* Another of their many creations, the short-lasting *Stone* (1980), featured Dennis Weaver as a cop—much like Joseph Wambaugh—who wrote popular detective novels while still on the force. The team had also written and executive produced such well-received, innovative TV movies as *That Certain Summer, The Gun* and *The Execution of Private Slovik.* Over the years, they had collaborated frequently on TV movies *(A Cry for Help)* and TV series *(The Adventures of Ellery Queen)* with Peter S. Fischer, an experienced scenarist and producer. The trio had been trying to sell CBS-TV on a detective series featuring a mature male magician. Instead, the network told them to fashion a whodunit vehicle around a female.

INITIAL PLANS FOR *MURDER, SHE WROTE*

According to Levinson (who would die of lung cancer on March 12, 1987) the idea for the new series came about as follows: "Helen Hayes as Miss Marple did well in the ratings. Bill and Peter Fischer and I got together and decided, 'Let's not do Miss Marple. Let's make her a mystery writer, like Agatha Christie.' Then it was a question of who could play Agatha Christie. Only one person—Jean Stapleton. CBS loved the idea. Jean loved the idea."

At the time, Emmy Award-winning Jean Stapleton was best known for her years as Edith "the dingbat," married to bigoted, irascible Archie Bunker on the hugely popular TV sitcom, *All in the Family.* After being with the series from 1971–1980, she left to expand her acting horizons. After that her TV ventures were mostly made-for-television movies, including *Eleanor, the First Lady of the World* (1982) which presented her as the steadfast, philanthropic wife of President Franklin D. Roosevelt. Now she was willing to consider a new weekly TV series.

With the blessing of CBS-TV, which approved the concept, Link, Levinson and Fischer began the creative process that led to *Murder, She Wrote.* The trio intended to profit from the mistakes they had made on *The Adventures of Ellery Queen.* That program, starring Jim Hutton and David Wayne, had struggled through a single season (1975–1976) on NBC-TV.

Levinson had a post mortem on that earlier series: "Our plots on *Ellery Queen* were too tricky. . . . We got a kick out of outsmarting the audience. That was a mistake. We also removed the show from reality by setting it in the 1940s. And Ellery Queen was a cerebral bumbler. It's difficult to keep a mystery show going when your leading character is a laid-back bumbler. Jessica is a dynamo. She never walks. She charges everywhere."

After Fischer drafted the two-hour pilot/TV movie for *Murder, She Wrote* they showed the results to Stapleton. Levinson remembered, "Jean didn't like the script. She didn't understand the character. I think after playing Edith Bunker she wanted something more sophisticated than this bicycle-riding widow from Maine." As such, Stapleton exercised her right to decline the project and dropped out of consideration for the series. Another reason given over the years for Stapleton's "wrong" decision was that William Punch, her husband of many years, had died recently. Reportedly, she was too much at loose ends to focus on a weekly shooting schedule. (Ironically, in 1986, Jean appeared in one of the CBS-TV Agatha Christie movies, *Dead Man's Folly*, featuring Peter Ustinov—who coincidentally was Angela Lansbury's ex-brother-in-law—as Belgian sleuth Hercule Poirot.)

Having lost the bankable Stapleton, Fischer, Levinson and Link conferred with Harvey Shephard, then senior vice-president of programming at CBS Entertainment. Shephard would recall that at that meeting everyone agreed that the "script was so well done that we asked, 'Who else can we cast?'"

The quartet soon came up with the name of Angela Lansbury. At first, it seemed a strange choice. After all, the three-time Oscar nominee and four-time Tony Award winner was best known for playing obsessive mothers on camera (e.g., *The Manchurian Candidate*, [1962]) and for her exuberant sophisticate on stage (i.e., the hit musical *Mame* [1966]). However, Angela already had a recent association with Agatha Christie and Miss Jane Marple. She had been among the all-star cast of *Death on the Nile* (1978), a popular movie based on a Christie novel. Two years later, she had actually played Miss Jane Marple in the not-so-successful feature film, *The Mirror Crack'd.*

Everyone liked the idea of casting British-born Lansbury, a talented, reliable Hollywood fixture who could play American as well as anyone. And the creators' timing was perfect. It was known that Angela, after years of refusing a TV series, was now at that career point (and age) where she would accept a weekly grind because it was "a mountain I had to climb." What made the challenge so appealing to her were (1) the prospects of a fat fee and (2) having the opportunity to reach a huge viewership.

On the down side, Lansbury was miffed that she hadn't been the creators' first choice for the series role. Thankfully, her husband/manager, Peter Shaw, convinced her to read the script. Angela has recalled, "I liked what I visualized her [Jessica] to be when I read the script. There was something about her quality that I felt I could adapt myself to very easily, and very comfortably, and hopefully she could be an attractive person even though I was playing a middle-aged widow. I felt she was courageous and full of excitement and energy about life and people. . . . This attracted me to her because that's my feeling about life and people. I don't have any feeling of being any age, and my enthusiasm for living and the prospect for the future never diminishes."

What also appealed to Angela, then in her late 50s, was the fact that her compassionate counterpart—if she accepted the acting assignment—would not be a carbon copy of the elderly Jane Marple she had admittedly overplayed in *The Mirror Crack'd.* Lansbury appreciated Peter S. Fischer's character creation because "He played up the fact that physically, Jessica was a very active woman—she rode a bicycle, she jogged, she looked after herself. She did not drive a car; I don't quite know why. . . . As it turned out, it was a very good thing she didn't because it precludes, in a sense, the need for car chases."

REFINING THE CHARACTER OF JESSICA FLETCHER

As negotiations with Angela proceeded, the creators refined their lead character. Levinson explained, "We wanted Angela to be herself—not eccentric Miss Marple, Mame, Mrs. Lovett [of her Broadway musical, *Sweeney Todd* (1978)]. People who are too hot wear out their welcome on television. They get on your nerves."

Fischer agreed on the need to keep the focal character toned down at all costs. Once the series was under way, he would remark, "It's hard for Angela because she can do 90% more than we ask. But the key to success in a series is a nice predictable character doing things in a predictable way. Actors who are bigger than the medium don't succeed. Angela can effortlessly project a warm and lovable human being."

For her part, Angela had a few creative demands regarding the show. "I stipulated that there should be no scenes of gratuitous violence, with blood and gore and car smashes. . . ." She told the production squad, "I also don't want the inevitable sidekick of a man behind the scenes manipulating me." Additionally, she emphasized that Jessica Beatrice Fletcher should never be a "knitting spinster." Her sensible requests were honored.

After Lansbury had been contracted—under a five-year pact—to star in *Murder, She Wrote*, the creative team reached yet another pivotal conclusion. It was one that both appealed to and a bit frightened Lansbury. It was decided to blend their concept of Jessica Fletcher with the real-life Angela Lansbury.

It would be the first time, really, that Angela would be "herself" in front of the cameras and not be "hiding" behind a fictional personality. As Fischer spelled it out, "Angela was filled with trepidation. She had always submerged herself into another character. She was nervous. If the audience didn't like her as herself, it would be devastating."

But who was the "real" Angela?

Those in the entertainment community who knew Lansbury best described her off-camera self as open-minded, compassionate and tenacious. Long after Angela and *Murder, She Wrote* had become an enduring hit, Lansbury's husband, Peter Shaw, observed of Lansbury and her TV alter ego, " . . . it's awfully hard to tell the difference between the two. Angela has that marvelous gumption, and that's one of the nice things that Jessica had."

As the two-hour telefilm/pilot was being shot in the spring of 1984, Levinson, Link and Fischer realized they had little time in which to pitch the project as a series for the upcoming 1984–1985 season. As Fischer would recall to the *Christian Science Monitor*, "We cast the show with such luminaries as Brian Keith, Arthur Hill, Ned Beatty, Anne Francis, and Bert Convy and then arranged the [shooting] schedule so certain key scenes would be shot first. We then wrote a short script that featured Angela (as Jessica) in the kitchen of her Cabot Cove house talking directly to the camera. This narrative was combined with selected scenes to bridge the plot, up until the discovery of the dead body. It also allowed us to show off Jessica's character in the best possible light without having to stumble through an excess of plot. . . . The twenty-five-minute presentation was shown simultaneously to the CBS affiliates and to the advertising community, and their reaction was almost unanimously favorable. . . . Buoyed by this outpouring of support, the network ordered thirteen episodes to start airing the following September."

The next—and very important—concern was *where* to position the series on the CBS-TV network lineup. Again, in retrospect, it seemed great luck that the new series was to follow the lead-in of CBS's popular *60 Minutes*. This particular sweetheart time slot (after a Saturday night berth was rejected) was chosen because the network's senior vice-president, Harvey Shephard, felt, "It was perfect. Both shows appealed to intelligent people and to people over thirty-five. NBC and ABC had escapist, youth-oriented programs with *Knight Rider* and *Hardcastle & McCormick* at eight P.M. That maximized our chances of success."

DEBUT PILOT SHOW A SUCCESS

Murder, She Wrote debuted on Sunday, September 30, 1984, as a 120-minute opener with the episode "The Murder of Sherlock Holmes." The show got a top-ten audience rating. *Variety* reported, "Thanks to Lansbury's polished performance, it did not become the Americanized Miss Marple vehicle it threatened to be. . . . The script's nicest touch was in having a menacing young black on a bus turn out to be a Lansbury fan in time to save her from a couple of punks on a dimly lit Manhattan street."

Variety judged of the star, "In the pilot she fleshed out a likable, bright woman, brimming with housewifely tidbits and perpetually civil with working-class people." The trade paper predicted, "If the plotting doesn't get too archaic to do her in, she seems to have the deft character actress's dexterity to make *Murder, She Wrote* an adult whodunit . . . that could hold a goodly number of *60 Minutes* viewers on CBS-TV each Sunday."

The *Chicago Tribune* enthused, "Wonderfully leisurely . . . with lots of time to ponder details, muse clues and get to know star Angela Lansbury. . . . This is a 'real-time' mystery. Lansbury gets her clues at the same time viewers do. There are enough red herrings to make an interesting fish boil, but what's even better is that the writers get through 120 minutes without a single car smash."

Tom Shales *(Washington Post)* pointed out that *Murder, She Wrote* "really is a mystery show, not a beat-'em-up show. . . . Most cop and detective shows don't even bother to hide the identity of the culprit from viewers anymore. . . . So *Murder, She Wrote* is refreshing on that score." Shales also noted, "It may be a class act, but it is also a quainter act than it needs to be. . . ." The *Washington Post* critic concluded, "It's just that *Murder, She Wrote* could have been more intelligent and more stylish and still not scared viewers off."

The following Sunday, October 7, 1984, *Murder, She Wrote* began its weekly run in its hour-long format. That October 7, 1984, episode, "Deadly Lady," further defined for viewers the who and what of Jessica Beatrice Fletcher of Cabot Cove, Maine. She is a middle-aged substitute school teacher, recently widowed, who has found a new career as the author of mystery novels and who moonlights as a detective. She is a contented New Englander, who lives in a rambling Victorian house and is proud to be Mrs. (not Ms.) Fletcher, with fond memories of a very happy marriage.

Simi Horwitz *(Washington Post)* noted that Jessica Fletcher was not a total goody-two-shoes: "This aging widow-woman from Maine . . . is the most intrusive buttinsky on prime-time television. In its ladylike way, her behavior is positively outrageous. . . . She insistently interrogates suspects, sets up stings to entrap wrong-doers, traipses across closed-to-the-public crime scenes in search of clues, and, most irritating—and wonderfully implausible—instructs the police in whatever city she finds herself. . . ."

If the new TV amateur sleuth didn't have a sidekick, there was the recurring presence of crabby Ethan Cragg (Claude Akins), a gruff fishing boat owner and a pal of industrious, but easy-going Jessica. There was also portly Sheriff Amos Tupper (Tom Bosley), a nice but not-so-smart law enforcer.

Before long in the first season, the Cragg character disappeared from the story line. Not only did the chemistry fail to jell between Jessica and Ethan, but actor Claude Akins, himself having starred in past series, didn't like being a second banana. On the other hand, Tom Bosley, best known for playing harassed Mr. Cunningham on TV's *Happy Days* had great on-camera rapport with Lansbury and remained a supporting staple of the show for the next few seasons.

From the start, the demands of filming twenty-two weekly installments per season was a tough adjustment for Lansbury. When not enduring long daily hours on the Universal Studios sound stages in Los Angeles, she was frequently on location in northern California. There, the coastal town of Mendocino stood in for Maine's Cabot Cove, where Jessica resided. The Victorian-style house used for establishing outside shots of Jessica Fletcher's home was the Blair House Inn, a bed-and-breakfast situated at 45110 Little Lake Street. Cabot Cove's Hill House Inn, featured on several *Murder, She Wrote* segments, was an actual Mendocino business. (Whenever the cast made location filming treks to Mendocino, they would stay at Hill House.) Additional "New England" backdrops were provided by location filming in other parts of northern California and Oregon.

As the year wore on, Angela learned what many others had before her: "When you're working in a series, there's no life outside it. Which is pretty stupid when you stop and analyze what you're doing—just running down corridors and things, to which they seem to attach importance. I sometimes feel I'm playing an older Nancy Drew."

One of Lansbury's rules for doing the program was having a closed set at Universal. She reasoned, "On a dramatic show such as this, it's very distracting to have people unrelated to the business around who just want to see how we do it. They puncture the bubble of work we try to surround ourselves with, particularly on this show. The kind of camaraderie between actors and audience that exists on a sitcom doesn't exist here, because there is no audience. The audience is the camera eye, and one is always working to it—not to the stagehands or anyone else."

She added, "Also, you need room to make mistakes, and you don't like making them in front of strangers if you think they're going to carry it home with them. People who visit sets think that it's all magic. They really don't know what goes into actually creating a scene—the interplay between the actors and director and so on."

ANGELA INFLUENCES DEVELOPMENT OF SHOW

Once having collaborated on the concept and the story of the *Murder, She Wrote* pilot, Richard Levinson and William Link remained only in a consulting capacity. On the other hand, before long, Angela was putting her own creative input into new scripts. This was merely an added function for the actress, who not only starred in the series, but did most of her own makeup, cut her own hair for the show, and sometimes offered casting suggestions.

As the weeks passed, Angela became more insistent that Jessica should follow less conventional guidelines. She "suggested" that Mrs. Fletcher, who has no vanity about wearing reading glasses, should not dress continuously in frumpy tweeds and sensible shoes, that she should be more progressive in her life-style and also not to be one who has given up on a love life. It was also clear to Lansbury that her alter ego should always display high-level energy, whether writing, detective snooping, painting a house, fishing. . . .

Angela told *TV Guide* her theories concerning Jessica Fletcher: "She's not an eccentric, not a busybody or a character. That's just what we didn't want. I think she's a very honest and straightforward person, very ethical, with an open mind. She's a good all-rounder. And she's an American. That's very important, she's very American." In short, "She is what most women of that age [about 60] would like to be. She is a cock-eyed optimistic romantic and so am I. And she is attractive, but in a feminine, nonthreatening way."

After the fact, Richard Levinson admitted that when *Murder, She Wrote* went on the air, "Everyone I knew in television was saying that we wouldn't last more than a few weeks. The best I was hoping for was a marginal success." To the surprise of most everyone, viewers responded as enthusiastically as critics to the new series.

Robert MacKenzie *(TV Guide)* summed up the consensus: "Jessica is a delightful creation, the more so for being played by Angela Lansbury. With her tall, sturdy frame and earnest English face, Lansbury can be impressive or amusing to look at, as she chooses. She knows to ride the edge of comedy without going over, and she has a smile that could toast bread. Television is lucky to get her."

Another ingredient that proved popular with viewers was the weekly guest cast of red herrings and murderers. Like past whodunit series *(Burke's Law, Columbo, The Adventures of Ellery Queen)*, the show used the audience-grabbing gimmick of employing veteran actors—very often stars from Hollywood's film and TV past—in offbeat casting assignments. As *TV Guide's* MacKenzie pointed out, "When a whodunit tries to cheap it on the acting budget it's always obvious that the killer is the most prominent of the guest actors. That's an important point [that this show is *not* doing], and another sign that the producers and the network intend for Lansbury to travel first class."

Peter S. Fischer explained why celebrity talent worked so well on *Murder, She Wrote.* "Every guest is paid a top fee in the low four figures, and all guests are billed alphabetically. . . . Other actors have said they wanted special billing or none. Then it's none. . . . Occasionally we run into people who demand star treatment, but not very often, because Angela is so professional. She comes in prepared, ready to go to work. She's not a prima donna. We've had stars with reputations of being monsters on other shows, and they're wonderful with us. . . ."

According to Fischer, few veteran performers over the years refused an offer to be on *Murder, She Wrote.* Two who declined—saying they were retired—were John Payne and John Lund. Sometimes a star would suggest another luminary. (For example, Van Johnson brought forth the idea of casting Joan Caulfield.) Fischer explained further, "The older stars love to come on the show because they get to work with old friends without any responsibility: If you're a guest you just have a good time. Nobody's looking to you to carry the show." Another policy inaugurated would be that if a name performer played a small role one time, he or she might well get a far more sizable role the next outing.

By the time the first season (1984–1985) of *Murder, She Wrote* ended, the show emerged as the #8 rated series on the air, with a 21.8% audience viewership. It was a spectacular victory. It had trounced its time slot competition, and had beaten out such popular nighttime TV series as *Knots Landing*, *Falcon Crest* and *Cheers*. The series had also spawned merchandising, ranging from a *Murder, She Wrote* board game to novelizations of series episodes (and later, original Jessica Fletcher novels authored by Donald Bain).

Realizing that her series was to go on—at least for a second season—Lansbury and her husband bought a Brentwood, California, home. The star herself enthused, "You have to be thrilled with the way we've gone over. Not only the critics, but the numbers. . . . I think it's the first time a show has really been aimed at the middle-aged audience. I never go shopping without some comfortable lady coming up and saying, 'Thank you for giving us something to watch.' Young people are coming around to it, too, when they see a story instead of a car chase."

THE SECOND SUCCESSFUL SEASON

During the second season (1985–1986) of *Murder, She Wrote* other refinements were made to the principal character and her supporting stock company. First of all, Angela vetoed having so many of the weekly guest murderers falling in love with her: "I said no to those slight romantic liaisons. It makes her seem as though she has round heels [i.e., a woman of loose virtues]."

With Claude Akins' character removed from the series, Fischer introduced a new recurring character to fit Lansbury's requirement that Jessica "must consort with people of a certain intellectual level." The new addition was Cabot Cove's widowed Dr. Seth Hazlitt, a bright if cantankerous man, with a natural curiosity about life. As Fischer reasoned, "We could do more with him [than with Ethan Cragg] because he was more Jessica's age and temperament. He was also the town doctor, which made it easy to get him into the show. When you're finding bodies, you need both a sheriff and a doctor." Another personality who popped up on the show infrequently was real estate broker Harry Pierce (played by John Astin of *The Addams Family* fame).

Lansbury told the media regarding season #2, "I think we're going to try to make it more interesting this year, by dint of making the plots a little more complex. It will take people a little longer to guess who the murderer is." She also predicted, "If we survive well this season and we keep our audience, and I think the chances are very good, we'll undoubtedly be asked to do a third season."

Now that *Murder, She Wrote* was proving itself, Universal relaxed the weekly pressure on Lansbury. When the series first went on the air, each episode (45 minutes and 45 seconds long) required seven days of preparation and seven twelve-hour (or more) days of production. Typically three days were spent on location, one on Universal's backlot and three on studio sound stages. Each episode in the early years cost about $1.3 million and involved a staff and crew of seventy-six.

To accommodate the now proven TV star, the show switched from a seven-day shooting schedule to an eight-day window. Thankful for the more "leisurely" pace, Angela admitted, "I could not have gone on. The work was making inroads on my emotional stability. I was getting crazy."

(Despite the expanded numbers of days allowed to film each segment, Angela remained firm on another point. "If I begin work at six in the morning, I quit at six in the evening. I leave. If I make an exception for one scene, they'll say, 'You did it last week, so why can't you stay over now?' I have to be bullheaded—which is very much against my grain.")

Yet another concession was reducing the number of different directors used on the hit series. The first season had employed thirteen; the second year utilized only five. In choosing such talent, Angela stated, "I prefer directors with stage experience who know something about actors and acting and who don't make you feel like a piece of furniture to be moved around."

By now there was no question that the show would alter its plot format. Why should it? It was a major reason, besides the consummate Miss Lansbury and the tasteful production values, which drew viewers to the program week after week. Later, John O'Connor *(New York Times)* would assess in retrospect that *Murder, She Wrote's* very familiarity and consistency combined to make the show "a cup of hot Ovaltine to help the weary unwind." He neatly summarized the program's unyielding plot, "Somewhere around 8:45 she suddenly realized, 'That's it!' . . . And just before the final batch of commercials, the culprit, confronted with Jessica's deductive powers and a flashback showing where a mistake had been made, blurted out a complete confession. A final freeze-frame caught Jessica in close-up wearing an inevitably fetching expression."

To compete against *Murder, She Wrote* in 1985–1986, rival NBC-TV scheduled two new half-hour programs: Steven Spielberg's *Amazing Stories* and a new edition of *Alfred Hitchcock Presents.* In the same 8–9 P.M. hour slot, ABC premiered a new action series, *MacGyver,* starring Richard Dean Anderson. These counter-programming moves were to no avail. *Murder, She Wrote* ended its second year on the air as the #3 series, now with a 25.3% audience viewership. (Interestingly, it was also doing better than its lead-in show, *60 Minutes.)*

Lansbury could personally attest to the show's increased popularity. "When we were filming in Oregon, we found there were a lot of bars where the proprietors set up a pool among the customers, the prize money going to the person who guessed the identity of the murderer before the pool closed at the end of the first act. That kind of audience interest, I guess, is what brings in the ratings."

It also didn't hurt the series' appeal that Jessica Fletcher had become less frumpy and "a bit more real, closer to me than when we started out." By now Lansbury, who had gained weight during the first season (due to nibbling during the endless waiting between scene shots), had slimmed down from a size 14 to what the show's costume designer, Alfred E. Lehman, referred to as "an expensive [size] 10."

Another factor for the show's accelerating popularity was that Lansbury was exercising more clout on the series. She was the first to admit, "I'm a hard person to please. My standards are awfully high, and I never want to let the audience down. I know what they expect. I know what they want from the show, and I know what they expect from me as an actress; and anything less than that, I am highly embarrassed."

With her new-found leverage, Angela found that the show's staff was listening more closely to her suggestions. Then executive producer and frequent episode scripter Peter S. Fischer allowed, "Angela's tough, but she's usually right. Besides, when you have a star in a series with a [frequent] 27 rating, it's like having an 800-pound gorilla. It can do anything it wants."

SUCCESS, BUT WITHOUT MAJOR EMMY AWARDS

One thing Angela could *not* do was win an Emmy Award for herself or for the overall show. In its first season, John Addison had won an Emmy for *Murder, She Wrote* in the category of Outstanding Music Composition for a Series. In the second year, the show's costumer, Alfred E. Lehman, won one for Outstanding Costume Design for a Series.

Those two trophies proved to be the show's only Emmy wins. It became an annual event for Angela to be nominated for Outstanding Lead Actress in a Drama Series. Being a bridesmaid and never the bride at the Emmys has always irked Lansbury. As late as 1991 she bridled, "Nobody in this town [Los Angeles] watches *Murder, She Wrote.* Only the public watches. The industry is barely aware the show exists. They think it's made back east, I think. . . ."

Even before *Murder, She Wrote* began its third season (1986–1987), Angela was voicing concerns about whether to continue onward with her hit vehicle. She said, "It doesn't draw on my abilities beyond knowing how to learn my lines, understanding the character and putting myself in the situation. . . . It's very enjoyable work in the sense that I don't have to do any digging down. I certainly couldn't do it forever, because it doesn't stretch me at all."

In the 1986–1987 season, to combat *Murder, She Wrote* in its Sunday evening 8 P.M. time slot, NBC chose two sitcoms, *Easy Street* (with Loni Anderson) and *Valerie* (with Valerie Harper). ABC opted for a Sunday Night Movie. Once again, *Murder, She Wrote* swamped the competition by maintaining its 25.4% viewership (although it was now #4, bested by *The Cosby Show, Family Ties* and *Cheers*).

An unusual promotional ploy during the third season demonstrated just how potent Angela's showcase had become for CBS-TV. Another of the network's established shows, *Magnum, P.I.*, was faltering during its seventh season. CBS arranged to have a cross-over double episode. As such, Lansbury's Jessica Fletcher and Tom Selleck's Thomas Magnum appeared in a two-part story whose first half began on *Magnum, P.I.* (November 19, 1986) and concluded on *Murder, She Wrote* (November 23, 1986). It perked up Selleck's viewership. However, Lansbury was uncomfortable with forcing her show's format into another's premise. Thus, the gimmick was never employed again for *Murder, She Wrote.*

For its fourth season (1987–1988), the other networks again worked hard to unseat *Murder, She Wrote.* ABC had its detective series *(Spencer: For Hire);* NBC tried two half-hour sitcoms *(Family Ties* and *My Two Dads).* The new Fox network offered *Werewolf* and *Married . . . with Children.* This time the oppositions' strategy had a marked effect. *Murder, She Wrote* slipped to #9 and only averaged a 20.2% audience viewership for the season.

In the next year (1988–1989), *Murder, She Wrote* moved back up a notch (to #8) but lost a few percentiles in the viewership race (down to 19.9%). The most noticeable fifth season change was that Tom Bosley was no longer playing Sheriff Amos Tupper. He had left the program to star in his own detective series, *Father Dowling Mysteries.*

To replace the well-liked Bosley, the show hired Ron Masak, a Lou Costello look-alike. He was assigned to play Sheriff Mort Metzger, an ex-New York City cop who seeks a quieter work life in countrified Cabot

Cove. Among the differences between Jessica's old and new law officer cohort, Metzger was a far brighter criminal investigator. (Nevertheless, he was still much in need of Mrs. Fletcher's expert assistance.)

FIVE SEASONS: TO CONTINUE OR LEAVE?

If CBS seemed to have forgotten the fact that Lansbury's five-year pact was due to expire at the end (May, 1989) of this, the show's fifth season, she had not. She was already telling the press, "I think at my time of life I need more time for myself. I have a lot of projects and things I can do."

Angela also hinted about being bored with her acting chore. "Jessica is a listener, a questioner. She's a cerebral soul. She's seldom emotionally involved in the plots. That's up to the guests. They get to play the dramatic roles. I don't mind. It's fun. But you know, someone likened my job on *Murder, She Wrote* to being a horse pulling a milk wagon, while I'm ready to run the Grand National."

By early 1989, CBS realized that the star of its bread-and-butter series might fly the coop. Already rival networks were sounding out Lansbury about her joining their line-up, and at the moment, she held no special loyalty to her network. (Later, Angela publicly revealed her private feelings about the network's treatment of her during the first five seasons. She noted that CBS-TV "took us for granted for many, many years. This wasn't *Miami Vice*. It wasn't a hot half-hour sitcom. It was about a woman over sixty. And it took care of itself.")

In late January 1989, CBS president, Laurence Tisch, came courting Lansbury at her trailer home on the studio lot. Angela has recalled, "He was so dear. . . . He said, 'We really want to work with you and your company, and we very much want you to stay with CBS'." According to Lansbury, "Well, it made me feel very warm. I hadn't had a pat like that in a long time. It was terrific!"

Thus by mid-1989, CBS-TV could announce that it had worked out an agreement that assured Angela Lansbury and her Corymore production company a berth at CBS no matter what happened to *Murder, She Wrote.* Summing up these negotiations, the star said, "Money talked in that instance. CBS was really worried about me leaving, and they made me an offer which I certainly didn't refuse. It meant so much not to me personally but to my company, my kids and my grandchildren."

Reportedly, for the sixth season (1989–1990), Lansbury was to earn about $175,000 weekly or close to $4 million for the season. Her Corymore Productions, Inc., was to earn some $2 million to develop new series for future seasons. (One such program in which Corymore was involved became

Touched By an Angel, 1994–). And the residuals from past, present and the next year's episodes could gross her another $6 million.

In the 1989–1990 season, *Murder, She Wrote* was up against ABC's *Free Spirit* and *Hometown*, NBC's *Sister Kate* and *My Two Dads* and Fox's *America's Most Wanted* and *Totally Hidden Video.*

"ONLY" HOSTING SOME SEGMENTS PROVES UNPOPULAR

The main format change—and it was a major one—on the sixth year of *Murder, She Wrote* was that Angela only appeared in thirteen of the twenty-two segments. In the other nine, she served as host, opening and closing the story (usually featuring ex-jewel thief Dennis Stanton played by Keith Michell). The reduced work schedule not only permitted her a breather, but allowed her to accept other assignments (TV movies, etc.). However, audiences didn't respond well to Lansbury's frequent absence from the stories, and the series dropped to #13 for the year with only a 17.7% audience viewership.

Nevertheless, CBS picked up Angela's option for the seventh (1990–1991) season. She was to earn a reported $350,000 per *Murder, She Wrote* episode. By now the network was suggesting that Lansbury develop a new (less expensive) property to substitute for her weekly whodunit. CBS even agreed to pay $3.6 million for the creation of this vehicle, and it guaranteed that it would air nine episodes of the creation. If the new entry reached into the top thirty programs, CBS would pay an additional $6 million for another thirteen episodes.

If the proposed new sitcom was renewed for a second season, CBS was to pay $11 million for the new season. With other perks, the new project could be worth $19-$20 million to Lansbury and her production company. However, at this point, Angela was reluctant to test the waters with a new concept. (Later, there was talk of her doing a half-hour weekly show based on the play and movie *Driving Miss Daisy*, and still later, a spy series based on Dorothy Gilman's book character, Mrs. Emily Pollifax. Neither property materialized.)

For the seventh (1990–1991) season, it was agreed that Angela would appear fully in seventeen of the twenty-two installments. However, fans were still miffed. Lansbury's husband and manager, Peter Shaw, acknowledged, "We've gotten so many letters from fans who don't like it when Angie's not in the show. They feel it's false advertising."

What also hurt the show's rating in its seventh year was the defection of William Windom, who went over to a new sitcom, *Parenthood.* As a substitute, Joe Dorsey was brought in as Ben Devlin, the new owner of the *Cabot Cove Gazette.* However the chemistry was just not there, and he eventually faded from the program. When *Parenthood* flopped after three months on the air, Windom returned to his Dr. Hazlitt character on *Murder, She Wrote.*

Already it was a yearly ritual for Angela to announce that the current season would be her final one as Jessica Fletcher. This time, she was a bit earlier in speaking her mind. It happened in the fall of 1990. "It is the last season. I don't want to continue with a weekly show. I don't want to say goodbye to Jessica. I would like to make TV movies with her."

Meanwhile, CBS worked with Lansbury to develop other alternative, less expensive properties to substitute for *Murder, She Wrote.* However, nothing could be agreed upon. *Murder, She Wrote* ended the 1990–1991 season at #12 and with only a 16.4% audience viewership. (One of its time spot rivals, ABC's *America's Funniest Home Videos,* finished the year tying for #7.)

By now, in the spring of 1991, it was agreed that despite Angela Lansbury and its proven format, *Murder, She Wrote* was in danger of dying of old age. At this juncture, at the end of the seventh season, executive producer/cocreator Peter S. Fischer left the program. He was replaced by David Moessinger.

MAJOR CHANGES IN EIGHTH SEASON

As part of the new regime for its eighth season (1991–1992), Angela would work four twelve-hour days per week. As part of the new look (and as an economy save), it was decided to downplay the use of veteran names on the series and to employ younger talent in the supporting parts. Doing so helped to improve viewership among under-thirty TV watchers.

To brighten the established story line, it was decreed that the character of Jessica Fletcher would now be spending three to four days each week in New York City at her new part-time apartment. She would be teaching criminology at Manhattan University as well as working with inner city young adults in creative writing courses. She would return to Cabot Cove on weekends.

These concept changes allowed for the flexibility (and better credibility) of contrasting urban and rural settings. It also permitted Jessica to become more actively involved with the younger generation. Additionally, to emphasize that Mrs. Fletcher was "with it," she abandoned her manual typewriter for a home computer. Observant viewers also noted that Angela's hairstyle and wardrobe were more fashionable and that Lansbury had undergone cosmetic surgery to give herself a more youthful look.

With these important changes in the works, Angela told the press that she felt "challenged to turn the show around because we'd been taken for granted so much. I'm putting in more than I've ever done before because of my real involvement with the scripts, with casting, with the direction we're going. I had no input before, none whatsoever."

The revamped *Murder, She Wrote* did far better in the ratings during its eighth season of 1991–1992. It trounced several of its Sunday night competition, including NBC's *Man of the People* (with James Garner) and *Pacific Station* (with Robert Guillaume). Happy with the changes, by late January 1992, Angela renewed her pact for the series' ninth season. She was to receive a reported $400,000 per episode for 1992–1993.

As part of the sweet deal for the 1992–1993 season, Lansbury became executive producer of *Murder, She Wrote,* replacing David Moessinger. She reasoned to her network bosses, "I felt that if I was going to continue with the show, I must then take the responsibilities—and also take the blame if it wasn't coming off."

Angela was reinvigorated by her new position of power. And it showed. For example, in December 1992, *TV Guide's* Mary Murphy reported from the show's set, "This is Angela Lansbury at work: tough, vibrant, and very much in control of what goes on in the production of *Murder, She Wrote*. . . . Indeed, watch her on the set and one thing is immediately clear: Lansbury is nothing like the sweetly eccentric New England mystery novelist she portrays in the show."

MURDER, SHE WROTE NOW A FAMILY MATTER

By now, *Murder, She Wrote* had become a true family affair. In contrast to most in the entertainment industry who downplayed nepotism on projects, Lansbury was proud of being associated with her relatives. Her husband, Peter Shaw, was her manager and frequent on-set advisor. Son Anthony, who had begun on the series as a dialogue director, was now one of the recurring segment directors, while her stepson, David Show, was president of Corymore Productions. In addition, Bruce Lansbury, one of Angela's younger, twin brothers, and himself a TV veteran (producer of *Mission: Impossible,* etc.) became a producer on the show and a frequent scripter. Moreover, David Lansbury, Angela's nephew, became an occasional guest performer on the series.

During the ninth season of 1992–1993, *Murder, She Wrote* broke the usual industry tradition. It jumped back *up* in the ratings, making it to the top five! Angela reacted with, "I'm glad this locomotive is getting back on the track. It was too valuable to let it fall by the wayside."

In January 1993, Angela signed for two more seasons (#10 and #11) on the show. Reflecting on the number of her relatives involved on the series, Lansbury joked, "Other actresses get up in the morning and kiss their kids and their husband goodbye. I get up in the morning to meet and go to work with my family. . . . If I quit, I put my family out of work. I won't do that. Not until we all agree it's time."

How was the long-lasting series holding up? *Variety* reviewed the January 17, 1993, segment. It reported, "You can't put it out of the ballpark every time at bat. *Murder, She Wrote,* now halfway through its ninth season, has more homers than strikeouts even if latest seg, 'Double Jeopardy,' doesn't quite make it to the fence. . . . The plotting on the series is usually more complex than this one; fault here lies largely in character development. . . . [Nevertheless] It's just fun watching Lansbury pick up the clues and piece the deed together. Lansbury's a delight, showing terrific concentration with inner workings."

Murder, She Wrote began its tenth season on September 12, 1993. Among its competition was NBC's *SeaQuest DSV,* ABC's *Lois & Clark: The New Adventures of Superman* and Fox's *Martin* (with Martin Lawrence). Even Angela was concerned by the tough opposition: "I thought, boy, this is really some stiff competition. I figured we had to be prepared to take our lumps and just hope we could survive." Not to worry. Lansbury's show did just fine, maintaining itself in the top nine—and often higher—for the whole year; far better than its rival programs.

During the tenth season, *Murder, She Wrote* celebrated the taping of its 200th shot episode ("Bloodlines"). The segment reunited Angela with Mickey Rooney, with whom she had costarred in MGM's *National Velvet* back in 1944 (!). Reviewing this milestone installment, *Daily Variety's* Tony Scott reported approvingly, "Secret of the success of [*Murder, She Wrote*], besides its cozy appeal to older generations, is the Lansbury touch. And it's a descendant of 1930s and 1940s second-bill theatrical mysteries whose plots were basically clustered around a Philo Vance or a Charlie Chan. Their dialogue was direct, characters little more than devices, and the solution, usually sprung at a gathering of suspects, was fanciful. . . . Formula still works if shrewdly applied—and if it offers Lansbury as its central figure."

Launching into its eleventh season in September 1994, it was not easy for Lansbury to keep her characterization of Jessica Fletcher fresh and dimensional. Angela shared her own theory for keeping her pivotal character interesting: "Every eight days I get to work with an entirely new group of actors in a new setting. It's not like I'm stuck in the same old place day after day, even if I do have to find a corpse everywhere I go." Of course, it didn't hurt that television's Queen Bee had every imaginable perk on and off the set. According to *Globe,* "The veteran actress demanded—and got—a black Lincoln Town Car parked on the set at all times. . . . 'Angela likes to sit in the quiet of the enclosed car with tinted windows in between takes,' reveals an insider on the show. And while she's relaxing in there, two professional English tea servers are at her beck and call in case she gets thirsty!"

During the 1994–1995 season, *Murder, She Wrote* found itself pitted against ABC's *Lois & Clark: The New Adventures of Superman*, NBC's *SeaQuest DSV* and Fox's two half-hour sitcoms: *The Simpsons* and *Hardball* (a short-lived baseball comedy). Nevertheless, *Murder, She Wrote,* according to Nielsen Media Research, ended in #9 position (tying with *Roseanne*) in the chart of the year's most popular TV shows. Once again, it had been touch-and-go whether Lansbury would renew for yet another go-round of *Murder, She Wrote*. However, by January 1995, she had committed to the 1995–1996 season. Yet she let it be known, as she had so many times before, that this would (*most likely*) be the swan song of the weekly episodes.

MURDER, SHE WROTE MOVED BY STUDIO

Then, in May 1995, without prior notification, CBS-TV announced publicly that it was pulling *Murder, She Wrote* from its long-established Sunday night (family entertainment) time spot to Thursdays at eight P.M. where it would have to complete against NBC's very high performing half-hour sitcom *Friends* and a new youth-oriented comedy, *The Single Guy* (starring Jonathan Silverman). As Lansbury recalled to the *Los Angeles Times,* she was informed of the decision by phone by CBS Entertainment president Peter Tortorici. Per Angela, he "simply said that they were very grateful for all the years and for our contribution in keeping CBS alive when it was foundering. I personally felt very heartbroken." Angela told the press, "I really feel angry for all the people who watched us. . . . I felt desperate about it [at first]. I now feel we can go forward on Thursday and take our chances. It's probably our last year anyway, but I just feel badly for all those people who built their Sunday nights around us." The programming battle between CBS-TV and *Murder, She Wrote* became a cause célèbre, much discussed by the media for months to come.

In making this time shift, CBS-TV had to know that it would almost certainly prompt Lansbury not to renew the program for further weekly episodes, although the possibility of two-hour telefeature follow-ups had long been considered a possibility. Indeed, shortly after the 1995 season began, Angela confided to Susan King of the *Los Angeles Times,* "I don't think I would have ever agreed to do this twelfth season if I knew this was going to happen. I just couldn't understand. I couldn't find any logic to their thinking and neither could anybody else."

For its part, the network may have reasoned that phasing out *Murder, She Wrote* was not such a bad idea after all. Not only was the show starting to run out of creative ways to keep its formula fresh, but there was the matter of its high production costs. Whereas most weekly drama hour shows cost $1.2 or $1.3 million, *Murder, She Wrote* now required a $1.8

million budget per episode shot. (It was rumored that if the series should come back for 1996–1997, the network (1) wanted to pay a lower per episode fee reflecting the show's lower rating and (2) would not guarantee a return to the Sunday night berth which was now the property of Cybill Shepherd's sitcom, *Cybill.* The matter became academic when during the 1995–1996 season, *Murder, She Wrote,* unable to complete with the enormously successful *Friends,* slipped in the viewership charts beneath the top fifty shows watched each week.

By early 1996 it was accepted that May would see the end of *Murder, She Wrote* on a weekly basis. (It was also agreed that while not exclusive to CBS, Lansbury would give the network first offer on any *Murder, She Wrote* telefeatures or her long-projected new sitcom.) Deciding it could afford the luxury, the whodunit show took occasion to satirize *Friends,* the Generation X comedy that was murdering the veteran series in the ratings. On the February 8, 1996, episode, "Murder Among Friends," Jessica Fletcher is caught up in a homicide investigation on the set of the TV show *Buds,* whose characters, plot line and even theme song are immediately reminiscent of *Friends.*

In an ironic bid to end the brouhaha between CBS-TV and *Murder, She Wrote,* the network announced that the detectives series would move *back* to Sunday nights at 8 P.M. for its four final episodes (April 28 through May 19, 1996), although it had occasionally done so before during the season when it was a sweeps rating week.

With both parties now committed to ending the weekly *Murder, She Wrote,* Lansbury and her production team decided it would *not* end its run with a high-profile finish. The star's stepson, David Shaw, co-executive producer of the show and head of Lansbury's Corymore Productions, explained, "We've been working on these scripts all season, and we're going to do them as planned. We'll give the show as good a sendoff as we can . . . but I think we want to keep this a quiet time. I think Angie would like to just go out quietly."

The series' finale, "Death By Demographics," was its own telling jibe at CBS and the television industry's fixation on wooing 18- to 49-year-old viewers at the expense of other audience segments who, contrary to the belief of the advertising community, are actually bigger and who have and do spend money. The segment was set at a San Francisco radio station that altered its programming format to appeal to younger listeners.

Murder, She Wrote ended its weekly tenure with a gentle note and soft ratings. (It received a 20% in the major market overnight Nielsen rating, compared to 29% for its NBC network competition, the sitcom *Mad About You.*) Behind the scenes, the veteran show also wrapped up on a low key. As Angela prepared to shoot the final installment, she informed the media with her trademark grace, "I would rather not talk with any press [on the sound stage]. I would rather not have people on the set filming [candid shots]. I just want to spend this last episode with the friends I have worked with for twelve years. And some have really been there for twelve years." Angela even arranged not to have to be part of the filming on the final day of production. She felt it would be too emotional for her. However, she did host a "fabulous" lunch on the last day for cast and crew. When the Emmys were announced for the 1995–1996 season, Angela received her twelfth and final Emmy nomination for *Murder, She Wrote* in the category of Lead Actress in a Drama Series. At the September 8, 1996, Emmy ceremonies, she again lost.

A SUMMING UP FOR THE SERIES

With *Murder, She Wrote* now part of TV history, John S. O'Connor *(New York Times)* took occasion to pay tribute to the long-running, so highly rated, classy series: "For twelve seasons, Ms. Lansbury's Jessica has been a wonderfully engaging woman, managing to be the soul of propriety, clearly signaling her disapproval of unseemly behavior, while getting into all sorts of hairy situations—she was once taken hostage at a women's prison—and splendidly retaining her infectious charm. Week after week, often traveling abroad, she brought us clever beginning-middle-end tales with tidy solutions and comforting morality. Evil was always punished."

In a postscript penned for *TV Guide,* Lansbury offered her own valentine to the show's most important ingredient—its audience. She wrote:

> But mostly I remember and thank you, the viewers—you who sustained me through those early years when I was still finding my way in television, you who have stayed true to the series for twelve seasons, you who honored us by allowing *Murder, She Wrote* into your homes every week. My dearest wish is that those who enjoyed Jessica's adventures will remember her as I do: an active, mature woman, possessed of courage, independence, and wit, broad-minded and young at heart, a champion of the wrongfully accused. I suspect there are some fascinating two-hour mysteries for her to solve yet.

Summing up the show's enduring success, producer Bruce Lansbury analyzes, "It's Angie and her expression of Jessica Fletcher as a real human being, someone people trust and have confidence in, a mature woman who is up with the times. The mystery is the fun part, the puzzle part, and for us it's the repetition of the familiar, which television really thrives on. You find a good joke and you play it every week. But really, much bigger than our format, it's the star."

ABOUT ANGELA LANSBURY

> "[Acting] is the one area—touch wood—where I have never had any doubt that I could deliver the goods. That has been the grace note in my sonata of life, the thing that has absolutely seen me through thick and thin, and even saved my sanity on a number of occasions."
>
> (Angela Lansbury, 1980s)

Before she became a TV mega star in the mid-1980s as Jessica Fletcher of *Murder, She Wrote,* genteel and civilized Angela Lansbury had already enjoyed three distinctive show business careers. In the 1940s—when not yet twenty—the 5'9" actress was a MGM contract player and earned two Oscar nominations for playing characters far older than her actual years. By the early 1960s, Angela had created a brand new screen forte. As the cinema's most overpowering mother, she won another Academy Award bid for her horrendously warped mama in *The Manchurian Candidate* (1962). Four years later, she captured audiences' fancy in yet another entirely different mode. She was now the sparkling *Mame,* the toast of a Broadway musical and the proud winner of her first of four-to-date Tony Awards!

If the public was surprised by Lansbury's "rebirth" as the chic dancing and singing Mame Dennis, she wasn't. According to Angela, "All those years I had this vision that someday I'd blossom forth.... I could see myself singing, dancing, carrying on, being the life of the party, hogging the limelight—the works. Nobody knew—not even my family—but I knew."

For Angela, it was a brand new experience being *the* star of a production, rather than the expert supporting performer. "My emergence as a Broadway luminary in *Mame* suddenly made me everybody's property. When you've got a hit on Broadway and you walk down the street, man, everybody lets you know that you're the queen of the town for that brief period in which your star is glaring in the firmament."

After *Mame,* Angela starred in several other Broadway vehicles, including a high-voltage revival of *Gypsy* (1974) and the tour-de-force *Sweeney Todd* (1979). However, sensing it was time to "open a new window," she gravitated to a medium she had long mainly ignored.

She had been hesitant about trying TV as a full-fledged star because, "I always thought if you went into television, you'd burn yourself out and you'd never be able to get a job in movies or theater again, and I didn't want to jeopardize that part of my career. That's why I didn't do television for years." She adds, "I was offered series, but the role would always be as a member of some ensemble group in a situation comedy. As I told my agent, I didn't work forty years to come along and support someone I don't even know."

Again, to everyone's amazement, Angela beat the odds by turning *Murder, She Wrote*—a show predicted not to last one season—into a major ongoing success. For most of its twelve years on the air (1984–1996) as a weekly series, the show enjoyed a tremendously high and loyal viewership. (And it's likely that the two-hour *Murder, She Wrote* TV movies planned for the future will continue to be an audience pleaser.) As a result of this starring vehicle, Lansbury became one of the 1990s most powerful, highly paid female performers on American TV.

Of her enduring TV alter ego, Jessica Fletcher, the novelist turned amateur sleuth, Angela has noted, "I'm delighted when women of my age stop and tell me how grateful they are that they are represented by a character like Jessica Fletcher who embodies such 'with it' qualities. They're very interested in watching a woman of middle years acting like an energetic, bright, intelligent person and not like somebody who's on her way to crockdom—which we, those ladies of my age, certainly are not. We're bouncing and bounding around, along with everybody else. . . ."

A FUTURE STAR IS BORN

Angela Bridgid Lansbury was born in London, England, on October 16, 1925. She was the daughter of Edgar Isaac Lansbury, a lumber merchant, and Moyna MacGill, a stage actress.

In turn, Edgar was the son of George Lansbury, one of the founders of the British Labor Party. Moyna, born Charlotte ("Chattie") McIldowie in Belfast, Ireland, was the daughter of William McIldowie, the director of the Belfast Opera and a lawyer. Adopting the stage name of Moyna MacGill, she made her professional acting debut on the London stage in *Love in a Cottage* (1918) followed by roles on the London stage in *As You Like It* (1920), *Success* (1923) and *The Fairy Tale* (1924). (Meanwhile, she made her motion picture debut in the British-made silent film *Garryowen,*

1920.) Moyna's previous marriage—to actor, director and playwright Reginald Denham—had produced a daughter, Isolde, four years Angela's senior.

As a toddler, Angela was very close to Isolde, and they would perform imitations and dances for the family. The sisters were separated later when Isolde went to stay with her father. (Isolde would eventually become an actress herself and, at one time, was married to performer Peter Ustinov.)

Recalling her childhood, Angela has vivid impressions of her mother's special look. "Her beauty absolutely dazzled me.... I would help her get dressed; then she'd go out in a flurry of powder and perfume and get herself up to go to the theater. She'd say, 'I'm going to cut a bit of a dash.'"

At the time, Angela was unusually *un*concerned with her own physical appearance. "I never thought I was pretty. I was always self-conscious. I had a very beautiful mother.... Maybe the psychiatrists would say that's why I felt that way about myself." By the 1960s, having blossomed as the smart Broadway star, Lansbury noted, "I like the way I look now more than I did when I was younger. I think I've grown into myself. I found a style that's right for me. In the past, I always felt I had to look like someone else."

Since Angela's paternal grandfather, George Lansbury, was a famous politician of the day, his granddaughter got a solid taste of politicking in her childhood. She often accompanied him to political rallies and returned home to mimic the speakers she had heard. (Years later, in 1996, she would tell Larry King on his cable TV talk show, "I have a parrot's propensity for picking up accents. It's been very useful.") Sometimes young Angela fantasized about becoming a politician herself; on other occasions, she thought she might be a concert pianist.

Like most youngsters, Angela enjoyed the magic of going to the movies. However, she recalls, "I never wanted to be an actress when I was young. I actually wanted to be the characters I saw up there." She also remembers, "I was a morose little girl at times. I was very sensitive, very easily hurt, and I would cry when my mother left me to go to the theater."

In 1930, when Angela was five, her mother gave birth to identical twin boys, Bruce and Edgar. It was at this point that Mrs. Lansbury retired, temporarily, from the stage.

DRASTIC CHANGES AT HOME

The Lansburys were financially comfortable, often spending time at their farm in Berrik-Salmone, near Benson, which they purchased in 1931. However, the Great Depression caught up with them and the family went bust. "But," remembers Lansbury, "my mother had done a marvelous thing. Unbeknownst to my father, she had put away money that she earned in a couple of very successful shows. She bailed out the family."

In 1935, Mr. Lansbury died. In describing this traumatic period, Angela says that until then, she had been a "skirt hider-behinder." She was shy and overly sensitive. ("When he died, I was shattered. As a child you recover quickly. But as years went by, I realized there was a tremendous void in my life.") With Moyna now a single parent, the Lansburys' lifestyle changed radically. Moyna moved the family to more modest digs in Hampstead, on the outskirts of London, and Angela was enrolled at the South Hampstead High School for Girls.

Of the times following her dad's death, the star says, "I was an old lady at ten. . . . I became the partner with my mother in bringing up my brothers. I had to grow up fast." She also has commented, "I began to come out of my shell. My sister, Isolde, would organize family theatricals with my twin brothers and me. In those performances, Mother recognized that I had a natural ability to take on attitudes, that I was observant—which one has to be if one is to be a character actress."

Angela has a special memory of this transitional period. "One of the most liberating experiences of my life had been when I was eleven and went to Ireland alone with my sister. I had such a wonderful time that my whole life from then on was devoted to getting back to Ireland. That was my Shangri-la." She also would say, "It was among the Irish that I developed my sense of comedy and whimsy. My English half is my reserved side, but just put me onstage and the Irish comes out."

WORLD WAR II STRIKES THE LANSBURYS

With the outbreak of World War II, most London school children were evacuated to the country to avoid being victims of anticipated Nazi bombing raids. Angela abhorred the thought of being sent away to "boarding" school and convinced her mother to allow her to study at home with a tutor. It was then that Angela decided upon a stage career.

With Moyna's blessing, the youngster began studying dance, diction and singing under her mom's tutelage. Six months later, thanks to a scholarship, Angela was enrolled in the Webber-Douglas School of Singing and Dramatic Art in Kensington. Her first stage role at school was as a lady-in-waiting in *Mary of Scotland,* followed by playing a country bumpkin in Shakespeare's *As You Like It.* Says Angela, "I realized I enjoyed playing characters rather than worrying about looking gorgeous as the leading lady."

As the threat of German bombing of England became a reality in August of 1940, Moyna, who was working as an ambulance driver, chose to follow the advice of a distant cousin from Brawley, California. Thus, in August 1940, Moyna, Angela and the twins boarded the Canadian Pacific liner, *Duchess of Atholl,* and set forth in a convoy to Montreal, Canada, from which they took a train to New York City.

Once in New York City, the Lansburys stayed for a time with their sponsors, Wall Street businessman Charles T. Wilson and his wife, at their Lake Mahopac, New York, summer home. That September, Angela auditioned for the Feagin School of Drama and Radio in Manhattan, and was accepted there on a scholarship.

Arrangements were made for Angela to board at the East 94th Street house of Mr. and Mrs. George W. Perkins. Looking back, Angela reflects, "I was fifteen and very grown up. English girls are, for the most part." By the fall of 1941, Angela was back living with her mother in a forty-two-dollar-a-month one-room apartment in Greenwich Village, while the twin boys were at the Choate School in Wallingford, Connecticut.

Arthur Bourbon was a classmate of Angela's at the Feagin School. He encouraged her to develop her knack of mimicry into an act. After rehearsing an imitation of Beatrice Lillie singing Noel Coward's "I Went to a Marvelous Party," Lansbury auditioned for Bourbon's agent in a showcase at One Fifth Avenue, a small but popular Manhattan nightclub. The agent approved and soon arranged for his client to appear, at sixty dollars a week, at the Samovar, a little club in Montreal. Her summer 1942 job lasted for six weeks.

THE ROAD TO HOLLYWOOD

By this point, Moyna had joined a touring Canadian variety show (*Celebrity Parade*) that was entertaining the troops. Thereafter, Moyna gravitated to Los Angeles, hoping to break into American movies. When that didn't work out, she found work with a small Hollywood theater group, often serving as a ticket taker. Meanwhile, she suggested that Angela join her on the West Coast. Thus, Lansbury came to Los Angeles, while the twins remained at school in Connecticut.

Living in a twenty-eight-dollar-a-month one-room apartment, mother and daughter made the rounds of the studios but met with no success. Then, near Christmas, both obtained jobs at Bullock's Wilshire Department Store. After a brief period in the wrapping department (at eighteen dollars weekly), Angela became a salesgirl in the cosmetics department (at twenty-six dollars weekly). Bullock's offered to enroll the teenager in the buyers' training program, but her poor math skills ended that thought. (As for Moyna, she had been assigned to the toy department. However, she was fired for spending too much time playing with the games.)

Moyna knew many of the English colony of actors working in Hollywood movies. Through one, Michael Dyne, a struggling young actor, Angela got her movie career break. As Angela describes it, "He was being considered for a part in a film [*The Picture of Dorian Gray*, 1945] MGM was going to make. He took me along to the studio, and they gave me a test. He didn't get the part, but they gave me a contract starting at five hundred dollars a week. I never went back to the store."

Once on the MGM lot, she was spotted by an associate of director George Cukor who, in turn, had her test, instead, for *Gaslight* (1944), a thriller scheduled to go into production before *Dorian Gray*. Although Angela proved satisfactory in her screen audition as the cockney maid, studio executives thought her too young for that part or for *Dorian Gray*. However, studio mogul Louis B. Mayer, after seeing the test, voted to place Lansbury under a seven-year studio contract.

WORKING AT MGM

Angela was soon put to work on the Culver City sound stages. She celebrated her eighteenth birthday in 1943 on the set of *Gaslight* (1944), which starred Ingrid Bergman and Charles Boyer. In this period piece melodrama, Lansbury was the snitty parlor maid, Nancy Oliver. Says Angela of director George Cukor, "He knew what I could do as an actress ... and he cashed in on it like gangbusters. And if he hadn't, I wouldn't have got off the ground."

Gaslight opened in May 1944, and Lansbury, among others, received glowing reviews. The *New York Post* championed that Angela "calls to mind one of Bette Davis's most famous efforts in *Of Human Bondage* [1934]." Lansbury was nominated for a Best Supporting Actress Oscar, but lost to veteran star Ethel Barrymore (of *None But the Lonely Heart*).

From *Gaslight*, the studio put Angela into *National Velvet* (1944). That successful family picture featured Elizabeth Taylor as a British teenager who rides her beloved horse in the Grand National steeplechase race. Lansbury played Taylor's physically mature older sister, while Mickey Rooney was the ex-jockey who trains Taylor to ride to victory.

More important to Angela's career was *The Picture of Dorian Gray* (1945). Based on Oscar Wilde's elegant but horrific novel, Lansbury was seen as a virginal East End music hall singer who's drawn to handsome, mysterious Dorian Gray (Hurd Hatfield). With its risqué subject matter and low-budget look, the arty movie wasn't appreciated in its time. However, Angela received positive reviews as the ill-fated young woman. She was the frail creature who sang "Goodbye, Little Yellow Bird." Lansbury was again Oscar-nominated. Ironically, she lost the prize to Anne Revere, who won for playing Angela's mother in *National Velvet*.

With such a strong beginning in movies, Angela should have been content. However, she felt intimidated at being surrounded on the studio lot by such glittering figures as Greer Garson, Hedy Lamarr, Judy Garland and Lana Turner, as well as such up-and-coming personalities as Esther Williams, June Allyson and Ava Gardner.

Looking back at her MGM days, Lansbury analyzes, "I never had those chocolate-box looks they wanted for romantic leads in those days." However, she admits that being a slightly pudgy, "average-looking" young woman had its benefits: "As a character actor I achieved two things—first, a healthy sense of my offscreen self and my private life, which I learned to keep separate from my screen characters. And second, a longevity of career that has outlasted many of the leading ladies who relied on their looks."

Thinking back on the Angela Lansbury of the mid-1940s, she observes, "I wasn't American. I was English, and I think that prevented me from getting into the social life. I was very shy, very trepidatious of moving into the stream of Hollywood social life." In fact, she mostly avoided the nocturnal social swim, a habit which has remained over the decades. Her reasoning has always been, "I don't really know how to play that scene. If you write it for me, I can play it. But as Angie, I can't. To do it, you have to work at it, and I felt my responsibility was to the work: the acting, the doing better, the growing."

FIRST MARRIAGE . . . AND DIVORCE

By 1945, Lansbury had settled into her career, and her family was reunited in Los Angeles. (Louis B. Mayer even offered the twins acting contracts, but Moyna said no.) Also by then, Angela had met screen actor Richard Cromwell. She was nineteen and he was thirty-five. The handsome performer had made his screen debut in *Tol'able David* (1931) and became a leading man of 1930s features. However, by the 1940s, his career was fast on the decline. Nevertheless, he was exceedingly good looking and charming. On September 27, 1945, Angela and Richard married.

It proved to be a mistake from the start. For one thing, she had gone into the union for the wrong reasons: "I was a young woman looking for glamour and attention, and I didn't really get it. So what did I do? I got married at nineteen." For another, "Because I had matured so fast I had missed that whole coming awareness of boys and dates and the breathless excitement of being on the threshold of womanhood. That maturity welded atop the child wreaked havoc with my marriage to dear Roy [her pet name for her husband who had been born Roy Radabaugh]." Stated another way, "I was just starting out and trying to be the person that I thought the magazines and the studios expected me to be. But I couldn't pull it off."

Far more damaging to the newlyweds' relationship was the fact that Cromwell was homosexual. Not long ago, Lansbury admitted to the press, "I didn't know until after we were separated that he was gay. My first great, great romance. It was a terrible tragedy. The desperate part was that I was so in love with him." Thus, after nine months of marriage, the

Cromwells separated and divorced. However, they remained on friendly terms. When he died of cancer in October 1960, the very loyal Angela sent a large pillow of white gardenias to the mortuary. He was buried with his head resting on her pillow of flowers.

In late 1945, Angela began the legal procedure to become an American citizen, a status she achieved in 1951.

In the well-regarded Judy Garland musical, *The Harvey Girls* (1946), Angela played the icy dance hall queen who locks horns (and has a marvelous barroom brawl) with Garland. Much to her chagrin, the studio had Virginia Rees dubbed in Lansbury's song numbers because, as Angela said later, "I didn't have that deep, throaty voice that they wanted." In a far lesser feature, *The Hoodlum Saint* (1946), in which Esther Williams abandoned swimming pools for heavy dramatics, Lansbury was a blond torch singer involved with much older William Powell.

In the studio's musical extravaganza, *Till the Clouds Roll By* (1946), Angela performed "How'd You Like to Spoon with Me" on a gigantic swing. Because she was considered a character player, she was in the "also" category listed beneath the revue's main attractions (Judy Garland, Van Johnson, Dinah Shore, Lena Horne, Frank Sinatra, *et al.*).

THE ON-SCREEN DOMESTIC

It was back to celluloid domestic service when Angela was loaned to United Artists for another period drama, *The Private Affairs of Bel Ami* (1947). She played a parlor maid (what else?) drawn to the roguish George Sanders. (Ironically, the studio had earlier vetoed loaning Lansbury to Warner Bros. for a very important Bette Davis vehicle, *The Corn Is Green,* [1945], in which Angela would have played the part of a flirtatious domestic. Angela had also wanted to test for the saucy lead in *Forever Amber* [1947] at Twentieth Century-Fox, but MGM refused to heed her request.)

Returning to MGM for *If Winter Comes* (1947), Lansbury was made up and coifed to be a woman of thirty-five who makes life miserable for her stalwart husband (Walter Pidgeon) and the latter's new-found love (Deborah Kerr). Angela despised that film. Next, Angela shared screen time with Margaret O'Brien in the overly melodramatic *Tenth Avenue Angel* (1948). In a far classier venture, *State of the Union* (1948), Lansbury was the seductive forty-six-year-old daughter of a newspaper tycoon who tries to woo away a presidential candidate (Spencer Tracy) from his wife (Katharine Hepburn). Angela was excellent as the mild villainess.

Increasingly anxious to channel her screen career in more rewarding directions, Angela continuously begged the studio to give her more substantial roles. She wanted parts closer to her real-life age and ones that would allow her—at least occasionally—to be warm-hearted. Her pleas were continually ignored.

For example, when it was announced that Metro-Goldwyn-Mayer was mounting a new version of *The Three Musketeers* (1948), Angela made it known that she wanted to portray the glamorous if evil Milady de Winters. However, the studio selected Lana Turner (a much bigger box-office draw) for the key role in the costume drama, as they had earlier given Turner the part Angela tested for opposite Spencer Tracy in *Cass Timberlane* (1947). Instead, in the Technicolor *The Three Musketeers*, Angela was stuck with the subordinate part of being Queen Anne of Austria, wife of France's King Louis XIII (Frank Morgan). Looking back, Lansbury sums up, "I kept wanting to play the Jean Arthur roles, and Mr. Mayer kept casting me as a series of venal bitches. . . ."

FINDING TRUE LOVE

In 1947, actor Hurd Hatfield, who had become a good friend, invited Angela to a weekend party at a friend's house in the Ojai Valley, northwest of Los Angeles. The man who drove Angela to the gathering was another MGM contract player, Englishman Peter Pullen Shaw. He was seven years her senior and had spent several years in the British military during World War II. "We were so pleased to meet fellow countrymen that we became incredible friends very quickly." Like Lansbury, Shaw had been married previously; in fact he had a little boy, David, by that union.

They began a slow courtship. "We became friends, then lovers—and then we got married." The couple went to England intending to wed in her family church. However the vicar of the Church of England refused them since both had been divorced. Instead, the two wed in London on August 12, 1949, at St. Columba's, a Scottish Presbyterian Church. Her half sister, Isolde, was the matron of honor, while Peter's brother Edgar gave Angela away. Peter's brother Patrick was the best man. Also in attendance were Angela's mother, Moyna, and Peter's father, Walter.

Back in Hollywood, Angela returned to her (increasingly frustrating) acting assignments. However, she had a heart-to-heart talk with Peter about his stagnating performing career. She said, "Darling, I don't think you're an actor. You should do something else." He fully agreed and turned to becoming a talent agent, soon going to work for the William Morris Agency. Later, he became an executive assistant to Robert Weitman and Benjamin Thau at MGM, and still further on, would return to William Morris in an executive capacity.

Angela had a thankless role in MGM's *Red Danube* (1949), a message picture set in 1945 Vienna, with Lansbury as the junior subaltern (dressed in uniform throughout the film). Much more impressive was Paramount's biblical spectacular *Samson and Delilah* (1949). Victor Mature and Hedy Lamarr had the leads, but producer-director Cecil B. DeMille cast Angela as the aristocratic Semadar. In reviewing this big box-office hit, the *New York Times* described Lansbury as "a plump and pouting doll."

By 1950, Hollywood was feeling the pinch of competing free television. The studios economized by retrenching, cutting back their roster of players. One of Angela's final MGM pictures was *Kind Lady* (1951). In this period melodrama, Lansbury was the amoral cockney who helps Maurice Evans steal the assets of elderly Ethel Barrymore.

Set loose by MGM and no longer made secure by a weekly salary, Angela and Peter Shaw went to London. They hoped that the work scene there might be more favorable. However, after three unpromising months, they returned to California.

NO LONGER UNDER STUDIO CONTRACT

While Peter gravitated back to studio administrative duties, Angela functioned as a free-lance actress. She did episodes of TV anthology dramas and accepted film work wherever she found it. Roles in such slim vehicles as *Mutiny* (1952), *Remains to Be Seen* (1953—made way earlier at her alma mater, MGM) and *Life at Stake* (1954) might have permanently discouraged other Oscar nominees, but not Lansbury. She plowed onward. ("I didn't quit because that's not in my nature.") Meanwhile, in early 1952, Angela gave birth to Anthony Peter Shaw; eighteen months later, Deirdre Angela was born.

Angela regards her two 1955 movies as the lowest point of her screen career. *A Lawless Street* was a Randolph Scott Western in which she was a dance hall entertainer in Medicine Bend, Colorado. In *The Purple Mask*, a juvenile swashbuckling entry starring Tony Curtis, she was stuck in a subordinate role as a milliner. Looking back, she's said, "I wish I had spent more time with my family and less time making mediocre movies in those days."

Lansbury's career perked up with Danny Kaye's *The Court Jester* (1956), a high-caliber burlesque set in medieval England. In this spoof, she was delightful as the stubborn princess. The low-budget *Please Murder Me!* (1956), featuring Raymond Burr, returned Lansbury to the type of evil role she had done so well a decade earlier. Increasingly, she relied on guest-starring parts in TV dramas because, as she said, "It paid awful well and didn't take me away from home."

GIVING BROADWAY A TRY

It was British director Peter Glenville, a family friend, who broke Angela out of her career rut. He offered her a top-featured role in the Broadway version of *Hotel Paradiso* (1957). The opportunity intrigued her because, "I adore comedy. Such a change after the harpies and heavies Hollywood cast me in." Bert Lahr was top-starred in this French bedroom farce.

The period comedy barged onto Broadway on April 11, 1957, at the Henry Miller Theatre. The play and Lahr received high praise from the critics, while Angela, as the almost-bedded Marcelle, got sterling notices. The *New York Herald-Tribune* labeled Angela "ravishing" and applauded her for being "a very crisp chick with a snappish line." The comedy ran for only 108 performances. However, it taught the actress a great deal about her acting craft. It also marked the first time she and actor William Windom worked together. They would be reunited decades later when he joined the TV series *Murder, She Wrote* in 1985 in the recurring role of Cabot Cove's Dr. Seth Hazlitt.

Back in California at the Malibu home the Shaws owned, Angela found her Broadway venture had made her a more bankable screen name. In *The Long Hot Summer* (1958), starring Paul Newman and Joanne Woodward, she was the Southern hotel keeper who's been Orson Welles' mistress for years and yearns to become his wife. In complete contrast was MGM's *The Reluctant Debutante* (1958). Headlining Rex Harrison and his wife Kay Kendall, this sparkling British drawing room comedy featured Lansbury as a bitchy, snobbish aristocrat pushing her daughter into high society.

It was in mid-1960 that Angela agreed to return to the stage in *A Taste of Honey*. Her part was that of a slutty, selfish forty-year-old mom who ditches her daughter (Joan Plowright) to wed a drunken playboy (Nigel Davenport). When it opened on Broadway in October 1960, the *New York Morning Telegraph* lauded, "Angela Lansbury fairly drenches the role of the mother in perfection of characterization." (Few noted that in real life, Joan Plowright was only four years younger than Angela, her onstage mother.)

During the engagement, Angela once again sublet a Fifth Avenue apartment. This time she brought her children Anthony and Deirdre to be with her, although Peter Shaw remained on the West Coast. The show ran for 376 performances, with Lansbury leaving the cast in the spring of 1961.

While Angela had been on Broadway, she had two further movie releases. She was the widow who runs a beauty parlor and is drawn to married man Robert Preston in *The Dark at the Top of the Stairs* (1960). Far less solid was the fluffy *A Breath of Scandal* (1960), a costume picture starring Sophia Loren as a wayward princess, and Angela as a chic courtesan. These were followed by an overly low keyed drama, *Season of Passion* (1961), filmed on location in Australia.

A NEW MOVIE MOLD

Although few realized it at the time, it was an Elvis Presley musical that gave Angela a new lease on cinema life. In *Blue Hawaii* (1961), she was signed to play the singer's possessive Southern belle mother. (Actually, Elvis was only ten years her junior.) According to the actress, "The role intrigued me; it's a kind of comedy I'd never done before . . . and it takes me out of the British things."

Next, Angela was heard but *not* seen, when she dubbed in the dialogue of too heavily accented Swedish actress Ingrid Thulin in *The Four Horsemen of the Apocalypse* (1962). Then, for Angela, it was back to her new forte, the suffocating mama. In *All Fall Down* (1962), she pampers and even craves her spoiled son (Warren Beatty).

Her next feature presented her as the most horrendous mother since Medea. *The Manchurian Candidate* (1962) showcased Angela as an enemy operative (of the Russians) in America who directs her brainwashed son (Laurence Harvey) to assassinate the top presidential candidate at a Madison Square Garden rally. In this gripping picture, Lansbury was nominated for her third Academy Award, but lost the Best Supporting Actress trophy to Patty Duke (*The Miracle Worker.*) Strangely, after her acting peak in *The Manchurian Candidate,* Angela's screen career took a downward spiral. She was wasted in a Jane Fonda tearjerker (*In the Cool of the Day,* 1963).

A BROADWAY SONG-AND-DANCE STAR

When asked why she accepted the top starring role in the Broadway-bound musical *Anyone Can Whistle* (1964), Angela said, "I always fancied I had a sexy singing voice, but no one would let me use it. When *Whistle* was offered to me, I grabbed it." In this theater-of-the-absurd musical, Lansbury was cast as a small town mayor, with Lee Remick the head nurse of the local insane asylum and Harry Guardino as a practicing idealist.

Anyone Can Whistle debuted on Broadway on April 4, 1964. *Newsday* observed, "That skillful comedienne, Angela Lansbury, scores heavily in two numbers and in several scenes. However, Mr. Laurents has allowed her to press far too hard for her comic effects, so that she becomes after a while a caricature on one monotonous note." The show folded after nine performances. Soon afterward, Lansbury could be seen on-screen in *The*

World of Henry Orient (1964). In this Peter Sellers comedy, she was the adulterous mother of a fourteen-year-old, and Tom Bosley (later her *Murder, She Wrote* coplayer) was her meek spouse.

Two projects that did not come to pass for Lansbury might have moved Angela's career into fresh directions. She was to star in the London company of *Hello, Dolly!*, but production delays forced her to drop out. The other was a deal to star in the London stage, the Broadway stage and the movie version of *The Prime of Miss Jean Brodie.* The package fell apart, and Zoe Caldwell went on to gain acclaim in the Broadway version, while Maggie Smith won an Oscar for her performance in the screen adaptation.

Angela had a cameo in the biblical epic *The Greatest Story Ever Told* (1965), as Claudia, the wife of Pontius Pilate (Telly Savalas). Next, she was the manipulative widow who loses Glenn Ford to Geraldine Page in *Dear Heart* (1965). In *The Amorous Adventures of Moll Flanders* (1965), Angela was a titled lady of eighteenth century London who helps a buxom wench (Kim Novak) in her employ. Then it was back to form as the calculating mother of a 1930s movie star in *Harlow* (1965).

MAME BRINGS FAME

Anyone Can Whistle had whet Angela's appetite for another musical vehicle. Thus, her desire made her very cooperative with Broadway producers. Long before it was announced (December 15, 1965) that she would star in *Mame*, a musical version of Rosalind Russell's stage hit *Auntie Mame* (1956), she had campaigned actively for the part. It was a rare approach for Lansbury. "[Acting] has never been the driving thing with me. . . . I am strictly practical and won't lift a finger unless I get paid for it. . . . I don't indulge myself in the enjoyment of acting." Before she finally won the coveted part, she had flown to New York four times (at her own expense) to audition for director Gene Saks, composer Jerry Herman and the others.

Mame was launched on Broadway on May 24, 1966. She galvanized critics and audiences alike as swank Mame Dennis of Beekman Place who, in 1928, finds herself supervising her precocious nephew. During the course of the show, Angela did a tango, a cakewalk, and the Charleston, and modeled twenty-four costume changes. For *Mame*, she won a Tony Award as the best musical actress of the year.

Angela played *Mame* for 418 performances and then took the show on a national tour. She made sure of a lengthy engagement in Los Angeles. She wanted executives at Warner Bros.-Seven Arts, who had acquired the screen rights, to see how zesty a leading lady she was. (Unfortunately, when the movie was eventually made in 1974, it was a miscast, too old

Lucille Ball who inherited Lansbury's part. To this day, Lansbury refuses to see the movie *Mame.*)

Summing up her *Mame* experience, Angela observed, "*Mame* saved me. I would have become a second string character actress. I never had a driving show business ambition. That's why *Mame* was so important; it made me able to embody feelings I had about myself. I had this jangling feeling in the back of my head that I could do a musical. I knew I could do it, which is odd because I'm an awful stick in the mud."

Meanwhile, *Mister Buddwing,* made on location in New York in 1965, was finally released in October 1966. James Garner was the amnesiac who becomes involved with several women, including a drunken tart, Angela.

POST-*MAME* PROJECTS

As a follow-up stage vehicle to *Mame,* Angela starred in *Dear World.* It was a musicalized version of Jean Giraudoux's play *The Madwoman of Chaillot.* When the poetic/comic fable tried out in Boston in November 1968, it was found drastically wanting. However, Angela as the dotty old crone, garbed in a red wig, blackened eyes and wearing a big floppy hat, got impressive notices.

Pre-Broadway production problems continued to plague *Dear World,* and Lansbury wanted to drop out. She was persuaded to remain, part of the argument being her $11,000 weekly salary. The show bowed on Broadway on February 6, 1969, to very qualified reviews. Although she won another Tony Award, the show folded in May 1969 after only 132 performances and at a loss of $720,000.

To offset this misadventure, Angela starred in the black comedy movie *Something for Everyone* (1970), shot in Bavaria in the late summer of 1969. Lansbury had a tour-de-force part as a calculating countess down on her luck. In the Hal Prince-directed story, she is hoodwinked by an amoral, bisexual con man (Michael York) who nearly takes over her life, as well as that of her son and daughter. The R-rated feature was too arty for general consumption, but became a cult favorite in subsequent years.

The early 1970s continued to be unfortuitous for Angela. By now, she was well aware that her two teenage children increasingly were having a difficult time. Anthony, in particular, was getting more deeply involved in drugs, a situation which counseling, drug treatment, and the like did not remedy. As far back as 1966, when she was doing *Mame* on Broadway, Angela recalled, "I'd find Anthony in my dressing room, tormented, asking for an advance on his allowance. We both knew what it was for." She admits, "There was a time when I wanted to throw him out." Angela further reasoned, "Perhaps my preoccupation with my work, my success, gave them [Anthony and Deirdre] a false standard, led them to misunderstand how they fitted in, forced them to think that they somehow had to match my success."

FATE DECREES A LIFE-STYLE CHANGE

Things came to a crisis in the late summer of 1970. Angela's mother, Moyna, was suffering from cancer. (She had already lost her larynx and would die in 1975 from the disease.) Then one September day, a huge brush fire in Malibu, California, destroyed the Shaws' home.

Meanwhile, during this traumatic period, Anthony was hospitalized for an overdose of drugs. Per Lansbury, "It brought the crisis to a head. I threw aside the fancy shrinks and knew I couldn't rest, or work again, until drastic measures were taken. I had to find a place where my children could be safe and free, mentally and physically, from all the turmoil and tragedy."

Then it occurred to her that her childhood dream of one day living again in Ireland might be the answer. Angela reasoned, "It was one of the last places on earth that was fairly drug-free." Thus, the Shaws purchased a big stone farmhouse in County Cork. They took their two troubled children there. "It was one of the happiest decisions of my life. . . ." She has recalled, "The fresh air and hard work turned him into a completely different young man. Meanwhile, Deirdre apprenticed as a cook in a nearby restaurant, and studied art." Angela continued, "I took long walks with my children in the lovely Irish countryside. I seriously thought I would give up my career and just enjoy life." For a while, Shaw commuted from the U.S. to Ireland, but eventually (1972) he quit his outside business activities to concentrate on being Angela's full-time agent.

During this period of her children's recovery, Angela was involved in a pre-Broadway mishap, *Prettybelle*. The musical, staged by Gower Champion, opened and closed in Boston in early 1971. It presented Angela as a sexually obsessed Southern belle who, while a mental hospital patient, writes her memoirs. For Walt Disney Studio, she starred in a screen musical, *Bedknobs and Broomsticks* (1971), which was touted as the successor to the film company's *Mary Poppins* (1964). Unfortunately, the candy-coated new entry, in which Angela played an apprentice witch, never found its audience.

By late 1971, Angela's son was studying drama in London, and Lansbury agreed to return to the stage early the next year. This time it was the London version of Edward Albee's *All Over*, a talky drama that failed to impress theatergoers.

BACK ON BROADWAY

A year later, she was back on Broadway for the March 13, 1973, showcase *Sondheim: A Musical Tribute,* and then returned to London to star in a new British mounting of *Gypsy.* When the classic musical opened on May 29, 1973, the *London Mail* insisted, "The London musical stage belongs to only one woman from this very second; a rose by any other name is now Angela Lansbury!" The star brought the show to Broadway in September 1974, where she enjoyed a personal triumph.

Thereafter, after playing the queen to Albert Finney's *Hamlet* (1975), Angela did a 1976 tour of *Mame* in Florida. In April 1978, on Broadway, she and Michael Kermoyan took over for three weeks for Constance Towers and Yul Brynner in *The King and I.* Of this brief assignment, the star said, "I regard it as a heaven-sent opportunity to get my motor running for the next musical I'm to do."

MEAT PIES AND A TONY

The "next" proved to be *Sweeney Todd* which debuted on Broadway on March 1, 1979. It was a dark, macabre piece about cutthroats and bloody bodies and doctored-up meat pies, as well as having more operatic than musical comedy. Angela was the practical, if slovenly, Mrs. Lovett, who becomes the mistress of the demon barber of Fleet Street (Len Cariou; later George Hearn).

In performing the exhausting Stephen Sondheim score, Angela had to do coloratura and dramatic soprano singing. Her bravura performance won her another Tony Award. During the show's run, she and Peter Shaw lived in a Manhattan high-rise apartment. (Son Tony was still living at the family farmhouse in Ireland, buying and selling cattle and working in England as an actor. Deirdre, then in her mid-twenties, was a model and part-time actress.)

By this point, Angela had returned to filmmaking. She joined an all-star cast (David Niven, Bette Davis, Maggie Smith) for a screen version of Agatha Christie's *Death on the Nile* (1978). It was a stylish period whodunit with Peter Ustinov (her ex-brother-in-law) as Inspector Hercule Poirot. Then, *The Lady Vanishes* (1979), unfortunately, was a dreary remake of the classic Alfred Hitchcock thriller from 1938. Angela inherited the role so brilliantly played by Dame May Whitty in the earlier edition. Lansbury was the elderly (!) Britisher who turns out to be a spy for the Allies.

JANE MARPLE ENTERS THE SCENE

Angela made another Agatha Christie vehicle—*The Mirror Crack'd* (1980). Fitted out in heavy makeup and powdered gray hair, she was transformed into amateur sleuth Jane Marple. The accidentally campy movie—with unintentionally laughable performances by Elizabeth Taylor, Rock Hudson and Kim Novak—was not a success. Its lack of popularity halted any plans for Lansbury to perform in further Miss Marple adventures.

Failing to find a new musical comedy (plans to star in an adaptation of the movie *Sunset Boulevard* never materialized), Angela tried a comedy. In *A Little Family Business*, she was cast as a New England society matron who turns the tables on her explosively bigoted, two-timing spouse (John McMartin). The show, which featured son Anthony in a supporting role, opened and closed on Broadway in short order in late 1982.

Wanting to relight old fires, Angela agreed to a major revival of *Mame*. After an out-of-town tour, it opened in New York on July 24, 1983. Despite a solid production, the vehicle had lost the edge and surprise of the 1966 original. Moreover, now nearing sixty, Lansbury could not provide the same high-voltage performance she had done nearly twenty years before. The New York engagement was not the long-running, profitable hit anticipated.

TV OR NOT TV

At this juncture, it was becoming increasingly hard for her to find stage or motion picture roles that suited her star standing, talents and age. She found herself gravitating more and more to TV, particularly to miniseries. In *Little Gloria—Happy at Last* (1982), she had a showy role as Gertrude Vanderbilt Whitney, the aunt who challenges Gloria's mother (Lucy Gutteridge) for control of the mega-rich child. Angela received an Emmy nomination for her performance as the snob full of moral hypocrisy.

This TV success led to Lansbury reuniting with Lee Remick for the touching TV movie *The Gift of Love: A Christmas Story* (1983) and for Angela teaming with Sir Laurence Olivier in *A Talent for Murder* (1984). The latter was a below-par cable TV movie in which Angela played an eccentric, wheelchair-bound mystery writer involved in a real whodunit.

Lansbury followed this misfire with oversized cameos in two 1984 miniseries: *Lace* and *The First Olympics: Athens 1896*. By now, she had also returned to theater screens, first in the cartoon feature *The Last Unicorn* (1982), as a singing off-camera voice. In another musical, *The Pirates of Penzance* (1983), a screen adaptation of the enduring Gilbert and Sullivan operetta, she was zesty as the off-kilter nanny, Ruth. Next, she was in

Company of Wolves (1984), a very Gothic rendition of the Little Red Riding Hood fairy tale.

Having rejected offers of TV series (mostly sitcoms) for years, Angela now had a change of heart. The first script offered her was a soap opera. "I think I was to be the cook. So I called my agents and I said, 'If I'm going to make the grand step into television, I don't want to play the cook. I want to play the leading role. It's all or nothing at all.'" Another potential was to costar in a TV comedy with actor Charles Durning for highly successful television producer Norman Lear. Again, Lansbury said no.

MURDER, SHE WROTE BRINGS TV STARDOM

In 1984, when Jean Stapleton, who had just lost her husband, turned down the lead in a proposed new weekly TV series, Lansbury accepted. The role was of Jessica Fletcher, a middle-aged widow who has great success as a mystery writer and finds herself solving real-life homicides. As Lansbury admitted of her turn-about decision, "Primarily, I was motivated by ego. I wanted to play to that huge audience just once."

Murder, She Wrote premiered on CBS-TV on September 30, 1984. No one, least of all Angela, expected the weekly whodunit series to outlast its first season. However, thanks to her sturdy performance, the high caliber production values, and its time slot just after the popular *60 Minutes*, the hour-long drama series proved to be a surprise Sunday night winner.

One of the toughest adjustments for Angela doing this weekly series was to learn to pace herself properly. Midway through the first season, she admitted, "I have been running from location to location, from Seattle to Mendocino and all over Southern California. Every day I get up at 5:45 A.M., and start learning new lines to replace the ones I fell asleep memorizing the night before. This is such an insular existence—constantly thinking about this series and the lines I have to learn—that I get bored with myself."

It was not until the spring of 1986 at the end of her second series season (under a five-year contract) that Angela herself accepted that *Murder, She Wrote* was a resounding hit. She and her husband had been renting a Brentwood, California, home, but now they wanted to own a homestead. The house they chose was up a canyon in Brentwood, north of Sunset Boulevard. It was an airy, three-bedroom place, with tile floors, four fireplaces, and a swimming pool. (Angela's stepson, David, a prosperous builder, and later involved in an executive capacity on *Murder, She Wrote* and for Lansbury's production company, Corymore, lived nearby.)

As if not busy enough on her starring show, Angela thirsted for other acting outlets to stretch her talents. She was featured in a miniseries, *Rage of Angels: The Story Continues* (1986), starring Jaclyn Smith. In 1988, she headlined the dramatic TV movie *Shootdown*. It was the real-life story of a U.S. government employee demanding to know why her son's passenger plane was shot down by the Russians.

This was followed by the tender *The Shell Seekers* (1990), in which a British woman revisits her childhood haunts to find fresh meaning to her life. Angela has confided, "I went after this role, indeed I did. I could see myself there and I could see my childhood."

In the telefeature *The Love She Sought* (1991), she was a feisty spinster teacher at a Midwestern Catholic school who visits Ireland. There she receives a surprise revelation from the man with whom she has been so long corresponding. Said Lansbury of this venture, "Some of the best work I've done on TV—and it went completely by the board! They [NBC-TV] put it on a Sunday night opposite *Murder, She Wrote* and The World Series."

JESSICA FLETCHER MOONLIGHTS

The same year, 1991, Angela could be heard as the voice of Mrs. Potts, a gentle teapot (who sang the title tune) in Disney's *Beauty and the Beast*. Regarding her involvement in this smash-hit feature-length theatrical cartoon, Lansbury noted, "As a woman who has played some of the most despicable mothers in her time . . . it's a wonderful sort of coming-around for me . . . being accepted as a lovable woman on-screen." Next, Angela was showcased to good advantage in the whimsical, romantic *Mrs. 'Arris Goes to Paris* (1992), a made-for-television movie directed by son Anthony, and costarring Omar Sharif and Diana Rigg.

As if all this professional activity wasn't enough, Angela starred in a workout video *(Angela Lansbury's Positive Moves)* which later appeared in book form. Additionally, the star did TV commercials (for an aspirin manufacturer) and was active in charity work. She frequently was a host on the annual Tony Awards, and, for one year, on the Emmys. She also was active in various AIDS charities.

As *Murder, She Wrote* progressed successfully from season to season, its formula whodunit proved unbeatable. (The only fly in the ointment was that although nominated twelve times, Lansbury never won an Emmy for her work on the mystery series.) The network insured Angela's good spirits during the first five seasons by giving her an increasingly beneficial revamped contract. When her initial tenure ended in the spring of 1990, Lansbury—and everyone else—fully expected her to seek new challenges elsewhere. As such, competing NBC offered Angela a $20 million pact to move over to their fold.

However, negotiations with CBS-TV were so lucrative that Lansbury returned year after year to the adventures of Jessica Fletcher. It became an annual "game" of Lansbury announcing that she was quitting the show at season's end, and then suddenly agreeing to a revamped, lucrative pact. She almost did quit being television's Jessica Fletcher at the end of the 1991–1992 season to star in a new half-hour CBS-TV project based on the play/movie of *Driving Miss Daisy*. Plans for this half-hour comedy-drama program were later abandoned after a test script was drafted.

When *Murder, She Wrote* launched into its ninth season in the fall of 1992, it had a new executive producer—Angela Lansbury. She reasoned to *USA Today*, "After eight years, I thought darn it. I'd love to have a crack at being the selector, being the person who makes the decisions about the scripts and the look of the show."

A FAMILY AFFAIR

Beyond the financial rewards (she was earning approximately $500,000 per episode) and other perks, there was another major reason why Lansbury remained loyal to *Murder, She Wrote*. The hit show had become a family affair. Peter Shaw was her personal advisor/agent, while son Anthony, married and a father, rose from dialogue director to frequent episode director on the program. Stepson David, now a divorced parent, headed Angela's Corymore Productions which coproduced the show. Lansbury's brother, Bruce, an established TV executive in his own right, was both a producer and frequent scripter on *Murder, She Wrote*. Later, Angela's nephew, David (who married and later divorced actress Ally Sheedy) was a frequent guest star on the series.

As for daughter Deirdre, by the early 1990s she and her Italian husband, Vincenzo Dattarra, who had owned a restaurant in Rome, had moved to Los Angeles where they opened an eatery, Positano, in Santa Monica.

On January 1, 1993, Angela was the grand marshal of the 104th Tournament of Roses Parade. That December, she joined other celebrities who honored Stephen Sondheim, one of the recipients of the televised The Kennedy Center Honors. A few weeks earlier, at the Beverly Hilton Hotel, Angela had received the American Ireland Fund's 1993 Heritage Award.

THE TENTH SEASON MILESTONE

In early 1994, as she concluded filming her tenth season of *Murder, She Wrote*, Angela made a pact for two TV films for the CBS network. One would be *Mrs. 'Arris Goes to New York*, to be directed by son Anthony. The other picture would be based on short stories by Ray Sipherd. In mid-May 1994, having already filmed a few episodes for the 1994–1995 *Murder,*

She Wrote season, Angela underwent replacement surgery on her left hip. The two-hour operation was to correct a problem that had been plaguing Angela for years and, in recent times, had been exceedingly painful. Hardly had she revived from the surgery than Lansbury was boasting, "The surgery may slow me down, but it isn't going to stop me! . . ." She added, "If I need a cane for the first few shows, the writers will just write it in."

In June of 1994, Angela was made a Commander of the British Empire. That same month, *TV Guide,* in a poll of cast and crew of TV series, named Angela the "Best-Loved Star in Hollywood" who's "quick to compliment good work, and she pays attention to details that make people feel special." The magazine ended its profile on "heavenly" Angela with the query, "Has anybody thought of turning this woman into a miniseries?" Later in the summer of 1994, Lansbury and Shaw flew to their home in Ireland, where she recuperated from the hip surgery before returning to her TV series filming. In November of that year, Peter Shaw underwent double bypass and heart valve replacement surgery at a Santa Monica, California, hospital. For three weeks, production on *Murder, She Wrote* was shut down, so that Angela and the family could be at his side at St. John's Hospital.

During its eleventh season on the air, *Murder, She Wrote* dipped out of the top ten most-watched TV series on the air, falling to position twelve or sometimes thirteen in the weekly rating. It was certainly no cause for network alarm. However, at the time, CBS-TV was launching a new attack to recapture the much-prized youth segment of TV viewers. Thus, in late May 1995, Lansbury received unexpected news—her series would be *moved* to Thursday evenings so that the network's comedy *Cybill* with Cybill Shepherd could have a Sunday berth. *Murder, She Wrote* was now scheduled to air opposite *Friends,* a twentysomething comedy that had tied with the whodunit program for eighth spot in the 1993–1994 season and was constantly gaining in popularity. "I'm shattered," Angela told the *Los Angeles Times'* Rick Du Brow of the unceremonious shift. "I just felt so disappointed that after all the years we had Sunday night at eight, suddenly it didn't mean anything. It was like gone with the wind."

Already committed to the show's twelfth season, Angela carried on in trouper fashion. However, in going against the increasingly trendy *Friends* on Thursday evenings, *Murder, She Wrote* was trounced in the audience ratings. It often ranked *beneath* the top fifty most popular shows on the air. Interestingly, for the last four episodes of *Murder, She Wrote's* final season, CBS-TV, without ever officially admitting it had made a programming misjudgment, repositioned *Murder, She Wrote* back to its traditional Sunday night time spot. Speaking for his stepmother, David Shaw told the *New York Post,* "I suppose in a way we feel vindicated by the fact that it's done so well when it's been back on Sunday night." He added, "It's no secret Angie was unhappy with the move [to Thursdays] and felt disconnected from her audience. I suppose we were all very annoyed, but she got over that very quickly." He insisted that Lansbury "doesn't have any bitter feelings" regarding the contretemps with CBS.

On April 11, 1996, twelve years exactly from the first day of shooting on *Murder, She Wrote*, the series wrapped up production of its weekly episodes at Universal Studio lot in Los Angeles. Regarding the finale to the weekly grind, Lansbury has described, "It was the most devastating experience that I've ever had to go through. . . . I got through it, heaven knows how. I felt so cut off, so bereft that I couldn't imagine that it could ever be over after twelve years. . . . So many friends . . . a family." The last first-run sixty-minute episode ran on May 19, 1996. In many ways, it was the end of an era. (Ironically, when the Emmy nominations for 1995 were announced in July 1996, Angela received her sixteenth overall and twelfth and final *Murder, She Wrote* Emmy bid in the Lead Actress in a Drama Series category. She reacted with, "This is my last chance, my last hurrah. . . . I'm very proud to be nominated again." At the September 1996 Emmy Awards, Angela once again lost out in the prize race. The industry slight rankled her so deeply—along with the past hurt of having lost out to star in the movie version of *Mame*—that when interviewed on TV's *60 Minutes* in November 1996, Lansbury broke into tears during her taped segment with reporter Lesley Stahl.

However, Angela Lansbury has no intention of retiring. As part of her ongoing CBS-TV pact, she filmed *Mrs. Santa Claus*, a made-for-television movie musical with a score by *Mame's* Jerry Herman. The old-fashioned "tune fest" costarred Charles Durning as Santa and Michael Jeter as the head elf. (The whimsical two-hour show aired on December 8, 1996, and did extremely well in the ratings. Lansbury gave her usual solid, professional performance which compensated for the rather mundane score and constricted choreography.)

In her acting future, Angela still hopes to shoot the long-delayed sequel to *Mrs. 'Arris Goes to Paris*. Meanwhile, she has contributed her voice to an animated, feature-length version of *Anastasia* (1997), based on the play and the 1956 movie starring Ingrid Bergman and Yul Brynner. Angela is to be heard as the Dowager Empress. And then, of course, there are the projected *Murder, She Wrote* TV movies slated to begin production in mid 1997. (Lansbury told the *Los Angeles Times* in December 1996 that she plans to do the two-hour episodes ". . . as long as I can keep walking. Contractually, we are obligated to do two a year for two years and we will see how it goes. If I can handle more and they want more, then we will do it.") Meanwhile, her Corymore Productions has signed a development deal with Universal Television for other potential projects.

As a balance to work, there are the periods that Angela and her husband spend in Ireland at their new home. (The Shaws had sold the old Parsonage in 1979 when they returned to California on a full-time basis.) In late July 1996, Angela, along with Edward Asner, Charles Kuralt and five others were elected into the Academy of Television Arts & Sciences' Hall of Fame. The induction ceremony took place at the institution's facility at Disney-MGM Studios (near Orlando, FL) on October 5, 1996.

ANALYZING THE PAST TO SEE INTO THE FUTURE

Evaluating her acting technique, which has been such an anchor over the decades, she says, "I'm a voyeur, a sponge. The qualities which I imbue into my characters are absorbed from other people. They aren't me, Angie. For somebody in show business, I don't play the 'game,' if you know what I mean. I'm not 'show biz' to any degree at all unless it is called for. If it is, then I will entertain you in that fashion. For charity or promotion, those are the times when one is expected to become this dizzy, glamorous person. And I do it, but it isn't really me, you see."

Looking back on her family life, she admits, "I guess my children got the short end of the stick, not my husband. The marriage has always been sound, simply by mutual awareness—he of my requirements, freedoms . . . and I'm not talking of sexual freedoms, but time spent in pursuit of being myself as an actress, not just a star. He has been of inordinate help, and my versatility stems from him. When I wanted to go off to garden in the country, he would be the one who kept my nose to the grindstone, the one who would advise me to stretch my talents in a challenging role. It has been a marvelous, strong relationship."

Further regarding her supportive spouse, she says, "I feel very blessed that we've managed to come this far. At home I've always had total support, total reassurance. I think that's why I've managed to get so much work done. I suppose if I'd had a lot of romances and marriages and so forth, I couldn't have done so much."

As to her active life-style, she explains, "When I'm busy I seem to find so much more time to do the things I enjoy. I love to cook and do housework. I'm the kind of person who enjoys doing the dishes. . . . When I come home at night I relax by cooking for myself and my husband, rather than have a tray brought to me in bed." She does acknowledge, "I'm more disorganized [at home]. I'm driven to do twenty different things at a time. Like so many women who are high achievers, one never feels they've done enough at home." Regardless, her philosophy is, "It's terribly important that women of my age maintain their vigor and their energy. I have a regimen; I have a point of view and a very positive attitude."

As to the continued importance of acting in her life, "I need it desperately. I need that outlet in my life. I need to perform very much or I'm just not happy. I often try to describe what it is that I want to share with the audience. I want to achieve those high, screaming moments in theater which you can't always hit but which, when you do, there's no experience in the world that can match it."

Lansbury acknowledges one nontheatrical goal: "My last great ambition in life is to create a garden from scratch. I want to prepare the soil and just watch my flowers grow. One of the problems in my business is that we are all gypsies. But stability is the thing I yearn for most. To be a good gardener you have to stick with your plants."

Looking ahead, Angela says, "I want to maintain my career through the latter years of my life on my own terms. I don't want to become an old actress who occasionally works. And I don't want to work nonstop forever; I want to have time to do some of the things I haven't done, like travel." She sums up the future with "I love acting. I love to be busy. . . . I love what I do. I hope I'll never have to stop."

ABOUT THE SUPPORTING CAST REGULARS

Tom Bosley

(Sheriff Amos Tupper)

He was born on October 1, 1927, in Chicago, Illinois. During World War II he served in the U.S. Navy. While attending De Paul University in Chicago, Tom made his stage debut in *Our Town* in 1947 with the Canterbury Players at the Fine Arts Theatre. His off-Broadway bow came in 1955 in a production of *Thieves' Carnival.* Tom's breakthrough stage part was as New York's Mayor Fiorello H. LaGuardia in the long-running Broadway musical *Fiorello!* (1959) for which he won a Tony Award. Other Broadway assignments included *Nowhere to Go But Up* (1962), *Catch Me If You Can* (1965) and *The Education of H*Y*M*A*N K*A*P*L*A*N* (1968).

Bosley's first feature film was *Love with a Proper Stranger* (1964), followed by parts in such movies as *The World of Henry Orient* (1964—in which he played Angela Lansbury's husband), *Yours, Mine and Ours* (1968), *Gus* (1976), *O'Hara's Wife* (1982), *Million Dollar Mystery* (1987), *Wicked Stepmother* (1989—with Bette Davis) and the 1996-made *Big Foot: The Long Journey Home.*

Tom started in TV in 1952. His initial series work was on *The Debbie Reynolds Show* (1968–1970), followed by such vehicles as *The Sandy Duncan Show* (1972) and *Wait Till Your Father Gets Home* (1972–1974). From 1974–1983, the rotund performer played Howard Cunningham, the harassed hardware store owner coping with family, boarders and friends in the classic sitcom *Happy Days.* It insured his position in pop culture/TV history. Meanwhile, Tom played Benjamin Franklin both on *The Bastard* (1978) miniseries and its follow-up, *The Rebels* (1979).

After being with *Murder, She Wrote* from 1984 to 1988, playing the congenial, none-too-bright Sheriff Amos Tupper, Bosley left to star as Father Frank Dowling, the inquisitive Chicago priest, on the lighthearted series *Father Dowling Mysteries* (1989–1991). His more recent TV movies include *Fire and Rain* (1989) and *The Love Boat: A Valentine Voyage* (1990). In addition, Bosley had a guest starring role on the revived *Burke's Law* TV series.

Tom's most recent stage assignment was in the hit Broadway stage version of *Beauty and the Beast* (1994), playing Belle's dad, Maurice. He repeated the role in the subsequent extended Los Angeles stage edition of *Beauty and the Beast* which closed in mid-1996.

Bosley married Jane Eliot on March 8, 1962, and they have one child, Amy (who now has three children). Two years after Jane's death from cancer in 1978, Tom wed actress Patricia Carr on December 21, 1980.

Ron Masak

(Sheriff Mort Metzger)

He was born July 1, 1936, in Chicago, Illinois, the son of a salesman/musician and a mother (Mildred Alice Rudy) who was a merchandise buyer. Ron attended Chicago City College, as well as studying theater at the local C.T.C. and the Drama Guild. After a stint in the army as an entertainer, he made his acting debut with the Drama Guild in Chicago in *Stalag 17* in 1954. From 1962–1966, Ron was the resident leading man with the Candlelight Dinner Theatre in Summit, Illinois.

Masak's movie debut occurred in Rock Hudson's *Ice Station Zebra* (1967), followed by such movies as *Daddy's Gone A-Hunting* (1968), *Tora! Tora! Tora!* (1970), *Evel Knievel* (1971) and *Harper Valley, P.T.A.* (1979).

On television, Masak has done nearly 2,000 TV commercials, including many for Budweiser Beer, voice-overs for Vlasic Pickles, and several as a look-a-like to Lou Costello of the comedy team Abbott and Costello. Ron's dramatic appearances include his debut on *The Twilight Zone* (1959) and, later, *Police Story* (1976, 1977), and *Rockford Files* (1977), among others. He has been in such TV movies as *Heat of Anger* (1972), *In the Glitter Palace* (1977), *Pleasure Cove* (1979), *World War III* (1982) and *The Neighborhood* (1982).

Ron's initial TV series as a regular were *The Good Guys* (1968–1970) and *Love Thy Neighbor* (1973). In 1976, Masak starred in an unsold CBS-TV series pilot, *Jeremiah of Jacob's Neck,* in which he played a police chief who moves into a New England mansion with his family and must cope with the troublesome ghost (Keenan Wynn) of a smuggler. By the time Masak was cast on *Murder, She Wrote* in 1989 in the recurring role of Cabot Cove's new sheriff, Mort Metzger, he had already made two appearances on the whodunit series in nonassociated guest roles. In the 1985 episode "Footnote to Murder," he played a New York City police lieutenant, and in 1987's "No Accounting for Murder," also set in Manhattan, he was cast as a duped investor.

Masak married Kay Frances Knebes on September 23, 1961. They have six children: Tammy, Debbie, Kathy, Mike, Bobby and Christine. Masak's daughter Kathy (now billed as Kathryn Masak) appeared in small guest roles on two episodes of *Murder, She Wrote* during its twelfth and final season (1995-1996).

Keith Michell

(Dennis Stanton)

He was born on December 1, 1928, in Adelaide, South Australia. The son of a furniture manufacturer, Keith was educated at Adelaide Teachers' College (School of Arts and Crafts) and at Adelaide University. For a time he taught art.

Michell made his first stage appearance at the Playbox Theatre in Adelaide in *Lover's Leap* (1947). Later, in England, he trained at the Old Vic Theater School. As a member of the Young Vic Theater Company, he played Bassanio in *The Merchant of Venice* (1950–1951). He made his West End debut in the musical *And So to Bed* (1951). Keith was a member of the repertory theater company at Stratford-on-Avon in 1954 and, two years later, joined the Old Vic Company. There he performed in a number of productions, including *Much Ado About Nothing* and *Anthony & Cleopatra.* His first Broadway stage appearance was as Nestor/Oscar in *Irma La Douce* (1960). Thereafter, Michell was a frequent performer on both sides of the Atlantic, notable for appearances on Broadway in *Man of La Mancha* (1969) and *Abelard and Heloise* (1971).

Keith's many movie roles include *True as a Turtle* (1957), *The Gypsy and the Gentleman* (1958), *Hell Fire Club* (1961), *Prudence and the Pill* (1968), *Moments* (1973), *Julius Caesar* (1979) and *The Deceivers* (1988). Among his several TV roles have been key parts in *The Six Wives of Henry VIII* (for which he won an Emmy in 1972), *An Ideal Husband* and *Dear Love.* He is the illustrator of a book of poems and has had frequent exhibitions of his paintings. Keith has also recorded several albums, including *Captain Beaky and His Band* (Vol. 1 and 2). In 1987, Michell authored a cookbook entitled *Practically Macrobiotic.*

Keith married Jeanette Laura Sterke, an actress and art instructor, on October 18, 1957. They have two children: Paul Joseph and Helena Elizabeth.

William Windom

(Dr. Seth Hazlitt)

He was born on September 28, 1923, in New York City. The son of an architect, William attended several educational institutions, including Williams College, the Citadel, Antioch College and the University of Kentucky. During World War II, he served in the U.S. Army with the 508th parachute infantry. After the armistice, he studied at both Fordham University and Columbia University in New York City.

Windom made his stage debut as the Duke of Gloucester in a production of *Richard III* in Biarritz, France, in 1937. Back in the United States, he was in the off-Broadway production of *Henry VIII* in 1940 and, after years of stock work, appeared on Broadway—as a telephone voice—in *A Girl Can Tell* (1953). Additional Broadway appearances included *Mademoiselle Colombe* (1954), *The Grand Prize* (1955) and *Double in Hearts* (1956). Still later, William toured in one-man shows about humorist James Thurber and World War II combat reporter Ernie Pyle.

Windom's principal theatrical film appearances include *To Kill a Mockingbird* (1962), *The Americanization of Emily* (1964), *Hour of the Gun* (1967), *The Detective* (1968), *Escape from the Planet of the Apes* (1971), *Echoes of a Summer* (1976), *Grandview U.S.A.* (1984), *Planes Trains and Automobiles* (1986), *Sommersby* (1993), and *Miracle on 34th Street* (1994).

William's TV debut was in the title role of *Richard III* on an anthology show in 1950. A tremendously prolific television actor, his series before *Murder, She Wrote* have included *The Farmer's Daughter* (1962–1965), *My World and Welcome to It* (1969–1970—for which he won an Emmy Award), *The Girl with Something Extra* (1973–1974) and *Brothers and Sisters* (1979).

Windom first appeared on *Murder, She Wrote* in the April 1985 episode "Funeral at Fifty-Mile." He was cast as one of the four heavies in that segment. The next fall, as of episode #24 ("Joshua Peabody Died Here—Possibly"), he joined the whodunit series as a regular, in his recurring role of irascible Dr. Seth Hazlitt. (William had first worked with Angela Lansbury in 1957 when he appeared with her in the Broadway comedy *Hotel Paradiso.)* He dropped out of *Murder, She Wrote* in 1990 to become a key member of the TV sitcom *Parenthood.* That program, however, lasted only three months. Thereafter, as of episode #141 ("Family Doctor") in January 1991, Windom rejoined *Murder, She Wrote* in his occasional part of Doc Hazlitt. He has been in such recent made-for-television movies as *Velvet* (1984), *Dennis the Menace* (1986), *There Must Be a Pony* (1986), *Back to Hannibal: The Return of Tom*

Sawyer and Huckleberry Finn (1990) and *Attack of the 50-Foot Woman* (1993).

Windom has been married five times, most recently (December 31, 1975) to writer Patricia Veronica Tunder. William has six children: Rachel, Heather, Juliet, Hope, Rebel and Russell.

SEASON ONE

1984–1985

1. "The Murder of Sherlock Holmes"

(9/30/84) 120 mins.

Director: Corey Allen **Story:** Richard Levinson, William Link and Peter S. Fischer **Teleplay:** Fischer

Regular: Angela Lansbury (Jessica Fletcher)

Recurring Characters: Paddy Edwards (Lois Hoey); Arthur Hill (Preston Giles); Michael Horton (Grady Fletcher)

Guest Law Enforcers: Ned Beatty (Police Chief Roy Gunderson); Hap Laurence (Young Deputy); Beau Starr (Cop on the Beat)

Guest Cast: Eddie Barth (Bernie); Peter Boyle (Marvin, the Talent Agent); Stanley Brock (Marvin); Jessica Browne (Kitty Donovan); David Byrd (Davis); Dan Chambers (New Holvang Cab Driver); Bert Convy (Peter Brill); Russell Curry (Black Youth); Herbert Edelman (George, the Bus Driver); Richard Erdman (Eggman); Donald Elson (Bookstore Owner); Jay Fenichel (Celturi); Anne Lloyd Francis (Louise McCallum); Andy Garcia (1st Tough); Ellen Greenwood (Murlie); John Hancock (Daniel, the Train Porter); Billie Hayes (Peter Pan at the Party); Jimmy Joyce (Tom, the Building Security Guard); Brian Keith (Caleb McCallum); Larry McCormick (TV Reporter); Ken Olfson (TV Book Critic); Tricia O'Neil (Ashley Vickers); Cathy Paine (Young Woman); Dennis Patrick (Dexter Baxendale); Anne Ramsey (Derelict Woman on Bus); Raymond St. Jacques (Local Doctor); Kat Sawyer-Young (Feminist Interviewer); Paula Victor (Agnes Peabody); Danny Wells (Talk Show Host); Sally Young (Performer); Daniel Zippi (Mailman)

The Settings: Cabot Cove, Maine; New York City; New Holvang, New York

The Case: Widowed Jessica Fletcher is an avid reader of murder mysteries. Now only an occasional (substitute) English teacher at Cabot Cove High School, she writes a whodunit, *The Corpse Danced at Midnight*, strictly for her own amusement. However, her well-meaning nephew, Grady, a struggling young accountant in New York City, brings the manuscript to the attention of Manhattan-based Covington House Press. Much to Jessica's surprise, that company's president, Preston Giles, publishes the manuscript.

When her novel becomes an overnight best-seller, Jessica takes the train to Manhattan to promote her book on TV and radio talk shows. Giles, who takes an immediate romantic interest in Mrs. Fletcher, invites her to his country estate in New Holvang for a "come-as-your-favorite-fictional-character" costume ball. Jessica, emotionally drawn to her publisher, accepts the offer.

At the party she dresses as Cinderella's godmother, while Giles dons the outfit of the Count of Monte Cristo. Among the many others at the festivities is Caleb McCallum, a vicious tycoon. He owns a chain of fast food restaurants, for which Grady Fletcher is a corporate headquarters accountant. During the evening, Caleb's unhappy wife, Louise, is infuriated to see Ashley Vickers, McCallum's former mistress, at the gala. (Later, the drunken Louise angrily drives off into the night.) Yet another invitee is off-Broadway producer Peter Brill.

In the early morning after the lavish party, Jessica, who has been out jogging, finds a corpse floating—facedown—in Giles' swimming pool. Although clothed in Caleb's Sherlock Holmes costume, the victim proves to be Dexter Baxendale, a sleazy New York private investigator. As police chief Roy Gunderson determines—with more than a little assist from the astute Mrs. Fletcher—no one had heard the fatal shots fired because of a nearby airfield. The constant sonic booms that emanate from there sound very much like gunfire, so no one had paid any attention to the real shots.

Jessica returns to the Big Apple and quickly decides she belongs back in Cabot Cove. However, she keeps getting drawn back into the Baxendale murder case. Meanwhile, Gunderson appears on the urban scene. Although out of his jurisdiction, his pride demands that he explore the homicide case further. And, because he respects Mrs. Fletcher's powers of observation, he frequently turns to her for advice. Later, going aboard McCallum's yacht *(The Chowderking)*, Gunderson discovers the skipper's corpse among the stored sails. Finding the mogul's murderer will not be easy, because, as one observer already noted of Caleb, "Half the country had reason to kill him. The other half didn't know him."

Before long, due to circumstantial evidence, Grady is arrested for McCallum's murder. To clear her nephew, Jessica traipses in and around Manhattan (which, on one occasion, results in her being mugged). She also goes by cab to Bayside, Long Island, to check out clues at a yacht club. The trail leads to Ashley, who, besides once dallying with Caleb, worked at the company's headquarters. The path also takes the New England matron to the Serendipity Theatre where Brill, another likely suspect, is casting his new show. Finally, the evidence draws Jessica back to New Holvang and the scene of the initial homicide. There, in a near-deadly encounter, she confronts the killer.

Highlights: Because the plot has modest Jessica becoming an instant celebrity, there is ample opportunity for a study in contrasts. One minute she is a Cabot Cove (ex)school teacher wearing tweed skirts, cardigans sweaters and pedaling around the coastal Maine town on her bicycle. The next, as a hot new author, she is the smartly dressed darling of the TV talk show circuit. Very quickly, she is caught up in a whirl of yachts, costume parties and a nightmarish round of discovering dead bodies.

Once in the Big Apple, new elements rapidly enter Jessica's life. Although a contented widow, she responds romantically to her charming publisher.

Also, as would become customary in the weekly episodes, civilian Jessica is partnered with a local law enforcer. Here her cohort is police chief Roy Gunderson. At first, he scoffs at her sleuthing skills because (1) she is "merely" a successful novelist and *not* a professional law enforcer and (2) she is a woman. However, as she would demonstrate weekly thereafter, Jessica has superb "real-life" detection skills beyond her literary creativity. Her deductive skills eventually earn her Gunderson's admiration.

Other elements that would continue throughout the *Murder, She Wrote* series were the running gags and humorous moments woven into each episode. Here, it's Jessica's effort to leave New York City. Twice, she reaches the station and boards the home-bound train. However, each time—as Daniel the porter wryly observes—something prevents Mrs. Fletcher from remaining aboard.

Another aspect of this premiere segment are the several scenes that focus on Mrs. Fletcher dispensing folksy advice and home remedies to sophisticated urban types, cynical city dwellers, *et al.* They represent both character development and comic relief. As the series progressed through its first years, these countrified ways of Mrs. Fletcher would be downplayed, and eventually, she would transform into a very polished, globe-trotting person.

Additionally, as happens now with Preston Giles and would occur occasionally in later installments, Jessica encounters (potential) romance. Typically, as she does here, she eventually brushes off the advances. Here, she reasons to her publisher, "This is all moving too fast for a widow lady from Maine." In future episodes, it would be her loyalty to the memory of her late husband, Frank, that makes her reject any nonplatonic relationships.

Still further on in the series, when she has become an international celebrity famed for best-sellers and crime-solving, she is a self-sufficient notable who has no place in her full life for domestic responsibilities. (And, of course, having no marital ties allows the unencumbered Mrs. Fletcher to pursue new [weekly] adventures at a moment's notice.)

Trivia: Because this episode was both the pilot and series' premiere of *Murder, She Wrote,* it was allotted a lengthy two-hour time period and a higher budget for guest stars and production values. Later, in trimming the footage to manageable size, some roles were (greatly) diminished. For example, the part of the New Holvang physician/coroner (played by well-established actor Raymond St. Jacques), ended as a walk-on in the final print. Peter Boyle (as the crummy talent agent, Marvin) did not fare much better.

Michael Horton made the first of several appearances as Jessica Fletcher's nephew, a naive young accountant who is constantly losing his job and always falling in love with pretty young women. He was seen previously as Harvey Winchell on *The Eddie Capra Mysteries* (1978–1979).

As would also become habit, many of the segment's guest stars—including Bert Convy and Raymond St. Jacques—would reappear in later series installments in contrasting roles. One of them, Herbert Edelman (1930–1996) would be especially noteworthy in his future occasional recurring part as New York City police lieutenant Artie Gelber. On the other hand, Arthur Hill (who had several TV series on his resume: *Owen Marshall, Counselor at Law, Glitter,* etc.), would resurface on *Murder, She Wrote* in 1990's "The Return of Preston Giles" (#137), again playing the sophisticated Manhattan publisher. Bert Convy (1933–1991) had won an Emmy as Best Host of a Game Show in 1977 for *Tattletales.* On *Rawhide,* Raymond St. Jacques (1930–1990) played the mess wagon cook Solomon King. Brian Keith was a veteran of several TV series: *Crusader, Family Affair, Hardcastle & McCormick,* etc. Ned Beatty's first series work was a sitcom, *Szysznyk* (1977–1978). John Hancock's teleseries credits would include *Hardcastle & McCormick* and *Houston Knights,* among others.

To be noted in the cast ensemble is Anne Ramsey, best known for the title role in *Throw Momma from the Train* (1987), in a bit as a bag lady on the bus driven by Herbert Edelman. In the sequence in which Jessica Fletcher is (nearly) mugged, the first thug is played by Andy Garcia, who would go on to be Oscar-nominated for *The Godfather, Part III* (1990) and make such other features as *When a Man Loves a Woman* (1994), and *Things to Do in Denver When You're Dead* (1995).

2. "Deadly Lady"

(10/7/84) 60 mins.

Director: Corey Allen **Teleplay:** Peter S. Fischer

Regulars: Angela Lansbury (Jessica Fletcher); Tom Bosley (Sheriff Amos Tupper)

Recurring Character: Claude Akins (Captain Ethan Cragg)

Guest Law Enforcer: Carol Swarbrick (Deputy Emma)

Guest Cast: Robert Beecher (Elizah Cobb, the Mortician); Tom Bower (Jonathan Bailey, Editor of the *Cabot Cove Gazette*); Doran Clark (Nancy Earl); Howard Duff (Ralph [Stephen Earl]); Marilyn Hassett (Maggie Earl); Richard Hatch (Terry Jones); Anne Lockhart (Grace Earl Lamont); John Petlock (Nils Andersen); Dack Rambo (Brian Shelby); Cassie Yates (Lisa Earl Shelby)

The Setting: Cabot Cove, Maine

The Case: A yacht from Bridgeport, Connecticut, seeks refuge from a hurricane at Cabot Cove. According to the boat's passengers—sisters Nancy, Maggie, Grace and Lisa—their father, Stephen Earl, was swept overboard and lost during the storm. When local Sheriff Amos Tupper investigates the case, he is perplexed because no body can be found.

Meanwhile, Earl turns up in town disguised as a hobo named Ralph and does handyman's work for Jessica Fletcher in exchange for food. He admits his true identity, and having provided adequately for his daughters, he intends to see America on his own. However, he is later found shot to death on a deserted piece of the town's ocean front.

Suspicion falls on the deceased's four now-wealthy daughters: drab Maggie, who self-sacrificingly kept house for her dad and who later insists that she killed him; Grace, who blamed her father for breaking up her marriage; Nancy, whose former beau, Terry Jones, had once been bought off by Stephen, but who now has mysteriously turned up in Cabot Cove; and Lisa, who is constantly bickering with her grasping spouse, Brian.

The perplexed sheriff, aided by Jessica and crusty Captain Ethan Cragg—who owns charter fishing boats—combine forces to solve the mystery.

Highlights: Still defining Jessica Fletcher's character for TV viewers, this episode demonstrates the depth of the resourceful woman. When not pounding out chapters of her latest murder mystery on her manual typewriter, she maintains her house, jogs daily and runs errands on her trusty bicycle. She also plays frequent host to gruff townsman Ethan Cragg, whose knowledge of the sea and weather conditions prove useful to sleuthing Jessica. (She and Ethan enjoy occasional deep-sea fishing excursions together.)

In this episode, gracious Jessica is so taken by her temporary helper, Stephen Earl, that she gives him her late husband's favorite meerschaum pipe. She also dispenses advice to friends and strangers alike.

By this segment, Jessica is not only a prominent mystery writer, but also has a growing reputation for solving real-life crimes. As such, Amos Tupper, Cabot Cove's not-so-swift law enforcer, welcomes the chance to utilize Jessica's detecting skills. A born diplomat, she leads slow-thinking Amos in the right direction, but allows him to believe he is controlling the investigation.

Trivia: This episode introduces two new recurring characters: Claude Akins as brusque Captain Cragg, who has a possible romantic interest in Jessica, and Tom Bosley's amiable but rather inept sheriff, who is better at snacking and gossiping than in ferreting out criminals. While Sheriff Tupper's staff are mostly men, this segment provided a one-shot appearance by Carol Swarbrick as Deputy Emma.

This was the second and final series segment directed by Corey Allen, a veteran character actor. In future seasons, the *Cabot Cove Gazette* would have several other editors and/or owners beyond Tom Bower's Jonathan Bailey.

Howard Duff (1917–1990) made a name in 1940s radio starring as private eye Sam Spade. Screen jobs included *Brute Force* (1947), *Naked City* (1948), *Women's Prison* (1954—with his actress wife Ida Lupino), *Kramer vs. Kramer* (1979), *No Way Out* (1987). Claude Akins (1918–1994), from Nelson, Georgia, had been the (co)lead in several TV series, among which were *Movin' On* (1974–1976) and *Legmen* (1984).

Richard Hatch replaced Michael Douglas as Karl Malden's partner for the last season (1976–1977) of *Streets of San Francisco* and later participated on *Battlestar Galactica* (1978–1979). Anne Lockhart, the granddaughter of actors Gene and Kathleen Lockhart and the daughter of actress June Lockhart, had also costarred on *Battlestar Galactica,* playing Sheba. The career of Dack Rambo (1941–1994) included daytime TV soap operas (*All My Children, Another World*) and such series as *Sword of Justice* (1978–1979).

3. "Birds of a Feather"

(10/14/84) 60 mins.

Director: John Llewellyn Moxey **Teleplay:** Robert E. Swanson

Regular: Angela Lansbury (Jessica Fletcher)

Recurring Characters: Jeff Conaway (Howard Griffin); Genie Francis (Victoria Brandon)

Guest Law Enforcer: Harry Guardino (Lieutenant Floyd Novak)

Guest Cast: Brian Avery (Master of Ceremonies); Robin Bach (Maitre d'); Tony Ballen (Waiter); Bart Braverman (Bill Patterson); Dick Gautier (Mike Dupont); Herndon Jackson (Waiter #2); Gabe Kaplan (Freddy York); Martin Landau (Al Drake); Carol Lawrence (Candice Drake); John O'Leary (Minister); Gary Pagett (Security Guard); William Edward Phipps (Charlie); Barbara Rhoades (Barbara Stevenson); Nick Savage (Leather Guy)

The Setting: San Francisco, California

The Case: By now the author of several successful murder mysteries, Jessica is promoting her latest novel in San Francisco. While in the Bay City, she visits her niece, Victoria Brandon. The latter is puzzled because her fiancé, Howard Griffin, a one-time struggling actor, claims to be too busy selling life insurance to find time for her.

One night, Vicki takes Aunt Jessica to the L'Campion Club for dinner and to see ventriloquist Freddy York perform. The evening goes awry when the cabaret's sleazy owner, Al Drake, is shot. A woman is apprehended fleeing from the backstage murder scene and proves to be Howard—dressed in drag! He explains that he had secretly given up his sales job to return to show business, albeit temporarily as a female impersonator. His story does not impress grumpy police detective Lieutenant Floyd Novak who books him on a murder charge.

Convinced that Howard is not guilty, Jessica sets out to prove his innocence so that he and Vicki can marry. In the process, Jessica uncovers several legitimate suspects: Freddy York, who connived to break his long-term contract with the deceased so he could accept a lucrative Las Vegas booking; the victim's discontented widow, Candice, who has been having an affair with club performer Mike Dupont; and Bill Patterson, Freddy's unscrupulous agent.

Highlights: Jessica has ample opportunity to be a doting aunt. She not only plays mediator between her neglected niece and the latter's fiancé, but she also offers the couple a free trip to Hawaii. However, her "meddling" presence is less welcome to Lieutenant Novak, who wonders aloud, "What is there about that woman that makes me nervous?"

By now the segment finale was frozen in format to contain Jessica's confrontation with the suspect(s): once the killer has been tricked into revealing his/her guilt, the culprit confesses—with an accompanying flashback—as to how and why the homicide(s) took place. The episode coda had also been standardized with a final light moment in which Jessica is caught smiling and/or surprised in freeze-frame at an amusing turn of event involving fellow characters.

Trivia: Angela Lansbury and Harry Guardino (1925–1995) had appeared together in the short-lived Broadway musical *Anyone Can Whistle* (1964). Guardino would return in several subsequent *Murder, She Wrote* episodes. Genie Francis had gained TV fame in the early 1980s as Laura on the daytime soap opera *General Hospital.* Jeff Conaway had been seen as another would-be actor when he played cabbie Bobby Wheeler on the TV sitcom *Taxi* (1978–1981). Dick Gautier, who had starred as rock star Conrad Birdie in *Bye, Bye Birdie* (1960) on Broadway, made his TV series debut as a robot on *Get Smart* (1966–1969).

In this segment, comedian Gabe Kaplan (*Welcome Back, Kotter,* 1975–1979) portrayed the ambitious ventriloquist. In a 1991 *Murder, She Wrote* episode—"Where Have You Gone, Billy Boy?" (#148)—actor Grant Shaud (*Murphy Brown,* 1988–1996) would appear as a shy, dummy-obsessed voice-thrower. The two parallel installments were both scripted by series producer Peter S. Fischer.

4. "Hooray for Homicide"

(10/28/84) 60 mins.

Director: Richard Colla **Teleplay:** Robert Van Scoyk

Regular: Angela Lansbury (Jessica Fletcher)

Recurring Character: Claude Akins (Captain Ethan Cragg)

Guest Law Enforcers: Erik Hollen (Detective Mack Brody); Jose Perez (Lieutenant Mike Hernandez)

Guest Cast: R. J. Adams (TV Newsperson #2); Melissa Sue Anderson (Eve Crystal); John Astin (Ross Hayley); Barbara Block (TV Newsperson); Samantha Eggar (Marta Quintessa); James MacArthur (Allan Gebhart); Virginia Mayo (Elinor); Marianne McAndrew (Sunny Finch, Mr. Lydecker's Secretary); Richard Milhoan (Security Guard); Ron Palillo (Norman Lester, Esq.); Wayne Powers (1st Assistant Director); Hank Rolike (Paddy); Lisa Hope Ross (Tour Guide); Paul Ryan (Ted Lafferty); John Saxon (Jerry Lydecker); Jack Scalici (TV Newsperson #1); Morgan Stevens (Scott Bennett); Lyle Waggoner (Strindberg)

The Settings: Cabot Cove, Maine; Los Angeles, California

The Case: Jessica Fletcher flies to Hollywood to protest the flimsy filming of her novel, *The Corpse Danced at Midnight,* by trash movie producer Jerry Lydecker. Meeting him on the studio lot, she is incensed at his callousness. She threatens to do whatever (!) is necessary to prevent this shoddy screen adaptation from materializing. However, she discovers from her publisher's lawyers that she has innocently signed away all rights to control the movie version of her book.

When Lydecker is later found dead on a movie set, Jessica is the prime suspect. Working around and with police lieutenant Mike Hernandez, she uncovers several more likely candidates. They include Marta Quintessa, the picture's unappreciated costume designer; has-been screenwriter Allan Gebhart, a recovering alcoholic who was humiliated by the late filmmaker into writing the schlock adaptation; curvaceous leading lady Eve Crystal, who had been unfaithful to her late mentor; and harassed movie director Ross Hayley, who stands to succeed Lydecker in the lucrative capacity of the movie's producer.

Highlights: In her first trip to tinseltown, Jessica Fletcher is only momentarily impressed by the film colony's rich life-style. She is far more concerned with protecting the integrity of her literary work, even if it costs her valuable future movie deals.

In contrast to the law officers in many other episodes who regard Jessica as a busybody nuisance, the vastly overworked Lieutenant Hernandez craftily maneuvers her into helping him solve the case. Her helper in this adventure is Norman Lester, a young attorney at her publisher's Los Angeles law firm.

Trivia: Virginia Mayo, a 1940s and 1950s Hollywood leading lady, was the first of many former screen beauties to make cameo appearances on *Murder, She Wrote.* She is seen here in the unglamorous role of a stout wardrobe lady. John Astin, famous as Gomez on TV's *The Addams Family* (1964–1966), would jump from his guest role here as an opportunistic film director to a briefly recurring part as real estate broker Harry Pierce in the series' second season.

5. "It's a Dog's Life"

(11/4/84) 60 mins.

Director: Seymour Robbie **Teleplay:** Mark Giles, Linda Shank

Regular: Angela Lansbury (Jessica Fletcher)

Guest Law Enforcers: Byron Cherry (Deputy Will Roxie); Robert Cornthwaite (Coroner); Roger Miller (Sheriff)

Guest Cast: Cherie Currie (Echo Cramer); Cathryn Damon (Morgana Cramer); James Hampton (Veterinarian); Dean Jones (Marcus Boswell, Esq.); Lenore Kasdorf (Trish Langley); Donna Anderson Marshall (Miss

Sampson); Jared Martin (Spencer Langley); Bernard McDonald (Master of the Hunt); Brian Mozur (Anthony); Greg Norberg (Gary); Dan O'Herlihy (Denton Langley); Lynn Redgrave (Abby Benton Freestone); Gregory Walcott (Isaiah Potts); Forrest Tucker (Tom Cassidy); Sandy Ward (Barnes)

The Setting: Greenville, Virginia

The Case: Jessica Fletcher travels down south to visit her cousin, Abby Freestone. The latter, who hails from Kent, England, is a horse trainer working at Langley Manor, the plush estate owned by Denton Langley. When Denton is "accidentally" killed during a fox hunt celebrating his eightieth birthday, the family is shocked that the majority of the $15 million estate has been left to Teddy—the eccentric man's favorite dog!

Meanwhile, the deceased's drunk daughter, Trish, is crushed to death at the property's electronic front gates. The finger of guilt points to Teddy, who was seen pushing the gate button in the estate guard house. Now Jessica must convince the sheriff that animal expert Abby did not train the canine to "kill." The clues lead either to the dead man's son, Spencer, who has heavy stock market debts, or Tom Cassidy, Denton's longtime friend and neighbor, or Denton's bizarre daughter Morgana, who is deeply immersed in astrology and psychic readings, or congenial Marcus Boswell, the family's longtime lawyer.

Highlights: As an estate guest, Jessica rides in the episode's opening fox hunt. (Her athletics are mostly handled by a stunt double.) By this juncture, the inestimable Mrs. Fletcher has gained confidence as a crime-solver and is anything but meek in pointing out to the local lawman his faulty detecting logic. In the segment's climactic courtroom trial, Jessica, as a friend of the court, demonstrates who actually trained the star witness—Teddy the dog—to hit the gate button on cue.

Trivia: This was the first episode to feature one of Jessica Fletcher's relatives from across the Atlantic Ocean. While Angela Lansbury had comically ridden to the fox hunt in her Broadway hit *Mame* (1966), her episode costar, Forrest Tucker, had played the hunt-riding husband of Mame Dennis in the earlier, nonmusical film version of the property, *Auntie Mame* (1958). Britisher Lynn Redgrave, the star of *Georgy Girl* (1966), had lead jobs on TV's *House Calls* (1979–1981) and *Teachers Only* (1982–1983), to name a few.

Dean Jones was a veteran lead of TV series: *Ensign O'Toole* (1962–1963), *Chicago Teddy Bears* (1971) and *Herbie, the Love Bug* (1982), etc. James Hampton began his TV series work with *F Troop* (1965–1967) as bugler Hannibal Dobbs. Irish-born Dan O'Herlihy numbered *The Travels of Jaimie McPheeters* (1963–1964) and *A Man Called Sloane* (1979–1980) among his TV series jobs.

6. "Lovers and Other Killers"

(11/18/84) 60 mins.

Director: Allen Reisner **Teleplay:** Peter S. Fischer

Regular: Angela Lansbury (Jessica Fletcher)

Guest Law Enforcer: Greg Morris (Lieutenant Andrews)

Guest Cast: Grant Goodeve (Jack Kowalski); Peter Graves (Dean Edmund Gerard); Lois Nettleton (Amelia); Andrew Prine (Professor Todd Lowery); Andrew Stevens (David Tolliver); Lorry Walsh (Lila Schroeder Kowalski)

The Setting: Seattle, Washington

The Case: Jessica Fletcher has come to Seattle to lecture at the city's university. Her academic sponsor is longtime friend Dean Edmund Gerard. He arranges for a grad student to provide secretarial support for Jessica during her campus visit. Her young helper is efficient David Tolliver, who has a charming way with older women. However, Jessica insists that their relationship remain strictly professional.

Lila, the estranged wife of the school's swimming coach, Jack Kowalski, is found murdered. The killing parallels that of several previous Seattle homicides—all of older, well-to-do women. Because David had been involved with one of these victims, police lieutenant Andrews tags him as a key suspect in the new killing. Although Jessica mistrusts the manipulative David, she ponders other possible suspects. They include hot-tempered Jack Kowalski, who was jealous of his philandering mate; Professor Todd Lowery, a married man with a roving libido; and widowed Dean Gerard, who had been seen frequently with pretty Lila. In addition, there's Amelia, Dean Gerard's office assistant who has a crush on her employer.

Highlights: By now, Jessica is considered an expert in her writing specialty. She demonstrates her flair with students by giving an enthusiastic seminar series on "Murder in Literature." As well-prepared for danger as any of her fictional sleuths, Jessica carries mace in her handbag. However, it doesn't save her from a nasty physical confrontation with the segment's killer.

Unlike most *Murder, She Wrote* installments, this one ends on an ambiguous note. The viewer, like Jessica, is left uncertain whether one cleared suspect might not be guilty of other nonrelated murders!

Trivia: This entire episode was shot on location in Seattle. It also provided a reteaming of Peter Graves and Greg Morris, both veterans of TV's classic *Mission: Impossible* (1966–1973). Grant Goodeve had played David Bradford on *Eight Is Enough* (1977–1981). Andrew Stevens had made his feature film debut in *Las Vegas Lady* (1976), which starred his mother, Stella

Stevens. His other movies have included *The Fury* (1978), *Ten to Midnight* (1983) and *Night Eyes* (1990). Lois Nettleton had costarred with Peter Graves in the movie *Valley of Mystery* (1966).

7. "Hit, Run and Homicide"

(11/25/84) 60 mins.

Director: Alan Cooke **Teleplay:** Gerald K. Siegel

Regulars: Angela Lansbury (Jessica Fletcher); Tom Bosley (Sheriff Amos Tupper)

Recurring Characters: Claude Akins (Captain Ethan Cragg); Paddy Edwards (Lois Hoey)

Guest Law Enforcer: G.R. Smith (Deputy)

Guest Cast: Edward Albert (Tony Holiday); June Allyson (Katie Simmons); David Ashrow (Umpire); Dee Croxton (Cora McIntyre); Patti D'Arbanville (Leslie); Lois Foraker (Elizabeth Andler Bowles); Bruce Gray (Dean Merrill); Van Johnson (Daniel O'Brien); Ed Morgan (Local #2); Roger Price (Local #1); Harry Stephens (Doctor); Douglas Stephenson (Gas Station Attendant); Stuart Whitman (Charles Woodley)

The Setting: Cabot Cove, Maine

The Case: All Cabot Cove is excited about the annual Founder's Day picnic. More importantly, a stranger in town, Charles Woodley, owner of a Boston electronics firm, is run down by a remote-controlled car. While hospital-bound, Woodley insists he came to town as a guest of his old employee, Daniel O'Brien. However, Daniel, an absent-minded inventor, denies that he ever issued an invitation. (In fact, O'Brien mentions he once lost an expensive legal action attempting to reclaim designs and patents from his ex-boss Woodley.) Meanwhile, Dean Merrill, a partner in Woodley's firm, appears in town only to be murdered by the same driverless vehicle.

Puzzled Sheriff Amos Tupper is thankful for Jessica Fletcher's aid. She is further encouraged to solve the baffling crime by Katie Simmons, who once worked with Daniel in Boston and who has long loved him. Other interested parties include Tony Holiday, O'Brien's nephew, and the latter's girlfriend, Leslie.

Highlights: While solving the killing, Jessica is locked in the remote-control station wagon which "drives" out of control. After being rescued, she sighs to onlookers, "And you wonder why I don't drive a car."

Trivia: While under Metro-Goldwyn-Mayer contract in the 1940s and early 1950s, June Allyson and Van Johnson had been a very popular screen love team in such vehicles as *Two Girls and a Sailor* (1944), *The Bride Goes Wild* (1948) and *Too Young to Kiss* (1951). When Allyson and Johnson paired for *Till the Clouds Roll By* (1946) and *Remains to Be Seen* (1953), Angela was a featured coplayer. Edward Albert, the son of actors Eddie Albert and Margo, made his screen debut in *The Fool Killer* (1965) followed by major roles in *Butterflies Are Free* (1972), *The Greek Tycoon* (1978) and *Wild Zone* (1989).

8. "We're Off to Kill the Wizard"

(12/9/84) 60 mins.

Director: Walter Grauman **Teleplay:** Peter S. Fischer

Regular: Angela Lansbury (Jessica Fletcher)

Guest Law Enforcers: John Schuck (Captain Davis); James Stephens (Detective Lieutenant Bert Donovan)

Guest Cast: Christine Belford (Erica Baldwin); James Coco (Horatio Baldwin); Kim Darby (Laurie Bascomb); George DiCenzo (Michael Gardner [Micky Baumgarden]); Gene Evans (Nils Highlander); Vincent Howard (Second Guard); Anne Kerry (Carol Donovan); Laura Leyva (Clerk); Leaf Phoenix (Billy Donovan); Summer Phoenix (Cindy Donovan); Henry G. Sanders (Skycap); Richard Sanders (Arnold Megrim); Ivan Saric (Security Guard); Eric Server (Ned O'Brien, the Park Security Officer); James Stephens (Bert Donovan); Kristoffer Tabori (Phillip Carlson)

The Setting: Suburb of Chicago, Illinois

The Case: Tyrannical Horatio Baldwin owns several theme parks across the U.S. He invites Jessica Fletcher to his amusement facility outside of Chicago, hoping she will join his creative team in mapping out a new House of Horrors. She is enticed neither by his proposal nor by his dictatorial behavior. While in the Windy City, she visits her niece, Carol, who is married to a suburban police lieutenant, Bert Donovan.

Just as Jessica is about to depart town, she learns that Baldwin has died mysteriously behind the locked doors of his theme park office suite. Intrigued by the puzzling death which the police label a suicide, Jessica puts her deductive skills to work. She is helped by her nephew, Bert. Before long, Baldwin's business associate, Michael Gardner, tumbles from a building balcony.

In short order, Jessica discovers that Baldwin's key staff had been blackmailed into staying at their jobs by their late employer. There is Phillip Carlson, Baldwin's right-hand man who hoped to become the enterprise's corporate vice-president; Arnold Megrim, the firm's shifty bookkeeper; Nils Highlander, the park's construction foreman; and Laurie Bascomb, Horatio's meek private secretary. Also involved is Erica, Baldwin's attractive widow, a former showgirl whose several past spouses have all conveniently died.

Highlights: With a theme park backdrop and an oversized performance by James Coco as the deadly tycoon, the resultant proceedings are pleasantly offbeat. Jessica proves to be far more than a sedate armchair detective as she employs high concept office technology to trap the crafty killer.

Trivia: This unusual segment was the first of a great many to be directed by Walter Grauman. Besides featuring Emmy Award winner James Coco (1929–1987), the show offered appearances by Kristoffer Tabori and James Stephens, both of whom returned to the series on several occasions in new roles. Playing Jessica's grandnephew and grandniece were Leaf and Summer Phoenix, the siblings of the late actor River Phoenix. Rotund James Coco (1928–1987) won a Best Supporting Actor Oscar bid for his performance in *Only When I Laugh* (1981). His TV series were *Calucci's Department* (1973) and *The Dumplings* (1976).

9. "Death Takes a Curtain Call"

(12/16/84) 60 mins.

Director: Allen Reisner **Teleplay:** Paul W. Cooper

Regulars: Angela Lansbury (Jessica Fletcher); Tom Bosley (Sheriff Amos Tupper)

Recurring Character: Claude Akins (Captain Ethan Cragg)

Guest Law Enforcers: Dane Clark (FBI Agent O'Farrell); William Conrad (Major Anatole Kossoff); Read Morgan (Sergeant Kevin Hogan)

Guest Cast: Kerry Armstrong (Irina Katsa); Steve Arvin (TV Reporter); Courtney Burr (Dewey Johnson); George de la Pena (Alexander Masurov); Anthony DeLongis (Serge Berensky); Adam Gregor (Nagy); Hurd Hatfield (Leo Petersen [Leon Petrovitch]); James Carroll Jordan (Fleming, the Stage Manager); Vicki Kriegler (Natalia Masurov); Jessica Nelson (Velma Rodecker); Paul Rudd (Palmer Eddington)

The Settings: Boston, Massachusetts; Cabot Cove, Maine

The Case: Jessica Fletcher is invited to a special performance of the Rostov Ballet, the Russian company now performing in Boston. She is the guest of her Cabot Cove neighbor and longtime friend Leo Petersen. While at the performance, which is interrupted by a protest demonstration, a KGB watch guard is murdered, and two of the lead dancers, Alexander and Natalia Masurov, defect. It develops that Leo was involved with the escape plan, and he now asks Jessica to hide the fleeing dancers in Cabot Cove.

Meanwhile, both FBI agent O'Farrell and KGB officer Major Anatole Kossoff investigate the high-profiled case. In particular, Jessica matches wits with the Russian investigator, who labels Alexander the killer, since the dagger he used on stage in the ballet proves to be the murder weapon.

When not stalked by Kossoff's Soviet underlings both in Boston and in Cabot Cove, Jessica copes with several very involved parties. There is Fleming, the ballet's stage manager, who is deeply attracted to Natalia; Irina Katsa, the Masurovs' fellow dancer and passionate friend; Velma Rodecker, an agitated protester; and Palmer Eddington, whose U.S. military father helped Leo escape from East Berlin at the end of World War II.

Highlights: Providing an early example of détente, Jessica and the equally astute Major Kossoff not only learn to appreciate each other's deductive skills, but also develop a healthy—almost romantic—rapport.

On the other hand, Sheriff Tupper is overwhelmed by the burgeoning international conflict in Cabot Cove. In one of Amos's most endearingly dumb moments, he conducts a one-sided conversation dockside with Alexander (who is posing as one of Cragg's new crew members). The gullible sheriff leaves the "interrogation" site oblivious that he was just face-to-face with the Russian being sought by both the KGB and the FBI.

Trivia: This was the fourth and final series appearance by Claude Akins (1918–1994) as Captain Ethan Cragg. Also, this episode was a professional reunion for Angela Lansbury and Hurd Hatfield, who had first performed together in the MGM movie *The Picture of Dorian Gray* (1945). This segment introduced a Russian motif that would reappear in following seasons. A more elaborate ballet sequence would be featured in the 1992 episode "Danse Diabolique" (#163).

Paul Rudd was featured in the movie *The Betsy* (1978). James Carroll Jordan played Billy Abbott in the miniseries *Rich Man, Poor Man—Book II* (1976–1977). Among Hurd Hatfield's more recent film parts were *King David* (1985) and *Crimes of the Heart* (1986).

10. "Death Casts a Spell"

(12/30/84) 60 mins.

Director: Allen Reisner **Teleplay:** Steven Hensley, J. Miyoko Hensley

Regular: Angela Lansbury (Jessica Fletcher)

Guest Law Enforcers: Lee Duncan (Cop #1); Robert Hogan (Lieutenant Bergkamp)

Guest Cast: Elvia Allman (Elderly Lady); Robert Balderson (Hypnotized Person #1); Diana Canova (Joan Germaine); Joy Ellison (Hypnotized Person #5); Jose Ferrer (Cagliostro); Gay Hagen (Hynoptized Person #3); Murray Hamilton (Bud Michaels); Rance Howard (Fillmore); Conrad Janis (Dr. Yambert); Elaine Joyce (Sheri Diamond); Mary Lou Kenworthy (Liz); Brian Kerwin (Andy Townsend); Robert Loggia (Joe Kellijian); Ritchie Montgomery (Busboy); Max Nutter (Zack Bernard); Michelle Phillips (Regina Kellijian); Alex Reebar (Jay Colucco, the Hypnotist); Bill Shick (Hypnotized Person #4); Hartley Silver (Hynotized Person #2); Kathy Stangel (Hypnotized Person #6); Dianne Turley Travis (Helsema); Bob Tzudiker (Clerk)

The Setting: Lake Tahoe, Nevada

The Case: Joan Germaine, a novice staff member of Jessica's publisher, invites Jessica to Lake Tahoe at company expense. She intends to discuss an idea she has developed for Mrs. Fletcher's next book, which would involve the Amazing Cagliostro. He is the master hypnotist who has just invited a group of skeptical journalists to attend a demonstration to prove that his talents are legitimate.

Jessica and Joan arrive late to the special performance. When the guards open the room (locked from the inside), Cagliostro is found dead from a knife wound. The hypnotized witnesses in the room—the six media guests—can recall nothing of the killing.

Pairing up with Lake Tahoe police lieutenant Bergkamp, Jessica focuses on several suspicious parties. There is angry Joe Kellijian, whose wife, Regina, had been having an affair with the hypnotist. Also involved are veteran reporter Bud Michaels, now a drunkard working for a supermarket tabloid, who had known the dead man years before. Additionally, there is young Andy Townsend, whose dad was once a news service bureau chief in London. Low-life Zack Bernard is blackmailing Regina about her affair with the deceased, and, finally, there is Sheri Diamond, who once worked for the murder victim and more recently undertook a trapeze strip act.

Highlights: In a sequence where Jessica is hypnotized by Yambert, a rival of Cagliostro, she is made to describe the man's office first as a barfly would and then as a Park Avenue social snob. Later, when Jessica tracks a suspect who has just driven off, she enterprisingly hitches a ride on a passing motor scooter.

Trivia: Diana Canova, the actress daughter of comedian Judy Canova, found success on TV playing Corrine Tate on the sitcom *Soap* (1977–1980). She would next return to *Murder, She Wrote* in the 1990 episode "Murder—According to Maggie" (#125), a projected series spin-off that never materialized. Rance Howard is the father of actors Ron and Clint Howard.

Jose Ferrer (1912–1992) had several memorable screen roles: *Joan of Arc* (1948—as the Dauphin), *Cyrano de Bergerac* (1950—for which he won an Oscar), *Moulin Rouge* (1952—as Toulouse Lautrec), etc. Robert Loggia was the star of the TV series *T.H.E. Cat* (1966) and made such movies as *Somebody Up There Likes Me* (1956) and *Jagged Edge* (1985—for which he was Oscar-nominated). Brian Kerwin played the bi-sexual lover of Matthew Broderick in *Torch Song Trilogy* (1988) and had roles in *Murphy's Romance* (1985) and *Hard Promises* (1992).

11. "Capitol Offense"

(1/6/85) 60 mins.

Director: John Llewellyn Moxey **Teleplay:** Peter S. Fischer

Regular: Angela Lansbury (Jessica Fletcher)

Guest Law Enforcer: Herschel Bernardi (Detective Lieutenant Avery Mendelsohn)

Guest Cast: Edie Adams (Kaye Sheppard); Frank Aletter (Congressman Wendell Joyner); Colby Chester (Harold DeWitt); David Hooks (Representative Ronald Olsen); Linda Kelsey (Diana Simms); Stephen Macht (Congressman Dan Keppner); Nicholas Pryor (Harry Parmel, Esq.); Mitchell Ryan (Ray Dixon); Gary Sandy (Joe Blinn); Mark Shera (Thor Danziger)

The Settings: Cabot Cove, Maine; Washington, D.C.

The Case: When Maine's Congressman Joyner dies suddenly, Jessica is asked to fill the interim vacancy until a new election is held. Reluctantly agreeing, Jessica flies to Washington, D.C., where she is guided through the bureaucratic jungle by her inherited aides, Diana Simms and Joe Blinn. Soon, she is courted by Harry Parmel, a determined lobbyist who, along with the equally conniving Ray Dixon, want her to support a pending Congressional bill. The legislation would allow construction of a new cannery near Cabot Cove, despite its antienvironmentalist implications.

Meanwhile, Marta Craig, a young woman entangled in a Congressional blackmailing scheme, is found murdered, and suspicion points to Congressman Dan Keppner. Having met the latter, Jessica is convinced of his innocence. As such, she works with Detective Lieutenant Avery Mendelsohn to prove Dan's innocence. Meanwhile, she learns about the ways of the nation's capital from Thor Danziger of the Ecological Foundation and from Kaye Sheppard, a veteran political gossip columnist.

Highlights: One of the many virtues of *Murder, She Wrote* is that no matter how "far out" an episode's plot premise, it always retains sufficient plausibility, especially when the story line is twisted to bring Jessica into the heart of the action. For example, here, when asked why she has been selected to replace the late senator, Jessica is told she has three prized virtues: (1) no political ambition, (2) she is well-known and (3) her integrity is not in question. It makes sense.

True to her well-known spunk, Jessica refuses to be a lame duck replacement and immediately adapts to the rigorous Washington scene. Paralleling Jimmy Stewart's classic filibuster in *Mr. Smith Goes to Washington* (1939), Jessica is an able, informed orator at the special committee hearing on the cannery.

If Mrs. Fletcher is a quick learner at political life, she is an old hand—by now—in dealing with law enforcers with whom she must work. More so than in many of the series' offerings, Lieutenant Mendelsohn is a full-bodied characterization, a humanitarian police officer who balances experience with intuition. Jessica and the Jewish lawman strike an instant rapport, and he soon compliments her with the comment, "Maybe you should have been a cop."

Trivia: Herschel Bernardi (1923–1986) was no stranger to playing a law enforcer, having been Lieutenant Jacoby on TV's *Peter Gunn* (1958–1961). Edie Adams, the widow of comedian Ernie Kovacs, had made several movies: *The Apartment* (1960), *Love with the Proper Stranger* (1964), *Adventures Beyond Belief* (1987), etc. Stephen Macht played Joe Cooper on *Knots Landing* and David Keeler—Sharon Gless's boyfriend—on *Cagney & Lacey.*

Linda Kelsey is still best known for her work as reporter Billie Newman McCovey on *Lou Grant* (1977–1982). Angela Lansbury had previously co-starred in two feature films dealing with the political scene: *State of the Union* (1948) and *The Manchurian Candidate* (1962).

Astute viewers will note a rare sloppiness in production values in this episode. In the D.C. scenes, Jessica's hotel room is labeled #2560. However, it is very obvious that the prop department had inadequately painted over a set door which had once read room #332.

12. "Broadway Malady"

(1/13/85) 60 mins.

Director: Hy Averback **Teleplay:** Tom Sawyer

Regular: Angela Lansbury (Jessica Fletcher)

Recurring Character: Michael Horton (Grady Fletcher)

Guest Law Enforcer: Gregory Sierra (Detective Sergeant Moreno)

Guest Cast: Ed Bakey (Monsignor Kelly); Milton Berle (Lew Feldman); Vivian Blaine (Rita Bristol); Dante D'Andre (Captain); Elaine Giftos (Lonnie Valerian); Bob Gorman (Jimmy Finley); Sharee Gregory (Kate Metcalf); Victoria Harned (Newscaster); Gregg Henry (Barry Bristol); Bert Hinchman (Carlin Nahs); Lorna Luft (Patti Bristol); Robert Morse (Marc Faber); Joe Nesnow (Doorman); Patrick O'Neal (Si Parrish); Robert Roman (Taki); Johnny Seven (Man); Edison Stroll (Dr. Peter Weber); Barbara Whinnery (Gretchen Pashko)

The Settings: Cabot Cove, Maine; New York City

The Case: When Grady Fletcher is hired as accountant for an upcoming Broadway musical, *Always April*, he invites Jessica Fletcher, his visiting aunt, to attend rehearsals. There the author meets the show's star, the legendary Rita Bristol, who is making a long-awaited comeback.

Also involved in the stage project are Rita's son, Barry, who helped package the show; Patti, Rita's daughter, who is featured in the cast; Kate Metcalf, who is Rita's understudy and Grady's new romance; insensitive show director Marc Faber, who wants his West Coast-based girlfriend, Lonnie Valerian, to inherit the star role; and producer Si Parrish, who has sold 200% of the show to investors.

One day after a tense rehearsal, Patti is ambushed by a mugger in the stage alleyway. Barry reacts immediately by shooting the assailant. Later, an attempt is made on Rita's life. Jessica becomes involved in the backstage mystery, despite the frigid reception she receives from apathetic Sergeant Moreno. The investigation leads Jessica to old-time talent agent Lew Feldman and to the truth behind Rita's quitting show business three decades earlier.

Highlights: Although Jessica may be a newcomer to the show business world, she develops an immediate rapport with stellar entertainer Rita Bristol. Usually Jessica dispenses worldly advice—especially on romance—to younger individuals. However, here she proves admirably supportive of a peer who is coping badly with love of her offspring, love of performing and a diminishing love of staying alive.

When not helping the Bristol clan, Jessica must deal with Detective

Sergeant Moreno, a man numbed to his job. To spark him out of his lethargy, Jessica constantly challenges and battles him.

Trivia: This was Michael Horton's second appearance as nephew Grady Fletcher. For the episode's opening scene of Vivian Blaine's character watching one of her old films *(Moon Over Rio)* on TV, clips from Blaine's movie *Doll Face* (1946) were used. Blaine (1921–1995) had made a big hit on Broadway in the musical *Guys and Dolls* (1950) as marriage-minded club performer Miss Adelaide, a role she repeated on-screen (1955). Lorna Luft is the daughter of Judy Garland and the half sister of Liza Minnelli, while Milton Berle, once "Mr. Television," was making a rare appearance in a dramatic role. Gap-toothed Robert Morse gained prominence in the Broadway musical *How to Succeed in Business Without Really Trying* (1961) and made a startling Tony Award-winning 1990s comeback on the stage with *Tru,* a one-man show about author Truman Capote. Patrick O'Neal (1927–1994) was an alumnus of such TV series as *Dick and the Duchess* (1957–1958), *Diagnosis: Unknown* (1960) and *Emerald Point NAS* (1983).

13. "Murder to a Jazz Beat"

(2/3/85) 60 mins.

Director: Walter Grauman **Story:** Paul Savage, David Abramowitz **Teleplay:** Paul Savage

Regular: Angela Lansbury (Jessica Fletcher)

Guest Law Enforcer: Bradford Dillman (Detective Lieutenant Simeon Kershaw)

Guest Cast: Wally K. Berns (Proprietor); Michael Caravan (Dr. Allan Collyer, the Queen of Mercy Hospital Intern); Robert Clarke (Actor); Olivia Cole (Callie [Carol] Coleman); Elaine Hobson (Lisa); Jackie Joseph (Actress); George Kirby (Eubie Sherwin); Mario Machado (TV Announcer); Bruce Marchiano (Assistant Director); Cameron Mitchell (Aaron Kramer); Garret Morris (Lafayette Duquesne); Ed Nelson (Carl Turnball); Clive Revill (Jonathan Hawley); Stan Shaw (Eddie Walters); Bobby Sherman (Jimmy Firth); Glynn Turman (Ben Coleman); David Whitfield (Hec Tattersal)

The Setting: New Orleans, Louisiana

The Case: WBBX-TV talk show host Jonathan Hawley invites Jessica Fletcher to appear on his local program, *New Orleans Today.* By error she arrives in town two days early and has lots of free time for taxi driver Lafayette Duquesne to show her the city's sights. Later, Hawley takes

Jessica to a Bourbon Street jazz club, Poule Rouge. There she meets talented clarinetist Ben Coleman, his devoted wife Callie and Ben's manager, Aaron Kramer. Jessica witnesses a confrontation between Coleman and three members (Eubie Sherwin, Jimmy Firth and Eddie Walters) of his band whom Ben is discarding now that he has an upcoming Las Vegas gig.

During an impromptu jazz jam session, Ben keels over dead from a supposed heart attack. However, Jessica is certain the man was poisoned and persuades Detective Lieutenant Kershaw to delve deeper. Before long, she uncovers tie-ins to a smuggling operation and to repercussions from Coleman's years-long habit of philandering.

Highlights: For music and travel aficionados, this segment provides jazz performance sequences, as well as atmospheric location shots of New Orleans landmarks.

Trivia: This installment featured two of the series' favored gimmicks. One was presenting Jessica as an astute student of rare poisons because of her mystery book writing (in particular for *Murder on the Amazon).* As such, she spots telltale evidence on a corpse (e.g., slight color drain around the lips, blue tinge around fingernails). The other often-used series conceit was the "fortuitous" circumstance that the death/murder had been captured on video tape. It allows super observant Mrs. Fletcher to study the evidence for helpful clues.

New Zealand-born Clive Revill has spent much of his professional career in Great Britain and in portraying buffoons: *Fathom* (1967), *The Private Life of Sherlock Holmes* (1970), etc. Robert Clarke was in many 1940s' RKO features: *The Falcon in Hollywood* (1944), *The First Yank into Tokyo* (1945), etc. Stan Shaw, an alumnus of Hollywood's black exploitation features, has appeared in such other features as *Rocky* (1976), *The Great Santini* (1979) and *Fried Green Tomatoes* (1991).

In 1961, Twentieth Century-Fox contractee Bradford Dillman costarred with his real-life wife, actress/model Suzy Parker, in *Circle of Deception.* Cameron Mitchell (1918–1994) performed in several major features early in his career: *They Were Expendable* (1945), *Death of a Salesman* (1952), *The Robe* (1953—the voice of Christ), etc. Later he was reduced to junk entries such as *Bloodlink* (1986) and *Terror in Beverly Hills* (1990).

14. "My Johnny Lies over the Ocean"

(2/10/85) 60 mins.

Director: Seymour Robbie **Teleplay:** Peter S. Fischer

Regular: Angela Lansbury (Jessica Fletcher)

Guest Cast: Paul Carafote (Ramon, the Steward); Don Dubbins (Dr. Carmichael); Jason Evers (Dr. Marshall Fletcher); Rosemary Forsyth (Dr. Andrea Jeffreys Reed); Kay Freeman (Nurse); Lynda Day George (Diane Shelley); Michael G. Hawkins (Dr. Ross); Vicki Lawrence (Phoebe Carroll); Don Matheson (Oklahoma Cowboy); Leslie Nielsen (Captain Daniels); Belinda J. Montgomery (Pamela Crane); Andrew Parks (Russell Tompkins); Mark Pilon (Ship's Officer #2); Lawrence Pressman (George Reed); George Marshall Ruge (Morley, a Ship's Officer); Byron Webster (Maitre d'); JoAnne Worley (Carla Raymond)

The Settings: The high seas; St. Thomas, Virgin Islands

The Case: Jessica Fletcher's niece, Pamela Crane, has been released from a mental sanitarium. She had suffered a nervous breakdown following the death of her husband Johnny from a self-inflicted gunshot wound. Dr. Marshall Fletcher, a surgeon, asks his sister-in-law, Jessica, to accompany Pamela on an all-expenses-paid, two-week cruise in the Caribbean.

Among the 680 passengers aboard the posh S. S. *Cristallino* are two midwestern insurance company workers, Phoebe Carroll and Carla Raymond, as well as the recently married George Reed and his doctor wife, Andrea. Before long, Pamela receives a series of gifts, telegrams and calls which suggests that the late Johnny Crane—or at least his spirit—is anxiously contacting his wife. The frightening effects of these strange occurrences push Pamela into hysterics.

Jessica receives the cooperation of the ship's captain, Daniels, and the ship's purser, Diane Shelley, to provide the distraught Pamela with twenty-four-hour security. Meanwhile, Andrea Reed is found dead in her stateroom, apparently the victim of self-induced barbiturate poisoning. Mrs. Fletcher believes otherwise and quickly ties the murder to Pamela's persecutor(s).

Highlights: Having established Jessica's impressive detecting traits, the series occasionally gave the character room to expand when she playacts in order to tip a suspect's hand. Herein, Jessica has a marvelous "drunk" scene in which she staggers about the ship sipping and spilling her glass of champagne while catching an involved party off guard.

Trivia: This episode was a rare instance in which, before the required showdown with the gallery of suspects, Jessica alerts another character to the identity of the likely killer. As in each *Murder, She Wrote* episode, Jessica next admits aloud that now she must prove her murder theory.

Bubbly Vicki Lawrence gained prominence as a variety troupe regular on *The Carol Burnett Show* (1967–1979). Leslie Nielsen starred in many TV series roles, including the police actioner *The New Breed* (1961–1962) and the cop spoof *Police Squad* (1982—which led to his starring in several movies based on the television series). Fractious JoAnne Worley had been a member of *Rowan & Martin's Laugh-In* (1968–1970). Lawrence Pressman was cast as Bunky Thurston in the miniseries *The Winds of Wars* (1983).

15. "Paint Me a Murder"

(2/17/85) 60 mins.

Director: John Llewellyn Moxey **Teleplay:** Peter S. Fischer

Regular: Angela Lansbury (Jessica Fletcher)

Guest Law Enforcer: Ron Moody (Inspector Henry Kyle)

Guest Cast: Fernando Allende (Miguel Santana); Alma Beltran (Rosa); Capucine (Belle Chaney); Judy Geeson (Elaine McComber); Robert Goulet (Willard Kaufmann); Stewart Granger (Sir John); Pepe Hern (Antonio); Steven Keats (Stefan Conrad); Christina Raines (Margo Santana); Cesar Romero (Diego Santana)

The Setting: A remote Mediterranean isle

The Case: Famous painter Diego Santana invites several friends, including Jessica Fletcher, to his island retreat to celebrate his sixtieth birthday. Among those coming to the island are Diego's ex-wife, Belle Chaney; a has-been playwright, Willard Kaufmann; a London art gallery owner, Sir John; a Scotland Yard Inspector, Henry Kyle; and Elaine McComber, the head of a charity. Already at the villa are Santana's current wife, Margo, Diego's son, Miguel, and a young sculptor, Stefan Conrad, whom Santana is training.

Diego confides to Jessica that he fears death is stalking his island. His prediction proves true when an urn "accidentally" falls from a ledge and nearly kills the host. Later, the alcoholic Kaufmann suffers a heart attack and is flown off the island. Still later, Santana is fatally shot with an arrow. As Jessica and Inspector Kyle piece together the evidence, they discover that not only did several parties stand to benefit greatly from Diego's death—which would increase the value of his art work enormously—but that Stefan is strongly attached to Margo Santana.

Highlights: The plot line here is a variation of the classic whodunit movie *And Then There Were None* (1945)—itself based on a prior Agatha Christie novel (1939) and play (1943). This installment uses its picturesque but claustrophobic locale to fine advantage, allowing few distractions from the small gathering of guests and/or murder suspects.

Trivia: French-born actress Capucine (1933–1990) was an exotic screen personality noted for roles in *Song Without End* (1960), *The Pink Panther*

(1964) and *What's New Pussycat?* (1966). As part of her 1980s comeback, she appeared on *Murder, She Wrote*. In March 1990 she committed suicide by jumping from the window of her attic apartment. On TV's *Flamingo Road* (1981–1982), Christina Raines played Lane Ballou.

Dapper Britisher Stewart Granger (1913–1993) had a long film career, including many features costarring his off-camera wife, Jean Simmons: *Adam and Evelyne* (1949), *Young Bess* (1953), *Footsteps in the Fog* (1955), etc. Canadian-born singer Robert Goulet made a 1960s fling into Hollywood movies: *Honeymoon Hotel* (1963), *I'd Rather Be Rich* (1964), etc. Cesar Romero (1907–1994), whose early features included *The Thin Man* (1934) and *The Return of the Cisco Kid* (1939), was featured in the TV series *Passport to Danger* (1956).

16. "Tough Guys Don't Die"

(2/24/85) 60 mins.

Director: Seymour Robbie **Teleplay:** Peter S. Fischer

Regular: Angela Lansbury (Jessica Fletcher)

Recurring Character: Jerry Orbach (Harry McGraw)

Guest Law Enforcer: Paul Winfield (Lieutenant Starkey)

Guest Cast: Barbara Babcock (Priscilla Daniels); Conrad Bachmann (Office Manager); Janna Brown (Receptionist); John Furey (Larry King); Nancy Grahn (Erin Kerry); Rosanna Huffman (Mrs. Connie Miles); Tina Lafford (Leora Cargill); Floyd Levine (Archie Miles); John McMartin (Gavin Daniels); Margery Nelson (Alma Leonard, the Secretary); Gerald S. O'Loughlin (Ray Kravitz); Alex Rocco (Ernie Santini); Fritz Weaver (Judge Carter Lambert)

The Settings: Boston, Massachusetts; Cabot Cove, Maine

The Case: In researching her next book, Jessica Fletcher hires a Boston private detective, Archie Miles, to investigate the 25-year-old Danbury scalpel murder. Before Miles can drive to Maine to interrogate a witness in that long-ago case, he is murdered in his office.

Jessica feels that her having hired Archie may have led to his death. Her guilt prompts her to investigate and bring the killer to justice. Meanwhile, Archie's partner, the disorganized and irritable Harry McGraw, wants revenge for his partner. McGraw uncovers that Miles had been working on three cases. One was Jessica's research; another involved a local contractor, Ernie Santini, suspected of cheating on his wife; and the third dealt with

Priscilla Daniels. She is the editor of *Femininity* magazine who remains close with her ex-husband, Gavin Daniels, a university official.

Meanwhile, Jessica discovers that Judge Lambert, who presided over the Danbury murder case many years before, is now a close friend of Priscilla Daniels. Jessica also talks with Ray Kravitz, who works for Harry McGraw. Ultimately, she has to make a decision on the propriety of using the old murder case for her next novel.

Highlights: Although they are direct opposites in many ways, Jessica Fletcher and Harry McGraw are both determined fact-chasers, unmindful of dangerous obstacles. Each is wont to use—as McGraw does here when posing as a Texan—a character-disguising ruse to gain needed information. As reluctant crime-solving partners, each grudgingly gains respect for the other. By the fade-out, brash Harry gives Jessica the ultimate compliment. He offers her a job with his private detective firm!

Trivia: This was the first of several appearances of Jerry Orbach—then starring on Broadway in the musical *42nd Street*—as the irrepressibly irresponsible Harry McGraw. On September 27, 1987, Orbach debuted in CBS-TV's *The Law and Harry McGraw.* The detective series featured Barbara Babcock, not in her *Murder, She Wrote* role of the magazine editor, but as Ellie Maginnis, an attorney with an office across the hall from McGraw's detective agency. The spin-off program lasted but one TV season. John McMartin played Julian J. Roberts on the nighttime soap opera, *Falcon Crest* (1985–1986). He costarred with Lansbury on Broadway in *A Little Family Business* (1982).

17. "Sudden Death"

(3/3/85) 60 mins.

Director: Edward M. Abroms **Teleplay:** Robert E. Swanson

Regular: Angela Lansbury (Jessica Fletcher)

Guest Law Enforcer: Tim Thomerson (Detective Lieutenant Clyde Pace)

Guest Cast: Wyatt Anderson (Football Player); John Beck (Web McCord); Warren Berlinger (Pat Patillo); Dick Butkus (Tank Mason); David Doyle (Brad Lockwood); Bruce Jenner (Zak Farrell); Gary Lockwood (Commissioner Harris Talmadge); Albert Lord (Baxter, the Houseman); James McEachin (Grover Dillon); Allan Miller (Phil Kreuger); Elizabeth Savage (Mavis Kreuger); Jan Smithers (Cathy Farrell); Arnold Turner (Security Guard); Marcianne Warman (Jill Farrell)

The Setting: Not stated

The Case: When she attends the funeral of her eccentric Uncle Cyrus, Jessica Fletcher learns that she has inherited a share in the Leopards, a professional football team. As such, she visits the Leopards' headquarters. There, its owner, Phil Kreuger, who intends to relocate the team to a larger city, offers to buy Jessica's stock. She declines the bid.

When Kreuger is found dead in the training room whirlpool bath, several individuals are suspects. There is Zak Farrell, a benched quarterback whose wife, Jill, is keeping a secret; the team's manager, Pat Patillo; the deceased's business associate, Web McCord; crafty attorney Brad Lockwood; and football commissioner Harris Talmadge. Other suspicious individuals are the victim's widow, Mavis, then separated from her husband, and embittered Grover Dillon, who had once been a star athlete until Kreuger, then a coach, had made him play ball too soon after he sustained an injury.

Highlights: Few *Murder, She Wrote* episodes showcased Jessica Fletcher in such an athletic workout or allowed her to cut loose so frequently. Here she is given *carte blanche* for her investigation, not because of her mystery writing fame and being a real-life crime-solver, but because she is a team stockholder. Thus, the resolute lady pops up on the football practice field, queries a squad member while he's taking a locker-room shower and, during a team party, bounces gleefully around the room in rhythm to the hip music beat.

Trivia: Guest stars included Olympic Decathlon gold medalist Bruce Jenner as well as one-time Chicago Bears football hero Dick Butkus and other gridiron names. Warren Berlinger had begun his TV series work on *The Joey Bishop Show* (1961–1962). John Beck had been on the Western program, *Nichols* (1971–1972). James McEachin had had the lead in TV's *Tenafly* (1973–1974). Gary Lockwood had notched several guest assignments on such 1970s TV series as *Barnaby Jones* and *Police Story.*

Unfortunately, this episode relied on a too often repeated *Murder, She Wrote* crime-solving gimmick. Jessica entraps the killer by letting it be known that she has found a missing button that obviously came from a piece of clothing worn by the murderer at the time of committing the crime.

18. "Footnote to Murder"

(3/10/85) 60 mins.

Director: Peter Crane **Teleplay:** Robert E. Swanson

Regular: Angela Lansbury (Jessica Fletcher)

Guest Law Enforcers: Ron Masak (Lieutenant Meyer); Biff Yeager (Donovan, the Cop)

Guest Cast: Vincent Baggetta (Frank Palinski); Talia Balsam (Debbie Delancey [Palinski]); Josh C. Becker (Optometrist); John Brandon (Ernie); Morgan Brittany (Tiffany Harrow); Constance Forslund (Lucinda Lark); Pat Harrington (Mel Comstock); Mark Harrison (Assistant District Attorney); Michael Kearns (Reporter); Nancy Marlow (Lady); Kenneth Mars (Hemsley Post); William McDonald (Bailiff); Diana Muldaur (Alexis Post); Robert Reed (Adrian Winslow); Paul Sand (Horace Lynchfield); Lana Schwab (Clerk)

The Setting: New York City

The Case: In Manhattan for the prestigious Gotham Book Awards, Jessica Fletcher attends a prize nomination reception with Horace Lynchfield, an impoverished poet she had met the previous summer in Cabot Cove. Others at the conclave are awards coordinator Tiffany Harrow; snobbish Adrian Winslow, a prize-winning author; and Hemsley Post. The latter confides that he has just written a Vietnam War novel.

When the abrasive Post is found dead in his hotel room with a dagger in his chest, ambitious assistant district attorney Mel Comstock concludes that Lynchfield is the culprit. Jessica believes otherwise. Her probe leads to Alexis, the victim's estranged wife who had loaned her spouse a great deal of money; Winslow, who once worked for the deceased; Lucinda Lark, the author of popular romance novels; Frank Palinski, an ex-G.I. and would-be novelist; and Debbie Delancey, an autograph hound with a penchant for writing.

Highlights: With so many characters and story lines woven into the plot, Jessica's on-camera time is more limited than usual. Particularly effective in the episode is Robert Reed as the prissy, tweedy author with a waspish personality.

Trivia: Ron Masak makes his *Murder, She Wrote* series debut here, playing a low-keyed police investigator. He would make another guest appearance before joining the series in the fall of 1989 in the newly conceived role of Cabot Cove's Sheriff Mort Metzger. Robert Reed (1932–1992) is indelibly associated with being Mike Brady the all-knowing dad on TV's *The Brady Bunch* (1969–1974) and its many follow-up series. Vincent Baggetta had played the lead role on the drama series *Eddie Capra Mysteries* (1978–1979). Kenneth Mars had been a regular on *The Don Knotts Show* (1970–1971) and *Sha Na Na* (1977–1978). New York-born Pat Harrington (Jr.) won an Emmy in 1984 for playing the talkative janitor, Dwayne Schneider, on the sitcom *One Day at a Time* (1975–1984).

19. "Murder Takes the Bus"

(3/17/85) 60 mins.

Director: Walter Grauman **Teleplay:** Michael Scheff, Maryanne Kasica

Regulars: Angela Lansbury (Jessica Fletcher); Tom Bosley (Sheriff Amos Tupper)

Guest Cast: Charles Bazaldua (Man); Linda Blair (Jane Pascal); John Chandler (Gilbert Stonner); Michael Constantine (Ben Gibbons, the Bus Driver); Terence Knox (Steve Pascal); Larry Linville (Associate Professor Kent Radford); Rue McClanahan (Miriam Radford); Albert Salmi (Joe Downing); Don Stroud (Carey Drayson); Mills Watson (Ralph Leary, the Diner Owner); David Wayne (Cyrus Lefingwell)

The Settings: Cabot Cove, Maine; Maine's Route 1 between Cabot Cove and Portland

The Case: On a rainy night in Cabot Cove, Amos Tupper boards a Portland-bound bus to attend a dinner meeting of the New England Sheriffs' Association. He is joined by Jessica Fletcher, who has agreed to deliver a banquet speech there. Other passengers include Joe Downing, the owner of a Gloucester fishing trawler; librarian Miriam Radford and her husband, Kent, an associate professor at St. Usus College; an aged widower named Cyrus Lefingwell; a tense married couple, Steve and Jane Pascal; and the substitute driver, Ben Gibbons. En route, the bus stops near the state prison, where Gilbert Stonner comes aboard. Later, Carey Drayson, a jewelry salesman who had been tailing the bus in his car, boards the vehicle.

Because of the worsening storm, the bus stops at the Kozy Korner Kitchen, a roadside diner operated by Ralph Leary. Unable to reach help because the phone lines are down, the group waits out the storm. Later, Jessica discovers Stonner's corpse on the bus. He has been stabbed in the neck. Not only is his travel bag missing, but so is the rare book (*The Night the Hangman Sang)* he was reading.

Although Amos Tupper points out that he is outside his legal jurisdiction, he joins Jessica in examining the facts and the suspects. Before long, they discover a deadly connection between a long-ago unsolved bank robbery in Danvers, Massachusetts, and the present-day murder victim.

Highlights: There are many parallels between this segment and classic movie whodunits set at a spooky old mansion on a stormy night. Whether on the bus or at the little diner, the group is cut off from the outside world, which means the murderer must be one of those present. This adds delicious tension to the puzzle. If anyone in the group is different from the usual suspect it is gabby Miriam Radford, a busybody college librarian who compliments Jessica by telling her that she is among the top ten authors whose books are stolen at the library.

Trivia: Among the guest cast were several notable TV series veterans: Larry Linville ("M*A*S*H"), Rue McClanahan (*Maude, Mama's Family, The Golden Girls)*, Terence Knox (*(St. Elsewhere, Tour of Duty)*, and David Wayne (1919–1995) (*The Adventures of Ellery Queen, House Calls)*. Linda Blair, Oscar-nominated for her role as the possessed youngster in *The Exorcist* (1971), has more recently starred in low-budget exploitation features (e.g., *Bedroom Eyes* [1989] *Sorceress* [1994]).

20. "Armed Response"

(3/31/85) 60 mins.

Director: Charles S. Dubin **Teleplay:** Gerald K. Siegel

Regular: Angela Lansbury (Jessica Fletcher)

Guest Law Enforcer: Bo Hopkins (Lieutenant Ray Jenkins)

Guest Cast: Eddie Bracken (Barney Ogden); Victoria Carroll (Melanie Barker); Denise Cheshire (Candy Striper); Stephen Elliott (Dr. Samuel Garver); James Gammon (Billy Don Barker); Sam Groom (Dr. Wes Kenyon); Martin Kove (Dr. Ellison); Kay Lenz (Nurse Jennie Wells); Kevin McCarthy (Milton Porter, Esq.); Lucille Meredith (Mrs. Bundle); Susan Oliver (Head Nurse Marge Horton); Martha Raye (Sadie Winthrop); Lavelle Roby (Nurse); Fred D. Scott (Harlan, the Chauffeur); Paul Tuerpe (1st Security Guard); Gerald York (Security Guard #2)

The Setting: Dallas, Texas

The Case: When an author friend is sued for plagiarism, Jessica is flown to Texas to testify on his behalf, arrangements being made by the defendant's ostentatious attorney, Milton Porter. At the Dallas airport, she is accidentally thrown off balance by two rambunctious youths and injures her leg. Porter insists the mishap has the makings of a great negligence lawsuit and arranges for Jessica to recuperate at a plush local clinic operated by Dr. Samuel Garver. There she meets fellow patients, boisterous rich Sadie Winthrop and embittered widower Barney Ogden. She also observes the arguments between Dr. Kenyon and Dr. Ellison, two highly competitive rivals to becoming Garver's successor.

When Dr. Garver is shot to death in his fish pool at home, the police, including Lieutenant Ray Jenkins, pick nurse Jennie Wells as their prime suspect. After all, she was seen fleeing from Garver's home shortly before the killing. However, Jessica thinks otherwise.

Highlights: Always a very mobile individual, Jessica refuses to allow a leg injury to stop her from snooping. Whether from her hospital bed, in a wheelchair or hobbling on crutches, she pursues her leads. Adding energy to this segment are delightful performances by Kevin McCarthy as the rambunctious, glib lawyer and loud-mouthed Martha Raye as a wealthy matron with an eye for romance and a fondness for card playing.

Trivia: Susan Oliver (1927–1990), a movie and TV starlet of the 1950s and 1960s who gained more fame as a real-life aviatrix, had recurring roles on two soap operas, *Days of Our Lives* and *Peyton Place.* Eddie Bracken had costarred with Betty Hutton in several Paramount features: *The Fleet's In* (1942), *The Miracle of Morgan's Creek* (1943), etc. For wide-mouthed comedian Martha Raye (1916–1994), screen assignments had ranged from the sublime (*Monsieur Verdoux* [1947]) to the fun (*Artists and Models* [1937]) and down to the ridiculous (*The Concorde—Airport 79* [1979]).

21. "Murder at the Oasis"

(4/7/85) 60 mins.

Director: Arthur Allan Seidelman **Teleplay:** Robert Van Scoyk

Regular: Angela Lansbury (Jessica Fletcher)

Guest Law Enforcers: Mark Costello (Motorcycle Officer); Ken Howard (Detective Sergeant Barnes)

Guest Cast: Ed Ames (Johnny Shannon); Joey Bishop (Buster Bailey); Joseph Bottoms (Mickey Shannon); David Bowman (Chico Miller); Joseph Cali (Vic LaRosa); Michael Griswold (Guard); Piper Laurie (Peggy Shannon); John Miranda (Gus); Jack O'Halloran (Lou Ross); Frederick Ponzlov (Waiter); Linda Purl (Terry Shannon)

The Setting: Desert Palms, California

The Case: At the Desert Palms Tennis Club, Jessica has a reunion with Peggy Shannon, a college classmate. The latter is long-divorced from pop singer Johnny Shannon, though they remain close because of their children who live at his nearby compound. Son Mickey is a frustrated jazz musician employed as a music arranger by his father. The more rebellious offspring, Terry, holds a grudge against her dad for having chased off the boy she married when she was seventeen.

One day Johnny is found dead in his den seated in his chair facing a blank TV screen. Adding to the complications, the room had been locked from the inside.

Because police sergeant Barnes is new to the area, he agrees to the Shannons' plea that Jessica help decipher the baffling killing. As she assesses clues, she learns from the victim's friend and stooge, comedian Buster Bailey, that the singer's organized crime connections had threatened retaliation for a past slight. Jessica also finds out that Johnny had fought with Terry's latest romance, tennis professional Vic LaRosa, and that the latter has tried to skip town.

Highlights: When not interacting with this expert cast of characters, Jessica demonstrates her abilities of observation, here regarding a closed-circuit TV security system which proves to have been a key element in Shannon's murder. Despite the alacrity with which she solves this case, Jessica remains humble. At one point, she modestly tells Barnes, "My occasional exploits are grossly exaggerated."

Trivia: Comedian Joey Bishop gained his professional reputation not only as a stand-up comic, but also as a member of Frank Sinatra's Rat Pack and as a 1960s TV talk show host. Ed Ames, one of the four singing Ames Brothers, had gone on to become a solo recording artist. Additionally, he had played the Indian Mingo on TV's *Daniel Boone* (1964–1968).

Piper Laurie, born Rosetta Jacobs, had won Oscar nominations for *The Hustler* (1961) and *Carrie* (1976). Among Joseph Bottoms' many films are *The Black Hole* (1979) and *Inner Sanctum* (1991). Linda Purl has acted in several TV movies: *Testimony of Two Men* (1977), *The Night the City Screamed* (1981), *Pleasures* (1986), etc.

22. "Funeral at Fifty-Mile"

(4/21/85) 60 mins.

Director: Seymour Robbie **Teleplay:** Dick Nelson

Regular: Angela Lansbury (Jessica Fletcher)

Guest Law Enforcer: Cliff Potts (Sheriff Ed Potts)

Guest Cast: Brooke Alderson (Alice); Noah Beery (Doc Wallace); Kathleen Beller (Mary Carver); J.D. Cannon (Bill Carmody); Edith Diaz (Emma); Efrain Figueroa (Hay-Soos, the Ranch Hand); Clu Gulager (Carl Mestin); Donald Moffat (Timothy Carver); Jeffrey Osterhage (Art Merrick); Stella Stevens (Sally Mestin); William Windom (Sam Breen, Esq.)

The Setting: Fifty-Mile, Wyoming

The Case: Jessica is in Wyoming for the funeral of her friend, John Carver. Among those at the service are the dead man's daughter, Mary, and her husband-to-be, Art Merrick; John's younger brother, Tim; and three of the deceased's close pals: attorney Sam Breen, Doc Wallace and Bill Carmody. Because Carver died intestate, his entire estate, including the ranch, is expected to go to Mary.

The calm is interrupted by the arrival of outspoken Sally Mestin and her husband, Carl. They produce Carver's will which states that everything goes to Mestin. The beneficiary claims that in the Korean War he had once saved Carver's life.

After Mestin is found hung in the barn, novice Sheriff Ed Potts asks Mrs. Fletcher's help. Jessica's sleuthing uncovers several people with a motive and/or opportunity to kill Carl, including ranch foreman Art Merrick, powerfully muscled Sally and several of the townspeople who want revenge for a past crime.

Highlights: Perhaps in no other *Murder, She Wrote* episodes is Jessica Fletcher more petulant, but then this is one of the most dour episodes of the entire series. Then, too, she is quite heavy-handed in her detecting chores, underlining each deduction very broadly. Thankfully, the outsized shenanigans of Sally Mestin provide a much-needed lighter tone. This segment concludes with a rarity. Jessica agrees *not* to reveal to one of the others the full truth in order to protect that person's peace of mind.

Trivia: This episode marked William Windom's debut performance on *Murder, She Wrote.* However, his role as a conscience-plagued Wyoming lawyer proved to be a far cry from his forthcoming role—at the start of season two in 1985's "Joshua Peabody Died Here—Possibly" (#24)—in which he becomes Cabot Cove's own cantankerous Dr. Seth Hazlitt.

Noah Beery, Jr., (1913–1994) came from a distinguished acting family and was active in movies from the 1920s: *The Mark of Zorro* (1920), *Rocketship X-M* (1950), *The Spirit of St. Louis* (1957), *Walking Tall* (1973), etc. He played James Garner's father on TV's *The Rockford Files* (1974–1980). Kathleen Beller's movie roles encompass *Godfather II* (1974) and *Time Trackers* (1988). Born Estelle Eggleston, Stella Stevens's early feature assignments encompass *Li'l Abner* (1959) and *The Nutty Professor* (1963). On *The Tall Man* (1960–1962) TV Western series, Clu Gulager played the outlaw Billy the Kid.

SEASON TWO

1985–1986

23. "Widow Weep for Me"

(9/29/85) 60 mins.

Director: Michael Hoey **Teleplay:** Peter S. Fischer

Regular: Angela Lansbury (Mrs. Marguerite Canfield [Jessica Fletcher])

Recurring Character: Len Cariou (Michael Haggerty)

Guest Law Enforcers: Emmett Dennis (Sergeant Darcy); Raymond St. Jacques (Police Chief Claude Rensselaer)

Guest Cast: Jerry Boyd (Doorman); Cyd Charisse (Myrna Montclair LeRoy); Claude Cole (Bellman); Marilyn Conn (Secretary); Ektarce (Desk Clerk); Mel Ferrer (Eric Brahm); Geoff Heise (Barnes); Howard Hesseman (Sheldon Greenberg); John Phillip Law (Sven Torvald); Anne Lockhart (Veronica Harrold); Ed Randolph (Croupier); Reggie Savard (Antoinette Farnsworth); Mary Wickes (Mrs. Alva Crane)

The Setting: Brittany Bay, Jamaica

The Case: Jessica Fletcher receives a desperate letter from Antoinette Farnsworth, a very wealthy middle-aged widow, saying that she fears for her life. Responding to the urgent plea, Jessica flies to the exclusive Brittany Bay Hotel in Jamaica disguised as a rich, eccentric recluse, Mrs. Marguerite Canfield of Lincoln, Nebraska. Jessica arrives too late to save Antoinette from being murdered. The island's police chief, Rensselaer, warns the upset "Mrs. Canfield" not to take matters into her own hands. However, Jessica is determined to capture her friend's killer.

Still in disguise, Jessica talks with the hotel staff, including suave manager Eric Brahm, who is desperate for ready cash; glamorous social events coordinator Myrna LeRoy, a former movie actress hiding a forbidden relationship; and security controller Sheldon Greenberg, who has a shady past. Jessica mingles with the guests: in particular wealthy Alva Crane; Veronica Harrold, a midwestern schoolteacher who mysteriously won a supermarket sweepstakes vacation; charming European Sven Torvald, who survives on women's kindness and, since Antoinette is dead, now has his eye on Veronica; and Irishman Michael Haggerty, who takes a keen interest in "Mrs. Canfield," and repeatedly appears at the most exasperating moments for Jessica.

Highlights: While posing as the recklessly lavish Mrs. Canfield, Jessica has ample occasion to wear a glamorous wardrobe and to playact as a frivolous eccentric. She also indulges her penchant for theatrics by flirting with the key male suspects at the hotel, including dapper Eric, gigolo Sven and the maddeningly intrusive Michael. When her identity as the Maine mystery novelist is discovered—gleaned from the dust jacket of one her books (*Dirge for a Dead Dachshund*)—she blithely flatters her discoverer by promising to feature him as a character in a forthcoming murder mystery.

Trivia: Location filming for this second season opener was done at the Turtle Bay Hilton & Country Club in Jamaica. Len Cariou, Lansbury's Tony Award costar of Broadway's *Sweeney Todd* (1979), made his first of several series appearances as the charming rogue Michael Haggerty. In further episodes, his amazing career in the British Secret Service would be delineated.

While at MGM, leggy dancer Cyd Charisse appeared in such movies as *The Harvey Girls* (1946—along with Angela Lansbury), *Singin' in the Rain* (1952) and *Party Girl* (1958). Mel Ferrer, another Metro-Goldwyn-Mayer graduate, appeared for that studio in *Knights of the Round Table* (1953) and *Saadia* (1954), among others.

Howard Hesseman is best known as the frantic disc jockey, Dr. Johnny Fever, on *WKRP* in *Cincinnati* (1978–1982). Sharp-featured Mary Wickes (1916–1996) played nurses on-screen in *The Man Who Came to Dinner* (1941) and *Now, Voyager* (1942). She was an on-camera nun in *The Trouble with Angels* (1966), *Where Angels Go—Trouble Follows* (1968), *Sister Act* (1992) and *Sister Act II* (1994). Raymond St. Jacques (1930–1990), who made his big screen debut in *Black Like Me* (1966), was in *Mister Buddwing* (1966) with Angela Lansbury. John Phillip Law's screen assignments covered a blind angel (*Barbarella* [1968]) and a wandering adventurer (*The Golden Voyage of Sinbad* [1973]).

24. "Joshua Peabody Died Here—Possibly"

(10/6/85) 60 mins.

Director: Peter Crane **Teleplay:** Tom Sawyer

Regulars: Angela Lansbury (Jessica Fletcher); Tom Bosley (Sheriff Amos Tupper); William Windom (Dr. Seth Hazlitt)

Recurring Character: John Astin (Harry Pierce)

Guest Law Enforcer: Chuck Connors (FBI Agent Fred Bemis)

Guest Cast: Robin Bach (Ellsworth Buffum); Jody Carter (Olive Newton); John Ericson (Henderson Wheatley); Meg Foster (Del Scott); Barbara Ann Grimes (Sarah Harris); Sandra Hawthorne (Mavis Gillam); Bruce Lawrence (Earthworm Driver); Ed Morgan (Austin Bailey); Roger Price (Eli Harris); Michael Sarrazin (David Marsh); David S. Sheiner (Arthur Griswold); Ken Swofford (Leo Kowalsi); Deborah White (Matty Marsh)

The Setting: Cabot Cove, Maine

The Case: Cabot Cove is up in arms! Local real estate broker Harry Pierce has engineered a major deal on behalf of tycoon Leo Kowalsi, who is planning a high-rise hotel project on Main Street. Henderson Wheatley's construction company begins excavating the property site. Meanwhile, David Marsh, an environmental activist who runs a local antique shop, leads a protest against this potential destruction of the town's quaint charm.

When a skeleton is found on the excavation site, the remains are speculated to be those of Joshua Peabody, Cabot Cove's most famous Revolutionary War figure. However, Jessica Fletcher and several others are skeptical of this hypothesis. By now, the media, including TV reporter Del Scott, are having a field day with the discovery, while Marsh obtains a court order to halt the building.

The building controversy becomes a murder investigation when Wheatley is murdered on the "historical" site. Jessica is drawn into the case when circumstantial evidence makes it seem—especially to newly arrived FBI agent Fred Bemis—that Marsh is the killer.

Highlights: In one of her most active adventures, Jessica literally digs into the case. Not only does she join the townsfolk in sifting through the earth for centuries-old relics at the building site, but she strikes pay dirt while researching the surprising backgrounds of several of the suspects.

Trivia: William Windom, who performed in the closing episode (#22) of the first season of *Murder, She Wrote*, returned to the show as a newly conceived character. He is featured as quirky Dr. Seth Hazlitt, the widowed local doctor with a penchant for good food, plain talk and self-reliance. He also has a soft spot for Jessica Fletcher.

John Astin, who had earlier (episode #4) handled a nonrelated role on *Murder, She Wrote*, made his debut appearance here as the hyperactive real estate agent Harry Pierce. Ken Swofford, who had made his mark as school figure Quentin Morloch on TV's *Fame* (1983–1985), would later return to *Murder, She Wrote* in a recurring part as San Francisco police officer Lieutenant Catalino in the segments featuring Keith Michell's Dennis Stanton.

25. "Murder in the Afternoon"

(10/13/85) 60 mins.

Director: Arthur Allan Seidelman **Story:** Paul W. Cooper **Teleplay:** Paul Savage

Regular: Angela Lansbury (Jessica Fletcher)

Guest Law Enforcers: George Murdock (Sergeant Kaplan); Robert Walden (Lieutenant Antonelli)

Guest Cast: William Atherton (Larry Holleran); Paul Burke (Herbert Upton); Nicholas Hammond (Todd Worthy); Elven Havard (Guard); Terry Kiser (Gordon La Monica); Alice Krige (Nita Cochran); Robert Lipton (Martin Grattop); John Muanda (Prop Man); Lloyd Nolan (Julian Tenley); Tricia O'Neil (Bibi Hartman); MacKenzie Phillips (Carol Needham); Lurene Tuttle (Agnes Cochran); Jessica Walter (Joyce Holleran)

The Setting: New York City

The Case: In Manhattan on publishing business, Jessica Fletcher visits her actress niece, Nita Cochran, at the bequest of her Aunt Agnes. Nita is employed on a daytime TV soap opera, *Our Secret Lives*. When Jessica arrives on the set, everyone is in an uproar because Joyce Holleran, the program's aggressive new producer/head writer, intends to revamp the show.

When Joyce is shot to death, there are a legion of suspects. Lieutenant Antonelli insists Nita is the most likely suspect. On the other hand, Jessica has faith in her relative's innocence, and draws up her own list of suspects. They range from actor Todd Worthy, who had fought with Joyce to cancel his show contract so he could work elsewhere, to Julian Tenley, who had played Dr. Goodman on the soap for thirty years but now fears dismissal, as does actor Martin Grattop. There is also Larry Holleran, Joyce's younger husband whom she had kept on a financial leash, and Carol Needham,

Joyce's efficient assistant who craved her boss's job. Another suspect is soap actress Bibi Hartman, who has been having an affair with Larry.

Highlights: With its setting of on- and off-camera activity at a daytime soap, much is made of showing how such entertainment programming is produced.

Trivia: One *Murder, She Wrote* producer would relate later, "I'll never forget when we used Lloyd Nolan as a guest star. Lloyd was eighty-two years old and, though we didn't know it at the time, quite ill. In fact, it was the last picture he did before he died [September 27, 1985]. On our show, his memory was gone and he simply couldn't handle his lines. Other actresses would have walked off, saying, 'Call me when he's ready.' But not Angela. . . . She coached him, whispered his cues, even took him by the hand at one point and said, 'Don't get upset, Lloyd. I blow lines, too.' Somehow, she got him through his scenes and it turned out all right. I'll remember that little episode as long as I live."

Acting veteran Paul Burke had costarred in such TV series as *Harbourmaster* (1957–1958) and *Dynasty* (1982–1984—as Congressman Neal McVane). William Atherton's more recent screen roles—in which he's usually a villain—include *No Mercy* (1986), *Die Hard 2* (1990) and *The Pelican Brief* (1993). Lurene Tuttle (1906–1986), a former 1930s radio actress and Hollywood character actress, had coleads on such TV fare as *Life with Father* (1953–1955) and *Father of the Bride* (1961–1962). MacKenzie Phillips, a costar of *One Day at a Time* (1975–1983), made such features as *American Graffiti* (1975) and *Love Child* (1982). Terry Kiser was the dead title figure in *Weekend at Bernie's* (1989) and *Weekend at Bernie's 2* (1993). Jessica Walter began in films in *Lilith* (1964) and hit her acting stride as the pathological antagonizer in Clint Eastwood's *Play Misty for Me* (1971).

26. "School for Scandal"

(10/20/85) 60 mins.

Director: Arthur Allan Seidelman **Teleplay:** Robert E. Swanson

Regular: Angela Lansbury (Jessica Fletcher)

Guest Law Enforcer: Jack Kehoe (Chief Griffen)

Guest Cast: Ron Asher (Student #1); John C. Becker (Station Master); Polly Bergen (Dr. Jocelyn Laird); Gary Bisig (Will Small); Darlene Carr (Trish Mercer); Dean Dittman (Faculty Man); Jim Greenblatt (Student #3); June Lockhart (Beryl Hayward); Roddy McDowall (Alger Kenyon); Mary Kate McGeehan (Daphne Clover); Kerry Noonan (Student #2); Craie Simmons (Faculty Wife); Morgan Stevens (Nick Fulton); James Sutorius (Ron Mercer); John Vernon (President Henry Hayward)

The Setting: Crenshaw City, New England

The Case: Jessica is scheduled to deliver the commencement address at New England's Crenshaw College. Once there, she has a reunion with her old college chum, Beryl Hayward, and the latter's husband, Henry. That evening, Jessica attends a party at the home of Jocelyn Laird, the head of the college's English department. Others in attendance include Ron Mercer, who badly wants to be named the English department's new assistant, and his wife, Trish; poetry specialist Alger Kenyon, who is Mercer's rival for the post and who is coping with his dying mother in Boston; Daphne Clover, Jocelyn's headstrong daughter, who is the New York-based author of popular romance novels; and handsome Nick Fulton, a former dismissed student from Crenshaw College and now Daphne's unemployed boyfriend.

The next day Nick's corpse is found at a nearby construction site. At first it's assumed he died accidentally, but this verdict is soon changed to murder. What complicates matters is that both Daphne and Jocelyn confess to the crime. It develops that mother and daughter share overlapping secrets as well as a relationship with the duplistic dead man (who had had other past affairs on campus).

Highlights: Not only are there strong performances by Polly Bergen, Roddy McDowall and James Sutorius, but there is the titillation of Mary Kate McGeehan's Daphne swimming "naked" in her mother's outdoor pool. A major highlight occurs when Jessica, having solved the mystery at hand, is nearly late for the commencement exercises. Dressed in cap and gown, she bicycles furiously through the campus to reach her destination.

Compared to many segments in which the antagonism or camaraderie between Jessica and the police investigator is strained, here it works well. Chief Griffen, who is taking a home study program in criminology, is thrilled to be handling his first homicide case. He welcomes Mrs. Fletcher's expertise in helping to solve the puzzle.

Trivia: Polly Bergen's professional career includes being a movie lead (*Kisses for My President*, 1964), a Broadway musical comedy star (*First Impressions*, 1960) and a stint as TV quiz show panelist (*To Tell the Truth*, 1956–1961). British-born Roddy McDowall, an excellent photographer, began his screen chores as a child actor in London: *Murder in the Family* (1936), *This England* (1940). Lois Nettleton's movie career includes Frank Sinatra's *Dirty Dingus Magee* (1970) and Burt Reynolds' *The Best Little Whorehouse in Texas* (1982). After playing the boy's mother on TV's *Lassie* (1958–1964), June Lockhart joined *Lost in Space* (1965–1968).

27. "Sing a Song of Murder"

(10/27/85) 60 mins.

Director: John Llewellyn Moxey **Teleplay:** Peter S. Fischer

Regular: Angela Lansbury (Jessica Fletcher)

Recurring Character: Angela Lansbury (Emma Macgill)

Guest Law Enforcers: David Grant Hayward (Sergeant); Barrie Ingham (Inspector Roger Crimmins); Ron Southart (Plainclothes Officer)

Guest Cast: Kenneth Danziger (Archie Weems); Richard L. Davies (1st Tough); Sarah Douglas (Violet Weems); Gillian Eaton (Landlady); Neil Hunt (2nd Tough); Olivia Hussey (Kitty Trumbull); Glynis Johns (Bridget O'Hara); Patrick Macnee (Oliver Trumbull); Greg Martyn (Danny Briggs); Terence Scammell (Director); Kristoffer Tabori (Ernest Fielding)

The Setting: London, England

The Case: English music hall trouper Emma Macgill has been a victim of several "accidents" at her Chelsea Road flat and at the theater. Fearing for her safety, she urges her American cousin, Jessica Fletcher, to come to the rescue. Jessica flies to London, but is too late. Her relative has suffered a fatal mishap.

In unmasking her cousin's murderer, Jessica teams with Scotland Yard Inspector Roger Crimmins. Those figuring in the case are Bridget O'Hara, Emma's longtime dresser; conniving stage manager Archie Weems, co-owner of the Mayhew Theatre with Emma; Violet, Archie's money-hungry wife; genteel solicitor Ernest Fielding, Emma's randy beau; Oliver Trumbull, a former Shakespearean actor now an unfunny comic at the Mayhew; and Kitty, Oliver's attractive daughter and his staunchest protector.

Highlights: With Angela Lansbury cast as both the refined, successful American author and her down-to-earth, cockney-accented, British look-alike cousin, this episode is a marvelous showcase for the actress, especially in those moments when both appear together face-to-camera. Interestingly, British-born Lansbury is more adept at capturing her American character than in fleshing out her veteran English music hall relative. The episode captures the London ambiance, especially in the moments on- and offstage at the Mayhew.

Trivia: The *Murder, She Wrote* scripters used the maiden surname of Angela Lansbury's actress mother (Moyna MacGill) when conceiving the character of Jessica's British relative. In the story, Emma Macgill performs "Goodbye, Little Yellow Bird," a plaintive number that Angela Lansbury had first sung in *The Picture of Dorian Gray* (1945), a movie for which she received a Best Supporting Actress Oscar nomination.

In this episode, Inspector Crimmins is stated to be a coworker and friend of Inspector Henry Kyle (Ron Moody) who solved a mystery with Jessica in the 1985 episode, "Paint Me a Murder" (#15).

Patrick Macnee is best-known to TV viewers for playing Jonathan Steed in the British drama series *The Avengers* (1966–1969) and *The New Avengers* (1978–1980). Kristoffer Tabori had been in such TV movies as *The Glass House* (1972) and *The Chicago Story* (1981). Glynis Johns and Angela Lansbury had appeared together in the TV miniseries *Little Gloria—Happy at Last* (1982). Olivia Hussey, who played one of the doomed lovers in *Romeo and Juliet* (1968), was once married to Dean Martin's son, Dean Paul.

28. "Reflections of the Mind"

(11/3/85) 60 mins.

Director: Seymour Robbie **Teleplay:** Robert E. Swanson

Regular: Angela Lansbury (Jessica Fletcher)

Guest Law Enforcer: Martin Milner (Sheriff Bodine)

Guest Cast: Ann Blyth (Franchesca Lodge); Janet DeMay (Brooke Devon); Wings Hauser (Carl, the Gardener [Carson Todd]); Steven Keats (Dr. Victor March); Ben Murphy (Scott Lodge); Stacey Nelkin (Cheryl); Frannie Parrish (Nurse); Esther Rolle (Margaret)

The Setting: Cincinnati, Ohio

The Case: Well-to-do Franchesca is married to a younger man, Scott Lodge, though she still grieves over her late first husband, Ross. More recently, she has begun feeling his presence—and even hearing his voice—in her River Road home. Frightened by the mounting evidence of Ross's "return," she becomes emotionally unstable. One day Scott finds her cowering in the closet, and she attacks him with a pair of scissors. Thereafter, she is temporarily confined to the psychiatric ward of a local hospital under Dr. Victor March's care. Upon release, she beckons her old friend, Jessica Fletcher, to Cincinnati to help her sort out her life.

Hardly has Jessica reached Franchesca's house, than Scott leaves for a Chicago business meeting. Soon after, the police report that he died when his car went over a cliff.

Aided by Sheriff Bodine, Jessica explores Franchesca's ghost-ridden home and promptly discovers several "skeletons" in the closets. Scott had been having an affair with his secretary, Brooke Devon. Franchesca's relative, Cheryl, has a troubled past, including drug use and emotional instability. Then, too, there is Carl, the devious gardener who is far more creative away from his daily chores.

Highlights: Set in a "haunted house" full of hidden passages and shadowy rooms, the sinister mood is emphasized by a sudden thunderstorm. Ann Blyth, the singing and dramatic star of 1940s and 1950s Hollywood features (*Mildred Pierce* [1945], *Rose-Marie* [1954]), gives a solid performance as the tormented wife/widow.

Trivia: The driving-the-heroine-out-of-her-mind plot gambit was made popular in the MGM movie *Gaslight* (1944), for which Angela Lansbury received an Oscar nomination as the underhanded cockney maid. Martin Milner had earlier played a law enforcer as Officer Pete Malloy on TV's *Adam 12* (1968–1975).

A one-time original member of the Negro Ensemble Company, Esther Rolle gained fame as Florida Evans on *Maude* (1972–1974) and *Good Times* (1974–1979). Wings Hauser has made a specialty of starring in low-budget action features: *Vice Squad* (1982), *Watchers 3* (1994), etc. Steven Keats's screen credits include *Black Sunday* (1977) and *Eternity* (1990). One of Ben Murphy's earliest screen roles was in *The Graduate* (1967); he was Will Chisolm on the Western TV series *The Chisholms* (1979–1980).

29. "A Lady in the Lake"

(11/10/85) 60 mins.

Director: Walter Grauman **Teleplay:** Robert Van Scoyk

Regulars: Angela Lansbury (Jessica Fletcher); Tom Bosley (Sheriff Amos Tupper); William Windom (Dr. Seth Hazlitt)

Recurring Character: John Astin (Harry Pierce)

Guest Law Enforcer: Johnny Crawford (Deputy Noah Paisley)

Guest Cast: Susan Blanchard (Caroline Nester Crane); William Christopher (Burton Hollis); Charles Frank (Lyle Jordan); Laurence Luckinbill (Howard Crane); Lee Meriwether (Grace Overholtz); Lee Purcell (Joanna Benson); Charles Taylor (Jack Turney); Lauren Tewes (Betty Jordan)

The Setting: Stone Lake, Maine

The Case: In the midst of writing a new novel, *Murder at the Inn*, Jessica Fletcher asks real estate broker Harry Pierce to find her northwoods atmospheric lodging to aid in her research. He takes her to Stone Lake in Maine, to a place operated by the dour Grace Overholtz. There, Jessica meets Jack Turney, the woman-chasing young man in charge of the inn's boats, who has ties to Grace. Among the Stone Lake Inn guests is nagging Howard Crane married to put-upon Caroline, as well as another unhappily married couple, Lyle and Betty Jordan. Pompous Burton Hollis, an avid bird watcher, reminds Jessica that they once took a writing seminar together. For some reason, the arrival of Joanna Benson upsets Howard.

Everything turns topsy-turvy early one morning when Jessica walks down to the lake. She spots Howard and Caroline fighting in a boat, from which Mrs. Crane jumps overboard. Later, Caroline is found drowned. Now, wonders Jessica, was the victim, an expert swimmer, pushed or did she jump? And how did her body end up on the north side of the lake? Helping her solve the mystery are Cabot Cove's very own Sheriff Amos Tupper and Dr. Seth Hazlitt.

Highlights: The special merit of this episode is the surprising plot twists provided by the suspects' complex relationships. Of note is the growing friendship between Jessica and Seth. By now, the eccentric, but good-hearted family physician calls his pal "Jess," and she relies on his medical knowledge far more than Sheriff Tupper's limited detecting acumen to solve the crime.

Trivia: Still favoring guest stars with high audience identification, this episode utilized several past TV favorites: Johnny Crawford of *The Rifleman* (1958–1963), Lee Meriwether of *Barnaby Jones* (1973–1980) and Lauren Tewes of *Love Boat* (1977–1984).

When characters are first introduced to Jessica Fletcher, they almost invariably recite a shopping list of her best-sellers, including *The Killer Called Collect.* Most remembered by characters is Jessica's first book, *The Corpse Danced at Midnight.* (In this segment the title is stated to be *The Corpse Danced Till Midnight.*)

30. "Dead Heat"

(11/24/85) 60 mins.

Director: Peter Crane **Teleplay:** J. Miyoki Hensley, Steven Hensley

Regular: Angela Lansbury (Jessica Fletcher)

Guest Law Enforcer: Roy Thinnes (Lieutenant Misko)

Guest Cast: Tony Ballen (Bookie #1); Priscilla Barnes (Vicky Gallegos); Ramon Bieri (Pat Phillips); Jack Carter (Cliff Carpenter); Freddy Chapman

(Nurse); Lonny Chapman (Jack Bowen); Carole Cook (Christine Carpenter); Tom Dresen (Ernie); Robert Ellenstein (Mr. P.); Joe Faust (Security Guard); Norman Fell (Vince Shackman); Stu Gilliam (Ernie, the Taxi Driver); Linda Grovenor (Tracy Macgill); Clu Gulager (Mike Gann); Derrel Mawry (Cookie Milford); Don Matheson (Chief Steward); Richard Paradise (Bookie #2); Alex Rebard (Guzmann, the Gunsel); Bert Rosario (Carlos Gallegos)

The Setting: The Hibiscus Racetrack in Southern California

The Case: En route to San Francisco, Jessica Fletcher spends a day at a Southern California racetrack visiting her niece. The latter, Tracy Macgill, is a novice jockey. Later, when jockey Carlos Gallegos develops food poisoning, horse owner Jack Bowen substitutes Tracy as the rider of Anchors Ahoy in the upcoming race.

Tracy wins the event, but her joy is short-lived when Bowen is found dead in the stables, a tranquilizer dart lodged in his neck. In short order, Tracy is suspended from further racing because of irregularities surrounding her riding a potentially medicated racer. In addition, she is police lieutenant Misko's prime candidate as Bowen's killer.

Although Jessica is inexperienced with the world of horse racing, she quickly takes control of the situation at the track. Her attention turns to Vicky Gallegos, the wife of the ailing jockey who happens to be an illegal alien. Then there are Dr. Mike Gann, an unscrupulous veterinarian; blustering bookie Vince Shackman; and suspicious track security person Pat Phillips.

Highlights: With its murderous overtones, this is anything but a typical light racetrack story. To lighten the mystery, there is Cliff and Christine Carpenter, passionate but superstitious track gamblers, each of whom has an unique "winning" system. Their enthusiasm for horse betting is so infectious that Jessica is soon attracted to the betting habit as well.

Trivia: Both Norman Fell and Priscilla Barnes were veterans of the long-running TV sitcom *Three's Company*. However, their show tenures (Fell: 1977–1979, Barnes: 1981–1984) didn't overlap. Character actor Lonny Chapman worked in *Young at Heart* (1954) and *Norma Rae* (1979). Brash comedian Jack Carter's early TV series cover *American Minstrels of 1949* (1949) and *Cavalcade of Stars* (1949–1950). Ramon Bieri was a veteran of TV's *Bret Maverick* (1981–1982) and *Joe's World* (1979–1980).

31. "Jessica Behind Bars"

(12/1/85) 60 mins.

Director: John Llewellyn Moxey **Teleplay:** Carelton Eastlake

Regular: Angela Lansbury (Jessica Fletcher)

Guest Cast: Margaret Avery (Dixie); Adrienne Barbeau (Kathryn); Barbara Baxley (Amanda Debs); Diane Bellamy (Head Guard); Darlene Conley (Mims); Yvonne DeCarlo (Miss Springer); Kiristall Eklund (Prisoner); Gay Hagen (1st Guard); Linda Kelsey (Mary Stamm); Janet MacLachlan (Dr. Irene Matthews); Faith Manton (2nd Guard); Vera Miles (Warden Elizabeth Gates); Susan Oliver (Louise); Susan Peretz (Bertha): Eve Plumb (Tug); Donna Ponterotto (Jamie); Jan Stratton (Gate Guard); Mary Woronov (Brady)

The Setting: A prison in Maine

The Case: Jessica agrees to substitute teach a class in creative writing at a state prison for women. While instructing her students, the riot alarm sounds. She, Warden Elizabeth Gates and several other administrators and female guards are taken hostage. The rampaging prisoners are led by Kathryn. When the prison physician, Dr. Irene Matthews, is found dead, it is assumed to be murder. Since prisoner Mary Stamm, serving time for killing her wife-beating spouse, was observed leaving the infirmary moments before the doctor's body was discovered, she is the major suspect.

Jessica persuades the rioting convicts—who are threatening a bloody breakout—to allow her to investigate the killing and to abide by her findings. Among those she questions are several of the not-so-honest staff, including Miss Springer, in charge of the kitchen, and Amanda Debs, the administrative deputy. There is also uncertainty about the prison chief, who is more focused on running for the U.S. Senate than on bettering jail conditions. Moreover, several prisoners confide that Gates and Dr. Matthews had fought bitterly not long before the latter died. Meanwhile, a second murder takes place behind the prison bars.

Highlights: Taking its cues from a long line of Hollywood women-behind-bars movies (*Women Without Names* [1940], *Caged* [1950] *Women's Prison* [1954]), this episode relies heavily on genre clichés and stereotypes. However, even the tough prisoners are no match for Jessica Fletcher, who gains their respect while unraveling the facts behind the morphine-induced death of Dr. Matthews. Especially effective among the convict population are Adrienne Barbeau's tough babe and Susan Peretz' (Big) Bertha.

Trivia: In the 1940s and 1950s Yvonne DeCarlo had been a voluptuous star at Universal Pictures (where *Murder, She Wrote* was produced). She starred in exotic sand-and-sandal adventures (*Salome, Where She Danced* [1945], *The Desert Hawk* [1950] and the prison drama *Brute Force* [1947]). She returned to Universal for the TV series *The Munsters* (1964–1966), playing the vampirish Lily.

Janet MacLachlan was Polly Swanson on *Archie Bunker's Place* (1980–1981). Adrienne Barbeau was Bea Arthur's daughter, Carol, on *Maude* (1972–1978). After being sweet Jan Brady on TV's *The Brady Bunch* (1969–1974), Eve Plumb played a prostitute in the TV movie *Dawn: The Story of a Teenage Runaway* (1976). Best known as Janet Leigh's surviving sister in *Psycho* (1960), Vera Miles was cast opposite Jimmy Stewart in *The FBI Story* (1959) and *The Man Who Shot Liberty Valance* (1962). Margaret Avery was Shug in *The Color Purple* (1985).

32. "Sticks and Stones"

(12/15/85) 60 mins.

Director: Seymour Robbie. **Teleplay:** Linda Shank, Mark Giles

Regulars: Angela Lansbury (Jessica Fletcher); Tom Bosley (Sheriff Amos Tupper); William Windom (Dr. Seth Hazlitt)

Recurring Character: John Astin (Sheriff Harry Pierce)

Guest Law Enforcer: Philip Brown (Deputy Willard)

Guest Cast: Paul Benedict (Frederick Hoffman); Cecil Cabot (Mabel Bemish); Joseph Campanella (George Knapp); John David Carson (Larry Burns); Marsha Hunt (Elvira Tree); Evelyn Keyes (Edna); Danny McCoy, Jr. (Waiter); Denny Miller (Nils Anderson); Betsy Palmer (Lila Norris); Ken Samson (Man); Garnett Smith (Mel); Parker Stevenson (Michael Digby); Christopher Stone (Adam Forbisher); Kristy Syverson (Beverly Forbisher); Bob Tzudiker (Agent); Howard Witt (Bart Nelson)

The Setting: Cabot Cove, Maine

The Case: Beverly Forbisher, a Cabot Cove homeowner who is planning to sell her property, is electrocuted while taking a bubble bath. Not long afterward, travel writer Michael Digby appears in town. He intends to write a book alerting the world that Cabot Cove is an undiscovered tourist gem. Meanwhile, the town is flooded with hate mail which turns neighbor against neighbor, including sharp-mouthed Edna, who accuses Jessica of breaking up her marriage. Before long, Elvira Tree, who admits to having sent only one of the spite letters, is found hanging from a tree outside her home.

As chaos spreads through the town, Jessica sifts through the clues. Because Sheriff Tupper has retired, she must deal with—and help—Amos's replacement, real estate broker Harry Pierce. Needing a more pliable sidekick, Jessica turns to Michael Digby. Through him, she learns about the local planning commissioners (George Knapp, Lila Norris and Bart Nelson) and their scheme regarding a Cabot Cove condo development project.

Highlights: This is one of the most heavily plotted excursions, with several intriguing sub-stories, an abundance of local color and many red herrings. If Tom Bosley's Sheriff Amos had been a bumbling delight before, he takes on very human shading here. Discovering that retirement ill suits him, he eagerly collaborates with Jessica to assist dumbfounded Harry Pierce dealing with his law enforcement duties.

Trivia: Parker Stevenson costarred with Shaun Cassidy in *The Hardy Boys Mysteries* (1977–1979). This was John Astin's third and final appearance as Harry Pierce. John David Carson had acted in *The Savage Is Loose* (1974) and *Empire of the Ants* (1977). Former 1940s MGM starlet Marsha Hunt, blacklisted during the House Un-American Activities Committee's Communist witch hunt of the late 1940s, had played with Wendell Corey and Patty McCormack in the TV sitcom *Peck's Bad Girl* (1959).

Denny Miller was *Tarzan, the Ape Man* (1959). Before appearing as Vivien Leigh's sister in *Gone with the Wind* (1939), Evelyn Keyes had been in *Artists and Models Abroad* (1938) and *The Buccaneer* (1938). Betsy Palmer's movie credits encompass *The Long Gray Line* (1955), *The Last Angry Man* (1959) and *Friday the 13th* (1980). Christopher Stone (1940–1995) had been a guest performer on such TV series as *Bionic Woman*, *Dallas* and *Spencer's Pilots.*

33. "Murder Digs Deep"

(12/29/85) 60 mins.

Director: Philip Leacock **Teleplay:** Maryanne Kasica, Michael Scheff

Regulars: Angela Lansbury (Jessica Fletcher); William Windom (Dr. Seth Hazlitt)

Guest Cast: Cecile Callan (Karen Parks); Robert Dryer (Guard); George Grizzard (Dr. Aubrey Benton); David Groh (Dr. Garfield); Randolph Mantooth (Raymond Two Crows [De Marco]); Stephen Shortridge (Steve Gamble); Connie Stevens (Cynthia Armstrong); Robert Vaughn (Gideon Armstrong)

The Setting: Grand Cadera, New Mexico

The Case: At the suggestion of vacationing Dr. Seth Hazlitt, Jessica joins him at an archaeological dig eighty miles east of Santa Fe, New Mexico. She hopes the experience will be useful in researching her new book, *Murder at the Digs.* The accommodations in the desert heat are austere, and things quickly boil over. First, there are mysterious Indian drumbeats, supposedly due to the expedition violating sacred Native American territory. Then, Raymond Two Crows, a young Indian who has opposed the excavation, is murdered under weird circumstances.

Wealthy Gideon Armstrong, who financed the dig, convinces the group not to call in the police—yet—because it will cause the site to be closed down. With only a weekend to solve the murder, Jessica, with Seth in tow, undertakes the challenge. Others involved include Gideon's disgruntled, spoiled wife Cynthia; two rival grad students, Karen Parks and Steve Gamble; a condescending TV commentator/author, Dr. Aubrey Benton; and a university professor, Dr. Garfield.

Highlights: Under the best of circumstances Dr. Seth Hazlitt loves his creature comforts and his daily rituals. However, he is surprisingly complacent about his volunteer desert work and the onslaught of adversities. Combining her intuitive knack with her researching skills, Jessica—who seemingly can adapt to any situation or culture—soon overcomes her unfamiliarity with Indian customs and the world of archaeology to spot the killer.

Trivia: During Robert Vaughn's years (1964–1968) starring in the spy/action series *The Man from U.N.C.L.E.*, Angela Lansbury guest-starred on the series in the November 12, 1965 episode, "The Deadly Toys Affair." Randolph Mantooth, the son of a full-blooded Seminole Indian, appeared in such teleseries as *Emergency* (1972–1977), *Operation Petticoat* (1978–1979) and the daytime soap opera *Loving* (1987). David Groh was Valerie Harper's perplexed but understanding spouse on *Rhoda* (1974–1977). Connie Stevens costarred with Troy Donahue in a trio of features: *Parrish* (1961), *Susan Slade* (1961) and *Palm Springs Weekend* (1963).

34. "Murder by Appointment Only"

(1/5/86) 60 mins.

Director: Arthur Allan Seidelman **Teleplay:** Jerry Ross

Regular: Angela Lansbury (Jessica Fletcher)

Recurring Character: Michael Horton (Grady Fletcher)

Guest Law Enforcer: Herbert Edelman (Lieutenant Varick)

Guest Cast: Christine Belford (Fiona Keeler); Robert Culp (Norman Amberson); Robert Desiderio (Roger Adiano); Ann Dusenberry (Liz Gordon); Leigh McCloskey (Todd Amberson); Jayne Meadows (Lila Lee Amberson); Millie Perkins (Glenda Vandevere)

The Setting: New York City

The Case: Between a hectic schedule of Manhattan publishing appointments, Jessica Fletcher visits with her favorite nephew, Grady Fletcher. Always between jobs and girlfriends, he now hopes that a college classmate, Todd Amberson, can wrangle him an accounting job with Lila Lee Cosmetics. The firm is run by iron-handed Lila Lee Amberson and her less adept brother, Norman. Currently, they are hosting the company's annual sales convention.

Jessica is pleased to discover that Norman's much-younger fiancée is none other than Liz Gordon, one of her former creative writing students. Later, when Liz misses a dinner engagement, Norman and Jessica rush to the girl's apartment. There they find her strangled corpse and notice that her portrait has been viciously damaged.

Determined to bring Liz's killer to justice, Jessica works hand-in-hand with Detective Lieutenant Varick. Getting over the shock of learning that the victim had once been a call girl, Jessica targets several likely suspects: the volatile, controlling Lila Lee; Norman's son, Todd, who is frustrated from years of being in his relatives' shadows; Glenda Vandevere, Norman's loyal and love-struck secretary; and Roger Adiano, who has his own ax to grind.

Highlights: Jayne Meadows provides a devastating satirical caricature of a cosmetics mogul. Meadows's oversized performance is in sharp contrast to Angela Lansbury's sensible Jessica Fletcher. The latter shines with maternal radiance as she bunks out at her nephew's modest New York City digs, advises the ingenuous young man on the ways of business and love, and builds his confidence by having him do legwork for her sleuthing.

Trivia: Married to talk show veteran Steve Allen, Jayne Meadows had been a 1940s MGM contract player along with Angela Lansbury. Veteran character actor Herbert Edelman (1930–1996), making his second *Murder, She Wrote* appearance, was in transition to his eventual Lieutenant Arnie Gelber characterization (another New York cop) that would become his series specialty. Sequences for the Lila Lee Cosmetics convention were shot at Los Angeles's venerable Ambassador Hotel. Leigh McCloskey's feature film credits boasted *Fraternity Vacation* (1985) and *Hamburger . . . the Motion Picture* (1986). Millie Perkins had starred in *The Diary of Anne Frank* (1959).

35. "Trial by Error"

(1/12/86) 60 mins.

Director: Seymour Robbie **Story:** Scott Shepherd **Teleplay:** Paul Savage

Regular: Angela Lansbury (Jessica Fletcher)

Guest Cast: David Ackroyd (Tom Casselli); R.J. Adams (Victor Assmussen); Tony Bill (Mark Lee Reynolds); Norman Burton (Drew Narramore); Virginia Capers (Margo Webster); Macdonald Carey (Oscar Ramsey, Esq.); Robert Casper (Arthur Jasper); John Chandler (Johnny Detweiler); Doran Clark (Becky Anderson); Jon Cypher (Max Flynn); Gene Evans (Otto Fry); Tom Ewell (Josh Corbin); Gary Frank (Lee Callahan); Arlene Golonka (Sally Conover); Javier Grajeda (Paramedic); Alan Hale (Fenton Harris); James Hampton (Jerry Burns, the Bartender); Lenore Kasdorf (Ally Collins); Warren Kemmerling (Dr. Maurice Webster); Diane Lander (Stephanie Reynolds); Vicki Lawrence (Jackie MacKay); Walter Mathews (Judge Philo Walker); Allan Miller (Frank Lord); Brock Peters (Thornton Bentley); Richard Sanders (Gerald Richard); Michael Swan (Cliff Anderson); Gregory Walcott (Willie Patchecki)

The Setting: Cabot Cove's County Seat, Maine

The Case: As jury foreman, Jessica Fletcher refuses to yield to her impatient fellow jurors—including Jackie MacKay, Sally Conover and Oscar Ramsey—who insist that the case is open and shut. She persuades them to reevaluate all the facts.

Mark Reynolds is charged with what he claims is the self-defense murder of Cliff Anderson. The latter surprised Mark and Cliff's soon-to-be ex-wife, Becky, at her apartment, making love. Complicating the situation is the fact that earlier that day, Mark and his wife, Stephanie, had been involved in a traffic accident when he swerved their car to avoid hitting a youngster who had carelessly ridden his bicycle into their path. Mark escapes uninjured, but Stephanie suffers a broken collarbone and other internal injuries. She is rushed to the hospital, where much later that day she dies.

As Jessica and her fellow jurors scrutinize the testimony, intriguing facts come to light, leading to an amazing outcome.

Highlights: This episode boasts one of the largest casts assembled for a Jessica Fletcher hour-long adventure. Because there are so many diverse personalities—among the jurors, in the flashbacks of events leading up to the victim's death, etc.—few of the guest stars have occasion to shine. However, Allan Miller, as juror Frank Lord, makes a strong impression as an annoying radio talk show host who cannot outtalk or outmaneuver Jessica.

Trivia: Among the acting ensemble, stage and film star Macdonald Carey was best known for his role as Dr. Tom Horton on the TV soap opera *Days of Our Lives*, from 1965 until his death in 1994. As an actor Tony Bill costarred in several features: *Come Blow Your Horn* (1963), *Shampoo* (1975), etc. As a movie director, his credits include *Five Corners* (1987) and *A Home of Our Own* (1993). Comic actor Tom Ewell (1909–1994) began his screen career with *Adam's Rib* (1949) and went on to *The Seven Year Itch* (1955) opposite Marilyn Monroe and *State Fair* (1962) with Alice Faye. Brock Peters built a screen career on *To Kill a Mockingbird* (1962), *The L-Shaped Room* (1962) and *The Pawnbroker* (1964).

36. "Keep the Home Fries Burning"

(1/19/86) 60 mins.

Director: Peter Crane **Teleplay:** Philip Gerson

Regulars: Angela Lansbury (Jessica Fletcher); Tom Bosley (Sheriff Amos Tupper); William Windom (Dr. Seth Hazlitt)

Recurring Character: Orson Bean (Ebeneezer McEnery)

Guest Cast: Sharon Acker (Wilhelmina Fraser); Norman Alden (Hawthorne); Gary Crosby (Ted Stully); Anne Lloyd Francis (Margo Perry); William Lucking (Bo Dixon); John McCook (Harrison Fraser, III); Donna Pescow (Cornelia); Henry Polic II (Alan Dupree); Marcia Rodd (Betty Fiddler); Alan Young (Floyd Nelson)

The Setting: Cabot Cove, Maine

The Case: To Bo Dixon's consternation, his diner is losing business to the newly refurbished restaurant at the Joshua Peabody Inn. Moreover, the inn's boastful owner, Floyd Nelson, has also stolen away Bo's mainstay, waitress Cornelia. The enraged Dixon becomes a diner at the inn to analyze just what is attracting the Cabot Cove crowd. He happens to pick the morning that an epidemic of apparent food poisoning at the inn leads to the hospitalization of several patrons, including Wilhelmina Fraser, and the death of one of them, Betty Fiddler.

While Jessica is sorting out the facts with Sheriff Amos Tupper and overworked Dr. Seth Hazlitt, she deals with officious Margo Perry, an expert from the State Health Department. The investigators not only focus on Alan Dupree, the heavy-drinking, supercilious new inn chef, but on Floyd Nelson's business rival, Bo Dixon.

Highlights: In a battle of wits and experience, Jessica proves a match for the highly efficient but jaded Margo Perry. Thus, there are several amusing interchanges as each tries to rule out the other's case theories. Meanwhile, Amos Tupper is left in the dust. Not only is he embarrassed that the offer of complimentary meals led him to switch his dining loyalties from Dixon's Diner to the Joshua Peabody Inn, but he becomes frantic because he was gobbling a huge breakfast at the inn on that fateful day. As such, he turns into a comically classic hypochondriac. In this posture he is a perfect foil for Dr. Hazlitt's biting witticisms. This setup allows both Cabot Cove favorites to reveal new personality traits.

Trivia: As with many episode titles of *Murder, She Wrote,* this one is not only a pun on a popular saying, but it provides a useful plot line reference. Comedian Alan Young, who plays the inventive new proprietor of the inn, had starred as befuddled Wilbur Post on TV's classic *Mr. Ed* (1961–1966).

For the record, in an earlier second season episode, "Joshua Peabody Died Here—Possibly" (#24), the stubborn Dr. Hazlitt insisted—in opposition to more skeptical Jessica Fletcher—that the legendary Joshua Peabody was a real human being. However, in this new installment, Seth changes his mind about the actuality of Cabot Cove's most famous Revolutionary War soldier.

Orson Bean, of the mid-1990s *Dr. Quinn, Medicine Woman,* had played Reverend Brim on *Mary Hartman, Mary Hartman* (1977–1978). Bing Crosby's son, Gary (1933–1995), had a middling screen career which began with bits in his dad's *Star Spangled Rhythm* (1942) and went on to *Mardi Gras* (1958), *Operation Bikini* (1963) and *Which Way to the Front?* (1970). At the time of his death, he was planning to record an album of "duets" with his late father. Among Anne (Lloyd) Francis's screen work are *Bad Day at Black Rock* (1954), *Forbidden Planet* (1956) and *Funny Girl* (1968).

37. "Powder Keg"

(2/9/86) 60 mins.

Director: John Llewellyn Moxey **Teleplay:** Peter S. Fischer

Regular: Angela Lansbury (Jessica Fletcher)

Guest Law Enforcers: Dorian Harewood (Sheriff Claudell Cox); W.K. Stratton (Deputy Morgan)

Guest Cast: Dan Adams (Barfly); John Alvin (Dr. Frazier); Pat Corley (Frank Kelso); Mariclare Costello (Cassie Latham Burns); Debra Dusay

(Desk Clerk); Cindy Fisher (Linda Bonner); Brian L. Green (Matthew Burns); Jackie Earle Haley (Billy Willetts); John Dennis Johnston (Peter Fargo); Bill McKinney (Demsey); Muriel Minot (Woman); Jeffrey Osterhage (Ed Bonner); Hartley Silver (Man); Craig Stevens (Professor Ames Caulfield); Stuart Whitman (Phil Bonner); Larry Wilcox (Andy Crane)

The Setting: Hoopville, Alabama

The Case: After attending an exhausting writers conference in Alabama, Jessica Fletcher and fellow author/teacher Ames Caulfield, a widower, are stranded in a sleepy town when Caulfield's car breaks down. They stay at the Hotel Imperial operated by Cassie Burns, who is the mother of Matt, a young adult. Before long, Jessica and Ames discover that Hoopville is a hotbed of trouble.

Town bully Ed Bonner, who had recently and unexplainably come into some money, is knifed to death. The prime suspect is Matt, Cassie's son, who is a singer/musician at Reese's, a local roadhouse run by Frank Kelso. The evening of Bonner's death, Ed and Matt had fought in front of many witnesses. Later, the murder weapon is unearthed at Matt's place, and he is taken into custody. Caulfield begs Jessica to help young Burns, admitting that years ago he knew Cassie, who was then one of his students.

Thereafter, local redneck ruffians—including Ed's pals Billy Willetts and Andy Crane—lead a rioting crowd to the jail, demanding that Matt be turned over to them. Sheriff Claudell Cox and his men barely hold off the mob from lynching the prisoner. Meanwhile, the trail leads Jessica to the dead man's father, Phil Bonner, and to the deceased's sister, Linda, a waitress at Reese's.

Highlights: Because Hoopville and its folk are so different from Cabot Cove and its inhabitants, the contrast makes a fascinating change of pace for the series. Adding to the tension in this very Southern town is the fact that Hoopville's sheriff is an African-American.

Trivia: The country western ambiance of the roadside club in this episode would be replicated in later installments. Rotund Pat Corley would play another type of club operator when he was cast later as the owner of Phil's Restaurant on the TV sitcom *Murphy Brown* (1988–1996).

Craig Stevens had been the lead in TV's *Peter Gunn* (1958–1961) while Dorian Harewood had been a cast regular of *Strike Force* (1981–1982) and *Trauma Center* (1983). Before *CHiPs* (1977–1982), Larry Wilcox had been in such made-for-TV movies as *The Great American Beauty Contest* (1973), *Sky Heist* (1975) and *Restless* (1977). Veteran film star and ex-boxer Stuart Whitman had been U.S. Marshal Jim Crown on *Cimarron Strip* (1967–1968).

38. "Murder in the Electric Cathedral"

(2/16/86) 60 mins.

Director: John Llewellyn Moxey **Teleplay:** Dick Nelson

Regular: Angela Lansbury (Jessica Fletcher)

Guest Law Enforcer: Dick Van Patten (Fred Whittaker, the District Attorney)

Guest Cast: Jack Bannon (Dr. Mark Brady); Barbi Benton (Sue Beth); Frank Bonner (Earl Fargo); Steve Forrest (Reverend Willie-John Fargo); Judy Geeson (Sister Ruth Fargo); Richard Herd (Harvey McKittrick); Art Hindle (Sam McKittrick); Mildred Natwick (Carrie McKittrick); Jeannie Wilson (Alice McKittrick)

The Setting: Cherokee Flats, Oklahoma

The Case: Not having seen her old teacher in over thirty years, Jessica jets to Oklahoma to pay her a visit. She is surprised to discover that Carrie McKittrick, now a very wealthy widow, is extremely ill. When Carrie suffers a heart attack she is rushed to the hospital.

While Jessica keeps a vigil outside Carrie's room, the news of the patient's critical condition brings visitors to her bedside. Among those are Harvey McKittrick, Carrie's stepson; Sam McKittrick, Carrie's grandson and a wife beater; and Alice McKittrick, Sam's well-meaning wife. The mercenary Harvey and Sam hope to convince Carrie to change her will yet again. As it stands now, almost all her fortune is to be left to TV evangelist Reverend Willie-John Fargo, who owns the clinic where Carrie is a patient.

When Carrie passes away, Jessica is uncertain whether it was from natural causes. After all, she had seen a nurse rushing from the patient's room a brief time before Carrie died. Her hunch proves right when an autopsy reveals Mrs. McKittrick died of cyanide poisoning. However, District Attorney Fred Whittaker, who cares more about keeping the good will of the influential Fargos and McKittricks, refuses to press an investigation. As such, Jessica takes charge.

The clues lead Mrs. Fletcher back and forth between the McKittrick household and Reverend Fargo's group. The latter includes the proselytizer's relatives, Earl and Sister Ruth. Others implicated in the setup are the clinic's Dr. Mark Brady and his nurse assistant, Sue Beth.

Highlights: Usually Jessica Fletcher is the senior adult of the story line, but here she is almost schoolgirlish in her scenes with her elderly mentor, Carrie McKittrick. The latter has a very impressive moment when, fearing she will not long survive her heart problems, she begs Jessica not to let her will be changed.

Trivia: Veteran actor Dick Van Patten had a long run as Nels on TV's *Mama* (1949–1957). In *Eight Is Enough* (1977–1981) he was Tom Bradford, the model father. Barbi Benton had been a regular on TV's *Hee Haw* (1971–1976). Steve Forrest had a featured role on *Dallas* in 1986. Sterling actress Mildred Natwick (1905–1994), had been Oscar nominated for her role as Jane Fonda's mother in *Barefoot in the Park* (1967) and won an Emmy as an amateur sleuth in the series *The Snoop Sisters* (1973–1974), which costarred Helen Hayes.

39. "One Good Bid Deserves a Murder"

(2/23/86) 60 mins.

Director: Seymour Robbie **Teleplay:** J. Miyoko Hensley, Steven Hensley

Regular: Angela Lansbury (Jessica Fletcher)

Recurring Characters: Ray Girardin (Lieutenant Casey); Jerry Orbach (Harry McGraw)

Guest Law Enforcer: Sterling Swanson (Hogan, the Desk Sergeant)

Guest Cast: David Ankrum (Young Doctor); Karen Black (Dr. Sydney Dunn); Nancy Grahn (Sheila Saxon); Robert Gray (Albert "Bert" Cromwell, the Auction House Worker); Hurd Hatfield (William Radford); Edward Mulhare (Richard Bennett); Cotter Smith (Robert Rhine, Esq.); Rebecca Street (Deborah Chase, Sal Domino's Secretary); Vic Tayback (Sal Domino)

The Setting: Boston, Massachusetts

The Case: Jessica Fletcher comes to Logan Airport to greet her friend Richard Bennett. She agrees to do a favor for the movie star who is flying that day to Spain. He asks her to visit a Boston auction house five days hence and bid on the diary of the late movie star Evangeline. Once she acquires it, he instructs Jessica to destroy it. To accomplish her mission, he gives her one million dollars!

At the auction house, Jessica meets its owner, William Radford, and discovers that several others have a deep interest in the screen star's diary. They include Dr. Sydney Dunn, a Beverly Hills psychiatrist, who was the sex symbol's therapist; as well as Sal Domino, who used to make porno films; and Sheila Saxon, a former agent turned producer. Before the coveted diary can be sold, Bennett's body is discovered in an antique armoire that was not initially planned to be auctioned.

While at the Boston police station for questioning, Jessica encounters Harlan A. McGraw, better known as Harry McGraw, private detective. He agrees to help the baffled Jessica solve this latest case. Before long, a $300 chess set she purchased for Dr. Seth Hazlitt at the auction house is stolen from her Back Bay hotel room. Meanwhile, several important pages from Evangeline's impounded diary are removed from the evidence room at the police precinct. This discovery draws several interested parties back to Jessica, as they are convinced that she must have a full copy of the document. They include a fanatical fan, Bert Cromwell and Robert Rhine, the assistant of a former ambassador who has political ambitions but fears what the diary says about his connection to Evangeline.

Highlights: With the story's Evangeline being a carbon copy of real-life sex symbol Marilyn Monroe, the episode takes on a greater dimension. The rapport established between Harry McGraw and Jessica Fletcher in 1985's "Tough Guys Don't Die" (#16) is further embellished here. The duo's (mis)-adventure fleshes out the budding chemistry between these very diverse characters. At times, Jessica is amused by the street-smart, but life-foolish Harry. However, there are moments when this free-wheeling soul exasperates her. But, as would become customary on their joint sleuthing, they realize that each brings something different and vital to the case, and together they make an admirable team.

On the deficit side, Karen Black's absurd performance as a psychiatrist reduced a lot of the episode's credibility.

Trivia: Bronx-born Jerry Orbach had begun his career as a stage actor *(The Fantasticks)* and debuted on TV on *The Jack Paar Show* (1960). Irishman Edward Mulhare, who bore a resemblance to Rex Harrison, often followed in the latter's career path. Mulhare took over on stage for Harrison as Professor Henry Higgins in *My Fair Lady.* Later, Mulhare inherited the part of the ghostly sea captain in TV's *The Ghost and Mrs. Muir* (1968–1970), a role which Harrison had performed in a 1947 movie. Vic Tayback's (1929–1990) movies included *Bullitt* (1968) and *Alice Doesn't Live Here Anymore* (1974—which led to his ongoing role on the TV spin-off *Thunderbolt and Lightfoot* [1975]), among others.

40. "If a Body Meets a Body"

(3/9/86) 60 mins.

Director: Peter Crane **Teleplay:** Steve Stoliar

Regulars: Angela Lansbury (Jessica Fletcher); Tom Bosley (Sheriff Amos Tupper); William Windom (Dr. Seth Hazlitt)

Guest Cast: Robert Donner (Silas Pike); Ella R. Edwards (Townsperson); Timothy Jecko (Townsperson); Anne Jeffreys (Agnes Shipley); Audrey Landers (Phyllis Walters); Lori Lethin (Christy Olson); Monte Markham (Ned Olson); Joe Maross (Henry Vernon); Rex Smith (Stew Bennett); Carrie Snodgress (Connie Vernon); Richard Stahl (Reverend Matthews); Robert Sterling (Ben Shipley)

The Setting: Cabot Cove, Maine

The Case: Cabot Cove is shocked when financial advisor Henry Vernon dies while on vacation with his wife, Connie. Three days later, many townsfolk, including Jessica Fletcher, turn out to pay their last respects. However, no one is prepared for the chaos at the funeral service. First, Phyllis Walters, a truck stop waitress, interrupts the church proceedings with her allegation that she loved the deceased and that Connie knows dark secrets regarding Henry's death. In the ensuing confusion, the closed coffin topples open, and everyone is aghast to discover that the corpse is not Henry's!

Sheriff Amos Tupper is baffled as to the actual identity of the embalmed victim. For that matter, he has no idea what happened to Vernon's remains, nor does Connie Vernon—at first. Matters take a new twist when Henry's body and some partially burned stacks of money are located in the back of Stew Bennett's stolen van. An autopsy reveals that Vernon was murdered less than a day before.

While the criminal investigation proceeds, several Cabot Cove citizens—including Jessica, Amos and Mr. and Mrs. Shipley—learn from Henry's partner, Ned Olson, that the Pheasant Ridge Medical Clinic project is bankrupt and that their invested funds have vanished. Ned blames the fiasco on Henry.

Highlights: In episodes such as this, one gets a fully realized picture of small-town life with its strata of society and intermingled connections between assorted households. As would prove true throughout the series, Jessica's nosing into a criminal case meets with far less resistance on her home turf. Unsurprisingly, she is far less intrusive in her handling of suspects in Cabot Cove than she is when on one of her many incident-filled treks to big cities.

Trivia: Anne Jeffreys and Robert Sterling, married in actual life, had co-starred in two TV series: *Topper* (1953–1956) and *Love That Jill* (1958). Richard Stahl was chef Howard Miller on the 1980s TV sitcom *It's a Living*. Monte Markham's television acting resume includes starring as the sleuthing lawyer on the revived *Perry Mason* (1973–1974).

41. "Christopher Bundy—Died on Sunday"

(3/30/86) 60 mins.

Director: Peter Crane **Teleplay:** Gerald K. Siegel

Regular: Angela Lansbury (Jessica Fletcher)

Recurring Character: Michael Horton (Grady Fletcher)

Guest Law Enforcers: Robert Costanza (Detective Lieutenant Greco); Charles Sweigart (Uniformed Officer)

Guest Cast: Bert Convy (Christopher Bundy); Bobby Di Cicco (Antonio D'Argento); Josh Gordon (Announcer); Robert Hooks (Everett Charles Jensen); Carol Lawrence (Rachel D'Argento); Katherine Moffat (Millicent Moor); Michele Nicastro (Vanessa); Alex Rocco (Bert Yardley); Eric Server (Pete Morgan, the Security Guard); Robert Stack (Chester Harrison)

The Setting: Near Poughkeepsie, New York

The Case: Jessica Fletcher is horrified to learn that *Literary Lions Monthly*, for whom she has written a short story, has just been purchased by girlie magazine mogul Christopher Bundy. Bundy's representatives refuse to release her from her author's contract. An angered Jessica, with her obliging nephew Grady Fletcher in tow, storms Bundy's estate fortress in upstate New York.

Bundy, the country's most eligible bachelor, charms Jessica and Grady into staying the night at the family compound. The next morning, Bundy's bullet-ridden body is found upstairs in the mansion.

Detective Lieutenant Greco immediately seizes on Chester Harrison as the logical suspect. After all, this publisher, who owed the victim a great deal of money, had stayed at the lush house overnight and had sped off in his car shortly after the body was discovered.

Jessica, on the other hand, who had previously met Harrison at a Texas book fair, feels differently. She concentrates on the houseful of grasping relatives and brooding retainers: the deceased's sister, Rachel D'Argento; Rachel's son, Antonio by her first marriage; and her daughter, Vanessa, by a second union. Then there is Bundy's longtime subordinate, Bert Yardley; a shapely magazine "model," Millicent Moor; and Bundy's houseman, Charles Jensen.

Highlights: While many of the visiting cast provide unmemorable cameos, Michael Horton shines as overly trusting Grady Fletcher. Although constantly in Aunt Jessica's shadow (isn't everyone?), he is unmindful because he knows she cares about his welfare. An example of Grady's vulnerability occurs when he discovers that Millicent was only playing up to him to gather a particular suspect's attention.

Trivia: Once again, the solving of the crime hinges on Jessica's astute observation in (re)watching the VCR tape of a closed-circuit surveillance system.

Robert Stack's very lengthy show business career is highlighted by his lead role of Eliot Ness in *The Untouchables* (1959–1963) and hosting *Unsolved Mysteries* (1988–1994). Robert Hooks gained recognition during the 1970s black exploitation film cycle: *Trouble Man* (1972), *Aaron Loves Angela* (1975), etc. Game show host Bert Convey (1933–1991) had once been a professional baseball player as well as a pop singer. Carol Lawrence made her name on Broadway in the 1950s' *West Side Story*. Alex Rocco has been a mainstay of budget action pictures: *Detroit 9000* (1973), *Return to Horror High* (1987), etc.

42. "Menace Anyone?"

(4/6/86) 60 mins.

Director: Arthur Allan Seidelman **Teleplay:** Robert B. Sherman

Regular: Angela Lansbury (Jessica Fletcher)

Guest Law Enforcers: Richard Jacobson (Patrolman); Barry Primas (Detective Berger); David Spielberg (Lieutenant Travis)

Guest Cast: Harold Ayer (Sexton); Helen Baron (Reporter #1); Dennis Cole (Mitch Mercer); Gus Corrado (Paramedic); Bryan Cranston (Brian East); Karlene Crockett (Barbara McDermott); Lawrence Haddon (Judge); Linda Hamilton (Carol Atkinson McDermott); Van Johnson (Elliot Robinson); Kelli Maroney (Cissy Banes); Doug McKeon (Donny Harrigan); Rod Porter (Reporter #2); Betsy Russell (Doris Robinson); Kerry Sherman (Rosie, a Patient at Overview Sanitarium)

The Setting: Boston, Massachusetts

The Case: Jessica Fletcher is honorary chairperson of a charity tennis tournament in Boston. The matches are held at Elliot Robinson's swank tennis club. One of Elliot's assistants is Carol Atkinson, a former student of Jessica's.

In short order, trouble erupts courtside. Ace tennis player Donny Harrigan angers Elliot when he balks at playing in the tournament. Things do not improve when Donny's manager, Mitch Mercer, supports his immature client. Meanwhile, Robinson's daughter, Doris, admits to her dad that she strongly resents losing to Carol the post as his special assistant.

Disaster strikes when Brian East dies in a car bombing most probably intended for the vehicle's owner, his fiancée Carol. Further on, police lieutenant Travis is murdered at Carol's apartment. Despite all evidence, Jessica is certain that the young woman is innocent.

As Jessica picks her way through the maze of information, she focuses on a tragedy three years ago when Elliot's other daughter, Barbara, died in a plane crash. The loss left Robinson permanently grief-stricken, while Doris, who felt responsible for her sister being on the plane that fateful day, has been emotionally unstable ever since. To make matters worse, Doris insists now that the dead Barbara has come back to life!

Highlights: The obvious rapport between Angela Lansbury and Van Johnson—both veterans and costars of 1940s and 1950s MGM movies—makes their scenes together a special treat. One of the surprises of this installment is the series precedent breaker of having the police investigator murdered. Jessica takes his death personally because she had become friendly with Travis when they had taken a criminology seminar at Boston College the prior year.

Trivia: A buffed-up Linda Hamilton would later costar with Arnold Schwarzenegger in *The Terminator* (1984) and *Terminator 2: Judgment Day* (1991), while Betsy Russell had already starred on the big screen in *Avenging Angel* (1985) as a teenage hooker. Dennis Cole was Detective Jim Briggs on *Felony Squad* (1966–1969) and Johnny Reach on *Bearcats* (1971). Freckle-faced Van Johnson rejected the role of Eliot Ness on *The Untouchables*—a part taken by Robert Stack—but Johnson did play a character called The Minstrel on the mid-1960s *Batman.*

43. "The Perfect Foil"

(4/13/86) 60 mins.

Director: Walter Grauman **Teleplay:** Robert E. Swanson

Regular: Angela Lansbury (Jessica Fletcher)

Guest Law Enforcer: Cesare Danova (Lieutenant Edmund Cavette)

Guest Cast: Barbara Babcock (Rosaline Gardner); Guerin Barry (Costumed Sir Walter Raleigh); Peter Bonerz (Calhoun Fletcher); Richard Brose (Headsman); George DiCenzo (Johnny Blaze); Robert Forster (Gilbert Gaston); Wendy Gates (Costumed Madame Dracula); David Hedison (Mitch Payne); Lisa Langlois (Kitty Manette); Rafael Mauro (Costumed Napoleon); Sherry McFarland (Receptionist); Joe Ross (Desk Clerk); Hank Rolike (Taxi Driver); Penny Singleton (Aunt Mildred); Granville Van Dusen (Brad Garner)

The Setting: New Orleans, Louisiana

The Case: At the request of her Aunt Mildred, Jessica detours from her business traveling to stop in New Orleans to look up cousin Calhoun Fletcher. Jessica is aghast to discover that Calhoun's home has been converted into the notorious Lafite Sporting House.

It happens to be the last night of Mardi Gras and the club is hosting a wild masquerade party. Jessica mingles with the masked guests, hoping to find Calhoun. Instead, she is present when the gambling club's owner, Johnny Blaze, dies in his office. Several witnesses swear that just before his murder, the victim had been sword fighting with a masked Calhoun.

Calhoun protests that he was home in a drunken sleep at the time of the party. Nevertheless, he is arrested. Jessica comes to his aid, assisted by Calhoun's pal, corporate attorney Mitch Payne. It's learned that police lieutenant Edmund Cavette is pleased that Blaze is dead, for the late crook was implicated (but never convicted) in the death of Cavette's son, the latter having accused Blaze of cheating at cards.

Others who had a stake in Johnny's death are Washington, D.C., politician Brad Gardner and his domineering wife Rosaline because of Brad's gambling debts to Blaze. Additionally, club workers Kitty Manette and Gilbert Gaston were having an affair which the deceased had threatened to destroy.

Highlights: The hour's smartest moments occur when Jessica weaves her way through the costumed party, chatting with guests, and commenting wittily on their finery.

Trivia: Making a one-shot appearance as Aunt Mildred was Penny Singleton, the dimpled entertainer who had played Dagwood Bumbstead's scatterbrained wife in the long-lasting (1938–1950) *Blondie* movie series. Peter Bonerz gained prominence as the unorthodox dentist Jerry Robinson on TV's *The Bob Newhart Show* (1972–1978). More recently he has become a major TV sitcom director. Once performing in major features such as *Reflections in a Golden Eye* (1967) and *Medium Cool* (1969), Robert Forster's recent efforts have been B movies like *The Banker* (1989).

44. "If the Frame Fits"

(5/18/86) 60 mins.

Director: Paul Lynch **Teleplay:** Philip Gerson

Regular: Angela Lansbury (Jessica Fletcher)

Guest Law Enforcer: Cliff Gorman (Police Chief Cooper)

Guest Cast: Deborah Adair (Ellen Davis); Christopher Allport (Donald Granger); John De Lancie (Binky Holborn); Gordon Jump (Frank Tilley); Norman Lloyd (Lloyd Marcus): Audrey Meadows (Mildred Tilley); Andra Millian (Sabrina Marcus); Michael Morgan (Young Man); Aubrey Morris (Forbes, the Houseman): Merritt Russell (Waiter); Anne Schedeen (Julia Granger)

The Setting: Cedar Heights, Connecticut

The Case: At the request of retired publisher friend Lloyd Marcus, Jessica Fletcher has flown to his suburban town for the weekend. The well-to-do widower wants Jessica's opinion of a murder mystery manuscript he has in hand. (Actually Marcus wrote the novel, but is too sensitive to admit to the fact.)

While Jessica and Lloyd attend a dull dinner party, his house is robbed of a valuable painting, which proves to be the latest in a series of art robberies in this fashionable neighborhood. Matters become more serious the next night when Julia, Marcus's snobbish daughter, is found murdered in the living room of her nearby home. Police chief Cooper deduces that she died while preventing a robbery.

Astute Jessica reasons otherwise, as the clues seem all too neatly set forth. Since Cooper is so blasé about the crime, she is left to her own devices to follow up her hunch. She learns about the wealthy locals from Forbes, Marcus's houseman, as well as from Ellen Davis, an employee at the swank local country club. Chats with Frank Tilley, the town's mayor and chief insurance agent, and his wife, Mildred, prove revealing, as do conversations with an effete dilettante, Binky Holborn, and Lloyd's other daughter, Sabrina, who has had a long-time crush on her brother-in-law. The least cooperative information givers are Lloyd, who despises his son-in-law, and Donald Granger, the victim's not so grieving widower.

Highlights: There are several amusingly drawn characters who interact with probing Jessica. There is a delicate moment as Jessica must gently tell Marcus that "his" mystery novel is no good. On the other hand, the amateur sleuth uses sarcasm to force Ellen Davis to reveal truths. Most amusing are the interchanges between Jessica and materialistic Mildred Tilley in which Jessica, arching her eyebrows and inflecting her voice, shows that she finds this woman's shallow life-style a great pity.

Trivia: Nowhere in the annals of *Murder, She Wrote* is there such a disgruntled—albeit laid back—police officer as Chief Cooper. After seventeen discouraging years on the Manhattan police force, he accepted a tedious post in suburban Cedar Heights. Now he plans to join his brother-in-law's more lucrative plumbing business. As such, whenever Jessica wants this police officer's assistance, he is busily tinkering with a customer's kitchen sink drain, or some other task.

Norman Lloyd's show business career includes helping Orson Welles to form the Mercury Theatre Group in late 1930s New York City. Later, besides acting on TV (e.g., *St. Elsewhere*) he was a producer and director in the medium. Audrey Meadows (1924–1996), born to missionary parents in China, gained fame as Jackie Gleason's TV wife on *The Honeymooners* in the 1950s. Gordon Jump was Arthur Carlson on *WKRP in Cincinnati* (1978–1982).

SEASON THREE

1986–1987

45a. "Death Stalks the Big Top: Part One"

(9/28/86) 60 mins.

45b. "Death Stalks the Big Top: Part Two"

(10/5/86) 60 mins.

Director: Seymour Robbie **Story:** Peter S. Fischer **Teleplay:** Paul Savage

Regular: Angela Lansbury (Emmeline Polsby [Jessica Fletcher])

Guest Law Enforcers: Gregg Henry (Sheriff Len Childs); Greg Norberg (Cop #1)

Guest Cast: Martin Balsam (Edgar Carmody); Roz Bosley (Housekeeper); Susan Brown (Audrey Bannister); Jackie Cooper (Carl Schulman [Neil Fletcher]); Alex Cord (Preston Bartholomew); Courtney Cox (Carol Fletcher); Ronny Cox (Mayor Anson Powers); Joey Cramer (Charlie McCallum); Laraine Day (Constance Fletcher); Joe Dorsey (Harry Kingman); Greg Evigan (Brad Kaneally); Florence Henderson (Maria Morgana); Dennis Howard (Howard Bannister); Charles Napier (Hank Sutter); Dan Priest (Doctor); Lee Purcell (Maylene Sutter); Ken Sansom (Bert, the Front Desk Man); Mark Shera (Raymond Carmody); Harry Stephens (Ned); Pamela Susan Shoop (Katie McCallum); Barbara Stock (Daniella Morgana Carmody); Harry Woolf (Ms. Morgana's Driver)

The Settings: Catlinburg, Arkansas; Pullman City, Arkansas; Washington, D.C.

The Case: Jessica Fletcher is on hand in Washington, D.C., for the pending marriage of her favored niece, Carol, although she has little in common with the bride-to-be's imperious grandmother, Constance. In a private moment, Carol shows Jessica a leprechaun statuette she has just received in the mail with a postmark from Catlinburg, Arkansas. She is convinced that it is from her grandfather, who presumably died in a boating mishap years ago. To soothe both Carol's and her own curiosity, Jessica follows up on the lead.

Once in Arkansas, the trail takes Jessica to a traveling circus which is performing in Catlinburg. Before long her suspicions lead her to the town's jail where Carl Schulman, a clown, is being held for the death of Hank Sutter, the circus foreman, who was bludgeoned with a juggler's club. As she feared, the prisoner is none other than her long-lost brother-in-law, Neil Fletcher. He explains why, years ago, he had abandoned his suffocating wife, Constance, and their foolish, empty-headed daughter, Audrey, and later found peace of mind entertaining others as Blinky the Clown. Neil begs Jessica to leave matters be. He is content to take the blame for the alleged homicide.

Regardless of his wishes, Jessica pursues the case. Her private investigation—which finds her imperiled in a deadly fire—involves several members of the accident-prone Carmody Circus. There is ailing Edgar Carmody, struggling to keep his financially strapped circus going and arguing with his son, Raymond, over the best way to run the operation. Raymond's marriage to Daniella is floundering because she wants him to quit the circus. Also a suspect is equestrienne Maylene Sutter, who isn't sorry that her bullying husband, Hank, is now dead, allowing her to quit the show to raise horses. She wants Brad Kaneally to join her in the new venture, but he refuses because he loves high wire artist Katie McCallum.

Meanwhile, Katie, the widowed mother of young Charlie, had blamed Sutter, who was lusting after her, for the death of her husband in a high wire "accident" a year ago. At that time, the McCallums had been working for a rival circus, owned by Harry Kingman. The latter is now pressuring beleaguered Edgar Carmody to sell out to him. The late Hank Sutter had been on Kingman's payroll to create "accidents" on the Carmody Circus grounds and was, before his death, demanding that Kingman pay up the rest of the payoff he was due—or else. Later Kingman is strangled in his motel room.

Other suspects in the two murders include domineering Maria Morgana, the wealthy fashion designer, who has come to town to convince her daughter, Daniella, to return to the West Coast—with or without her husband Raymond. Also not to be ignored are self-absorbed ringmaster Preston Bartholomew, who claims he is expecting a sudden windfall, and Brad Kaneally, the circus roustabout, who has been hiding a troubled past as a lawbreaker.

As the facts fall into place, Jessica cannot forget her promise to Carol to return in time for the wedding, hopefully with Neil at her side.

Highlights: In this two-part, third season premiere, there are many offbeat moments with the array of cameo artists. Thankfully, the ambiance allows one to overlook the several hammy performances, especially by Alex Cord as the predatory ringmaster. Without doubt the highlight in this two-hour excursion is Jessica's impersonation of the gossipy, blue-collar Emmeline Polsby of Polsby General Store & Dry Goods. Sporting outrageous heart-shaped sunglasses, a wide-brim straw hat and a t-h-i-c-k Arkansas accent, she does her best to gain the confidence of circus roustabouts, in order to learn Neil Fletcher's whereabouts.

Another memorable scene is the touching reunion of Jessica and Neil in his prison cell. Both are teary-eyed as they bridge the missing years and cope with his present circumstances. It is a rare occasion to see cheerful, resilient Jessica crying as they recall the funeral of Jessica's husband, Frank, and why Neil could not make his presence known at the cemetery services for his brother.

Trivia: Jackie Cooper and Laraine Day were fellow MGM alumni but had left the lot before Angela began her studio tenure in 1943. Cooper had starred on such TV series as *The People's Choice, Hennesey,* and *Mobile One.* Day was a regular on television's *Day Dreaming with Laraine Day, I've Got a Secret* and *Masquerade Party.* Martin Balsam (1919–1996), both an Oscar (*A Thousand Clowns* [1965]) and Tony Award winner (*You Know I Can't Hear You When the Water's Running* [1967]), was a TV series veteran of *Valiant Lady, The Greatest Gift* and *Archie Bunker's Place.* In addition, the cast boasted Florence Henderson *(The Brady Bunch),* Greg Evigan *(B.J. and the Bear, My Two Dads),* Mark Shera *(Barnaby Jones),* Barbara Stock *(Spenser: For Hire),* Alex Cord *(Airwolf)* and Ronny Cox *(Apple's Way, Spencer, St. Elsewhere, Cop Rock).* Ingenue Courtney Cox *(Family Ties, Misfits of Science),* would make her show business mark in the ensemble cast of *Friends* (1994–).

46. "Unfinished Business"

(10/12/86) 60 mins.

Director: Walter Grauman **Teleplay:** Jackson Gillis, Peter S. Fischer

Regulars: Angela Lansbury (Jessica Fletcher); Tom Bosley (Sheriff Amos Tupper); William Windom (Dr. Seth Hazlitt)

Guest Law Enforcers: James Bartz (Deputy #2); J.D. Cannon (Sheriff Bill McCoy); Philip Clark (Deputy Roy)

Guest Cast: E. Erich Anderson (Gary Roberts); Lloyd Bochner (Dr. Terence Mayhew); Armand Cerami (Searcher); Don DeFore (Jake Sanford);

Pat Hingle (Barney Kale); Hayley Mills (Cynthia Tate); William Mims (Mayor); Erin Moran (Maggie Roberts); Connie Sawyer (Ethel, the Housekeeper).

The Setting: Juniper Lake, Maine

The Case: Although police lieutenant Barney Kale has finally retired, he is not at peace. He is haunted by a decade-old unsolved murder involving a county prosecutor who drowned at a mishap at Juniper Lake near Cabot Cove. Barney heads out to the lake to finally solve the case. At the now dilapidated lodge, he has a nasty encounter with manager Jake Sanford, who once owned the land but had to mortgage the property in order to get the lodge going.

Others drawn to the premises include Dr. Terence Mayhew, who had invested $200,000 in the pie-in-the-sky project ten years ago; Cynthia Tate, who had been Mayhew's secretary then; and Dr. Seth Hazlitt, who at that time had just lost his wife, had spent all his savings on her medical care, and had gambled wrongly on the investment to restore his depleted bank account.

When Kale's reopening of the case had come to Seth's attention, he suddenly left Cabot Cove for Juniper Lake without any explanation. A worried Jessica convinces Sheriff Amos Tupper to join her on a search party. Once Seth is located, Tupper returns to Cabot Cove, but Jessica remains at the lodge. Before long, young Gary Roberts is shot in cabin #30. His disinterested wife, Maggie, tells Jessica that her husband had just been released from a Massachusetts prison and that she was planning to leave him.

The homicide brings unorthodox Sheriff McCoy onto the scene. As such, Jake's enmity for the man is renewed as McCoy had trampled over the rules of evidence in handling the decade-ago murder investigation. Dictatorial McCoy demands that everyone stay put on the premises until the new killing is solved—or else!

Highlights: Occasionally when pushed, Jessica Fletcher relies on more than just her quick wits and sharp deductive powers to gain the truth. Here, when coping with know-it-all McCoy, she finally (1) tells him off and (2) threatens to call her pal, the governor of Maine. It gets results!

Trivia: If anything could make mature viewers feel ancient, it was seeing 1950s Disney moppet star Hayley Mills and 1970s *Happy Days* adolescent Erin Moran playing (very) mature adults. Canadian Lloyd Bochner had been a regular on *One Man's Family* (1952), *Hong Kong* (1960–1961), and *Dynasty* (1981–1982). Don DeFore (1917–1993) is best remembered as hearty Thorney Thornberry on *The Adventures of Ozzie & Harriet* (1952–1958) and as good-natured George Baxter on *Hazel* (1961–1965).

47. "One White Rose for Death"

(10/19/86) 60 mins.

Director: Peter Crane **Teleplay:** Peter S. Fischer

Regular: Angela Lansbury (Jessica Fletcher)

Recurring Character: Len Cariou (Dennis McKelvey [Michael Haggerty])

Guest Cast: Jenny Agutter (Margo Claymore); Michael Anderson, Jr. (Dr. Lynch); Julian Barnes (British Sergeant); Tony Bonner (Henry Claymore); Eric Braeden (Gerhardt Brunner); Bernard Fox (Andrew Wyckham); John Glover (Franz Mueller); Maria Mayenzet (Greta Mueller); Warwick Sims (Jack Kendall)

The Setting: Washington, D.C.

The Case: Jessica is in the nation's capital to meet with her British publisher. When her contact is suddenly summoned out of town, his duties are turned over to hale and hearty Andrew Wyckham. The latter escorts Jessica to a high-profile concert by two East Germans, violinist Greta Mueller and her accompanist brother Franz. Afterward Jessica and Wyckham are to attend a gala party for the prime minister.

However, at intermission, Michael Haggerty, who has been posing as Dennis McKelvey of the London *Evening Sentinel,* forces Jessica and Wyckham at gun point to leave the concert. They race by car across town, pursued by Gerhardt Brunner of the East German secret service. Once at the British Embassy, Michael demands that Henry Claymore, the 1st Secretary, give them sanctuary. Once in the compound, Michael, who was wounded at the concert hall, helps Greta and Franz from the limousine's trunk.

Later that night, Jack Kendall, whom Haggarty is replacing on a dangerous mission, is found dead in the embassy garden. As Jessica points out, one of the few people in this government house must be the killer. Could it be Claymore's recent bride, the South African-born Margo, with a covert past, or Franz who has been working undercover for the British in East Berlin? Or might it be the horrified Greta, whose loyalties lie with her homeland? Another possibility is the efficient Dr. Lynch, who had access to the poison that killed Kendall.

Highlights: Since their first meeting in 1985's "Widow Weep for Me" (#23), the relationship of Jessica Fletcher and Michael Haggerty has taken on a far more intimate tone. Although she knows that he lives a hazardous life, is prone to putting his mission above anyone's safety, and can't be taken at face value, she nevertheless responds to his roguish charm. Even when real danger looms, she believes that her resourceful collaborator, with a boost from her own ingenuity, will save the day.

Trivia: German-born Eric Braeden first acted under his given name (Hans Gudegast) when he was Captain Hauptman Hans Dietrich in TV's *The Rat Patrol* (1966–1968). As Eric Braeden, he began a long run in the role of Victor Newman on the daytime TV soap opera *The Young and the Restless.* Michael Anderson, Jr., the son of director Michael Anderson, had played Angela Lansbury's son in *Dear Heart* (1964).

48. "Corned Beef and Carnage"

(11/2/86) 60 mins.

Director: John Llewellyn Moxey **Teleplay:** Robert E. Swanson

Regular: Angela Lansbury (Jessica Fletcher)

Recurring Characters: Jeff Conaway (Howard Griffin); Genie Francis (Victoria Brandon Griffin)

Guest Law Enforcer: James Sloyan (Lieutenant Spoletti)

Guest Cast: Susan Anton (Christine Clifford); Warren Berlinger (Jim Ingram); Russ Fega (Pizza Delivery Man); Peter Haskell (Leland Biddle); Richard Kline (Larry Kinkaid); Bill Macy (Myron Kinkaid); Marletta Marrow (Receptionist); Phil Rubenstein (Delicatessen Clerk); David Ogden Stiers (Aubrey Thornton); Ken Swofford (Grover Barth); Marcia Wallace (Polly Barth)

The Setting: New York City

The Case: While on business in Manhattan, Jessica has a reunion with her niece Victoria and the latter's struggling actor husband, Howard Griffin. Victoria is employed at a Madison Avenue ad agency, and before long, Jessica finds herself enveloped in the advertising world.

Victoria's ruthless boss, Larry Kincaid, is in danger of losing a major account—the fast-food franchise owned by demanding Polly and Grover Barth. Kincaid thinks nothing of suggesting to a horrified Victoria that she put her body on the line with an attracted Grover to keep both the account and her job. Meanwhile, Myron, the firm's controller and Larry's overshadowed brother, insists that Larry's extravagant life-style is breaking the company. At the same time, Larry is pressuring burned-out Aubrey Thornton to break his employment contract, but the man refuses to leave his lucrative post. That evening Larry Kincaid is murdered in his office, ironically hit over the head with one of his industry trophies.

Abrasive police lieutenant Spoletti, definitely not one of New York City's finest, has little use for Jessica, who insists that her niece should not be one of the murder suspects. With few more clues than an uneaten corned beef sandwich (delivered to the victim's office shortly before his death), Jessica sets out to nab the real culprit.

Among those drawn into the case are Jim Ingram, the portly night security guard at the Kinkaid Ad Agency; Leland Biddle, the cagey owner of a rival ad agency; and statuesque Christine Clifford, Leland's aggressive spy link into the Kinkaid camp.

Highlights: In marked contrast to the vicious competition depicted in the advertising world are the scenes of newlyweds Howard and Victoria stabilizing their fragile marriage. Sensible Aunt Jessica is forced to mediate between the two young lovers who lack the art of communication. If Bill Macy chomps the scenery as the harried force behind the scenes, Richard Kline is on target as the despicable agency head, as mean a man in the ad game as Sydney Greenstreet was in *The Hucksters* (1947).

Trivia: The characters of Howard Griffin and Victoria Brandon had first appeared in 1984's "Birds of a Feather" (#3).

Richard Kline had played neighbor Larry Dallas on *Three's Company* (1978–1984). Marcia Wallace was the man-hungry receptionist on *The Bob Newhart Show* (1972–1979) while Massachusetts-born veteran Bill Macy had labored as overwhelmed Walter Findlay married to *Maude* (1972–1976). David Ogden Stiers, a veteran of *M*A*S*H* (1977–1983), would turn up in the 1996 final weekly episode (#260) of *Murder, She Wrote.* After leaving the cast of *General Hospital* in 1982, Genie Francis returned to the daytime TV soap opera in the fall of 1993, again reteamed with Anthony Geary, the latter as Luke Spencer.

49. "Dead Man's Gold"

(11/9/86) 60 mins.

Director: Seymour Robbie **Teleplay:** Robert Van Scoyk

Regulars: Angela Lansbury (Jessica Fletcher); Tom Bosley (Sheriff Amos Tupper); William Windom (Dr. Seth Hazlitt)

Recurring Character: Robert Hogan (Dr. Wylie Graham)

Guest Cast: Grant Goodeve (Larry Gaynes); Wendy Kilbourne (Susan Ainsley); John Laughlin (Bill Ainsley); Julia Montgomery (Alexandra Bell); Sean McClory (Ross Barber); Leslie Nielsen (David Everett); J. Eddie Peck (Coby Russell); Ian Ruskin (Gregory Small)

The Setting: Cabot Cove, Maine

The Case: It has been thirty-five years since Jessica Fletcher last saw her high school flame, David Everett. Since then he has become a global jet-setter who has married and divorced four times. He now returns to Cabot Cove because of a treasure chart he obtained which details the whereabouts of a British merchant ship that sank in the local harbor in 1777. To locate that vessel's valuable cargo, Everett has organized a team of young divers: Bill and Susan Ainsley, as well as Larry Gaynes and Alexandra Bell.

Flattered by David's attention, Jessica invites him to stay in the guest room of her house. Before long, bizarre circumstances force her to reevaluate her opinion of the seemingly glamorous visitor. First, she is informed by Dr. Wylie Graham, a new doctor in town, that David has a reputation for being involved in scams. Later, Everett admits that two men (Gregory Small, Ross Barber) are after him because he owes them a great deal of money that he borrowed to finance the treasure search. Still later, when Alexandra dies—the victim of a hit-and-run killing—Jessica must stop being "the romantic fool" and ask David some hard questions. After all, he is a suspect in the homicide case.

Highlights: Overwhelmed by her charming house guest and by old memories, Jessica Fletcher becomes almost kittenish as she renews her relationship with David Everett. Breaking all her sensible rules, she invites the newcomer to stay at her home and even loans him money. Despite the chaste nature of Jessica's flirtation with David, Dr. Seth Hazlitt becomes increasingly jealous of the stranger. In contrast to his typical behavior, Seth is amazingly civil to Dr. Graham, the rival new physician in Cabot Cove. (Part of Seth's "generosity" to Graham is due to the fact that he has known his peer, recently retired from the navy, for thirty years.)

With such shaded performances by the seasoned older cast members, the shallow characterizations by the younger cast members here is glaring.

Trivia: Prolific actor Leslie Nielsen, who gained universal recognition for his *Naked Gun* movie spoofs in recent years, had starred as a lawman in several police TV series: *The New Breed* (1961–1962), *The Protectors* (1969–1970) and *Police Squad* (1982).

50. "Deadline for Murder"

(11/16/86) 60 mins.

Director: Seymour Robbie **Story:** John Kennedy, Michael McGough, Tom Sawyer **Teleplay:** Tom Sawyer

Regular: Angela Lansbury (Jessica Fletcher)

Recurring Character: Harry Guardino (Haskell Drake)

Guest Law Enforcers: Gretchen Corbett (Lieutenant Caruso); Morgan Jones (Sergeant Tierney); Lisa Nelson (Police Officer)

Guest Cast: Barbara Allyne Bennet (Secretary); Katherine Cannon (Eleanor Revere); Ervin Fuller (Harry); Tom Henschel (Dr. Framer); Dorothy Meyer (Nurse O'Hanlon); Tim O'Connor (Walter Revere); Ken Olin (Perry Revere); Peter Mark Richman (Lamar Bennett); Eugene Roche (Billy Simms); Matt Roe (Guard); William Smith (Clyde Thorson); Glynn Turman (Lassiter); Sydney Walsh (Kay Garrett); Mary Wickliffe (Nurse Phillips)

The Setting: Boston, Massachusetts

The Case: Eccentric veteran reporter Haskell Drake has fallen on rough times. As such, he now works in Boston for *The Sentinel,* suffering under an unimaginative boss, Billy Simms and the whims of a crass publisher, Lamar Bennett, the latter having turned the publication into a supermarket tabloid.

When Haskell is bed-ridden at Westside Memorial Hospital due to a heart attack, he loses his will to live. However, Jessica Fletcher, who years before served a newspaper summer internship under Drake, gives the irascible bachelor a pep talk. He challenges her to become his "legs" to help him investigate the sudden, mysterious death of the hated Bennett. Jessica accepts the dare, still smarting from the "hatchet job" the sleazy publication had recently published about her.

Following Haskell's barking commands and using her own intuitive skills, Jessica investigates the staff and guests who attended the newspaper's office party, during which Bennett had collapsed and died of an apparent massive cerebral hemorrhage. Among those with motives are the publication's managing editor, Billy Simms; the victim's most pressured flunky, Clyde Thorson; the deceased's bodyguard, who inherits $25,000 from the dead man's will; Walter Revere, the too genteel former publisher of *The Sentinel,* who hopes to reclaim the paper; Revere's materialistic offspring, Eleanor and Perry; Lassiter, a disgruntled staff reporter; and Kay Garrett, a determined new *Sentinel* employee.

Highlights: With growling, demanding Haskell Drake in the driver's seat, Jessica Fletcher becomes amazingly meek, subdued by her desire to pamper and reinvigorate her old friend, but also respectful of his fine reporting skills. An extremely touching moment occurs when she and cigar-chomping Haskell reminisce about the old days when she was Drake's star helper. (She had given up the newspaper world to marry Frank Fletcher.) In the present, Jessica can think of no finer compliment to her than when, at the end of the case, Haskell admits she is a pretty darn good newsperson in digging up the truth.

Lieutenant Caruso is like most *Murder, She Wrote* distaff law enforcers. She bridles at Jessica's interference in the case, not only because the mystery writer is butting into police business, but also because this outsider is "merely" a middle-aged, female busybody. This is ironic since Caruso constantly complains of sex discrimination on the police force.

Trivia: Harry Guardino's (1925–1995) character, Haskell Drake, would return in 1991's "Moving Violation" (#143). Ken Olin made a career mark as one of the *thirtysomething* (1987–1991) TV acting ensemble. Gretchen Corbett had enjoyed a recurring role on *The Rockford Files* (1974–1978) playing attractive attorney Beth Davenport always ready to help James Garner's character.

51. "Magnum on Ice"

(11/23/86) 60 mins.

Director: Peter Crane **Teleplay:** Robert E. Swanson

Regular: Angela Lansbury (Jessica Fletcher)

Guest Law Enforcers: Ramon Bieri (Captain Frank Browning); Kwan Hi Lim (Lieutenant Tanaka); Turner Pe'a (Police Officer)

Guest Cast: Rhonda Aldrick (Maid); Winston Chase (Houseboy #2); Harry Emdo (Desk Clerk); Stephanie Faracy (Amy Sayler); Keah Farden (Bellboy); John Hillerman (Jonathan Quayle Higgins, III); Dorothy Loudon (Pamela Bates); Jared Martin (Arthur Houston); John McMartin (Jason Bryan); Byron Ono (Houseboy #1); Andrew Prine (Victor Sayler); Tom Selleck (Thomas Sullivan Magnum); Jessica Walter (Joan Fulton)

The Setting: Oahu, Hawaii

The Case: Jonathan Higgins, manservant to wealthy writer Robin Masters, meets three women at the airport: wealthy Joan Fulton, Joan's secretary, Amy Sayler, and Joan's friend, Pamela Bates. Joan's husband had died a few months earlier, leaving her with a business to run, while Pamela is searching for her missing sister. Later, Amy temporarily disappears.

Thomas Magnum, a private eye who lives at Robin Masters's lush estate on Oahu's north shore, points out that he had seen a man, Paul Mayfield, following the vanished young lady. Meanwhile, at a party hosted by wealthy Jason Bryan, Mayfield is shot and Magnum is arrested for the homicide. Later, after Thomas is released, he learns that the dead man had actually been a hit man on assignment. His mission had been to kill one of the female trio. But which one?

Pamela, meanwhile, contacts her old friend Jessica Fletcher to help with the out-of-hand situation. Almost from the start, Jessica is hampered by the impulsive Magnum, who has no use for this danger-prone, too logical mainland woman. Mrs. Fletcher also has difficulties with stern police officer Captain Frank Browning, who doesn't want civilians interfering in police business.

Before long, another victim, Arthur Houston, dies, and Amy's dominating spouse, Victor Sayler, has turned up on the island.

Highlights: With so many forces hostile to Jessica's investigation, it's little wonder that she responds favorably to the cultured, if stuffy, Higgins who respects her reputation as a novelist and sleuth. Higgins's cordiality is in great contrast to her lack of rapport with laid-back, womanizing Thomas Magnum. The latter scoffs at Jessica's pesky snooping. Besides, embarrassingly, she is always one step ahead of Magnum in following up clues. Predictably by the finale, the two have gained a grudging respect for one another. Magnum promises Jessica, "If you don't take out a private investigator's license, I won't buy a typewriter."

Trivia: By its seventh season on the air, ratings for *Magnum, P.I.* had eroded. CBS-TV hoped to re-charge the show's viewership with a two-part episode which would bring Thomas Magnum in contact with Jessica Fletcher of the highly rated *Murder, She Wrote.* Each camp wanted the two-parter to end on their own program to insure the expected high viewership. (CBS-TV decided to air part one on *Magnum, P.I.* on November 19, 1996, with the conclusion shown on *Murder She Wrote* four days later.) With two such disparate characters (and actors) working together, the end results were more gimmicky than satisfying. It was the only occasion that *Murder, She Wrote* was used in tandem with another teleseries. (*Magnum, P.I.* would last yet another TV year, going off the air at the end of the 1987–1988 season.)

Back in 1979, when Angela Lansbury had left her Tony Award-winning role in the Broadway musical *Sweeney Todd,* she had been replaced by actress Dorothy Loudon. Loudon's series work involved *It's a Business?* (1952), *The Garry Moore Show* (1962–1964) and *Dorothy* (1979).

Among Tom Selleck's early movie roles were *Myra Breckinridge* (1970) and *Terminal Island* (1973). John Hillerman's other TV series include *Ellery Queen* (1975–1976), *One Day at a Time* (1977–1980) and *The Hogan Family* (1990–1991). On John McMartin's roster of features are *What's So Bad about Feeling Good* (1968), *Sweet Charity* (1969) and *Brubaker* (1980). Kwam Hi Lim played his recurring role of police lieutenant Tanaka on the full run of *Magnum, P.I.* (1980–1988). Andrew Prine was a regular on such TV shows as *The Wide Country* (1962–1963), *The Road West* (1966–1967) and *The Final Battle* (1984). Stephanie Faracy was featured in such weekly entries as *The Last Resort* (1979–1980) and *True Colors* (1990–1992). Jared

Martin had a lead role as Dr. Harrison Blackwood in TV's *War of the Worlds* (1988–1990).

52. "Obituary for a Dead Anchor"

(12/7/86) 60 mins.

Director: Walter Grauman **Story:** Bob Shayne **Teleplay:** Robert Van Scoyk

Regulars: Angela Lansbury (Jessica Fletcher); Tom Bosley (Sheriff Amos Tupper)

Recurring Characters: Robert Hogan (Dr. Wylie Graham); Richard Paul (Mayor Samuel Booth)

Guest Cast: Frank Anneses (Ronald Ross); Abby Dalton (Judith Keats); Chad Everett (Kevin Keats); Patti Karr (Claire Polsby, Society Editor of the *Cabot Cove Gazette*); Robert Lipton (Richard Abbott); Kathleen Lloyd (Paula Roman); Robert Pine (Doug Helman); Rex Robbins (George Fish, Manager of Hill House Hotel); Paul Ryan (TV Commentator); Erik Stern (Gerald Foster); Mark Stevens (Nick Brody)

The Setting: Cabot Cove, Maine

The Case: Kevin Keats, the controversial anchorman of a national TV news magazine, causes considerable consternation when he arrives in Cabot Cove with a camera crew to tape Jessica Fletcher for a segment of his *Scrutiny* program. Within days, Keats is dead, the victim of a boating explosion. Later, it is discovered that the recovered corpse is actually that of a man with only eight toes.

As Jessica searches for answers, she must deal with Paula Roman and Nick Brody, the cohosts of *Scrutiny*, as well as the program's producer, Robert Pine, and the vice-president in charge of network news, Robert Lipton. Then there is Judith Keats, the wife of the missing supposed victim, as well as sinister art collector Ronald Ross, the latter having been a target of Keats's hard journalism.

Highlights: This is one of the infrequent occasions when Jessica Fletcher has no argument with Sheriff Amos Tupper's theories on the murder case. However, she does take exception when the oblivious Amos accidentally steps into camera range while she is taping a TV interview on the streets of Cabot Cove.

With Dr. Seth Hazlitt temporarily out of town, Jessica finds a new friend in Dr. Wylie Graham, who also enjoys good conversation and a game of chess. On the other hand, she must cope with pompous, do-little Mayor Samuel Booth.

Even in the show's third season, the scriptwriters were still insistent on overexplaining why civilian Jessica Fletcher is delving into yet another homicide case. Equally obvious was the effort to paint the citizens of Cabot Cove as quaint characters boasting very Down East accents.

Trivia: This was the second and final appearance of Robert Hogan as Dr. Wylie Graham. In contrast, it was the first of many visitations by Richard Paul as self-aggrandizing Samuel Booth, the C.P.A. turned inefficient town mayor. A native of Los Angeles, Paul began his acting career performing Shakesepearean plays.

Abby Dalton's initial TV series was Jackie Cooper's sitcom *Hennesey* (1959–1962). Robert Pine toiled for years as a supporting player before rising to prominence as Sergeant Joe Getraer on *CHiPs* (1977–1983). One-time movie star Mark Stevens (1919–1994) played a two-fisted newsman on TV's *Big Town* (1952–1957).

53. "Stage Struck"

(12/14/86) 60 mins.

Director: John Astin **Teleplay:** Philip Gerson

Regular: Angela Lansbury (Jessica Fletcher)

Guest Law Enforcer: John Schuck (Chief Merton P. Drock)

Guest Cast: Shea Farrell (Larry Matthews); Annie Gagen (2nd Reporter); Bob Hastings (Eddie Bender); Richard Hoyt-Miller (Young Reporter); Donald Most (T.J. Holt); Edward Mulhare (Julian Lord); Christopher Norris (Pru Mattson); Daniel O'Herlihy (Preston); Eleanor Parker (Maggie Tarrow); John Pleshette (Nicky Saperstein); Ann Turkel (Barbara Bennington); Jeffrey Uppa (1st Reporter)

The Setting: Applewood, New England

The Case: Famous stage and screen stars Maggie Tarrow and Julian Lord, who once had been married, are appearing in a pre-Broadway version of a drawing room comedy, *Finders Keepers, Losers Weepers.* For the tryout, they have selected the Applewood Playhouse, now owned by Preston, because it was at this summer theater that they had first met. Jessica Fletcher, who had been a backstage apprentice crew member that long-ago summer, is invited to the show's special opening night.

It develops that Maggie, recently treated at an Arizona health clinic for a drinking problem, is jittery about her stage return. A mysterious note found in her makeup box scares her from appearing onstage opening night. Her understudy, Barbara Bennington, a TV daytime soap opera actress, takes her place. Barbara's success, however, is short-lived, as she soon dies, a victim of cyanide poisoning.

Far quicker than the unassuming police chief Drock, Jessica picks up the scent of the guilty party. Among those suspected are T. J. Holt, a New York reporter who claims the victim was his fiancée; Larry Matthews, a cast member who has had a very close personal relationship with Maggie; Nicky Saperstein, the play's concerned producer; Bob Hastings, a local druggist who does props at the theater; Pru Mattson, the show's stage manager and the object of Matthews's romantic interest; and Julian Lord, who has had a long history of battling with his highly emotional (ex)wife.

Highlights: Whenever Jessica Fletcher meets friends from her past, she is prone to nostalgic reminiscences, especially when it deals with her late husband, Frank Fletcher. Here, there is a telling recounting of how she first met Frank backstage.

Not since Peter Sellers's bumbling police detective in the *Pink Panther* movie series has there been such a clumsy lawman as Chief Merton P. Drock. At the playhouse to fill the brief acting role of onstage valet, he is totally unable to handle a murder investigation. He admits to Jessica that without her expertise, he wouldn't know where to begin. If Drock is amusingly awkward in front of the footlights, he is nothing short of hilarious when he adopts a Hercule Poirot posture and accent in the "real-life" murder case.

Trivia: Astute viewers will note that the LaRue Pharmacy exterior set used in this segment turns up in future episodes, but now as a Cabot Cove business locale!

Actor John Astin, who had appeared previously on *Murder, She Wrote* in the recurring role of realtor Harry Pierce, directed this segment. Donny Most was known to TV viewers as Ralph Malph on *Happy Days* (1974–1980). John Schuck had been Sergeant Charles Enright on *McMillan and Wife* (1971–1977) and had been Murray on *The New Odd Couple* (1982–1983). Ireland's Daniel O'Herlihy had been Oscar-nominated for his role in *The Adventures of Robinson Crusoe* (1952) and starred in a remake of *The Cabinet of Caligari* (1962). Warner Bros. leading lady Eleanor Parker made her screen bow in *They Died with Their Boots On* (1941) and was Oscar-nominated for *Caged* (1950) and *Interrupted Melody* (1955). Edward Mulhare was in *Von Ryan's Express* (1965), *Our Man Flint* (1965) and *Caprice* (1967).

54. "Night of the Headless Horseman"

(1/4/87) 60 mins.

Director: Walter Grauman **Teleplay:** R. Barker Price

Regular: Angela Lansbury (Jessica Fletcher)

Guest Law Enforcers: Doug McClure (Sheriff Rankin); Tom Ohmer (Deputy Charlie); Gary Pagett (Deputy)

Guest Cast: Thom Bray (Dorian Beecher); Sanford Clark (1st Man); Karlene Crockett (Sarah Dupont); Brandon Douglas (Todd Carrier); John England (3rd Man); Adam Ferris (Brendan); Judy Landers (Bobbie, the Inn Waitress); Hope Lange (Charlotte Newcastle); Charles Siebert (Dr. Penn Walker); Forry Smith (2nd Man); Guy Stockwell (Dorn Van Stotter); Donald Thompson (Robert); Fritz Weaver (Edwin Dupont); Barry Williams (Nate Findley); Brad Zerbst (4th Man)

The Setting: Wenton, Vermont

The Case: Dorian Beecher, the newly appointed poetry teacher at Wenton Academy, is desperate to impress his girlfriend, Sarah Dupont, and her status-conscious father, Edwin Dupont. Thus he pretends that Jessica Fletcher, a writer friend who is now visiting town, is actually his dutiful mother.

Meanwhile, Dorian competes with Nate Findley, the academy's horse master, for Sarah's affections. One night, the two men fight at the inn's restaurant. Later, Nate is found dead, and peculiarly, not only is his decapitated head missing, but his boots are on his wrong feet.

Sheriff Rankin jails Beecher when the teacher's sword proves to have been the murder weapon. Fully knowing that her young friend could not do such a horrendous deed, Jessica must prove his innocence. Her investigation leads to Charlotte Newcastle, the academy's administrator, who is suspected of embezzling school funds; as well as Edwin Dupont, Sarah's overprotective father, who is furious that she had been intimate with the victim; and Dr. Penn Walker, the lusty local dentist.

Highlights: Occasionally, Jessica Fletcher finds it expedient to bend the truth a bit to make a guilty party confess. However, she is embarrassed when circumstances force her to pretend to be Dorian Beecher's mother. Too honest to blatantly lie, she merely chooses her words carefully, allowing listeners to assume what they will. Thanks to Angela Lansbury's expertise as a farceur, the gambit works exceedingly well.

Using Washington Irving's "The Legend of Sleepy Hollow" (1820) as a basis, this modern version of the famous ghost story parallels the original in many plot points, even to having the lead character—Dorian Beecher—being a gawky, love-struck pedagogue like Irving's Ichabod Crane.

Trivia: Doug McClure (1936–1995) played Trampas on the Western TV series *The Virginian* (1962–1971). His last show was the syndicated comedy *Out of This World* (1987–1991). Thom Bray, costar of *Riptide* (1984–1986), was a last-minute replacement for actor Paul Sand, who was committed to another series. Barry Williams was an alumnus of *The Brady Bunch* (1969–1974), where he had played Greg, the eldest of the six children. Hope Lange had dealt previously with specters as Mrs. Carolyn Muir on TV's *The Ghost and Mrs. Muir* (1968–1970). Judy Landers, the younger sister of Audrey Landers (see #40, 255), had been a regular on TV's *Vega$* (1978–1979), *B.J. and the Bear* (1981) and *Madame's Place* (1982). Charles Siebert was known for playing another type of doctor—Dr. Stanley Riverside, II—on *Trapper John* (1979–1986).

55. "The Corpse Flew First Class"

(1/18/87) 60 mins.

Director: Walter Grauman **Teleplay:** Donald Ross

Regular: Angela Lansbury (Jessica Fletcher)

Guest Law Enforcers: Ron Basker (Mark, the British Chief); David Hemmings (Inspector Errol O. Pogson)

Guest Cast: Mary Jo Catlett (Mrs. Metcalf); Charles Davis (Mr. Stegmeyer); Robin Dearden (Kay Davis); Pat Harrington (Gunnar Globle); Ian Howard (Security Man); Vince Howard (Blanton); Charles Hoyes (Carney); Crystal Jenious (Mrs. Miley); Don Maharry (Mr. Miley); Kate Mulgrew (Sonny Greer); Gene Nelson (Louis Metcalf); Andrew Parks (Fred Jenkins); John S. Ragin (Dr. Cliff Strayhorn); Chris Robinson (Captain Whetsel); Lee Sargent (Elizabeth Welch); James Shigeta (John Kitamura); John Straightley (Customs Man); Mark Venturni (Leon Bigard); Robert Walker (Otto Hardwick); Gerald York (Man on Phone)

The Settings: Boston, Massachusetts; over the Atlantic Ocean

The Case: Jessica Fletcher is on an airplane from Boston's Logan Airport to England to research a grizzly turn-of-the-century murder case for her new book. Others on the flight include a jet-setting movie star, Sonny Greer, who is traveling with her lover, Leon Bigard. There is also Boston plastic surgeon Dr. Cliff Strayhorn; Inspector Errol O. Pogson, twenty-five-year man with Scotland Yard; and hustling movie producer, Gunnar Globle, who is looking for production financing.

During the transatlantic flight, Leon is killed in the first-class compartment. It is discovered that he is actually Sonny's bodyguard, responsible for protecting her jewelry. Now her fabled Empress diamond necklace is missing! Disgruntled that he has been passed over for many promotions at the Yard, Pogson is determined to make his mark by unraveling this whodunit before the plane lands at Heathrow. In tandem with Jessica, he discovers the connections between the deceased and Otto Hardwick, a man with a criminal record; Mr. Kitamura, a diamond cutter; and the Metcalfs, who are jittery about the mysterious contents of a bag they are clutching; as well as the edgy steward, Kay Davis.

Highlights: With its expansive cast and plot elements borrowed from Elizabeth Taylor-Richard Burton's *The V.I.P.s* (1963) as well as many plane disaster movies, this installment strives for an elegant, brisk tone.

Trivia: As in 1985's "My Johnny Lies over the Ocean" (#14), part of Jessica Fletcher's deductive reasoning involves determining just when several key passengers aboard actually booked their reservations.

David Hemmings, the British-born leading man of *Blow Up* (1966), *The Charge of the Light Brigade* (1968) and *The Love Machine* (1971), later turned to directing: *Just a Gigolo* (1978), *The Survivor* (1981) and *Dark Horse* (1992), among others. Pat Harrington, as a scrambling moviemaker here, had a change-of-pace assignment from his long-running role as Dwayne Schneider, the opinionated building superintendant on TV's *One Day at a Time* (1975–1984). Gene Nelson had been the dancing star of such movies as *Tea for Two* (1951) and *Oklahoma!* (1955). Chris Robinson was Tech. Sergeant Sandy Komansky on TV's *Twelve O'Clock High* (1965–1967). Mary Jo Catlett appeared as Pearl Gallagher on *Diff'rent Strokes* (1982–1986). Kate Mulgrew's TV starring series work has ranged from *Kate Loves a Mystery* (1979) to *Star Trek: Voyager* (1995–) as resolute Captain Kathryn Janeway, the spaceship captain.

56. "Crossed Up"

(2/1/87) 60 mins.

Director: David Hemmings **Teleplay:** Steven Long Mitchell, Craig W. Van Sickle

Regulars: Angela Lansbury (Jessica Fletcher); Tom Bosley (Sheriff Amos Tupper); William Windom (Dr. Seth Hazlitt)

Recurring Character: Michael Horton (Grady Fletcher)

Guest Law Enforcer: James McIntire (Deputy Charlie Wells)

Guest Cast: Henry Brandon (Abel Gorcy); Colleen Camp (Dody Rogers); Tony Dow (Gordon Rogers); Stephanie Dunnam (Leslie Cameron); James

Carroll Gordon (Adam Rogers); Giselle MacKenzie (Mona); Sandy McPeak (Morgan Rogers); Yolanda Nava (TV Announcer)

The Setting: Cabot Cove, Maine

The Case: Things couldn't be worse for Jessica Fletcher. She has thrown out her back and is confined to bed, and storm warnings are up for Hurricane Ida. Then, through crossed telephone wires, she overhears a conversation between two men who are plotting to murder an old man on his estate. Neither Dr. Seth Hazlitt, who is constantly checking on Jessica, nor Grady Fletcher, who has come up from New York to tend to his aunt, take her "real-life" murder plot seriously. Sheriff Amos Tupper decides that her concerns result from cabin fever. However, they change their tune when wealthy old Jebidiah Rogers is found murdered.

Frustrated that she can't snoop on her own, Jessica uses Grady as her eyes and ears. She directs him to nose around and provides questions for him to ask the deceased's heirs, including pretty Leslie Cameron, orphaned years before and now living at Jebediah's spacious house. (Grady finds a romantic rapport with this recent college graduate whom he had first met several summers ago.) There are also the dead man's three sons: the no-nonsense Morgan, the hard-working Gordon, who is married to the materialistic Dody, and the youngest sibling, the playboy Adam. Rounding out the gallery of suspects is Abel Gorcey, a man recently out of jail, who has sworn vengeance on the murdered man, who once was his employer.

When a second murder occurs, Jessica predicts correctly that she might well be victim #3.

Highlights: Expanding on the underlying premise of the classic radio drama "Sorry, Wrong Number" (which became a 1949 movie with Barbara Stanwyck), no *Murder, She Wrote* episode has ever presented Jessica in such a vulnerable, immobile state. As she fidgets unhappily in bed, much is made of her coping with overly solicitous friends and the limited cooking skills of well-meaning nephew Grady. Predictably the plot climaxes with Jessica caught alone at home and at the mercy of the killer.

Trivia: England's David Hemmings, who had costarred in 1987's "The Corpse Flew First Class" (#55), directed this segment. Canadian-born singer and actress Giselle MacKenzie, once the colead of TV's *Your Hit Parade* (1953–1957), was spotlighted here as the owner of a local diner, who used to teach tango classes in Cabot Cove. Henry Brandon had often played menacing characters in movie serials of the 1940s, as well as strong supporting roles in features: *Edge of Darkness* (1943), *Canon City* (1948), *The Searchers* (1956), etc. Tony Dow is forever associated with his role as Wally Cleaver, the clean-cut older brother in *Leave It to Beaver* (1957–1963), a role he continued in *The New Leave It To Beaver* (1985–1989).

Colleen Camp, who had substituted briefly for Mary Crosby in 1979 as Kristin Shepard on *Dallas*, later was featured on the brief-running sitcom *Tom* (1994), starring Tom Arnold.

57. "Murder in a Minor Key"

(2/8/87) 60 mins.

Director: Nick Havinga **Teleplay:** Arthur Marks, Gerald K. Siegel, Peter S. Fischer

Regular: Angela Lansbury (Jessica Fletcher/Narrator)

Guest Law Enforcer: William Hubbard Knight (Lieutenant Perkins)

Guest Cast: Rene Auberjonois (Professor Harry Papazian); Shaun Cassidy (Chad Singer); Paul Clemens (Michael Prescott); Herbert Edelman (Max Hellinger); Alexander Folk (Hargrove, the Security Man); Karen Grassle (Christine Stoneham); George Grizzard (Professor Tyler Stoneham); Tom Hallick (Alexander Simon); Alexander Henteloff (Ray Parnell, of the Public Defender's Office); Jennifer Holmes (Reagen Miller); Scott Jacoby (Danny Young); Dinah Manoff (Jenny Coopersmith); Stephen Swofford (Templeton); Brenda Thompson (Pianist); Paris Vaughn (Pauline)

The Setting: a Southern California college

The Case: Jessica Fletcher narrates her latest murder mystery. On a Southern California college campus, arrogant Professor Tyler Stoneham, of the music department, is overbearing to everyone. His victims include a hapless teaching associate, Harry Papazian, whom he exploited when they once wrote a music dictionary together; a talented student, Michael Prescott, from whom Tyler plagiarizes songs; and Christine, Stoneham's ignored wife.

One day Stoneham is stabbed to death. Because a campus security guard surprises Prescott at the murder scene, Lieutenant Perkins arrests the young man. Michael's friend, Chad Singer, a law student, works to free Prescott. He is aided by another of their crowd, New Yorker Jenny Coopersmith, with whom Singer shares living quarters. Together, Chad and Jenny track the actual killer, who just might be (1) Max Hellinger, a Broadway producer who had contracted for Stoneham's stolen songs, (2) Reagen Miller, a student with a talent for lyrics who had been bamboozled by the dead man, or (3) Christine, the teacher's unhappy spouse.

Highlights: Without Jessica Fletcher's buoyant presence to patch together the plot mechanics, the story sags in too many places. On a positive note,

Herbert Edelman's show business character adds much-needed levity to the proceedings.

Trivia: This was the first of several upcoming episodes in which Jessica Fletcher does not participate in the main story line. Here she opens the segment with a brief introduction and is seen, in a narrator's capacity, when the show returns from each commercial break.

The guest cast included three children of celebrity performers: Shaun Cassidy, the son of singer/actress Shirley Jones and the late Jack Cassidy; Paul Clemens, the offspring of actress Eleanor Parker (who had appeared in episode #53); and Dinah Manoff, the daughter of actress/director Lee Grant, and a costar of *Soap* and *Empty Nest.* Tony Award winner Rene Auberjonois had been Clayton Endicott, III, on *Benson* (1980–1986) and would be Constable Odo on *Star Trek: Deep Space Nine* (1993–). Brooklyn's Herbert Edelman (1930–1996) was a graduate of such series as *The Good Guys, Strike Force, 9 to 5* and would be Beatrice Arthur's needy ex-husband on *The Golden Girls* (1985–1992). George Grizzard's extensive TV career includes such shows as *The Adams Chronicle* (1976) and *Studio 5-B* (1989).

58. "The Bottom Line Is Murder"

(2/15/87) 60 mins.

Director: Anthony Shaw **Teleplay:** Steven Long Mitchell, Craig W. Van Sickle

Regular: Angela Lansbury (Jessica Fletcher)

Guest Law Enforcers: Barry Corbin (Lieutenant Lou Flanningan); Mark Phelon (Cop)

Guest Cast: Adrienne Barbeau (Lynette Bryant); Judith Chapman (Jayne Honig); William Ian Gamble (Security Guard); Pat Klous (Clare Henley); Robert F. Lyons (Steve Honig); Brian Matthews (Ryan Monroe); Rod McCary (Kenneth Chambers); Joe Santos (Joe Rinaldi); Morgan Stevens (Robert Warren); George Takei (Bert Tanaka, the Janitor); Paul Tompkins (Reporter)

The Setting: Denver, Colorado

The Case: As part of a promotional book tour, Jessica Fletcher stops in Denver, Colorado. She is to appear on a book review program on HBLR-TV. It is the same studio where opportunist consumer activist Kenneth Chambers telecasts his highly rated, exploitive show.

When the much-disliked Chambers is murdered, no one is sorrier than officious Lieutenant Lou Flannigan, who had enjoyed the prestige and salary of being Kenneth's unofficial police expert. As such, the obnoxious policeman is especially impolite to Jessica when she steps into the criminal investigation.

Suspects abound at the station. There is the victim's producer, Steve Honig; the victim's harassed assistant, Ryan Monroe; slick station manager Robert Warren; tough Lynette Bryant, who was Chamber's research associate and now will take over his program; and pretty blonde Clare Henley, who is suddenly cast as hostess of the station's replacement program, *The New Bottom Line.* Additionally, toy manufacturer Joe Rinaldi, whose unsafe teddy bears were one of Chambers's targets, is delighted to see the activist dead.

Highlights: Usually during the course of solving a case, Jessica gains inspiration from something someone says or from suddenly realizing that a casual item left at the murder scene is actually a valuable clue. Here, in a well-handled sequence, she hits pay dirt from a conversation with the TV station's night janitor, Bert Tanaka. George Takei neatly underplays his part as the minor functionary who takes great pride in his work and in maintaining order.

Trivia: This was the first of many episodes to be directed by Angela Lansbury's son, Anthony Shaw, who had previously been a dialogue director on the program. This segment's police detective is played by Barry Corbin, who went on to play former astronaut Maurice Minnifield on *Northern Exposure* (1990–1995). George Takei was an original crew member of *Star Trek* (1966–1969), playing the role of Sulu.

59. "Death Takes a Dive"

(2/22/87) 90 mins.

Director: Seymour Robbie **Teleplay:** Peter S. Fischer

Regular: Angela Lansbury (Jessica Fletcher)

Recurring Characters: Ray Girardin (Lieutenant Casey); Jerry Orbach (Harry McGraw)

Guest Cast: John Amos (Doc Penrose); Richard Balin (TV Sports Commentator); Ernest Borgnine (Cosmo Ponzini); Richard Bravo (Sanchez); LeVar Burton (Dave Robinson); Bill Capizzi (Doorman); Bradford Dillman (Dennis McCullough); Caren Kaye (Lois Ames); Lynne Moody (Pam Collins); Michael McGrady (Sean Shaleen); Marcia Moran (Waitress); Harold Sylvester (Blaster Boyle); Adam West (Wade Talmadge)

The Settings: Boston, Massachusetts; Cabot Cove, Maine

The Case: Boston private eye Harry McGraw summons his old friend, Jessica Fletcher, to Boston. He is in a tight spot. A dead pal has left Harry a controlling interest in a boxer, Blaster Boyle. Meanwhile, McGraw's gambling habit has indebted him to a tough loan shark. Harry's only chance of surviving this scrape is to have Blaster win an important match against Sean Sheleen. To train Boyle for the ring event requires seed money which he doesn't have. Harry persuades Jessica to loan him five thousand dollars.

Soon thereafter, crooked fight promoter Wade Talmadge is found murdered. Harry is arrested as the #1 suspect because he had had a major argument with Talmadge when the latter told him Blaster better lose the match to Sheleen—or else. To save her friend and her investment, Jessica leaps into the world of boxing.

Before long, Jessica finds herself locking horns with tough Cosmo Ponzini, who owns the Ninth Street gym, and Dennis McCullough, Sean's determined manager. She also must compete for clues with ambitious newspaper reporter Dave Robinson and the latter's comely photographer, Pam Collins. Simultaneously, Jessica contends with unyielding Boston police detective, Lieutenant Casey, who remembers her and Harry unkindly from a past case.

Highlights: Jessica Fletcher had before—and would again—be involved in the colorful world of sports. However, never had she participated in such a grimy level of athletics as that of the bare-bones Boston gym run by Ponzini. In a salute to Sylvester Stallone's *Rocky* movies, a montage features Jessica taking over from a jailed Harry to help Doc Penrose train Blaster Boyle for the crucial match. In the process, Mrs. Fletcher gets far more of a physical workout than she ever anticipated, all of which proves exceedingly diverting for viewers.

Trivia: This first and only ninety-minute episode of *Murder, She Wrote* served as another pilot for the forthcoming spin-off CBS network series *The Law and Harry McGraw* (1987–1988). That upcoming TV program also featured Jerry Orbach as the disheveled, disorganized Beantown private eye with a great reluctance to ever tell the "straight skinny" (i.e., the whole truth). Jerry Orbach had appeared in such TV specials as *Twenty-Four Hours in a Woman's Life* (1961—with Ingrid Bergman) and *Annie Get Your Gun* (1967—with Ethel Merman).

Academy Award winner Ernest Borgnine had starred in several TV series: *McHale's Navy* (1962–1965), *Future Cop* (1976), *Airwolf* (1984–1986) and, more recently, in *The Single Guy* (1995–). LeVar Burton made his mark playing the young Kunta Kinte on the TV miniseries *Roots* (1977) and later returned to prominence as Lieutenant Geordi La Forge on *Star Trek: The Next Generation* (1987–1994). The costar of such films as *A*

Certain Smile (1958), *A Rage to Live* (1965), Bradford Dillman played John Wilkes Booth in *The Lincoln Conspiracy* (1977). Adam West had once been Gotham's own Bruce Wayne in TV's *Batman* (1966–1968).

60. "Simon Says, Color Me Dead"

(3/1/87) 60 mins.

Director: Kevin G. Cremin **Teleplay:** Robert E. Swanson

Regulars: Angela Lansbury (Jessica Fletcher); Tom Bosley (Sheriff Amos Tupper); William Windom (Dr. Seth Hazlitt)

Guest Law Enforcer: Phillip Clark (Deputy Collins)

Guest Cast: Diane Baker (Eleanor Thane); Foster Brooks (Simon Thane); Ann Dusenberry (Carol Selby); Leonard Frey (Felix Casslaw); Tess Harper (Irene Rutledge); Chris Hebert (Tommy Rutledge); Steve Inwood (Cash Logan); Dick Sargent (George Selby, Esq.); Daryl Wood (Martha Sommers, the Bike's Owner)

The Setting: Cabot Cove, Maine

The Case: Venerated painter Simon Thane lives reclusively in Cabot Cove during the summer. One day he surprises Jessica Fletcher by inviting her to a small dinner party, noting that his wife Eleanor, who has been away in the city decorating their new condo, is back in town.

That evening, Jessica joins the Thanes at their house for the get-together, along with George and Carol Selby. The Selbys, also summer season residents from Boston, own several works by their host and prod him to have a new exhibit (which would enhance the value of their own collection). This idea is seconded by another dinner guest, Felix Casslaw. He is a prissy New York art gallery owner visiting in Cabot Cove.

By the following day, Simon is dead, stabbed in the chest in his work studio, and the innovative new painting he was working on is missing. The murder weapon proves to be the kitchen carving knife used by part-time domestic Irene Rutledge to cut the meat dish at the previous night's party. Additionally, Irene's work dress has blood stains on it. When the police come to question her, she is hastily packing to leave for Portland and happens to have two valuable sketches by Simon in her bag.

Jessica cannot believe that hard-working, single mother Irene is guilty of the homicide and does her best to resolve the killing. She is given token support by George Selby, a Boston lawyer. Adding to the mystery is recently apprehended Cash Logan, a man with a criminal record. The police discover the missing Thane painting in the back of his van. However, for some baffling reason, the face on the nude portrait has been slashed out of the canvas.

Highlights: Being childless, Jessica reserves her maternal instinct for her nephews and nieces, but they are mostly grown adults. Here, when she volunteers to look out for Irene's young son, Tommy, while Irene is in police custody, Mrs. Fletcher has a rare opportunity to display her motherly side. In another telling sequence, Jessica comforts Eleanor Thane on the loss of her husband. She relates—in an admirably controlled performance—how one must wait for the pain of losing a loved one to subside and then somehow manage to put away the grief and hold on to good memories.

Trivia: Dick Sargent (1930–1994), whose feature films included *Operation Petticoat* (1961) and *The Ghost and Mr. Chicken* (1966), had replaced Dick York as Samantha's (Elizabeth Montgomery) husband, Darrin Stephens, on TV's *Bewitched* from 1969 to 1972. Leonard Frey (1938–1988) gained recognition as part of the original off-Broadway cast (1968) and the film version (1970) of *Boys in the Band.* Foster Brooks was formerly of *The New Bill Cosby Show* (1972–1973) and *Mork & Mindy* (1981). Ann Dusenberry had been aboard the short-lasting *Life with Lucy* (1986). Diane Baker's movies spanned *The Best of Everything* (1959), to *Krakatoa, East of Java* (1968) and on to *The Pilot* (1982) and *Imaginary Crimes* (1994).

61. "No Laughing Matter"

(3/15/87) 60 mins.

Director: Walter Grauman **Teleplay:** Tom Sawyer

Regular: Angela Lansbury (Jessica Fletcher)

Guest Law Enforcer: David Knell (Wylie B. Ledbetter, Acting Chief of Police)

Guest Cast: Daniel Chodes (Al); George Clooney (Kip Howard); Pat Crowley (Edie Howard); Pat Delaney (Ms. Kline); George Furth (Farley); Paul Ganus (Man); Buddy Hackett (Murray Gruen); Arte Johnson (Phil Rinker); Steve Lawrence (Mack Howard); Sheree North (Norma Lewis); Alice Nunn (Henrietta, the Cook); Beth Windsor (Corrie Gruen)

The Setting: The Catskills, New York

The Case: For over twenty-five years, the former comedy team of Murray Gruen and Mack Howard has been feuding. Because Murray's daughter, Corrie, and Mack's son, Kip, intend to marry, the duo call a temporary truce. They agree to celebrate the engagement party at the Hiawatha

Lodge, the modest Catskills hotel that Gruen has recently purchased. As Corrie's godmother, Jessica is invited to the gathering.

Others attending the festivities are Norma Lewis, Murray's ever-patient girlfriend; Phil Rinker, who used to be the team's agent; Farley, who handles the two performers' accounting; and Edie, Mack's loving wife.

From the start, overly sensitive Murray and stubborn Mack argue continuously. Matters turn ominous when Gruen is literally stabbed in the back in the bathroom. Later, Rinker's corpse is found hanging in the storage room.

The police are summoned, but it is novice Wylie Ledbetter who arrives, since the local police chief is having elective surgery. Thus it is up to Jessica to sort through the cross-motives and old grudges of the assemblage to find the murderer.

Highlights: Never noted for subtlety, Buddy Hackett tears through his role of the blustery comedian who craves the show business limelight still enjoyed by his ex-partner. As a refreshing change, the law enforcer on tap is not a cynical old hand, but a dedicated young man, who welcomes Jessica's intelligent participation in the inquiry

Trivia: Although Steve Lawrence's wife, Edyie Gorme, wasn't available to play Lawrence's on-camera spouse, a nod was made in her direction by naming her fictional counterpart "Edie." George Clooney, the actor nephew of singer Rosemary Clooney, would later rise to stardom on TV's *ER* (1994–) as Dr. Douglas Ross. Dancer/actress/acting coach Sheree North had succeeded for a time in 1950s Hollywood as a threat/substitute to Marilyn Monroe. Arte Johnson is best recalled as a troupe member of *Rowan & Martin's Laugh-In* (1968–1971). For the TV cameras, Buddy Hackett had starred in *Stanley* (1956–1957) and was the host of the post-Groucho Marx and pre-Bill Cosby version of *You Bet Your Life* (1980).

62. "No Accounting for Murder"

(3/22/87) 60 mins.

Director: Peter Crane **Teleplay:** Gerald K. Siegel

Regular: Angela Lansbury (Jessica Fletcher)

Recurring Characters: Michael Horton (Grady Fletcher); Barney Martin (Lieutenant Timothy Hanratty)

Guest Law Enforcer: Charles Walker (Sergeant Joe)

Guest Cast: Paul Comi (The Phantom); Peggy Doyle (Edna); Dorothy Lamour (Sophie); Geoffrey Lewis (Lester Grimshaw); Michael J. London

(Seller); Ron Masak (Marty Giles); Patricia McCormack (Lana Whitman); Thom McFadden (Harry Caldwell); James Noble (Allen Carlisle); Michael Tolan (Ralph Whitman); Kate Vernon (Connie Norton)

The Setting: New York City

The Case: Jessica Fletcher couldn't be happier for her nephew, Grady Fletcher. He has a responsible position as a rising executive in a Manhattan accounting firm. While visiting the city, she comes to the offices of Paul Carlisle & Assoc. to meet his employers, as well as secretary Connie Norton, on whom Grady has a crush. However, before long, all hell breaks loose in this office building which is supposedly haunted by a stalking ghost.

First, Ralph Whitman, a principal at the firm, is found dead in his office suite. A message scrawled on the dead man's office wall reads "Leave me alone or I'll kill again." Many assume that it was written by "The Phantom." However, police lieutenant Timothy Hanratty is definitely not so sure. Meanwhile, hard-nosed Internal Revenue Service auditor Lester Grimshaw arrives at the accounting firm. He is investigating Neptune Ventures, a tax shelter venture which, according to filed papers, was Grady's responsibility.

While overwhelmed Grady, who knew nothing of the Neptune scam, is coping with the skeptical IRS man, Jessica and the congenial police lieutenant look into the homicide. The evidence leads them to Whitman's adulterous wife, Lana, who had been missing for several hours after her husband's death; as well as Allen Carlisle, the deceased's money-hungry partner; and Marty Giles, one of several coerced investors in the Ventures.

Highlights: In this very unusual episode, which has touch of the blarney to it, Jessica Fletcher is quite aggressively authoritative. For once, she is receiving unusually full cooperation from the sympathetic police lieutenant.

Trivia: Dorothy Lamour (1914–1996), the former sarong girl of 1930s and 1940s movies, was cast here in an irrelevant subplot cameo. Patricia McCormack had starred on TV as a child in *Mama* (1953–1957) and during that period had been in the Broadway and Hollywood version of *The Bad Seed.* From 1979–1980, she appeared in the TV sitcom *The Ropers*, a spin-off of *Three's Company.* Stage, screen and TV actor Michael Tolan had appeared with Angela Lansbury in *The Greatest Story Ever Told* (1965); his cameo was as Lazarus, Lansbury's as the wife of Pontius Pilate (Telly Savalas).

63. "The Cemetery Vote"

(4/5/87) 60 mins.

Director: Seymour Robbie **Teleplay:** Robert Van Scoyk

Regular: Angela Lansbury (Jessica Fletcher)

Guest Law Enforcers: Zale Kessler (Coroner); Ed Lauter (Sheriff Orville Yates); Mitchell Ryan (State Police Officer Ernest Lenko); Jeff Yagher (Deputy Wayne Beeler)

Guest Cast: Dick Balduzzi (Gil Stokes); Ellen Bry (Linda Stevens); Joe Campanella (George McDaniel); Bruce Davison (David Carroll); Katherine DeHetre (Rita); John McLiam (Harry Stevens); Neal Penso (Paramedic); Charlene Tilton (Cindy March); Marie Windsor (Kate Gunnerson)

The Setting: Comstock, Idaho

The Case: When Jessica Fletcher learns of the death of a former student's husband, she pays a sympathy visit to Comstock, Idaho. There she hears from young Linda Stevens that her husband, Jimmy, died in a bizarre car accident six weeks ago. Jimmy's father, Harry, reports that local sheriff Orville Yates has destroyed the victim's impounded vehicle.

Jessica's investigation reveals a hotbed of corruption, including Sheriff Yates, who is not above using a "cemetery" vote (i.e., copying dead names off tombstones to create additional voters) to win his elected post. Yates's married deputy, Wayne Beeler—no innocent himself—is having an affair with Cindy March, a city hall secretary. She frequently provides others with confidential municipal documents and information. Then there is the tough cafe proprietor, Kate Gunnerson, who is allowed by the Comstock police to run a local gambling operation.

Jessica finds support from deputy mayor, David Carroll, and from George McDaniel, a councilman pal of David's. However, after disgruntled Harry Stevens is murdered, Mrs. Fletcher turns to state police officer Ernest Lenko for backup support. In the meantime, she repeatedly puts her life in peril.

Highlights: Relying on typecasting to establish immediate character impressions, the story benefits from audience identification with the cast in their typical screen roles: a righteous force (Bruce Davison), a sneering villain (Ed Lauter), a tough broad (Marie Windsor), a trampy young woman (Charlene Tilton). Also emphasized in this installment is the mistaken myth that vice and violence are part of urban life, *not* small-town America.

Trivia: Joe Campanella earned his acting stripes as a regular on such vintage TV series as *The Nurses, Mannix* and *The Lawyers.* Bruce Davison, whose acting achievements include recurring roles in TV series *(Hunter* and *Harry and the Hendersons),* made his mark in such features as *Last Summer* (1969), *Willard* (1971), and his Oscar-nominated performance in *Longtime Companion* (1990). Veteran actress Marie Windsor has been especially efficient in *film noir* roles: *The Narrow Margin* (1951) and *The Killing* (1956). From 1978 to 1985, Charlene Tilton was Lucy Ewing Cooper on the nighttime TV soap opera *Dallas.*

64. "The Days Dwindle Down"

(4/19/87) 60 mins.

Director: Michael Lynch **Teleplay:** Philip Gerson

Regular: Angela Lansbury (Jessica Fletcher)

Guest Law Enforcers: Art Hindle (Policeman Rod Wilson); Russ Marin (Lieutenant Sharp); Harry Morgan (Retired Police Lieutenant Webb)

Guest Cast: Emory Bass (Hotel Manager); Richard Beymer (Sidney Jarvis); Tom Dresen (Peabody); June Havoc (Thelma Vate); Cynthia Leighton (Secretary); Jeffrey Lynn (Sam Wilson); Martita Palmer (Nurse); Mark Pilon (Secretary); Martha Scott (Georgia Wilson); Susan Strasberg (Dorothy Davis); Gloria Stuart (Edna Jarvis); Debbie Zipp (Jerry Wilson)

The Setting: Los Angeles, California

The Case: While in Los Angeles, Jessica Fletcher, who has recently written *The Stain on the Stairs,* is approached by restaurant hostess Georgia Wilson. Georgia begs Mrs. Fletcher to hear her husband's sad story. Sam Wilson is a broken old man recently released from prison, where he wrongly served thirty years for a homicide. Now he wants his name to be cleared.

In the late 1940s, Sam had just lost his bookkeeping job. He had agreed to take a $10,000 payoff from his former boss, Mr. Jarvis, to make the latter's planned suicide look like murder so the Jarvis family could collect the needed insurance. However, Wilson had a change of heart, but, when he reached Jarvis's house, his ex-employer was already dead. In a panic, Sam stole the money. Later, he was arrested by Lieutenant Webb and eventually convicted of the killing on circumstantial evidence.

Her curiosity aroused, Jessica investigates, assisted by Sam's policeman son, Rod. She visits those involved in the long-ago killing: the dead man's widow, Edna, now an emotional cripple confined to a rest home; the deceased's wealthy son, Sidney, who doesn't want the long-ago tragedy revived; Thelma Vate, the dead man's former secretary, who seems to know a great deal about the truth; Dorothy Davis, the proud granddaughter of the deceased's partner; and wheelchair-bound Webb, retired from the police force but still haunted by the strange facts of the old case.

Highlights: With such an array of mature acting professionals, this entry boasts superior performances that rise above the curiosity factor of seeing old favorites anew.

Trivia: The very unique gimmick of blending the story line and footage from an old movie with a plot update was the concept of series cocreator and executive producer Peter S. Fischer. Before selecting *Strange Bargain* (1949)—with Martha Scott, Jeffrey Lynn and Harry Morgan—as the film to use, Fischer had viewed hundreds of black-and-white movies, looking not only for a *film noir* tale that warranted a "sequel," but one in which several of the main players were still living and would agree to appear on *Murder, She Wrote.* According to Fischer; "John Payne was in three of our proposed movies, but he said no. Alice Faye was in another. She told us, 'That's the worst damned movie I ever made. I don't even want to think about it!' "

June Havoc is the actor/director sister of famed stripper Gypsy Rose Lee. Richard Beymer had first gained note in the movie *West Side Story* (1961). Harry Morgan made his deepest impressions as Officer Bill Gannon in *Dragnet* (1967–1970) and as Colonel Sherman Potter on *M*A*S*H* (1975–1983). Jeffrey Lynn (1909–1995) and Gloria Stuart had been 1930s movie stars, while Martha Scott made her screen debut in *Our Town* (1940). Susan Strasberg had been a leading player dating back to *Picnic* (1956). Cast in a small role as one of the Wilsons' family was Debbie Zipp. In the 1987–1988 season, she became a recurring regular on *Murder, She Wrote* playing Grady Fletcher's bride-to-be, Donna Mayberry.

65. "Murder She Spoke"

(5/10/87) 60 mins.

Director: Anthony Shaw **Teleplay:** Si Rose

Regular: Angela Lansbury (Jessica Fletcher)

Guest Law Enforcers: G.W. Bailey (Lieutenant O. Faraday); Mark Neely (Sergeant)

Guest Cast: William Atherton (Greg Dalton); Michael Callan (Carl Anglin); Michael Cole (Earl Tuchman); Charlie Daniels (Stoney Carmichael); Trish Garland (Secretary); Austin Kelly (Cabbie); Jonna Lee (Sally Carmichael); Fredric Lehne (Al Parker); Wendy Phillips (Nancy Dalton); Constance Towers (Margaret Witworth); Patrick Wayne (Randy Witworth)

The Setting: Nashville, Tennessee

The Case: Jessica is recording one of her novels for the Mystery Books for the Blind. In a nearby studio, Stoney Carmichael, one-time country music great, is finishing his comeback album. During a power blackout, Randy Witworth, an owner of the Red Rivers Recording Studios, is stabbed in his office and dies en route to the hospital.

According to Lieutenant Faraday, the finger of guilt points to Greg Dalton, the blind producer, who was angry with Randy that his books-on-tape series was being canceled. However, Jessica agrees with the suspect's wife, Nancy, that her husband is innocent, despite the murder weapon being a steak knife that belonged to Greg.

To prove Dalton's innocence, Mrs. Fletcher questions several interested parties. They include Margaret Witworth, the victim's older and jealous widow; sound engineers Earl Tuchman and Al Parker, who may be involved in selling bootleg tapes of studio recordings; Carl Anglin, who, now that Randy is dead, can take over the recording facility; Stoney Carmichael, who wanted to get out of his recording contract with Randy; and Sally Carmichael, Stoney's niece, who craves a singing career and who is the object of Anglin's lust.

Highlights: Having the chief homicide suspect be an embittered blind man lends an interesting edge to the plot, as does the country music flavor in the recording studio segments.

Trivia: Charlie Daniels is a real-life country music star. Michael Cole is an alumnus of *The Mod Squad* (1968–1973), while former dancer Michael Callan earned screen experiences in *Gidget* (1959) and *Cat Ballou* (1965). Actress/singer Constance Towers is the wife of former actor-turned-ambassador John Gavin. Professionally, Patrick Wayne followed in the footstep of his actor father, John Wayne, with whom he acted in *The Searchers* (1956), *The Alamo* (1960) and *McLintock* (1963), among others.

SEASON FOUR

1987–1988

66. "A Fashionable Way to Die"

(9/20/87) 60 mins.

Director: Nick Havinga **Teleplay:** Donald Ross

Regular: Angela Lansbury (Jessica Fletcher)

Guest Law Enforcers: Michael Voletti (Officer Lutes); Fritz Weaver (Inspector Panassie)

Guest Cast: Lee Bergere (Maxim Soury); Bill Beyers (Peter Appleyard); Danielle Brisebois (Kim Bechet); Randi Brooks (Lu Watters); Louise Dorsey (Dede); Bonnie Ebsen (Yvette, the Maid); Taina Elg (Claudia Soury); Karen Hensel (Marie, the Maid); Juliet Prowse (Valerie Bechet); Barbara Rush (Eva Taylor); Alain St. Alix (Billman); Julie Silliman (Margo); Jean-Paul Vignon (Emcee)

The Setting: Paris, France

The Case: At the invitation of Eva Taylor, Jessica Fletcher departs for Paris where her old friend is launching her new Tailored Look clothing line at an upcoming fashion show. Meanwhile, well-heeled roué Maxim Soury cheats on his wife, Claudia, with his latest mistress, Valerie Bechet, a songstress who owns a bistro. Soury, an entrepreneur and blackmailer on the fringes of the Paris underworld, has loaned Eva money for her venture. Now, before the crucial unveiling of her collection, he demands a 50% stake in her business.

Shortly after the successful showing, Maxim is shot to death in his hotel room. Gallant, self-important Inspector Panassie thinks the murderer is probably Eva Taylor. However, Jessica is unconvinced that her friend could be the woman in the long white coat seen leaving the victim's room about the time of his death.

Jessica's inquiry leads her to two maids at the Hotel Inter-Continental, as well as to Eva's assistant, Peter Appleyard. Additionally, Mrs. Fletcher questions fashion models Lu Watters and Kim Bechet, one of whom has a secret past and the other a hidden love affair, as well as Soury's wife, Claudia, and his mistress, Valerie.

Highlights: Set in the glamorous world of haute couture, the episode boasts glimpses of a stylish fashion show, as well as song interludes by Juliet Prowse's Valerie Bechet. Seldom has Jessica met such a self-satisfied police official as Inspector Panassie, who assumes that every woman of a certain age—including Mrs. Fletcher—must find his charms irresistible. During the course of the proceedings, the viewer is treated to a brief sightseeing tour of Paris, including Jessica and Eva dining at the Jules Verne Restaurant at the Eiffel Tower.

Trivia: Once again, a clothes button provides a pivotal clue for the ever-observant Jessica Fletcher. Both Finnish Taina Elg (*Les Girls* [1957], *Watusi* [1958] and South African Juliet Prowse (1937–1996) (*Can Can* [1959], *G.I. Blues* [1960]) had been dancers who turned to acting careers in 1950s Hollywood films. Former child actor Danielle Brisebois, now a chanteuse, had appeared on Broadway in *Annie* and, later, was Archie Bunker's street-wise niece on TV's *All in the Family* (1978–1983). Randi Brooks had appeared on *Brothers and Sisters* (1979), *Renegades* (1983) and *Rituals* (1984–1985).

67. "When Thieves Fall Out"

(9/27/87) 60 mins.

Director: Seymour Robbie **Teleplay:** Arthur David Weingarten

Regulars: Angela Lansbury (Jessica Fletcher); Tom Bosley (Sheriff Amos Tupper)

Guest Cast: John Glover (Andrew Durbin); Michael Lembeck (Arnie Wakeman); Kenneth McMillan (Kevin Cauldwell); Caitlin O'Hearney (Tara Sillman); John Bennett Perry (Judge Harry Sillman); Dack Rambo (Bill Hampton); Shelley Smith (Alison Hampton); Mark Voland (Dan Pulling); Charles Summers (Doc Mathews)

The Setting: Cabot Cove, Maine

The Case: In the small town of Cabot Cove events crowd on top of one another. Dan Pulling is fired from his sales job by car lot owner Bill Hampton. Meanwhile, Kevin Cauldwell is retiring as the local high school's football coach. Then there is Andrew Durbin who has recently returned to Cabot Cove, where he rents Leila Small's home for a few weeks. Wheelchair-bound Arnie Wakeman, a stock market investor, hopes to sue Hampton, claiming the latter sold him a "lemon" car which resulted in Wakeman's car mishap. As for Judge Harry Sillman, he insists he cannot hear the pending negligence case because he was a childhood friend of both parties.

When Hampton is found shot to death, Sheriff Amos Tupper concludes it is suicide. However, more alert Jessica Fletcher notes that the victim was left-handed, yet he was shot in the right temple. As she marshals the facts, Jessica discovers that Bill's killing is tied to a strange twenty-year-old murder and theft.

Highlights: For a few scenes, Jessica Fletcher yields the limelight to Kevin Cauldwell, her longtime school associate and friend. In telling moments, he admits to thirty years of frustration at never having had a gridiron team that was a major winner.

Trivia: Michael Lembeck, the actor son of Harvey Lembeck (*Stalag 17* [1954] and TV's *The Phil Silvers Show* [1955–1959], etc.) had played Bonnie Franklin's son-in-law on *One Day at a Time* (1979–1984) and later turned to directing TV sitcoms (*Coach*, *Major Dad*, etc.). Kenneth McMillan (1932–1989) was Valerie Harper's boss on *Rhoda* (1977–1978). John Bennett Perry had played Sheriff Gilmore on *Falcon Crest* (1985–1986). John Glover's movie credits contain *Annie Hall* (1977), *White Nights* (1984) and *In the Mouth of Madness* (1995).

68. "Witness for the Defense"

(10/4/87) 60 mins.

Director: Seymour Robbie **Teleplay:** Robert E. Swanson

Regular: Angela Lansbury (Jessica Fletcher)

Guest Cast: Christopher Allport (Jim Harlan); Dori Arnold (Secretary); Ivan Bonar (His Lordship); Charlie Brill (Rudy); Richard Cox (Clay McCloud); Stefan Gierasch (Plansky, the Private Detective); Dean G. Griffin (Klebber); Marilyn Hassett (Patricia Harlan); Simon Jones (Barnaby Friar); Dianne Kay (Monica Blaine); Patrick McGoohan (Oliver Quayle); Juliet Mills (Annette Pirage); James Staley (Mr. Fouchet); Claire Trevor (Judith Harlan)

The Setting: Quebec, Canada

The Case: Jessica is summoned to Quebec to testify at the trial of author Jim Harlan. His wife, Patricia, had died in a tragic fire while Mrs. Fletcher was visiting wealthy matriarch Judith Harlan. Now, according to flamboyant defense attorney Oliver Quayle, Jim is being charged with having murdered his wife prior to covering up her death by setting a fire. With determined Annette Pirage representing the Crown, Quayle pulls out all his theatrical tricks to win the case for Harlan.

Unable to make any accommodation with the immoderate Quayle, Jessica must assess the case on her own. Posing as a naive reporter from a small town in Maine, she gathers the buried facts in a particularly ingenious fashion. She finds out that the murder victim had been a Las Vegas showgirl who once spent a year in an Arizona jail for embezzlement. Moreover, it turns out that Monica Blaine was not a college friend of Patricia's, that the gardener, Clay McCloud, has a criminal record, that domineering Mrs. Harlan is obsessed with family pride, and that a seedy private detective, Plansky, has uncovered amazing new evidence.

Highlights: Always an enemy of pompous authority, Jessica is forced to endure a battle of wills with self-opinionated Oliver Quayle. Their engaging tug-of-war climaxes in a heated courtroom hassle in which the lawyer seeks to discredit the hostile witness (i.e., Jessica Fletcher) by twisting truths. As an example, he cites her stay at a mental sanitarium. An annoyed Jessica explains in court that it was merely to research her book *Sanitarium of Death.*

Trivia: Once again, a piece of jewelry proves to be a vital clue in wrapping up the case at hand. Proficient actress Claire Trevor, making a rare TV appearance, had won a Best Supporting Actress Academy Award for *Key Largo* (1948). American-born Patrick McGoohan, reared in England, had gained prominence with several TV series: *Danger Man, Secret Agent, The Prisoner* and *Rafferty.* Britisher Juliet Mills, who earned an Emmy as Best Supporting Actress in a Drama Special for *QB VII* (1975), had starred as Phoebe Figalilly in TV's *Nanny and the Professor* (1970–1971).

69. "Old Habits Die Hard"

(10/11/87) 60 mins.

Director: John Llewellyn Moxey **Teleplay:** Chris Manheim

Regular: Angela Lansbury (Jessica Fletcher)

Guest Cast: Eileen Brennan (Marion Simpson); Fay DeWitt (Sister Mary-Margaret); M'el Dowd (Sister Margaret-Mary); Cindy Fisher (Nancy

Bates); Caroline Gilshian (Sister Anne); Clu Gulager (Ray Carter); Evelyn Keyes (Sister Emily); Mark Keyloun (Mike Phelps); Ed Nelson (Mayor Albert Simpson); Scott Paulin (Dr. Marshall); Jane Powell (Reverend Mother Claire); Robert Prosky (Bishop Shea); Sherri Stoner (Sarah Martino); Carol Swarbrick (Sister Margaret-Marie); Audrey Totter (Sister Paul)

The Setting: Bergen Falls, Louisiana

The Case: Near Shrevesport, Louisiana, Jessica is enjoying a restful reunion with her old college chum and Kappa Delta sorority sister, now Reverend Mother Claire. Soon, the tranquillity at the Bergen Falls convent is shattered when aged Sister Emily dies at the dining table. Bishop Shea insists that the devout Sister killed herself with an overdose of medication. As such, he refuses to permit a church burial. However, both Jessica and Reverend Mother know that Sister Emily never would have taken her own life.

To get at the truth, Jessica confers with the convent's substitute physician, Dr. Marshall, as well as with Marion Simpson, the activist wife of the local mayor, Albert Simpson. Then there is rebellious Mike Phelps, a pharmacy delivery truck driver, who is angry that the nuns are supporting his girlfriend, Sarah Martino, in her desire to join the order.

Later, Jessica uncovers that Sister Emily once had a hand in the arrest of Nancy Bates, who is now back in town after a prison stay. In addition, there is private detective Ray Carter, who had been pressuring Sister Emily, who kept a case history of convent students, to help him solve a final case before he retires.

Highlights: In a well-established Hollywood tradition, it was considered an intriguing bit of casting to have actresses as pious nuns. While most of the cast—especially Jane Powell—are busy being theatrically reverent, efficient Jessica Fletcher bridges the secular and religious worlds. Meanwhile, there's frenetic Marion Simpson, a tightly fisted, controlling woman with an excessive gift for gab.

Trivia: Like Angela Lansbury, Jane Powell (*Holiday in Mexico* [1946] and *A Date with Judy* [1948]) and Audrey Totter (*Her Highness and the Bellboy* [1945] and *The Lady in the Lake* [1946]) were alumnae of MGM's 1940s golden era. (Lansbury and Totter were both in *Tenth Avenue Angel* [1948].)

Robert Prosky spent well over two decades as a stage actor in Washington, D.C., before coming to TV (e.g., Sergeant Stanislaus Jablonski on *Hill Street Blues*).

70. "The Way to Dusty Death"

(10/25/87) 60 mins.

Director: Nick Havinga **Teleplay:** Philip Gerson

Regular: Angela Lansbury (Jessica Fletcher)

Guest Law Enforcer: Nat Brant (Lieutenant Grayson)

Guest Cast: Joanna Barnes (Lydia Barnett); Richard Beymer (Morgan McCormack); Lynn Carlin (Nicole); E.R. Davies (Board Member #2); Flo DiRe (Josette, the Maid); Nancy Dussault (Kate Dutton); Jenilee Harrison (Serena); Richard Jaeckel (Dr. Chatsworth); Andrea Marcovicci (Anne Hathaway); Sandy McPeak (Spruce Osborne); Joanna Pettet (Virginia McCormack); Lawrence Pressman (Tom Dutton); Jay Robinson (Paddock); Bob Sneed (Board Member #1); Ray Walston (Q.L. Frubson); Cornel Wilde (Duncan Barnett).

The Settings: New York City; suburban New York

The Case: As a member of the board of directors of Barnett Industries, Jessica Fletcher is invited along with the other directors to Duncan Barnett's suburban New York home. Others "asked" to the country estate for the weekend are the firm's top executives. Everyone anticipates that the tycoon will name his successor at this get-together. Instead, the ailing Barnett announces that he doesn't intend to retire. The next morning, he is found dead of an apparent heart attack in his Jacuzzi.

With little help from police lieutenant Grayson, Jessica determines that it was murder most foul. That decided, she interrogates the assemblage. She learns that overly aggressive Morgan McCormack and his wife, Virginia, badly wanted Barnett out of the way. Q.L. Frubson is found to be on several boards of directors and has a reputation for shady dealings. Tom Dutton, another top Barnett executive, would do almost anything to be the victim's successor, while his frustrated wife, Kate, has long hated the pressures of corporate life. Spruce Osborne is revealed to be grabbing company stock in a takeover bid. Others playing the executive suite game are Barnett's widow, Lydia, as well as Anne Hathaway, a company officer, and Nicole, Duncan's long-enduring secretary.

Highlights: This episode takes a cue from two 1954 Hollywood movies: *Executive Suite* and *A Woman's World* (in which Cornel Wilde had played a corporate president hopeful). This segment brings together a diverse group of high motivated suspects, each with a strong reason to eliminate the victim, thus making this a challenging whodunit.

Trivia: For a nice change of pace, the police *do not* provide an alter ego to Jessica Fletcher's sleuthing. Here it is Dr. Chatsworth who serves as Mrs. Fletcher's sounding board.

Joanna Barnes had costarred in the TV series *21 Beacon Street* (1959) and *The Trials of O'Brien* (1965–1966) Baby-faced Richard Jaeckel had been working in a movie studio mailroom when he was discovered for such movies as *Guadalcanal Diary* (1943), *Sands of two Jima* (1949), *The Violent Men* (1955) and *Black Moon Rising* (1986).

Before continuing roles on *Berrenger's* (1985) and *Trapper John, M.D.* (1985–1986), Andrea Marcovicci had been featured on the daytime soap opera *Love Is a Many Splendored Thing* in the early 1970s. Joanna Pettet's early screen roles include *The Group* (1966), *Night of the Generals* (1967) and *Robbery* (1967). Feisty Ray Walston recreated his Broadway roles in the movie versions of *South Pacific* (1958) and *Damn Yankees* (1958) and went on to award-winning prominence as Judge Henry Bone in TV's *Picket Fences* (1992–1996). One-time swashbuckling screen lead Cornel Wilde (1915–1989) directed and costarred with his wife Jean Wallace in several pictures: *Storm Fear* (1955), *Sword of Lancelot* (1963), etc.

71. "It Runs in the Family"

(11/1/87) 60 mins.

Director: Walter Grauman **Teleplay:** Peter S. Fischer

Regular: Angela Lansbury (Emma Macgill)

Guest Law Enforcer: Anthony Newley (Inspector Frost)

Guest Cast: Ian Abercrombie (Dr. Ernest Blandings); Peter Ashton (Burt Hawkins, the Chauffeur); John David Bland (Derek Constable); Mark Lindsay Chapman (Johnny); Lester Fletcher (Reverend Twilley); Christopher Hewett (Humphrey Defoe); Richard Johnson (Geoffrey Constable); Pamela Kosh (Mrs. Dexter Hundley); Jane Leeves (Gwen Petrie); Rosemary Murphy (Sybil Constable); Carolyn Seymour (Pauline Constable); John Standing (Arthur Constable)

The Settings: English countryside; London, England

The Case: In London, retired music hall star Emma Macgill receives a surprise visit from solicitor Humphrey Defoe. He informs her that his friend and client, Geoffrey Constable, wishes her to have a thousand pounds, a small house in Tuxford and, most of all, to have his World War II love pay a visit to his country estate. It has been over forty years since Emma last saw Constable. Since then, Geoffrey has endured a long-standing, loveless marriage and is now widowed. Defoe alerts Emma that Geoffrey has only months to live.

Arriving at the country house, down-to-earth Emma makes a bad impression on Geoffrey's snobbish sister, Sybil. Equally inhospitable are Constable's sons, Johnny and Arthur, as well as the latter's social-climbing wife, Pauline. Arthur and Pauline's spendthrift son, Derek, is vaguely amused by the socially "inferior" Emma. On the other hand, Emma's presence is a wonderful tonic for ailing Geoffrey, the current Viscount of Blackraven.

As part of their reunion, Emma and Geoffrey embark on a picnic where he proposes marriage to her. While eating the pickled herring she has prepared, he is fatally stricken. Labeled the chief suspect in the case, Emma must prove to Inspector Frost and the others that she is innocent. In the process, she uncovers the facts surrounding the mysterious death—a few weeks earlier—of Geoffrey's aged father. Before long, the killer's murderous scheme becomes all too clear. By the finale, when the Scotland Yard authority compliments her on her knack for detecting, Emma can proudly boast, "Let's just say, it runs in the family."

Highlights: Unlike 1985's "Sing a Song of Murder" (#27), Angela focuses on her zestful characterization of unbridled, redheaded Emma Macgill, a trouper from the old school. Having mastered the cockney character, Lansbury plays up the strong contrast between her natural woman and the artificialities of the class-conscious Constables, thus creating an entertaining study of opposites.

Trivia: During an after-dinner entertainment at the country estate, Emma sings "How'd You Like to Spoon with Me." It was a number Angela had earlier performed in the MGM musical *Till the Clouds Roll By* (1946). Angela Lansbury and Richard Johnson had costarred previously in *The Amorous Adventures of Moll Flanders* (1965). Anthony Newley, a former child movie star (*Oliver Twist* [1948]) in England, wrote and directed the autobiographical *Can Hieronymus Merkin Ever Forget Mercy Humpe and Find True Happiness?* (1969) which costarred his then wife, Joan Collins.

More frequently a stage actress, Rosemary Murphy's movie parts encompass *To Kill a Mockingbird* (1962), *Any Wednesday* (1966) and *September* (1987). Broadway's Christopher Hewett had played domestics on two TV series: *Fantasy Island* (1983–1984) and *Mr. Belvedere* (1985–1990).

72. "If It's Thursday, It Must Be Beverly Hills"

(11/8/87) 60 mins.

Director: Peter Crane **Teleplay:** Wendy Graf, Lisa Stotsky

Regulars: Angela Lansbury (Jessica Fletcher); Tom Bosley (Sheriff Amos Tupper); William Windom (Dr. Seth Hazlitt)

Recurring Characters: Julie Adams (Eve Simpson); Gloria DeHaven (Phyllis Grant); Kathryn Grayson (Ideal Molloy); Sally Klein (Corinne, the Beauty Shop Helper); Ruth Roman (Loretta Spiegel)

Guest Law Enforcer: Rick Lenz (Deputy Jonathan Martin)

Guest Cast: Antoinette Bower (Mrs. Audrey Martin); Ray Girardin (George Tibbits, the Postman); Dody Goodman (Beverly Hills)

The Setting: Cabot Cove, Maine

The Case: No one in Cabot Cove seems to be making a killing in the new state lottery. However, murder comes to town when extremely unhappy Audrey Martin is found dead. At first it seems a suicide, but it is soon declared a case of homicide. The chief suspect is her widower, Jonathan, the unassuming night deputy for Sheriff Amos Tupper.

Having great faith in Jessica Fletcher's skills, Jonathan begs her to prove his innocence. Before long, Jessica and Amos discover that the love-starved deputy has been romancing several Cabot Cove women, allotting them each a weekly night when he would abandon his police rounds to pay a call at their homes. Among the courted were such local divorcees and/or widows as real estate agent Eve Simpson, pampered housewife Ideal Molloy and travel agent Phyllis Grant. To Dr. Seth Hazlitt's amazement, his long-time nurse, Beverly Hills, is Jonathan's Thursday night regular.

Highlights: Every small town has its favored hangouts. For the middle-aged women of Cabot Cove it is Loretta Spiegel's beauty shop where a customer's hair may sooner curl from blunt gossip than from a permanent wave solution. Now established as the center of all news and rumors in Cabot Cove, the shop and its colorful habitués would be featured in future installments.

Trivia: Like Angela Lansbury, both Gloria DeHaven (*Best Foot Forward* [1943], *Summer Holiday* [1948]) and Kathryn Grayson (*Anchors Aweigh* [1945], *The Kissing Bandit* [1948]) had been MGM players during the 1940s. During the same period, Ruth Roman was building her screen career which would peak with a prolonged stay at Warner Bros. (*Three Secrets* [1950], *Strangers On a Train* [1951], etc.). Dody Goodman, a former Broadway dancer, made a sharp impression as a regular cut-up on TV's *The Jack Paar Show* (1956–1958). Rick Lenz, a veteran of such movies as *Cactus Flower* and *Little Dragons* (1980), had been in the Richard Boone Western TV series *Hec Ramsey* (1972–1974), playing Sheriff Oliver B. Stamp.

73. "Steal Me a Story"

(11/15/87) 60 mins.

Director: John Llewellyn Moxey **Teleplay:** Peter S. Fischer

Regular: Angela Lansbury (Jessica Fletcher)

Guest Law Enforcers: Joe Horvath (Sergeant Gates); Chris Hubbell (Cop); Yaphet Kotto (Lieutenant Bradshaw)

Guest Cast: Jeff Abbott (Attorney); Vincent Baggetta (Bert Puzo); Bradford Dillman (Avery Stone); Bill Dunham (Heavy); Fionnula Flanagan (Freida); Lenore Kasdorf (Brenda Blake, who plays Nurse Steele); Scott Laurence (Assistant Director); Doug McClure (Gary Patterson, who plays Dr. Valiant); Kim Miyori (Gayle McGiveny); Barry Pearl (Publicity Staffer); Jay Roberts (2nd Assistant Director); Matt Stetson (Secretary); Gail Strickland (Kate Hollander); Ken Swofford (Sid Sharkey); Kate Williamson (Lady Customer); Gail Youngs (Diane Crane)

The Setting: Los Angeles, California

The Case: In Southern California to promote her latest novel, *Calvin Canterbury's Revenge,* Jessica is visited by Gayle McGiveny. The fledgling scriptwriter tells Mrs. Fletcher that an unscrupulous TV executive producer, Sid Sharkey, has ordered Gayle to rip off one of Jessica's novels as material for an episode of his TV series, *Danger Doctor.*

The aghast mystery writer offers to collaborate with timid Gayle on a fresh segment idea. Later, Jessica storms into Sharkey's office to voice her strong objections to his intended literary piracy. Soon thereafter, Sid is killed when a package he is opening explodes. Thus Jessica becomes one of Lieutenant Bradshaw's prime suspects.

To prove her innocence to the gruff law officer, Jessica takes up her detective mantle once again. Her exploration is made all the tougher because Sharkey had so many enemies. For example, Brenda Blake—Nurse Steele on the show—had been trying unsuccessfully to buy out of her contract. Also, there was little love lost between the deceased and actor Gary Patterson, the latter starring as the program's Dr. Valiant, or, for that matter, director Bert Puzo and producer Avery Stone. Power-hungry United TV Network executive Kate Hollander had been battling Sid, and Freida, Sharkey's much-suffering secretary, had long harbored hatred for her exploitive boss.

Highlights: A favorite motif on *Murder, She Wrote* was exploring behind-the-scenes activities in show business. This excursion offers a particularly incisive study of the TV industry where rating points and salaries are prized higher than integrity and talent. Jessica learns much about the inner workings of the television business when she craftily agrees to work in story development for Gary Patterson so she can have a legitimate reason to wander around the studio.

Trivia: A constant *Murder, She Wrote* character theme is that Jessica Fletcher will never knowingly do anything even remotely unethical or immoral if she can possibly avoid it in solving a caper. Thus here, as in several other installments, just before putting her master plan in action to wrap up the whodunit, she confides to a fellow conspirator, "I don't know how legal this is or if it will work. . . ."

Doug McClure (1936–1995), the (co)star of many TV series (e.g., *The Overland Trail, Checkmate, Out of This World*) made his strongest impression as Trampas on *The Virginian* (1962–1971). Vincent Baggetta found success as Dr. Peter Chernak on the daytime TV soap opera *Love Is a Many Splendored Thing* in the early 1970s. Yaphet Kotto, who directed the movie *Nightmares of the Devil* (1988), had played a law enforcer on screen in *Report to the Commissioner* (1974). Gail Strickland's TV series number such entries as *The Insiders* (1985–1986) and *What a Country* (1986–1987).

74. "Trouble in Eden"

(11/22/87) 60 mins.

Director: Nick Havinga **Story/teleplay:** John D.F. Black, Paul Savage

Regular: Angela Lansbury (Jessica Fletcher)

Guest Law Enforcer: Roy Thinnes (Sheriff Landry)

Guest Cast: Macdonald Carey (Dr. Lynch); Joan Caulfield (Mary Rose Welch); Thom Christopher (Reverend Willard Manchester); Tom Fitzsimmons (Lewis Framm, Esq.); Betty Garrett (Martha Neilson); Rosanna Huffman (Mrs. Dora Manchester); Tricia O'Neil (Lila Benson); Mills Watson (Snooks Sitwell); Stuart Whitman (C.J. Dobbs)

The Settings: New York City; Eden, Oregon

The Case: One day Mary Rose Welch has lunch with her friend Jessica Fletcher in Manhattan. Mary Rose mentions that her sister, Charlotte, who operated a hotel in Eden, Oregon, had passed away recently. She also relates that she has received an anonymous letter from Oregon suggesting that Mary Rose's death from a heart attack was actually murder and that she should check into why the body was so hastily cremated. Mary Rose asks Jessica to go with her to Eden to investigate. Before they can depart,

Mary Rose is hospitalized as the result of a suspicious hit-and-run car accident.

Posing as Mary Rose, Jessica arrives in Eden. At the Garden of Eden Hotel, now managed by Lila Benson, Mrs. Fletcher discovers that the deceased had been operating a bawdy house! From the talkative maid, Martha, Jessica learns more details of Charlotte's death, including the fact that right after Charlotte's murder, the dead woman's will and money had vanished from her strongbox hidden beneath her bedroom floor rug.

Before long, ever-curious Jessica has aroused a great deal of animosity from certain townsfolk, including Dr. Lynch, local businessman C.J. Dobbs, mortician Snooks Sitwell, Reverend Manchester and Sheriff Landry (who had been receiving a thousand-dollar monthly payoff from Charlotte).

Highlights: The plot line of Jessica Fletcher having to deal with a (temporary) madam and her flock of prostitutes creates entertaining segment moments, as opposed to the ominous scenes in which the mystery writer snoops into dangerous territory.

Trivia: Both Joan Caulfield (1922–1991) of *Dear Ruth* (1947) and *The Sainted Sisters* (1948) and Macdonald Carey (1913–1994) of *Dream Girl* (1947) and *Streets of Laredo* (1949) had been contract lead actors at Paramount Pictures in the 1940s. Betty Garrett (*Words and Music* [1948], *On the Town* [1949]) had been at MGM with Angela Lansbury in the late 1940s. Roy Thinnes was a seasoned TV series star: *The Long Hot Summer, The Invaders* and *The Psychiatrist.* Veteran screen, stage and TV actor Stuart Whitman had such movie credits as *When Worlds Collide* (1952), *Ten North Frederick* (1958) and *The Mark* (1961) for which he was Oscar-nominated.

75. "Indian Giver"

(11/29/87) 60 mins.

Director: Walter Grauman **Teleplay:** Gerald K. Siegel

Regulars: Angela Lansbury (Jessica Fletcher); Tom Bosley (Sheriff Amos Tupper); William Windom (Dr. Seth Hazlitt)

Recurring Character: Richard Paul (Mayor Sam Booth)

Guest Law Enforcer: Otto Felix (Deputy)

Guest Cast: Theodore Bikel (Professor Harold Crenshaw); Heidi Bohay (Donna Crenshaw); Terry Burns (TV Reporter); Lonny Chapman (Addison Langley); Jack Colvin (Harris Atwater); Maggie Kederon (2nd Reporter);

Gary Lockwood (Tom Carpenter); Ralph Meyering, Jr., (Reporter); Jennifer Salt (Helen Langley); Charles Siebert (Norman Edmonds); Bernie White (George Longbow); Gerald York (Bully)

The Setting: Cabot Cove, Maine

The Case: The good citizens of Cabot Cove are taken aback when their annual Founders Day celebration is disrupted. Ironically, the intruders are descendants of Chief Manatoka and the Algonquin Indian tribe who used to roam the area. Their representative, George Longbow, insists that his people are the rightful claimants to a 1758 land grant from the British which encompasses all of Cabot Cove. Mayor Sam Booth appoints Jessica Fletcher and Dr. Seth Hazlitt to study the legitimacy of this claim.

Jessica calls upon Professor Harold Crenshaw, an expert in Indian history, to provide advice. (It develops that Crenshaw's daughter, Donna, and George Longbow are past college friends.) Meanwhile, at a hastily convened town meeting, anger mounts at Longbow's persistent demands. If the Indian grant theory is upheld, it could mean disaster for Addison and Helen Langley, who have optioned part of the territory in question. Addison intends to sell the property to wealthy Harris Atwater who, in turn, hopes to construct a resort hotel there. Adding to the complex situation, Norm Edmonds, who is fostering his own interests, offers Crenshaw a $50,000 bribe to come up with "proof" discrediting the Native Americans.

Later, Addison Langley is found dead at the town hall—with a lance sticking out of his body. Before Sheriff Amos Tupper can take action, a faction composed of prejudiced locals led by Tom Carpenter track down George Longbow, a suspect in the homicide, and beat him up. It is up to Jessica to stop further mayhem in Cabot Cove by finding the true killer.

Highlights: The joy of this installment is Richard Paul's amusing sketch of the do-nothing, but loud-mouthed Cabot Cove mayor. He gives new meaning to the expression "passing the buck."

Trivia: Austrian-born Theodore Bikel, an international stage, TV, film and cabaret performer with a penchant for playing roles of diverse nationalities, gained a latter-day reputation for starring as Tevye in stage productions of *Fiddler on the Roof.* Richard Paul had played Mayor Teddy Burnside on *Carter Country* (1977–1979) and was Reverend Billy Joe Bickerstaff on *Hail to the Chief* (1985).

Gary Lockwood's movies range from *Splendor in the Grass* (1961) to *Firecreek* (1967) and *The Wild Pair* (1987) and include his most famous screen work: *2001: A Space Odyssey* (1968). Jennifer Salt, the daughter of screenwriter Waldo Salt, had been in *Midnight Cowboy* (1969), *Play It Again Sam* (1972), among others.

76. "Doom with a View"

(12/13/87) 60 mins.

Director: Walter Grauman **Teleplay:** Kenneth A. Berg

Regular: Angela Lansbury (Jessica Fletcher)

Recurring Character: Michael Horton (Grady Fletcher)

Guest Law Enforcers: Monte Markham (Inspector Donald Matheney); Macon McCalman (Hotel Detective Fritz Rice)

Guest Cast: Tony Batten (Workman); John Callahan (Garrett Harper); Kenny Davis (Husband); Robert Desiderio (Mark Havlin); Jennifer Holmes (Sandra); Lynn Holt (Aquarium Lady); Juli Reding Hutner (Mrs. Townsend); Mary Ingersoll (Cashier); Judy Kerr (Wife); Janet Leigh (Cornelia Montaigne Harper); Charlotte Rae (Nettie Harper); Sheila Shaw (Maid); Steve Tschudy (Somnelier)

The Setting: New York City

The Case: Struggling New Yorker Grady Fletcher is in a predicament. His aunt, Jessica Fletcher, is arriving in town for a visit, but his apartment is being fumigated. A fraternity pal from Purdue University saves the day. Garrett Harper invites the Fletchers to stay at the city's plush Montaigne Plaza Hotel.

Once there, the Fletchers meet Garrett's wife. She is the ultrawealthy and much older Cornelia Montaigne Harper who owns the hotel. Very soon, Cornelia displays her jealousy when computer operator Sandra Clemens, a cheerleader from Garrett's past campus days, arrives from Fort Wayne, Indiana, for another of her frequent stays at the hotel.

Rainy weather isn't the only thing that turns the weekend sour. Sandra is found dead in her room, apparently having tripped and, in the fall, having fatally hit her head on the dresser. When Grady is found in the victim's room—retrieving a certain bracelet at Garrett's request—he is marked as the chief homicide suspect.

While proving Grady's innocence, Jessica crosses swords with Inspector Donald Matheney, who can scarcely be bothered to tear himself away from society functions. On the other hand, sleazy hotel detective Rice is always looking for skeletons in closets about the premises. Meanwhile, Jessica evaluates what role Garrett's overprotective mother, Nettie Harper, or Cornelia's ambitious right-hand man, Mark Havlin, have in the killing.

Highlights: Janet Leigh has a showcase caricaturing a Leona Helmsley-type hotel mogul. A particularly entertaining sequence is the intimate hotel dining room dinner party where catty remarks, questioning looks, and diplomatic smoothings run rampant as Nettie and Cornelia battle over pampered Garrett. Later, in a rare moment of bad temper, Jessica Fletcher loses patience with naive Grady, accusing him of being a pawn to any "friend's" demands or a pretty woman's smile, which frequently gets him and Mrs. Fletcher into deep water with the law.

Trivia: As fellow MGM contract players in the 1940s and early 1950s, Angela Lansbury and Janet Leigh costarred in *If Winter Comes* (1947) and *The Red Danube* (1949). Later, they appeared together in the memorable *The Manchurian Candidate* (1962). Bronx-born Robert Desiderio was Ted Melcher on *Knots Landing* (1988–1989). Charlotte Rae played Edna Garrett on both *Diff'rent Strokes* (1978–1979) and *The Facts of Life* (1979–1986).

77. "Who Threw the Barbitals in Mrs. Fletcher's Chowder?"

(1/3/88) 60 mins.

Director: John Llewellyn Moxey **Teleplay:** Robert Van Scoyk

Regulars: Angela Lansbury (Jessica Fletcher); Tom Bosley (Sheriff Amos Tupper); William Windom (Dr: Seth Hazlitt)

Guest Law Enforcers: Dennis Bailey (Deputy Grover); Colleen Camp (Deputy Marigold Feeney)

Guest Cast: Henry Gibson (Harold Banner); Geoffrey Lewis (Kenny Oakes); Anne Meara (Winnie Tupper Banner); Joseph V. Perry (Ralph); Barbara Rhoades (Flo Oakes); Donnelly Rhodes (Ed Bellamy); Guy Stockwell (Elmo Banner)

The Setting: Cabot Cove, Maine

The Case: Things have never been more problematic for Cabot Cove's Sheriff Amos Tupper. His latest deputy has quit, and the only new applicant is Marigold Feeney, a former meter maid from Augusta, Maine. Under the law, the somewhat chauvinistic Amos has no choice but to hire her. At the same time, another female (re-)enters his life—his sister Winnie from Kentucky. The hysterical woman has left her stern husband, Elmo Banner, and seeks refuge with Amos.

Soon thereafter, Elmo, who owns a drugstore chain back home, arrives in town. (He has learned of Winnie's whereabouts from Donnelly Rhodes, the Louisville, Kentucky, private detective he hired.) Banner is accompanied by his sister, Flo Oakes, his brother-in-law, Kenny Oakes, and his brother, Harold Banner. Hoping to soothe over the tense reunion of Winnie and her relatives, Jessica Fletcher cooks a lobster dinner at her house and serves her famous clam chowder. Dr. Seth Hazlitt and Amos are also invited to the gathering.

At the fateful meal, Winnie whines and Elmo remains gruff, while the other relatives bicker. Suddenly, Elmo keels over dead at the dinner table. The subsequent autopsy proves he died of a special ingredient in the chowder—barbital!

Extremely embarrassed that a guest should die at her dining table—while eating her cooking!—Jessica is determined to find the killer. Doing so will serve a dual purpose: clearing herself of a potential homicide charge and restoring her now besmirched culinary reputation.

Highlights: Since Amos Tupper is such an oddball character—even in quirky Cabot Cove—the townsfolk are exceedingly curious about his relatives. As such, a good deal of the episode's humor springs from the good sheriff, adrift at handling usual everyday events, trying to deal with a family crisis. Meanwhile, the old-fashioned law enforcer is struggling with the concept of a woman deputy.

Trivia: Anne Meara, a fine farceur and adept actress—*Fame* (1980)—is the wife of her long-standing comedy partner, Jerry Stiller. The latter, who gained new laurels in the 1990s as Frank Costanza, the cantankerous dad of Jason Alexander's character George on the TV sitcom *Seinfeld,* would himself appear on *Murder, She Wrote* in 1989's "When the Fat Lady Sings" (#116). The Stillers are the parents of actor Ben Stiller, who directed *Reality Bites* (1994) and *The Cable Guy* (1996). Diminutive Henry Gibson has appeared in several Robert Altman-directed features: *Nashville* (1975), *A Perfect Couple* (1979), *Health* (1980), etc.

78. "Harbinger of Death"

(1/24/88) 60 mins.

Director: Anthony Shaw **Teleplay:** R. Barker Price

Regular: Angela Lansbury (Jessica Fletcher)

Guest Law Enforcer: George DiCenzo (Sergeant Kettler); Kirk Thornton (Forensic Man)

Guest Cast: Armand Asselin (Max, the Security Guard); Steven Ford (Drake Eaton); Robin Gammell (Dr. Thor Lundquist); Karen Grassle (Fay Hewitt); Dean Jones (Leonard Palmer); Kate McNeil (Carrie Palmer); Marcia Rodd (Madeline DeHaven); Jeffrey Tambor (Russell Armstrong)

The Setting: Upstate New York

The Case: Jessica Fletcher heads to upstate New York to help her niece, Carrie, celebrate her third wedding anniversary. Carrie is married to the older Leonard Palmer, an astronomer at the Astro-Physic Institute. When Jessica arrives, Leonard tells her that Carrie suddenly left for Ithaca to help out ailing Aunt Edna. Mrs. Fletcher finds this odd, since she knows for a fact that Edna is in fine health.

While awaiting her niece's return, Jessica learns more about Leonard's work, including his hatred of his employers' spending so much time chasing contracts for government weaponry and war research. Palmer is far more interested in tracking a mysterious comet which is scheduled for reappearance in the galaxy at any time.

Meanwhile, Madeline DeHaven, a director of the Defense Spending Review Board, arrives in town with her good-looking assistant, Drake Eaton. She has come for meetings with the Institute's head, Russell Armstrong. Discussions take a back seat when Drake is found shot to death in his hotel room.

To Jessica's dismay, her "missing" niece is a murder suspect. Mrs. Fletcher discovers that the deceased was an old beau of Carrie's and that the young woman had scheduled a rendezvous with him. However, Leonard also had an excellent motive for homicide—jealousy.

Others caught in the web of intrigue include Madeline, angered that her underling was deeply interested in Carrie. In addition, Fay Hewitt, a veteran Institute worker, turns out to be in love with Leonard, and she may be throwing a false finger of guilt at Carrie to free Palmer of his matrimonial entanglements. Then, there is high-achieving Thor Lundquist, Leonard's work rival, who is more in tune with the Institute's policies than Palmer.

Highlights: This episode gives glimpses into the world of astronomy, and reintroduces another favored series gambit. It features a police investigator, Sergeant Kettler, who, upon discovering that Jessica Fletcher is a famed novelist, asks her to collaborate on rewriting his manuscript about his most startling cases. To avoid antagonizing her investigation partner, she must stall for time before refusing the "honor." The twist to the situation here is that before Jessica can reject the rewrite offer, Kettler's manuscript is optioned by a Hollywood producer. Now it's Kettler's turn to say no to the proposed collaboration.

Trivia: Steven Ford, the actor son of President Gerald Ford, had spent over six years playing Andy Richards on the daytime TV soap opera *The Young and the Restless.* Dean Jones, a cast member of several Walt Disney movies including *That Darn Cat* (1965) and *The Ugly Dachshund* (1966), had starred on Broadway in *Company* (1970). Marcia Rodd had been a regular on *The David Frost Revue* (1970–1971) and was Alice Kovacs on *Flamingo Road* (1981–1982).

79. "Curse of the Daanu"

(2/7/88) 60 mins.

Directors: Walter Grauman **Teleplay:** Chris Manheim

Regulars: Angela Lansbury (Jessica Fletcher); William Windom (Dr. Seth Hazlitt)

Guest Law Enforcers: Larry Linville (Lieutenant Steven Ames); Michael McNab (Police Officer); Kres Mersky (Police Officer)

Guest Cast: Jane Badler (Carolyn Hazlitt); Doug Barr (Mark Hazlitt); Kabir Bedi (Vikram Akbar); Michael Blue (Explorer in Prologue); Richard Bradford (Richard Hazlitt); Clive Revill (Bert Davies); Jane Windsor (Alice Davies Hazlitt)

The Setting: Suburban Maryland

The Case: After conferring with their congressman in Washington, D.C., Jessica Fletcher and Dr. Seth Hazlitt visit Hazlitt's long-estranged sibling, Richard, in Maryland. The very wealthy Richard is Seth's only brother and has recently remarried. His bride is the far younger Alice Hazlitt. The wedding has badly upset Richard's grown-up children, Carolyn and Mark, who fear that they will lose their "rightful" portion of the estate to their stepmother.

At a party, with Alice's father, Bert Davies, in attendance, Richard presents his spouse with an enormously expensive gift. It is a rich ruby which once was the demon eye of a statue of Daanu in India. The gem, now part of a necklace, is said to bear an ancient curse. In addition, Richard and Seth reconcile.

That evening, Alice nearly dies of carbon monoxide poisoning when someone locks her in her home garage with a car's motor running. The next morning, Richard is found dead—strangled—in his study. Oddly, the doors to the room were locked from the inside!

While Seth copes with his brother's death, practical Jessica, in association with police lieutenant Stephen Ames, works through the sea of clues. Besides the victim's two avaricious offspring, there is also Vikram Akbar, mysterious cultural attaché at his country's Washington, D.C., embassy. He had offered the deceased twice the purchase price if he would sell Akbar the gem so it could be returned to India. It is also known that Bert Davies is in financial straits and that Alice persuaded Richard to take out large life insurance policies with her as beneficiary.

Highlights: This episode mingles superstition and suspense involving a cursed jewel, with its mood established in the opening prologue set in a dank cave in India. In the other main plot line, testy Seth Hazlitt reveals another side of himself during his reunion—after thirty years—with his brother. Seth proves to be a vulnerable soul as he and his sibling discuss the reason for their estrangement. In a touching coda, Hazlitt ponders the quirk of fate that took away his brother just as they patched up their differences.

Renown as a novelist and crime-solver, Jessica Fletcher is many things to many people. The running gag of this installment is when the police detective assumes that because Jessica has just left the nation's capital and is constantly referencing business in D.C., she must be a secret government agent. As such, the lawman shows her a deference not usually accorded a lay person in a homicide investigation.

Trivia: Richard Bradford had starred in the teleseries *Man in a Suitcase* (1968). Doug Barr had participated on TV's *When the Whistle Blows* (1980) and *The Fall Guy* (1981–1986). Clive Revill was seen on *Wizards and Warriors* (1983) as Vector the Wizard.

80. "Mourning among the Wisterias"

(2/14/88) 60 mins.

Director: Walter Grauman **Teleplay:** Scott Anderson

Regular: Angela Lansbury (Jessica Fletcher)

Guest Law Enforcer: Rene Auberjonois (Captain Walker Thorn)

Guest Cast: James L. Brown (Dr. Church); Penny Fuller (Grace Banfield); Frank Gorshin (Arnold Goldman); Matt McCoy (Todd Wendle); Barry Nelson (Eugene McLaughlin); Lois Nettleton (Deidre French); Linda Purl (Crystal Wendle); Elliot Reid (Jonathan Keller, Esq.); Beah Richards (Ola Mae)

The Setting: Suburban Savannah, Georgia

The Case: Pulitzer Prize-winning playwright Eugene McLaughlin invites his good friend Jessica Fletcher to visit his plantation in Georgia. Not only has he finally written a new drama which he wishes Jessica to read, but he also hopes to wed her. The ailing Eugene admits having ulterior motives. After he dies he wants Jessica to supervise any rewrites and oversee the rehearsals of his new work. Jessica declines the flattering offer.

When McLaughlin's lawyer and business advisor, Jonathan Keller, is shot to death in an upstairs room, Eugene is found standing over the victim's body, holding the murder weapon. Jessica cannot accept the conclusion that her friend is guilty, even when it is made known that the deceased had been misappropriating his client's funds for years.

With police captain Thorn of Savannah, Jessica sifts through the facts. There is young Todd Wendle, Eugene's nephew, who recently married Crystal and who is employed at Keller's law firm. Also on hand are Arnold Goldman, an avaricious play producer, as well as fading actress Deidre French, who would kill for a good role. Not to be overlooked is Grace Banfield, a love-hungry woman whom Eugene once thought of marrying.

Highlights: With its pseudo-Georgian atmosphere and many of the characters dripping thick Southern accents, this installment plays like a road company tour of an inferior Tennessee Williams play. In contrast, Jessica Fletcher emerges as the piece's most legitimate personality, an intriguing mix of practicality, an artist's creative temperament, and a female soul buoyed by a marriage proposal (no matter what its nature).

Trivia: Impressionist/comic/actor Frank Gorshin is best remembered for his guest villain role of The Riddler in the 1960s *Batman* TV series. Rene Auberjonois, who once taught acting at the college level, had appeared in such features as *M*A*S*H* (1970), *The Hindenberg* (1976) and *The Player* (1992). Barry Nelson, the 1950s' star of TV's *The Hunter* and *My Favorite Husband*, had been the first actor to ever play superspy James Bond, doing so on a 1954 TV adaptation of *Casino Royale*. Lastly, Linda Purl had the role of Andy Griffith's perky lawyer/daughter in *Matlock* (1986–1987).

81. "Murder through the Looking Glass"

(2/21/88) 60 mins.

Director: Seymour Robbie **Teleplay:** Robert Van Scoyk

Regular: Angela Lansbury (Jessica Fletcher)

Guest Law Enforcers: Rosemary Alexander (Cop); Laurence Luckinbill (Sergeant Milton Cooper); Kirk Scott (Adams)

Guest Cast: Brian Carpenter (Desk Clerk); Cliff DeYoung (Father Francis); Wayne Heffley (Guard); Elizabeth Kent (Admirer #1); Hugh McPhillips (Father Francis Kelly); Kerry Leigh Michaels (Admirer Chairperson); Mark Shera (Van Buren); Dan Shor (Pierce); Gregory Sierra (Sanchez, the Bodyguard); Karen Valentine (Ellen Cosgrove); Ken Zavayna (Admirer #2)

The Settings: Hartford, Connecticut; Farmington, Connecticut

The Case: In town for the New England Booksellers Convention, Jessica emerges from a hotel seminar meeting to witness the crash of a runaway car. Before the driver dies, he tells Jessica and a nearby priest, Father Francis, that he is a hit man who has just killed Carl Cosgrove. When she insists that bombastic police sergeant Milton Cooper investigate, he grudgingly drives Jessica to the Cosgrove home in Farmington. There, Ellen Cosgrove insists that her spouse is very much alive! Still unconvinced, Jessica later demands to see Mr. Cosgrove, who is allegedly recuperating in his upstairs bedroom.

The puzzle takes on added dimension when Jessica becomes involved with several people other than Father Francis, who may or may not be a priest. There is Jackson, a senior group leader in the Department of Special Security; Van Buren and Pierce, two of Jackson's subordinates; and Sanchez, the bodyguard for Dino Delgado, a Latin American witness for a pending congressional hearing.

Highlights: With its intricate plot of intrigue, double agents, and corruption within a highly sensitive government agency, this segment abounds in red herrings and situations that are not at all what they seem.

Trivia: Perky Karen Valentine starred as Alice Johnson in *Room 222* (1969–1974). Gregory Sierra was Carlos "El Puerco" Valdezon on *Soap* (1980–1981). On the miniseries *Centennial* (1978–1979), Cliff DeYoung was seen as John Skimmerhorn.

82. "A Very Good Year for Murder"

(2/28/88) 60 mins.

Director: Walter Grauman **Teleplay:** Peter S. Fischer

Regular: Angela Lansbury (Jessica Fletcher)

Guest Law Enforcers: Arlen Dean Snyder (Chief Thadius Kyle); Rob Zapple (Deputy)

Guest Cast: Jeff Albert (Guest #2); Kristen Alfonso (Michele Gambini); Ina Balin (Stella Gambini); Bibi Besch (Fiona Gambini); Tom Byrd (Paul Gambini); Grant Goodeve (Ben Scuyler); Paul Lyell (Guest #1); John C. Mooney (Doctor); Robert O'Reilly (Stephen Ridgely); John Saxon (Marco Gambini); Eli Wallach (Salvatori Gambini); Billy Zane (Tony Gambini)

The Setting: Sonoma County, California

The Case: As a dear friend of the Gambini family, Jessica Fletcher is invited to the wine country of northern California. The occasion is Salvatori's seventy-fifth birthday party. Among the patriarch's other relatives present are Stella, his sister and housekeeper; Marco, his son and next-in-charge to running the famed Gambini Winery; and Fiona, Marco's unhappy wife. Also in attendance are Salvatori's other offspring Paul, a professional football player; Tony, a playboy with a penchant for gambling; and Michele, a fickle young woman who has brought along her latest boyfriend, Ben Scuyler.

Before long, Jessica learns that Salvatori is very ill, a condition worsened by the pressure of an eastern syndicate wanting to buy out his business. Meanwhile, Tony takes a tumble on a "broken" step going into the wine cellar. Investigation proves that it was no accident. Later, Ben is found dead at the bottom of the same cellar steps. He may have been poisoned. Things become more complex with the arrival of Stephen Ridgely, an investment advisor, who insists he is an old friend of Paul's.

In tandem with smartly dressed police chief Thadeus Kyle, Jessica unwraps the vineyard mystery. In the process, Mrs. Fletcher weighs an ethical choice, which is truly a matter of life or death.

Highlights: With most of the cast working hard to maintain their Italian ethnicity, seasoned actor Eli Wallach easily walks away with the honors as the family elder. He provides a needed strong force, especially in his scenes with Jessica Fletcher.

Trivia: Eli Wallach, who made his screen bow in *Baby Doll* (1956), had played Sons of Italy roles in *Crazy Joe* (1974) and *The Godfather, Part III* (1990). John Saxon, born Carmen Orrico in Brooklyn, New York, made his mark in baby-faced roles of the late 1950s, thereafter starring as Dr. Ted Stuart on *The New Doctors* (1969–1972). Ina Balin (1937–1990), nee Ina Rosenberg, had lead parts in *The Black Orchid* (1959) and *From the Terrace* (1960). Bibi Besch (1940–1996) had been a regular on TV's *The Secret Storm* and *The Edge of Night*. Kristen Alfonso achieved fame on the daytime soap *Days of Our Lives* in the 1980s as part of supercouple Bo and Hope. She returned to *Days* in the early 1990s. She also starred in the prime-time soap *Falcon Crest* as Pilar Oretega.

83. "Benedict Arnold Slipped Here"

(3/13/88) 60 mins.

Director: Seymour Robbie **Story:** Wendy Graf, Lisa Stotsky **Teleplay:** Robert Van Scoyk

Regulars: Angela Lansbury (Jessica Fletcher); Tom Bosley (Sheriff Amos Tupper); William Windom (Dr. Seth Hazlitt)

Recurring Character: Julie Adams (Eve Simpson)

Guest Cast: Brian Bedford (Alastair Andrews); Barbara Cason (Emily Goshen); David Clennon (Wilton Tibbles); Shea Farrell (Kevin Tibbles); Lois Foraker (Liza Adams); Katherine Moffat (Lauren Hastings); Dick O'Neill (Benny Tibbles)

The Setting: Cabot Cove, Maine

The Case: When Tillie Adams, an elderly Cabot Cove recluse, passes away, Jessica Fletcher is named executor. Before Jessica can fully inventory the house, a battle royal erupts. Benny Tibbles, a local antique dealer who had catered to Tillie, is the beneficiary of the home's many valuable heirlooms. He is at odds with the departed's only living relative, her middle-aged hippie grandniece. It is Liza who inherits the house itself.

Meanwhile, local real estate agent Eve Simpson announces she has a hot prospect to buy the run-down Adams place. It is Britisher Alastair Andrews, an expert on Revolutionary War figure General Benedict Arnold. He's convinced Tillie's home holds evidence that Arnold was a hero not a traitor.

Soon thereafter, Benny is found dead in the Adams home, having been bludgeoned with a fireplace poker. Perplexed Sheriff Amos Tupper is helped once again by Jessica. In the process, she deals with the dead man's avaricious brother, Wilton Tibbles, a Boston antique dealer; Lauren Hastings, Wilton's beautiful girlfriend, who lusts after Kevin Tibbles, the deceased's strapping son; and weird Emily Goshen, Tillie's nosy, one-time cleaning lady.

Highlights: The scenario provides several rich character studies, especially Eve Simpson. She is a shrewd real estate person with a sharp knack for making any property—no matter what its deficits—seem like a wonderful steal. Her (lack of) ethics continually clash with Jessica's sense of fair play. There is a simultaneous tug-of-war between Amos and Dr. Seth Hazlitt, the latter missing no opportunity to poke fun at the sheriff's several professional shortcomings.

Trivia: David Clennon made his mark as smarmy ad executive Miles Drentell on *thirtysomething* (1989–1991). Dick O'Neill played the occasional role of Chris Cagney's retired policeman father on *Cagney & Lacey* (1982–1988). Brian Bedford of Yorkshire, England, was Anthony on *Coronet Blue* (1967). Barbara Cason was a veteran of *Temperatures Rising* (1973–1974) and *Carter Country* (1977–1979).

This was Tom Bosley's final appearance as Sheriff Amos Tupper. He left his recurring role to star in *Father Dowling Mysteries* (1989–1991). Not until 1988's "Mr. Penroy's Vacation" (#90) would a new Cabot Cove sheriff (Mort Metzger) be introduced into the series.

84. "Just Another Fish Story"

(3/27/88) 60 mins.

Director: Walter Grauman **Teleplay:** Philip Gerson

Regular: Angela Lansbury (Jessica Fletcher)

Recurring Characters: Michael Horton (Grady Fletcher); Debbie Zipp (Donna Mayberry)

Guest Law Enforcers: Elkanah Burns (Medical Examiner); Norman Fell (Lieutenant Rupp)

Guest Cast: Sonny Bono (Valentino Reggiore); Jack Carter (Harry Finlay); Dick Gautier (Chaz Crewe); James Carroll Jordan (Doug Brooke); Valerie Landsburg (Alice Brooke); Valchik Mangassarian (Chef); Richard Molenare (Cabbie); Jack Tate (Yuppie); Brenda Vaccaro (Mimi Harcourt)

The Setting: New York City

The Case: At her nephew Grady's urging, Jessica Fletcher invests in Alice's Farm Restaurant, a trendy new Manhattan eatery. She dines there with Grady to check out the enterprise and, more importantly, to meet the young man's new fiancée, Donna Mayberry. While there, Jessica is introduced to the establishment's owners: Doug Brooke, the financial overseer; his sister, Alice, who is in charge of the kitchen; and Chaz Crewe, the glib maitre d'.

Some hours later, Chaz is found dead in the kitchen's meat locker, having been stabbed and slashed with a sharp object. Lieutenant Rupp arrives and commandeers Grady and Donna—both of whom are accountants—to examine the restaurant's books. Because there are rumors of grand theft of food from Alice's kitchen, he hopes the ledgers will reveal a clue to the murder.

Meanwhile, Jessica takes matters into her own hands. The trail leads her to rival restaurateur, Valentino Reggiore, for whom the three Alice owners once worked. Then there is manipulative newspaper columnist Mimi Harcourt, a silent partner in the new yuppie hangout, as well as a quipster bartender, Harry Finlay, a man who doesn't miss a thing.

Highlights: Whenever vivacious, shrewd Mimi Harcourt bursts onto the scene, she commands full viewer attention. However, a close second are the two young lovers, Grady and Donna. Although they are two peas in the same pod—analytical, shy, sincere—they fear commitment. Grady also fears his future father-in-law, a man who owns the third largest accounting firm in New York state and the employer who fired him five years earlier.

Trivia: Emmy Award-winning Brenda Vacarro—also a Tony Award nominee—was a frequent *Murder, She Wrote* guest participant. She had played lead roles in such short-lived TV series as *Sara* (1978), *Dear Detective* (1979) and *Paper Dolls* (1984). Sonny Bono, once half a singing team with his then wife, Cher, later became mayor of Palm Springs, California.

85. "Showdown in Saskatchewan"

(4/10/88) 60 mins.

Director: Vincent McEveety **Teleplay:** Dick Nelson

Regular: Angela Lansbury (Jessica Fletcher)

Guest Law Enforcer: Lance LeGault (Inspector Roger McCabe)

Guest Cast: Rosana DeSoto (Consuela Schaeffer); Joe Dorsey (Doc Schaeffer); Michael Frederic (Medic); Patrick Houser (Marty Reed); Terry Kiser (Wally); Paul LeMat (Luke Purdue [Carl Mattson]); Lisa Long (Flirtatious Girl); Ed McCreary (Bartender); Kristy McNichol (Jill); Thomas H. Middleton (Warden Burns); Richard Molner (Intern); George Okunett (Man); Eileen T'Kaye (Secretary); Ron Troncatty (Public Address System Announcer); Larry Wilcox (Boone Talbot); Devon Williams (Mona); Cassie Yates (Carla)

The Setting: Queensbridge, Saskatchewan, Canada

The Case: Concerned about her niece, Jessica pays an unannounced visit to Jill, who is spending the summer on the Canadian rodeo circuit to be near her boyfriend, rider Marty Reed. Arriving in Queensbridge, Jessica is quickly drawn into the world of steer roping and bronco riding.

She meets Wally, a one-time rodeo rider reduced by an accident into becoming a rodeo clown. Then there's also veteran performer Boone Talbot, who is envious of Marty, the hotshot circuit newcomer. Another show star, Luke Purdue, is injured while competing in the bull-riding event. Ill-tempered Doc Schaeffer sidelines Luke for the next day's important event.

Shortly thereafter, Schaeffer, who suffers from emphysema, dies of smoke inhalation when his trailer is mysteriously set on fire. Roger McCabe, an inspector with the Royal Canadian Mounted Police, joins forces with Jessica to ferret out the killer. Others caught up in the murder case are the victim's relieved wife, Consuela, and Carla, a friend of Boone and Jill. Another twist to the situation is the sudden arrival of a young woman from Miles City, Montana, who has a baby boy, Buster, in tow. She proves to be the wife of supposed bachelor Marty.

Highlights: In a very relaxed excursion, Jessica Fletcher adapts readily to the outdoors. She takes part in country dancing and even drinks a beer!

When not interacting with the very civilized law enforcer, McCabe, Jessica is dispensing romantic advice to her infatuated niece.

Trivia: As a youngster, Emmy Award-winning actress Kristy McNichol had starred in such TV series as *Apple's Way* (1974–1975) and *Family* (1976–1980). In the late 1980s, she began a several seasons run on *Empty Nest.* Larry Wilcox had been Dale Mitchell on *Lassie* (1972–1974) and Officer Jon Baker on *CHIPS* (1977–1982).

86. "Deadpan"

(5/1/88) 60 mins.

Director: E.W. Swackhamer **Story:** Arthur Weingarten
Teleplay: Maryanne Kasica, Michael Scheff

Regular: Angela Lansbury (Jessica Fletcher)

Guest Law Enforcers: R.J. Arterburn (Sergeant); Eugene Roche (Lieutenant Aloyius Jarvis)

Guest Cast: Philip Abbott (Ed Cullen); Michael Ashe (Businessman); Barbara Beckley (Sophisticated Lady); Lloyd Bochner (Jason Richards); Sue Brigden (Wife); Miles Chapin (Walter Knapf); Carole Cook (Shayne Grant); Don Correia (Shayne's Assistant); John DiSanti (Danny O'Mara); Marcy Goldman (Assistant); Marilyn Hassett (Barbara Blair); Rich Little (Barney Mapost); Christopher Norris (Denise Quinlan); Robert Rigamonti (Maitre d'); Penny Santon (Mrs. Rizzo, the Neighbor); Dean Stockwell (Elliot Easterbrook)

The Setting: New York City

The Case: To Jessica Fletcher's dismay, great liberties have been taken with her novel, *A Murder Comes to Maine*, en route to the Broadway stage as *Mainely Murder*. She is embarrassed to tell playwright Walter Knapf, a former student, her true opinion of the ludicrous adaptation. On the other hand, experienced Broadway producer Shayne Grant is convinced the revamped show will be a sizable hit. Meanwhile, director Jason Richards makes crucial last-minute cast changes.

On opening night, Danny O'Mara, the *New York Chronicle's* drama critic, gives the production a surprising rave review. In contrast, snide Elliot Easterbrook destroys the show in his TV critique. Not long after, O'Mara is found dead.

At first, the victim's arch rival, Easterbrook, is Lieutenant Jarvis's prime suspect. Later, when a neighbor, Mrs. Rizzo, reports she saw Knapf outside the dead man's door the night of his demise, the limelight shifts to the bewildered playwright. Meanwhile, at the *Chronicle*, Jessica questions the deceased's boss, Ed Cullen, and assistant-turned-replacement, Denise Quinlan, as well as pressured stage press agent, Barney Mapost. Then there is Barbara Blair, who had given a script to one of the suspects.

Highlights: Between delightful moments of Broadway backstage intrigue, Jessica Fletcher more than holds her own. She is in fine form when she diplomatically lashes out at the transgressors of the travesty, her every remark full of biting double meaning.

Trivia: As in other episodes, a crucial plot point is exactly when the murder took place, not when investigators think it may have occurred. Yielding to the high tech age, Jessica's search for answers leads her into the world of computers and modem transfer of data.

Comedian Rich Little, best known as an impressionist with an uncanny knack for imitating President Richard M. Nixon, had appeared as a regular in such TV series as *Love on the Rooftop, The John Davidson Show* and *The Julie Andrews Hour.* One-time child star Dean Stockwell, who had been at MGM in the 1940s along with Angela Lansbury, had recurring success as the adult star of *Compulsion* (1959), *Long Day's Journey into Night* (1962) and *Blue Velvet* (1986), as well as the TV series *Quantum Leap* (1989–1993). Penny Santon made a specialty of ethnic types on TV sitcoms: *Don't Call Me Charlie* (1962–1963), *Matt Houston* (1982–1983), etc.

87. "The Body Politic"

(5/8/88) 60 mins.

Director: Anthony Shaw **Teleplay:** Donald Ross

Regular: Angela Lansbury (Jessica Fletcher)

Guest Law Enforcers: Robert Louis Cameron (Fingerprint Man); Neal Kaz (Cop #1); David O'Karski (Cop #2); Harrison Page (Lieutenant Gowans)

Guest Cast: Eddie Albert (Jackson Lane); Robin Bach (Clerk); Marie Chambers (Cass Malone); Peter Fox (Bud Johnson); Robert Fuller (Arthur Drelinger); George Grizzard (Edmund Hall); Anthony S. Johnson (Reporter); Shirley Jones (Kathleen Lane); Daphne Maxwell Reid (Nan Wynn); Scott Segall (Staffer); James Sloyan (C.W. Butterfield)

The Setting: California

The Case: Financially and emotionally supported by her wealthy husband Jackson Lane, Kathleen Lane is in a hot run-off with Arthur Drelinger in the primaries for a major political office. Kathleen begs her old friend, Jessica Fletcher, to pitch in as a last-minute speech writer on environmental issues.

Just as Kathleen's cause gains momentum, rumors circulate that she has been having an affair with her married campaign manager, Bud Johnson. She strongly denies the charges, but things turn sour when Bud tumbles to his death from the balcony of Kathleen's suite at the Hotel Excalibur. Worse, the corpse is found wearing her hotel robe, and it develops the victim was pushed from the height.

Coming to her friend's defense, Jessica assesses the suspects. They include Kathleen's political rival Arthur Drelinger, as well as his grasping campaign controller, C.W. Butterfield. There is also Kathleen's political pollster, Nan Wynn, who has been offered a job with the opposition; Kathleen's staff worker Cass Malone, who had been involved romantically with the deceased; and slimy muck-raking TV reporter Edmund Hall, the host of TV's *Face the Issues.*

Highlights: With especially strong performances by the lead guest cast, this is a superior *Murder, She Wrote* segment. Once again, Jessica Fletcher is drawn into a new milieu where she proves highly adaptable, all the time protesting her inexperience.

Trivia: Wholesome Shirley Jones of Rodgers and Hammerstein movie musical fame *(Oklahoma!, Carousel)* won a Best Supporting Actress Oscar playing a prostitute in *Elmer Gantry* (1959). She cemented her place in TV history by starring as the ever-chipper mother in *The Partridge Family* (1970–1974). At the time this episode was filmed, Daphne Maxwell Reid was costarring with her real-life husband, Tim Reid, in the TV sitcom *Frank's Place* (1987–1988). Veteran screen, stage and TV star Eddie Albert obtained special immortality as Oliver Wendell Douglas, the beleaguered gentleman farmer spouse of Eva Gabor in the bucolic comedy *Green Acres* (1965–1971). George Grizzard won an Emmy for his performance in the 1980 TV movie *Attica.*

SEASON FIVE

1988–1989

88. "JB as in Jailbird"

(10/23/88) 60 mins.

Director: Anthony Shaw **Teleplay:** Robert E. Swanson

Regular: Angela Lansbury (Jessica Fletcher)

Recurring Characters: Len Cariou (Derrick Dawson [Michael Haggerty]; Michael Horton (Grady Fletcher); Debbie Zipp (Donna Mayberry)

Guest Law Enforcers: Greg Barnett (Police Officer); Michael Callan (Sergeant Nash); Ron O'Neal (Sergeant Joe Santiago)

Guest Cast: Maureen Arthur (Veronica); Sam Behren (Kevin Styles); Maxwell Caulfield (Roger Travis); John Rhys-Davies (Lancaster); Leslie Easterbrook (Glenda); John Hanagel (Clerk); Joseph Ruski (Ivanov)

The Settings: Berkeley, California; San Francisco, California

The Case: At the San Francisco Airport, British foreign agent Michael Haggerty offers his old acquaintance, Jessica Fletcher, a ride to her Bay City hotel. Just when she thinks that trouble-prone Michael has reformed, he detours their car into a squalid back alley. There he has a shoot-out with a Bulgarian political assassin and then disappears. The police arrive, and a bewildered Jessica is jailed on a murder charge. She cannot convince Sergeant Nash of her true identity because someone has reported Mrs. Fletcher's purse and passport as stolen.

When her nephew, Grady Fletcher, whom she was to meet at the Royal Imperial Hotel, arrives at the police station, he insists she is not his famous aunt! Stuck behind bars, Jessica chats with a floozy, Veronica, in the next cell and passes time reading a paperback novel that the dead killer had been carrying. Finally, Haggerty shows up at the precinct, posing as Jessica's lawyer, Derrick Dawson. He confides a few details to her and advises the angry Mrs. Fletcher that for the time being, she is safer in jail.

However, danger follows Jessica to the cell block as visitors and interrogators abound, none of whom she is sure is legitimate. They comprise Sergeant Joe Santiago on special business for the Miami police department; Glenda Morrison, who pretends to be a reporter for the *San Francisco Chronicle;* Kevin Styles, a special attorney for the State Department; and Roger Travis, another British operative who, like Haggerty, reports to the aloof Mr. Lancaster.

Highlights: Despite the array of red herrings and a sequence in which Michael Haggerty cavorts in drag, this installment is very slow going. A bright moment is provided by Maureen Arthur's Veronica, a frequent jailbird who is impressed that Jessica is being charged with a murder rap.

Trivia: If Grady Fletcher's romance with Donna Mayberry had taken a rocky turn in the past, matters were not improved here where Donna calls Grady from back East and becomes jealous when he tries to explain why another young woman is in his hotel room. Ron O'Neal was a veteran of Hollywood's 1970s black exploitation film cycle: *Superfly* (1972), *Superfly TNT* (1973), *The Final Countdown* (1980), etc. English actor Maxwell Caulfield played in Hollywood's *Grease 2* (1982), *The Boys Next Door* (1985) and *In a Moment of Passion* (1993).

89. "A Little Night Work"

(10/30/88) 60 mins.

Director: Walter Grauman **Teleplay:** Peter S. Fischer

Regular: Angela Lansbury (Jessica Fletcher)

Recurring Character: Keith Michell (Dennis Stanton)

Guest Law Enforcers: Joe Santos (Lieutenant Bert Alfano); Gerald S. Sharp (Cop)

Guest Cast: Frances Bergen (Janice Darrow); Harry Cason (Reporter #2); Armand Cerami (Security Guard); Jensen Collier (Joanna); Bill Cort (Ray); John Dye (Andy Broom, the Hotel Busboy); Jamie Farr (Theo Wexler); Leann Hunley (Shannon McBride); Conrad Janis (Miles Hatcher); Rick Jason (Axel Weingard); Julie Parrish (Marta Weingard); Rhonda Pierson (Reporter #1)

The Setting: New York City

The Case: Jessica Fletcher attends a swank Manhattan fund-raiser for Axel Weingard, a publisher with political goals. There, an aggressive literary agent, Theo Wexler, campaigns to make Jessica one of his clients. Mrs. Fletcher is also courted by Dennis Stanton, a debonair stranger.

Later, Weingard is found strangled, the victim of an apparent jewel heist. As Lieutenant Bert Alfano points out, Jessica is in a peculiar situation. At about the time of the murder, Stanton had climbed down to her balcony from the floor above, which is where Weingard was killed. Then there is Jessica's acquaintanceship with Andy Broom, a writer employed as a hotel busboy. Broom admits that he submitted a novel to the dead man a year before only to see the publisher print a very "similar" book thereafter.

Soon more parties become entwined in the case. There is Shannon McBride, a special claims adjuster for an insurance company, who is willing to pay—with no questions asked—$100,000 to retrieve Marta Weingard's stolen necklace. In addition, real estate speculator Miles Hatcher had an ax to grind against the victim, for Weingard had threatened to cancel his huge investment in Hatcher's new project.

Highlights: To properly introduce viewers to jewel thief Dennis Stanton, he has several engaging sequences with Jessica. In one, he explains how his wife's protracted illness left him hugely in debt. After her death six years ago, he sought revenge against the Susquehanah Fire & Casualty Insurance Company which had denied his medical claims. He has attacked them by stealing only jewelry that is insured by that firm (the same outfit which had issued a policy for Marta Weingard's jewelry).

Trivia: Jamie Farr gained popularity as cross-dressing Corporal Maxwell Klinger on *M*A*S*H* (1973–1983) and in its staid sequel, *AfterMASH* (1983–1984). Frances Bergen, the widow of ventriloquist Edgar Bergen and the mother of actress Candice Bergen, found her dialogue scenes deleted at the last minute to trim the running time. Thus, she remains in the episode as a silent walk-on. Joe Santos was very familiar with police roles, having been Detective Dennis Becker on *The Rockford Files* (1974-1980) and Lieutenant Frank Harper on *Hardcastle & McCormick* (1985–1986).

90. "Mr. Penroy's Vacation"

(11/6/88) 60 mins.

Director: Anthony Shaw **Teleplay:** Robert E. Swanson

Regulars: Angela Lansbury (Jessica Fletcher); Ron Masak (Sheriff Mort Metzger); William Windom (Dr. Seth Hazlitt)

Recurring Characters: Willie Nye (Deputy Floyd); Richard Paul (Mayor Sam Booth)

Guest Cast: Norman Alden (Bart Kapper); Candice Azzara (Marilee Penroy); Don Calfa (Clifford Coleson [Reverend Wilfred Smythe]); Tim Choate (Daryl Croft); Henry Jones (Morris Penroy); Joan Leslie (Lillian Appletree); Robert Moberly (Clyde, the Mailman); Al Pugliese (Ole Korshack); Deborah Rose (Sue, the Bank Clerk); Teresa Wright (Helen Appletree)

The Setting: Cabot Cove, Maine

The Case: Cabot Cove has a new sheriff. Amos Tucker has retired to Kentucky to live with relatives. His replacement is Mort Metzger, who has abandoned New York City police work to enjoy a more leisurely pace in the country with his wife, Adele.

Many of the town's locals attend the birthday party Lillian and Helen Appletree host for their star boarder, Morris Penroy, a retired railroad baggage clerk. Peculiarly, the guest of honor is absent. The agitated Appletree women claim he went away and may never return. Meanwhile, Mayor Sam Booth's bulldog, Winston, sniffs out a partially buried item in the Appletrees' backyard, which turns out to be a corpse. Before long, bodies are found everywhere at the Appletrees' leading the new sheriff and ever-helpful Mrs. Fletcher on a perplexing merry-go-round.

Among the many dubious personalities involved are Bart Kapper, a special investigator for the Boston & Western Railroad chasing the perpetrators of a $5 million armed robbery; Marilee Penroy, who claims to have married Morris shortly before he left for Cabot Cove a year ago; a crook named Ole Korshak; and Clifford Coleson, a suspicious man of many aliases who hails from Brockton, Massachusetts.

Highlights: Despite the prevalence of corpses, this is a lighthearted whodunit revolving around the two pixilated Appletree sisters. (These spinsters bring to mind the two similar fey personalities from that stage and film classic *Arsenic and Old Lace.*)

As Jessica Fletcher's new comrade-in-arms, city-wise Mort Metzger has mistakenly thought his new post would allow leisure days to play golf and fish. He clearly underestimates the village locals both as to potential culpability in committing murder and in solving homicides. It will take several upcoming episodes for this newcomer to appreciate fully the astute Jessica.

Trivia: Much is made of Mort Metzger being wed to Adele, a talkative, energetic ex-marine. She is often talked about but *never seen* in the series. Before being hired to play Sheriff Metzger, Ron Masak had made two previous *Murder, She Wrote* appearances—(#18, 62)—in nonassociated roles. Another fresh face on the show is Will Nye in the recurring role of not-so-swift Deputy Floyd. His countrified ways also prove a shock to cynical Metzger. Nye previously appeared in such unsold TV pilots as the drama *Farrell: For the People* (1992), starring Valerie Harper, and *The Family Martinez* (1986), created by Tommy Chong.

Teresa Wright won an Academy Award for her performance in *Mrs. Miniver* (1942). Joan Leslie, the ingenue of such movies as *Sergeant York* (1941), *Yankee Doodle Dandy* (1942) and *Cinderella Jones* (1946), came out of semiretirement for this *Murder, She Wrote* episode. Veteran character actor Henry Jones appeared in such movies as *The Bad Seed* (1956) and *Nine to Five* (1980), as well as the TV series *Channing* (1963–1964) and *Phyllis* (1975–1977).

91. "Snow White, Blood Red"

(11/13/88) 60 mins.

Director: Vincent McEveety **Teleplay:** Peter S. Fischer

Regular: Angela Lansbury (Jessica Fletcher)

Guest Law Enforcer: Barry Newman (Ex-Lieutenant Ed McMasters)

Guest Cast: John Aindt (Parker); Craig Branhem (Skier); Kenny Davis (Lead Performer); Ronnie Claire Edwards (Sylvia McMasters); Eric Allan Kramer (Gunnar Tilstrom); John Laughlin (Mike Lowery); Tony O'Dell (Larry Mclvor); Cyril O'Reilly (John Dowd); Jamie Rose (Anne Lowery); Emma Samms (Pamela Leeds); Bo Svenson (Karl Andersson); George Wyner (Dr. Lewis)

The Setting: Sable Mountain, New England

The Case: At the last minute, Grady Fletcher must bow out of a long-planned ski weekend with his Aunt Jessica. Nevertheless, his intrepid relative follows through with the trip. Arriving at Sable Mountain Lodge, she finds the resort crowded with contenders for the upcoming World Cup ski team, including Gunnar Tilstrom, John Dowd and Larry Mclvor. Others on the premises are the owners, Mike and Anne Lowery; a sports merchandising agent, Pamela Leeds; a physician, Dr. Lewis, and a New York couple, Ed and Sylvia McMasters.

In the highly competitive environment, tempers rise, leaving demanding Swedish skiing coach Karl Andersson to referee. Moreover, pushy Pamela Leeds argues fiercely with playboy skier Gunnar Tilstrom. The latter's failure to win championships lately is damaging his endorsement value. Mike Lowery, bitter that a past accident ended his career on the slopes, is jealous of Gunnar's attention to Lowery's wife, Anne. Meanwhile, argumentative Anne is fed up with her spouse and her unglamorous life as a small hotel co-owner.

During the weekend, the body of a Cup contender is found in the women's shower room. Since the raging storm has temporarily shut the lodge off from civilization, Jessica undertakes the homicide investigation. She is joined in her efforts by ex-cop Ed McMasters. Another guest, gynecologist Dr. Lewis, is recruited as a medical examiner.

Before long, another victim is claimed. Jessica soon uncovers that one of the homicide victims had been dallying with the wife of a Las Vegas mobster, and that another of the resort survivors is not what he or she claims.

Highlights: With most of the action confined to the interior of the ski lodge and the adjacent buildings, an appropriate claustrophobic atmosphere is established for this whodunit. In sharp contrast are the sequences of various characters skiing, including game Jessica trying her skill on the intermediate slopes. Once again, it is astute Mrs. Fletcher who realizes that the (first) murder happened in one spot, but that the killer had carted the body to another location, to throw investigators off the scent.

Trivia: Angular-featured Barry Newman starred in the TV movie *Fatal Vision* (1984). In addition he had recurring roles on the daytime TV soap opera *The Edge of Night* (1964–1965) and in the short-lived *Nightingales* (1989). Jamie Rose's credits included on-going stints on *Falcon Crest* (as Victoria Gioberti Hogan) and *St. Elsewhere* (as Dr. Susan Birch), as well as her starring series, *Lady Blue* (1985–1986) in which she was police detective Katy Mahoney. British-born Emma Samms replaced Pamela Sue Martin as Fallon Carrington Colby on *Dynasty* and the spin-off series, *The Colbys.*

92. "Coal Miner's Slaughter"

(11/20/88) 60 mins.

Director: Walter Grauman **Teleplay:** Chris Manheim

Regular: Angela Lansbury (Jessica Fletcher)

Guest Law Enforcer: Hoyt Axton (Sheriff Tate)

Guest Cast: Barbara Bain (Nora Morgan); Chuck Connors (Tyler Morgan); Cliff De Young (Carlton Reid); Marilyn Jones (Bridie Harmon); William R. Moses (Reese Morgan); Megan Mullally (Molly Connors); Denver Pyle (Eben Connors); Jared Rushton (Travis Harmon)

The Setting: Colton, West Virginia

The Case: In the mining community of Colton, West Virginia, young lawyer Molly Connors is caught trespassing on the premises of Tyler Morgan, the gruff local mine owner. (Molly is searching for evidence dealing with the decade-old death of her miner father.) Tyler has her arrested. Because her countrified grandfather, Eben Connors, is too poor to help, Molly turns to her former teacher, Jessica Fletcher, to arrange bail.

Upon arriving in the gloomy town, Jessica finds lodging at a boardinghouse operated by Bridie Harmon and her young son, Travis. (Bridie's husband had died in the same bizarre mine explosion that killed Molly's dad.) Jessica learns a great deal about the townsfolk from Molly as well as from Carlton Reid, the cooperative local representative for the miners' union.

Later, Tyler's body is discovered at his remote mountain cabin, a place no one visits without a special invitation. The murder weapon, a shotgun, is soon found stashed under the front seat of Molly's car.

As the mood in town turns ugly, Jessica works—not always hand-in-hand—with Sheriff Tate. Her inquiries lead her to bitter Nora Morgan, a once crack sharpshooter, who was well aware of her husband's many infidelities over the years. Another suspect is the victim's aggressive adult son, Reese, who had long fought with his father over how best to operate the mining operation. Additionally, there is feisty Eben Connors, who has never forgotten the mine-based death of his son.

Highlights: Several *Murder, She Wrote* episodes were similarly set in a small Southern town where pessimism abounds, no one keeps secrets, and the locals never forgive past transgressions.

Trivia: Ex-professional baseball player Chuck Connors (1921–1992) was featured in several TV series, including *Arrest and Trial* and *The Yellow Rose.* In *The Rifleman* (1958–1963) he was do-gooder Lucas McCain. Barbara Bain costarred on TV with her then husband, Martin Landau, in *Mission: Impossible* and *Space 1999.* William R. Moses was featured on both *Falcon Crest* and in the Perry Mason TV movies, while in the early 1980s folk singer Hoyt Axton was part of *The Rousters* and *Domestic Life.* Veteran actor Denver Pyle has long been identified with his role of Uncle Jesse Duke on *The Dukes of Hazzard* (1979–1985).

93. "Wearing of the Green"

(11/27/88) 60 mins.

Director: Seymour Robbie **Teleplay:** Peter S. Fischer

Regular: Angela Lansbury (Jessica Fletcher)

Guest Law Enforcer: Lucie Arnaz (Detective Bess Stacey); Patricia McCormack (Sergeant Kathleen Chadwick); Harry Moses (Police Officer)

Guest Cast: Thomas Bellen (Superintendent); Barbara Bosson (Diane Raymond); Michael Constantine (Laszlo Dolby); Erin Gray (Andrea Deane); John McMartin (Hudson Blackthorn); David Naughton (Ken Parrish); Jean Peters (Siobhan O'Dea); David Sage (Stavros); David Sheiner (Leo Selkirk)

The Setting: New York City

The Case: Jessica Fletcher's next novel is to feature a swank jewelry store. To research the project, she receives the full cooperation of Hudson Blackthorn to tour his fashionable Manhattan gem emporium. While Hudson is showing Jessica around after hours, a bomb explodes on the premises. Thereafter, it's discovered that the fabled Queen of Tara diamond tiara—only partially insured—is missing from its elegant display case.

Detective Bess Stacey and Sergeant Kathleen Chadwick interrogate witnesses, but have little luck in solving the heist. Meanwhile, Jessica studies the facts at hand which lead her to the store's diamond cutter, Laszlo Dolby. This refugee from Budapest had once dreamed of becoming a playwright. Later, he is found stabbed to death in his Greenwich Village apartment.

Next, the trail leads Jessica to reclusive, retired stage/film star Siobhan O'Dea, who had once owned the missing tiara. Others tied into the caper include Ken Parrish, an overly ambitious TV news man, as well as several employees at Blackthorn's plush emporium. The latter are Diane Raymond, who is Hudson's right-hand helper; Andrea Deane, a creative jewelry designer who feels stifled at work; and Leo Selkirk, chief of store security.

Highlights: Viewers who, like Jessica Fletcher, thrive on learning tidbits of offbeat information can appreciate the on-screen explanation of how an elaborate security system works. While some of the characters are agog at the legendary entertainer Siobhan O'Dea, down-to-earth Jessica treats her as a sad woman, not as a bizarre living legend. Thus Mrs. Fletcher's sympathetic approach to the troubled recluse makes their scenes together come vividly alive.

In complete contrast is the episode's joyful spoofing of the TV series *Cagney & Lacey* (1982-1988). Lucie Arnaz's Bess Stacey and Patricia McCormack's Detective Chadwick are broad take-offs on the roles played on that police detective show by Tyne Daly and Sharon Gless. Much is made of these two cops being so preoccupied with their personal lives that they have scant time to accomplish their jobs, let alone help Jessica.

Trivia: Jean Peters, long semiretired, starred in such feature films as *Viva Zapata!*(1952), *Three Coins in the Fountain* (1954) and *A Man Called Peter* (1955). However, she is best known for being the last wife (1957-

1971) of eccentric billionaire Howard Hughes. (The reason Peters accepted the role was "It was my mother's very favorite program . . . and I figured she'd be very angry if I didn't do it. It was fun going back to work.")

Lucie Arnaz is the actress daughter of Lucille Ball and Desi Arnaz. Michael Constantine won an Emmy Award for his role of school principal Seymour Kaufman of *Room 222* (1969-1974).

94. "The Last Flight of the Dixie Damsel"

(12/18/88) 60 mins.

Director: Vincent McEveety **Teleplay:** Peter S. Fischer

Regular: Angela Lansbury (Jessica Fletcher)

Recurring Characters: Martin Milner (Clint Phelps); Dale Robertson (Lee Goddard)

Guest Cast: Michael Ansara (Nicholas Rossi); Jane Greer (Bonnie Phelps); Clifton James (Ray Dressler); Richard Roundtree (Major Cooper); Robin Strasser (Sylvia Gagliano); Efrem Zimbalist, Jr. (General Havermeyer)

The Setting: An Air Force base in California

The Case: Back in the early 1950s, during the Korean War, Jessica Fletcher's husband, Frank, had served in the military. Suddenly, after all these years, the past comes all too vividly alive for the widowed Mrs. Fletcher. In 1952, an air force cargo plane had been abandoned during a fierce storm over Alaska. The downed plane had fallen onto an ice floe where it had been absorbed as part of an ice field. Now, years later, the craft has been found. Inside the vintage craft is the preserved corpse of a crew member who had been shot. Because records show that Frank Fletcher was the final person to parachute from the ill-fated C97, he is presently the chief suspect in the murder investigation.

When Jessica learns the dismaying details, she flies to the California air force base where the inquiry is being held. Because Frank cannot defend himself, she intends to clear his name. In the process, she deals with antagonistic Major Cooper as well as staunch, retired General Havermeyer. In addition, she mingles with several old acquaintances, including the survivors and relatives of that long-ago mishap: pilot Lee Goddard, Ray Dressler, Clint and Bonnie Phelps, Sylvia Gagliano and Nicholas Rossi.

Highlights: Nothing can bring tears to Jessica Fletcher's eyes more quickly than memories of her departed spouse. Here, she must not only relive trying episodes from her past, but have the heavy burden of defending a man no longer alive. Thus, there is an even deeper resonance to Mrs. Fletcher's very personal search for the truth. En route, she finds the spark of a new romance with self-reliant Lee Goddard.

Trivia: Jane Greer, once married to crooner Rudy Vallee and also a Howard Hughes protégée, had scored in several 1940s *film noir* movies: *They Won't Believe Me* (1947), *Out of the Past* (1947), *The Big Steal* (1949), etc. Other veteran performers included such past TV favorites as Michael Ansara *(Broken Arrow)*, Martin Milner *(Route 66, Adam 12)*, Efrem Zimbalist, Jr., *(77 Sunset Strip, The F.B.I.)*, Richard Roundtree *(Shaft)* and Dale Robertson *(Tales of Well Fargo, Death Valley Days)*.

95. "Prediction: Murder"

(1/1/89) 60 mins.

Director: Walter Grauman: **Teleplay:** Richard Stanley, Ralph Meyering, Jr.

Regular: Angela Lansbury (Jessica Fletcher)

Recurring Character: Dale Robertson (Lee Goddard)

Guest Law Enforcer: David Mack (Police Officer); Geoffrey Scott (Lieutenant Turner)

Guest Cast: Melody Anderson (Katherine Aaron); David Birney (Franchesco [Conrad Stiegler]); Steve Kahan (Roy Parks, the Ranch Hand); Michael Parks (Ben Aaron, Esq.); Lisa Pelikan (Jill Goddard); Lena Ponsette (Greta Olson); Michael Spound (Del Goddard)

The Settings: Rimrock Canyon, Arizona; (near) Tucson, Arizona

The Case: Having discovered a possible romance with former military pilot Lee Goddard (see #94), Jessica Fletcher visits his Arizona ranch situated not far from Tucson. There she reencounters Del, Lee's impetuous son, whom she had not seen in years. Del had once had a promising career at a Chicago ad agency until he married the ethereal Jill. Now, he is back home with his equally restless wife.

To celebrate Jessica's arrival, Lee hosts a barbecue. Among the invited guests are the unhappily married couple, Katherine and Ben Aaron. The evening's entertainment is a performance by Franchesco, a psychic. He makes several dire predictions involving Jill, including that there is death from fire in her future. The prognosis badly upsets Jill, but Del orders the forecaster to leave before his wife can ask the psychic further questions.

By the next day, Franchesco's foretellings start coming true when Jill chokes on a piece of toast. She is saved by quick-acting Jessica. Later, Jill is kidnapped. Distraught Lee quickly agrees to the ransom amount and his daughter-in-law is released. On the way home, her car goes over an embankment and explodes in flames.

Lieutenant Turner, aided by resourceful Jessica, sorts out the facts. It seems that Franchesco has had several prior arrests (but no convictions) on bunco charges. And what of the Swedish maid, Greta Olson, who hastily left the ranch to return to Sweden? Not to be overlooked is the fact that jealous Katherine was convinced that Ben had been having an affair with the eccentric victim.

Highlights: Beyond the splendid scenery and the novelty of a psychic going through his paces, the segment boasts the courtship of Jessica by Lee Goddard. In his direct way, the well-to-do widower proposes marriage. Gently, she declines the offer, insisting that she is not yet ready to consider a new relationship. However, she adds, that does not rule out the possibility in the future.

Trivia: Dale Robertson, who played the same role in 1988's "The Last Flight of the Dixie Damsel" (#94), was one of the few *Murder, She Wrote* performers to question the show's policy of listing the guest stars in the credits in alphabetical order. According to then executive producer and cocreator Peter S. Fischer, "This arrangement didn't sit well with Dale Robertson, who allowed as how he would just as soon have no billing. . . . This was okay with us. He did two shows, we didn't break our top fee and he didn't get billing. That was his choice and I never knew why."

David Birney was once married to Meredith Baxter, his *Bridget Loves Bernie* (1972–1973) costar, and had major roles in several TV series, including *Serpico, St. Elsewhere* and *Glitter.* Canadian-born Melody Anderson once starred as police officer Brooke McKenzie on *Manimal* (1983). Geoffrey Scott's TV series work includes *The Secret Empire* and *Dynasty.* Michael Parks, the 1960s answer to James Dean, played a nude Adam in *The Bible* (1966) and starred in TV's *Then Came Bronson* (1969–1970).

96. "Something Borrowed, Someone Blue"

(1/8/89) 60 mins.

Director: John Llewellyn Moxey **Teleplay:** Philip Gerson

Regular: Angela Lansbury (Jessica Fletcher)

Recurring Characters: Michael Horton (Grady Fletcher); Debbie Zipp (Donna Mayberry)

Guest Law Enforcer: Rick Hurst (Sheriff Slocum)

Guest Cast: Frank Arno (Tableman); Patricia Barry (Mrs. Pentworth); Ray Buktenika (Kyle Laughlin); David Byrd (Minister); Ralph M. Clift (Wedding Guest); Trent Dolan (Chairman); Conchata Ferrell (Harriet Lundgren, the Maid); Jay Lecky (Brat #2); Michael Leopard (Ice Bucket Delivery Man); Vicki Lucachick (Wedding Guest); Bill Macy (Uncle Ben); Paul Marin (Florist Delivery Man); Mark McGee (Florist); Howard Morris (Uncle Ziggy); Zachary O'Hearn (Brat #1); Betsy Palmer (Valerie); Frank Pangborn (Very Important Man); Jean Pfleiger (Wedding Guest); Eugene Roche (Franklin Mayberry); David Stenstrom (Photographer); Gale Storm (Maisie Mayberry); Barbara Townsend ("Cousin" Clara); Parker Whitman (Security Guard)

The Setting: Fishkill, New York

The Case: At long last, Grady Ambrose Fletcher and Donna Marie Mayberry are to wed. Jessica Fletcher arrives at the Mayberry estate in upstate New York where her nervous nephew ponders his fate. Meanwhile, the household is in an uproar as last-minute deliveries are made prior to the arrival of guests. Overseeing the chaos are the bride's parents: pompous Franklin and flighty Maisie Mayberry.

Events turn ominous when the Mayberrys' feisty maid, Harriet Lundgren, is found in the garden with a meat thermometer plunged into her back. To avoid canceling the ceremony, the corpse is shifted from spot to spot. Obsequious Sheriff Slocum regretfully seals off the estate, trapping gate-crashers, delivery folks and the murderer within the gated premises.

In between soothing the jittery newlyweds-to-be, Jessica reviews the situation. Pivotal figures include Maisie's lascivious brother Ben, who is in financial trouble; Maisie's other brother, the mother-fixated Ziggy; Valerie, the fading Southern belle fiancée of Ziggy; the impostor, Cousin Clara; the imposing Mrs. Pentworth; and Wilfred, once the "perfect" choice to marry Donna, but now a motorbike dude.

Highlights: Certainly this ranks as the daffiest episode of *Murder, She Wrote*, a fast-paced excursion modeled on 1930s Hollywood screwball comedies. The subordinate characters remain caricatures, which fits this zany plot line. On the other hand, Jessica is the venerable rock of Gibraltar as she dispenses practical advice and performs the sleuthing that the socially overwhelmed sheriff can't accomplish.

Trivia: Gale Storm is best remembered from two starring vehicles from the Golden Age of TV: *My Little Margie* (1952–1955) and *The Gale Storm Show/Oh, Susanna!* (1956–1960). Much of Betsy Palmer's fame derived from her TV game show outings: *Masquerade Party, I've Got a Secret*, etc. Howard Morris was a regular on *Your Show of Shows* (1951–1954) and *Caesar's Hour* (1954–1957). Among the younger players, Ray Buktenika appeared as the manipulative ad agency owner on *Life Goes On*, while portly Conchita Farrell played an aggressive show business attorney on the staff of *L.A. Law*.

97. "Weave a Tangled Web"

(1/15/89) 60 mins.

Director: Seymour Robbie **Teleplay:** Robert E. Swanson

Regulars: Angela Lansbury (Jessica Fletcher); Ron Masak (Sheriff Mort Metzger); William Windom (Dr. Seth Hazlitt)

Recurring Character: Will Nye (Deputy Floyd)

Guest Cast: Pamela Bellwood (Vivian Proctor/Vivian Austin); Lisa Brinegar (Debbie Proctor); George Chakiris (Eric Bowman); Scott Curtis (Danny Proctor); Mel Ferrer (Miles Austin); Charles Haid (Augie Specter); Stanley Kamel (Frankie, the Bartender); Gloria Loring (Margo Bowman); James Sutorius (Ralph Proctor)

The Settings: Cabot Cove, Maine; New York City

The Case: Cabot Cove widower Ralph Proctor, a tax accountant, works at home so he can care for his two young children, Danny and Debbie. His second wife of three years, Vivian, is a sales executive who spends much of her time on business trips around the U.S. One evening, while in New York on business, Jessica Fletcher attends a high-toned social function hosted by charming Miles Austin. She is amazed when she meets Miles's wife who is none other than Vivian. After explaining how she got herself into this strange situation, Vivian swears Jessica to secrecy.

Meanwhile, back in Cabot Cove, compulsive gambler Eric Bowman has divorced his wife, Margo, in a nasty break-up. Currently, he desperately needs $50,000 which he owes Boston bookie Augie Specter. Later, Eric is stabbed to death in room #6 at the Starlite Motel. Because Vivian was seen leaving the murder site, Sheriff Mort Metzger obtains a warrant for her arrest.

Drawn into the inquiry, Jessica deduces that the homicide can best be solved once she chats with the elusive Augie. She adopts a disguise and encamps at the Starlite Motel bar, becoming friendly with Specter's go-between, Frankie the bartender.

Highlights: With its subplot of bigamy, this risqué episode has a sophisticated edge. However, not everyone who learns of Vivian's dual life takes it as casually as Jessica, leading to an amazing sequence with Dr. Seth

Hazlitt. Another entertaining interlude involves Mrs. Fletcher masquerading as a barroom floozy with a penchant for betting long shots at the horse races. As she swigs down drinks, gossips with the bartender and sways in rhythm to the jukebox music, Jessica takes on a whole new persona.

Trivia: Dancer/actor George Chakiris had won a Best Supporting Actor Oscar for *West Side Story* (1961). Pamela Bellwood had been Claudia Blaisdel on *Dynasty* (1981–1986), while Charles Haid had been cast as Officer Andy Renko on *Hill Street Blues* (1981–1987). Just as Angela Lansbury was leaving her contract berth at MGM in the early 1950s, Broadway actor/director Mel Ferrer had begun his stay at the same studio, with such pictures as *Scaramouche* (1952) and *Lili* (1953).

98. "The Search for Peter Kerry"

(2/5/89) 60 mins.

Director: Walter Grauman **Teleplay:** Peter S. Fischer

Regular: Angela Lansbury (Jessica Fletcher)

Guest Law Enforcers: Sam Bottoms (Sergeant Joe Rice); Wren Brown (Uniformed Cop); John Petlock (Medical Examiner); Lane Smith (Police Chief Underwood)

Guest Cast: Mason Adams (Roger Philby, Esq.); Michael Beck (Danny Schubert); Vanessa Brown (Alma Goodrich); Anita Morris (Leona Schubert); James O'Connell (Minister); Lorna Patterson (Edie Lorraine, the Pianist); William Prince (Andrew Kerry); Marc Singer (Rick Barton)

The Setting: New York City

The Case: Jessica Fletcher attends the Manhattan funeral of widow Evelyn Drake Kerry, whom she has known for years. The deceased had spent much of the past twenty years searching for her long-lost son, Peter, who had disappeared during a Chicago riot in the summer of 1968.

Later, while Mrs. Fletcher is having dinner with Peter's long-ago college roommate, real estate developer Danny Schubert, Danny hears a song being played that he is convinced was composed by Peter Kerry. They locate the composer, Rick Barton, an artist, and it seems he might be Peter. The latter claims to be an amnesia victim, brought about by a car accident in the late 1960s. When told the news, wheelchair-bound patriarch Andrew Kerry invites Banner and his girlfriend, Edie Lorraine, to the family home.

During the weekend at the Kerrys', Danny is found in the garage, having been stabbed to death and with an unexplainable burn on his hand.

Working at odds with condescending police chief Underwood, Mrs. Fletcher interrogates the others. They include attorney Roger Philby, who has been manipulating the Kerrys' estate; Alma Goodrich, the Kerrys' longtime housekeeper; as well as Leona, the victim's long-dissatisfied spouse.

Highlights: With its intricate plot of past and present deceptions, the story line hinges on the credibility of the two potential relatives, Andrew Kerry and Rick Barton. The question of whether the latter is or is not the real Peter Kerry is properly, and tantalizingly, kept unanswered until the episode's final moments.

Trivia: Marc Singer is best known for his TV series work *(The Contender, V)* as well as his sword-and-sorcery pictures which began with *The Beastmaster* (1982). Michael Beck starred in the teleseries *Houston Knights* (1987–1988), while both Vanessa Brown and William Prince were senior veterans of the Broadway and Hollywood (sound)stages. (Prince costarred with Angela Lansbury in *Counting the Ways* and *Listening*, two one-act plays by Edward Albee, presented at the Hartford [Connecticut] Stage Company in repertory in January 1977.) Lane Smith was featured in the 1984–1985 sci-fi TV series *V* and was to become *Daily Planet* editor Perry White in *Lois & Clark—The New Adventures of Superman* (1993–).

99. "Smooth Operators"

(2/12/89) 60 mins.

Director: Anthony Shaw **Teleplay:** Gerald K. Siegel

Regular: Angela Lansbury (Christina Chesterton [Jessica Fletcher])

Recurring Character: Barney Martin (Lieutenant Timothy Hanratty)

Guest Law Enforcer: Ray Donateli (Cop); Peter Van Norden (Dr. Sid Lantz); Ed Winter (Captain E. Larson)

Guest Cast: Dirk Benedict (Dr. David Latimer); Orlando Bonner (Charlie); Brenneman Carroll (Young Guy); Rudy Challenger (Dr. Lowell Wheatley); Nicolas Coster (Dr. Craig Zachary); Lise Hilboldt (Stephanie Holtz); Shirley Knight (Grace Fenton); Greg Lewis (Phil Cashman, the Reporter); Michael McGrady (Leon Schnable); Dennis Patrick (Dr. Robert Markle); Marco Roccuzzo (Wino)

The Setting: New York City

The Case: While attending publisher meetings in Manhattan, Jessica stops by to see her friend, Lieutenant Timothy Hanratty. He is upset because precinct superior Captain Larson has demanded that he stop wasting time on low-profile homicides. Nevertheless, Timothy remains intrigued with the puzzling murder of a wino found lying in rubble wearing only one shoe.

Buoyed by supportive Jessica, Hanratty pursues his hunches—rather than new-fangled scientific methods—to track the victim's identity. His guesswork leads him and Jessica to a West 78th Street apartment building where the deceased had resided. A neighbor, Grace Fenton, directs them to the Olde Yorke Hospital where the dead man had been the accountant.

Posing as swank Christina Chesterton, Jessica invades the hospital where she uncovers that its three physician partners (Latimer, Zachary and Markle) have been fleecing unsuspecting patients with unnecessary medical attention. In the process of solving the murder, widower Timothy and spinster Grace fall in love. As for Jessica, she has the pleasure of proving that snide Captain Larson was very wrong about the sleuthing skills of both Hanratty and herself.

Highlights: As always, Angela Lansbury shines when required to adopt a disguise on-camera. Here, her poodle-carrying Park Avenue matron is a gem. However, as in many other similar plot situations, her charade is spotted due to her fame as a leading mystery writer. One of those she is attempting to fool matches her profile with the photograph on the dust jacket of a Jessica Fletcher best-seller.

A contrasting sequence occurs in the hospital's basement file room as snooping Jessica is stalked. In addition, thanks to credible performances by Barney Martin and Shirley Knight, their respective characters falling in love creates a strong subplot.

Trivia: Barney Martin had earlier played Lieutenant Timothy Hanratty—with the twinkly-eyes and Irish brogue—in 1987's "No Accounting for Murder" (#62). Shirley Knight had appeared in many movies: *Sweet Bird of Youth* (1962), *The Group* (1966), *Endless Love* (1981), etc. She had co-starred with Angela Lansbury in *The Dark at the Top of the Stairs* (1960). Ed Winter, adept at sneering roles, had been a law officer previously in *Hollywood Beat* (1985).

100. "Fire Burn, Cauldron Bubble"

(2/19/89) 60 mins.

Director: John Llewellyn Moxey **Teleplay:** Tom Sawyer

Regulars: Angela Lansbury (Jessica Fletcher); Ron Masak (Sheriff Mort Metzger); William Windom (Dr. Seth Hazlitt)

Recurring Character: Will Nye (Deputy Floyd)

Guest Cast: Pat Crawford Brown (Woman); John Bryant (Man); Colin Campbell (Simon); Patience Cleveland (Harriet, the Garden Club Member); Jill Donald (Irene Torhune); Brad Dourif (Dr. Overman); Bruce Gray (R.L. Pearson, Esq.); Sally Hughes (Dora); Bill Maher (Rick Rivers); Roddy McDowall (Gordon Fairchild); Russell Nype (Reverend Fordyce); Jane Marla Robbins (TV Reporter); Christopher Stone (Adam); Dee Wallace Stone (Mildred Torhune); John J. York (Jonas Holt, the Taxi Driver)

The Setting: Cabot Cove, Maine

The Case: Spooky coincidences are plaguing Cabot Cove. While making his nightly rounds, Dr. Seth Hazlitt insists he saw a woman in a Puritan outfit making a witch's curse in a nearby yard. Another local, Harriet, is convinced that it's the spirit of Patience Torhune—burned 300 years ago as a witch—who has returned to claim justice. As the neighborhood buzzes with excitement, author Gordon Fairchild arrives to promote his new book on apparitions. Fairchild is accompanied by Rick Rivers, a media consultant.

While Rivers attempts to draw the media to Cabot Cove to exploit Fairchild's book, Irene Torhune, after years of being away, returns to town to see her sister, Mildred, the town librarian. Mildred and her fiancé, Adam, attempt to make the unhappy Irene comfortable, but the latter is absorbed in carrying out witches' rituals which confound the town. Eventually, an exorcist is summoned, but to no earthly avail. Later, Irene's body is located in the burned remains of a barn. An autopsy reveals she had been hit over the head before the fire was set.

Highlights: With its supernatural flavor, this installment certainly evokes the passions surrounding witchcraft hysteria of colonial days in Salem, Massachusetts. What makes the atmosphere relevant is how the townsfolk react to the superstitions. Unlike Seth, level-headed Jessica Fletcher refuses to be caught up in the frenzy. On another level, Jessica has a particularly engaging encounter with the punctilious Gordon Fairchild, who dismisses Mrs. Fletcher as a small-town nobody until he is advised of her international reputation. She is unimpressed by his belated efforts at flattery.

Trivia: Both Britishers and both MGM alumni of the 1940s, Angela Lansbury and Roddy McDowall did not make a film together until *Bedknobs and Broomsticks* (1971). At the time of filming this episode, Dee Wallace (the mother in *E.T.: The Extraterrestrial* [1982]) was married to coplayer Christopher Stone (1940–1995). Wallace and Stone costarred in the syndicated TV series *The New Lassie* (1989–1991).

101. "From Russia with Blood"

(2/26/89) 60 mins.

Director: Vincent McEveety **Teleplay:** Donald Ross

Regular: Angela Lansbury (Jessica Fletcher)

Guest Law Enforcers: Jack Bannon (Chief Inspector Bernicker); Anthony Geary (Lieutenant Theodore Alexandrov of the KGB)

Guest Cast: Eve Brenner (Irina); Christina Cardan (Writer); Michael Chieffo (Nikolai); Oliver Darrow (Driver); Peter Donat (Sergei Chaloff); Jeremy Kemp (Minister Melnikov); Milos Kirek (Dukhov); Johnny Lykes (Alexei); David McCallum (Cyril Grantham); Judy Parfitt (Peggy Brooks); Christine Rose (Mrs. Hayes, at the American Embassy); Erik Siljir (Guard); Adrian Zmed (Bert Firman)

The Setting: Moscow, Russia

The Case: In the spirit of glasnost Jessica Fletcher is Russia-bound for an international artists league conference. Sergei Chaloff, who had been out of favor with the former Communist regime for his outspoken writings, is Jessica's artist host for the cultural exchange program. At an elaborate state function, Mrs. Fletcher's purse is stolen by a fake waiter. The latter is gunned down by the police. Meanwhile, a roll of microfilm is found in her retrieved purse, and despite protestations of innocence, her passport is confiscated. She must remain in Moscow.

Caught in the midst of a power struggle between the Ministry of Culture and the KGB, Jessica taps into her ingenuity to bring the true facts to light, matters which go back to World War II and the Nazi invasion of Russia. In the process, she calls upon Bert Firman, an American with the National Press Association, and Cyril Grantham, a cultural attaché to the British Embassy. Others involved in extricating Mrs. Fletcher from her predicament are literary agent Peggy Brooks with a suspect past, as well as Chief Inspector Bernicker.

Highlights: As this expansively produced segment illustrates, Jessica Fletcher is a devout fighter for the cause of right no matter where she may be. (This impassioned American berates one duplistic bureaucrat, "With all your departments, I have yet to encounter justice!")

Trivia: David McCallum enjoyed great popularity as Ilya Kuryakin in the spy adventure series *The Man from U.N.C.L.E.* (1964–1968). In 1965, Angela Lansbury appeared on a segment of that TV show, "The Deadly Toys Affair." Anthony Geary is most closely associated with the role of Luke Spencer on daytime TV's *General Hospital.* Adrian Zmed went from playing Officer Vince Romano on *T.J. Hooker* (1982–1985) to hosting the arcane *Dance Fever* (1985–1987).

102. "Alma Murder"

(3/12/89) 60 mins.

Director: Anthony Shaw **Teleplay:** Chris Manheim

Regular: Angela Lansbury (Jessica Fletcher)

Guest Law Enforcers: Lee De Broux (Sergeant Trask); Robert Hackman (Cop)

Guest Cast: Jason Bighe (Steve Chambers); Owen Bush (Hank Pruett, the Plumber); Felicia Lansbury (Sara Haines); E.G. Marshall (Professor Leon Walker); Kevin Michaels (Secretary); Janice Rule (Margaret Stone); Dinah Shore (Emily Dyers); Dana Sparks (Karen Chambers); Kate Vernon (Rhonda Sykes); Ralph Waite (District Attorney Paul Robbins); David Wilson (Waiter)

The Settings: Cabot Cove, Maine; Green Falls, New Hampshire

The Case: Jessica Fletcher returns to her alma mater, Harrison College, under peculiar circumstances. She has come to Green Falls, New Hampshire, upon learning that her former professor, Leon Walker, has confessed to the killing of an undergraduate student with a dubious reputation and a rich life-style. Jessica cannot accept that Walker would commit such a crime. With the help of two old friends—Emily Dyers, a sorority house mother, and Margaret Stone, who works with Professor Walker—Jessica examines the complex situation.

District Attorney Paul Robbins, whom Jessica dated in her college years, also finds the situation incredible. However, he must abide by the volunteered confession. Later, Steve Chambers, a young teacher at Harrison, insists that it was he, not his mentor (Walker), who was responsible for the young woman's death. Before the truth becomes evident, Jessica delves into decades-old events, including a pregnant classmate who never graduated.

Highlights: With Jessica Fletcher back at her college stamping grounds, one can almost envision her as a carefree, albeit serious, coed. Once again, the spark of a past romantic flame shines forth, as Jessica and Paul Robbins—he now romantically involved with Margaret Stone—reminisce about the good old days.

Trivia: Singer and talk show host Dinah Shore (1917–1994), a multi Emmy Award winner, made a rare dramatic appearance in this segment. Ralph Waite gained his repute as father Ben Walton on *The Waltons* (1972–1981), while Emmy Award winner E.G. Marshall had headlined such series as *The Defenders* (1961–1965) and *The New Doctors* (1969–1973).

103. "Truck Stop"

(4/2/89) 60 mins.

Director: Vincent McEveety **Teleplay:** Philip Gerson

Regular: Angela Lansbury (Jessica Fletcher)

Guest Law Enforcer: Ken Swofford (Sheriff Tugman)

Guest Cast: Elizabeth Ashley (Vera Gerakaris); Mike Connors (Walter Murray); Peter Haskell (Terence Locke, the Insurance Man); Ron Karabatsos (Pete Gerakaris); Andrew Prine (Roscoe); Jill Schoelen (Flora Gerakaris); Kristoffer Tabori (Desmond); Isaac Turner (Grange)

The Setting: California (near the Nevada border)

The Case: Screenwriter Walter Murray confers with Jessica Fletcher in Las Vegas, Nevada, to discuss his current assignment, a screen adaptation of one of her novels. They continue their work session as they drive from the gambling capital to Los Angeles. En route, near the California border, their car breaks down close to a dilapidated desert motel and diner. They are forced to spend the night there until the auto repairs can be completed.

During the next hours, tempers flare between the motel's owner, crude Pete Gerakaris, and his bored, younger wife, Vera, when it appears Vera and Walter are renewing a relationship begun many years ago. Matters get worse as Vera's daughter, Flora, fights with her mother, and pursues a reckless romance with a biker, Grange. Before long, Pete is murdered, followed by another killing, which leaves yet a third party near death's door.

Highlights: In tribute to the classic *film noir* movie *Double Indemnity* (1944), this complex exercise shifts back and forth from the actual story to variations of the plot line told in the cynical gumshoe style of a pulp detective novel. To help the viewer differentiate between the alternating narratives, the "real" one was filmed in color, while the fictional variation is presented in black-and-white cinematography.

Much of the action centers around Jessica Fletcher and insensitive Sheriff Tugman listening to a tape recorded confession made by a dying man. Upon hearing the full chronology, Jessica arranges the climactic showdown to trap the actual killer.

Trivia: Born Kreker Ohanian, Mike "Touch" Connors built his acting reputation on three TV series: *Tightrope* (1959–1960), the super violent *Mannix* (1967–1975) and *Today's F.B.I.* (1981–1982). Tony Award-winning Elizabeth Ashley revived her once promising acting career with a continuous role on TV's *Evening Shade* (1990–1994). Kristoffer Tabori, the son of actress Viveca Lindfors and director Don Siegel, acted in such movies as *The Sidelong Glances of a Pigeon Kicker* (1970) and *Girlfriends* (1978).

104. "The Sins of Cabot Cove"

(4/9/89) 60 mins.

Director: John Llewellyn Moxey **Teleplay:** Robert Van Scoyk

Regulars: Angela Lansbury (Jessica Fletcher); Ron Masak (Sheriff Mort Metzger); William Windom (Dr. Seth Hazlitt)

Recurring Characters: Julie Adams (Eve Simpson); Gloria DeHaven (Phyllis Grant); Kathryn Grayson (Ideal Malloy); Sally Klein (Corinne, the Beauty Shop Helper); Will Nye (Deputy Floyd); Ruth Roman (Loretta Spiegel)

Guest Cast: Luke Askew (Noah Harwood); Frederick Coffin (Tim Mulligan); Page Hannah (Sybil Reed); Rosanna Huffman (Miriam Harwood); Graham Jarvis (Ellis Holgate, the Bookstore Owner); Stuart Nisbet (George Greer); Joan Roberts (Janet Paisley, the TV Interviewer); Fran Ryan (Rose Mulligan)

The Setting: Cabot Cove, Maine

The Case: The good people of Cabot Cove are abuzz when Sybil Reed, a former student of Jessica Fletcher's, returns to town. Word is out that she has written a just-published, ultra-spicy novel. However, once the townsfolk read the scandalous roman à clef, *The Sins of Cabot Cove*, they are shocked to discover that the fiction bears a too tantalizing resemblance to reality, and their praise turns to rage. Soon neighbors are up in arms against neighbors, as guilty consciences over past transgressions and imagined slights rile most everyone in town. Even Jessica is miffed at her house guest, Sybil, who has made unflattering references to Mrs. Fletcher in her novel.

Life turns topsy turvy in Cabot Cove as dastardly events seem to follow a blueprint established in Sybil's book. First the Castle Cove bookstore is arsoned. Then Miriam Harwood, who had been having an affair with butcher

Tim Mulligan, is murdered with a frying pan. The immediate assumption is that the victim's crusty spouse, Noah, is the guilty party. Things take a wicked turn when it is discovered that Corinne, the assistant at Loretta Spiegel's beauty salon, has been feeding overheard gossip to Sybil, her school chum from years ago.

Highlights: The fantasy that small-town life is idyllic is dashed in this wryly humorous installment. Whether it be the "girls" at Loretta's Beauty Shop or town character Rose Mulligan protesting the moral virtues of her butcher son, no one is above having secrets or being quick to (mis)judge his/her neighbors.

Trivia: This episode marked the first return of the regulars from Loretta's Beauty Shop, introduced in 1987's "If It's Thursday, It Must Be Beverly Hills" (#72). The never seen, but much discussed Adele, wife of Sheriff Mort Metzger, is said now to be teaching a self-defense class for locals. This new knowledge seems to strengthen Mort's prior intimations to Jessica Fletcher of who wears the pants in the sheriff's household.

Staunch-looking Fran Ryan was a veteran of such TV series as *Green Acres*, *Gunsmoke* and *The Wizard*. While under MGM contract, Kathryn Grayson costarred with singer Mario Lanza in *The Midnight Kiss* (1949) and *The Toast of New Orleans* (1950). Gloria DeHaven, the daughter of (assistant) director Carter DeHaven, made her screen debut in Charles Chaplin's *Modern Times* (1936). In her lengthy career, Ruth Roman has appeared in the movie serial *Jungle Queen* (1945), the Marx Brothers movie *A Night in Casablanca* (1946) and the TV series *Knots Landing* (1986). In an earlier TV show, *The Long Hot Summer* (1965–1966), Roman played the same role—Minnie Littlejohn—that Angela Lansbury had created in the 1958 movie, *The Long Hot Summer*. One of Julie Adams's best-remembered roles as a 1950s Universal Pictures contractee was as the harassed heroine in *The Creature from the Black Lagoon* (1954).

105. "Trevor Hudson's Legacy"

(4/16/89) 60 mins.

Director: Walter Grauman **Story:** Evie Houston **Teleplay:** Paul Savage

Regular: Angela Lansbury (Jessica Fletcher)

Guest Law Enforcers: Steve Forrest (Sheriff Hank Masters); Jay Horton (Deputy)

Guest Cast: David Bradley (Adam Perry, a Drifter); Georgia Brown (Dorothy Westerfield); Raymond Davis (Doctor); Don Galloway (Andrew Hudson); Robert Klein (Barney Drake); Michael Learned (Maria Hudson); Yvette Nipar (Cat Hudson Drake); Robin Strand (Bob Jarrett); Barrie Youngfellow (Livvy Hudson)

The Setting: (Near) Custer's Creek, Montana

The Case: Jessica Fletcher, president of the Trevor Hudson Foundation, heads to Custer's Creek, Montana, to attend a celebration involving the forthcoming posthumous publication of Hudson's final novel. Since the great man's passing a year ago, young writer Bob Jarrett, hired at Jessica's recommendation, has been editing the dead author's notes.

When Jessica arrives at Hudson's home, a distressed Jarrett confides that Trevor's notes were merely the ramblings of a dying man. He adds that members of Hudson's family have pressured him to create a fiction in Trevor's style. Those suggesting that he take such unethical liberties include Hudson's sisters, Maria and Livvy, and, to a far lesser degree, the dead man's painter son, Andrew. Meanwhile, another relative, movie star Cat Hudson Drake, arrives. She has in tow her henpecked, minor talent agent husband, Barney.

Jarrett's moral dilemma becomes academic when he is found dead in Trevor's library. He had been hit over the head as he was working on the book galleys. In short order, Sheriff Hank Masters, a lifelong friend and admirer of Trevor's, arrests Adam Perry, a hitchhiker Cat had picked up for a brief romantic fling. According to the hot-headed Masters, the evidence against Perry is conclusive.

Mrs. Fletcher has an alternative theory about who might be the actual killer. It requires her to quiz Hudson's immediate family, including the tag-along, jealous Barney, as well as the grandiose Dorothy Westerfield, Hudson's longtime publisher.

Highlights: Always the voice of moral conscience, Jessica has a field day coping with the grasping writer's family and associates, all of whom have a financial stake in seeing the fabricated, posthumous novel published. This battle of wills between moral integrity and crass profiteering reveal the essence of Jessica Fletcher's goodness.

Trivia: Kentuckian Don Galloway is most noted for his Detective Sergeant Ed Brown on Raymond Burr's *Ironside* (1967–1975). Multiple Emmy Award winner Michael Learned earned three trophies for *The Waltons* (1972–1980) and one for *Nurse* (1981–1982). Barrie Youngfellow played one of the sexy young waitresses in the sitcom *It's a Living* (1980–1982; 1985–1989).

Skilled stand-up comic Robert Klein, who also scored in a Broadway musical *(They're Playing Our Song)*, made his network TV debut on *The Tonight Show with Johnny Carson* in January 1968. British-born Georgia

Brown (1933–1992) reached a peak in the 1960s stage musical *Oliver!*, while Steve Forrest, the actor brother of Dana Andrews, had a trio of TV series leading assignments: *The Baron*, *S.W.A.T.* and *Dallas*.

106. "Double Exposure"

(4/30/89) 60 mins.

Director: Anthony Shaw **Teleplay:** Robert E. Swanson

Regular: Angela Lansbury (Jessica Fletcher)

Recurring Character: Jerry Orbach (Harry McGraw)

Guest Law Enforcers: Earl Boen (Sergeant Howard Sternhagen); Allan Browne (Sergeant Frank Coyle); Robert Hogan (FBI Agent Guilfoyle); William Lucking (Lieutenant Roy Quinlan)

Guest Cast: Christine Belford (Maude Paulson Winslow); Jon Cypher (Nathan Swarthmore, Esq.); Justine Darby (Ralphie); Marty Davis (Cookie, the Bartender); Louise Fitch (Nosy Neighbor); John Furlong (John Wilson [John Winslow]); Louis Herthum (Wilber); Wendy Hoffman (Hotel Clerk); Joshua Peevy House (Tommy); Jack Jozefson (Taxi Driver); Karen Morrow (Gladys); Danny Murphy (Sloane); Melanie Noble (Receptionist); Barry O'Neill (Boy #4); Andrew Stevens (Dr. Adam Paulson); Scotty Williams (Boy #3)

The Settings: Boston, Massachusetts; Chicago, Illinois

The Case: While shopping in Boston, Jessica Fletcher encounters an old Cabot Cove neighbor, John Winslow. However, he later denies having ever met her. Very confused, Jessica phones the man's wife, Maude, in Chicago, only to be told that her husband died a few weeks earlier. Her concern and curiosity aroused, Jessica asks out-of-work Harry McGraw, her Boston private eye pal, to locate the evasive Winslow.

While Harry is doing his job, Jessica flies to Chicago where she talks with Maude and the widow's doctor brother, Adam. The latter had signed Winslow's death certificate. Mrs. Fletcher also meets with attorney Nathan Swarthmore, who represents the computer firm for whom Winslow had worked.

Meanwhile, back in Boston, Harry is arrested for the murder of Winslow, whom he had tracked to a run-down apartment building. To prove McGraw's innocence, Jessica must do battle with McGraw's old nemesis, Lieutenant Roy Quinlan.

Highlights: The beauty of this episode is that the people who seem to be criminals are not, and those who are assumed to be law-abiding citizens are just the reverse. A good deal of flavor is provided by the scenes at Gilhooley's, Harry McGraw's favorite Beantown bar and eatery.

Trivia: Jon Cypher was a veteran of several TV series: *Hill Street Blues* as the manipulative Chief Fletcher Daniels, *Knots Landing* as Jeff Munson, and *Major Dad* as Major General Marcus Craig.

107. "Three Strikes You're Out"

(5/7/89) 60 mins.

Director: Seymour Robbie **Teleplay:** Donald Ross

Regulars: Angela Lansbury (Jessica Fletcher)

Guest Law Enforcers: Dave Elliott (Police Officer); Reni Santoni (Lieutenant Caceras)

Guest Cast: Beau Billingslea (Kel Murray); Todd Bryant (Johnny Eaton); Bernie Casey (Doc Evans); Rick Dean (Mike Warlop); Tim Dunigan (Charley Holcomb [Freddy Masters]); Vince Edwards (Harry Dial); Shea Farrell (Pete Briggs); Terri Garber (Loretta Lee); Ed Hooks (Bellman); Jake Jacobs (Avery Burns); Anne Lockhart (Roz Briggs); Robert Mandan (Irving Randolph); Roxanne Reese (Nancy Murray); Harry Robinson (Umpire); Paul Sorvino (Al Sidell); Harry Woolf (Fan)

The Setting: Scottsdale, Arizona

The Case: In Arizona for a writers' conference, Jessica Fletcher takes the opportunity to visit her nephew, Johnny Eaton. He and fellow baseball player Charley Holcomb have just been traded from the Titans to the Comets. It's a further career step upward in professional baseball for Johnny. However, he's fearful about the showing he will make in spring training on the pitcher's mound and asks Jessica to provide moral support.

While watching the action from the sidelines, Jessica meets Al Sidell, an ex-sports writer turned manager for Eaton and Holcomb. She also chats with Roz, the wife of another nervous player, Pete Briggs. Hanging around the practice field, Jessica learns that team owner Irving Randolph is having financial problems and that Harry Dial, the Comets' gruff manager, is apprehensive about his players' chances in big league action.

Loretta Lee, the new TV pre-game hostess, is found dead in her hotel room from a blow to her head. Circumstantial evidence points to Charley

Holcomb as the culprit. However, Jessica is soon convinced that Holcomb is innocent.

The list of suspects is large. Besides assorted Comets members, there is jittery Mike Warlop, who had been traded to the Titans in exchange for Eaton and Holcomb, based on discoveries that Doc Evans is covering up a medical secret about one of the players. Moreover, one hot-headed athlete is hiding from a past assault charge, while yet another team member is afraid to admit where he was the night of the homicide.

Highlights: This was certainly not the first or the last time Jessica Fletcher would cross over into the world of athletics. Each of her excursions allows the literate but folksy Jessica to mingle with sports players and fans alike. Here, she can relax, enjoy learning more about the sport at hand and soak up the new atmosphere—all grist for her future novels.

Accustomed to barging in on the action, Jessica meets a near defeat in tough Harry Dial. He's the confirmed chauvinist who derogatorily refers to Mrs. Fletcher as "Aunt Minnie." On one occasion, when the amateur sleuth traps Harry into a quizzing session in the men's locker room, Dial threatens to drop his towel. It works. Jessica quickly beats a hasty retreat.

Trivia: Vince Edwards (1928–1996) is fondly remembered as TV physician *Ben Casey* (1961–1966). Brooklyn-born Paul Sorvino, the father of Oscar-winning actress Mira Sorvino and who has an aspiring career as an opera singer, was the (co)star of such 1970s TV short-lived series as *We'll Get By* and *Bert D'Angelo/Superstar* and was to costar in the 1990s *Law and Order*. A very prolific actor, Robert Mandan's best credit still remains pompous Chester Tate on the satirical *Soap* (1977–1981).

108a. "Mirror, Mirror on the Wall: Part One"

(5/14/89) 60 mins.

108b. "Mirror, Mirror on the Wall: Part Two"

(5/21/89) 60 mins.

Director: Walter Grauman **Teleplay:** Peter S. Fischer

Regulars: Angela Lansbury (Jessica Fletcher); Ron Masak (Sheriff Mort Metzger); William Windom (Dr. Seth Hazlitt)

Recurring Character: Will Nye (Deputy Floyd)

Guest Cast: Richard Anderson (Lew Bracken); William Bryant (Gadge); Michael Doven (Joey); Robert Dryer (Arnie); Richard Erdman (Jonathan); Shelley Fabares (Liza Caspar); Ken Gerson (Willie); David Hedison (Victor

Caspar); Ken Howard (Hank Shipton); Daniel McDonald (Bobby Shipton); Lisa Nelson (Nurse); Edward Penn (Doctor); Jean Simmons (Eudora McVeigh); Scott Stewart (Maitre d'); Richard Wieand (TV Reporter)

The Setting: Cabot Cove, Maine

The Case: Eudora McVeigh, the enduring queen of mystery writers, arrives in Cabot Cove. She appears unannounced on Jessica Fletcher's doorstep, with a basket of luscious apples in hand. Soon, gracious Jessica is inviting the author to be her house guest.

Unknown to Jessica, Eudora has a treacherous ulterior motive. Her position in the writing world is slipping. Her publisher keeps pointing out that what Mrs. Fletcher writes is "in," while what Eudora is turning out is "out." The embittered Eudora is determined to study her rival firsthand and, at the same time, use devious means to overcome her writer's block.

Before long, things go amuck at Jessica's. Crucial notes for her new novel disappear. Biting into an apple destined for Jessica, Dr. Seth Hazlitt suddenly collapses (from what turns out to be poisoned fruit). Earlier, a corpse was found on the rocky Maine coastline. The dead man proved to be a New York-based private detective who had been on Eudora's trail.

The most likely culprit in the homicide case is envious Ms. McVeigh. However, fair-minded Jessica takes into account other recent arrivals in Cabot Cove. They include the suspect's estranged husband, Hank Shipton; Eudora's stepson, Bobby; as well as the mystery maven's agent Liza Caspar, and the latter's husband, Victor.

Highlights: Rarely has Jessica Fletcher encountered such a staunch adversary, ironically one from her own writing world. Each is expert in the cat-and-mouse game of false leads, framed innocent suspects and useful clues buried in the obvious.

The well-crafted story line takes on added dimension when it is understood that the two-part drama (an oddity on this weekly program) was conceived originally as both the finale to the show's fifth season and to the series itself. Angela Lansbury's initial five-year pact was nearly over, and she had said she did not plan to continue with the series. However, at the last minute she was tempted into renewing her weekly show via a new lucrative deal. Thus Peter S. Fischer, program cocreator, executive producer and author of this two-part segment, had to do a "frantic, last-minute rewrite of the whole script." This explains why there are many changes in the recurring characters' personalities here, items not resolved or ignored when the series resumed production for season #6.

For example, there are several instances in this two-parter in which Jessica and Seth *almost* bridge their sterling platonic alliance into a near-romantic rapport. This would have been a logical outcome had the series been actually ending. The same goes for Hazlitt's persistent needling of

Mrs. Fletcher to stop being so obsessed with her novel writing. He urges her to take more opportunity to enjoy all the wonderful things around her: i.e., her good friends, the beauty of nature, etc. As such, the double episode concludes with Jessica putting aside her book writing—for the time being—to join Seth on a fishing excursion. This same let's-wrap-up-the-characters'-story-lines finds Sheriff Mort Metzger in this outing being extremely exasperated by the growing siege of murders in Cabot Cove. There is a suggestion that he could easily decide to abandon his disheartening profession. However, in the script rewrite he remains in his chosen career.

Trivia: British-born Jean Simmons, once married to actor Stewart Granger and then to director Richard Brooks, starred in such features as *Hamlet* (1948), *The Robe* (1953), *Elmer Gantry* (1960) and *How to Make an American Quilt* (1995). On TV she won an Emmy for her performance in the miniseries *The Thorn Birds* (1983). She and Angela Lansbury costarred in the James Garner MGM movie *Mister Buddwing* (1966).

The other guest artists were all TV series veterans: Richard Anderson *(The Six Million Dollar Man, The Bionic Woman)*, Shelley Fabares *(The Donna Reed Show, One Day at a Time, Coach)*, David Hedison *(Five Fingers, Voyage to the Bottom of the Sea)* and Ken Howard *(The Manhunter, The White Shadow, The Colbys)*. William Bryant had been a part of *Hondo* and *Switch,* among others. Richard Erdman participated on *The Ray Bolger Show, Saints and Sinners, From Here to Eternity,* etc.

SEASON SIX

1989–1990

109. "Appointment in Athens"

(9/24/98) 60 mins.

Director: Vincent McEveety **Teleplay:** Tom Sawyer

Regular: Angela Lansbury (Jessica Fletcher)

Recurring Character: Len Cariou (Michael Reardon [Michael Haggerty])

Guest Law Enforcer: Steve Inwood (Sergeant Petrakas)

Guest Cast: June Chadwick (Pamela Drake); Thom Christopher (Dimitri Popadopalous); Anthony Gordon (Monsieur Le Bon); Thom Keane (Hotel Clerk); Sybil Lines (Madge Scofield); John McCafferty (Laddie Fairchild); Rosie Malek-Yoan (Air Levant Clerk); Miguel Marcott (Airline Clerk); Ian Ogilvy (Harold Baines); Richard Todd (Colonel Alec Scofield); Peter Van Norden (Henryk Stuyvesant); George Zaver (Bellhop)

The Settings: Athens, Greece; Paris, France

The Case: As part of her international book tour, Jessica Fletcher is about to leave Paris for Cairo. However, her Egyptian flight announces a several-hours delay. Her old associate, British secret agent Michael Haggerty, who has shown up mysteriously, suggests that Jessica, instead, fly with him to Athens and then book a connecting flight on to Cairo. Although suspicious of her elusive and trouble-prone friend, she agrees to the plan. Next, Haggerty vanishes.

Once in Athens, she finds that flights to Cairo are overbooked until at least the next day. Not yet comprehending that her travel problems were engineered by Haggerty, she accepts the kindness of Harold Baines, the local representative of a global conglomerate. He offers her their corporate suite at a city hotel.

When Michael does reappear, Jessica forces a bit of the truth from him. It turns out that against the orders of his superior, Colonel Alec Scofield, Michael hopes to free fellow M16 agent Laddie Fairchild, who was kidnapped while trailing an international arms smuggler. Haggerty convinces Jessica to pretend to be Mrs. Michael Reardon, a rich lumber heiress, to help him save the kidnapped victim from the terrorists.

Making matters more complex, a woman is found murdered in Jessica's suite. She proves to be Pamela Drake, an actress pal of Haggerty's, whom he had first asked to play his dangerous charade but who had been detained in England. Now enmeshed in a murder case, Mrs. Fletcher is ordered by the police, Sergeant Petrakas, not to leave town. Others playing key roles in the international intrigue are Madge, Scofield's adulterous wife; Henryk Stuyvesant, a private investigator; and Dimitri Popadopalous, a mystery man.

Highlights: Boasting beautiful Mediterranean scenery, this James Bond-like escapade allows Jessica a fitting showcase. She befuddles her targets while impersonating the quarrelsome wealthy woman, she assembles clues as a shrewd observer, and she risks her life once again as the unwitting partner of charming Michael Haggerty.

Trivia: Englishman Richard Todd, the Academy Award-nominated star of *The Hasty Heart* (1949), appeared in such diverse movies as *Robin Hood* (1952), *A Man Called Peter* (1955) and *Operation Crossbow* (1965). Ian Ogilvy, also a Britisher, performed in such films as *Wuthering Heights* (1970) and *Death Becomes Her* (1992). He was the star of the TV series *The Return of the Saint* (1978).

110. "Seal of the Confessional"

(10/1/89) 60 mins.

Director: Vincent McEveety **Story:** Whitney Wherrett Roberson **Teleplay:** Lynne Kelsey

Regulars: Angela Lansbury (Jessica Fletcher); Ron Masak (Sheriff Mort Metzger); William Windom (Dr. Seth Hazlitt)

Recurring Character: Will Nye (Deputy Floyd)

Guest Cast: Bonnie Bartlett (Marilyn North); Hunt Block (Father Donald Barnes); Jon Cedar (Evan West); Kathy Christopherson (Girl); Mimi Cozzens (Owner of Jimmie's Restaurant); Cal Evans (Boy); Allan Feinstein

(George Woodward, Esq.); Robert Horton (Jack Hutchings); Lance Kerwin (Eddie Frayne); Steve Peterson (Investigator); Jerry Potter (Joe); Madlyn Rhue (Doris Barrett West); Jennifer Runyon (Kelly Barrett)

The Setting: Cabot Cove, Maine

The Case: Wheelchair-bound Doris West is devastated when her husband, Evan, is stabbed to death on the Cabot Cove beach. However, the victim's stepdaughter, Kelly, home on summer vacation from boarding school, sheds no tears at his passing.

As evidence is gathered in the homicide case, retarded young Eddie Frayne is brought into custody by Sheriff Mort Metzger because he had the bloody murder weapon (a knife) in his possession. Jessica Fletcher cannot fathom why good-natured Eddie would kill anyone. Another person convinced of the youth's innocence is Father Donald Barnes, the temporary pastor at St. Joseph's Church. A few hours earlier, he had heard a confessional from a parishioner who admitted to having killed Evan West. The priest is deeply troubled because the seal of the confessional forbids him to reveal the damning truth.

To solve the murder, Jessica meets with Marilyn North, the private nurse who had been attending Doris. Then there is the widow herself, who knew of her husband's many indiscretions and who had been supporting him for years. Additionally, there is George Woodward, the lawyer defending confused Eddie. George was a longtime friend of the deceased and knew many of his secrets.

Highlights: The plot gambit of relying on the seal of the confessional, employed in Alfred Hitchcock's *I, Confess* (1953) and several other movies, is woven into this scenario but with an added twist. More than one person legitimately believes he or she is responsible for the victim's end.

Trivia: Madlyn Rhue, a longtime sufferer of multiple sclerosis, had a tailored-made part as the handicapped character. She had been featured in such TV series as *Bracken's World* (1969–1970) and *Executive Suite* (1976–1977). Lance Kerwin had been the child star of *James at 15* (1977–1978).

111. "The Grand Old Lady"

(10/8/89) 60 mins.

Director: Vincent McEveety **Teleplay:** Peter S. Fischer

Regular: Angela Lansbury (Jessica Fletcher/Narrator)

Guest Law Enforcer: John Karlen (Lieutenant Martin McGinn)

Guest Cast: Gregg Binkley (Copy Boy); Mark Lindsay Chapman (Paul Viscard); Dane Clark (Henri Viscard); Donald Craig (Nicholas Crane); June Havoc (Lady Abigail Austin); Gary Kroeger (Christy McGinn); Floyd Levine (Harry Krumholtz); Joan McMurtrey (Eleanor); Aubrey Morris (Mr. Bellows); Wolf Muser (Peter Daniken); Derek Partridge (Doctor); Henry Polic, II (Arthur Bishop); Lisa Ryan (Woman); Michael Douglas Scott (2nd Officer); Terry Sheppard (Busboy); Joe Staton (Nurse); James Stephens (Lennihan); Gordon Thomson (Major McGuire); Robert Vaughn (Edwin Chancellor); Paxton Whitehead (Captain Oliver)

The Setting: New York City

The Case: Reading of the death of Lady Abigail Austin, the grand dame of murder mystery writers, Jessica Fletcher reflects back on a real-life case that happened some fifty years ago.

The *Queen Mary*, with Lady Abigail Austin aboard, is in New York harbor, and Captain Oliver has a serious situation. A passenger, who proves to be a former gestapo officer, is stabbed to death while on the huge ship. Coming aboard to investigate is New York police officer Lieutenant Martin McGinn. He is joined in the case by his determined son, Christy, a Manhattan crime reporter. While they look for clues, Lady Abigail, by virtue of her expertise in the whodunit field, begins her own interrogation of the likely suspects. Before the killer is unmasked, another murder occurs, and several suspicious persons must establish their alibis. With the complex case resolved, the titled writer disembarks, convinced that she resolved the case. Actually, it is Christy who turned the spotlight on the killer.

Highlights: This was the first of many episodes in the next few seasons of *Murder, She Wrote* in which Angela Lansbury's Jessica Fletcher would only narrate the opening and closing "bookends" to the story. While many subsequent such stories clearly were not scripted with Jessica in mind for the lead role, that is not the case here. One notes the strong parallels between Jessica and the venerated fiction writer who carries her deductive talents over into "real life." Obviously, it was intended that originally Lansbury's Mrs. Fletcher would be the focal crime-solver in this escapade.

Trivia: June Havoc once starred on TV in *Willy* (1954–1955). Brooklyn-born John Karlen had been a cast member of the Gothic soap opera *Dark Shadows* (1966–1971). Robert Vaughn, who later turned to a succession of villain roles in films and TV, earned his acting stripes as Napoleon Solo of the espionage action series *The Man from U.N.C.L.E.* (1964–1968). Dane Clark, a Warner Bros. utility leading man in the 1940s, participated in such 1950s TV series as *Wire Service* and *Bold Adventure* and the 1973 TV revival of *Perry Mason*.

112. "The Error of Her Ways"

(10/15/89) 60 mins.

Director: Anthony Shaw **Teleplay:** Donald Ross

Regular: Angela Lansbury (Jessica Fletcher)

Guest Law Enforcers: Elliott Gould (Lieutenant Hanna); Louis Herthum (Officer Kreuger)

Guest Cast: Elvia Allman (Elderly Lady #1); Monty Bane (Emmett Barry, the Private Investigator); Terence Beasor (Fontana); Susan Blakely (Pauline Byrne); Kathy Cannon (Marian Randall); Ruth Engel (Elderly Lady #2); Paul Gleason (Sterling Rose); Robin Gordon (Employee); Marilyn Jones (Linda Dixon); Peter MacLean (Alden); Thomas H. Middleton (Doctor); Barbara Parkins (Kay Weber); Edmund L. Shaff (Banker); Marshall Thompson (Ward Silloway)

The Setting: Palm Springs, California

The Case: Some months before, Marian Randall had been charged with killing her unfaithful husband, Clark Randall, a Palm Springs, California, real estate developer. She insists she is innocent. However, when freed on bail, she commits suicide. This cycle of events leads Jessica and Lieutenant Hanna, both involved in the original investigation, to question the facts surrounding Clark's murder. Mrs. Fletcher is particularly puzzled why Marian consumed a large dosage of a drug to which she was allergic just before locking herself in the garage and succumbing to carbon monoxide poisoning.

Meanwhile, Linda Dixon, the dead woman's angry sister, initiates a class action wrongful death suit, naming Jessica and others as defendants. Before long, the facts fall into place for Jessica and the badgered police lieutenant. Implicated in the final situation are attractive bank official Kay Weber, real estate salesperson Sterling Rose, accountant Ward Silloway, and love-hungry Pauline Byrne.

Highlights: It is a singular turn of events for Jessica to ever question her deductive powers, especially in a clear-cut case. However, here she wonders whether she was guilty in a possibly innocent woman's death. It lends an intriguing slant to the proceedings, part of which are related through flashbacks.

Trivia: Louis Herthum, who had already appeared in a prior *Murder, She Wrote* segment, would begin, during the 1991–1992 season, his recurring role of Cabot Cove's Deputy Andy Broom. Elliott Gould, once married to Barbra Streisand, made his movie reputation playing smarmy big-screen characters: e.g., *M*A*S*H* (1970), *The Long Goodbye* (1972) and *Busting* (1973). In the 1980s, he had little luck with his TV series *E/R* and *Together We Stand.*

Former model Susan Blakely starred in *Report to the Commissioner* (1975), as well as the TV miniseries *Rich Man, Poor Man* (1976). Barbara Parkins, of *Valley of the Dolls* (1967), made her show business breakthrough as Betty Anderson Harrington Cord on the TV nighttime soap opera *Peyton Place* (1964–1969). Marshall Thompson (1925–1992), another MGM alumnus like Angela Lansbury, was featured on TV's *Daktari* (1966–1969).

113. "Jack and Bill"

(10/29/89) 60 mins.

Director: Chuck Bowman **Teleplay:** Peter S. Fischer

Regular: Angela Lansbury (Jessica Fletcher/Narrator)

Guest Law Enforcers: Pat Harrington (Lieutenant Lou Brickman); Paul Lyell (Cop); Bob Roitblat (Police Sergeant)

Guest Cast: Susan Anton (Celia Jainter); Max Baer (Johnny Wheeler [Bruce Forrester]); Warren Berlinger (Sugarman); Lisa Donaldson Bowman (Sportscaster); Carlos Cervantes (Heavy #1); Sandra Cornwall (1st Beauty); Claude Dunkelman (Andy Brickman); Nate Esformes (President Ruiz); Alexander Folk (Cricket, the Bartender); Ken Howard (Bill Boyle); Rosanna Huffman (Marge Brickman); Dennis Madalone (Thug #2); Marji McKelvey (2nd Beauty); Milt Oberman (Vet); Rose Portello (Maria); Whitney Rydbeck (Hastings); Jessie Scott (Beautiful Young Thing); Courtney Sonne (Brenda Brickman); Viola Kates Stimpson (Elderly Lady); Elizabeth Sung (Lip Reader); John Tayloe (Actor in 16mm Film); Ellen Travolta (Mona); Glynn Turman (Earl Browder); Duane Whitaker (Drunk)

The Setting: Los Angeles, California

The Case: Congenial Bill Boyle, a former professional football linebacker, is now a laid-back Los Angeles private investigator. His old pal, Johnny Wheeler, asks him to dog-sit a white French poodle named Jack. When Wheeler is murdered, Bill is left caring for the precocious, lovable dog. Meanwhile, mayhem ensues as various strangers attempt to steal Jack. However, the latter proves quite resourceful in helping Boyle survive attacks by thugs and others.

Eventually, the perplexed Boyle discovers that Johnny had been working with a global government agency and was involved in thwarting a plot to assassinate an international figure, President Ruiz, at the Los Angeles

Coliseum. Buoyed by his statuesque girlfriend, Celia, his flippant secretary, Mona, and working with his policeman brother-in-law, Lieutenant Lou Brickman, Bill and the ever-faithful Jack crack the case.

Highlights: With Jessica Fletcher here sidelined to a mere hosting chore, this entry lacks the personality and point of view of a typical *Murder, She Wrote* entry. Despite the charm of Ken Howard's Bill Boyle and the cuteness of the canine costar, the segment plays like an unsold TV series pilot.

Trivia: Ken Howard, who made his screen debut in Liza Minnelli's *Tell Me That You Love Me Junie Moon* (1970), had revealed a singing flair in the screen musical *1776* (1972). Pat Harrington, Jr., the son of a vaudeville trouper, began his TV career in the NBC-TV network mailroom. Besides the long-running sitcom *One Day at a Time* (1975–1984), Harrington supplied the voice of the befuddled inspector in the 1970s TV children's program *Pink Panther Show.* Statuesque Susan Anton's prominence began with her late 1970s Muriel Cigars commercials.

114. "Dead Letter"

(11/5/89) 60 mins.

Director: Anthony Shaw **Teleplay:** Paul Schiffer

Regulars: Angela Lansbury (Jessica Fletcher); Ron Masak (Sheriff Mort Metzger); William Windom (Dr. Seth Hazlitt)

Recurring Characters: Will Nye (Deputy Floyd); Richard Paul (Mayor Sam Booth)

Guest Cast: Susan Anspach (Lois Fricksey); Steve Bean (Young Man); Kevin Bourland (Everett); Lynn Clark (Young Girl); Rosemary DeCamp (Agnes); Peter Fox (Ron Stiller); George Furth (Fred Owens); Max Gail (Stanley Holmes); Jonathan Goldsmith (Bud Fricksey); Stuart Nelson (Jack); Richard Riehle (Aaron); Robin Riker-Hasley (Connie Kowalski); Al Waxman (Carl Wilson)

The Setting: Cabot Cove, Maine

The Case: At a Cabot Cove rummage sale, Jessica Fletcher buys an antique bureau. Little does she know that her acquisition will snowball into murder and arson.

Trouble starts when Mrs. Fletcher opens a drawer of her new purchase and discovers an undelivered letter stuck behind a drawer. She takes it to the addressee, Bud Fricksey. Later, when Owens Furniture Store burns,

Fricksey's body is discovered in the rubble. An autopsy proves that he died from foul play!

In fast order, Jessica and Sheriff Mort Metzger, as well as a cynical insurance claims adjuster, Connie Kowalski, are involved in the mystery. They puzzle through the evidence which brings them to the dead man's wife, Lois, who badly wanted to end her unhappy marriage to jealous Bud. There's also Ron Stiller at the gas station who's infatuated with Lois, as well as the financially plagued owner (Fred Owens) and bookkeeper (Stanley Holmes) of the incinerated furniture emporium. Also suspect is Carl Wilson, the fire chief and his men.

Highlights: Once again, this entry boasts the fine local color and offbeat characterizations that make the series so popular. It uses the familiar ploy of a running subtheme in the story line finale. Here the story opens with a large yard sale to help finance Cabot Cove's new fire engine. The episode concludes with the dedication of the new equipment, only to have the proud onlooking Cabot Cove notables—including Jessica Fletcher—sprayed by an out-of-control burst of water.

Trivia: Performing here in a rare recent acting assignment, 1940s character actress Rosemary DeCamp had previously been a backbone of such pre-1970s TV series as *The Life of Riley*, *Bob Cummings Show* and *That Girl*. Canadian-born Al Waxman had scored as Lieutenant Albert Samuels on *Cagney & Lacey* (1982–1988). Among Richard Paul's earlier TV series were *Match Game, P.M.* (1975–1982—as a panelist), *One in a Million* (1980) and *Herbie, the Love Bug* (1982).

115. "Night of the Tarantula"

(11/12/89) 60 mins.

Director: Vincent McEveety **Teleplay:** Chris Manheim

Regular: Angela Lansbury (Jessica Fletcher)

Guest Law Enforcer: Darrow Igus (Sergeant Jones)

Guest Cast: Obaka Adedunyo (Dr. Hayes); Cheryl Arutt (Michelle Dusant); Grand L. Bush (George Gordon); Hurd Hatfield (Jean-Pierre Dusant); Ji-Tu (Calder Williams); James Lancaster (Mark Waverly); Patrick Masset (Adam Waverly); John Rhys-Davies (Harry Waverly); J. Christopher Sullivan (Servant); Nancy Valens (Selina Williams Waverly); Shani Wallis (Olivia Waverly)

The Setting: Jamaica in the Caribbean

The Case: During a childhood summer spent with cousin Emma Macgill in London, Jessica Fletcher became friendly with Olivia Waverly. Now, years later, Jessica visits the widowed Olivia in Jamaica. The occasion is the thirtieth birthday celebration for Mrs. Waverly's son, Adam. Others at the festivities are Olivia's bachelor brother-in-law, Harry Waverly; Olivia's younger son, Mark; and the Waverly's impoverished neighbor, aristocratic Jean-Pierre Dusant. It is understood that Dusant's pretty daughter, Michelle, will one day marry Adam—who is to inherit control of the estate—although it is Mark who really loves the young woman.

When Adam returns after weeks away on business, he has surprising news. He has married Selina, the daughter of Calder Williams, an island voodoo priest. The practical Harry suggests that Michelle should now wed Mark, while the angered Calder puts a curse on his daughter's white family. Later, Harry is found dead, with a boa constrictor wriggling over his corpse. What puzzles Jessica is that the murder room was locked from the inside and that the snake is so small.

Further on, Adam nearly dies from ingesting rat poison. By combining forces with a local policeman, Lieutenant Jones, and George Gordon, the publisher of the island's newspaper, Jessica pierces through voodoo and black magic rituals to unmask the killer.

Highlights: Taking Jessica Fletcher far afield from Maine to an exotic tropical locale provides its own novelty. This foreign flavor is heightened by weaving native rituals and voodoo curses—not to mention a secret passageway—into the mystery.

Trivia: John Rhys-Davies of Salisbury, England, starred in the 1982 TV series *The Quest*, as well as being featured in many films. British cabaret singer Shani Wallis appeared in such features as *A King in New York* (1957), *Oliver!* (1968) and *Round Numbers* (1992).

116. "When the Fat Lady Sings"

(11/19/89) 60 mins.

Director: Walter Grauman **Teleplay:** Peter S. Fischer

Regular: Angela Lansbury (Jessica Fletcher)

Recurring Character: Keith Michell (Dennis Stanton)

Guest Law Enforcer: Jerry Stiller (Lieutenant Birnbaum)

Guest Cast: Kathleen Beller (Maria Dexler); Theodore Bikel (Rosanno Bertolucci); Leo Damean (Giorgio Russo); David E. Elliott (Paramedic);

Mark Herrier (Barry Sanderson); Lila Kaye (Teresa Mancini); Tom Kendall (Stage Manager); Carol Lawrence (Silvana Bertolucci); Walter Olkewicz (Howard); James Short (Lou Faraday); Tom Tarpey (Doctor); Tom Van Hoof (Customs Agent Dixon)

The Setting: San Francisco, California

The Case: Jessica is in San Francisco for a mystery writers' convention. Her old chum, Dennis Stanton, a former jewel thief who has gone legitimate, insists upon taking her to meet world-acclaimed opera tenor Rosanno Bertolucci. He, in turn, provides tickets for them to attend the star's gala opening performance for the season. After the charity event, Jessica and Dennis go backstage. There they find Rosanno arguing with a man named Lou Faraday. The portly singer chases the intruder out of the building and into an adjacent alleyway where he shoots him dead.

For contentious Lieutenant Birnbaum, it's an open-and-shut case against Bertolucci, who is now under police custody at the hospital where he is recovering from a heart attack. However, the facts don't add up for Jessica. She had heard *two* shots being fired when Rosanno cornered the victim in the alley. And what happened to the dead man's gray windbreaker?

Joined by equally astute Stanton, Jessica questions several suspects: Silvana, Bertolucci's volatile wife of thirty years; Maria Dexler, the star's pretty but not so proficient opera protégée; Teresa Mancini, the accused's aunt who now knows her nephew's deeply buried secret. Meanwhile, there is another murder victim, this time young journalist Barry Sanderson, who had a crush on Maria. With the help of Custom Agent Dixon, Mrs. Fletcher solves the murders.

Highlights: With its backstage ambiance, operatic background and oversized performances, this episode was a little operetta unto itself. Contrasted with the unsubtle opera people and the argumentative police investigator is the growing bond between Jessica and the suave Dennis. Now that he has abandoned his criminal ways, Mrs. Fletcher finds him a most endearing companion and cosleuth.

Trivia: Keith Michell's Dennis Stanton had debuted on *Murder, She Wrote* in 1988's "A Little Night Work" (#89). Since then, the characterization had undergone changes. Now Dennis uses his burglary expertise on the *right* side of the law, working as a claims investigator for a Bay area insurance firm. Lila Kaye, a member of England's Royal Shakespeare Company, had appeared on Broadway in the musical *The Life and Adventures of Nicholas Nickelby* (1981) and had starred on TV in *Mama Malone* (1984). Kathleen Beller had been Kirby on the nighttime soap opera *Dynasty* (1982–1984). Broadway singing star Carol Lawrence had once been married to singer/actor Robert Goulet.

117. "Test of Wills"

(11/26/89) 60 mins.

Director: Anthony Shaw **Teleplay:** Robert E. Swanson

Regular: Angela Lansbury (Jessica Fletcher)

Guest Law Enforcers: Jeremy Roberts (Sergeant Stokley); Morgan Woodward (Sheriff Brademus)

Guest Cast: Philip Abbott (Dr. Hubbard Dabney); Gene Barry (Henry Reynard); Victoria Booth (Mrs. Forrest, the Maid); John Callahan (Preston Howard); Jill Carroll (Kimberly); Keir Dullea (Jason Reynard); Marj Dusay (Alice Carson); H. Ray Huff (Pilot); Curt Lowers (Forrest, the Butler); Cassie Yates (Valery Renard)

The Setting: Mount Tyler, a private island

The Case: A month earlier, Jessica had met multimillionaire Henry Reynard at the Annual Book Awards in Chicago. Now he has invited her to be his weekend guest at his isolated island retreat. Upon arrival, the tycoon confides that he is in grave danger and tells her of the several attempts that have been made on his life. However, he is fearful of alerting the police because, if the news should leak out, it could ruin his financial empire.

Henry offers Jessica a million-dollar check to her favorite charity if she'll focus her prized detecting skills on this matter. While she refuses his financial proposition, she agrees to study the situation. Later that day, Reynard advises his family that he's made a new will. The news does not sit well with his mostly self-absorbed, mercenary family. They include his daughter Alice, his low-achieving son Jason, the latter's wife, Valery, and the apple of Henry's eye, his granddaughter, Kimberly.

A storm breaks over the island, and soon, the lights go out in the house. Thereafter, Henry is shot dead with a revolver. His relatives locate a copy of the new will and learn the bulk of Reynard's $50 million estate has been left to Mrs. Fletcher. During the night, Preston Howard, the boyfriend of shy Kimberly, is gunned down in the pool house.

With the powerboat disabled, everyone is stuck on the island, and it's up to Jessica to unmask the killer(s). Others on the premise include Dr. Hubbard Dabney, and thc domestics, Mr. and Mrs. Forrest.

Highlights: With its premise grounded in the tradition of *The Cat and the Canary* (1939) and *And Then There Were None* (1944), the virtue of this episode is the compact story line which confines the suspects to a self-contained arena. If the subordinate characters tend to be stereotypical, both Jessica Fletcher and the crafty Henry Reynard provide strong focal points. Employing a favorite device of the whodunit, the story line has a very surprising twist which is capped by a wry, philosophical finale.

Trivia: Gene Barry, who gained initial TV popularity in the Western *Bat Masterson* (1959–1961), enjoyed greater fame as dapper law enforcer Captain Amos Burke in *Burke's Law* (1963–1966). Like the subsequent *Murder, She Wrote,* one of the key gimmicks of *Burke's Law* was using a different array of show business veterans for each week's guest assignments. Barry revived *Burke's Law* in an unsuccessful new edition (1994–1995). Keir Dullea's acting reputation was built on *David and Lisa* (1962) and *2001: A Space Odyssey* (1968).

118. "Class Act"

(12/3/89) 60 mins.

Director: Allen Reisner **Teleplay:** Peter S. Fischer

Regular: Angela Lansbury (Jessica Fletcher/Narrator)

Guest Law Enforcers: Barry Newman (Lieutenant Amos Jason "Jake" Ballinger); Gerald S. O'Loughlin (Captain Joe Rawlings); Brett Stimely (Patrolman); Garry Walberg (Sam Kendall, at the Forensic Lab)

Guest Cast: William Brocktrup (Leo Gunderson); Robert Casper (Dean Howard Cogden); Robin Claire (Secretary); Holly Clark (Girl); Gloria Cromwell (Anna Gunderson); Vicki Lynne Davis (Grainger's Secretary); Christina Hart (Sister Maria); Grant Heslov (Bernie Berndlestein); Lise Hilboldt (Elizabeth Mills); Robert Lipton (Colin Hale); Heather McAdam (Jane Ballinger); Elinor O'Connell (Joanne Summerfield); Robert Pine (Senator Andrew Grainger); Hallie Todd (Moira McShane, Student Secretary)

The Settings: Los Angeles, California; Sacramento, California

The Case: Los Angeles police detective Lieutenant Jake Ballinger is convinced that the murder of a young woman was not committed by Leo Gunderson, who is now serving five to ten years for involuntary manslaughter. However, his supervisors order him, now six years away from retirement, to let matters lie. When he refuses, he is shunted off to teach a course at Los Angeles's Freemont University.

Undaunted by the demotion, Jake converts the few students who sign up for Criminology 240 to assist him on the stalled case. They are divorcee Elizabeth Mills, the assistant to a chief claim adjuster of a major insurance company, and geeky taxi driver Bernie Berndlestein, a would-be private eye.

New evidence is turned up by Jake's ingenious helpers, and with this ammunition, he questions anew the suspects in the case. They include Sacramento-based state senator Andrew Grainger, his aide, Colin Hale, as

Angela Lansbury as Jessica Fletcher.

Angela Lansbury and Arthur Hill (as her publisher and beau) in a romantic interlude from the segment, "The Murder of Sherlock Holmes" (1984).

Angela Lansbury and Claude Atkins (as Captain Ethan Cragg) wharf-side in Cabot Cove, Maine for the episode, "Deadly Lady" (1984).

Angela Lansbury as Jessica Fletcher.

Claude Atkins (as Captain Ethan Cragg) and Tom Bosley (as Sheriff Amos Tupper), two first season (1984-1985) regulars on *Murder, She Wrote.*

Robin Bach (in profile), Genie Francis (as niece Victoria Brandon) and Angela Lansbury in the San Francisco-set segment "Birds of a Feather" (1984).

Lynn Redgrave (as cousin Abbie Freestone) and Angela Lansbury ride to the hounds in the installment "It's a Dog's Life" (1984).

Angela Lansbury, June Allyson and Van Johnson banter in the "Hit, Run and Homicide" episode (1984).

Vivian Blaine and Angela Lansbury in the 1995 segment "Broadway Malady."

Bruce Jenner and Dick Butkus make a gridiron hero of Angela Lansbury on the set of the "Sudden Death" segment (1985).

Len Cariou (as British undercover operative Michael Haggerty), Cyd Charisse, Mel Ferrer, Angela Lansbury, Mary Wickes, John Phillip Law, Anne Lockhart and Howard Hesseman in the Caribbean resort-set "Widow Weep For Me" (1985).

Angela Lansbury teaching a creative writing class to prisoners in "Jessica Behind Bars" (1985).

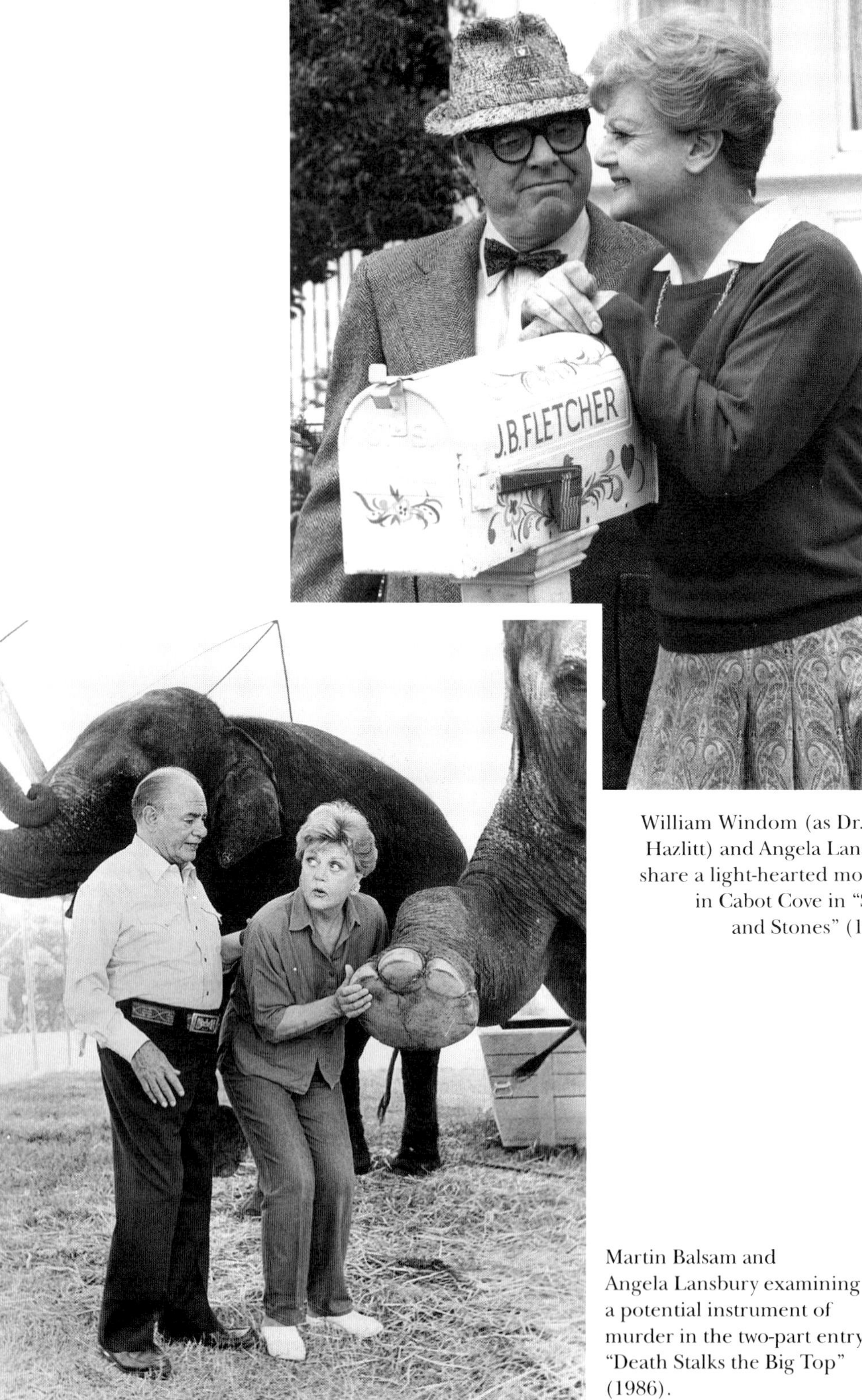

William Windom (as Dr. Seth Hazlitt) and Angela Lansbury share a light-hearted moment in Cabot Cove in "Sticks and Stones" (1985).

Martin Balsam and Angela Lansbury examining a potential instrument of murder in the two-part entry, "Death Stalks the Big Top" (1986).

Jerry Orbach (as Boston private eye Harry McGraw) and Angela Lansbury partner for "One Good Bid Deserves Another" (1986).

Angela Lansbury and Tom Selleck (as Honolulu private investigator Thomas Sullivan Magnum) share detecting honors and billing on the cross-over segment "Magnum on Ice" aired on *Magnum, P.I.* (1986).

Juliette Prowse and Angela Lansbury encounter homicide in chic Paris during "A Fashionable Way to Die" (1987).

Angela Lansbury (as her British cousin Emma Macgill) and Anthony Newley harmonize on the set of the "It Runs in the Family" segment (1986).

Eli Wallach (as a Napa Valley vintner) and Angela Lansbury dance away their cares in "A Very Good Year for Murder" (1988).

Angela Lansbury and Keith Michell (as soon-to-be-reformed jewel thief Dennis Stanton) have a close encounter in "A Little Night Work" (1988).

Angela Lansbury and Jean Peters ponder a bejeweled clue in "The Wearing of the Green" (1988).

Angela Lansbury and Richard Roundtree face tough facts in the episode "The Last Flight of the Dixie Damsel" (1988).

Debbie Zipp (as Donna Mayberry Fletcher), Michael Horton (as nephew Grady Fletcher) and Angela Lansbury at the belated wedding ceremony for "Something Borrowed, Someone Blue" (1989).

Ron Masak (as Sheriff Mort Metzger) and Angela Lansbury compare notes in the two-part episode "Mirror, Mirror on the Wall" (1989).

Angela Lansbury ponders the truthfulness of tale-spinner Len Cariou (as British secret agent Michael Haggerty) in "Appointment in Athens" (1989).

Angela Lansbury, Winifred Thayer (back row, far left) and the regulars down at the local beauty shop. Front row: Gloria De Haven (as travel agent Phyllis Grant), back row: Ruth Roman (as beautician Loretta Spiegel), Julie Adams (as realtor Eve Simpson) and Kathryn Grayson (as Ideal Malloy) in the Cabot Cove segment "Town Father" (1989).

Diane Baker, Angela Lansbury and Larry Wilcox deal with a holiday mystery in 1992's "A Christmas Secret."

Angela Lansbury as amateur crime-solver Jessica Fletcher.

well as the senator's playboy son who is a medical student at Freemont University.

Highlights: Typically, whenever Jessica Fletcher is not featured as the segment heroine, the installment lacks bite and depth. However, thanks to a deftly exploited plot premise, this hour is memorable. Barry Newman shines as the obsessed, rebellious lawman, a widower who finds romance during the course of his investigation.

Trivia: Robert Lipton had been featured in *The Survivors* (1969–1970). Heather MacAdam, playing Newman's waifish daughter here, later shined as Sela Ward's daughter, Cat Margolis, on *Sisters* (1991–1996). Hallie Todd, cast as the segment's bright student secretary, would return later in the season in the recurring role of Rhoda Markowitz, the smart office helper of Dennis Stanton.

119. "Town Father"

(12/17/89) 60 mins.

Director: John Llewellyn Moxey **Teleplay:** Philip Gerson

Regulars: Angela Lansbury (Jessica Fletcher); Ron Masak (Sheriff Mort Metzger); William Windom (Dr. Seth Hazlitt)

Recurring Characters: Julie Adams (Eve Simpson); Orson Bean (Ebeneezer McEnery); Gloria DeHaven (Phyllis Grant); Kathryn Grayson (Ideal Malloy); Sally Klein (Corinne, Helper at the Beauty Shop); Richard Paul (Mayor Sam Booth); Ruth Roman (Loretta Spiegel)

Guest Cast: John Considine (Horton Thayer); Phyllis Franklin (Mabel, the Mayor's Secretary); Basil Hoffman (Milton Overguard); William Lanteau (Howard); Courtney McWhinney (1st Lady); Sheila Pinkham (2nd Lady); Barbara Perry (Party Guest); Lee Purcell (Annie Mae Chapman); Holland Taylor (Winifred Thayer); Charlie Woolf (Fulton, the Store Man)

The Setting: Cabot Cove, Maine

The Case: Even in Cabot Cove, politics make strange bedfellows. Do-nothing Mayor Sam Booth is running for reelection against overzealous Milton Overguard. The race is especially tough because Overguard has the financial support of Jason Vernon, a wealthy New York City lawyer who has been paying hefty sums for Cabot Cove real estate.

In waging his electoral race, Booth hasn't counted on the arrival of young Annie Mae Chapman of Casper, Wyoming. She claims that Sam is the father of her five children, a result of his yearly vacations out west, but he won't marry her. Booth strongly denies the scandalous accusations. Nevertheless, he is in very hot water when Annie Mae is shot to death in her room at the nearby Paradise Motel.

To prove Sam's innocence, Jessica teams with Sheriff Mort Metzger and Dr. Seth Hazlitt, as well as Loretta Spiegel and the gossipy customers at her beauty shop. Others drawn into the case include the bickering Horton and Winifred Thayer, as well as ambitious real estate agent Eve Simpson.

Highlights: One of the joys of *Murder, She Wrote* is its ongoing revelations about the quirky citizens of Cabot Cove. Paralleling the murder investigation is an amusing depiction of hot-headed locals embroiled in self-importance when running for municipal office. Meanwhile, the often greedy townsfolk must balance whether quick profits from real estate deals are worth the dangers of Cabot Cove becoming overbuilt and urbanized.

Trivia: Vermont-born comedian Orson Bean, in the occasional role of cantankerous Ebeneezer McEnery (see #36), had been a permanent panelist on many 1950s and 1960s TV quiz shows.

120. "Good-Bye Charlie"

(1/7/90) 60 mins.

Director: Anthony Shaw **Teleplay:** Robert Van Scoyk

Regular: Angela Lansbury (Jessica Fletcher/Narrator)

Guest Law Enforcers: Robin Bach (Lon Ainsley, the Assistant Coroner); Bill Mayer (Sheriff Ed Ten Eyck); Clyde Kusatsu (Jack Imoto, the Coroner)

Guest Cast: Don Brunner (Lyle Coogan); Michael Callan (Buck Mahoney, Esq.); Bryan Cranston (Frank Albertson); Lise Cutter (Tillie Bascomb); John Finnegan (Man); Faith Ford (Sunny Albertson); Ronny Graham (Clarence Dobkin); Stanley Grover (Businessman); Elizabeth Holmes (Bimbo); David Huddleston (Charles Kenneth Albertson); Ernie Lively (Jake); Bill Maher (Man); Lisa Melilli (Marcia Mae Bailey); Scott Palmer (Raymond Fleischer, Esq.); Tessa Richards (Doreen Albertson)

The Settings: Hollywood, California; Huckabee, Nevada

The Case: Attorney Raymond Fleischer has interesting news for Frank Albertson. He informs the struggling Los Angeles private detective that a wealthy Detroit woman has left her entire estate to his Uncle Charlie, a former boyfriend of hers. The bad news for Frank and his wife, Sunny, is that their now-wealthy bachelor relative, who once lived with them for quite a spell, was last seen two years ago in Reno, Nevada.

Desperate for money, the Albertsons hatch a scheme to cash in on Charlie's inheritance. Since they are his only living relations, they must prove that the beneficiary is indeed dead. The ruse takes the inventive couple to Huckabee, Nevada, where an unidentified mangled body has been found on the railroad tracks. The Albertsons insist the deceased was Charlie.

The local sheriff finds the Albertsons' allegation intriguing because several others have already made counter claims as to whom the John Doe corpse was. They include shyster lawyer Buck Mahoney, who insists the dead party is the father of his client, Marcia Mae Bailey. (Once that is accepted, Buck intends to institute a large wrongful death suit against the railroad.) There is also Tillie Bascomb, who insists the corpse is that of her missing husband, Mort, an insomniac who frequently took nocturnal walks along the railroad tracks.

To prove whom the mysterious victim really is, the bewildered Albertsons turn amateur detectives.

Highlights: With its shaggy-dog-story approach, this lighthearted entry zips along at a fast clip. Whenever the facts appear to be clear-cut, a fresh development pushes the plot into new areas. With its neat story twists, this segment provides solid entertainment.

Trivia: Since the late 1950s, Michael Callan, a one-time dancer, had been appearing in mostly fluffy movie and TV assignments, including his sitcom *Occasional Wife* (1966–1967). In casting that foreshadowed her breakthrough role as TV newscaster Corky Sherwood Forrest on *Murphy Brown* (1988–), Faith Ford played her specialty, the perky but flighty blonde. Ronny Graham, as a jailbird here, was a regular on many TV series: *The New Bill Cosby Show, Chico and the Man,* etc.

121. "If the Shoe Fits"

(1/21/90) 60 mins.

Director: Anthony Shaw **Teleplay:** Lynne Kelsey

Regulars: Angela Lansbury (Jessica Fletcher); Ron Masak (Sheriff Mort Metzger); William Windom (Dr. Seth Hazlitt)

Recurring Character: Will Nye (Deputy Floyd)

Guest Cast: Jonathan Brandis (Kevin Bryce); Bruce Glover (Jack Franzen); Bridget Hanley (Gloria Franzen); John Harkins (Owen Brownwell); Season Hubley (Marla Bryce); Lorna Luft (Patsy Dumont); Kiel Martin (Danny Snow); Edwina Moore (Nurse); Paige Pengra (Lee McAdam); Teri Ralston (Lydia Johansen); Dane Winters (Post Office Clerk)

The Setting: Cabot Cove, Maine

The Case: Owen Brownwell, the owner of a local shoe factory, is having great difficulty meeting the steep monthly rent on his manufacturing building. His landlord is womanizing Jack Franzen, a married man who also owns the small house rented by Marla Bryce and her boy, Kevin. Marla works on the production line at Brownwell's shoe plant. She devotes her free time to searching for a better-paying job and fending off Franzen's sexual advances.

One day, Franzen disappears from town. Later, his body is found. His skull had been bashed in with a heavy object. The evidence of guilt points to Marla because the deceased had visited her house shortly before his death. When Sheriff Metzger jails the suspect, Jessica Fletcher takes young Kevin into her house while she searches for the actual killer.

Jessica questions Owen Brownwell and several shoe factory workers, including earthly Patsy Dumont and delivery man Danny Snow. Then there is the murder victim's chic widow Gloria, now freed from dealing with a cheating spouse. Meanwhile, temporary foster parent Mrs. Fletcher must contend with Lee McAdam, the social worker assigned to Kevin's case.

Highlights: Sexual harassment is a strong plot element in this segment. In another story angle, Jessica displays a strong maternal sense in dealing with troubled young Kevin. The situation also allows her to question the town's—and her own—complacent blindness to the financial plights of others (i.e., Marla Bryce).

Trivia: Season Hubley had a brief tenure (1976–1977) on *Family* and appeared in such features as *Lolly Madonna XXX* (1973) and *Escape from New York* (1981—with her then husband, actor Kurt Russell). Lorna Luft, the singer/actor daughter of Judy Garland, played nurse Libby Kegler on *Trapper John, M.D.* (1985–1986). Jonathan Brandis gained stature as a teenage heartthrob in *seaQuest DSV* (1993–1996).

122. "How to Make a Killing Without Really Trying"

(2/4/90) 60 mins.

Director: Walter Grauman **Story:** Charles Leineweber **Teleplay:** Robert E. Swanson

Regular: Angela Lansbury (Jessica Fletcher)

Guest Law Enforcers: Nigel Gibbs (Policeman); Rob Narita (Forensics Man); Kevin Tighe (Lieutenant Moynihan)

Guest Cast: Vinny Argiro (Superintendent); Tony Brafa (Gino); Morgan Brittany (Candice Ashcroft); Edd Byrnes (Sid Hooper); John Calvin (Philip Royce); Connie Danese (Receptionist); Farley Granger (Jerome Ashcroft); David Groh (Gordon Tully); Lela Ivey (Norma Pulaski); Joe Maruzzo (Rudy Bianco); Barry Van Dyke (Buddy Black, the Golf Pro)

The Setting: New York City

The Case: Jessica has been a longtime client of Ashcroft and Royce, a prestigious Manhattan stock brokerage firm. When she visits their offices she discovers that Norma Pulaski, the assistant of playboy Philip Royce, has been doing most of her boss's client work, including Jessica's. Later, Philip is found dead—his skull cracked by a golf club. Suddenly, Mrs. Fletcher finds herself engulfed in the investigation.

At odds with Lieutenant Moynihan, Jessica, nevertheless, pieces together the situation which involves $2 million missing from the dead man's office safe. It turns out that the lazy victim had been having an affair with Candice Ashcroft, the daughter of the firm's co-owner, Jerome Ashcroft, but had refused to marry her. In addition, he had been thinking of selling his share of the business, much to Jerome's consternation.

As Jessica musters the facts, she interacts with wealthy Gordon Tully, who had been hoping to purchase the brokerage firm and golf pro/hustler Buddy Black, who knew one too many of the deceased's secrets. Also caught up in the crime scene is hot-shot stock broker Sid Hooper.

Highlights: Not surprisingly, many *Murder, She Wrote* episodes feature female characters who are extremely competent in the business world, as here with Norma Pulaski. However, what was becoming a stronger motif on this series was the inclusion of a romantic subplot featuring the story line's young people. In this instance, it's Rudy Bianco who works for his family's bakery and loves Norma. Another familiar series trend is providing the guest police investigator-of-the-week an offbeat character trait to make the role more dimensional. Here, Lieutenant Moynihan, having been burned once by a bad stock investment, has automatic antipathy to anyone involved in the world of finance.

Trivia: Relatively early in his career, handsome Farley Granger had starred in two Alfred Hitchcock features: *Rope* (1948) and *Strangers on a Train* (1951). Morgan Brittany had been Katherine Wentworth on *Dallas* (1981–1984). Edd Byrnes's claim to trivia immortality was playing Kookie, the jive-talking parking lot attendant of TV's *77 Sunset Strip* (1958–1963). His character was forever combing his mop of hair and inspired the million-selling novelty song "Kookie, Kookie, Lend Me Your Comb."

123. "The Fixer-Upper"

(2/11/90) 60 mins.

Director: John Llewellyn Moxey **Story:** Paul Schiffer **Teleplay:** Oliver Hailey

Regular: Angela Lansbury (Jessica Fletcher)

Recurring Characters: Dean Butler (Howard Griffin); Genie Francis (Victoria Griffin)

Guest Law Enforcers: Chad Everett (Detective Lieutenant Redick); Murray Leaward (Police Doctor); Jonathan Palmer (Medical Examiner)

Guest Cast: R.J. Adams (Rent-a-Cop); Sally Champlin (Woman Client); Jode Winter (Deborah Tarkington); Mitchell Edmonds (Buyer); Vicki Frederick (Claire Hastings); Marty Ingels (Seymour Densch); Andrea King (Maid); George Maharis (Alex Burton); Ken Olandt (Kevin Tarkington); Dack Rambo (Arnold Hastings); Robert Rigamonti (Director); David Stenstrom (Husband); Carol Swarbrick (Wife); Brenda Vaccaro (Didi Blair)

The Setting: Los Angeles, California

The Case: In Los Angeles to promote her new book, Jessica Fletcher has a reunion with her niece, Victoria Griffin. The latter has relocated to Southern California with her husband, Howard, a struggling actor. Victoria is now in the real estate business, working with a high-powered mentor, Didi Blair.

Victoria's exclusive listing to sell Deborah Tarkington's Beverly Hills mansion is fast running out. Very much a novice, Victoria is quickly learning that the real estate game is quite ruthless. Her joy at the news that broker Arnold Hastings has a client who will meet Deborah's asking price is short-lived. When Deborah discovers that Hastings is working with Alec Burton, the crass entrepreneur who once dumped her, she vetoes the sale.

Later, Deborah turns up dead while Victoria is found by the authorities holding the murder weapon, a fireplace andiron. Jessica steps in to convince the law that her niece is innocent, especially when it's determined that the deceased had been drinking heavily and taking pills before her death.

Mrs. Fletcher's inquiries bring her to Kevin Tarkington, the deceased's pampered, sole offspring. In addition, there is Seymour Densch, who claims that Burton had asked him to buy Deborah's house, a fact that Alec hotly denies; as well as Claire, Arnold's castrating wife.

Highlights: This segment, with its focus on the glib barracuda of Didi Blair, provides an insightful, if satirical, depiction of the wheeler-dealer real estate game in Southern California when the marketplace was reaching a high point. It also reveals Jessica's skills as arbitrator for her niece and nephew who have yet to adjust fully to married life.

Trivia: As Buzz Murdock, George Maharis plied *Route 66* (1963–1966). After acting in such TV sitcoms as *I'm Dickens—He's Fenster* (1962–1963), Marty Ingels turned to talent brokering and married actress Shirley Jones, who later divorced him. Andrea King, as the victim's close-lipped maid, was a sharp Warner Bros. contract lead in the 1940s, often teamed on-screen with Helmut Dantine.

In this segment, Dean Butler replaced actor Jeff Conaway in the role of Victoria's husband, Howard Griffin.

124. "The Big Show of 1965"

(2/25/90) 60 mins.

Director: Jerry Jameson **Teleplay:** Robert Van Scoyk

Regular: Angela Lansbury (Jessica Fletcher)

Guest Law Enforcers: Michael Cole (Lieutenant John Meyerling); Sheldon Leonard (Retired Sergeant Bulldog Kowalski)

Guest Cast: Isabel Cooley (Head Nurse); Anne Francis (Lee Haley); Joy Garrett (Sharon King); Elaine Joyce (Cathy Haley); Gavin MacLeod (Art Sommers); Don(ny) Most (Ozzie Gerson); Donald O'Connor (Barry Barnes); John Rubinow (Joel Roth); Connie Stevens (Marge Haley); Kim Strauss (Richie King); Timothy Williams (Sid Lyman); Jeff Yagher (Scott Fielding)

The Setting: New York City

The Case: Scott Fielding, vice-president of Marketing and Development at Reynolds & Company, Publishers, talks to Jessica Fletcher about his late uncle, Richie King. Fielding details how this celebrity crooner died twenty-five years ago under bizarre circumstances and suggests that Mrs. Fletcher solve the old case and write a book about it.

Jessica visits the TV studio where Richie died decades ago. She meets big-time entertainer Barry Barnes, who is rehearsing a reunion special of acts with whom he had worked in 1965—the year King died. Among those recruited for the nostalgia outing are the singing Haley Sisters: Lee, Cathy and Marge. Lee is married to writer Art Sommers, a man she had once disliked. However, she had wed him two weeks after Richie's death, much to the dismay of her then boyfriend, Barry Barnes.

The rehearsals are fraught with problems, not the least of which is Marge's emotional instability. Later, the jittery Barnes suffers a heart attack, convinced he has seen a stalking woman veiled in black, the same specter that had haunted him back in 1965. Meanwhile, a new homicide occurs, and the suspects include two young writers, Sid Lyman and Joel Roth, with whom the dead man had just fought, and the TV show's music director, Ozzie Gerson.

Needing further background on the old case, Jessica turns to retired police detective Bulldog Kowalski, who has never abandoned hope of solving the baffling crime.

Highlights: Having a nostalgia musical revue within a sentimental segment adds an intriguing touch to this outing. So many familiar faces crop up that one is distracted from the heavy-handed whodunit structure, especially when Donald O'Connor or Sheldon Leonard are front and center.

Trivia: Concetta Rosalie Ann Ingolia, better known as Connie Stevens, got her big acting break as Cricket Blake on TV's *Hawaiian Eye* (1959–1963). Anne Francis, who began as a teen on TV in the late 1940s, had a starring television series in *Honey West* (1965–1966). Emmy Award-winning actor, producer and director Sheldon Leonard (1908–1997) excelled playing Damon Runyonesque characters on the big screen and made his fortune producing, among others, TV's *The Danny Thomas Show* and *I Spy*. Between ocean-going gigs in *McHale's Navy* (1962–1964) and *The Love Boat* (1977–1986), Gavin McLeod was big-hearted Murray Slaughter on *The Mary Tyler Moore Show* (1970–1977). Donald O'Connor, a trouper since infancy, enjoyed great popularity as the human partner of a talking mule in the Francis movie series (1949–1955), as well as a dancer and singer in many musicals, such as *Singin' in the Rain* (1952) and *Call Me Madam* (1953).

125. "Murder—According to Maggie"

(3/4/90) 60 mins.

Director: John Llewellyn Moxey **Teleplay:** Peter S. Fischer

Regular: Angela Lansbury (Jessica Fletcher/Narrator)

Guest Law Enforcers: Denis Arndt (Lieutenant Vincent Palermo); Paul Ganus (2nd Uniformed Cop); Myles O'Brien (1st Uniformed Cop)

Guest Cast: Talia Balsam (Julie Pritzer); Diana Canova (Margaret Mary McCauley); Miriam Flynn (Vi, the Secretary); Ann Morgan Guilbert (Harriet De Yol); Dwayne Hickman (Brian Thursdan); Vince Howard (Projectionist); Leann Hunley (Dana Darren); Bruce Kirby (Andy Butler); Paul Kreppel (Leo Kaplan); Greg Norberg (Phil Dooley); Gary Sandy (Keith

Carmody); Ben Slack ("Burnsie" [Burnsale]); Tim Thomerson (Bert Rodgers); Tom Troupe (Al, the Director)

The Setting: Los Angeles, California

The Case: Jessica relates the peculiar circumstances surrounding a homicide case set at a West Coast TV studio. It involves Margaret Mary McCauley, one of Jessica's former students. Maggie had become a TV writer whose series, *Beat Cop*, was a major hit. However, Keith Carmody, the new head of programming for the Federated Television Network, decrees that the popular program is to be canceled.

Carmody is persuaded to reevaluate his decision, but, while in the company's screening room viewing *Beat Cop* footage, he is shot dead. Few mourn his passing. Certainly not Julie Pritzer, who replaces the dead man at the network, nor Bert Rodgers, the series' ego-driven star. On the other hand, there is Rodgers' colead, Dana Darren, who was anxious to leave *Beat Cop* for a new series to be packaged by Leo Kaplan.

Meanwhile, with Lieutenant Vincent Palermo (on whom love-struck Maggie had fashioned her TV hero) nosing around the set, Brian Thursdan, president of the studio that produces *Beat Cop*, urges Maggie to solve the crime, so everything can return to "normal."

Highlights: As in other episodes that are set behind-the-scenes at a TV show, the Hollywood on Hollywood slant enhances this murder caper. While Diana Canova, the daughter of film, stage and radio comedian Judy Canova, provides a more active younger heroine than Angela Lansbury's Jessica Fletcher, the Maggie character lacks sufficient individuality to be memorable. This, perhaps, explains why this spin-off pilot did not sell as a new series.

Trivia: Ex-child actor Dwayne Hickman was a veteran of *The Bob Cummings Show* and *The Many Loves of Dobie Gillis*. Ann Morgan Guilbert, seen here as a major studio stockholder, played next-door-neighbor Millie Helper on the classic *The Dick Van Dyke Show* (1961–1966) and reemerged as Yetta, Fran Drescher's grandmother on *The Nanny* (1993–). Guilbert's actress daughter, Hallie Todd, would have the recurring role of Rhoda Markowitz, the San Francisco-based secretary of insurance investigator Dennis Stanton (played by Keith Michell), in later *Murder, She Wrote* installments. Talia Balsam is the daughter of actor Martin Balsam.

126. "O'Malley's Luck"

(3/25/90) 60 mins.

Director: Michael J. Lynch **Story:** Gerald K. Siegel **Teleplay:** Lynne Kelsey

Regular: Angela Lansbury (Jessica Fletcher/Narrator)

Guest Law Enforcers: Jay Acavone (Detective Sergeant Vinnie Grillo); Stacy Edwards (Officer Frances Xavier Rawley); Pat Hingle (Lieutenant James Ignatius O'Malley); Phillip Sterling (Captain Sam Cohen); Howard Schechter (Detective Rush)

Guest Cast: Brian Avery (Reporter); Ellen Barnett (Gretchen Trent); Pamela Bowen (Cindy Marsh); James Carroll Jordan (Paul G. Abbott); Ron Leibman (Roland Trent); Tiiu Leek (Reporter); Nicholas Pryor (David Kingston); Valerie Redding (Reporter); Francesca P. Roberts (Ruth, the Secretary); Carolyn Seymour (Alice Montrose); Steve Whiteford (Reporter)

The Setting: New York City

The Case: Now a major player in the police department, Lieutenant Jim O'Malley pulls strings to have Officer Frances Xavier Rawley, the daughter of his old partner, assigned to him as a special assistant. Together they work on a puzzling case involving Gretchen Trent. She had leaped to her death from the upper terrace of her husband's high-rise office building.

O'Malley has a hunch that the victim's spouse, Roland Trent, a wealthy real estate developer, knows far more than he is telling about the supposed suicide. The victim's personal assistant, Alice Montrose, recalls that Trent had stopped by the office the night of his wife's death to pick up his briefcase. Then there is a homeless person who had been sleeping in the alley near the building and never heard the jumper scream. Jim and Stacy also make note of Roland's new girlfriend, a very attractive part-time model.

Highlights: Buoyed by Pat Hingle's flavorful performance as an independent, old-fashioned police detective, the story is far more entertaining than the formula whodunit parameters might have allowed normally. If murder suspect Roland Trent is presented in too heavy handed fashion, the ingénue police investigator adds a light counterpart.

Trivia: Broadway and film actor Ron Leibman, the ex-husband of actress Linda Lavin, starred in the TV drama series *Koz* (1978–1979) and would later portray a megalomaniac media tycoon in *Central Park West* (a.k.a. *CPW*) (1995–1996). Pat Hingle played Chief Paulton on *Stone* (1980). Nicholas Pryor was Laurie Walters' boyfriend in later installments of *Eight Is Enough* (1977–1981) and was Jack Felspar on *The Bronx Zoo* (1987–1988).

127. "Always a Thief"

(4/8/90) 60 mins.

Director: Walter Grauman **Teleplay:** Peter S. Fischer

Regular: Angela Lansbury (Jessica Fletcher/Narrator)

Recurring Characters: Keith Michell (Dennis Stanton); James Sloyan (Robert Butler); Ken Swofford (Lieutenant Perry Catalano); Hallie Todd (Rhoda Markowitz, the Secretary)

Guest Cast: Ipale Aharon (Mahmoud Amini); E.E. Bell (Delivery Man); Lisa Blount (Andrea Bascomb Douglas); Roscoe Born (Lanny Douglas); Mitch Hara (Photographer); Virginia Hawkins (Phyllis, the Housekeeper); Jill Jaress (Deirdre); Shirley Knight (Grace Lambert); Marco Lopez (Pedro, the Gardener); Dina Merrill (Monica Douglas); Chris Mulkey (Joey Freeman); Ed Nelson (Ray Bascomb)

The Setting: San Francisco, California

The Case: Dennis Stanton, a reformed jewel thief, now works as an insurance claims adjuster for Consolidated Casualty in San Francisco. He mails his old friend Jessica Fletcher a tape about his latest adventure.

Events swirl around a valuable coin, an 1804 Gilbert Stuart silver dollar owned by Monica Douglas. Middle Eastern rug merchant Mahmoud Amini offers Lanny Douglas $200,000 if he will persuade his mother to sell the collectible. Lanny is intrigued, as his chain of Pepperport Cafe restaurants is not doing well. Moreover, Douglas is having great difficulty with his high-living wife, Andrea. Before long, two murders occur, including the death of Pedro, Monica's gardener.

Competing with gruff Lieutenant Perry Catalano to solve the dual homicides, Dennis mingles with several case suspects: Ray Bascomb, the overprotective father of Andrea; Joey Freeman, the victim's rather immoral business associate, and Grace Lambert, Monica's spinster sister.

Highlights: With Dennis Stanton launched as an ongoing lead figure on non-Jessica Fletcher episodes of *Murder, She Wrote,* he is showcased in his own special world. As a bay city bon vivant, he nimbly outwits his office boss, Robert Butler, at every turn, often abetted by Stanton's inventive secretary, Rhoda Markowitz.

By truly knowing how the criminal mind works, Dennis has an enormous advantage over the police. Moreover, being unorthodox, Stanton relies on his ingenuity to circumvent stumbling blocks, such as scaling the outer wall of a house to "drop in" on a suspect. On the other hand, he cannot resist flirting with a lead (such as Grace Lambert) whether or not it is relevant to his current case. In fairness, once one recovers from the disappointment of viewing installments not featuring bright and witty Jessica Fletcher, Dennis Stanton has a charming quality all his own.

Trivia: For the record, dapper Dennis, who favors a British-style golf visor cap, always carries an umbrella, which he uses as a multipurpose weapon.

Dina Merrill, formerly married to actor Cliff Robertson, is the daughter of millionairess Marjorie Merriweather Post. She began on TV in the mid-1950s, later featured as Estelle Modrian on *Hot Pursuit* (1984). Chris Mulkey played Hank Jennings on *Twin Peaks* (1990–1991). Among the features of Shirley Knight are *Dutchman* (1967), *Beyond the Poseidon Adventure* (1979) and *Hard Promises* (1991). Hallie Todd is the daughter of actress Ann Morgan Guilbert (next-door neighbor Millie Helper on *The Dick Van Dyke Show*).

128. "Shear Madness"

(4/29/90) 60 mins.

Director: Walter Grauman **Teleplay:** Chris Manheim

Regular: Angela Lansbury (Jessica Fletcher)

Guest Law Enforcers: Cody Glenn (Policeman); William Lucking (Sheriff Barnes)

Guest Cast: Barbara Babcock (Rosemary Taylor); Loren Blackwell (Professor Nathan Rollins); Daniel Bryan Cartmell (Bus Driver); Dennis Christopher (Dr. Henry Carlson); Ben Ryan Ganger (2nd Boy); Anne Marie Gillis (Mother); Joseph Gordon-Levitt (1st Boy); Linda Grovenor (Meg Taylor); Jon Huffman (Hearty Male); Shirley Jones (Ann Owens Arden); Yolanda Lloyd (Caterer); Sandy McPeak (Bill Spencer); Bryan O'Byrne (Reverend Simmons); Doris Roberts (Helen Owens); Freyda Thomas (Coquette); Robert Walker (George Owens)

The Setting: Fairville, Texas

The Case: Jessica Fletcher flies to the Lone Star state to attend the wedding of her cousin, Ann Owens. The latter has had very bad luck in the matrimonial arena. Her first husband died twenty-eight years ago in an accident. Fifteen years later, Ann had been engaged to remarry, but her fiancé had been murdered. Ann's brother, George, was charged with that crime. However, on an insanity plea he had been confined to a mental institution. Now he has been released and is heading home.

At a prewedding party, Ann's suitor, Bill Spencer (who had made his fortune in Alaska), is killed in the basement of the Owens' house. He is murdered with clipping shears just like Ann's intended had been fifteen years earlier.

There are several (potential) suspects wandering in and out of the Owens' house. They include the dazed George Owens, who has a memory gap covering the time that Spencer died; Helen Owens, who lives at the house but has felt herself an intruder once her sister announced her wedding plans; and Dr. Henry Carlson, the concerned psychiatrist who supervised George's treatment at the institution. Then, too, there is Rosemary Taylor, the owner of the *Fairville Gazette*, and her equally intrusive daughter, Meg.

Highlights: Veteran series director Walter Grauman intelligently uses special lighting (for menacing shadows) and sound effects (to suggest the thunderstorm) to create a marvelous mood of pending doom in the gloomy Owens house.

Trivia: Robert Walker (Jr.) is the son of actors Jennifer Jones and Robert Walker, the latter two having costarred in *Since You Went Away* (1944). Doris Roberts, who counts *The Honeymoon Killers* (1970) among her movie credits, won an Emmy Award for her guest role on a 1983 episode of *St. Elsewhere.* She also spent several seasons (1983–1987) as Mildred Krebs, the ex-IRS agent turned office manager on *Remington Steele.* Dennis Christopher's recent movies include *Doppelganger* (1992). Barbara Babcock's resume includes movies like *Heaven with a Gun* (1968), *Bang the Drum Slowly* (1973) and *The Lords of Discipline* (1981). Linda Grovenor played Jessica Fletcher's niece, Carol, in 1985's "Dead Heat" (#30).

129. "The Szechuan Dragon"

(5/6/90) 60 mins.

Director: Kevin G. Cremin **Teleplay:** Tom Sawyer

Regulars: Angela Lansbury (Jessica Fletcher); Ron Masak (Sheriff Mort Metzger); William Windom (Dr. Seth Hazlitt)

Recurring Characters: Michael Horton (Grady Fletcher); Will Nye (Deputy Floyd); Debbie Zipp (Donna Mayberry Fletcher)

Guest Cast: Belinda Bauer (Carla Thyssen); Ramon Bieri (Nick Zavakis); Bernie Coulson (Stanley Lewis); Elinor Donahue (Connie Lewis); Doug DuVal (Fred); James Lew (Cambodian); Cliff Osmond (Kris Karas); Gordon Ross (Captain Malachi); Maura Spencer-Reed (Phoebe); David Warner (Justin Hunnicut)

The Settings: Cabot Cove, Maine; New York City

The Case: While she is in England visiting cousin Emma Macgill, Jessica Fletcher's nephew, Grady, and his pregnant wife, Donna, house-sit in Cabot Cove. What is anticipated as a quiet retreat proves to be a wild nightmare.

It all starts when Captain Malachi disembarks from a ship at a Manhattan pier. He barely escapes from the gun-wielding Carla Thyssen, who is after a priceless, 400-year-old statuette from the Tang dynasty known as the Szechuan Dragon. Later, when the peg-legged seafarer heads for Cabot Cove, Carla and her confederate, the sinister Justin Hunnicut, follow him.

Days later, Malachi is found dead on the living room floor at Jessica's. Grady and Donna are as puzzled as Sheriff Mort Metzger as to how the intruder had a key to Mrs. Fletcher's front door. A letter written in Greek is found on the corpse. The sheriff asks a local, Nick Zavakis, to translate the contents, but the wordage makes no apparent sense.

As lying strangers and devious natives fight over the missing statuette, Metzger, aided by Grady and Donna, deals with additional participants: a sinister Cambodian; Jessica's next-door neighbor, Connie Lewis; and the latter's motorcycle-riding son, Stanley.

Highlights: In this entry, Jessica Fletcher literally phones in her appearances as she frequently contacts Grady and only belatedly gets a sense of the chaos transpiring at home during her absence. With its homage to *The Maltese Falcon* (1941), the narrative benefits from the low-keyed presence of Grady and his zany wife, Donna, as well as from Dr. Seth Hazlitt's frequent, sly observations.

Trivia: This proved to be the final series appearance of the Donna Fletcher character, although Grady Fletcher—after a long absence—would return to *Murder, She Wrote* for the 1995 segment "The Dream Team" (#235). Former child actress Elinor Donahue is best remembered for playing the older daughter of Robert Young and Jane Wyatt on *Father Knows Best* (1954–1960). David Warner, who had handled classical roles in his native England, developed a Hollywood screen specialty of villainy: *Time After Time* (1979), *The Island* (1980), *Tryst* (1994), etc.

130. "The Sicilian Encounter"

(5/20/90) 60 mins.

Director: Kevin G. Cremin **Teleplay:** Robert E. Swanson

Regular: Angela Lansbury (Jessica Fletcher/Narrator)

Recurring Character: Len Cariou (Michael Haggerty)

Guest Law Enforcer: John Standing (Chief Daniel Trent)

Guest Cast: Daniel Douglas Anderson (Korstrack); Vincent Baggetta (Antonio); Marianne Bergonzi (Woman); Joseph Cali (Priest); Anthony DeFonte (Tailor); Ralph DeLia (Pilot); George DiCenzo (Mario Carboni); James Garrett (Llewelyn); Deidre Hall (Claudia Carboni [Jennifer Page]); Ralph Manza (Father Anselmo); Gina Minervini (Maid); Robert Miranda (Gino Carboni); Jovin Montanaro (Bellman); Steve Nataloe (Waiter); Ian Ogilvy (Peter Baines); Stephen Poletti (Bank Clerk); Daniel Trent (Barton)

The Settings: Geneva, Switzerland; Palermo, Sicily

The Case: Returning to Cabot Cove from publisher meetings, Jessica Fletcher reads a letter from her friend Michael Haggerty in which he recounts his latest counter-espionage exploit.

The recently widowed Claudia Carboni has flown from Boston to Sicily to pay respects to her late husband's hot-blooded family. She is traveling with Britisher Peter Baines, a charming fortune hunter, whom she intends to marry. Unknown to Claudia, she is being trailed by an Englishman who is connected to the British M16 secret service. When this spy is murdered by Mario Carboni's thugs, Michael Haggerty steps into the action. Disguised as the Boston clergyman who is to officiate at Claudia's wedding, he arranges a daring escape which leads her, Baines and Haggerty on a wild trek to Geneva. Meanwhile, another intruder, who claims to be Gino Carboni, is greeted in a most unfriendly way by his Sicilian hosts.

Once in Geneva, the madcap cat-and-mouse game focuses on a sought-after black book filled with information about the mob organization recently headed by Claudia's late husband in America. As rival CIA and M16 agents draw the underworld figures into their net, the stakes change from moment to moment, depending on who has possession of the prized notebook.

Highlights: From scene to scene, this episode switches from mock serious gangster antics to zany James Bond-style escapades. Played with tongue-in-cheek panache, the story pulsates at a merry pace, evolving into a three-way competition between charming Michael Haggerty, resourceful Claudia and materialistic Peter Baines.

Trivia: A graduate of daytime soap operas *(The Young and the Restless, Days of Our Lives)*, Deidre Hall later starred in *Our House* (1986–1988). In this, the closing episode of the 1989–1990 *Murder, She Wrote,* season, Britisher Ian Ogilvy plays the brother of Harold Baines, a character Ogilvy had portrayed in "Appointment in Athens" (#109), the sixth season's opening installment. Character actor George DiCenzo had contrasting ongoing roles as Lieutenant Edward DeNisco on *McClain's Law* (1981–1982) and Charles the butler on *Dynasty* (1984–1985).

SEASON SEVEN

1990–1991

131. "Trials and Tribulations"

(9/16/90) 60 mins.

Director: Vincent McEveety **Teleplay:** Peter S. Fischer

Regular: Angela Lansbury (Jessica Fletcher)

Guest Law Enforcers: Richard Camphius (Prison Guard #2); Stephen Furst (Sergeant Paulsen); Vincent McEveety (Prison Guard #1); Lance E. Nichols (Policeman)

Guest Cast: Michael Beck (Justin Fields); Molly Cheek (Anne Stevenson, Esq.); Carrie Hamilton (Geraldine Stone); George Hearn (Elliott Von Steuben); Richard Hoyt-Miller (Fred, the 1st Waiter); Kim Hunter (Beatrice Vitello); Darlene Kardon (Mrs. Torgeson); Thom Keane (3rd Waiter); George Maharis (Charlie Cosmo, Esq.); Ben Masters (Ray Dandridge); Molly McClure (Hestor, the Process Server); Joe Nesnow (Cab Driver); Gerry Okuneff (Eddie Stone); Mary Angela Shea (Secretary); Ron Tron (Driver); Jerry Tullos (2nd Waiter)

The Settings: New York City; New York state

The Case: Six years ago, Jessica Fletcher assisted the authorities in a murder investigation which led to Eddie Stone's arrest and conviction. Recently, that convict has died while attempting a prison break. Now, in Manhattan, his daughter, Geraldine, has filed a $50 million wrongful death suit, naming Jessica Fletcher and others as defendants. Ray Dandridge, an executive with the insurance company drawn into the liability case, suggests Mrs. Fletcher settle out of court. She refuses to yield so easily.

Taking matters into her own hands, Jessica gains the cooperation of Sergeant Paulsen, whose late partner had worked on the long-ago case.

One of their first targets is Charlie Cosmo, Geraldine's shyster lawyer, who won't put them in touch with Angelo Vitello, the taxi driver witness in the old case who now claims that Jessica bribed him with $5,000 to doctor his testimony at Stone's trial. Mrs. Fletcher visits the Vitellos where the man's forlorn wife, Beatrice, confides that her husband is deathly ill. Later, a diabetic attack triggers Angelo's death (or murder) and a resentful Beatrice becomes strangely silent.

Others caught in the tightening web are Justin Fields, Geraldine's overly ambitious pastry chef boyfriend, and Elliott Von Steuben, Justin's demanding restaurant employer. There is also Anne Stevenson of the District Attorney's office who prosecuted the original case and can't let go now, as well as the troubled Geraldine herself.

Highlights: Seldom has a Jessica Fletcher adventure been populated with so many grasping parties. Drawn into the morass as a suspect, Jessica is even forced to parade through a police line-up!

Of special interest in the appealing characterization of Sergeant Paulsen, a good-hearted soul whose wife has left him, who has been passed over for promotions three times and, now in total frustration, has eaten his way into bulkdom.

Trivia: Kim Hunter, an Academy Award winner for *A Streetcar Named Desire* (1951), had been blacklisted in Hollywood during the 1950s Senator McCarthy Communist witch hunt. She authored a most unique autobiography, *Loose in the Kitchen* (1975), one combined with a cookbook. Portly Stephen Furst, a graduate of TV's *Delta House* had played Dr. Elliot Axelrod on *St. Elsewhere* (1983–1988). Utility leading man Ben Masters had been a member of TV's *Heartbeat* (1988), while Michael Beck had costarred in *Houston Knights* (1987–1988).

Frequent *Murder, She Wrote* director, Vincent McEveety, appears in this episode briefly as a prison guard.

132. "Deadly Misunderstanding"

(9/23/90) 60 mins.

Director: Anthony Shaw **Teleplay:** Robert E. Swanson

Regulars: Angela Lansbury (Jessica Fletcher); Ron Masak (Sheriff Mort Metzger)

Recurring Characters: Joe Dorsey (Bennett J. Devlin); Will Nye (Deputy Floyd)

Guest Cast: David Chrisman (Young Intellectual in Writing Class); Lise Cutter (Melissa Maddox); Geoffrey Lewis (Hank Crenshaw); Janet Margolin (Rita Garrison); David McCallum (Drew Garrison); David Oliver (Jeff Ogden); Mary Ann Pascal (Trudy, the Waitress); Cliff Potts (Ralph Maddox); Bette Rae (Earnest Grandmother in Writing Class); Robina Suwol (Coffee Shop Patron)

The Setting: Cabot Cove, Maine

The Case: Bennett J. Devlin is the new editor of the *Cabot Cove Gazette,* with earnest Jeff Ogden as his young helper. Jeff is infatuated with flirtatious Melissa Maddox. She is unhappy being wed to meat-and-potatoes Ralph, who is overly consumed with his construction business. In turn, Ralph is tempted by Trudy, a pert waitress at the local coffee shop. Meanwhile, the bored Melissa and Jeff take a local creative writing class taught by Drew Garrison.

With her broken arm (from an accident) in a cast, Jessica has hired Melissa to type her latest murder mystery manuscript. Later, when Melissa's husband is found stabbed to death at the lumberyard, Jessica feels compelled to help her bewildered typist. Before long, sensitive Jeff is accused of homicide, while Mrs. Fletcher wonders why Drew Garrison, married to Rita, has burned Melissa's short story, "Daggers of Love." There is also vengeful Hank Crenshaw, the former coffee shop cook, who had a strong grudge against the victim.

Highlights: The introduction of intellectual Ben Devlin, a Pulitzer Prize-winning journalist from Washington, D.C., provides Jessica with a potential new suitor. However, self-sufficient Mrs. Fletcher finds the newcomer far too blunt, while he has grave problems adjusting to small-town life and to Jessica's no-nonsense attitude, especially about her privacy. Throughout this episode, the two "adversaries" spar, each setting strict limits to their platonic acquaintanceship. As the tale progresses, he develops an appreciation for Mrs. Fletcher's fact-gathering skills.

Trivia: Janet Margolin, whose screen credits included *David and Lisa* (1962), had been a costar of TV's *Lanigan's Rabbi* (1977). At the time of her death (1993) she was married to actor Ted Wass of *Blossom* (1991–1995). Cliff Potts had been featured on such television series as *Once an Eagle, Lou Grant* and *For Love and Honor.*

William Windom was on sabbatical from *Murder, She Wrote* to handle a recurring featured role on the TV series *Parenthood.* When that sitcom quickly failed in the fall of 1990, his character—explained to have been away on vacation—returned to *Murder, She Wrote* as of episode #141, "Family Doctor."

133. "See You in Court, Baby"

(9/30/90) 60 mins.

Director: Vincent McEveety **Teleplay:** Peter S. Fischer

Regular: Angela Lansbury (Jessica Fletcher/Narrator)

Recurring Characters: Keith Michell (Dennis Stanton); Ken Swofford (Lieutenant Perry Catalano); Hallie Todd (Rhoda Markowitz, the Secretary)

Guest Law Enforcer: Alexander Folk (Desk Sergeant)

Guest Cast: Victoria Boa (Joyce); Heidi Bohay (Amy Sue Kriegler); Judith Chapman (Karen Davies); Charles Haid (Joe Briscoe); Christopher Halsted (Ernie, the Waiter); Tom Isbell (Ed Kriegler); Peter Kowanko (Johnny Trixler [Jason Thompson]); Ed McCready (Guard); Vera Miles (Charmaine Thompson); Robert Reed (Truman Calloway, Esq.); Nana Visitor (Marcia McPhee)

The Setting: San Francisco, California

The Case: Boiling mad at his ex-wife, Amy Sue, wealthy Ed Kriegler steals back the expensive red sports car she gained in the divorce settlement. He shoves the vehicle over a cliff. Thereafter, Amy Sue's barracuda divorce lawyer, Truman Calloway, goes into action against Ed. Meanwhile, claims investigator Dennis Stanton is investigating his insurance company's potential liability in the matter.

Stanton is unwillingly drawn into a murder case when Calloway is found dead in his office, having been stabbed with a letter opener. Ed is the prime suspect, having been spotted at the scene of the crime. The jailed Kriegler advises Stanton that he won't sign a waiver statement releasing the insurance firm from liability on the car until Dennis helps to clear him of the homicide charge.

Dennis uncovers that the much-married victim had recently seen his first ex-wife, Charmaine Thompson, who tried to persuade well-heeled Calloway to pay the medical school tuition of their illegitimate son, Jason. The lawyer had refused any such assistance.

From Truman's longtime secretary, Karen Davies, Dennis learns that the victim had lately been threatened by Joe Briscoe, a former cop turned lawyer, who was to be Calloway's adversary in an upcoming high-profile case. Also part of the scene is Johnny Trixler, who was angered at the huge percentage fee Truman demanded to handle the young man's divorce from his ultra-wealthy spouse.

Highlights: One of the treats in *Murder, She Wrote* is the ingenuity with which the scripters continually find fresh plot ploys to involve Jessica Fletcher in the hunt for a murderer. For some reason, the gimmick works less well with the Dennis Stanton character. While he has charm, he, unlike

Jessica, has an unsavory past criminal record and is known to be deceitful with anyone, if it will lead him to his crime-solving goal. Thus, when Stanton is harassed by Lieutenant Catalano for interfering in police business and/or seeming to be the killer culprit, it's a logical reaction. As such, no real camaraderie can develop between two such disparate crime fighters.

Trivia: Vera Miles, a one-time protegée of director Alfred Hitchcock in *The Wrong Man* (1957) and *Psycho* (1960), has chalked up a huge volume of TV credits, but no ongoing series roles. While playing Rhoda Markowitz, Dennis Stanton's secretary, Hallie Todd was also handling a colead in the sitcom *Going Places* (1990–1991). Nana Visitor was later to have a starring role as Major Kira Nerys in the science fiction TV series *Star Trek: Deep Space Nine* (1993-).

134. "Hannigan's Wake"

(10/28/90) 60 mins.

Director: Vincent McEveety **Teleplay:** Peter S. Fischer

Regular: Angela Lansbury (Jessica Fletcher)

Guest Law Enforcers: Bradford Dillman (Bradley Folkes, Deputy Commissioner of Police); Guy Stockwell (Retired Detective Bert Kravitz)

Guest Cast: Emory Bass (Jonathan Barish, the Mortician); Kate Randolph Burns (Madge); La Reine Chabut (Madeline); Johnny Crear (Victor Impelleteri); Anthony Geary (Eric Grant); Cynthia Harris (Phyllis Thurlow); Van Johnson (Daniel Hannigan); Mala Powers (Dorothy Folkes); Raphael Sbarge (Stephen Thurlow); Isaac Turner (Eddie Folkes); Stephen Young (Ernie Dolan); Efrem Zimbalist, Jr. (Richard Thompson Grant)

The Settings: Cabot Cove, Maine; Philadelphia, Pennsylvania

The Case: When Pulitzer Prize-winning author Daniel Hannigan dies, Jessica Fletcher rushes to Philadelphia to attend the wake. Some time earlier, the wheelchair-bound Daniel had been digging into a sixteen-year-old murder case, prompted by Phyllis Thurlow. The latter had insisted to Daniel that her brother, Martin, who was sent to prison for allegedly killing his wife, was not guilty. Before he passed away, Hannigan had also become convinced of Martin's innocence, deducing that the victim's brother, Eric, was the guilty party. But Eric had been protected by his powerful, rich father, Richard Grant.

With Hannigan gone, Phyllis urges Jessica to pick up the threads of Daniel's research. Mrs. Fletcher agrees reluctantly, half-convinced that

Daniel had lost the power of objectivity in his final years. She is assisted by small restaurant owner Bert Kravitz, a former cop who had been briefly part of the original homicide investigation. Jessica receives less help from Bradley Folkes, the deputy commissioner of police. He claims to be fearful of upsetting the politically potent Grant. Unmindful of Grant's threats or an attempt made on her life, Jessica forces a confrontation with Grant's playboy son, Eric, who once had a bad drug problem.

Highlights: Talk about an actor lying down on the job. Van Johnson's Daniel Hannigan, except for a few flashback sequences, is mostly seen lying at rest in his coffin, while a joyful wake is conducted around him.

Trivia: Once a contract leading lady at Universal Pictures in the 1950s, Mala Powers had gone on to such TV series as *Hazel* and *The Man and the City.* Emmy Award-winning Bradford Dillman had starred in several teleseries: *Court-Martial, King's Crossing* and *Falcon Crest.* Guy Stockwell, the older brother of actor Dean Stockwell, had participated in the 1960s TV fare *Adventures in Paradise* and *The Richard Boone Show.* This segment was the third *Murder, She Wrote* appearance for ex-MGM star Van Johnson. Efrem Zimbalist, Jr., son of a concert violinist and an opera singer mother (Alma Gluck), is the father of actress Stephanie Zimbalist. This was his second *Murder, She Wrote* appearance.

135. "The Family Jewels"

(11/4/90) 60 mins.

Director: Jerry Jameson **Teleplay:** Tom Sawyer

Regular: Angela Lansbury (Jessica Fletcher)

Guest Law Enforcer: Charles Rocket (Lieutenant Stuyvesant)

Guest Cast: Joey Aresco (Rocco Pastolino); Deborah Benson (Barbara Loring); John Considine (Porter Finley, III); Richard Davalos (Man); Mike Farrell (Drew Borden); Marcy Goldman (2nd Reporter); Michael Halpin (Technician); Stanley Kamel (Sid Staples); Jonna Lee (Margaret Gable); Diana Lewis (TV Newscaster); Howard McGillin (Charles Lockner, Jewelry Shop Clerk); Doug Mears (Arthur Morris); Pamela Roylance (Olivia); Brenda Vaccaro (Sheila Kowalski Finley); Forrest Witt (1st Reporter)

The Settings: New York City; Westchester County, New York

The Case: Down-to-earth Jessica Fletcher rediscovers that the rich live by far different rules than the rest of humanity. Wealthy Sheila Finley shoplifts an expensive piece of jewelry from Beaumont's in plain sight of

Mrs. Fletcher. However, the exclusive Manhattan store merely adds the charge to her husband's monthly bill. It also turns out that Sheila is having an affair with her chauffeur, Rocco Pastolino, but Porter Finley, III, blithely turns the other cheek.

When Jessica attends a fund-raising charity event in suburban New York, her hosts are none other than the Finleys. Things get more surprising when the chauffeur is found dead in the estate garage and Sheila is singled out as a major suspect. However, by now, Jessica has come to like this frank and colorful woman. The latter tells Mrs. Fletcher of her impoverished upbringing, her intriguing later years, and how she came to be worth $40 million.

In short order, Jessica realizes that overly deferential Lieutenant Stuyvesant isn't going to be much help. Thus, she must piece together the information that the murder victim was Sheila's high school boyfriend whom Porter had hired a while ago as a surprise for his wife. Another questionable party is Margaret Gable, the pretty young maid who had planned to leave for South America with the driver. Adding to the puzzle is a masked man who steals into Sheila's bedroom one night and chloroforms her.

Highlights: There are few more engaging moments in a *Murder, She Wrote* story than those occasions when Jessica knows something to be true but cannot convince others of it. Such is the attraction of the opening sequence here. It foreshadows that few situations or individuals in this tale can be taken at face value. Most unexpected is the appeal of Sheila Finley, who accepts that her fortune is her best drawing card and who dismisses her one "harmless" vice—kleptomania. Thanks to high-energy Brenda Vaccaro, the character comes winningly alive.

Trivia: Richard Davalos, whose film acting credits date back to the mid-1950s, was part of TV's *The Americans* (1960). Brenda Vaccaro won an Emmy Award for Best Supporting Actress in a Variety Program for *The Shape of Things* (1974). Mike Farrell was a veteran of such TV fare as *Days of Our Lives* (1968–1970), *The Interns* (1970–1971) and, most notably, *M*A*S*H* (1975–1983).

136. "A Body to Die For"

(11/11/90) 60 mins.

Director: Anthony Shaw **Teleplay:** Donald Ross

Regulars: Angela Lansbury (Jessica Fletcher); Ron Masak (Sheriff Mort Metzger)

Recurring Characters: Julie Adams (Eve Simpson); Joe Dorsey (Ben Devlin); Will Nye (Deputy Floyd)

Guest Cast: Jason Beghe (Wayne Bennett); Michele Bernath (Woman); Katharine Durish (Receptionist); Ruta Lee (Renee); Ernie Lively (Joe Hardin); Paul Lueken (Paramedic); Patricia McPherson (Betty Bennett); Hugh O'Brian (Fred Keppard); James Olson (Clarence LaRue); Sally Struthers (Nancy LaRue)

The Setting: Cabot Cove, Maine

The Case: The women of Cabot Cove have found a new diversion, taking physical education at Wayne Bennett's local gym. Among the strongest devotees are real estate agent Eve Simpson and fitness-conscious Renee. Another exerciser is Nancy LaRue, the pudgy wife of druggist Clarence, who owns LaRue's Pharmacy.

Meanwhile, Eve is excited that Fred Keppard, a charming widower from Boston, intends to purchase an expensive piece of property in the vicinity. However, the deal turns sour when Keppard is found dead in Eve's home. Jessica not only invites the distraught Eve to stay at her place, but she assists Sheriff Metzger in resolving the killing.

In the process, Jessica discovers that more than one person in town is a con artist using assorted aliases. There are several open questions: why Joe Hardin broke into Wayne's gym, why a certain young woman is reluctant to admit her special relationship to Wayne and why Nancy LaRue's hasty out-of-town visit to a sick sister should so interest her husband.

Highlights: This episode delights in exposing the lust and envy created among the Cabot Cove women when muscular Wayne opens his gym. Everyone in town has a different reaction, including well-padded Sheriff Mort Metzger, who decides to embark—albeit briefly—on a fitness regimen himself.

Trivia: This episode marked the second of three appearances of Joe Dorsey as newspaperman Ben Devlin. Hugh O'Brian had been the gun-wielding lead of *The Life and Legend of Wyatt Earp* (1955-1961). In her thinner days, Sally Struthers had played Gloria Bunker Stivic, Carroll O'Connor's shrill daughter in *All in the Family* (1971–1978) as well as in the short-lasting spin-off, *Gloria* (1982–1983); and, more recently, she has appeared in TV commercials for *Save The Children.*

137. "The Return of Preston Giles"

(11/18/90) 60 mins.

Director: Walter Grauman **Teleplay:** Tom Sawyer

Regular: Angela Lansbury (Jessica Fletcher)

Recurring Character: Arthur Hill (Preston Giles)

Guest Law Enforcer: Todd Sussman (Detective Sergeant Jack Slocum)

Guest Cast: Lois Chiles (Millie Bingham Stafford); George Coe (Martin Bergman); Steven Connor (Assistant Manager); Michael Eugene Fairman (Cabby); Arlene Golonka (Gloria Winslow); Regina Leeds (Dorothy); Michael McKean (Ross McKay); Brynn Thayer (Linette McKay); Gordon Thomson (Kendall Stafford); Kriss Turner (Secretary)

The Setting: New York City

The Case: Hoping to revive failing Sutton Place Publishers, corporate raider Ross McKay pulls strings to have Preston Giles paroled from prison where he is serving a long sentence on a murder charge. As payback, Preston is ordered to woo best-selling mystery writer Jessica Fletcher back into the fold as a Sutton Place author. The big problem, of course, is that it was Jessica's sleuthing that put Preston—her first publisher and a romantic interest—behind bars a few years back.

Understandably leery of Giles, Jessica is supportive of the nearly broken man. However, all her past memories of betrayal rise again when Sutton Place's comptroller, Martin Bergman, is found dead at work and Giles is accused of the new homicide. Preston had a long-standing grudge against the devious executive and he had been at the office the night the victim was killed.

Jessica works through her misgivings in order to follow up those clues that seem unimportant to Detective Sergeant Jack Slocum. There is the matter of McKay's wife, Linette, a Wall Street investment banker. She is having an affair with fellow worker Kendall Stafford, whose wife, Millie, is the daughter of the firm's cofounder. Mrs. Fletcher's attention is also directed to glib Ross, who found it imperative to break into the crime scene after the murder.

Highlights: Picking up the story threads of the series' debut segment in September 1984, this follow-up uses clips from that two-hour premiere for flashbacks. As depicted, since Preston and Jessica first met, their positions have reversed. Now she is a well-to-do success and an international celebrity to boot. In the years since they romanced, she has become far better adjusted to her single life as a widow and no longer is easily captivated by a handsome, debonair suitor. These realizations provide a bittersweet tone to the whodunit at hand.

Trivia: In the years since he first performed on *Murder, She Wrote*, seasoned actor Arthur Hill had costarred in the TV series *Glitter* (1984–1985). In a far different characterization from here, Michael McKean had created an indelible impression with TV watchers for his eccentric blue collar worker

Lenny Kosnawski on *Laverne & Shirley* (1976–1983). Brynn Thayer has earned solid acting exposure as the attorney daughter of Andy Griffith's *Matlock* in its early 1990s revamped format. Todd Sussman, herein one of Jessica Fletcher's more adamant police detective non-supporters, had been a team member of TV's *The Bob Crane's Show, Spencer's Pilots* and *Goodnight, Beantown.*

138. "The Great Twain Robbery"

(11/25/90) 60 mins.

Director: Jerry Jameson **Teleplay:** Steve Brown

Regular: Angela Lansbury (Jessica Fletcher/Narrator)

Recurring Characters: Keith Michell (Dennis Stanton); James Sloyan (Robert Butler); Ken Swofford (Lieutenant Perry Catalano); Hallie Todd (Rhoda Markowitz, the Secretary)

Guest Law Enforcer: Stephen Prutting (Sergeant Oliver)

Guest Cast: Diane Baker (Anna Louise Barlow); David Birney (Lawrence Erlich); Lewis Dauber (Duke of Nonesuch); Freddie Dawson (1st Reporter); Roy Dotrice (Professor Chandler Fitzpatrick); Holly Gagnier (Lindsey Barlow); Jan Hoag (Book Lover); Russ Marin (Authenticator); Delana Michaels (2nd Reporter); Daniel Namath (Maitre d'); Nehemiah Persoff (Constantin Stavros); Susan Ware (Newscaster)

The Setting: San Francisco, California

The Case: Jessica Fletcher's latest mystery novel features gentleman thief Damian Sinclair. Besides having the same initials as Dennis Stanton, the character bears a close resemblance to her friend. The latter is still based in the bay city as an insurance claims investigator. As he tells book-touring Jessica over dinner in Carmel, California, he's had quite a time with his latest case. In fact, it caused him to be temporarily fired.

A former con artist associate, Lawrence Erlich, comes to Dennis at Consolidated Casualty Insurance Company, wanting to heavily insure a rare literary manuscript. The property is the long "missing" *The Wild and Wicked Wench,* attributed to Mark Twain. Stanton is rightly suspicious of Erlich, once considered a master forger. When the manuscript is supposedly totally destroyed in a fire, Dennis must determine whether there is any way in which his firm can avoid paying the $5 million claim.

Before long, homicide is a new ingredient in the case. Constantin Stavros, the authenticator Dennis had earlier hired to confirm or deny the manuscript's legitimacy, is murdered, before he can tell Dennis how he thought the book had been faked. Meanwhile, Dennis deals with Anna Barlow, the owner of the "Twain" work, and her daughter, Lindsey, a rebellious young adult. There is also Professor Chandler Fitzpatrick, who initially staked his reputation on the manuscript being genuine.

Highlights: Urbane and artful Dennis Stanton is in his element matching wits and skills with the likes of devious Lawrence Erlich, who once had a strong attraction for Dennis's wife, Elizabeth, now deceased. Also, a nice rapport develops between Stanton and his hard-working secretary, Rhoda Markowitz, a resourceful woman more loyal to her boss than to company policy.

Trivia: Diane Baker began her Hollywood film career in the late 1950s as a Twentieth Century-Fox contract player *(The Best of Everything, Journey to the Centre of the Earth,* etc.). She later starred in the sitcom *Here We Go Again* (1973). British stage actor Roy Dotrice made a specialty of playing senile old men on-camera *(Amadeus, The Lounge People,* etc.). Credits for Israeli-born Nehemiah Persoff include *On the Waterfront* (1954), *Fate Is the Hunter* (1964), *Voyage of the Damned* (1976) and as an off-camera voice in the animated feature *An American Tail: Fievel Goes West* (1991).

139. "Ballad for a Blue Lady"

(12/2/90) 60 mins.

Director: Jerry Jameson **Teleplay:** William Bigelow

Regular: Angela Lansbury (Jessica Fletcher)

Guest Law Enforcers: Brandon Maggart (Lieutenant Jackson); Cary Pitts (Guard); Bob Swain (Forensic Man)

Guest Cast: Daphne Ashbrook (Alice Diamond); Jimmy Dean (Bobby Diamond); John Christy Ewing (Dr. Benson); Jeri Gaile (Brittany Brown); Blake Gibbons (Garth); Mickey Gilley (Conrad Booker); Gary Grubbs (Mark Berringer); Tom Hallick (Preston Wardell); Florence Henderson (Patti Sue Diamond); Marji Martin (Mirabelle); Sheb Wooley (Billy Ray Hawkins)

The Setting: Nashville, Tennessee

The Case: It's been a decade since Jessica has seen her longtime friend, Patti Sue Diamond, a veteran country music star. Mrs. Fletcher flies to Nashville for a reunion, and discovers that Patti Sue is stuck in a troublesome domestic situation. Her husband, Bobby, is having problems at his record label Blue Lady and is having an affair with a young singer, Brittany

Brown. Meanwhile, Patti Sue and her stepdaughter, Alice, who also works at the record firm, are constantly bickering.

When Bobby Diamond is fatally poisoned with strychnine and his widow almost succumbs to a similar fate, Jessica steps in to entrap the killer. The line-up of suspects encompasses songwriter Garth, Brittany's jealous boyfriend, as well as Billy Ray Hawkins, a country singer and songwriter who is unhappily under contract to Blue Lady. There is also the question whether Bobby's death could have been suicide.

Highlights: In her Dolly Parton-like characterization, Florence Henderson brings verve to vulnerable Patti Sue Diamond, who has known Jessica Fletcher since their summer camp days forty years ago. Patti Sue is a mixture of self-assurance and fragility, and must contend with an adulterous husband as well as the crop of young singers seeking to steal her country music limelight. Of special interest is show business-oriented Lieutenant Jackson. Like thousands of others in Grand Ole Opry territory, he "just happens" to always have a pile of his compositions at hand to plug at the least encouragement.

Trivia: From 1950s Broadway musicals to a semiregular spot on TV's *The Jack Paar Show* (1958–1962), Florence Henderson leaped to becoming Carol Brady on the quintessential *The Brady Bunch* (1969–1974) which spawned *The Brady Bunch Hour* (1977), *The Brady Brides* (1981) and *The Bradys* (1990). In real life, Jimmy Dean, Mickey Gilley and Sheb Wooley were all country music performers. Daphne Ashbrook was featured on *Our Family Honor* (1985–1986) and *Fortune Dane* (1986).

140. "Murder in F Sharp"

(12/16/90) 60 mins.

Director: Kevin G. Cremin **Teleplay:** William Bigelow

Regular: Angela Lansbury (Jessica Fletcher/Narrator)

Recurring Characters: Joe Dorsey (Ben Devlin); Keith Michell (Dennis Stanton); James Sloyan (Robert Butler); Hallie Todd (Rhoda Markowitz, the Secretary)

Guest Cast: Anne Gee Byrd (Widow); Stephen Caffrey (Alex Seletz); Melinda Culea (Nicole Gary); Aaron Heyman (Mr. Morris); John Kerry (Security Guard); Dean R. Miller (Charlie, the Doorman); Ricardo Montalban (Vaclav Maryska); Patricia Neal (Milena Maryska)

The Setting: San Francisco, California

The Case: In the midst of a concert, renowned pianist Vaclav Maryska stalks offstage insisting the keyboard is out of tune. Hours later, he returns to his San Francisco apartment, apparently drunk. With Milena, his high-strung wife, in the bedroom, Maryska retires to the library. Later, a fire breaks out in the room and Vaclav badly burns his hands putting out the blaze.

Since Vaclav's world-famous hands are insured for $10 million, claim adjuster Dennis Stanton must assess the facts. Dennis's inquiry reveals that the remarkably well adjusted Vaclav plans to become a teacher, devoting himself to such gifted pupils as his lovely protégée, Nicole Gary.

However, the inquiry does a turnabout when Milena is found shot to death on the apartment floor. It is learned she had recently been arguing with Alex Seletz, her grown-up son from a prior marriage. As Stanton observes, Alex had a good motive. As beneficiary of his mother's $200,000 insurance policy, he could lead a very comfortable existence.

Highlights: Sometimes even the most experienced of actors cannot overcome a deficient script. Such was the case here where the plot loopholes, inconsistencies and the highly contrived characters left the stars little with which to work.

Trivia: This marked one of the few occasions in which a *Murder, She Wrote* episode contained a very graphic, gory scene—i.e., Vaclav Maryska holding up his badly charred hands in full camera view.

Latin America's Ricardo Montalban was one of Angela Lansbury's fellow alumni at late 1940s MGM. The brother-in-law of Loretta Young, Ricardo had the prominent role of mysterious Mr. Roarke of TV's *Fantasy Island* (1978–1984) as well as playing Zachary Powers on *The Colbys* (1985–1987). Winning an Academy Award for *Hud* (1963), stage and screen star Patricia Neal not only survived a siege of multiple strokes and family tragedies in the mid-1960s, but endured to star in *The Subject Was Roses* (1968), *Ghost Story* (1981) and *Caroline?* (1990).

141. "Family Doctor"

(1/6/91) 60 mins.

Director: Walter Grauman **Teleplay:** Robert Van Scoyk

Regulars: Angela Lansbury (Jessica Fletcher); William Windom (Dr. Seth Hazlitt)

Guest Law Enforcers: Newall Alexander (FBI Agent Zweiback); Michael Blue (1st Policeman); Joe Cortese (Lieutenant Jerry Marino); Howard

George (Desk Sergeant); Jay Hill (2nd Policeman); William Utay (FBI Agent Misch)

Guest Cast: Tige Andrews (Carmine Abruzzi); Cynthia Bain (Denise Abruzzi); David Ciminello (Salvatore Abruzzi); Robert Costanzo (Freddie); Diane Franklin (Phyllis Chase); Rose Gregorio (Rosa Abruzzi); Vincent Irizarry (Michael Abruzzi); Randall Jeffries (Bellhop); Linda Larkin (Karen Ann, the Waitress); Monte Markham (Andrew Chase, Esq.); Amy Yasbeck (Connie Canzinaro)

The Setting: Boston, Massachusetts

The Case: To cap a day of museum touring and shopping in Boston, Jessica Fletcher and Dr. Seth Hazlitt dine at the city's Clams and Claws Restaurant. During dinner, Seth is called away for a phone call and vanishes. A deeply disturbed Jessica consults the police.

Hours later, Seth reappears. He tells Jessica and the police that he was kidnapped and taken blindfolded to a mansion outside of Boston where he performed emergency surgery on an older man suffering from a bullet wound. After that, he had been let go. Jessica and Seth remain overnight in Boston because FBI agents want to talk to the physician about his mystery patient. The next morning, Seth, this time with Mrs. Fletcher in tow, is kidnapped yet again.

They are brought to the expensive home of slick attorney Andrew Chase, the mouthpiece of a local underworld organization. By now, Carmine Abruzzi, the mob boss patient of last night, has died: Abruzzi's hot-tempered son, Salvatore, insists Seth be executed in retribution for malpractice. However, his calmer brother, literate Michael, wants to reconsider the situation.

Caught in deadly peril, baffled Seth assists Jessica in reexamining the facts. They determine that the Godfather had died of a fatal dosage of digitoxin injected with one of Seth's now-missing syringes. The household is full of suspects. Besides the Abruzzi brothers, their thugs and the crooked lawyer, there is Carmine's strong-willed widow, Rosa. In addition, there is Denise, Michael's pregnant wife who abhors the idea that he might succeed his late father in the family business, as well as Connie Canzinaro, Sal's temperamental fiancée, and Phyllis Chase, who lusts after one of the Abruzzi brothers.

Highlights: In the opening sequences, there is a slam-bang shoot-out as Carmine falls prey to a hit man. Once surmounting the far-fetched premise, the cast plays to the hilt their Mafia family roles, especially Rose Gregorio as the matriarch who lives only for the day she has grandchildren. Monte Markham is quietly effective as the sinister lawyer.

With his ever-expanding waistline, Dr. Hazlitt provides the episode's comedy relief. He is the one who carps about the restaurant's poor service and high prices, while gobbling down his own and part of Jessica's lobster dinner. In a contrasting mood, the conscientious doctor turns grief-stricken over any possible negligence on his part that may have contributed to Carmine's death.

Trivia: This marked William Windom's return to *Murder, She Wrote,* his first series episode since the past season's "The Szechuan Dragon" (#129). Monte Markham was a veteran of several series: *The Second Hundred Years, Mr. Deeds Goes to Town, Rituals.*

142. "Suspicion of Murder"

(1/20/91) 60 mins.

Director: Vincent McEveety **Teleplay:** Peter S. Fischer

Regular: Angela Lansbury (Jessica Fletcher/Narrator)

Recurring Characters: Keith Michell (Dennis Stanton); James Sloyan (Robert Butler); Ken Swofford (Lieutenant Perry Catalano); Hallie Todd (Rhoda Markowitz, the Secretary)

Guest Law Enforcers: John Arndt (Cop #2); Ed Beechner (Officer Ishumi); Dennis O'Sullivan (Cop #1).

Guest Cast: Susan Blakely (Christine Hellinger); Sam Bottoms (Joe Hellinger); Lenny Citrano (Doorman); Dennis Cole (Ryan Donovan); Robert Donovan (1st Man); Paul Keith (Cashier); Judy Kerr (Hotel Housekeeper); Adam Silbar (Clerk) Robin Strand (Danny Hellinger)

The Setting: San Francisco, California

The Case: Between fighting the war of the roses with Japanese beetles at her Cabot Cove home, Jessica relates the latest caper of her San Francisco friend, ex-jewel thief, Dennis Stanton.

To celebrate his pending divorce, ex pro-tennis player Ryan Donovan hosts a party for friends. There Stanton encounters striking Christine Hellinger, whom he hasn't seen in a year. She confides that she and her roughneck husband, Ben, who was never accepted by her sophisticated crowd, have separated. Later that night, Christine seduces the willing Dennis. The next day, Christine calls from a San Raphael motel saying that Ben has again physically abused her. Now drawn into a domestic squabble, Stanton drives to the Hellinger home to confront the abusive husband. Soon thereafter, through circumstantial evidence, Dennis finds himself charged with Hellinger's murder.

To extricate himself from this latest scrape, Dennis must question the victim's hostile two sons who operate the family's moving and storage company. Danny is the responsible sibling, while the younger, Joey, hates being involved in the dreary business. It requires all of Stanton's resourcefulness to break this case.

Highlights: Rising above the pedestrian plot line, the segment's idiosyncratic recurring characters provide the viewer with diversion. For example, having gone honest in recent years, Stanton is nevertheless surprised to note that he is losing his touch when he accidentally trips a silent alarm while breaking into a business office. As for Rhoda Markowitz, Dennis's very competent secretary, she is dismayed to realize that she is about to attend her fourteenth wedding, once more as the bridesmaid and *not* the bride.

Trivia: Dennis Cole, once married to actress Jaclyn Smith, starred in TV's *Bracken's World* (1969–1970). Sam Bottoms, the third-born brother (after Timothy and Joseph) of the acting clan, costarred in the TV miniseries *John Steinbeck's East of Eden* (1981) and such TV movies as *Savages* (1974), *Desperate Lives* (1982) and *Island Sons* (1987), the latter with his actor siblings.

143. "Moving Violation"

(2/3/91) 60 mins.

Director: Anthony Shaw **Teleplay:** Robert E. Swanson

Regulars: Angela Lansbury (Jessica Fletcher); Ron Masak (Sheriff Mort Metzger)

Guest Law Enforcer: Robert Ginty (Lieutenant Avery Powell)

Recurring Characters: Harry Guardino (Haskell Drake); Will Nye (Deputy Floyd); Richard Paul (Mayor Sam Booth)

Guest Cast: Barbara C. Adside (Janet Costner); Susan Clark (Meredith Hellman); Jack Colvin (Chandler Hellman); Lois de Banzie (Phyllis Costner); Phyllis Franklin (Mabel); Philip Baker Hall (Len Costner); David Lansbury (Brad Hellman); Britt Leach (Arnold, the Front Desk Man at the Navarro Inn); Stephen Macht (Jason Farrell, Esq.); Jason Bo Sharon (Billy); Suzanne Snyder (Morgan Philips); Daniel Ben Wilson (Mickey)

The Setting: Cabot Cove, Maine

The Case: When Brad Hellman speeds recklessly through Cabot Cove, Sheriff Mort Metzger gives chase. When stopped, the offender attempts to bribe the law enforcer. The enraged Mort takes Brad into custody. Checking the prisoner's record, Metzger learns that Brad had been in a prior accident a few years back, one which killed four others. Meanwhile, Brad's father, Ambassador Chandler Hellman, arrives with a high-pressure lawyer, Jason Farrell, in tow. In a private meeting between father and son, Chandler hits Brad. Later, the young man insists it was Mort who had assaulted him.

The arrogant Chandler, accompanied by his imperious new wife, Meredith, appeals to wimpy Mayor Sam Booth to force Metzger to free Brad. Soon, Lieutenant Avery Powell of the state's criminal investigation division is summoned to Cabot Cove to study the facts. A disgusted Mort quits his post. Meanwhile, Brad, who had been freed on bail, is found dead, having been shot with two bullets.

At this point, Jessica Fletcher steps in to solve the murder and to get Mort back on duty. She learns a great deal of the victim's past from her old friend Haskell Drake, a New York newspaper reporter. Equipped with this knowledge, she confronts the suspects, which include, besides Brad's society parents, Morgan Philips, Brad's current girlfriend. Then there is crippled Janet Costner, an innocent passenger in drunken Brad's car that fateful day four years ago. She had wanted Brad jailed for his crime, but her parents preferred the Hellmans' lucrative settlement.

Highlights: A well-etched study of class consciousness, this episode proves that in Cabot Cove money can't buy everything. If Mort Metzger is stubbornly honest, so Jessica Fletcher remains her unflappable self. As such, her run-ins with snobbish, pushy Meredith Hellman are story highlights. Not to be overlooked are the amusing incidents involving cowed Mayor Sam Booth, who yields to the slightest pressure.

Trivia: Susan Clark, the Emmy Award-winning star of the TV movie *Babe* (1976), had costarred with her ex-football player husband, Alex Karras, in the sitcom *Webster* (1983–1987). Philadelphia-born Stephen Macht had played recurring roles on TV's *American Dream* and *Knots Landing.* Harry Guardino (1925–1995) recreated his newshound character (Haskell Drake) first seen in 1986's "Deadline for Murder" (#50). Angela Lansbury's nephew, David, here made the first of several *Murder, She Wrote* appearances.

144. "Who Killed J.B. Fletcher?"

(2/10/91) 60 mins.

Director: Walter Grauman **Teleplay:** Lynne Kelsey

Regular: Angela Lansbury (Jessica Fletcher)

Guest Law Enforcers: Max Baer (State Trooper Boone Willoughby); David Cowgill (Deputy); Earl Holliman (Sheriff Tanner)

Guest Cast: Janet Blair (Bertie); Curt Booker (Security Guard); Rod Britt (Hotel Clerk); Marvyn Byrkett (Technician); Betty Garrett (Kit Parkins); Michael Leopard (Cabbie); Mario Machado (Anchor); Marc Marcosi (Waiter); Jon Menick (Kennel Clerk); Terry Moore (Florence); Margaret O'Brien (Jane); Jamie Rose (Lisa McCauley); Tom Schanley (Rick, the Kennel Groomer); Lyman Ward (Mitchell Lawrence); Marie Windsor (Caroline); Jane Withers (Marge Allen)

The Settings: Bremmerton, Texas; Sunville, Texas

The Case: Marge Allen, an enthusiastic Texan, is a key member of the J.B. Fletcher Literary Society. Like Jessica Fletcher, whom she often impersonates on "sleuthing" excursions, Marge has a natural curiosity. It prompts her to break into a local kennel to learn why a certain pet owner wins every annual dog show competition. Later, she is the victim of a car "accident." Because she had been using her Jessica Fletcher alias at the time, news services around the world spread the information that J.B. Fletcher is dead.

Actually, Jessica is in Dallas, Texas, on a book promotion tour when a TV newscast alerts her that she (!) is dead. Thereafter, charge card companies and the bank, among others, cancel her accounts, believing her to be deceased. To restore her living person status, Mrs. Fletcher heads to Bremmerton, Texas and nearby Sunville.

First, Jessica meets with her Literary Society fans. The surviving members, Kit Parkins, Bertie, Florence, Jane and Caroline, excitedly help the real-life Mrs. Fletcher track clues in the bizarre homicide. As such, Jessica learns that Lisa McCauley, coowner of a local pet grooming business, has just lost her husband in a hunting "accident." It also turns out that Lisa is having an affair with Rick, a groomer at her business.

From insurance agent Mitchell Lawrence, Mrs. Fletcher is advised that Mrs. McCauley is the beneficiary of a large life insurance policy. Another person with an ax to grind is State Trooper Boone Willoughby, who wants to start a special canine unit.

Highlights: The zanies at the J.B. Fletcher Literary Society are a joyful lot, each having family or business connections who provide Jessica with useful information. Her shepherding of these young-at-heart women provides a springboard for delightful character sketches. The running gag of a frustrated Jessica vainly imploring The Establishment to accept that she is alive adds to the hilarity.

Trivia: Janet Blair, the 1940s star of *My Sister Eileen* (1942) and *The Fabulous Dorseys* (1948), had costarred in TV's *The Smith Family* (1971–1972). Marie Windsor had made several Westerns: *Dakota Lil* (1950), *The Tall Texan* (1953), *The Good Guys and the Bad Guys* (1969), etc. Terry Moore, who has long insisted she was once secretly wed to multimillionaire Howard Hughes, had won an Academy Award nomination for *Come Back, Little Sheba* (1952) and been featured in the 1962 Western TV series *Empire.* Former child star Jane Withers had teamed with screen rival Shirley Temple in *Bright Eyes* (1934) and made her own starring vehicles: *Ginger* (1936), *Boyfriend* (1939), etc. Withers's comeback as an adult actress included *Giant* (1956) and *Captain Newman, M.D.* (1963).

Having made two television Western series *(Hotel de Paree* and *The Wide Country)* Earl Holliman supported Angie Dickinson in *Police Woman* (1974–1978). Before becoming a film producer and director in the late 1970s, Max Baer, the son of a heavyweight boxing champ, had portrayed dumb Jethro—as well as the character's sister—on *The Beverly Hillbillies* (1962–1971). Margaret O'Brien, another 1940s MGM alumni like Angela Lansbury and Betty Garrett (the widow of actor Larry Parks), was the moppet star of such features as *Meet Me in St. Louis* (1944) and *Little Women* (1949). She had adult roles in *Heller in Pink Tights* (1960) and *Amy* (1981).

145. "The Taxman Cometh"

(2/17/91) 60 mins.

Director: Anthony Shaw **Teleplay:** Donald Rose

Regular: Angela Lansbury (Jessica Fletcher)

Guest Law Enforcers: John Christopher (Police Officer); Greg Allan (Police Officer); Fred Willard (Lieutenant Phillips)

Guest Cast: Joan Crosby (Maid); Robin Dearden (Gail Manning); Gregg Henry (Richard Wellstood); Phyllis Newman (Edna Hayes); Macon McCalman (Nolan Hayes); Kent McCord (George Harris); Annie O'Donnell (Mrs. Leeman); Dominic Oliver (Pizza Man); Roy Thinnes (J.K. Davern); Max Wright (George Yelverton, the IRS Man)

The Setting: Jonesburg, Missouri

The Case: While visiting Edna Hayes, a college chum, Jessica learns that her friend is divorcing her self-indulgent husband, Nolan, and that her company, Edna's Baked Goods, is having severe financial problems. Adding to Edna's stress is an audit, being conducted by IRS agent George Yelverton, regarding $2 million the firm owes in back withholding taxes.

When Lieutenant Phillips labels Edna a top suspect in the roadside murder of her ex-mate, Jessica feels obliged to pinpoint the real culprit. She learns a lot about the case from Edna's plant executives: head of accounting Gail Manning, sales and marketing chief J. K. Davern and in-house attorney Richard Wellstood. The crux of the case depends on Mrs. Fletcher locating two key people: (1) the mysterious outside auditor, Spencer Prinze and (2) the pizza delivery man who can substantiate Edna's alibi at the time of the homicide.

Highlights: More so than in many other *Murder, She Wrote* episodes, this segment has an engaging roster of red herrings. A humorous theme running throughout is the panic engendered whenever the all-powerful IRS agent comes into sight. Even Lieutenant Phillips has matters in his financial past that do not bear scrutiny, which makes him very obliging to the bullying government minion.

Trivia: Broadway performer Phyllis Newman had been featured in two 1960s TV series: *Diagnosis: Unknown* and *That Was the Week That Was.* B-movie actor Gregg Henry had been part of such TV movies/miniseries as *Rich Man, Poor Man—Book II, Pearl* and *The Blue and the Gray.* Clean-cut Kent McCord had been Officer Jim Reed on TV's *Adam 12* (1968–1975) as well as Captain Troy on *Battlestar Galactica* (1982). Roy Thinnes's television series and miniseries credits include *Code Name: Diamond Head, From Here to Eternity* and *Scruples.* Character actor Max Wright often played abrasive government officials and had a leading role in the TV series *Alf* (1986–1990).

146. "From the Horse's Mouth"

(2/24/91) 60 mins.

Director: Jerry Jameson **Teleplay:** Gerry Day

Regular: Angela Lansbury (Jessica Fletcher)

Recurring Characters: Richard Balin (Coroner); Jerry Orbach (Harry McGraw)

Guest Law Enforcer: Robert Donner (Sheriff Tyrone McKenna)

Guest Cast: Michael Ayr (Mark Mason, Esq.); James Bartz (Justin King); Melvin M. Belli (Judge Harley); Helena Carroll (Martha Jane Stokes, the Secretary); Maxwell Caulfield (Derek Padley); Patricia Charboneau (Diana Sterling); Nanette Fabray (Emmaline Bristow); Kathy Hartsell (Young Woman); Patricia Huston (Edie); Kevin McCarthy (Randolph Sterling); John Allen Nelson (Todd Sterling); Tricia O'Neil (Althea Mayberry); Debra Sandland (Dr. Christie Morgan); Gregory Walcott (Lamar Morgan)

The Setting: Peachtree, Kentucky

The Case: While in Kentucky on business, Jessica Fletcher fulfills her promise to her Boston pal, Harry McGraw. She bets $200 on a long shot for him at the racetrack. Unfortunately, the nag loses.

Meanwhile, Jessica gets entwined in problems at the track. A controversy rages between wealthy breeder Randolph Sterling and Lamar Morgan, the owner of Morgan Hills Farms. The two are in legal dispute regarding foals allegedly sired by Sterling's prize stud horse, King Paragon, and less pedigreed fillies owned by Morgan. The accelerating battle affects the growing romantic relationship between Randolph's son, Todd, and Lamar's daughter, Christie. Matters take a turn for the worse when Randolph is found clubbed to death at the stable and Sheriff Tyrone McKenna concludes that Lamar is the most likely suspect.

Recalling Harry McGraw's knowledge of the race world, Jessica hires the private eye to fly to Kentucky to help her sort out the truth. Together they interview Derek Padley, the victim's chief groomer, and comely Diana Sterling, whose past includes a marriage to a member of the British nobility. Also involved is pretty Althea Mayberry. Thanks to eccentric Emmaline Bristow, who claims she can talk to horses, Mrs. Fletcher wraps up the caper.

Highlights: Not since moviedom's Francis, the Talking Horse or TV's *Mr. Ed* has a "talking horse" played such a key role in a story line. With colorful Harry McGraw on hand to match wits and repartee with Jessica Fletcher, there is an abundance of flavorful dialogue and inventive sleuthing. Stealing the limelight is oddball Emmaline Bristow, a lady who knows her way around the track and has a special way with four-legged beauties.

Trivia: Emmy Award-winning Nanette Fabray was a veteran of Broadway musicals, films and TV. Her series work encompassed *Caesar's Hour*, and *One Day at a Time*. Kevin McCarthy, the brother of author Mary McCarthy, had been a TV performer since 1949. His feature film credits include performing in two versions (1956, 1978) of the sci-fi classic *Invasion of the Body Snatchers*. British-born Maxwell Caulfield, the husband of actress Juliet Mills, had been featured on TV's *The Colbys* (1985–1987). Famed real-life attorney Melvin M. Belli was cast here as the judge who must relocate the courtroom hearing to the stables.

147. "The Prodigal Father"

(3/10/91)60 mins.

Director: Anthony Shaw **Teleplay:** Maryanne Kasica, Michael Scheff

Regulars: Angela Lansbury (Jessica Fletcher); Ron Masak (Sheriff Mort Metzger)

Recurring Characters: Will Nye (Deputy Floyd); Richard Paul (Mayor Sam Booth)

Guest Cast: Claudia Christian (Bonnie Jenks Hastings); Don Galloway (Elton Summers); Robert Gordon (Linda); Gary Hollis (Antique Shop Customer); Robert Lansing (Herb Walsh); Mindy Ann Martin (Sally Hastings); Kathleen Nolan (Maxine Walsh); Andrew Prine (Gil Blocker); Donnelly Rhodes (Ned Jenks); Mark Roberts (Dr. Lyle Rush); Sarah Simmons (Antique Shop Customer); Abe Vigoda (George, the Desk Clerk at the Lighthouse Motel); Larry Wilcox (Dave Hastings)

The Setting: Cabot Cove, Maine

The Case: Years ago, Ned Jenks was thought to have drowned while escaping after a $200,000 bank robbery. However, he suddenly appears in Cabot Cove and registers at the Lighthouse Motel. Since no fugitive warrant had ever been issued on the assumed dead bank robber, the statute of limitations has expired.

Several locals have ties to the old heist. They are Elton Summers, president of the First Bank of Maine, whose career promotion was a result of his boss being fired after the robbery. Diner owner Gil Blocker had been a bank security guard then. For several years after the crime which he didn't halt, he was a drunk. Electronics business owner Herb Walsh has never fully recovered his health since being shot during the robbery.

When Jenks visits his daughter, Bonnie, Herb reacts very negatively. He fires Bonnie's electrician husband, Dave, who had been employed at Walsh's facility. Herb's wife, Maxine, who currently owns an antique shop, had been a good friend of Gil's in those bygone days and knew that he never carried a loaded gun while on security guard duty.

Some time later, Bonnie finds Ned shot to death at his motel room. According to George, the dour motel clerk, at the time Jenks died the victim had been phoning the local laundromat. Jessica Fletcher and Sheriff Mort Metzger also glean that, contrary to rumor, Jenks had only grabbed $20,000 not $200,000 in that long-ago bank job.

Highlights: A small town is a perfect setting to demonstrate how the past can catch up with the present. The stranger's arrival in Cabot Cove triggers a host of repercussions among individuals whose lives have been intertwined since that fateful day at the local bank.

Trivia: Kathleen Nolan, a starring member of TV's *Jamie*, *The Real McCoys* and *Broadside*, became the first woman president of the Screen Actors Guild in 1975. Robert Lansing (1929–1994) was featured in four 1960s TV series, including *87th Precinct* and *Twelve O'Clock High*, as well as the late 1980s' *The Equalizer*.

Don Galloway's many TV chores included hosting a quiz show, *The Guinness Game* (1979). Angular-faced Abe Vigoda played Detective Phil Fish on *Barney Miller* (1975–1977) and *Fish* (1977–1978). Andrew Prine's debut teleseries was the Western *The Wide Country* (1962–1963).

148. "Where Have You Gone, Billy Boy?"

(3/17/91) 60 mins.

Director: John Llewellyn Moxey **Teleplay:** Peter S. Fischer

Regular: Angela Lansbury (Jessica Fletcher/Narrator)

Recurring Characters: Keith Michell (Dennis Stanton); James Sloyan (Robert Butler); Ken Swofford (Lieutenant Perry Catalano); Hallie Todd (Rhoda Markowitz, the Secretary)

Guest Cast: Georgia Brown (Kate Kelley); Teri Copley (Brenda McCoy); Leslie Easterbrook (Sally Templeton); Jana Grant (2nd Insurance Company Worker); Marty Ingels (Gelardi); Jeffrey Jena (Comic); Mike Jolly (Elmo); Matt McCarter (3rd Insurance Company Worker); Kevin McCoy (1st Insurance Company Worker); Jim Metzler (Tom Benzinger); Grant Shaud (Woody Perkins); David Stenstrom (Budding Comic); Lyle Waggoner (Vic DeMarco); Susan Welby (4th Insurance Company Worker)

The Setting: San Francisco, California

The Case: While enjoying afternoon tea with Dennis Stanton, Jessica is told about his latest (mis)adventure as a San Francisco insurance company's claims adjuster.

Dennis is drawn into a peculiar situation when ventriloquist Woody Perkins claims that his insured dummy (Billy) has been kidnapped! As Stanton looks into the matter, he learns that Perkins is tied to an ill-advised work contract at Kate Kelley's comedy club. She won't let him out of his agreement so he can become the opening act for big-time Las Vegas entertainer Vic DeMarco.

Later, Kate Kelley's body is found in the club's basement. Not far from the corpse is the sought-after dummy, Billy. As such, according to Lieutenant Perry Catalano's logic, Woody is a major suspect. Stanton, as usual, believes otherwise, and he interrogates other interested parties.

They include Sally Templeton, a former headliner at the comedy club, who had turned to booze. Once dried out, she wanted a second career chance, but unsympathetic Kelley had vetoed a gig at her establishment. There is also impudent Brenda McCoy, an overly ambitious blonde in Woody's act, as well as Woody's manager, Tom Benzinger, who has his own agenda. Finally, there is Gelardi, Kate's unhappy club partner and master of ceremonies.

Highlights: This installment pales in comparison to most other *Murder, She Wrote* offerings. Not only is it lackluster and mechanical, but it's derivative. On the plus side is the interesting countercasting of Grant Shaud, best known for playing hyperactive, aggressive yuppies. He is effective as the exceedingly shy entertainer who can only voice his true feelings through his dummy, Billy.

Trivia: Grant Shaud earned a notch in TV history as Miles Silverberg, the neurotic young news show producer on *Murphy Brown* (1988–1996). Rugged Lyle Waggoner hit a career peak as a stock company member of *The Carol Burnett Show* (1967–1974) and as Major Steve Trevor on *Wonder Woman* (1976–1977). This was one of the last appearances of British stage *(Oliver!)* and film *(Lock Up Your Daughters)* actress Georgia Brown (1933–1992). Brooklyn-born Marty Ingels costarred with Phyllis Diller in the sitcom *The Pruitts of Southampton* (1967).

149. "Thursday's Child"

(4/7/91) 60 mins.

Director: Anthony Shaw **Teleplay:** Robert E. Swanson

Regular: Angela Lansbury (Jessica Fletcher)

Recurring Character: Martin Milner (Clint Phelps)

Guest Law Enforcers: Paul Gleason (Lieutenant Barney Claymore); Elven Havard (Duty Patrolman)

Guest Cast: John Anderson (Andrew Dixon, Esq.); John Beck (Ben Olston); Jim Boeke (Crocket); S. Scott Bullock (Taxi Driver); Fredric Cook (Aaronson); Lindsay Frost (Dawn Bickford); Alan Fudge (Councilman Axelrod); Richard Gilliland (Steve Landon); Vera Miles (Nancy Landon); Steven Novak (Roy Temple); Jennifer Warren (Cynthia Olston)

The Setting: (Near) Atlanta, Georgia

The Case: On a book tour stopover near Atlanta, Georgia, Jessica Fletcher receives an urgent phone call from Nancy Landon. The stranger tells Jessica that she had been stationed in South Korea in 1951 where she had met serviceman Frank Fletcher. Nancy then confides that she had Frank's love child, Steve, and the latter, now an architect, is in deep trouble.

Per Nancy, Steve had confronted contractor Ben Olston for using shoddy materials on a school project now under construction. When the work site was recently bombed, Olston and the police labeled Steve the prime suspect. Knowing Jessica's reputation for solving baffling crimes, Nancy begs Mrs. Fletcher, on behalf of her late husband's son, to help Steve out of this jam.

Although shocked by the revelation, practical Jessica, nevertheless, studies the case. Using a ruse, she questions Olston. Some days later, he is found shot to death on the floor of his home library. Because Nancy had been observed at the murder location at approximately the same time of the killing, she is taken into police custody.

Jessica's further search produces the fact that Olston had been having a special relationship with Dawn Bickford, the attractive assistant of Councilman Axelrod. There is also the matter of the victim's wife, Cynthia, who had gone out of town shortly before her husband's death to nurse a sick mother. Meanwhile, Mrs. Fletcher has attorney Andrew Dixon investigate Nancy's paternity claim.

Highlights: This is the most emotionally charged episode of *Murder, She Wrote*. It is a singular event to see Jessica Fletcher reduced to tears as she ponders the likeliness of Frank having betrayed her trust while he was on duty in the Korean War. Haunted by uncertainty, Jessica flies to Seattle, Washington, to meet with Clint Phelps who had served with Frank overseas. The visit results in high-voltage reminiscences, matched only by Jessica's confrontations with Nancy.

Trivia: Martin Milner here repeats his Clint Phelps' characterization first seen on 1988's "The Last Flight of the Dixie Damsel" (#94). Prolific actor Richard Gilliland had appeared in such TV series as *McMillan and Wife*, *Operation Petticoat* and *Just Our Luck*. Jennifer Warren had made her TV series debut as a regular on *The Smothers Brothers Comedy Hour* (1967–1969). Vera Miles had made her screen debut in *For Men Only* (1952) and recreated her *Psycho* (1960) leading lady role for its first sequel, *Psycho II* (1983).

150. "Murder, Plain and Simple"

(4/28/91) 60 mins.

Director: Vincent McEveety **Teleplay:** Chris Manheim

Regular: Angela Lansbury (Jessica Fletcher)

Guest Law Enforcer: John Ireland (Sheriff Haines)

Guest Cast: Todd Eric Andrews (Ethan Kaufmann); Hunt Block (Reuben Stoltz); Martha Bryne (Sarah Lapp); Ed McCready (Franz Kaufmann); Jay Robinson (Bishop Burkhardt); Jennifer Runyon (Rebecca Beiler); Michael Sarrazin (Jacob Beiler); Arlen Dean Snyder (Samuel Kaufmann)

The Setting: (Near) Lancaster, Pennsylvania

The Case: While in Philadelphia on book business, Jessica takes a relaxing Sunday drive into Amish country with her publisher's liaison man, Reuben Stoltz. It is a homecoming of sorts for young Stoltz, who had left the region years before to start his career.

Close to their destination, Reuben avoids hitting a recklessly driven buggy, and his car swerves into a ditch. Stoltz suffers a bad muscle spasm requiring bed rest, while the vehicle must undergo extensive repairs. Local Quakers at first refuse to help Reuben because he had turned his back on his religion. However, Bishop Burkhardt declares this a special exception and orders his congregation to extend proper hospitality.

Jessica and Reuben are given lodging by Jacob Beiler, a stern Quaker elder who is married to the much younger Rebecca. During the night, Jacob is stabbed with a pitchfork and tied to a scarecrow's cross. Sheriff Haines concludes that Reuben is the guilty party. It seems that Reuben and Rebecca were once sweethearts and, at the time of the murder, Stoltz had been seen heading to the barn where the victim had died.

In sorting out the neighbors' intricate relationships, Jessica talks with Sarah Lapp, a pregnant young woman working in the quilt shop. She has refused to name the biological father of her unborn baby and, as such, has been shunned by her congregation. Then there is rebellious Franz, the unhappy teenage son of heart-broken widower Samuel Kaufmann. Franz is the careless youth who had been driving the problem-causing buggy and who now is overly anxious to leave town.

Highlights: Obvious parallels exist between this episode and the much larger scale *Witness* (1985), the Harrison Ford feature film. Both focus on the clash of opposing cultures, and each deals with killings. In tearing away the layers of deceit here, Jessica Fletcher is once again the constant conciliator. She is always attentive to details, such as a misplaced cigarette lighter, or the fact that the corpse in question (as in several *Murder, She Wrote* segments) has been moved to disguise the time and place of death and to throw the law off the killer's trail. Another favorite show device used here was having the countrified sheriff be very astute and (almost) an equal match to the eagle-eyed Mrs. Fletcher.

Trivia: Jay Robinson, a specialist at eccentric roles, had gained major note playing the mad Caligula in *The Robe* (1953) and *Demetrius and the Gladia-*

tors (1954). Canadian-born Michael Sarrazin had made his mark as the young innocent of *The Flim Flam Man* (1967) and *They Shoot Horses, Don't They?* (1969). John Ireland (1914–1992) had been Oscar-nominated for *All the King's Men* (1949) and had been featured in the TV series *The Protectors* (1961).

151. "Tainted Lady"

(5/5/91) 60 mins.

Director: Vincent McEveety **Teleplay:** Robert Van Scoyk

Regular: Angela Lansbury (Jessica Fletcher)

Guest Law Enforcers: Karen Hensel (Deputy Mary Jo Rush); Gary Lockwood (Sheriff Deloy Hays); Javi Mulero (Deputy Ray Gomez)

Guest Cast: Marshall Colt (Ross Corman); Mary Crosby (Laura Corman); Nina Foch (Katie Emhardt); Sam Freed (Herb Apple, Esq.); Peter Gregory (Young Man); Jack Kruschen (Dr. John Logan); Laurie Prange (Doris Gerringer); Dee Wallace Stone (Ellen Wicker); Don Swayze (Edge Potter)

The Setting: Dry Wells, Texas

The Case: Ellen Wicker again calls upon Jessica Fletcher who, a few years back, had helped prove Ellen's innocence when she was charged with murdering her husband in Boston. Since then she had returned to Texas to her small hometown where she now runs the Desert Rose Cafe. However, her past reputation has followed her and no one will have anything to do with her socially.

Things get worse when Jake Gerringer dies of what Dr. John Logan labels a heart attack. However, further investigation reveals the cause of death to be poisoning, and it's also disclosed that the victim ate at Ellen's diner nightly and a box of arsenic has been discovered in her cafe storeroom.

As the townsfolk turn nasty, Jessica battles against time to prove her friend's innocence. She is helped by Ellen's lawyer, Herb Apple. In contrast, sinister Sheriff Deloy Hays does everything to harm Ellen's case, because of a past grudge.

The trail leads Jessica to Laura Corman, Dr. Logan's nurse, who had first alerted the authorities about Gerringer's "accidental" death. Mrs. Fletcher finds it more than coincidental that Laura's husband, Ross, had once seriously dated Ellen. There is also motorcycle punk Edge Potter who orders Jessica to discontinue her investigation.

Then there is Katie Emhardt, the widow of the owner of the town's tannery (which closed after a major earthquake ruined the building's structure). It seems that Mr. Emhardt recently died in a fashion similar to Gerringer. Finally, there is bored Doris Gerringer, who plans to relocate to Hollywood once her father's life insurance money is in hand.

Highlights: Bringing a 1990s sensibility to *Murder, She Wrote,* this complex (even confusing) segment makes ecology a focal issue. It also displays one of the most odious law enforcers in the whodunit TV series.

Trivia: Gary Lockwood, once a movie stunt man and a stand-in for Anthony Perkins, starred in TV's *Follow the Sun* (1961–1962) and *The Lieutenant* (1963–1964). Mary Crosby, the daughter of Bing Crosby and Kathryn Grant, made her reputation as Kristin Shepard, the woman on TV's *Dallas* who shot J.R. Ewing. Don Swayze is the actor brother of Patrick. Nina Foch, who won an Oscar nomination for *Executive Suite* (1954), was a regular on such TV series as *Two Girls Named Smith* (1951) and *Shadow Chasers* (1985–1986). Dee Wallace Stone appeared in such cult movie favorites as *The Hills Have Eyes* (1977), *The Howling* (1981), *Critters* (1986) and *Popcorn* (1991).

152. "The Skinny According to Nick Cullhane"

(5/12/91) 60 mins.

Director: Walter Grauman **Teleplay:** Tom Sawyer

Regulars: Angela Lansbury (Jessica Fletcher); Ron Masak (Sheriff Mort Metzger)

Recurring Characters: Will Nye (Deputy Floyd); Jerry Orbach (Harry McGraw)

Guest Cast: Leslie Easterbrook (Vikki Palumbo); Postmaster General Anthony Frank (Mailman); Pat Harrington (Nick Cullhane); Alex Hyde-White (Ogden Schmesser); Tony LoBianco (Phil Mannix); Tricia Long (Florence); Michael McGrady (Richard); Jameson Parker (Gordon Forbes, Esq.)

The Settings: Boston, Massachusetts; Cabot Cove, Maine

The Case: For fifteen years, Nick Cullhane, who used to write popular detective novels, has been the spokesperson for Boston-based Schmesser's Beer ("the working man's brew"). Now the brewery's playboy owner, Ogden Schmesser, announces he isn't renewing Cullhane's endorsement contract. This is bad news for Nick, who owes $150,000 to his bookie, Vikki Palumbo, who has taken over the family business.

Desperate for money, Nick hopes to sell his new novel, an explosive expose of Schmesser's unsavory exploits. Before Cullhane heads to his cabin retreat near Cabot Cove, he sends Jessica Fletcher a copy of the manuscript. She leaves a message on his answering machine expressing her delight with his writing.

When Nick vanishes, Vikki comes across Jessica's phone message at Cullhane's cabin. She orders seedy Boston private eye Harry McGraw, who owes Palumbo $800 in bad bets, to track down the voice and grab the manuscript. (In actuality, Jessica has turned over the novel to local newspaper editor Ben Devlin to read, but he's gone fishing in the Canadian wilds.)

Before long, a parade of determined individuals invade Cabot Cove. There's Vikki and her strong-arm boyfriend, Richard; Schmesser's slick lawyer, Gordon Forbes; and retired Boston cop Phil Mannix, now an unscrupulous private detective. Also Harry McGraw shows up. It's his bad luck to find Cullhane's bullet-ridden corpse at the *Cabot Cove Gazette.* Sheriff Mort Metzger, no friend of McGraw, is only too happy to arrest Harry on a murder charge.

Highlights: Any Jessica Fletcher caper involving irrepressible, sad-eyed Harry McGraw is always long on entertainment value. The well-paced segment alternates between the mock serious and the genuinely menacing. While many of the characters play their roles full tongue-in-cheek, Jessica finds nothing funny about the strangers' deadly mission.

Trivia: When this episode was written, Angela Lansbury had made it known that this seventh season was her final one on *Murder, She Wrote.* Thus the script ended with Harry McGraw's dialogue line, "And that's all she wrote." However, by the time the segment was taped in mid-March 1990, she was tempted into negotiation for an eighth starring season. That's when executive producer Peter S. Fischer added in a closing wink from Jessica Fletcher. Also to be noted is that this episode marks the final *Murder, She Wrote* appearances for the characters of Deputy Floyd and gumshoe Harry McGraw.

U.S. Postmaster General Anthony Frank has a cameo as a mailman. Tony LoBianco had his breakthrough role as one of *The Honeymoon Killers* (1970), a low-budget "classic" of sorts. Jameson Parker had impressed viewers as the clean-cut, conservative brother (as compared to Gerald McRaney as the grubby, laid-back sibling) on the popular TV detective series *Simon & Simon* (1981–1988).

SEASON EIGHT

1991–1992

153. "Bite the Big Apple"

(9/15/91) 60 mins.

Director: David Moessinger **Teleplay:** David Moessinger

Regulars: Angela Lansbury (Jessica Fletcher); William Windom (Dr. Seth Hazlitt)

Recurring Characters: Julie Adams (Eve Simpson); Jay Acavone (Sergeant Acosta); Andrew Brye (Ahmed Shankar, the Doorman)

Guest Law Enforcers: Darrell Harris (Detective); Eugene Roche (Lieutenant Jack Boyle)

Guest Cast: Rebecca Bush (Sharon Kingsley); John Considine (Harry Freelander); Alan Feinstein (Mike Freelander); Alexander Folk (Painter); Rosemary Forsyth (Estelle Freelander); Scott McGinnis (Scott Freelander); Julie Claire Paradis (Waitress); David Schall (Man at Party); Liz Sheridan (Rose Tessler)

The Settings: Cabot Cove, Maine; New York City

The Case: Prolific and popular mystery writer Jessica Fletcher accepts a post teaching criminology at Manhattan University in New York. Her weekly plan is to spend three or four days in the city at her new apartment, and to fly home to Cabot Cove for weekends. Nevertheless, her good friend, Dr. Seth Hazlitt, expresses concern at her moving to such a dangerous urban environment.

Hardly has Jessica reached Penfield House, her new apartment building home, than the doorman, Ahmed Shankar, advises her that Mike Freelander, the prior tenant of 4B, has been found murdered in the garage.

Soon, Mrs. Fletcher meets case investigators Lieutenant Jack Boyle and Sergeant Acosta.

Later, while unpacking, Jessica accidentally finds invoices from the dead man's import/export firm hidden in her bathroom's shower curtain rod. She brings the papers to Freelander's brother, Harry, and to Harry's son, Scott. As Jessica discovers, the invoices suggest that jewelry and other valuable stolen items were being shipped abroad through the company's business channels. Meanwhile, the late Mike's girlfriend, Sharon Kingsley, quits her job at the Freelanders' company.

That evening Jessica returns to 4B to discover her apartment has been rifled. Soon thereafter, Seth pays a surprise visit, insisting he will stay until everything is in order. Following the clues, Mrs. Fletcher revisits the Freelanders' office, where she is mugged. When she revives, she finds Harry's corpse. Further adding to the mystery, Seth locates a large uncut diamond in the clogged sink drain pipe at 4B.

Highlights: For its eighth season opener, *Murder, She Wrote* added a fresh wrinkle by having Jessica Fletcher reside part-time in Manhattan. The gimmick provides a serviceable springboard for different adventures, as well as permitting the increasingly chic Jessica to expand the range of her acquaintances and habitats.

Meanwhile, there are appearances by Cabot Cove's own Seth Hazlitt and man-chasing Eve Simpson. Each provides a comforting familiarity as viewers adjust to the premise alternation. If the episode's climactic plot ploy is a bit obvious, there are diverting story line pluses: the presence of a new regular, eager-to-please doorman, Ahmed Shankar, and the one-shot appearance of Jessica's nosy neighbor, Rose Tessler, who lives across the hall in New York City.

Trivia: Rosemary Forsyth had begun her filmmaking career as a Universal Studios contract ingenue where *Murder, She Wrote* was filmed. Her credits included *Shenandoah* (1965), *The War Lord* (1965) and *Texas Across the River* (1966). Boston-born Eugene Roche was a TV series veteran of *The Corner Bar* (1973), *Soap* (1978–1981) and *Webster* (1984–1986), as well as a frequent cast member of feature films. Jay Acavone had police officer parts on both *Hollywood Beat* (1985) and *Beauty and the Beast* (1987–1990).

154. "Night Fears"

(9/22/91) 60 mins.

Director: Anthony Shaw **Teleplay:** J. Michael Straczynski

Regular: Angela Lansbury (Jessica Fletcher)

Recurring Character: Alan Oppenheimer (Dr. Raymond Auerbach)

Guest Law Enforcers: Bobby Hosea (Officer Kevin Bryce); John Lavachielli (Officer David Morelli); Al Pugliese (Captain Jim Lupinski)

Guest Cast: Felicia Aechola (Teacher); Mark Auerwall (Teacher); Leesa Bryte (2nd Student); Tim Choate (Luke Philips); Tony Darren (Busboy); Mary Pat Gleason (Reference Librarian); Wings Hauser (Wallace Evans); Kelle Korbel (1st Student); Roxie Roker (Jennifer Bryce); Alina Rosario (Female Professor); Julie St. Claire (Rosalyn Aramendi)

The Setting: New York City

The Case: At Manhattan University, Jessica Fletcher meets her fellow teachers. One of them, Wallace Evans, a former police officer, is highly annoyed that Mrs. Fletcher has been handed "his" criminology class to teach. In the classroom, Jessica is disturbed when a demanding student, Luke Philips, insists that because he's a great fan and has bought all her novels, she "owes" him special gratitude. She much prefers earnest Kevin Bryce, a police officer studying for his sergeant's exam.

Later, Jessica learns that Rosalyn Aramendi, one of her brightest students, has become the latest victim of the campus mugger. The next day—with her class in progress—Evans challenges Mrs. Fletcher to a competition to see who will first nab the mugger. Although Jessica refuses the exploitive offer, Wallace leaks news of the contest to the campus paper. That evening, Jessica encounters Kevin Bryce at a campus crime scene. This time the mugger has killed his victim. Jessica feels obliged to step into the inquiry.

Although unimaginative Captain Jim Lupinski orders Kevin not to assist Jessica on her private investigation, Bryce refuses to be cowed—as his policeman father once had been—by departmental bureaucracy. In the process of entrapping the guilty party, Jessica is shot at three times on campus.

Highlights: In the new urban format of *Murder, She Wrote,* Jessica Fletcher meets brighter, younger friends and foes—all conveniently ethnically diverse. Additionally, the Big Apple locale provides a variety of menacing environments in which she is exposed to greater danger than in usually serene Cabot Cove, Maine.

To be noted here is a touching scene at Kevin Bryce's apartment when his mother tells Jessica how much becoming a law enforcer means to her son, and Mrs. Fletcher, in turn, becomes his free private tutor to pass the exams. Of equal substance are the sequences involving Jessica's outrage upon discovering that she was hired at the university not for her academic abilities, but for her celebrity status. The miffed author insists she will quit once they find a replacement. Later, her department chairman, Dr. Raymond Auerbach, apologizes and Jessica returns to the classroom.

Trivia: From 1975–1985, Roxie Roker (1929–1996) portrayed Helen Willis on TV's *The Jeffersons*. New York City-born Alan Oppenheimer gained initial recognition with small screen viewers as nerdish Dr. Rudy Wells on *The Six Million Dollar Man* (1974–1975). Earlier, he was featured on the TV sitcom *He and She* (1967–1968) and was an off-camera voice in the animated cartoon series *Inch High, Private Eye* (1967–1968). Wings Hauser was a cast member of the daytime soap opera *The Young and the Restless* in the late 1970s and early 1980s, followed by his Lieutenant Ronald Hobbs on *The Last Precinct* (1986).

155. "Unauthorized Obituary"

(9/29/91) 60 mins.

Director: Alex Singer **Teleplay:** Robert E. Swanson

Regular: Angela Lansbury (Jessica Fletcher)

Recurring Character: Andrew Brye (Ahmed Shankar, the Doorman)

Guest Law Enforcers: Mark Phelan (Policeman); David Spielberg (Lieutenant Henry Girard)

Guest Cast: Barbara Bain (Ellen Lombard); Sam Behren (Steve Lockner); Edward Bell (Barry McAdams, Esq.); Bradford Dillman (Arthur Brent); Edward Penn (Mr. Stearns); Cathy Podewell (Beth Dawson); Ron Recasner (Roger); Frank Telfer (Griswald); Andrea Thompson (Kristy Parrish); Jessica Walter (Jane Dawson)

The Setting: New York City

The Case: Best-selling author Jane Dawson specializes in tell-all biographies. This vicious predator is working on her next no-holds-barred project, an exploitive study of screen legend Ellen Lombard. The latter vanished from the limelight after a suicide attempt. One of the people Jane contacts for the lowdown on Ellen is Jessica Fletcher, a longtime friend of the reclusive movie star. Jessica refuses to cooperate in such a scurrilous project.

One evening the unscrupulous Jane is electrocuted in the hot tub of her Manhattan home. Arriving on the investigation scene, Jessica prevents Kristy Parrish, the victim's overly industrious assistant, from leaving the premises with valuable research papers on the Lombard project.

Later, Jessica delves into the complex background of Beth, the deceased's younger sister, and her years in Tupelo, Mississippi. Also to be considered is Steve Lockner, the victim's younger husband, whom Dawson intended to divorce. Moreover, Jessica must keep her objectivity about Ellen Lombard's husband, Arthur, a genteel man who would do anything to protect his wife's sanity. He had been seen leaving Jane's premises shortly before her corpse was discovered.

Highlights: It becomes a battle of the quills when Jessica Fletcher locks horns with fellow author Jane Dawson (an apparent caricature of gutsy biographer Kitty Kelly). The two writers square off at a restaurant meeting where Mrs. Fletcher proves she is just as tough as her mercenary adversary. In contrast are the serene scenes where Jessica soothes the disturbed Ellen Lombard and, later, proves the integrity of her friendship.

Trivia: Astute *Murder, She Wrote* viewers will note the similarity of the murder methodology here and in 1987's "The Way to Dusty Death" (#70).

Frequent series guest star Bradford Dillman achieved recognition for such diverse roles as the homosexual killer in *Compulsion* (1959) and the well-intentioned monk in *Francis of Assisi* (1961). Prolific performer Jessica Walter won an Emmy Award for her police series *Amy Prentiss* (1974–1975). Barbara Bain, who won three Emmy trophies for *Mission: Impossible* (1966–1969), made her TV series debut on *Richard Diamond, Private Detective* (1959).

156. "Thicker Than Water"

(10/6/91) 60 mins.

Director: Anthony Shaw **Teleplay:** Lawrence DiTillio

Regulars: Angela Lansbury (Jessica Fletcher); Ron Masak (Sheriff Mort Metzger); William Windom (Dr. Seth Hazlitt)

Recurring Character: Louis Herthum (Deputy Andy Broom)

Guest Cast: Bruce Abbott (Wayne Metzger); Luke Askew (Terry Montagne); Kenny Davis (Fisherman); Carol Gustafson (Waitress); Pat Hingle (Zach Franklin); Ted Markland (Ned Keller); Marjorie Monaghan (Elaine Franklin)

The Setting: Cabot Cove, Maine

The Case: Sheriff Mort Metzger is both upset and embarrassed when his younger brother, Wayne, arrives without notice in Cabot Cove. Wayne has just served three years in prison. Although Mort remains suspicious of his unreliable sibling, he finds him a job working on the *Gretchen*, a fishing boat owned by tough seaman Zach Franklin. Over Zach's objections, Wayne soon forms a close relationship with Elaine, Franklin's pretty young daughter.

One day, the *Gretchen* docks at Cabot Cove with Wayne the only person aboard. He tells the sheriff that the prior night, while he was asleep, Zach disappeared. Later, Wayne's bloody knife is found aboard, and it's discovered that $2,000 in cash is missing. Mort concludes instantly that Wayne has betrayed him yet again. Still later, Terry Montagne, co-owner of the *Gretchen*, is found dead, and Wayne vanishes.

Jessica Fletcher steps into this family matter, helping Mort to regain his objectivity. The trail leads to such evidence as the *Gretchen's* blueprints as well as the contents of a local warehouse, and to Ned Keller, the angry former owner of the *Gretchen*.

Highlights: Sheriff Mort Metzger is well showcased in this installment. The lawman has a highly effective scene in which he describes to Jessica Fletcher how, when he and Wayne had been orphaned in New York City, Mort had raised his sibling. He also relates how his brother got involved with the wrong crowd. This memorable recitation makes the ex-New Yorker a very dimensional person.

Trivia: This was Louis Herthum's first series appearance as Cabot Cove's Deputy Andy Broom, a far more sophisticated, albeit subservient, assistant to Sheriff Metzger. Herthum had previously played non-related assignments on *Murder, She Wrote.* Pat Hingle, who overcame a mid-life accident in which he lost digits of one hand and was permanently crippled in one leg, appeared in such feature films as *Splendor in the Grass* (1961), *Sudden Impact* (1983) and *Batman Returns* (1992).

For the record, in this story line, Jessica Fletcher is asked to autograph a copy of her newest book, *Ashes, Ashes, Fall Down Dead.*

157. "Lines of Excellence"

(11/3/91) 60 mins.

Director: Walter Grauman **Teleplay:** J. Michael Straczynski

Regular: Angela Lansbury (Jessica Fletcher)

Recurring Character: Alan Oppenheimer (Dr. Raymond Auerbach)

Guest Law Enforcers: Charles Cyphers (Lieutenant Timothy Chance); Randee Heller (Lieutenant Cynthia Devereaux)

Guest Cast: Mary Valena Broussard (1st Student); Carmine Caridi (Dominic Rossari); David Ciminello (Michael Rossari); Charles Frank (Alan

Miller); Alan Fudge (Derek St. James); David Groh (Henry Waverly); Conrad Janis (Jason O'Connell); Ivan Kane (Nero); Corinne Kason (Teresa); Karen Kondazian (Rosalee Rossari); Georgie MacMinn (2nd Student); Tricia O'Neil (Linda Truitt)

The Setting: New York City

The Case: Giving into the inevitable, Jessica Fletcher abandons her trusty manual typewriter for a state-of-the-art home computer. To learn more about her high tech equipment, the bewildered author enrolls in computer classes offered by Manhattan's Serious Cybernetics Corporation. The firm has three operational employees: instructor Alan Miller, a software designer; Derek St. James, in charge of installing and customizing customers' systems; and Linda Truitt, a free-lance computer designer who is having an affair with Miller. Another company worker is one of Jessica's bright criminology students, likable if rough Michael Rossari.

One day Jessica arrives at the midtown facilities to discover Alan Miller's corpse in the classroom. He has been strangled with a computer connector cord. Michael is branded the chief suspect because he had been seen arguing with the victim shortly before his death.

Certain that ingenious, hard-working Michael—whose goal is to become a writer—is innocent of the homicide, Mrs. Fletcher burrows into the case. She uncovers that the school has been selling stolen computer systems obtained by Michael. Also caught in the intrigue are Jessica's classmate, businessman Jason O'Connell, and Henry Waverly, a former student at Serious Cybernetics.

Highlights: As more and more high technology equipment and methodology creep into Jessica Fletcher's daily life, they provide useful new directions for episode locales and fresh ways for homicides to be committed and then be solved. With Jessica struggling (and usually succeeding) to be on life's cutting edge, she reveals a pleasing vulnerability—her realization that she has a lot of catching up to do to stay abreast of today's generation. Then, too, this segment allows Mrs. Fletcher to do what she does so well—interfering in characters' ways of being which leads to their reevaluating their life choices.

Trivia: Conrad Janis, who played music store owner Frederick McConnell on *Mork & Mindy* (1978–1979, 1980–1982), has had an alternate career as a jazz trombonist. Character actor Alan Fudge had been part of such TV series as *Man from Atlantis*, *Eischied* and *Paper Dolls*. Among Alan Oppenheimer's early feature films are *In the Heat of the Night* (1967), *Star!* (1968) and *Little Big Man* (1970).

158. "Judge Not"

(11/10/91) 60 mins.

Director: Chuck Bowman **Teleplay:** Gerald DiPago

Regular: Angela Lansbury (Jessica Fletcher)

Guest Law Enforcers: Randy Brooks (Detective John Coop, Jr.); William Lucking (Lieutenant Charles Foret); Bob Roitblat (Detective)

Guest Cast: William Atherton (Andy Henley); Olivia Cole (Melinda Coop); Julius Harris (Jack Lee Johnson); Tony Ralph-Wilson (Minister); Logan Ramsey (Judge Robert Henley); James Randolph (Gene); Beah Richards (Emma Coop)

The Setting: New Orleans, Louisiana

The Case: Daddy Coop, the "King of Rhythm and Blues," has died. Jessica Fletcher, who had done volunteer work for the United Negro College Fund with the musician's widow, Melinda, flies to New Orleans for the funeral. Later, she accompanies Melinda to the Possum Cafe. There, its owner, Jack Lee Johnson, has an exhibit of mementos from when he played bass in Coop's music group.

Scarcely do they reach the club than they find Jack Lee dead. Mrs. Fletcher notes that there's a peculiar square mark on the victim's neck. Later, Melinda confides to Jessica that she has been receiving frightening phone calls from an unknown party demanding a piece of evidence relating to the twenty-years-ago death of Luna Santee, a singer in Daddy's band.

While providing the police with her statement regarding Lee's death, Jessica meets prosecuting attorney Andy Henley. Later, he gives her a tour of the spooky old Henley mansion on the outskirts of town. There, Mrs. Fletcher notes an intriguing self-portrait by Andy's dad, Judge Robert Henley. From congenial Andy, Jessica learns how Luna was strangled two decades ago, but that her murder has never been solved. Meanwhile, Coop's son, John Jr., a police detective with a chip on his shoulder, trails the person responsible for the rash of menacing calls to his family. In the process, John is wounded, and, when he refuses to tell his superior officers why he had been injured, he is suspended.

Enmeshed in solving this mystery, Jessica learns further details from several other interested parties: Judge Henley, who was the district attorney in charge of prosecuting the Luna Santee murder case; Emma Coop, John Jr.'s grandmother; Gene, who had worked for the Coops for a long time and knows many of their secrets; and Melinda, who was long aware of Daddy's several extramarital affairs.

Highlights: This is one of the series' lesser episodes, with a thin, hackneyed plot barely sustaining the entry. It's also hampered by overly exaggerated

Southern accents, especially by the unrestrained Logan Ramsey and Olivia Cole. One of the segment's more invigorating scenes finds Jessica Fletcher losing her patience when uncooperative John Coop, Jr., tells her to leave town.

Trivia: Connecticut-born William Atherton turned from playing conventional young leading men in *The Sugarland Express* (1974) and *The Day of the Locust* (1974) to portraying offkilter on-screen characters in *Ghostbusters* (1984), *No Mercy* (1986) and *Die Hard 2* (1990). Beah Richards was Oscar-nominated for Best Supporting Actress for her role as Sidney Poitier's mother in *Guess Who's Coming to Dinner* (1967), while Olivia Cole won an Emmy Award for playing Mathilda in *Roots* (1977). Julius Harris was a veteran of Hollywood's black action film cycle: *Slaves* (1969), *Shaft's Big Score* (1973), etc. Both he and Atherton appeared in *Looking for Mr. Goodbar* (1977).

159. "Terminal Connection"

(11/17/91) 60 mins.

Director: Walter Grauman **Teleplay:** Robert E. Swanson

Regular: Angela Lansbury (Jessica Fletcher)

Guest Law Enforcer: Steve Forrest (Lieutenant Paul Stratton)

Guest Cast: Douglas Barr (Greg Franklin); Chad Everett (Clark Blanchard); Kerrie Keane (Margo Saunders, Esq.); Lois Nettleton (Ginny Blanchard); Jameson Parker (Dane Kenderson); Lisa Pelikan (Allison Franklin); Hank Stratton (Scott Blanchard)

The Settings: Los Angeles, California; Santa Barbara, California

The Case: Jessica Fletcher is invited to the fifth wedding anniversary party of Clark and Ginny Blanchard. Clark is an aggressive, jet-setter entrepreneur. Jessica first knew Ginny when the latter was the successful author of children's books. Ginny's son, Scott, by her first marriage, is a student at the University of Southern California.

Later that night, when a drunken Clark turns nasty, Jessica learns from distraught Ginny that she has long been a victim of wife abuse. While Clark is away on a business trip, Mrs. Fletcher urges her friend to leave him. However, Ginny refuses to abandon her husband or their life-style. The next morning, Clark's lifeless body is found in Ginny's car at their beach house and Ginny's blood-drenched purse is located inside. Although a sympathetic friend to Mrs. Blanchard, Lieutenant Paul Stratton has no option but to arrest the badly shaken Ginny.

Jessica is taken aback when Ginny's slippery lawyer, Margo Saunders, insists that her client plead guilty to the crime, reasoning that it will help Mrs. Blanchard obtain a better deal in court. Determined to substantiate Ginny's innocence, Mrs. Fletcher's spade work uncovers that Allison Franklin, the wife of the victim's chief executive, had been having an affair with Blanchard.

There is also the matter of Allison's husband, Greg, who supposedly was in San Francisco at the time of the foul play. Additionally, there is smarmy Dane Kenderson, who had been caught breaking into Clark's office to "borrow" files dealing with Blanchard's ruthless attempt to take over Kenderson's firm.

Highlights: If Jessica Fletcher can be engagingly down-to-earth among the unpretentious set, she is equally at ease as a celebrity among wealthy acquaintances. Here, whether at an upscale polo match or as a magnetic guest "working the room" at a fancy party, she is consistently chic and charming. Her serious-mindedness about abused wives, the subtext of the episode, imparts solid reality to the whodunit elements.

Trivia: A two-time (1977, 1983) Emmy Award winner, veteran Lois Nettleton began her film career with such features as *Period of Adjustment* (1962), *Come Fly with Me* (1963) and *Mail Order Bride* (1964). Chad Everett gained fame as Dr. Joe Gannon on *Medical Center* (1969–1976). Steve Forrest's early screen stints included *The Bad and the Beautiful* (1952), *Phantom of the Rue Morgue* (1954) and *Bedevilled* (1955). *Simon & Simon* veteran Jameson Parker had begun in movies with *The Bell Jar* (1979), *A Small Circle of Friends* (1980) and *White Dog* (1982).

160. "A Killing in Las Vegas"

(11/24/91) 60 mins.

Director: Anthony Shaw **Teleplay:** Bruce Lansbury

Regular: Angela Lansbury (Jessica Fletcher)

Recurring Character: Andrew Brye (Ahmed Shankar, the Doorman)

Guest Law Enforcer: Richard Portnow (Lieutenant Walt Murphy)

Guest Cast: Hal England (Bookseller); Bruce Gray (Ted Hartley); Wendy Hoffman (Waitress); Jeff Kaake (Eddie Wheaton); Andreas Katsulas (Jerry Pappas [Alex Rogas]); Howard Keel (Larry Thorson); Stephen Macht

(Frank Stinson); Joan McMurtrey (Alice Baxter); Lisa Melilli (2nd Waitress); Amy O'Neill (Susan Hartley); Connie Sawyer (Elderly Lady); Shelley Smith (Katherine McSorley); Jared Snyder (Wolf); David Soul (Wes McSorley)

The Settings: Las Vegas, Nevada; New York City

The Case: Since Jessica Fletcher is attending a Las Vegas book fair, her publisher's publicist/agent, Ted Hartley, asks her to check on his daughter, Susan, who is living in the gambling capital. She is working as a cocktail waitress at McSorley's Hotel and Casino where Jessica will be staying. According to Hartley, his daughter is spending more time with her boyfriend, Eddie Wheaton, a blackjack dealer, than in studying at college.

Immediately upon arriving in the gaming capital, Jessica meets Larry Thorson, the hotel's veteran security chief. The tough, honest man and Jessica quickly develop a strong rapport. From her new friend, Mrs. Fletcher learns that Wes McSorley, the resort's owner, has staked all his reserves on renovating the hotel so that in turn he could resell at a profit. However, his unsavory partner, the Seashore Properties Corporation, vetoes the crucial deal.

Later, Wes falls from the balcony of his penthouse suite and it is determined to be murder, not suicide. The police arrest Eddie Wheaton with good cause, as he has a record of assault and armed robbery. Besides, he had been caught skimming money from the casino. More importantly, hotel elevator surveillance tapes reveal the suspect going to and from the penthouse at the time of the murder.

A deeply alarmed Susan begs Jessica to intercede on Eddie's behalf. Mrs. Fletcher ascertains that not only was Eddie's pit boss, Frank Stinson, in on the skimming, but so was the hotel's casino manager, Jerry Archer. Also under suspicion is McSorley's liquor-dependent widow, Katherine, who has not always been discreet in her activities.

Highlights: In most *Murder, She Wrote* installments, Jessica Fletcher's worthy confederate in her crime-solving is often *not* the police investigator assigned to the case. Here, she teams with the astute hotel security chief, a solid citizen. The camaraderie between he and Jessica is one of the segment's treats. Another is the recurrent conceit that Mrs. Fletcher, so adept at so many things, is unknowledgeable and/or unskilled at an activity enjoyed by so many less-keen individuals. In this instance, it's gambling. There are fine moments as she lets down her reserve, and gives in to gambling fever.

Trivia: This was the first of many *Murder, She Wrote* scripts credited to Angela Lansbury's brother, Bruce. Booming Howard Keel, the bright star of several MGM musicals (*Annie Get Your Gun* [1950], *Kiss Me, Kate* [1953], etc.), later played the wealthy second husband of Barbara Bel Geddes on *Dallas* (1981–1991). Strong-featured Stephen Macht made his acting livelihood mostly in TV movies: *Amelia Earhart* (1976), *The Immigrants* (1978), *Stephen King's Graveyard Shift* (1991), etc. Jeff Kaake had played another gambling role when he was one of the young Las Vegas undercover vice cops in the short-lived (1990) *Nasty Boys* series.

161. "The Committee"

(12/1/91) 60 mins.

Director: Jerry Jameson **Teleplay:** J. Michael Straczynski

Regular: Angela Lansbury (Jessica Fletcher)

Guest Law Enforcer: John Kapelos (Lieutenant Howard Tartarus)

Guest Cast: Judy Jean Berns (Fund-raiser Organizer); Robin Dearden (Lisa Dutton, the Club Associate); Geoffrey Infeld (Messenger); Marabina Jaimes (Nurse); Randall James Jeffries (Valet); Elizabeth Kent (Young Woman); Norman Lloyd (Philip Arkham); John McMartin (Winston Devermore); Susan McWilliams (Fan); Nicholas Pryor (Theo Cayle); James Sutorius (Lawrence Cayle); Robin Thomas (Gerald Innsmouth); Ed Winter (Edward Dunsany); George Wyner (Harcourt Fenton); Darrell Zwerling (Doctor)

The Setting: New York City

The Case: Winston Devermore invites Jessica Fletcher to talk at the exclusive Avernus Club. She will be the first woman speaker at this old boys organization, composed of *the* wealthy, privileged and powerful. Her reading there is a great success.

Later that evening, Winston returns to the club for a covert meeting of the Committee, composed of himself, Philip Arkham, Edward Dunsany, Harcourt Fenton and Gerald Innsmouth. Guided by Arkham, the president, the group agrees to deal with Lawrence Cayle, a fellow member who is out of control. As is the custom, each committee member is given both a black (guilty) and white (innocent) marble for the voting. Arkham has his assistant, Lisa Dutton, collect the marbles in two pouches. The vote is 4 to 1 against Cayle. Fenton refuses to partake in punishing a peer and leaves. Meanwhile, Philip passes out another group of marbles. Whoever—and it is to be kept secret from the others—receives the gold one is to enforce the sanctioning.

The next evening, Lawrence responds to a message to appear at the Committee's room at midnight. There he is shot to death. Although Lieutenant Howard Tartarus is in charge of the homicide case, the Committee asks Jessica to investigate so that the organization's good name can be preserved.

Jessica is shocked by the club members' snobbish conceit that they are above the law. However, her curiosity is piqued and she follows through by questioning the dead man's subservient brother, Theo. Before long, another of the group is murdered, while yet another of them is severely injured in a car "accident."

Highlights: Because it deals with such a rarefied, self-impressed level of society, this segment has few characters with whom the viewer can empathize. Even Winston Devermore who is charming—especially to Jessica—is still far too much of a self-serving snob.

Trivia: Broadway musical performer John McMartin played Julian J. Robertson on *Falcon Crest* (1985–1986). Norman Lloyd, once associated with Orson Welles and then with Alfred Hitchcock, was avuncular Dr. Daniel Auschlander on *St. Elsewhere* (1982–1988).

162: "The List of Uri Lermentov"

(12/15/91) 60 mins.

Director: Anthony Shaw **Teleplay:** Tom Sawyer

Regular: Angela Lansbury (Jessica Fletcher)

Recurring Character: Len Cariou (Sir Michael Preston/a.k.a. Michael Reagan [Michael Haggerty])

Guest Law Enforcers: Louis Giambalvo (Lieutenant Blaisdell); David Starwalt (Policeman)

Guest Cast: Richard Beymer (Charles Lawton Standish); Theodore Bikel (Uri Lermentov); Michael Fawcett (Headwaiter); Spiros Focas (Constantin Kesmek); Janet Julian (Bonnie Hartman); Nicholas Kadi (Sergei Onyegin); Brian McNamara (Harry Neville); Mitchell Ryan (Congressman Arthur Prouty); Gwendolyn J. Shepherd (Dispatcher)

The Setting: Washington, D.C.

The Case: Congressman Arthur Prouty, no stranger to Cabot Cove, invites Jessica Fletcher to attend a reception during her visit to the nation's capital. At the gathering, she chances upon her nemesis/friend Michael Haggerty. This time the British secret service agent is posing as an affluent South African employed by a diamond cartel.

It develops that Michael is engineering a meeting with Uri Lermentov, a renegade KGB secret agent who is retiring to Kiev. Haggerty hopes to purchase from Uri a list of British undercover agents operating in Libya. Others who want the crucial names are manipulative lawyer Charles Lawton Standish and global arms dealer Constantin Kesmek. The coded document ends up in a book innocently handed to Jessica by Prouty.

Back at her hotel suite, two prowlers convene on her room to grab the document. Hours later, Mrs. Fletcher awakens to find the dead body of a bludgeoned Lermentov in her outer room. Before long, Michael has been arrested on a murder charge. Meanwhile, Standish offers Jessica $1 million in exchange for the vital paper. By now, she has shared information on the case with Prouty and his capable aide, Harry Neville. Thanks to Jessica's sleuthing, Lieutenant Blaisdell ends the winner—with the real culprit behind bars.

Highlights: By the 1990s, the overt cold war between Russia and the U.S. had ended. A side effect of this détente was to complicate the lives of script writers who had relied on Soviet/American antagonism to propel espionage plot lines; thus, the use of a less plausible story ploy in this episode (i.e., protecting the lives of British M16 agents in Libya).

More intriguing is the ongoing relationship between devil-may-care Michael and author/sleuth Jessica. She may protest that Haggerty and disastrous escapades are all too synonymous. However, she has an obvious underlying attraction for this dashing rogue which makes her incapable of rejecting his pleas for assistance. On a parallel level is Mrs. Fletcher's intriguing rapport with the capable, handsome politician and congressman. It speaks of future potential.

Trivia: Among Len Cariou's Broadway credits are such musicals as *Applause, Company, A Little Night Music* and *Sweeney Todd.* Theodore Bikel appeared on the New York stage in editions of *Cafe Crown, The King and I, My Fair Lady, Pousse-Cafe* and *The Sound of Music.*

163. "Danse Diabolique"

(1/5/92) 60 mins.

Director: Alexander Singer **Teleplay:** Jo William Philipp

Regular: Angela Lansbury (Jessica Fletcher)

Guest Law Enforcers: Ernie Lively (Lieutenant Martin Kinicki); Mark Costello (Sergeant O'Connor)

Guest Cast: Marisa Berenson (Claudia Cameron); Anthony Gordon (Backer); Stephen Nichols (Barry Carroll); Lindy Nisbet (Florist Shop Clerk); Adrian

Paul (Edward Hale); Daniel Pilon (Geoffrey Presser); Robert Torti (Damien Bolo); Nancy Valens (Lily Roland); Joel Weiss (Delivery Boy)

The Setting: San Francisco, California

The Case: On a book tour in San Francisco, Jessica Fletcher takes time out to join potential backers for a preview of a major revival of the ballet *Danse Diabolique*, a production which has a long history of being cursed. (The second time it was performed the lead ballerina had died!) The new rendition is sponsored by Mrs. Fletcher's old pals, producer Geoffrey Presser and prima ballerina Claudia Cameron, who offstage are husband and wife.

Before long, the curse seems to prove true yet again as backstage strife runs rampant. Young and ambitious Lily Roland persuades choreographer/principal dancer Edward Hale to have Geoffrey replace the mature Claudia in the lead part with her. Damien Bolo, assigned the male lead, is aggravated by the substitution. On the other hand, stage manager Barry Carroll, a dancer forced to retire due to a knee injury, is deeply in love with Lily and applauds the cast change—until he catches her in a compromising situation in her dressing room with Presser.

During the opening night Jessica and Claudia watch from their box seats. Suddenly, Lily dies onstage. Claudia and others blame the curse, but Jessica has spotted two puncture marks on Lily's palm. Before long, Jessica and crude Lieutenant Martin Kinicki are vying to solve the mystery. Two stage props (an artificial rose and a skull) become key elements in wrapping up the mystery.

Highlights: In this example of recurring "cultural" episodes, a good deal of attention is given to the ballet sequences, so much so that at times the murder plot seems almost forgotten.

Trivia: Actress/model Marisa Berenson, whose sister (Berry) had been married to actor Anthony Perkins (1932–1992), had been featured in such movies as *Death in Venice* (1971), *Cabaret* (1972) and *Barry Lyndon* (1975). Adrian Paul had been a cast member of TV's *The Colbys* (1986–1987) and *War of the Worlds* (1989–1990), but achieved far greater popularity with the syndicated teleseries *Highlander* (1992–).

164. "The Witch's Curse"

(1/12/92) 60 mins.

Director: Jerry Jameson **Teleplay:** Tracy Friedman

Regulars: Angela Lansbury (Jessica Fletcher); Ron Masak (Sheriff Mort Metzger); William Windom (Dr. Seth Hazlitt)

Recurring Character: Julie Adams (Eve Simpson)

Guest Law Enforcer: Louis Herthum (Deputy Dave Anderson)

Guest Cast: David Ackroyd (Nate Parsons); Carol Androsky (Anabelle Parsons); Kerry Brennan (Beth); Mary Crosby (Mariah Osborn [Mary Lynn Walker]); Lee DeBroux (Joe Hill); Rebecca Forman (Sherry); Linda Frasier (Arlissa Davenport); Marian Mercer (Penelope Hope Daniels); Ed Nelson (Judge Willard Clinton); Linda Porter (Clerk); Renata Scott (Charlotte); Marian Seldes (Lydia Winthrop); Robert Vaughn (Charles Winthrop)

The Setting: Cabot Cove, Maine

The Case: The townsfolk of Cabot Cove, under the direction of Dr. Seth Hazlitt, are recreating the 300-year-old burning at the stake of Rachel Abbot. At the auditions, Mariah Osborn, a mysterious newcomer to town, is handed the lead role. Her dramatic appearance at the tryouts attracts the attention of Charles Winthrop, whose wife, Lydia, has a supporting part in the production.

That night, someone breaks into the Winthrops' house, tampering with their safe, but strangely not stealing the valuable contents (jewelry). Rose petals are found strewn about the room, a symbolic reminder of Rachel Abbot's curse on Cabot Cove. Later, Judge Willard Clinton, who, in the pageant, is portraying the magistrate who sentenced Rebecca to her doom, is pushed from the top of the town hall.

As Jessica and Sheriff Mort Metzger piece together data on the murder, she ties together a note found in the judge's pocket with a traumatic incident that happened twenty-five years before. Meanwhile, Mort figures out the connection between the burning of insurance agent Nate Parsons' old files and a love affair that decades later inspires murder.

Highlights: By having the locals enthusiastically, if ineptly, participate in a play within the story, the viewer is treated to new aspects of familiar characters. Most of these Down Easterners are a superstitious, highly susceptible lot, which even includes the usually cynical Dr. Seth Hazlitt. With her orderly, practical mind, ever-vigilant Jessica Fletcher serves as a counterpoint to the more impressionable elements populating Cabot Cove.

Trivia: For some reason, Louis Herthum, already established as Deputy Andy Broom, did a temporary name change here to Deputy Dave Anderson, but in all other respects played the same part. Marian Mercer was a graduate of such TV sitcoms as *The Sandy Duncan Show* (1972), *Mary Hartman, Mary Hartman* (1975–1978) and *It's a Living* (1980–1982, 1985–1989). David Ackroyd played Dr. Boyer on TV's *AfterMASH* (1984).

165. "Incident in Lot #7"

(1/19/92) 60 mins.

Director: Anthony Shaw **Teleplay:** J. Michael Straczynski

Regular: Angela Lansbury (Jessica Fletcher)

Guest Law Enforcers: Ron Glass (Lieutenant Hanrahan); Christina Rich (Police Officer)

Guest Cast: Daniel Bardol (John Cavershaw); Larry Carroll (TV Anchorman); Jackie Gayle (Willy Montego); Henry Gibson (Oliver Thissle); Michelle Johnson (Monica Chase); Ron Leibman (Darryl Heyward); Lar Park Lincoln (Caroline Pryce); Paula Prentiss (Leonora Holt); Stuart Whitman (Ben Miller)

The Setting: Los Angeles, California

The Case: Jessica Fletcher arrives at Universal Studios in Hollywood for conferences about the screen adaptation of her novel, *Messenger of Midnight.* At the meeting are independent producer Darryl Heyward, as well as his longtime agent, Willy Montego, and screenwriter John Cavershaw. Later, while Jessica and John debate the merits of his adaptation, Darryl confronts his temperamental star, Leonora Holt. He also deals brusquely with his mistress, Monica Chase, the wife of his prime investor. Heyward breaks the news to Monica that their affair is over.

At the studio commissary, Darryl offers to give Jessica a behind-the-scenes tour of the famed *Psycho* house on the backlot. When she arrives there, she finds the producer lying on the floor, dead.

While Lieutenant Hanrahan pursues his avenue of inquiry, Jessica moves in different directions. She is handicapped by brash Leonora, who, since she will be playing a Jessica Fletcher-like character in the movie, thinks it would be fun and good publicity to try real-life sleuthing.

Meanwhile, there are plenty of suspects who disliked the late producer. Besides Leonora and Monica, there is Montego, whose agent's contract with Darryl wasn't being renewed. Additionally, there's Ben Miller, veteran head of the deceased's production unit, who knew he was being replaced by younger blood. And not least of all is bizarre Oliver Thissle, one of Leonora's more obsessive fans.

Highlights: For years after Alfred Hitchcock made *Psycho* (1960) at Universal Pictures, the famed Norman Bates house has been a featured attraction of the studio's backlot tour. In this episode, it became a plot line focal point. Counting on TV viewers to associate mayhem and murder with this famed spooky standing set, the story plays up its historical connection. On a lighter note is Jessica Fletcher's dismayed reaction to hyperactive, gurgly-voiced Leonora, a self-absorbed person Jessica desperately tries to avoid.

Trivia: Early in her career, tall, angular Paula Prentiss, married to actor/director Richard Benjamin, made a series of screen comedies in tandem with Jim Hutton: *Where the Boys Are* (1960), *Bachelor in Paradise* (1961), etc. She and Angela Lansbury costarred in *The World of Henry Orient* (1964). Henry Gibson appeared as a regular on *Rowan & Martin's Laugh-In* (1968–1971). Ron Leibman, more noted for dramatic screen roles (e.g., *Slaughterhouse Five* [1972] *Norma Rae* [1979]) was also an able farceur (e.g., *Zorro the Gay Blade* [1981]).

In recent years, veteran actor Stuart Whitman participated in several low-budget features: *Moving Target* (1989), *Omega Cop* (1990), etc. Ron Glass was a member of *Barney Miller* (1975–1982) and *The New Odd Couple* (1982–1983).

166. "The Monte Carlo Murders"

(2/2/92) 60 mins.

Director: Jerry Jameson **Teleplay:** Bruce Lansbury

Regular: Angela Lansbury (Jessica Fletcher)

Guest Law Enforcer: Patrick Bauchau (Inspector Charles Morel)

Guest Cast: Reuven Bar-Yotam (Chef Robert); Neill Barry (Richie Floret); David Birney (Earl Harper); Maryam D'Abo (Barbara Callaway); Lise Hilboldt (Cynthia Harper); Bo Hopkins (Scott Larkin); Jon Rashad Kamal (Gift Shop Proprietor); Diane Manzo (Desk Clerk); Dina Merrill (Annie Floret); Ian Ogilvy (Peter Templeton); Scott Strohmeyer (Henry); Victor Touzie (Armand Beauclaire); Gustav Vintas (Albert DeVere)

The Setting: Monte Carlo

The Case: Fatigued from her European book tour, Jessica Fletcher stops in Monte Carlo to visit college chum Annie Floret, the owner of L'Hotel Claudine. From Inspector Charles Morel, a good friend of Annie's, Jessica learns that Annie must immediately repay vicious businessman Earl Harper one million dollars, which she borrowed five years earlier, or she will lose her business. Annie is frantic over the matter, but her twenty-one-year-old son, Richie, is pleased by the turn of events. He hopes it will force his mother to adopt a more restful life-style.

Not long after, ruthless Harper is stabbed to death in his hotel suite. As the charming inspector and perplexed Jessica agree, the cast of suspects is indeed large. They include former jewel thief Peter Templeton, a hot-tempered man who now plays the piano in the hotel lounge; pretty Barbara Callaway, Peter's confederate who had been flirting with the victim; Scott

Larkin, a tough-minded business rival of the deceased; and Earl's wife, Cynthia; as well as Annie and Richie Floret.

Because the hugely valuable Alexandra diamond is missing from the dead man's suite, the police initially arrest Templeton. Hardly has he been released than Armand, officially a hotel waiter, is stabbed. Before he expires, he gives Jessica a clue—in French. The riddle leads Jessica on a wild chase through the hotel's five-star kitchen and, eventually, to trapping the actual killer.

Highlights: With its elegant setting and proficient cast, this episode is high-toned from start to finish. Its subthemes of misguided love and greed are reflected in the twisted relationships of several of its characters. The entry's running gag is Jessica's curiosity regarding the magic ingredients in Chef Robert's world-famous sauce. Before the finale, persistent Mrs. Fletcher charms the temperamental culinary whiz into giving her a special gift.

Trivia: Among Ian Ogilvy's first motion picture credits are *Stranger in the House* (1967), *The Sorcerers* (1967) and *Witchfinder General* (1968). Dina Merrill's initial movie appearances include *Desk Set* (1957), *Don't Give Up the Ship* (1959) and *Butterfield 8* (1960). David Birney's early big screen assignments encompass *Caravan to Vaccares* (1974) and *Knight's Work* (1976). Bo Hopkins began in Hollywood pictures with *The Bridge at Remagen* (1969), *The Wild Bunch* (1969) and *The 1,000 Plane Raid* (1969).

167. "Tinker, Taylor, Liar, Thief"

(3/1/92) 60 mins.

Director: Peter Salim **Teleplay:** Robert E. Swanson

Regular: Angela Lansbury (Jessica Fletcher)

Guest Law Enforcers: Elizabeth Anne Smith (Policeperson); Nick Tate (Inspector Stillwell)

Guest Cast: Sandy Allison (MacPherson); Lloyd Bochner (John Thurston); Kim Braden (Daisy Collins); Kenneth Danziger (Archie Potter); Richard A. Davies (Edward Cadwell); Peter Dennis (Albert, the Hotel Front Desk Man); Guy Doleman (Corsair); Trevor Eve (Julian Fontaine); Laurie Main (Man); Sharon Maughan (Penelope Cadwell); Derrick O'Connor (Mickey Dawks); Clement Von Franckenstein (Nigel Atkins); Diana Webster (Landlady)

The Setting: London, England

The Case: While visiting London, Jessica meets Nigel Atkins of the British Home Office. Thereafter, as Mrs. Fletcher returns to her hotel suite, she observes a redheaded young woman fleeing from the next room and vanishing down the service stairs. Inquisitive Jessica investigates and finds Atkins' corpse in Room 412. However, by the time the police arrive with Inspector Stillwell #412 is no longer in disarray and the body has vanished!

Later, Jessica finds the missing victim dumped into a service elevator. Again the police are summoned and again the cadaver disappears. By now, the exasperated authorities consider Jessica a scatter-brained American tourist. The merry-go-round concludes temporarily when witnesses report that a man has just leaped out of an upper window at the hotel. The corpse proves to be that of Atkins.

That evening, Mrs. Fletcher attends a chic party in Chelsea, hosted by Julian Fontaine, who is connected to the Home Office. There she encounters the fleeing woman, Penelope Cadwall, who is now accompanied by her husband, Edward. Later in the whirlwind of events, Jessica locks horns with Mickey Dawks, a tough-minded loan shark who is convinced that Mrs. Fletcher knows more about the "late" Mr. Atkins than she is admitting. Jessica follows leads to Daisy Collins, a prostitute who claims she can locate Atkins. Then there is Corsair, an executive in the espionage game, who controls many of the characters like puppets on a string.

Highlights: Many movies (*So Long at the Fair* [1950], *Frantic* [1988], etc.) have built a thrilling premise on a body that the hero(ine) has seen, but which the authorities claim is nonexistent. The mounting frustration of the plight allows Jessica Fletcher to be her persistent, analytic self—even in the face of the law officials' incredulity.

Trivia: In homage to Broadway composer Stephen Sondheim, in whose works (*Anyone Can Whistle, Gypsy,* etc.) Angela Lansbury had appeared on stage, one of the episode's opening sequences has a character bragging that he's just obtained two tickets to Sondheim's new West End stage hit. Early in his film career, Canadian-born Lloyd Bochner made such features as *Drums of Africa* (1963), *Harlow* (1965) and *Point Blank* (1967).

168. "Ever After"

(3/8/92) 60 mins.

Director: Anthony Shaw **Teleplay:** Robert Van Scoyk

Regular: Angela Lansbury (Jessica Fletcher)

Recurring Character: Andrew Brye (Ahmed Shankar, the Doorman)

Guest Law Enforcers: Robert Alan Browne (Officer Bronsky); Nada Despotovich (Deputy Ginger Billis); John DiSanti (Sheriff Elton Beals)

Guest Cast: Marcia Cross (Marci Bowman); Justin Dipego (Painter); Marj Dusay (Miriam Bowman); Elaine Welton Hill (Sheri Finestock); Maurice Hill (Irwin Fisk); Kevin McCarthy (Walter Bowman); Michael McGrady (Bo Wilder); Eda Reiss Merin (Dorothy Fremont); Richard Morse (City Clerk); Kate Mulgrew (Joanna Grimsky Rollins); Tony Roberts (Devon "Sonny" Lane); Mitchell Whitfield (Teddy Cardoza)

The Settings: Grill Harbor, Long Island, New York; New York City

The Case: Having been away on a weekend holiday, Jessica Fletcher returns to her Manhattan apartment and meets her new neighbor, Joanna Rollins. The latter is the star of the long-enduring daytime TV soap opera *Happily Ever After*. As Jessica unlocks her front door, she witnesses a fierce quarrel between Rollins and her lover, Devon "Sonny" Lane. An ex-child star, Lane has not only just been fired from the soap, but Joanna now dismisses him from her private life.

Some days later, amid a media splash, Joanna weds Walter Bowman, a wealthy older man. At once, she moves into his extravagant Long Island home. The new arrival is greeted coldly by Walter's spoiled daughter, Marci, and her tacky boyfriend, Teddy Cardoza. When Bowman's ex-first wife, Miriam, learns of Walter's nuptials, she turns bitchy. She informs Bowman that she had been having an affair with Bo Wilder, Bowman's "trusted" personal trainer. In turn, Walter fires Bo.

Meanwhile, a vandal slashes a valuable painting in Joanna's apartment. Jessica comforts the distraught actress and the two leave for dinner. While dining, Joanna phones her spouse. Later, Walter is found shot to death at his Long Island home.

Sheriff Elton Beals of the Grill Harbor police force and the just-arrived Jessica discover a shotgun under the victim's bed. It has two strange round marks on its stock. As the suspects are questioned, it develops that one (Devon) has a good alibi, while others (Miriam and Bo) don't. A hunch brings Mrs. Fletcher to theatrical casting agent Dorothy Fremont, who provides valuable insight into the case.

Highlights: Performing in exaggerated fashion, Kate Mulgrew and Tony Roberts turn in attention-grabbing characterizations. As such, even highly active Jessica Fletcher pales by comparison. It was a conceit of *Murder, She Wrote* that urban law enforcers are tough, cynical and fast-acting, while their suburban counterparts are the opposite. Here, the police officer definitely belongs to the latter category.

Trivia: Kate Mulgrew began her TV career playing Mary Ryan on *Ryan's Hope* (1975–1977). This was followed by her role as the snooping wife of police detective Columbo in *Kate Columbo* (1979). Broadway star and Woody Allen movie regular Tony Roberts had an early TV assignment in *The Edge of Night* (1965–1977). Later he (co)starred in *Rosetti and Ryan, The Four Seasons* and *The Lucie Arnaz Show.*

Marcia Cross is known to mid-1990s TV viewers as Kimberly Shaw, the vengeful physician on the prime-time soap opera *Melrose Place.*

169. "To the Last Will I Grapple with Thee"

(3/15/92) 60 mins.

Director: Walter Grauman **Teleplay:** J. Michael Stracyznski

Regular: Angela Lansbury (Jessica Fletcher)

Recurring Character: George Hearn (Sean Cullane)

Guest Law Enforcers: Ken Gerson (3rd Officer); Cliff Gorman (Lieutenant Jacoby); Donald Nardini (2nd Officer); Michael O. Smith (1st Officer)

Guest Cast: Dana Craig (Customer); Cameron Dye (Ian O'Connor); John Karlen (Patrick MacNair); Richard Lynch (Michael O'Connor); Sharon Mahoney (Kathleen Cullane); Mark Rolston (Finn Dawley); Matthew Saks (1st Student); Melissa Samuels (2nd Student)

The Setting: New York City

The Case: Sean Cullane, an Irish police officer, is in New York City on a professional exchange program. Currently, he's one of Jessica Fletcher's colleagues at Manhattan University. Now, he finds himself charged with murder. The victim is Michael O'Connor, a disreputable construction contractor who has been involved in many shady dealings. The deceased had recently moved to the U.S. from Dublin, Ireland. Back there, over past years, Sean Cullane had often arrested O'Connor on assorted charges.

The case seems stacked against Sean, as the fatal bullet had been fired from Cullane's service gun. Solidifying the case is the fact that Michael had made a videotape—shortly before his death and standing in the same location where he died—stating that if he should be found dead, the killer is Cullane.

Although Lieutenant Jacoby is satisfied that Sean is the murderer, Jessica isn't. In examining the circumstances, she turns her attentions to Finn Dawley, a loan shark to whom the victim owed money; as well as Ian O'Connor, the beneficiary of Michael's fortune; and Kathleen Cullane, the suspect's daughter. With help from Patrick MacNair, the owner of a local Irish pub where the accused and the deceased had often drunk, Mrs.

Fletcher studies the Irish background of all the parties and comes up with startling revelations.

Highlights: Obviously, the crux of each *Murder, She Wrote* episode is not only who the killer is, but how the homicide was committed. Here, so much effort is put into explaining the elaborate setup, that the gimmick loses credibility and interest for the viewer. With her own Irish heritage, Angela Lansbury favored episodes with a shamrock lilt. Here the bogus flavor and accents are too full of blarney.

Trivia: Broadway veteran George Hearn costarred with Angela Lansbury in an edition of the musical *Sweeney Todd,* one that was taped for TV in the early 1980s. Richard Lynch's television credits included series run in *Battlestar Galactica* (1980) and *The Phoenix* (1982). John Karlen won an Emmy Award as Tyne Daly's sympathetic spouse in 1986 for *Cagney & Lacey* in the Best Supporting Actor in a Drama category. Cliff Gorman gained early recognition as a costar of the original off-Broadway stage edition (1968) and film version (1970) of *Boys in the Band.* He also had the recurring role of Richard Crenna's associate in a series of TV movies dealing with the New York Police Department which began airing in the late 1980s.

170. "Programmed for Murder"

(4/5/92) 60 mins.

Director: Jerry Jameson **Teleplay:** Tom Sawyer

Regulars: Angela Lansbury (Jessica Fletcher); Ron Masak (Sheriff Mort Metzger); William Windom (Dr. Seth Hazlitt)

Recurring Characters: Julie Adams (Eve Simpson); Louis Herthum (Deputy Andy Broom)

Guest Cast: Hunt Block (Dr. Jonas Beckwith); Judith Chapman (Harriet Simmons Wooster); Tony Fields (Rudy Ortega); Boyd Gaines (John Halsey); Judith Hoag (Gretchen Price); Alex Hyde-White (Doug Simmons); Will Lyman (Allan Wooster); Amy Moessinger (Nurse); Stacy Ray (Laura Garrison)

The Settings: Boston, Massachusetts; Cabot Cove, Maine

The Case: Dr. Seth Hazlitt's professional reputation is in jeopardy. Harriet Wooster, a longtime acquaintance of both the good doctor and Jessica Fletcher, has expired in surgery. The death was apparently due to Seth's misdiagnosis. Adding to Seth's growing woes, several townsfolk have transferred their loyalty to young Dr. Jonas Beckwith, a bright if too clinical technician.

On the other hand, Jessica has a hunch that foul play entered into Harriet's death. Mrs. Fletcher knew that the deceased was about to sell her computer software firm in order to have more leisure time with her husband. The latter, Allan, operates a local plant nursery.

As Jessica snoops, she learns that the dead woman's attorney brother, Doug, had recently rejected a $5 million offer from John Halsey, a computer genius, to buy the business. It turns out that Doug, who was to receive a hefty finder's fee for the sale, had been using his fiancée, Gretchen Price, to persuade Halsey to substantially increase his bid. In addition, there is Rudy Ortega, a mean intermediary who has been pressuring the widower to approve the sale.

Highlights: In the 1990s, sophisticated lab tests are key to crime-solving. *Murder, She Wrote* takes this trend into account by having Jessica Fletcher rely increasingly on modern lab methodology to point her in the right direction. As she struggles to demonstrate Seth's innocence, she again acts as a buffer between two opposing parties. In this instance, she mediates between the old and new guard physicians, diplomatically finding a happy middle ground in which both can coexist contentedly. It is such little touches that give this series its warm, humane feeling.

Trivia: Hunt Block played Peter Hollister on the nighttime TV soap opera *Knots Landing* (1985–1987). Boyd Gaines was seen as Mark Royer on the sitcom *One Day at a Time* (1981–1984). Alfred Hyde-White, related to British character star Wilfrid Hyde-White, has made such recent feature films as *Loose Cannons* (1990) and *Pretty Woman* (1990).

171. "Day of the Dead"

(4/26/92) 60 mins.

Director: Anthony Shaw **Teleplay:** Mark A. Burley

Regular: Angela Lansbury (Jessica Fletcher)

Guest Law Enforcers: Ruben Amavizca (Guard); Geno Silva (Police Chief Quezada)

Guest Cast: Manuel Cabral (Clerk); Ismael Carlo (Juan Garcia); James Coburn (Cyrus Ramsey); Alex Colon (Ramirez); Miriam Colon (Consuella Montejano); Grant Cramer (Scott Baker); Kamala Lopez (Rosa Garcia); Tomas Milian (Enrico Montejano); Mike Moroff (Oso); Shelley Morrison (Maria); Cynthia Lee Santos (Girl); Gregory Sierra (Ramon)

The Setting: Mexico City, Mexico

The Case: To research a new book project, Jessica Fletcher flies to Mexico City. Hardly is she south-of-the-border than the gold Death Mask of Montezuma is stolen from the National Museum. Although deeply distracted by the loss, the archives' archaeologist curator, Cyrus Ramsey, shepherds Jessica around the city. Among those they encounter are rich Enrico Montejano who owns the hotel where Mrs. Fletcher is a guest. There is a great hostility between Cyrus and Enrico, because the former suspects the latter of dealing in stolen pre-Colombia artifacts.

Later, at the annual Day of the Dead celebration, a body, wearing the missing Death Mask of Montezuma, is discovered in nearby stables. The victim proves to be Enrico.

With the full cooperation of admiring Police Chief Quezada, Jessica confronts the list of potential killers, which includes hotel manager Juan Garcia, whose daughter, Rosa, was the victim's mistress. (Previously, the beautiful young woman had been involved with an American student, Jason Powell. He died in a peculiar car crash.) Also suspect is the menacing Ramirez, who had been following the dead man's every move. Then there is Ramon, a former circus entertainer who now owns a restaurant and had owed Enrico sizable back rent. Not to be overlooked is the deceased's widow, Consuella, who has taken charge already of her late husband's extensive business affairs.

Highlights: Family pride, professional honor and lust for wealth are all ingredients of this intricately woven episode. While the atmosphere smacks too much of artificial sound stage sets, a good deal of effort—at least by TV episode standards—was put into providing a proper Mexican ambiance. As in other segments where Jessica Fletcher tangles with another culture, she is on less sure footing here than when pursuing clues in a North American city.

Trivia: James Coburn of *Our Man Flint* (1966) spy movie fame starred in several TV series: *Klondike* (1960–1961), *Acapulco* (1961) and *Darkroom* (1981–1982), as well as playing Dashiell Hammett's Continetal Op character in the 1978 miniseries *The Dain Curse.* Gregory Sierra's many television series include *Sanford and Son* (1972–1975) and *Zorro and Son* (1983). Cuban-born Tomas Milian made his mark in several Italian-made screen vehicles: *The Big Gundown* (1967), *The Companeros* (1970), etc.

172. "Angel of Death"

(5/3/92) 60 mins.

Director: Walter Grauman **Teleplay:** Robert E. Swanson

Regular: Angela Lansbury (Jessica Fletcher)

Guest Law Enforcer: Noble Willingham (Sheriff Pat McAllister)

Guest Cast: Michael Canavan (Philip Stoddard); Doran Clark (Courtney Stoddard); Sondra Currie (Carol Kendall); Ken Kercheval (Alex Ericson, Esq.); Maria Mayenzet (Lisa Ryder); Darren McGavin (Martin Tremaine); Austin Pendleton (Barney Gunderson); Ray Reinhardt (General Avery Stark)

The Setting: Carmel, California; New York City

The Case: Jessica Fletcher is in Carmel, California, a house guest of Martin Tremaine. The well-established playwright, in the midst of rewrites on his new play, *Angel of Death,* is under great stress. He has never recovered emotionally from the suicide of his late wife, Vivian, and is convinced her ghost haunts this country mansion. Then, too, he is guilt-ridden about a car accident a year ago. He had been driving, and the injured passenger was Lisa Ryder, his typist, with whom he had been having an affair at the time of Vivian's death. Lisa is now blind and lives in an estate cottage where she sculpts.

Others tied to Martin's strained existence are Martin's stepdaughter, Courtney, as well as her protective uncle, attorney Alex Ericson. Additionally, there is demanding stage director Barney Gunderson and aging actress Carol Kendall, the latter badly wanting to star in Tremaine's new drama.

When Courtney's husband, Philip, is stabbed to death in Lisa's cottage, Sheriff Pat McAllister investigates the crime scene. As observant Jessica points out, several important clues (a bottle of "sleeping" pills, a new statue which Lisa is sculpting, and a barking dog belonging to Martin's neighbor, General Avery Stark) may lead to a solution of the homicide.

Highlights: Taking its cue from many ghost movies, this installment plays with the question as to whether an apparition is real or contrived. As had become standard in this series format, the blood linkage between characters plays a large role in many of their motivations, lies and actions. Always feeling an especial empathy with fellow writers, Jessica immediately makes herself at home at the playwright's estate, and refuses to relinquish her take-charge attitudes even in the face of homicide, spooks and determined law enforcers.

Trivia: Character actor Austin Pendleton, who made a specialty of playing nerdy kooks, appeared in such features as *Skidoo* (1968), *The Thief Who*

Came to Dinner (1973) and *My Cousin Vinny* (1992). Best known for playing Mike Hammer on TV's *Mickey Spillane's Mike Hammer* (1957–1959), prolific performer Darren McGavin won an Emmy Award in September 1990 for portraying Candice Bergen's dad on the sitcom *Murphy Brown*. Ken Kercheval was Cliff Barnes on *Dallas* (1978–1991).

173. "Badge of Honor"

(5/10/92) 60 mins.

Director: David Moessinger **Teleplay:** David Moessinger

Regulars: Angela Lansbury (Jessica Fletcher); Ron Masak (Sheriff Mort Metzger); William Windom (Dr. Seth Hazlitt)

Recurring Character: Louis Herthum (Deputy Andy Broom)

Guest Law Enforcer: Arlee Reed (Deputy)

Guest Cast: Tony Becker (Dave Sanders); Daniel Davis (Neal Dishman); Cliff DeYoung (Mason Porter); Robert Lansing (Lawrence Jarvis); Tom Nibley (Clerk); Gail O'Grady (Robin Dishman); Gerald S. O'Loughlin (Ben Oliver); Douglas Rowe (Proprietor of Wiggins Boat Shop); Pamela Susan Shoop (Dorothy Porter); Charles Stevenson, Jr. (Minister); John C. Tuell (Bus Driver)

The Setting: Cabot Cove, Maine

The Case: Dr. Seth Hazlitt is overjoyed when his long-lost World War II buddy, Ben Oliver, turns up in Cabot Cove. A jubilant Seth finds Ben employment as a maintenance man for Mason Porter, who builds and sells yachts. However, Hazlitt's joy is short-lived. Lawrence Jarvis, a private detective, arrives in town and announces that he has been tracking Oliver, convinced that he was responsible for an unsolved Detroit jewelry store robbery. Meanwhile, Porter is found murdered in his office while $60,000 in cash is missing from his wall safe. Sheriff Mort Metzger calls Ben in for questioning.

Seth cannot believe that his army buddy would commit such foul deeds. Jessica intercedes, and her queries lead her to wealthy Neal Dishman, who has just bought a new boat, and to his adulterous wife, Robin. Also involved is the dead man's nephew, Dave Sanders, a boat yard salesperson who resents his uncle's promotion of Ben. Added to the mix is a fire set at the Lighthouse Motel where Jarvis is a guest, as well as the presence of mind of one character in administering CPR to another.

Highlights: Beyond the intellectual exercise of pinpointing the culprit, this installment is an excellent character study. The viewer learns a good deal about seemingly self-reliant Seth Hazlitt, whose life was saved during the European campaign of World War II by his buddy, Ben Oliver.

Trivia: Extremely active character actor Gerald O'Loughlin, featured in such TV miniseries as *Wheels* (1978) and *The Blue and the Gray* (1982), acted in several feature films: *Twilight's Last Gleaming* (1976), *Frances* (1982), etc. Early in his screen career, Robert Lansing (1929–1994), born Robert H. Broom, made such feature films as *The 4-D Man* (1959), *A Gathering of Eagles* (1963) and *Under the Yum Yum Tree* (1964). Born in Inglewood, California, Cliff DeYoung appeared in such TV movies as *Terror on the Beach* (1973) and *I Love You Perfect* (1989).

174. "Murder on Madison Avenue"

(5/17/92) 60 mins.

Director: Jerry Jameson **Teleplay:** Bruce Lansbury

Regular: Angela Lansbury (Jessica Fletcher)

Guest Law Enforcer: Leo Rossi (Lieutenant Hornbeck)

Guest Cast: Robert Ackerman (Stromberg); Barbara Babcock (Meredith Delaney); Joel Fabiani (Boris Steloff); Shannon Fill (Reporter); Hallie Foote (Sylvia Moffett); John Hillerman (Edgar Greenstreet); Zale Kessler (Super); David Lansbury (Brian Singer); John Petlock (Miles Packard); Ben Slack (Frank Christy); Harley Venton (Devery McFarlane); Caroline Williams (Amanda North)

The Setting: New York City

The Case: In Manhattan, Jessica Fletcher is drawn to the corporate headquarters of the Marathon Toy Corporation by its eccentric chief executive officer, Edgar Greenstreet. He has lured Jessica into creating a new whodunit board game.

At the corporate facility, Jessica meets aggressive vice-president Meredith Delaney whose goal is to replace Edgar as the firm's top executive. Her battle plan involves choosing between two competing ad agencies who are campaigning hard for the lucrative Marathon account. At one agency are the quarreling Brian Singer and Amanda North, while the other is controlled by Boris Steloff, who is secretly Meredith's lover. The balance of power is shifted when Delaney learns that Boris is wooing Amanda to his team by romancing her.

During Marathon's 25th anniversary office gala, Meredith's bludgeoned corpse is found. Along with Lieutenant Hornbeck, Jessica becomes embroiled in the homicide misadventure. The roll call of possible culprits includes Devery McFarlane, the victim's long-suffering spouse who also works at Marathon, as well as Sylvia Moffett, the deceased's undervalued secretary, and reclusive toy designer Frank Christy. In addition, always making his presence felt is eccentric Edgar Greenstreet.

Highlights: Beyond the fast-moving executive suite battles, the perk of this segment is Edgar Greenstreet's high-security basement toy room/experimental lab. As the plot unfolds its murderous theme, this setting with its toys and games designed to amuse and divert takes on a sinister tone and unusual irony.

Trivia: John Hillerman first appeared on *Murder, She Wrote* when this costar of TV's *Magnum, P.I.* (1980–1988) was in a cross-over episode from that series (1986's "Magnum on Ice," #51). Barbara Babcock played Liz Craig on *Dallas* (1978–1982) and won an Emmy (1981) for a *Hill Street Blues* appearance. Again, Angela Lansbury's nephew, David, is featured in a guest role.

SEASON NINE

1992–1993

175. "Murder in Milan"

(9/20/92) 60 mins.

Director: Anthony Shaw **Teleplay:** Laurence Heath

Regular: Angela Lansbury (Jessica Fletcher)

Guest Law Enforcer: George DiCenzo (Inspector Lombardo)

Guest Cast: Susan Blakely (Catherine Webb); George Coe (Andrew Thayer); Robert Desiderio (Tom Heller); Paul Gleason (Steve Morrison); Robert Harper (Paul Crenshaw); Grace Kent (Maid); Gary Kroeger (Jim Randall); Barbara Pilavin (Countess); Leah Pinsent (Louise Thayer); Cesar Romero (Marcello Arbruzzi); Paul Ryan (Entertainment Reporter); Mary Wickliffe (Press Agent); Time Winters (Giorgio)

The Setting: Milan, Italy

The Case: Jessica Fletcher's novel *All the Murderers* has been translated into a movie by high-powered producer Catherine Webb and talented new director Jim Randall. As such, Jessica attends the Milan Film Festival where the picture is a big hit, prompting producer Steve Morrison to ask Randall to helm Morrison's upcoming screen project. However, Jim is under exclusive contract to Catherine and she refuses to release him.

Meanwhile, Catherine is studying cost overruns at her production company and informs her chief assistant, Tom Heller, she intends to fully investigate. Still fearful of losing Randall's services, she suggests to actress Louise Thayer that she'll have an important role in the company's forthcoming production. Since Louise is Jim's lover, Catherine hopes this will keep the filmmaker in tow. To tie the package together, Catherine lures Louise's father, Andrew, into the fold with a screenwriting offer that could be his comeback vehicle.

Later, Catherine is found dead in her office suite, with Jim standing over the corpse. She had been hit over the head with an onyx ashtray which Inspector Lombardo spots nearby. In the course of getting to the truth, Jessica questions several murder suspects. There is embittered Paul Crenshaw, the victim's former partner on *All the Murderers*, and Marcello Arbruzzi, the film's leading man, who offers some interesting insights. Also figuring into the deadly situation is Jim's decision to marry Louise, and the fact that a paparazzi was able to gain access to the second-story balcony of Catherine's suite.

Highlights: This segment smoothly mixes the glamour and back-stabbing competition that are requisite ingredients of any major international cinema festival. With an array of familiar old and newer performers, this entry creates a creditable backdrop for the not-so-formula whodunit. The chic settings permit the increasingly fashionable Jessica Fletcher to parade a high-style wardrobe and to bask—ever so modestly—in the glory of being a festival celebrity.

Trivia: As a surviving Latin lover from Hollywood's golden age, former dancer Cesar Romero went on to TV acclaim as the villainous The Joker on the mid-1960s *Batman* series. Already in his eighties at the time of making this episode, Romero died in 1994. Among his last movies were *Simple Justice* (1989) and *Mortuary Academy* (1991). Veteran trouper George Coe played in the TV sitcom *Goodnight, Beantown* (1983). Robert Desiderio had the lead role of Detective Wes Kennedy on TV's *Heart of the City* (1986–1987). George DiCenzo's movie appearances encompassed *The Frisco Kid* (1979), *Back to the Future* (1985), *Sing* (1989) and *Exorcist 3: Legion* (1990).

176. "Family Secrets"

(9/27/92) 60 mins.

Director: Walter Grauman **Teleplay:** Robert Hamner

Regulars: Angela Lansbury (Jessica Fletcher); Ron Masak (Sheriff Mort Metzger); William Windom (Dr. Seth Hazlitt)

Recurring Character: Louis Herthum (Deputy Andy Broom)

Guest Cast: Jeff Bankert (Owen Cooper in the Flashback); Michele Bernath (Customer); Richard Brestoff (William Bailey at the Sanatorium); Paul W. Carr (Businessperson); Beth Taylor Hart (Margaret Babbington in the

Flashback); Charley Lang (Arnold Lummis); Brian McNamara (Randall Sloan); David Newsom (Neal Latimer); Blair Sorby (Young George Latimer in the Flashback); Debra Stipe (Sally Bates); Phyllis Thaxter (Emily Weymouth); Richard Venture (George Latimer); Caroline Williams (Janet Weymouth)

The Setting: Cabot Cove, Maine

The Case: While researching a forthcoming novel at the Cabot Cove library, Jessica Fletcher says hello to Randall Sloan, a former student of hers and now a successful reporter at the *Portland Gazette.* He confides that he's investigating the "Mad Maggie" murder case of thirty years ago, the bloodiest killing in Cabot Cove's entire history.

In preparation for writing his book, Randall is investigating the Babbingtons and Weymouths, two of Cabot Cove's oldest families. According to Sloan, he's uncovered new data regarding the decades-old shooting of Owen Cooper by his lover, Margaret Babbington, and the circumstances surrounding her death in a mental institution months after the tragedy. News of Randall's project reaches Emily Weymouth, Margaret's rich reclusive cousin, and George Latimer, a local businessman who had been Emily's lover thirty years ago. Both of them had been with Margaret and Owen on a bird-watching expedition at the time of the fatality.

Later, Randall is found beaten to death in the library. Jessica and Sheriff Mort Metzger soon realize that the victim had a wealth of enemies. Besides Emily and George, there is librarian Arnold Lummis, a past schoolmate of the victim, who had been rejected in his bid to coauthor the project with Sloan. Then, there is Latimer's son, Neal, who is caught rifling through the reporter's motel room, looking for Sloan's research notes. Other interested parties are orphaned Sally Bates, who loves Neal, but does not meet George's social standards. Finally, there is Janet Weymouth, Emily's all too self-sufficient daughter.

Highlights: In most instances genealogical studies are educational not deadly. This excursion into family trees and individuals at cross purposes digs up more than one old scandal. It is a detection tale perfectly suited for history-drenched Cabot Cove. As Jessica interacts with the locals, Emily Weymouth proves to be underwhelmed with Jessica's international reputation—a rare situation indeed.

Trivia: Like Angela Lansbury, Phyllis Thaxter had been a contract screen player at 1940s MGM. At the time, she and Lansbury had costarred in *Tenth Avenue Angel* (1948). Brian McNamara had been a cast member of the very short lasting sitcom *The Nutt House* (1989). Richard Venture had appeared on the police series *Street Hawk* (1985).

177. "The Mole"

(10/4/92) 60 mins.

Director: Peter Salim **Teleplay:** Tom Sawyer

Regular: Angela Lansbury (Jessica Fletcher)

Recurring Character: Herbert Edelman (Lieutenant Artie Gelber)

Guest Law Enforcer: Lew Saunders (Plainsclothes Police Officer)

Guest Cast: John Allsopp (Jason Herd); Joseph Bologna (Bryan "Brynie" Sullivan); Lonnie Burr (Customer); Melinda Culea (Sara McCuthchen); Francis Guinan (Fred Chandler, Esq.); Ken Howard (Maxwell Hagen); William Brick Karnes (Sportscaster); Raymond Lynch (Coach Baker Davis); Robert Mangiardi (Cutter); Bruno Marcotulli (Bob Wilman); Siobhan McCafferty (Liz Foster); G.F. Smith (Assistant Manager); Lewis Smith (Louis Paloma, Esq.); Patty Toy (Airline Clerk); Ed Wasser (First Man)

The Setting: New York City

The Case: Jessica Fletcher is using ace Manhattan newspaperman Brynie Sullivan as a model for her new novel. After interviewing him, she heads to the airport to leave town. By error, she is given a plane ticket intended for Liz Foster. This, in turn, leads to Jessica being kidnapped by two men who work for wealthy Max Hagen, a businessman and owner of the Eagles basketball team.

The real Liz, an accountant for Hagen, had accessed confidential information about her crooked boss which she is willing to sell to federal prosecutor Louis Paloma for $100,000. Now knowing that hit men are on her trail, Foster demands an additional $100,000 for her dangerous data.

The thugs bring Jessica to Hagen who, upon realizing his error, releases her. The now-angered Mrs. Fletcher reports the incident to police lieutenant Artie Gelber. However, he's only a few days away from retirement and dreads getting entangled with the high-profile Hagen. Nevertheless, Jessica insists that Gelber investigate, all to no avail. Later, Mrs. Fletcher is whisked off by other men, this time to district attorney Paloma's office. Thereafter, Jessica tracks the real Ms. Foster to the Grand Palace Hotel. However, when the mystery writer arrives, there is Lieutenant Gelber investigating a homicide—Liz's.

Before Jessica and Gelber conclude their search, they must deal with a "mole" planted inside Hagen's organization, as well as a mysterious woman—Mrs. Phillips—who had recently checked out of the Grand Palace's room #1411.

Highlights: With her distinctive look and manner, one would hardly consider that the celebrated Jessica Fletcher might be mistaken by so many people for someone else. However, throughout much of this excursion, she is busy establishing her own identity, leading to merry mix-ups spiced with hazardous encounters. More so than with most *Murder, She Wrote* "guest" law enforcers, Jessica and the happily married grandfather, Gelber, develop a substantial accord. As such, he would return for several more (mis)adventures with the intrepid Maine widow.

Trivia: The husband of actress Renee Taylor, Joseph Bologna has starred in TV series, including *Rags to Riches* (1987) and *Top of the Heap* (1991). Lewis Smith's TV series exposure includes *Karen's Song* (1987), *Beauty and the Beast* (1989–1990) and the role of Charlie Main in the miniseries *North and South, Book II* (1989).

178. "The Wind around the Tower"

(11/1/92) 60 mins.

Director: Walter Grauman **Teleplay:** J. Michael Straczynski

Regular: Angela Lansbury (Jessica Fletcher)

Guest Law Enforcer: Richard Riehle (Police Sergeant Devon O'Malley)

Recurring Character: George Hearn (Sean Cullane)

Guest Cast: Michael Alldredge (Jason MacNamara); Pat Crawford Brown (Cashier); Mark Lindsay Chapman (Francis O'Reilly); Shay Duffin (Brian Mulrain); Shirley Anne Field (Anne Gillen); John Finnegan (Douglas Foudy); Carol Kiernan (Young Woman); Don Knight (Quint Sankey); Sarah MacDonnell (Claire Abbott); Nora Masterson (Carolyn Mulrain); Dakin Matthews (Neal Gillen); Mark Rolston (Liam Gillen)

The Setting: Aughrum, Ireland

The Case: In Ireland to research a new whodunit, Jessica Fletcher is met by Sean Cullane, her retired Dublin-based law enforcer friend. They are soon invited to the estate of wealthy real estate investor Neal Gillen near the charming village of Aughrum. Gillen is convinced that someone plans to murder him. He asks Sean to investigate the increasingly threatening situation. As they tour the estate, their host explains that the main house and its stone tower—looking out on the sea—were built two centuries earlier by a sea captain for his wife. The seaman's ship had smashed on the rocks and he had died as his spouse watched in horror from the tower. Recently, the whining sound of a crying woman has been heard coming from the tower. According to the superstitious villagers, someone will soon die!

The next night, Neal dies in his study. At first, it's judged that he died of natural causes, but further study proves that it was murder. The gallery of suspects encompass Anne, the victim's new wife; Gillen's cousin, Liam, who manages the estate's investments; and pretty Claire Abbott, the deceased's secretary, who lives in the main house and is attracted to Liam. Additionally, there is the Gillens' embittered neighbor, Jason MacNamara, who was forced to sell much of his land to Neal to raise cash, and woman-chasing Francis O'Reilly, the town's young pharmacist.

With Jessica, Sean and police sergeant Devon O'Malley on the killer's trail, the murderous path leads from the main house to the "haunted" clock tower.

Highlights: Buoyed by vivid on-location scenery and brogue-lilted dialogue, this is a flavorful exercise: If curses such as the Legend of the Crying Woman seem quaint to Jessica Fletcher, she is astute enough not to mock those who believe in the superstition. It is Jessica's intriguing mixture of practicality and open-mindedness that make her so believable as she moves back and forth from the expansive estate to the picturesque village. Again, there is a hint that her rapport with ex-lawman Sean goes beyond a mutual respect for the other's deductive powers. Cullane is solid as the grief-stricken Irishman, guilty that he couldn't prevent his friend's predicted death.

Trivia: George Hearn was repeating his heart-felt role of Sean Cullane, last seen in 1992's "To the Last Will I Grapple with Thee" (#169). British-born leading lady Shirley Anne Field had appeared in a variety of features: *Saturday Night and Sunday Morning* (1960), *My Beautiful Laundrette* (1985), *At Risk* (1994), etc. Mark Lindsay Chapman had been Brett Lomax on *Dallas* (1988) and Charley St. John on *Falcon Crest* (1989).

179. "The Dead File"

(11/15/92) 60 mins.

Director: Anthony Shaw **Teleplay:** Tom Sawyer

Regular: Angela Lansbury (Jessica Fletcher)

Recurring Character: Jon Polito (Lieutenant Peter DiMartini)

Guest Law Enforcers: David Ault (Officer Buckman); Susan Kellerman (Sergeant Martha Redstone)

Guest Cast: John Apicella (Sid the Doorman); Diana Bellamy (Paige Kindle); Harvey Fierstein (Stan Hatter); George Furth (Jerry Bozell); Robin Gammell (Roger Melton); Mark Eric Howell (Waiter); Rodney Kageyama (Ben Watanabe); Kris Kamm (Teddy Graves); Neal Kaz (Van Driver); Mell Lazarus (Cartoonist); Patrick Macnee (Dayton Whiting); Mark Roberts (Russell Yorke)

The Setting: New York City

The Case: Once more in Manhattan, Jessica Fletcher is dismayed that cartoonist Stan Hatter has caricatured her as a snooping animal—Jessica Fox—in his popular *Hatterville* comic strip. Another unhappy subject who compares notes with Mrs. Fletcher is Lieutenant Peter DiMartini. He's angered to find himself part of the politically oriented strip, cast as a lawman suspected of misconduct. (Three years earlier, DiMartini had been involved in the Three Musketeers case, in which he was accused of stealing $20 million in drugs.) Yet another victim of Stan's strip is Wall Street corporate raider Roger Melton, branded—in the strip—of stock fraud. Now Jessica must convince her fellow targets that she isn't responsible for digging up damaging information on them.

Meanwhile, hyperactive Stan, who has been married five times, lives on a precarious merry-go-round of alimony payments and near bankruptcy. His young assistant, Teddy Graves, helps Hatter maintain his frantic professional pace. Unknown to Stan, he is being trailed by Jerry Bozell, a shoddy journalist with a knack for gathering dirt. Jerry is being paid by Dayton Whiting, Hatter's ex-mentor, who is jealous of his protegé's success.

Soon thereafter, Ben Watanabe, a free-lance cartoon letterer for Stan, is found dead outside the cartoonist's apartment building. Apparently, he jumped from the window. When Sergeant Martha Redstone insists it's suicide, Jessica disagrees. In proving that it was indeed homicide, Mrs. Fletcher deals with Paige Kindle, the head of the newspaper syndication agency that boasts Hatter and Whiting as clients. Jessica also comes to believe Stan, who claims someone is tampering with his beloved cartoon scripts.

Highlights: This installment taps into the public's longtime fascination with the world of cartoon strips. With the majority of the focus on dedicated, eccentric cartoonist Stan Hatter, there is much to enthrall viewers, even when the employed whodunit formula becomes all too obvious.

Trivia: To be noted, the character of Ahmed Shankar has been replaced by Sid, a new front door employee at Jessica Fletcher's New York City apartment building. As the author and star of Broadway's *Torch Song Trilogy* (1982), gravel-voiced Harvey Fierstein won a Tony Award. He repeated his creative chores for the 1988 movie adaptation. Actor/writer George Furth had been a part of such TV series as *Broadside, Tammy* and *The Dumplings.* Screen acting credits for England's Patrick Macnee extend back to *The Life and Death of Colonel Blimp* (1943), *Hamlet* (1948) and *Flesh and Blood* (1951). Real-life cartoonist Mell Lazarus (creator of *Miss Peach*, etc.) made a cameo appearance here as himself.

180. "Night of the Coyote"

(11/22/92) 60 mins.

Director: Jerry Jameson **Teleplay:** Mark A. Burley

Regular: Angela Lansbury (Jessica Fletcher)

Guest Law Enforcers: Graham Greene (Sheriff Sam Keeyani); Roman J. Cisneros (Deputy)

Guest Cast: Frederick Coffin (Tony Sable); Steve Forrest (Max Teller); Mariette Hartley (Susan Lindsay); Gary Kasper (Earl); Joanelle Nadine Romero (Alice Chee); James Stephens (Charles Strickland); Nicolas Surovy (Ben Judson); Ernie Vincent (Mr. Wheatman); Laura Wernette (Betty); Floyd Red Crow Westerman (Uncle Ashie Nakai)

The Setting: Chaco Springs, New Mexico

The Case: Jessica Fletcher comes to Chaco Springs, New Mexico, to visit her longtime pal, Susan Lindsay, a painter. Nearby, in the ghost town of Silverville, Max Teller—on whom divorcée Susan has a crush—operates a museum and Old West show (featuring a reenactment of Cutter McGee's final hold-up before he was hung by the law in 1911). Rumor has it that before his capture, Cutter had buried his loot in Coyote Canyon. Among those believing the legend are historian Charles Strickland as well as Teller.

When Max's museum burns, Sheriff Sam Keeyani, a Native American, confirms that it was arson. Max believes that the crime was committed by Earl, a stuntman whom Teller had fired for stealing supplies. Later, Max is found dead in his office.

Jessica, as well as the sheriff, follows the killer's trail. Their investigation leads to Tony Sable, a newly released ex-convict who once ran a credit card scam when he and Max were partners in a mail order business. Now he wants to be part of the Silverville project. Then there is rancher Ben Judson, who had loaned Max necessary seed money to launch his tourist attraction. Judson had wanted to buy out his stubborn partner to gain water rights for his cattle herd, but Max had refused. Also engulfed in the situation is Betty, the victim's assistant.

Highlights: As part of the politically correct 1990s, *Murder, She Wrote* expanded its focus to include minority groups more frequently. Here the drama involves a soft-spoken, astute Native American law officer who uses his ancestors' traditional methods to find criminals. There is also the sheriff's uncle, Ashie Nakai. He's a curious mixture of the old world (he's a spiritual medicine man) and the new (as a devout reader of murder mysteries, he asks Mrs. Fletcher to autograph one of her books for him). On a different note, Jessica and Susan Lindsay have a revealing conversation on the pain of being middle-aged single women.

Trivia: Native American Graham Greene was Oscar-nominated for his pivotal role in *Dances with Wolves* (1990), later appearing in *Thunderheart* (1992) and *Maverick* (1994). Emmy Award winner Mariette Hartley, famous for her 1980s Polaroid TV commercials with James Garner, was a regular on such TV series as *Peyton Place* (1965), *The Hero* (1966–1967) and *Goodnight, Beantown* (1983–1984).

One of the several TV series in which Nicolas Surovy costarred was *Bridges to Cross* (1986). Among Steve Forrest's many TV movies are such Westerns as *Wanted: The Sundance Woman* (1976) and *Gunsmoke: Return to Dodge* (1987). James Stephens was in the made-for-television movies *The Death of Ocean View Park* (1979) and *Houston: The Legend of Texas* (1986).

181. "Sugar & Spice, Malice & Vice"

(11/29/92) 60 mins.

Director: Vincent McEveety **Teleplay:** Robert E. Swanson

Regular: Angela Lansbury (Jessica Fletcher)

Recurring Character: Len Cariou (Michael Haggerty)

Guest Cast: Donna Bullock (Laura Downing); James Handy (Pat Hogan); Gary Hollis (Brad Filmore); Patricia Idlette (Desk Person); Lenore Kasdorf (Cynthia Quatrain); Kevin Kilner (Paul Marlow); James Shigeta (Luc Lee); Beau Starr (Charlie Bennett); Steve Tschudy (Bartender); Kim Johnston Ulrich (Andrea Cromwell); Efrem Zimbalist, Jr. (Adam Quatrain)

The Setting: Hong Kong

The Case: Paul Marlow, a San Francisco banker, is hoping to marry. His fiancée is Andrea Cromwell, actually the daughter of British secret service agent Michael Haggerty. Unfortunately, Michael was so preoccupied with his M16 duties over the years that he never got to properly know his offspring. Now that Andrea is to wed, Haggerty has been investigating the groom-to-be. Michael isn't happy to find out that his future son-in-law may be involved in a pending merger with a Hong Kong financial institution operated by drug lords and arms smugglers.

When Michael is found standing over the bullet-ridden body of Paul, Andrea and others are convinced he is the murderer. On the other hand, Jessica Fletcher intuitively knows better. Soon she is on the trail of Hong Kong banker Luc Lee, an entrepreneur determined to retrieve incriminating data from the dead man's effects. Then there is also the victim's attractive assistant, Laura Downing, who is hunting for the same vital information. In addition, Mrs. Fletcher weighs the potential of Marlow's aggressive boss, Adam Quatrain, for being the murderer.

Highlights: As always, whenever Michael Haggerty is afoot, trouble surely follows. Here, however, he's the one at peril, not only to prove himself innocent of homicide, but also to regain his adult daughter's trust. Typically, Jessica Fletcher's experience and foresight give her the edge, even over self-reliant, charismatic Michael Haggerty.

Trivia: This was the first story line appearance of Michael Haggerty's grown-up daughter, Andrea. Blonde Kim Johnson Ulrich had been among those surviving the fiasco of *Nightingales* (1989) a variation on the old *Charlie's Angels* format. Hawaiian-born James Shigeta had often been cast as a Japanese on-screen: *Cry for Happy* (1960), *Bridge to the Sun* (1961), *Midway* (1976), etc.

182. "The Classic Murder"

(12/6/92) 60 mins.

Director: Walter Grauman **Teleplay:** Robert Van Scoyk

Regular: Angela Lansbury (Jessica Fletcher)

Guest Law Enforcers: Julian Barnes (Inspector Moss); John DiAquino (Sergeant Tom Jarrow); Anthony S. Johnson (Deputy)

Guest Cast: Charles Hoyes (Phil); Michael Knight (B.J. Wilson); Louise Latham (Mrs. Oates); Stephen Liska (Carl Graham); Lisa Melilli (Waitress); Natalija Nogulich (Marika Valenti); John Rubinstein (George Foster); Rita Taggart (Janine Foster); Wayne Tippit (Buck Wilson); Jessica Tuck (Sally Wilson)

The Settings: New York City; Westchester, New York

The Case: Rough-and-ready Buck Wilson is bargaining to buy the publishing house for which Jessica Fletcher writes mysteries. Buck's daughter, Sally, happens to be a young editor at the same establishment and is embarrassed by her dad's business intrusion. Later, Jessica meets Wilson at the opening of Buck's Buckaroos, the New York City outlet of Wilson's restaurant chain. During the party, the brash Buck disappears.

Back at Buck's Westchester house, two drink glasses are spotted in Wilson's bedroom, suggesting that the millionaire had an overnight guest. However, chauffeur Carl Graham insists he brought Buck home alone. Meanwhile, the press reports that the authorities will soon be investigating the Wilson empire for accounting discrepancies. By now, Sally's brother, B.J., has tapped into the firm's computer files and discovered that $150 million in cash is missing from company accounts.

Psychic Marika Valenti arrives at Buck's home where she demonstrates her skills. She divines that Wilson is dead and that his murderer has tossed the body into a deep shaft. However, the next morning, it is Marika who dies. She has been shot, and her corpse is now resting in a deep gully on the estate.

Determined to resolve the growing mysteries, Jessica relies on deductive rather than divining skills to properly analyze the situation. Conferring with both Scotland Yard—whom Marikia claimed she had once assisted—and local police sergeant Tom Jarrow, Mrs. Fletcher presses Buck's brother-in-law George Foster and sister Janine for more information on the missing millionaire. She also concludes that loyal household employee Mrs. Oates knows far more than she is willing to divulge—at first.

Highlights: With an overly theatrical performance by Natalija Nogulich as the psychic, this gambit never has the proper air of mystery to make the "unknown" creditable. In contrast, the astute, persevering Jessica Fletcher uses the emerging physical evidence to reach logical conclusions. On the plus side, the budding romance between Tom Jarrow and Sally Wilson has a ring of truth to it.

Trivia: John Rubinstein, the actor and composer son of classical pianist Artur Rubinstein, had been a TV series regular on both *Family* (1976–1980) and *Crazy Like a Fox* (1984–1986). Prolific character actress Louise Latham had appeared in the Western series *Sara* (1976). Rita Taggart had been part of the drama series *Almost Grown* (1988–1989).

183. "A Christmas Secret"

(12/13/92) 60 mins.

Director: Anthony Shaw **Teleplay:** Bruce Lansbury

Regulars: Angela Lansbury (Jessica Fletcher); Ron Masak (Sheriff Mort Metzger); William Windom (Dr. Seth Hazlitt)

Recurring Character: Louis Herthum (Deputy Andy Broom)

Guest Cast: Diane Baker (Mary Forsythe); Corinne Bohrer (Wanda Andrews); Amy Brenneman (Amy Wainwright); Craig Hamann (Bert Lazarus); Sean O'Bryan (Charlie McCumber); Eileen Seeley (Elizabeth "Beth" Forsythe); Ken Swofford (Alan Forsythe); Mary Tanner (Monica McCumber); Larry Wilcox (Floyd Bigelow)

The Setting: Cabot Cove, Maine

The Case: During the Yuletide season, former serviceman Charlie McCumber announces his engagement to Beth, the daughter of Alan and Mary Forsythe. Among those attending the Christmas party is hardware store owner Floyd Bigelow, a smooth playboy as well as city councilman. Other attendees include Cabot Cove newcomer Wanda Andrews, an employee of the mayor, and drab, color-blind Amy Wainwright, who operates the hardware store.

Thereafter, Wanda is found shot. Sheriff Mort Metzger arrests Charlie for the crime because McCumber's service revolver was determined to be the murder weapon. Meanwhile, Beth discovers an audio tape in her fiancé's bedroom. It contains a blackmailing message from an unknown woman. Although Wanda is still in a coma, Bigelow casts suspicion on the victim for recently discovered missing city pension funds. Regardless of all this evidence, Jessica Fletcher and Mort set a trap for the perpetrator, thus solving the mystery of another stranger in town.

Highlights: Like George Bailey of *It's a Wonderful Life* (1946), Dr. Seth Hazlitt has lost faith in the Christmas spirit and the good will of all. As this episode unfolds, the downhearted physician regains his enthusiasm for the holidays and for his fellow human being. As always, Windom makes what could be a throwaway cliché a telling situation.

Trivia: With his role as Lieutenant Perry Catalano (in the San Francisco-set Dennis Stanton segments) behind him, Ken Swofford returned to *Murder, She Wrote* in this new assignment. Diane Baker is not only a very experienced actress, but has directed TV shows and scripted such television entries as *One of a Kind* and a 1978 ABC *AfterSchool Special.* Larry Wilcox's made-for-TV movies include *Mr. and Mrs. Bo Jo Jones* (1971), *The Love Tapes* (1980), and *Perry Mason: The Case of the Avenging Ace* (1988).

184. "The Sound of Murder"

(1/3/93) 60 mins.

Director: Anthony Shaw **Teleplay:** Bruce Lansbury

Regular: Angela Lansbury (Jessica Fletcher)

Recurring Character: Michael Tolan (Lieutenant Allan Terwilliger)

Guest Cast: Richard Beymer (Richard Lefko); Edd Byrnes (Freddie Major); Mary Beth Evans (Julie Knight); Jonathan Goldsmith (Mitch Randall); Lori Hart (Member of Mirabilis Duo); Kevin Hicks (Willi Piper); Robert Knepper (Charles George Drexler); Jeffrey Steele Levasseur (Member of Mirabilis Duo); Kenny Long (Video Director); Miles O'Keeffe (Paul Atkins); Alexia Robinson (Holly Chase); Meadow Williams (Michele); Danny Woodburn (Giorgi Pappavasilopoulos)

The Setting: New York City

The Case: Jessica Fletcher is recording one of her novels, *The Corpse Danced at Midnight*, for the blind at Rojam Records. The label, owned by Freddie Major, is about to be merged into a conglomerate owned by Mitch Randall. Three contingencies for the sale are that Major fire vice-president Richard Lefko, who has underworld ties; that the firm's top recording group, Psi Phi, remain with the company, and that Michele, who is Mitch's girlfriend, be given a recording contract.

Meanwhile, Psi Phi's manager, Charles George Drexler, who had sold his shares in Rojam when he thought the firm was going bust, learns that the stock will go sky high if the merger goes through.

Jessica finds herself invited to the taping of a Psi Phi music video on Saturday. During the noisy shoot, full of sound and visual effects, Major is shot to death. Lieutenant Allan Terwilliger arrests studio sound engineer Paul Atkins because (1) he had disappeared from the sound truck at the time of the killing and (2) the murder weapon has been found in his car.

Another person entangled in the investigation is young musician Willi Piper. Once arrested for robbery, he suddenly has a chance at a big recording deal. In addition, there's label publicity person Julie Knight, who isn't allowed to forget her unsavory past, as well as Giorgi Pappavasilopoulos, a sleazy private eye.

Highlights: With its rock music ambiance and music video sequences, this was an instance of MTV coming to *Murder, She Wrote*, another example of the series reaching out to a younger audience. In usual fashion, Jessica Fletcher is nonplussed by her new environment, the hip music world, proving again that one of her most ingratiating traits is her desire to explore new trends and life-styles.

Trivia: Former beefcake artist Miles O'Keeffe made a strong impression in the title role of Bo Derek's *Tarzan, the Ape Man* (1981). Michael Tolan was in the TV series *The Nurses* (1964–1965) and *The Senator* (1970–1971).

185. "Final Curtain"

(1/10/93) 60 mins.

Director: Walter Grauman **Teleplay:** J. Michael Straczynski

Regulars: Angela Lansbury (Jessica Fletcher); Ron Masak (Sheriff Mort Metzger); William Windom (Dr. Seth Hazlitt)

Recurring Characters: Julie Adams (Eve Simpson); Louis Herthum (Deputy Andy Broom)

Guest Cast: Dennis Christopher (Lyman Taggart); Keene Curtis (Jerome Mueller); Bradford Dillman (Eric Benderson); Peter Donat (David North); John Gowans (1st Relative); Bonnie Hellman (2nd Relative); Barry Laws (John Koppel); Ed Morgan (Lighthouse Motel Manager); Maureen Mueller (Kathryn Evans); Don Perry (Patient); Bainbridge Scott (Hostess); Nicholas Shaffer (Bit Player)

The Setting: Cabot Cove, Maine

The Case: Cabot Cove is aflutter because veteran film star David North is coming out of a twelve-year retirement. He is to appear in a pre-off-Broadway tryout of *And Wept a Stranger* at the Cabot Cove community center where he had acted in his apprentice days. At the auditions, local real estate agent Eve Simpson is assigned a small role in the show, while Sheriff Mort Metzger is handed the part of a constable. However, Lyman Taggart of Bangor, Maine, is turned down. As such, this obsessive fan of North's creates a scene at the tryouts and, again, later on.

Another person who disturbs the rehearsals is Eric Benderson, David's one-time personal manager. He persuades North to promise him a substantial percentage of the play's grosses, a deal which upsets the investors. Meanwhile, Dr. Seth Hazlitt, who has known David since childhood, notices that his friend has become a heavy drinker and seems quite troubled. In discussing this with Jessica Fletcher, the physician recalls that years ago North had allowed a friend to borrow the actor's car. After the pal had died in a car accident, David had retired from acting.

Later, back at his motel, Eric Benderson is fatally struck over the head and his motel room is set ablaze. Because Lyman is at the murder scene, Mort arrests him. However, the facts don't add up for Jessica. While she begins to investigate, Seth stumbles upon David unconscious from gas fumes in his house.

Highlights: In its vignettes of little theater tryouts and rehearsals, this episode provides fine local color and comedy relief. Thanks to the vigor of Peter Donat's David North, the ambiguous celebrity comes to life. Dennis Christopher is equally riveting as the outraged stage wannabe. One particularly amusing moment in the proceedings is when Jessica Fletcher falls asleep at her computer!

Trivia: Chameleonlike character actor Peter Donat was a regular on *Flamingo Road* (1981–1982). Dennis Christopher of *The Boys in Company C* (1977) and *Breaking Away* (1979) played another disturbed soul in *Fade to Black* (1981), that time as a weirdo film enthusiast. Having made his Broadway debut in 1953 in Eugene O'Neill's *Long Day's Journey into Night*, Bradford Dillman costarred in such later features as *Treasure of the Amazon* (1985) and *Heroes Stand Alone* (1989).

186. "Double Jeopardy"

(1/17/93) 60 mins.

Director: Anthony Shaw **Teleplay:** Laurence Heath

Regular: Angela Lansbury (Jessica Fletcher)

Guest Law Enforcer: Julius J. Carry III (Sergeant Bill Davis)

Guest Cast: Robert Beltran (Father Michael); Ismael Carlo (Man); Larry Carroll (WROE-TV Telecaster); Raymond Cruz (Joseph [Jorge] Galvan); Rosana DeSoto (Maria Galvan); Valerie Dilman (Denise Dillers); Dan Ferro (Raymond Fernandez); Sonia Jackson (Librarian); Keri Johnson (Teen Boy); Judith Jones (Ruth Nelson); Tomas Milian (Frank Fernandez); Mark Juan A. Riojas (Manuel); Mark Adair Rios (Tony Galvan)

The Setting: New York City

The Case: As part of "giving back" to the community, Jessica Fletcher teaches a mystery writing class at St. Julian's, a Catholic church in an ethnically mixed neighborhood. The post has been arranged by impassioned Father Michael, a Hispanic activist. One of Mrs. Fletcher's most attentive students is Jorge. Some months earlier, Jorge's father, Councilman Roberto Galvan, had vanished. The chief suspect had been slum landlord Frank Fernandez. However, because no corpse was ever found, Fernandez had been acquitted.

After Father Michael chooses to run for councilman, Fernandez' son,

Raymond, suggests to his dad that the priest may end up missing like Roberto. Frank warns Father Michael, his illegitimate son, of the danger. Later, Galvan's corpse is found in a sewer. He had been shot through the heart. Because of the law against double jeopardy, Fernandez cannot be retried for the crime.

Sergeant Bob Davis of the New York Police Department warns Jorge and his brother Tony not to retaliate against Fernandez. Meanwhile Raymond and his men come gunning for the Galvan boys, but the latter escape. While this is occurring, the guilt-ridden Fernandez goes to confession, thinking Father Michael will be his confessor. While in the confessional, the penitent is sprayed with a poison mist and dies.

Already dragged into the case, Jessica realizes that she had discussed poisons in her class and had referred the students to *The Toxic Handbook*. When she reviews who had checked out the telltale volume, Mrs. Fletcher makes a startling discovery. Others who provide the amateur sleuth with vital background information are Denise Dillers, Raymond's girlfriend, as well as Galvan's widow, Maria, who runs a plant store.

Highlights: Increasingly, segments of *Murder, She Wrote* revolved around minority groups and their very real problems in coping with mainstream America. This social consciousness was another means for the series to appeal to a wider viewing audience.

Trivia: Rosana DeSoto had been a regular on the short-lasting *The Redd Foxx Show* (1986). Dan Ferro had been Tommy Ortega on *Falcon Crest* (1988–1989). Trained at New York's Actors Studio in the 1950s, Tomas Milan's later movie credits encompass *Salome* (1985), *Havana* (1990) and *Money* (1991). Raymond Cruz's film assignments numbered *Vietnam War Story 3* (1989) and *Clear and Present Danger* (1994). Robert Beltran would later have a costarring role as First Officer Chakotay on the TV series *Star Trek: Voyager* (1995–).

187. "Dead Eye"

(2/7/93) 60 mins.

Director: Jerry Jameson **Teleplay:** Tom Sawyer

Regular: Angela Lansbury (Jessica Fletcher)

Recurring Character: Wayne Rogers (Charlie Garrett)

Guest Law Enforcers: Julian Christopher (FBI Special Agent James Whitman); Ben Masters (Chief Thurman Gillis)

Guest Cast: Lonny Chapman (Frank Hemet); Martin Goslins (Houseman); Stewart Moss (Dr. Desmond Abner Farrow); Dennis Paladino (Bartender); John Petlock (Michael Malone); Linda Purl (Laura Ann Callan); Kevin Quigley (Bernard Philip Callan); Tom Alan Robbins (Assistant Manager); Al Ruscio (Santo Angelini); Jason Stuart (Motel Manager); Webster Williams (Hal Fredericks)

The Settings: Coral City, Florida; Miami, Florida

The Case: In Miami to deliver a lecture, Jessica Fletcher meets Laura Callan, a Denver district attorney. The remains of Laura's father, Bernie Callan, have been uncovered in a drain pipe in nearby Coral City. Callan, a private eye, had disappeared two days after President John F. Kennedy's 1963 assassination. Another party interested in the case is Chicago-based private investigator Charlie Garrett, a down-on-his-luck inveterate gambler. Reading that the dead man's wallet contains $10,000, he flies to Coral City and produces an old IOU from Bernie for $3,000. However, Chief Thurman Gillis is too preoccupied with the murder investigation to deal with Garrett's minor problem.

Soon after unsavory detective Frank Hemet breaks into both Charlie's and Laura's rooms, he is shot to death in his car. By now, Jessica has joined with Charlie and Laura to solve this complex case. Later, Laura shows her confederates surveillance photographs taken by her father not long before he disappeared. Jessica is amazed to spot Lee Harvey Oswald in the background of several photos. Standing next to Oswald is someone who resembles Mafia boss Santo Angelini. (When he was killed, Hemet had been working for Santo.) Later, the case takes another amazing turn when the police verify that the gun that killed Hemet was the same used on Bernie back in 1963.

Highlights: Creatively utilizing the public's persistent fascination with JFK's death, this episode craftily blends historical facts and footage with the segment's fiction. The early 1960s establishing sequences are lensed in contrasting black-and-white, giving those scenes the desired *film noir* look. As to the extraordinary historical photos—so important to the plot—they and the negatives disappear as quickly as they entered the narrative. For once, Jessica Fletcher is cowed by being momentarily so close to solving one of the twentieth century's great mysteries—the how, why and who of John F. Kennedy's murder in Dallas, Texas in November, 1963.

To be noted, the blasé local police chief of this adventure informs Jessica that he doesn't much like her detective fiction; he much prefers that of Agatha Christie!

Trivia: Wayne Rogers is still best known for his Captain John McIntyre on TV's *M*A*S*H* (1972–1975). Lonny Chapman was a veteran of *The*

Investigator (1956) and *For the People* (1965). From 1974–1975, Linda Purl was Gloria on *Happy Days*. She returned to the series as Ashley Pfister for the 1982–1983 season. Later, she was Charlene, the lawyer daughter of attorney *Matlock* (1986–1987). One of Ben Masters' earliest movie credits was *Mandingo* (1975).

188. "Killer Radio"

(2/14/93) 60 mins.

Director: Peter Salim **Teleplay:** Carlton Hollander

Regular: Angela Lansbury (Jessica Fletcher)

Guest Law Enforcers: William Lucking (Sheriff Leland Waterman); Tim Schnabel (Deputy Stallings)

Guest Cast: Victor Brandt (David Osterman); Stephen Caffrey (Jonathan Baker); Dallas Cole (Woman); Lindsay Crouse (Louise Anderson-Crowe); Georgia Emelin (Ronna Samuels); Harry Guardino (Danny Cochran); James Harlow (Alex Logan); Cynthia Harrison (Desk Clerk); Annie O'Donnell (Dr. Annie Farnum); Lyman Ward (Colin Crowe); Jeff Yagher (Marcus Rule)

The Setting: Easton, in the Midwest

The Case: At the request of a Park Avenue attorney, Jessica Fletcher includes the agricultural town of Easton on her midwestern book tour. She's been asked to check on her friend's son, Jonathan Baker. Rather than be a lawyer like his dad, Jonathan had "dropped out" and ended up in Easton as an engineer for the local radio station KGAB.

Jonathan is in love with the station's publicity head, Ronna Samuels. However, she is intrigued with Colin Crowe, who co-owns the station with his wife, Louise. The latter is about to divorce Crowe and to disassociate herself from KGAB. Meanwhile, vindictive Crowe plots to ruin a local politician, David Osterman, with the help of abrasive Marcus Rule, the station's acid-mouthed talk show host. Recently, Marcus has threatened to quit the station unless he receives a huge raise. To counter the threat, Colin indicates he will make known his foul-mouthed employee's special interest in young girls.

Later, at the outdoor party inaugurating the station's new transmitter, Crowe is discovered shot, hanging from a lower rung of the tower platform. The police, led by Sheriff Leland Waterman, find several bullets that missed their target. Apparently the killer was an amateur shot. Meanwhile, Ronna has disappeared.

As Jessica untangles the web of mystery, she deals with Danny Cochran, a longtime station engineer with a penchant for the racetrack, as well as beleaguered David Osterman and his campaign manager, Alex Logan.

Highlights: On many levels, this is one of the most satisfying *Murder, She Wrote* excursions. There is a wonderful rapport between chatty, old-fashioned Danny Cochran—a great admirer of J.B. Fletcher novels—and inquisitive Jessica.

A great moment of this segment—let alone the entire *Murder, She Wrote* series!—is Mrs. Fletcher's run-in with radio shock jock Marcus Rule. After suffering his ignorant abuse on air for a time, she retaliates in kind. She lets Rule and his listeners know exactly what she thinks of his low-brow psychobabble. Her tirade leaves this Howard Stern wannabe speechless.

Trivia: Viewers learn that *The Triple Crown Murders* was J.B. Fletcher's fourth novel and that another of her mysteries was *The Corpse at Vespers.*

Jeff Yagher had played Kyle Bates in the sci-fi series *V* (1984–1985). In the 1987 pilot to *21 Jump Street,* Yagher was Officer Tom Hanson, only to be replaced in the actual network series by Johnny Depp. Lindsay Crouse, daughter of famed playwright Russel Crouse, had been in such features as *All the President's Men* (1976), *Places in the Heart* (1985—winning her an Oscar nomination) and *Desperate Hours* (1990). Harry Guardino's (1925–1995) screen credits embodied several Clint Eastwood actioners: *Dirty Harry* (1971), *The Enforcer* (1976) and *Any Which Way You Can* (1980).

189. "The Petrified Florist"

(2/21/93) 60 mins.

Director: Anthony Shaw **Teleplay:** Donald Rose

Regular: Angela Lansbury (Jessica Fletcher)

Recurring Character: Gregory Sierra (Lieutenant Gabriel Caceras)

Guest Law Enforcers: Sandahl Bergman (Sergeant Daisy Kenny); James C. Bockelman (Officer)

Guest Cast: Gary Beach (Billy Kyle); Robert Firth (Davey Wells); Penny Fuller (Frances Hunt); John Gabriel (Dr. Johnny Windhurst); Richard Herd (Arnett Cobb); Carnetta Jones (Receptionist); Sally Kellerman (Junie Cobb); Marji Martin (Aggie Colbert); Denise Miller (Betty O'Hara); Taylor Nichols (George Erwin); Mort Sertner (Stan Hendricks); Elmarie Wendel (Nurse Receptionist)

The Setting: Los Angeles, California

The Case: In Beverly Hills, Jessica Fletcher is the house guest of chic Frances Hunt, editor of the *A-List* gossip tabloid. To celebrate her friend's visit, Frances hosts a smart party for Mrs. Fletcher. The guests include Junie Cobb, the *A-List* publisher; Arnett, Junie's husband who backs the publication; and George Erwin, one of Junie's prized editorial assistants. Others attending are gossip queen Aggie Colbert and handsome Dr. Johnny Windhurst. (This plastic surgeon to the stars is Frances's latest amour.) The belated floral arrangements for the get-together are delivered by an exhausted Billy Kyle, the extravagant owner of a trendy flower shop.

The next day, news spreads that Billy Kyle has been stabbed to death at his shop with a pair of his own shears. At the murder scene, the police discover an envelope—with George's fingerprints on it—containing $5,000. Erwin claims it was the *A-List*'s payoff to the dead man for celebrity tips. Frances becomes the major suspect when one of her gas charge receipts ties her to the vicinity and time of the killing.

Meanwhile, Jessica hopes to establish Frances's innocence by unearthing someone with a better motive. A prime candidate is football player Davey Wells, whom the publication had accused of substance abuse. There's also Junie, who has been hiding a close association with Dr. Windhurst. Another likely suspect is Betty, Frances's young cook who has been selling celebrity news to *Starscene*, the *A-List's* biggest competitor.

Highlights: The plot gimmick here ties Jessica to the title figure of the Danny Kaye movie *The Secret Life of Walter Mitty* (1946) and to Bobby Ewing of the nighttime soap opera *Dallas*. That aside, the plot is more fantastic than creditable, with the flamboyant personalities much too oversized to create viewer empathy.

Trivia: Before Loretta Swit gained fame as Major Margaret "Hot Lips" Houlihan on TV's *M*A*S*H* (1972–1983), Sally Kellerman had played the love-hungry head nurse in the 1970 film version. Sandahl Bergman, featured as the cop/would-be-actress in this segment, had been in several movies: *All That Jazz* (1979), *Stewardess School* (1986), *Hell Comes to Frogtown* (1988), etc. Gregory Sierra's credentials include *Papillon* (1972), *The Prisoner of Zenda* (1979) and *Honey I Blew Up the Kid* (1992).

190. "Threshold of Fear"

(2/28/93) 60 mins.

Director: Vincent McEveety **Teleplay:** James L. Novack

Regular: Angela Lansbury (Jessica Fletcher)

Recurring Characters: Eddie Barth (Richie Kanpinski, the Doorman); Herbert Edelman (Lieutenant Artie Gelber)

Guest Law Enforcers: Tom Isbell (Sergeant Grady); Whitney Rydbeck (Medical Examiner)

Guest Cast: Andrew Bloch (Ben Gotler); Joy Claussen (Patient); Dave Fennoy (TV Interviewer); Alexandra Kenworthy (Mrs. Eddington); Margot Kidder (Dr. Ellen Holden); David Lansbury (Peter Morgan); Cynthia Nixon (Alice Morgan); Jamie Rose (Laura Martin); David Soul (Jordan Barnett); Michael Zelniker (Henry Phelps)

The Setting: New York City

The Case: Alice Morgan, who lives in the same Manhattan apartment building as Jessica Fletcher, suffers from agoraphobia. Because she fears crowds, she hasn't left her apartment in several years. At the request of Richie Kanpinski, the doorman, Jessica checks on her isolated neighbor. The cowed young woman shows Mrs. Fletcher a telescope which she has pointed at a brownstone situated blocks away, which once was her home. Alice also has Jessica view a VCR tape of a recent TV interview featuring architect Jordan Barnett. According to the distressed Alice, he's the one who killed her mother, Lillian, five years ago.

When Barnett is later found stabbed through the heart, Jessica feels obliged to investigate, which brings her back into contact with Lieutenant Artie Gelber of Midtown Precinct South. The cast of potential villains encompasses Dr. Ellen Holden, Alice's manipulative psychiatrist, as well as Alice's stepbrother, Peter, who needs quick cash. As such, he demands that Dr. Holden persuade Alice to agree to the sale of the brownstone or he will reveal the physician's unorthodox treatment methods.

As for Barnett, the murdered architect, it turns out that five years earlier he knew both the Morgans and Dr. Holden. Recently, the latter had been jealous of Barnett's pretty associate, Laura Martin. Another concerned party is earnest Henry Phelps, who is Alice's neighbor in 10-B and has an abiding concern for the disturbed young woman.

Highlights: Bringing her small-town friendliness to the Big Apple, Jessica breaks through the emotional barriers of an overstressed neighbor. The bizarre personality of this disturbed young person adds a proper touch of eeriness to the story. It raises questions as to what is true and what is not as the characters and plot jump back and forth from a past trauma to the present day. In a different mood, Jessica's further collaboration with Lieutenant Gelber, a happily married grandfather, adds a much-needed frothiness to the plot.

Trivia: Angela Lansbury's nephew, David, returned to the program for another guest assignment. Margot Kidder gained a slice of show business immortality playing Lois Lane to Christopher Reeve's Clark Kent in *Superman* (1979) and in three of the sequels. David Soul's career breakthrough was joining with Paul Michael Glaser in the violent police action series *Starsky and Hutch* (1975–1979).

191. "The Big Kill"

(3/7/93) 60 mins.

Director: Jerry Jameson **Teleplay:** Mark A. Burley

Regulars: Angela Lansbury (Jessica Fletcher); Ron Masak (Sheriff Mort Metzger); William Windom (Dr. Seth Hazlitt)

Recurring Characters: Julie Adams (Eve Simpson); Louis Herthum (Deputy Andy Broom)

Guest Cast: Michael Beck (Brian Bentall); Chad Everett (Martin Fraser); Dana Gladstone (Walter Kurtz); Gregg Henry (Carl Ward); Hope Lange (Mary Lewis); Kathy Molter (Sarah Riddett); Richardson Morse (Charles Nielsen); Robert Patten (Russell); R. Leo Schreiber (Driver); Don Stroud (Phil Shannon); Toshi Toda (Japanese Fisherman); Lyle Waggoner (Ben Wright); Sandy Ward (Henry Riddett)

The Settings: Cabot Cove, Maine; New York City

The Case: The defense industry cutbacks imperil Pantechnics, which manufactures guided missiles. Its president, Martin Fraser, decides to lay off many workers at the Cabot Cove area plant. Then, Fraser plots to sell—illegally—surplus components. Using local trucker Phil Shannon and fisherman Henry Riddett, he plans to transfer the parts to a container vessel lying offshore. However, a bad storm forces Riddett back to shore with the contraband goods.

Meanwhile, Martin asks Wall Street financier Carl Ward for a loan, insisting that Pantechnics has a breakthrough underwater survey system ready for operation. Pantechnics' computer engineer, Brian Bentall, disagrees. Regardless, Martin pledges to demo the system for Ward on the coming weekend, relying on efficient worker Mary Lewis to keep everything humming. On another front, not long after Fraser gives Riddett's daughter Sarah $1,000 for her father's work, the seaman is found dead on his boat. Dr. Seth Hazlitt and Sheriff Mort Metzger label this death from asphyxiation as accidental.

However, before long, Jessica Fletcher is drawn into the case, because her real estate broker friend, Eve Simpson, is involved romantically with Fraser. When a second death occurs aboard Pantechnics' berthed craft,

Mrs. Fletcher investigates. It leads her and the others to realize that Riddett's passing was also a homicide.

Highlights: One of the several virtues of *Murder, She Wrote* is that even when the plot line is pedestrian, the tangy local color is a compensation. For example, Jessica currently is worrying about her leaking roof, Seth refuses to try the new chiropractor in Bar Harbor to remedy a bad back, and Eve boasts of her new beau. These vignettes from Cabot Cove daily life divert the viewer from the humdrum criminal scene at hand.

Trivia: Don Stroud began as Troy Donahue's stunt double on TV's *Hawaiian Eye* in the late 1950s. He moved on to playing law enforcers on *Kate Loves a Mystery* (1979) and *Mickey Spillane's Mike Hammer* (1984–1987). On the miniseries *Holocaust* (1978), Michael Beck was cast as Hans Helms. Gregg Henry was Wesley Jordache on the TV miniseries *Rich Man, Poor Man—Book II* (1976–1977). Hope Lange's early film credits include *Bus Stop* (1956), *The True Story of Jesse James* (1957) and *Peyton Place* (1957). Lyle Waggoner, of the matinee idol looks, was once a TV regular on *The Jimmie Rodgers Show* (1969). He also hosted a syndicated quiz program: *It's Your Bet* (1970). Chad Everett, born Raymond Lee Cramton, was the costar of TV series ranging from *The Dakotas* (1963) to *McKenna* (1994–1995).

192. "Dead to Rights"

(3/21/93) 60 mins.

Director: Anthony Shaw **Teleplay:** Tom Sawyer

Regular: Angela Lansbury (Jessica Fletcher)

Guest Law Enforcer: Richard Libertini (Lieutenant Gabriel Rodino)

Guest Cast: Ruth Anderson (Helen McCurdy); Sam Anderson (Carl Stevens); Christine Belford (Marissa "Missy" Stevens); Lorry Goldman (Saul Benson); Molly Hagan (Dana Ballard); Tom Henschel (Terence Gideon); Stephen T. Kay (Vincent Polaski); Evelyn Keyes (Wanda Polaski); Wallace Langham (Todd Merlin); Jeffrey Nordling (Bruce Hastings); Pamela Roylance (Gloria Jergens); Edward Winter (Baker Lawrence)

The Settings: Cabot Cove, Maine; Portland, Maine

The Case: Jessica Fletcher quickly realizes that her distracted research assistant, Dana Ballard, is a pathological liar. When Dana relocates to Portland, Maine, Jessica hopes that is the finish of the matter. However, Dana pretends to be the famed mystery writer and gives herself a wonderful job recommendation. Thereafter, Jessica comes back into Ballard's life when she shows up unexpectedly in Portland as part of her book tour.

Meanwhile, Dana is involved with Todd Merlin, a dishonest employee at a Portland securities brokerage firm. Todd maneuvers a secretarial job for Dana at the company where Carl Stevens is a partner and materialistic Marissa is the latter's wife.

Later, Dana is arrested for Stevens' murder. Her fingerprints are on the murder weapon, a gun, which is enough for Lieutenant Gabriel Rodino. Nevertheless, the suspect protests her innocence to Mrs. Fletcher. The latter concludes that for once the young woman may be telling the truth! Dana's public defender lawyer, Vincent Polaski, persuades Jessica to help with Dana's defense against self-serving Bruce Hastings, the prosecuting attorney.

Highlights: With a compulsive liar as the pawn in a murder setup, this imaginative segment has an intriguing, well-executed premise. When Jessica loses her temper with the scheming "heroine," a most diverting confrontation is put into motion. As the dedicated, optimistic lawyer, Vincent Polaski emerges as a refreshing "hero."

Trivia: Richard Libertini played The Godfather on *Soap* (1977–1978). Christine Belford's credits include *Banacek*, *Married: The First Year* and 1984's *Empire*. From 1986 to 1992 Sam Anderson was Sam Gorpley on the TV sitcom *Perfect Strangers*.

193. "Lone Witness"

(4/4/93) 60 mins.

Director: Walter Grauman **Teleplay:** Maryanne Kasica, Michael Scheff

Regular: Angela Lansbury (Jessica Fletcher)

Guest Law Enforcers: Laurence Luckinbill (Lieutenant Steve Warren); Clifton Powell (Detective Eddie Flowers)

Guest Cast: George Ede (H. Van Houle); Neil Patrick Harris (Tommy Remsen); Beth Howland (Sandy Oates); Sheila MacRae (Susan Wells); Joe Maruzzo (Fred Turner); John Bennett Perry (Dan Remsen); Kario Salem (Vic Gorman); Raymond Serra (Ben Eigers); Liz Vassey (Monica Evers)

The Setting: New York City

The Case: Jessica Fletcher is busy playing host to Susan Wells, a Cabot Cove friend who is writing a cookbook. Nervous Susan is preparing a gourmet feast for her would-be publisher, and Jessica must repeatedly order special ingredients from the nearby Angelo's Grocery Store. The latter's delivery boy is bright Tommy Remsen, who dreams of becoming a writer, despite the protests of his single parent father, Dan, a high school swim coach.

It is no secret that Tommy has a crush on pretty flight attendant Monica Evers, another tenant in Jessica's apartment building. (Others involved with Monica are her helpful but possessive neighbor, Sandy Oates, and lustful building manager Dan Remsen.) However, what isn't known is that Monica is a criminal go-between. She delivers diamonds stolen by Fred Turner to an Amsterdam fence and, in turn, brings the cash proceeds back from Holland to ruthless Fred in New York City.

Later, a near-hysterical Tommy claims that he's just seen Monica being murdered in the apartment building's basement and that her killer fired shots at the youth. However, the police's cynical lieutenant Steve Warren can't locate the corpse or any bullet holes from the supposed gunshots. Meanwhile, the concerned killer pursues Tommy, chasing him to his high school hideout.

Highlights: This installment boasts a well-executed boy-who-cried-wolf premise, a theme made popular by *The Window* (1949). Tension is built through the atmospheric settings, especially the eerie, empty school swimming pool. There is also the palpable anxiety of the frightened youth, when no one except Jessica and the murderer will believe his "wild" stories. In contrast is the lighthearted subplot in which excitable Susan Wells putters around in Jessica's kitchen while Mrs. Fletcher attempts, unsuccessfully, to concentrate on her book writing.

Trivia: Neil Patrick Harris, the star of *Doogie Howser, M.D.* (1989–1993), appeared in such features as *Clara's Heart* (1988). Beth Howland of Broadway's *Company* (1970) was vulnerable waitress Vera Louise Gorman on *Alice* (1976–1985). Sheila MacRae, who was a latter-day Alice Kramden on *The Jackie Gleason Show* (1966–1970), was once married to actor Gordon MacRae. Laurence Luckinbill of *The Delphi Bureau* (1972–1973) gained recognition in the off-Broadway (1968) and film (1970) versions of *Boys in the Band*. John Bennett Perry was a veteran cast member of several TV series: *240-Robert* (1979–1981), *Paper Dolls* (1984) and *Falcon Crest* (1985–1986).

194. "Ship of Thieves"

(5/2/93) 60 mins.

Director: Anthony Shaw **Teleplay:** Bruce Lansbury

Regular: Angela Lansbury (Jessica Fletcher)

Recurring Character: Keith Michell (Dennis Stanton)

Guest Law Enforcer: Sarah Partridge (FBI Agent Agnes Lowry)

Guest Cast: Dwier Brown (Philip Polachek); Jon Cypher (Captain Rory O'Neil); Kim Delgado (Purser); Jack Garner (Mr. Worthington); Sammy Goldstein (Comic); Michelle Johnson (Amber [Janet Fisk]); Sharon Lee Jones (Diana Peale); Walter Kelley (Passenger); Lee Meriwether (Leslie Hunter); Towers Monica (Seaman); Albie Selznick (Marvin Soble); J.R. Starr (Shopkeeper); Ellia Thompson (Molly Altrip); George Tovar (Roland Devereaux); Jane Withers (Alma Sobel); Michael Woods (Lance Brinegar)

The Setting: the Caribbean

The Case: Badly needing a rest, Jessica Fletcher takes a Caribbean cruise on the *Lady Wellington.* Aboard, she encounters college chum Leslie Hunter, who is now in the travel business. Leslie is seriously dating the ship's captain, Rory O'Neil. The latter plans to retire after this last voyage.

Others on the vessel include Roland Devereaux, a magician and con artist; Diana Peale, his accomplice; playboy thief Lance Brinegar and his girlfriend, Molly Altrip, a good-hearted soul who lacks self-esteem. Additionally there are gregarious Alma Sobel, a kleptomaniac; her watchdog son, Marvin; and Janet Fisk, who has just killed FBI agent Agnes Lowry and assumed her identity.

To her surprise, Jessica discovers that her good friend, Dennis Stanton, is in charge of security aboard ship. By now, Mrs. Fletcher has learned about a mysterious Caribbean money laundering scheme and heard rumors about an elusive crook named Amber. When the ship docks in Old Town, Captain O'Neil brings aboard a load of antique furniture, possessions he's acquired over the years. Meanwhile, Janet Fisk is found murdered in the ship's hold.

Highlights: In this travelers-in-peril narrative, there is ample room for a variety of character vignettes. More confident and sparkling than usual—thanks to the presence of charming Dennis Stanton—Jessica soon peels away the layers of secrets from her fellow passengers. With no law enforcer aboard, Jessica not only deals with Dennis, but copes with fledgling Philip Polachek, a ship steward who has been pressed into security work at the last minute.

Trivia: Former jewel thief Dennis Stanton has taken a leave of absence from his claims adjuster's post at a San Francisco insurance company. As he tells Jessica Fletcher, he craves more exciting adventures. This would be the suave actor's ninth and final *Murder, She Wrote* appearance.

Once Miss America (1955) and a former fashion editor on the *Today* show (1955–1956), Lee Meriwether spent several seasons (1973–1980) as a relative/helper on Buddy Ebsen's TV detective series, *Barnaby Jones.* Jon Cypher was the manipulative police chief, Fletcher P. Daniels, on *Hill Street Blues* (1981–1987). Former child star Jane Withers had a lucrative, long-running stint as TV commercials' Josephine the Plumber.

195. "The Survivor"

(5/9/93) 60 mins.

Director: Anthony Shaw **Teleplay:** Robert Van Scoyk

Regular: Angela Lansbury (Jessica Fletcher)

Guest Law Enforcers: Ned Bellamy (Captain Elgin Meyers); Wolfgang Bodison (John Andrew Beatty); Nigel Gibbs (Len Thomas); Stephen Mendel (Marv Goldman); James Pickens, Jr. (Sonny Greene); Stan Shaw (Sergeant Victor Lofton)

Guest Cast: Don Calfa (Vinnie); James E. Hurd, Jr. (Highjacker); Ken Kerman (Dock Boss); Kasi Lemmons (Paula Raynor); Monte Markham (Jimmy Haynes); Julio Oscar Mechoso (Dr. Luis Perez); Evan Millar (Buddy Walker); Ann Noel (Young Nurse); Ed O'Ross (Alex Walker); Nancy Sorel (Jill Walker); Glenn Taranto (Mechanic); Elayn Taylor (Alice)

The Setting: New York City

The Case: Sergeant Victor Lofton, one of New York's finest, has organized a sting operation to trap waterfront hijackers. However, there is a nasty leak in the setup. Lofton assigns John Beatty, a rookie police detective, to go undercover on the pier. John soon comes across Vinnie, a dock worker, who will squeal on the scam for a sizable fee. Meanwhile, Beatty's girlfriend, Paula Raynor, has become friendly with Jessica Fletcher, who has hired Paula as a free-lance computer consultant.

One evening, Paula and John attend a barbecue given for fellow members of the sting. The group includes Lofton, Len and Alice Thomas, Marv Goldman and Sonny Greene, as well as Alex and Jill Walker. Also there is Jill's congenial father, commercial real estate developer Jimmy Haynes. During the evening, a drunken Lofton picks a fight with John, who leaves the party in anger. John and Paula are involved later in a bad car mishap and John dies. At the hospital, a severely injured Paula confides to Jessica that the tragedy was no accident. Although suffering from shock, she recalls that before she lost consciousness she saw a wide vision of red, "a pool of crimson." Still later, an attempt is made on Paula's life in her hospital room.

Highlights: Reminiscent of such police thrillers as *Serpico* (1973) and *Prince of the City* (1983), this abbreviated version has an assortment of red herrings. It assumes the viewer is well familiar with the genre, and, as such, takes acceptable shortcuts in characterizations and plot motivation.

Trivia: Don Calfa participated in the TV sitcom *Park Place* (1981) and the drama series *Legmen* (1984). Frequent TV guest star Monte Markham was a cohost of the 1983 syndicated talk show *Breakaway.* Kasi Lemmons was part of the short-lasting television espionage series *Under Cover* (1991). Stan Shaw, another veteran of Hollywood's 1970s black exploitation film cycle, played Lafayette Tate in the TV drama series *The Mississippi* (1983–1984).

196. "Love's Deadly Desire"

(5/16/93) 60 mins.

Director: Robert M. Williams, Jr. **Teleplay:** Chris Manheim

Regulars: Angela Lansbury (Jessica Fletcher); Ron Masak (Sheriff Mort Metzger); William Windom (Dr. Seth Hazlitt)

Recurring Character: Louis Herthum (Deputy Andy Broom)

Guest Cast: Carroll Baker (Sibella Stone); John David Bland (Colin Burnham); Erwin Fuller (Mr. Turner); David Gail (Monroe Shepard); Robin Gordon (Sue, the Waitress); William Katt (Derek Hartman); Christopher Murray (Phil Coile); Jennifer Parsons (Peggy Reed); Andrea Roth (Valerie Hartman); Ian Ruskin (Smuggler); Yvonne Suhor (Marian King); B.J. Ward (Chairperson)

The Setting: Cabot Cove, Maine

The Case: Sibella Stone, the glamorous author of such popular Gothic romance novels as *Silence Parsenia,* is a temporary Cabot Cove resident, leasing Bay House which overlooks the ocean. Her entourage includes her younger husband, Derek, who is also her publisher; her spoiled stepdaughter Valerie; the arrogant Colin Burnham, a British race driver who is having an affair with willful Valerie; and Marian King, Sibella's pert research assistant who is romantically involved with Derek. Meanwhile, local carpenter Phil Coile warns Sibella that her house is unsafe because it's falling apart. (Actually, he fears one of the household may observe his ivory-smuggling operation headquartered on the beach below the house.)

Jessica Fletcher and grumbling Dr. Seth Hazlitt attend an evening party at Sibella's. When the hostess vanishes, a search party eventually locates her at the boat house where she had tumbled through the rotting floorboards and had become trapped below with the tide fast rising. The injured author is helped back to her house. The next morning, short order cook Monroe Shepard, a newcomer in town, finds Marian's body on the beach. The victim, wearing Sibella's hooded cloak, had been bludgeoned to death.

Sibella thinks the murderer may be her first husband, Joe, once jailed on an arson charge. He's out now and has been sending his ex-wife threatening notes. Sheriff Mort Metzger is more concerned with Coile, whom he surprises in the act of transporting the contraband ivory. Mort arrests him on several charges, including homicide.

However, Jessica has another theory on the case. Her deductions are triggered by the misspellings in the threat notes Sibella received.

Highlights: With the exception of Jean Simmons on the 1989 two-part segment "Mirror, Mirror on the Wall," rarely has *Murder, She Wrote* given an actress of Carroll Baker's stature such a meaty role. She shines as the controlling celebrity who fights to retain her grip on her parasitic retinue. Since they are fellow authors, Jessica and Sibella have an immediate rapport, one which produces several dramatic moments. Meanwhile, leave it to crabby Dr. Seth Hazlitt to find something anew to grouse about: i.e., the amoral renters at Bay House. For a change, his prejudice against newcomers is well-founded.

Trivia: Carroll Baker, the costar of *The Big Country* (1958) and *The Watcher in the Woods* (1980), was Oscar-nominated for *Baby Doll* (1956). In *Harlow* (1965) she played the ill-fated 1930s movie star, with Angela Lansbury cast as her manipulative mother! William Katt, son of actors Barbara Hale and Bill Williams, headlined TV's *The Greatest American Hero* (1981–1983). In the later 1980s, he was featured as Paul Drake, Jr., in a series of two-hour Perry Mason TV movies starring Raymond Burr and Barbara Hale, and then was in the short-lasting television series *Good Sports* (1991). David Gail gained TV exposure as Shannen Dougherty's short-term boyfriend on *Beverly Hills 90210* (1993–1994) and later on *Robin's Hoods* (1994) and *Savannah* (1995–).

SEASON TEN

1993–1994

197. "A Death in Hong Kong"

(9/12/93) 60 mins.

Director: Vincent McEveety **Teleplay:** Laurence Heath

Regular: Angela Lansbury (Jessica Fletcher)

Guest Law Enforcer: David Warner (Inspector McLaughlin)

Guest Cast: Teri Austin (Louise Walton); Barrie Ingham (Brian Dunbar); Calvin Jung (Chang); Raymond Ma (Mr. Li); Dustin Nguyen (David Kuan); France Nuyen (Emma Soon Dunbar); Jen Sung Outerbridge (Chinese Kidnapper); Soon-Teck Oh (Kai Kuan); James Sutorius (Mark Tower); Vivian Wu (April Dunbar)

The Setting: Hong Kong

The Case: In Hong Kong to lecture at the university, Jessica Fletcher is the house guest of Emma Soon Dunbar. Mrs. Fletcher had met the noted ceramic painter a few years back in Paris. Emma's Caucasian husband, Brian, is a wealthy industrialist who is being pressured to merge his operation with an unscrupulous Oriental combine.

While out shopping with Emma, Jessica is aghast when her friend is kidnapped. Mrs. Fletcher is further taken aback when everyone, including Inspector McLaughlin, accepts such a happening as "ordinary." Later, after Emma is ransomed, she, Brian and Jessica visit Shingo Po's nightclub where the Dunbars' daughter, April, is a vocalist.

Later, at a dinner hosted by the House of Dunbar, its founder, Brian, slumps over dead, poisoned, after sampling the appetizer of century-old eggs. Among the candidates as his killer are Kai Kuan, the deceased's business rival; Kuan's son, David, who is April's secret lover; ambitious

Mark Tower, an underling of the dead man's and a victim of gambling fever; and Louise Walton, another of Dunbar's executive associates, who will do anything to remain in a post of power.

Highlights: A major virtue of the tenth season opener of *Murder, She Wrote* is its splendid on-location scenery, an ingredient that would be increasingly utilized in the series' final years as a weekly entry. Using a strong cast of Orientals—many of whom are known to American film and TV viewers—the exotic ambiance distracts from the transparent whodunit.

Trivia: France Nuyen, who had a recurring role on the 1980s TV series *St. Elsewhere,* was featured in such movies as *South Pacific* (1958), *Diamond Head* (1962) and *The Joy Luck Club* (1993). Dustin Nguyen gained a foothold with TV viewers for his Officer Harry Truman Loki on *21 Jump Street* (1987–1990). James Sutorius was an alumnus of *The Bob Crane Show* and *The Andros Targets.* Barrie Ingham performed in *Dr. Who and the Daleks* (1965), *A Challenge for Robin Hood* (1968) and *The Day of the Jackal* (1973).

198. "For Whom the Ball Tolls"

(9/26/93) 60 mins.

Director: Anthony Shaw **Teleplay:** Donald Ross

Regular: Angela Lansbury (Jessica Fletcher)

Recurring Characters: Herbert Edelman (Lieutenant Artie Gelber); Leonard Lightfoot (Detective Henderson)

Guest Cast: Ray Abruzzo (Mike LaRocca, of Channel 6 News); Barbara Babcock (Carol Collins); Jeff Conaway (Nolan Walsh); Alex Courtney (Victor Barton); John Dennis (Pete, the Bartender); Lisa Dinkins (Reporter); Alexander Folk (Al, the Mailman); Hallie Foote (Margaret Johnson); Wendy Hoffman (Evelyn, Walter's Secretary); Lela Ivey (Nurse Josie Miles); Kevin Kilner (Eugene Gillrich); Robert Pine (Walter Gillrich); Jodi Russell (Peggy, Ms. Johnson's Assistant); Susan Walters (Lee Gillrich)

The Setting: New York City

The Case: So that the massive Gillrich Towers can be constructed, Gillrich Development Corporation is purchasing all available real estate in a particular section of Manhattan. One of the leaseholders refusing to sell is Nolan Walsh, who operates a local bar/restaurant where Ernest Hemingway and Eugene O'Neill once were patrons. In addition, Jessica Fletcher, who lives around the corner, is a frequent diner there.

Walsh's holdout is seconded by Carol Collins and Margaret Johnson of the City Preservation Committee. Besides the historical nature of the building, there is concern for the fate of an elderly tenant who lives above Nolan's eatery. As such, these anti- "progress" folk come into conflict with high-powered Eugene Gillrich and his older, wimpy brother, Walter.

The firmly established battle lines disintegrate when Walter is found shot to death in his brother's office. At first, Lieutenant Artie Gelber concludes that Margaret Johnson, who had an attraction for the victim, is the culprit. However, Jessica's observations point in a different direction.

Mrs. Fletcher uncovers that Eugene and Carol Collins had been having an affair and that Eugene's wife was aware of the betrayal. Intermingled in the caper is a Geraldo Rivera-type reporter, Mike LaRocca, who will do anything to dig up the restaurant's basement to determine whether racketeer Dutch Schultz's remains are buried there. Additionally, there is nurse Josie Miles from Queens, who knows the real truth about Mrs. Rhodes, Nolan's reclusive tenant.

Highlights: This lesser *Murder, She Wrote* episode is hampered by an unconvincing villain and an implausible finale. On the plus side, the entry brings out unexpected intimacy in the impersonal urban setting by focusing on a neighborhood watering hole. In addition, friendly Lieutenant Artie Gelber always brings out the whimsical in Jessica.

Trivia: Jeff Conaway, earlier (see #3) cast in *Murder, She Wrote* as the actor husband of Jessica Fletcher's niece, returns in a nonassociated role. Emmy Award-winning Barbara Babcock was a veteran of *Search for Tomorrow* (1976), *The Four Seasons* (1984) and the *Murder, She Wrote* spin-off, *The Law and Harry McGraw* (1987–1988). Wendy Hoffman appeared on *Makin' It* (1979); Lela Ivey participated on TV's *Knight & Daye* (1989). Robert Pine's movies range from *Munsters, Go Home* (1966) to *The Apple Dumpling Gang Rides Again* (1979).

199. "The Legacy of Borbey House"

(10/3/93) 60 mins.

Director: Walter Grauman **Teleplay:** Danna Doyle, Debbie Smith

Regulars: Angela Lansbury (Jessica Fletcher); Ron Masak (Sheriff Mort Metzger); William Windom (Dr. Seth Hazlitt)

Recurring Characters: Louis Herthum (Deputy Andy Broom); Madlyn Rhue (Jean O'Neill, the Librarian)

Guest Cast: David Birney (Lawrence Baker); Susan Christy (Carla Thompson, the Teenager); Roy Dotrice (Dr. Henry Sorenson); Richard Gilliland

(Charles Wetherly); Gary Hershberger (Dave Perrin); Steve Jackson (Jim Milio); Richard Jamison (Delivery Man); Donnie Jeffcoat (Billy, the Teenager); Judith Jones (Molly Holt); Christopher Neame (Peter Jatich); Lawrence Pressman (Philip Holt); Barbara Townsend (Mrs. Higgins)

The Setting: Cabot Cove, Maine

The Case: The good people of Cabot Cove wonder at the elaborate restorations that Lawrence Baker is making to the old Borbey house. It's a Victorian place on Oak Street reputed to have a history of housing vampires. Meanwhile, Jessica Fletcher is disturbed when contractor/electrician Charles Wetherly puts aside needed repairs to her home wiring in order to cater to Baker's expensive whims.

Also of interest to the townspeople is visiting Dr. Henry Sorenson who is researching a new book, *Middle European Natural Phenomenon in New England.* As for local car mechanic Dave Perrin, he's still haunted by his sister Laurel's disappearance eighteen months earlier. It has impaired his romance with Molly Holt, who works at her family's wallpaper shop. She wants to marry Dave so they can get on with their lives.

When the cryptic Baker is found dead with a stake driven through his heart, the townsfolk are in an uproar about this supposed vampire. To prove their case they point to teenagers who recently "saw" a shadowy figure rising from a grave in the cemetery and that a clove of garlic had been found nearby. Sheriff Mort Metzger has more earthly theories. He thinks that it was either Dr. Sorenson (who had been caught breaking into the Borbey house) or illegal alien Peter Jatich.

Less superstitious, more pragmatic Jessica has a better explanation—all based on a knotted rope found in the boat of the long-missing Laurel Perrin, as well as the architectural plans to the Borbey house.

Highlights: There are enough (sub)plots here to fill several episodes. With its alternating themes of superstition about vampires, romantic jealousy and missing relatives, the characters are pulled in several directions. With their zesty performances, Roy Dotrice and David Birney help to create a believable Gothic horror atmosphere.

Trivia: Madlyn Rhue, confined to a wheelchair because of multiple sclerosis, returned to *Murder, She Wrote* in a new role, that of librarian Jean O'Neill. (Hired after the episode had been completed so she could qualify for additional Screen Actors Guild insurance, her scenes were inserted into the finished segment.) British actor Roy Dotrice had been in such TV movies as *Family Reunion* (1982), *Harry Houdini* (1987) and *Carmilla* (1989) and had an ongoing role in the 1990s TV series *Picket Fences.* Lawrence Pressman had been featured in the teleseries *Mulligan's Stew* (1977) and *Ladies' Man* (1980–1981). Prolific performer Richard Gilliland had been one of Polly Draper's more enduring lovers on *thirtysomething* in the early 1990s.

200. "The Phantom Killer"

(10/24/93) 60 mins.

Director: Anthony Shaw **Teleplay:** Tom Sawyer

Regular: Angela Lansbury (Jessica Fletcher)

Recurring Characters: Herbert Edelman (Lieutenant Artie Gelber); Leonard Lightfoot (Detective Henderson)

Guest Cast: Vanessa Angel (Kathryn Scofield); Mark Barriere (Waiter); Christian Bocher (Dave Wolski); Janet Julian (Ellen Harper); David Kriegel (Ben Foreman/Gary Manyon); Jack Laufer (Carter Drummond); Reiner Schoene (Hans Dietrich); Alan Thicke (Harrison Kane); Scott Valentine (Dean Richards); Emily Warfield (Abby Peters)

The Setting: New York City

The Case: Ben Foreman, a nervous but brilliant free-lance writer, interviews Jessica Fletcher for an article in *Follies* magazine. The publication is edited and co-owned by highly competitive Dean Richards and his hard-nosed partner, Carter Drummond. *Follies'* gross is so marginal that Drummond must dip into his trust fund yet again to save the floundering magazine. Nevertheless, unscrupulous Harrison Kane makes it known that he wants to buy *Follies* or else!

When the despised Kane is found dead in his apartment sauna, Lieutenant Artie Gelber is assigned the case. Ben, who had been peddling a screenplay to Kane, was at the scene of the crime around the time of the murder and, as such, becomes the chief suspect. Jessica rushes to the young man's defense. Among those she queries are Kathryn Scofield, Dean's lady love; actress Abby Peters, who was almost seduced by the victim; high-style photographer Hans Dietrich; and Gary Manyon, an aggressive literary agent who remains unseen.

Highlights: It's a most unusual occasion when Jessica Fletcher despises anyone, no matter how slimy the individual. However, unscrupulous Harrison Kane is a different bird. Without her consent, he once peddled a Jessica Fletcher novel to the studios and networks. Not only didn't the pushy man get a sale, but he antagonized the studios to such an extent that all future legitimate offers for this J.B. Fletcher property were jeopardized.

That aside, this installment suffers from below par acting performances by many of the guest cast.

Trivia: This was the second time that Lieutenant Artie Gelber is partnered with Detective Henderson. Scott Valentine was best known as Mallory's Rocky-style artist boyfriend on *Family Ties* (1985–1989). Canadian-born Alan Thicke failed with a TV talk show, *Thicke of the Night* (1983–1984), but succeeded with two sitcoms, *Growing Pains* (1985–1992) and *Hope & Gloria* (1995–1996). Leonard Lightfoot played an attorney on *Silver Spoons* (1982–1983) and a police deputy on *She's the Sheriff* (1987–1989).

201. "A Virtual Murder"

(10/31/93) 60 mins.

Director: Lee Smith **Teleplay:** Carlton Hollander

Regulars: Angela Lansbury (Jessica Fletcher); William Windom (Dr. Seth Hazlitt)

Guest Law Enforcer: Sherman Augustus (Sergeant Rossi)

Guest Cast: Wayne Bolton (Colonel Fleming); Heaven Brooke (Servant Girl); Julia Campbell (Sharon Baskin); Arthur Cohan (Jeremy Hastings); Shoshana Henri (Carrie Brandeis); Kate McNeil (Kate Walden); Allan Miller (John Crowley [Charles Crowe]); Phil Morris (David Salt); Shawn Phelan (Alex Hooper); Thomas Ryan (Dan Porter); Kevin Sorbo (Michael Burke); Danny Woodburn (Mr. Townsend); Richard Yniguez (Ignacio Delcanto); Ramy Zada (James Lindstrom)

The Settings: Cabot Cove, Maine; Silicon Valley, California

The Case: Jessica Fletcher has written the script for a virtual reality murder mystery video game, *A Killing at Hastings' Rock*. She worked on the project with West Coast executive Michael Burke, whom she had known when he was a youngster in Kennebunkport, Maine. Now Jessica flies to Marathon Images, Inc.'s, northern California facility to try out the test module which is to be introduced to the trade in a few days.

During the run-through, bugs in the high-tech video game are discovered, leading Burke to blame team member James Lindstrom. Teenaged Alex Hooper, a computer programming whiz on the development team, saves the day by suggesting that the errors can be eliminated if Jessica does script rewrites. She agrees.

At the reception introducing the new product, Lindstrom is found shot dead in a virtual reality game booth, and confidential source codes for the new software, which he had on his person, are missing. Cynical Sergeant Rossi determines that Burke had the best motive and opportunity to commit the crime, so Michael is arrested. Jessica remains in town to clear Michael of the accusation.

Solving the mystery requires Jessica to snoop into secret transactions brewing between corrupt Marathon staffers (Lindstrom, David Salt) and John Crowley, head of Redwood Concepts, a rival firm. Then there is Sharon Baskin who, like Carrie Brandeis, has a crush on the murder suspect. Also tied into the caper is private detective Dan Porter, hired by Burke to tail Lindstrom, who is not above blackmailing his own clients.

Highlights: Pushing into very high tech frontiers, this *Murder, She Wrote* segment not only employs interactive virtual reality computer games as a gimmick, but makes them a key factor in solving the crime. When Jessica tests the intricate amusement (allowing the viewer to be drawn into the game), she discovers that clues to the murder have been worked into the software which features Colonel Fleming, Jeremy Hastings and a Servant Girl.

Trivia: Julia Campbell had been a member of TV's *Women in Prison* (1987–1988) as well as *Knight & Daye* (1989). In the brief 1991 series *Dark Justice*, Ramy Zada had played Judge Nicholas Marshall. Phil Morris, the son of actor Greg Morris (*Mission: Impossible*), had been a member of TV's *Marblehead Manor* (1987–1988), the revived *Mission: Impossible* (1988–1990) and *WIOU* (1990–1991). Richard Yniguez had played a priest on the sitcom *Mama Malone* (1984) and a police lieutenant on *O'Hara* (1987–1988). Kevin Sorbo was soon to become identified as the hunky hero of the syndicated TV series *Hercules: The Legendary Journey* (1995-).

202. "Bloodlines"

(11/7/93) 60 mins.

Director: Don Mischer **Story:** Michael Berlin, Eric Estrin **Teleplay:** Robert Hamner

Regular: Angela Lansbury (Jessica Fletcher)

Guest Law Enforcers: Blake Gibbons (Sheriff Clyde Benson); Scott Stevens (Deputy Vernon Kelly)

Guest Cast: Ami Dolenz (Tracey Noble); Frank Farmer (Dr. Garney); Tippi Hedren (Catherine Noble); Stephen Macht (Lloyd Mentone); Don Murray (Wally Hampton); Sean O'Bryan (Paul Hampton); Dave Powledge (Delivery

Driver); Mickey Rooney (Matt Cleveland); Shawnee Smith (Jill Cleveland); Don Swayze (Gus Tardio)

The Setting: (Near) Phillipsburg, Virginia

The Case: Swift Prince, a well-bred race horse which had been ridden in events on the West Coast, is purchased by two Virginians, Catherine Noble and Wally Hampton. Veteran trainer Matt Cleveland is in charge of Swift Prince. Matt's jockey daughter, Jill, is set to ride the prize horse at the Raleigh Handicaps.

Jessica Fletcher arrives in Virginia to research her upcoming book, which deals with the Virginia horse country. Naturally, she visits with her old friends Matt and Jill. (Jill is Mrs. Fletcher's godchild.) Jessica soon learns that Jill loves Wally's son, Paul, a banker, but that he's been pressured by his dad into marrying Catherine's daughter, Tracey, an empty-headed blonde. As the wedding plans become more elaborate, Catherine, hard pressed for funds, wonders how to meet the expense. Thus, winning her share of the Raleigh Handicaps purse is essential.

A few nights later, gruff old Matt is found lying dead by his truck. It appears he has been clobbered over the head while changing a flat tire. Distressed at losing her friend, Jessica competes with Sheriff Clyde Benson—a man sensitive to class distinctions—to solve the murder. Jessica interrogates Lloyd Mentone, a man with a shady past, who badly wanted to buy Swift Prince. Another suspicious character is redneck Gus Tardio, the embittered trainer who was passed over by the victim. In the nick of time, Mrs. Fletcher links a VCR tape (recently purchased by the deceased) on horse racing to the crime at hand.

Highlights: CBS-TV network publicity made much of this landmark episode (the 200th *shot*) which rematched Angela Lansbury with her MGM coplayer of fifty years earlier. At his salty best, Mickey Rooney brings verve to his characterization, unfortunately cut short by having him be the murder victim. Of note is the fact that Jessica, who a few years earlier had been computer illiterate, now travels with a state-of-the-art laptop computer.

Trivia: Within the segment it is mentioned that Jessica Fletcher is the author of the recently published *Triple Crown Murders*. Angela Lansbury and Mickey Rooney had costarred in MGM's *National Velvet* (1944). In that celebrated picture, young Rooney had also played a horse trainer. Don Murray, who played Sid Fairgate on *Knots Landing* (1979–1981), had earlier been a member of *Made in America* (1964) and *The Outcasts* (1968–1969). Tippi Hedren, the mother of actress Melanie Griffith, had been a star of Alfred Hitchcock's *The Birds* (1963) and *Marnie* (1964) and Charles Chaplin's *A Countess from Hong Kong* (1966). Shawnee Smith had been on the sitcom *All Is Forgiven* (1986). Stunt performer/actor Don Swayze had appeared in such features as *Edge of Honor* (1991) and did stunt work for *Point Break* (1991) which starred his older brother, Patrick.

203. "A Killing in Cork"

(11/21/93) 60 mins.

Director: Anthony Shaw **Teleplay:** Bruce Lansbury

Regular: Angela Lansbury (Jessica Fletcher)

Recurring Character: Mark Rolston (Sergeant Terence Boyle)

Guest Cast: Wendy Benson (Siobhan Kennedy); Michael Connors (Eric); Gordon Currie (Sean Griffith); Fionnula Flanagan (Fiona Delaney Griffith); Paul Ivy (Duffy); Lee Magnuson (Bar Person); Dakin Matthews (Dennis Moylan); Gerald S. O'Loughlin (Father Timothy); Cyril O'Reilly (Patrick Griffith); Udana Power (Una O'Reilly); Donnelly Rhodes (William Mahaffy); Andrew Robinson (Ambrose Griffith); Bridget Wilson (Emily Griffith)

The Setting: Kilcleer, Ireland

The Case: Jessica Fletcher is in County Cork, Ireland, where her mother's side of the family had once resided. She is visiting her longtime friend, Fiona Delaney Griffith, now the owner of Kilcleer Woolen Mills, and the author of four books on Irish myths.

Fiona was recently widowed when her husband, Robert, who had taken up masonry as a hobby, fell off the steeple he was repairing at St. Broderick's Church. However, according to family friend William Mahaffy, Robert had been murdered. But few people take Mahaffy's contention too seriously because he has a bad habit of drinking too much. (It later develops that William and Fiona had once had an affair.)

Days later, Ambrose Griffith, an American cousin, is found strangled to death at the local church. As Sergeant Terence Boyle gathers the facts, so does the very curious Jessica. She knows that Ambrose, who had a financial stake in the mills, wanted to move the operations to a third-world country. Then there is Fiona's son, Patrick, who dropped out of school ten years ago and disappeared (actually to Dublin). He has returned to town secretly and has been dating Siobhan Kennedy. Another of Fiona's sons, Sean, had been seen arguing with dictatorial Ambrose.

In addition, Dennis Moylan, the mills' vice-president, was no friend of Ambrose, for he and the deceased bitterly fought over the factory's relocation. Emily Griffith, the victim's widow, was in the process of being divorced by Ambrose who had discovered her indiscretions. There is also Una

O'Reilly, the slightly daft spinster lady from the village, who has not been the same since Robert died.

Highlights: Taking advantage of the Irish countryside where Angela Lansbury and her husband, Peter Shaw (and in the past her children, too), spent vacations, the star enjoyed filming this episode so close to "home." More so than 1992's "The Wind around the Tower" (#178), this entry captures the mood and spirit of its locale. On the downside, the script gets too caught up in Irish myths and notions as a plot device. Moreover, some of the cast (especially Gerald S. O'Loughlin as Father Timothy) tip the blarney a bit too often.

Trivia: Andrew Robinson, the memorable killer of *Dirty Harry* (1971), was featured in several action features: *Cobra* (1986), *Shoot to Kill* (1988), *Prime Target* (1991), etc. Gerald O'Loughlin's television series work included *Storefront Lawyers, The Rookies* and *Our House.* Dublin-born Fionnula Flanagan was a regular on such TV series as *How the West Was Won* (1978–1979), *Hard Copy* (1987) and *H.E.L.P.* (1990). Canadian Donnelly Rhodes participated on TV's *Soap, Report to Murphy* and *Double Trouble.*

204. "Love and Hate in Cabot Cove"

(11/28/93) 60 mins.

Director: Anthony Shaw **Teleplay:** Robert Van Scoyk

Regulars: Angela Lansbury (Jessica Fletcher); Ron Masak (Sheriff Mort Metzger); William Windom (Dr. Seth Hazlitt)

Recurring Character: Louis Herthum (Deputy Andy Broom)

Guest Law Enforcer: Matthew Flint (Deputy Ethan Loomis)

Guest Cast: Richard Beymer (Lou Keramides); Trent Dolan (Jason David); Wings Hauser (Sam Bennett); Jayson Kane (Waiter); Rick Scarry (Minister); Carrie Snodgress (Irene Macinoy); David Stenstrom (Craps Player); Adam Trese (Chad Macinoy); Liz Vassey (Candace Bennett); James Willett (Croupier); Penelope Windust (Laura Bennett)

The Setting: Cabot Cove, Maine

The Case: What is happening in once tranquil Cabot Cove? Jessica Fletcher is among several locals whose finances have been mismanaged by accountant Sam Bennett. In addition, someone has fired at Sheriff Mort Metzger at the police station. Now shady Lou Keramides is operating a private casino at the Timberline Inn. Every time Mort and his deputies raid the inn, Lou amazingly hides the gaming evidence before the law arrives.

While driving the sheriff's vehicle, Deputy Ethan Loomis is shot dead. Had the killer thought that Mort was behind the wheel? Not according to Jessica. Her queries lead to Sam Bennett, who had argued violently with the deceased because Loomis was dating Sam's daughter Candace. Then there's Keramides who had been bribing the deceased and who had voiced dissatisfaction with the results of his payoff. Not to be overlooked is Irene Macinoy, who operates the *Cabot Cove Gazette.* She is the overprotective mother of unruly Chad who loves Candace.

Highlights: Many staunch *Murder, She Wrote* fans favor the episodes set in Cabot Cove. In these, Jessica is at her most relaxed as she mingles with close friends and neighbors. A superior sequence here involves Jessica and food-loving Dr. Seth Hazlitt dining at the Timberline Inn to check out the rumors of a gambling operation on the premises. To gain entrance to the gaming rooms, Jessica pretends to be a bon vivant. Later, she has a memorable confrontation with hard-edged Keramides. To be noted is how modern the Cabot Cove police department has become, what with personal computers, cellular phones and police scanners.

Trivia: After her Oscar-nominated performance in *Diary of a Mad Housewife* (1972), Carrie Snodgress abandoned filmmaking for several years to raise her child by musician Neil Young.

205. "Murder at a Discount"

(12/5/93) 60 mins.

Director: Walter Grauman **Teleplay:** Rick Mittleman

Regular: Angela Lansbury (Jessica Fletcher)

Recurring Characters: Herbert Edelman (Lieutenant Artie Gelber); Leonard Lightfoot (Detective Henderson)

Guest Cast: Joseph Allsopp (Jed Collins); Sam Anderson (Neil Fraser); Jenny Burgess (Receptionist); James Daughton (Minister); John Enos (Rick Konig); Morgan Fairchild (Iris Novaro); Spencer Garrett (Aaron Woodman, Esq.); Bruce Gray (Ted Hartley); Darnell Harrison (Eli, the Video Director); Elaine Joyce (Lillian Conway); Sylvia Sage Lane (Bag Lady); Julianna Margulies (Rachel Novaro, Esq.); John Petlock (Man); Robert Rigamonti (Maitre d'); George Segal (Dave Novaro); Sandy Ward (Norman Trent)

The Setting: New York City

The Case: Jessica Fletcher's best-selling novel, *The Uncaught,* is just being released in a paperback edition. Before she can undertake a Hawaiian vacation, she and her publisher are sued for $10 million by Dave Novaro, the owner of a discount electronics store. He claims her book is a thinly disguised version of his first wife's murder. (Dave was accused of killing Janet, but found innocent by the jury.) Oddly, not until after he sues does Dave bother to read Jessica's novel.

When Dave is found murdered at his store, Jessica is a prime suspect. However, Lieutenant Artie Gelber, who had worked with Mrs. Fletcher on several past cases, knows she is innocent. Now Jessica and Artie must expose the real killer. The suspects include the victim's wife, Iris, who was in the process of divorcing her financially troubled spouse, and Neil Fraser, the dead man's partner, who was unhappy with Dave. As for the company bookkeeper, Lillian Conway, she had once thought Navaro would marry her. Also involved is Dave's lawyer daughter, Rachel, who had been representing her dad in his lawsuit, and, finally, there's Norman Trent, the father of Janet, who always thought Dave killed his daughter.

Highlights: Because this is such a fast-paced entry, plot loopholes and "coincidences" are cleverly disguised. And, as here, whenever Jessica is a murder suspect, she toils that much harder to solve the case, making such entries far more credible. A running gag here has Lieutenant Gelber eager to sell his old car. After his partner, Detective Henderson, buys the auto, Artie is forever rationalizing away the problems Henderson has with the vehicle.

Trivia: George Segal, has had a lengthy movie career: *Who's Afraid of Virginia Woolf?* (1966), *A Touch of Class* (1973), *Carbon Copy* (1981), *A Bear Called Arthur* (1992), etc. Morgan Fairchild's films include *The Seduction* (1982), *Campus Man* (1987) and *Body Chemistry 3: Point of Seduction* (1993). Elaine Joyce's debut TV series was *The Don Knotts Show* (1970–1971). Sandy Ward played Jeb Amos on *Dallas* (1978–1979). Julianna Margulies costars on *ER* (1994–)

206. "Murder in White"

(12/19/93) 60 mins.

Director: Vincent McEveety **Teleplay:** Peter S. Fischer

Regular: Angela Lansbury (Jessica Fletcher)

Guest Law Enforcers: Pauline Brailsford (Inspector Ellen Jarvis); Sean Francis Howse (Police Officer #1); Gale Van Cott (Police Officer); Jonathan Wood (Inspector Ernest Martindale)

Guest Cast: Davis Gaines (Peter Drew); Norman Lloyd (St. Cloud); Jean Marsh (Glenda Highsmith); Nick Meaney (Waiter at Binkie's); Anne Meara (Mae Shaughnessy); Ian Ogilvy (Lawson Childress); Michael Palance (Franklin Smith); Dedee Pfeiffer (Sally Briggs); Jim Piddock (Malcolm Brooker); Tim Ransom (Brett Dillon); Robin Sachs (Martin Kramer, the Producer); Edward L. Shaff (Lester Perth); G.W. Stevens (Oliver Hopkins)

The Setting: London, England

The Case: Jessica Fletcher is registered at London's Hyde Park Hotel because her novel *Murder in White* is being translated into a West End play. Neither director Davis Gaines nor producer Martin Kramer are happy with Mae Shaughnessy's adaptation. Then there's the matter of the cast, including too often drunk Lawson Childress and ineffectual Franklin Smith, both of whom fear they will be replaced. As for the leading lady, Glenda Highsmith, once a member of the Old Vic company, she's jittery during rehearsals.

When Kramer is stabbed to death, Glenda is the main suspect. However, Jessica, who has known Highsmith for years, can't believe her friend is guilty. In proving her theory, Mrs. Fletcher tangles with members of Scotland Yard who regard her as a nuisance. Nonetheless, there is young American Brett Dillon, who lives with Glenda, and cast member Sally Briggs, who despised the victim because he had attempted to seduce her. Competent stage manager Oliver Hopkins is also noted to be acting strangely. And what of the two private detectives—including bullying Malcolm Brooker—who had been investigating Glenda's background?

Highlights: With its atmospheric setting at London's Garrick Theatre as the cast prepares for opening night, this backstage entry has a ring of truth to it. An intriguing subtheme is the rivalry between two Scotland Yard investigators.

Trivia: Jean Marsh, who won several Emmy Awards for playing Rose the maid on *Upstairs, Downstairs* (1974–1977) was a cocreator of that series. Norman Lloyd, a barrister assisting Jessica Fletcher in this episode, had been the villain in Alfred Hitchcock's *Saboteur* (1942). When he starred in the 1978 TV series *Return of the Saint,* Britisher Ian Ogilvy followed in the footsteps of George Sanders and Roger Moore who appeared over the years as that stylish sleuth. Dedee Pfeiffer, the younger sister of actress Michelle Pfeiffer, was part of the ensemble on the teleseries *Cybill* (1995-), playing Cybill Shepherd's older daughter. Anne Meara's series roles include *The Paul Lynde Show* (1972–1973), *Rhoda* (1976–1977), *Archie Bunker's Place* (1979–1982) and *ALF* (1987–1990).

207. "Northern Explosion"

(1/2/94) 60 mins.

Director: Anthony Shaw **Teleplay:** Mark A. Butley

Regular: Angela Lansbury (Jessica Fletcher)

Guest Law Enforcers: Ana Alicia (Hilda Dupont, Royal Canadian Mounted Police); Matt McKenzie (Corporal Desmond O'Gara)

Guest Cast: Brian Frejo (George Quill); Alan Fudge (Brian Wade); Graham Greene (Peter Henderson, Esq.); Jerry Hardin (Hamish McPherson); Marilyn Jones (Marie Comouche); Ernie Lively (Rick Shipley); Shawyn Michael Perry (Bill Nahanee); Scott Plank (Buzz Berkeley); Ned Romero (Joe Quill)

The Setting: Dominion and Hobart Falls, British Columbia, Canada

The Case: En route to a friend's wedding in Vancouver, British Columbia, Jessica Fletcher's plane connection is grounded near Hobart Falls. There she finds herself in the midst of a squabble involving Rick Shipley, head of the Aurora Hills Company which is negotiating with government officials to start a mine near Hobart Falls. The local Indians, in particular, are angered by the project which will destroy their land.

During the weekend, obnoxious Hamish McPherson, a retired police officer, is murdered when unknown parties blow up a nearby bridge. Astute Jessica soon realizes that the homicide and a later second killing may be unrelated to the hotly contested environmental issues. She discovers that the first victim was on the trail of the perpetrator of a $500,000 bank robbery in Ottawa. The years-ago heist, involving a police officer's death, was never solved, and a $25,000 reward is still attached to the case.

Jessica's quest starts with First Nations leader George Quill, who belatedly acknowledges that he stole dynamite from Aurora Hills' stockpile. As the case proceeds, Mrs. Fletcher learns vital facts from Marie Comouche, the clerk at the hotel where the writer is staying. There's also pilot Buzz Berkeley, who loves Marie; peacemaker Joe Quill, the wise relative of George the agitator; and Peter Henderson, an upscale Toronto attorney who ignores his heritage.

Highlights: In one scene, a general store's book rack contains several J.B. Fletcher novels, including *The Corpse Danced at Midnight, The Umbrella Murders, The Dead Must Sing* and *The Killer Called.*

Murder, She Wrote continued to update its thematic material (here environmental issues) to be relevant for the 1990s. Open-minded Jessica, who cares nothing about the color of a person's skin, is the perfect, self-sufficient character to mingle with warring factions of various ethnic extraction in a backwoods setting.

Trivia: From 1991–1992, Native American Graham Greene was Leonard Quinhagak on the Alaska-set TV drama *Northern Exposure.* Ned Romero's early TV series included *Dan August* (1970–1971) and *The D.A.* (1971–1972). Alan Fudge counts among his feature film credits *Bug* (1975), *Capricorn One* (1978) and *Brainstorm* (1983). Jerry Hardin was Wild Bill Weschester on the TV sitcom *Filthy Rich* (1982–1983). Ann Alicia starred as popular villainess Melissa Agretti on *Falcon Crest.* When that personality was killed off and ratings plummeted, Alicia was brought back to the show as a look-alike character.

208. "Proof in the Pudding"

(1/9/94) 60 mins.

Director: Jerry Jameson **Teleplay:** Lisa Seidman

Regular: Angela Lansbury (Jessica Fletcher)

Guest Law Enforcer: Fran Bennett (Detective MacKenzie); Gene Ross (Desk Sergeant); Lew Saunders (Police Officer)

Guest Cast: Rachel Bailit (Stage Manager); Michael Brandon (Alex Weaver); Nick Corri (Manuel Ramirez); Bobby Di Cicco (Philip Bonelli); James Ingersoll (Timothy Milner, Esq.); Sal Landi (Sal Randazzo); Tony Lo Bianco (Paul Avoncino); John Saxon (Bernardo Bonelli); Liza Snyder (Jeannine Bonelli); Heidi Swedberg (Lorna Thompson); Tiffany Terry (Drip Stop TV Commercial Actor); Valerie Wildman (Diane Weaver)

The Setting: New York City

The Case: Author Jessica Fletcher is to be a celebrity guest on Diane Weaver's TV show, *Dining with Diane.* At the same Manhattan TV studio, Bernardo Bonelli has his own program, *Bonelli's Kitchen.* Meanwhile, domineering Bernardo is having problems opening his new restaurant. Gangster Paul Avoncino insists it would be healthier for Bernardo if he made Paul a partner. The latter agrees reluctantly.

In short order, the arrogant Bernardo is fatally stabbed in his kitchen on opening night. Later, Avoncino is shot to death. While unflappable Detective MacKenzie deals with the two crimes, Jessica embarks on her own clue-gathering expedition.

She first considers those who were involved recently with the late Bernardo. There's the victim's floundering nephew, Philip, who's the dead man's only heir. Aggressive Diane Weaver, unmindful of her husband Alex, had threatened Bernardo with giving his restaurant a bad review on her TV show if he didn't have an affair with her. Meanwhile, subservient Alex, desperate for money, told Bernardo he couldn't afford to invest $50,000 in the latter's culinary venture. As for Lorna Thompson, a TV station production worker, she not only invested in Bernardo's forthcoming eating establishment, but had taken out a hefty life insurance policy on the restaurateur.

Highlights: With a TV station and a restaurant alternating as backdrops, the viewer can't become bored with any one setting. As in so many show installments, Jessica gets a sudden insight into the murder at hand by observing a seemingly extraneous bit of action.

While Mrs. Fletcher is generally sympathetic or at least silently shocked when the revealed killer explains his/her reasoning for the crime, here, she breaks from tradition by being sarcastically outspoken to the disclosed killer. On another level, Jessica rarely receives sympathetic treatment from women police officers. Here her temporary nemesis is abrasive Detective MacKenzie.

Trivia: Angela Lansbury and John Saxon costarred in the screen comedy *The Reluctant Debutante* (1958). Tony Lo Bianco appeared in several police action films: *The French Connection* (1972), *The Seven Ups* (1973), *City Heat* (1984), etc. Michael Brandon, once married to actress Lindsay Wagner, had starred in the TV series *Emerald Point* and *Dempsey and Makepeace.* Fran Bennett had been head nurse Lenore Ritt on *Nightingales* (1989).

209. "Portrait of Death"

(1/16/94) 60 mins.

Director: Vincent McEveety **Teleplay:** Donald Ross

Regular: Angela Lansbury (Jessica Fletcher)

Recurring Characters: Herbert Edelman (Lieutenant Artie Gelber); Leonard Lightfoot (Detective Henderson)

Guest Cast: David Ackroyd (Bert Lown); Denise Gentile (Teddy Grace); Edward Hibbert (Philip Jovet, the Art Gallery Owner); Vincent Howard (The Real Dr. Swope); Jonathan Knopf (Art Dealer); Greg Lewis (Maintenance Man); Taylor Nichols (Mark Mitchell); Lee Purcell (Frances McNean, the Maid [Wanda Rae Skeetnik]); Diane Salinger (Mrs. Sondra Arthur); Bainbridge Scott (Dede Gorman); Loretta Swit (Kim Mitchell); Kristoffer Tabori (Dr. Swope)

The Setting: New York City

The Case: One day while visiting the Manhattan art gallery owned by Philip Jovet, Jessica encounters a familiar face from Cabot Cove. The latter is Kim Mitchell who—some months back—won $10 million in a magazine sweepstakes contest. Kim now lives in New York City where she hopes to become a professional sculptor. Meanwhile, Kim is dating handsome and congenial stock broker Bert Lown, as well as supporting her indecisive stepbrother, Mark.

A few days later, Jovet is found dead in his art gallery, having been stabbed with the sharp point of a metal statue. Coincidentally, at the time the snobbish gallery owner was murdered, he was talking on the phone with Jessica.

As the investigation proceeds, Jessica and her long-standing police cohort, Lieutenant Artie Gelber, evaluate the mounting list of those who despised the unscrupulous victim and had cause to eliminate him. They include Dr. Swope, the headmaster of Willow Gardens School for Boys, who is on a fund-raising mission involving a charity auction at Jovet's. There is also Mark, who had argued with the crafty gallery owner hours before the killing. It turns out that the hot-tempered adult had a police record for juvenile delinquency when he was a teenager in Cabot Cove.

Not to be overlooked is Teddy Grace, Mark's mercenary but unsophisticated girlfriend, who had accidentally bid on and won an art work at the auction that she can't pay for. Others tied into the case include Frances McNean, Kim's unassuming maid, as well as Mrs. Sondra Arthur, who had donated a painting for the fund-raiser, which is now missing.

Since Lieutenant Gelber is so fixated on locating his missing wallet—which may contain a big-prize winning lottery ticket—much of the investigation is left to the intrepid Mrs. Fletcher.

Highlights: In their several outings together, Jessica Fletcher and the balding, married Lieutenant Gelber have developed a shorthand for working in tandem. Their camaraderie is a buoyant plot line ingredient. On the other hand, the rapport between Gelber and Henderson (one tall and white, the other shorter and African American) is never sufficiently developed to pay dividends.

"Portrait of Death" is one of the more uninspired *Murder, She Wrote* entries. It's hampered by a pedestrian script and mechanical performances by most of the cast.

Trivia: Kristoffer Tabori made his film acting debut at age five, and by his mid-teens had small parts in *John and Mary* (1969) and *Dirty Harry* (1971—directed by his father, Don Siegel). Loretta Swit's occasional big screen assignments include *Stand Up and Be Counted* (1972), *Race with the Devil* (1975) and *S.O.B.* (1981). David Ackroyd had been a cast member of *A*

Peaceable Kingdom (1989), the brief-running Lindsay Wagner series, as well as *Studio 5-B* (1989) and *The Round Table* (1992).

210. "Deadly Assets"

(1/23/94) 60 mins.

Director: Anthony Shaw **Teleplay:** Tom Sawyer

Regulars: Angela Lansbury (Jessica Fletcher); Ron Masak (Sheriff Mort Metzger); William Windom (Dr. Seth Hazlitt)

Recurring Characters: Louis Herthum (Deputy Andy Broom); Wayne Rogers (Charlie Garrett)

Guest Cast: R.D. Call (Joseph Kempinsky); Frederick Coffin (Sanford Lomax); Rebecca Cross (Libby Terhune); Anthony Mangano (Oscar James Gandile); Matt Mulhern (Walter Perry); Eamonn Roche (Harvey Terhune); Millie Slavin (Celia Terhune)

The Setting: Cabot Cove, Maine

The Case: A nocturnal break-in at the Lomax Sheet Metal Company sets off a chain of unhappy events in Cabot Cove.

Sanford Lomax receives a threatening call from Chicago underworld figure Joseph Kempinsky asking whether Lomax still has on hand the $900,000 he's holding for the mob. Afraid to admit that the contents of his office safe have vanished, Lomax hires seedy Chicago private investigator Charlie Garrett to rush to Maine to locate the missing funds. Before long, the situation involves Oscar James Gandile, a worker at the local Hall of Records, when he is fatally clobbered with a hammer.

Jessica Fletcher, along with Sheriff Mort Metzger, probe the spiraling chaos in Cabot Cove. (At the same time, her old cohort, the down-at-the-heels private detective Charlie Garrett, weaves in and out of the complex action.) The path leads eventually to Celia Terhune, who owns a local antique shop, and her two offspring, Harvey and Libby. Libby works for the Hall of Records and is engaged to marry Walter Perry. The latter, as Mrs. Fletcher uncovers, had a grudge against Lomax for having done bad work for him.

Highlights: With out-of-state hoodlums and private eyes scampering through Cabot Cove on each others' trails, it is little wonder that the story line is confusing. This episode points up the dual sides of Mrs. Fletcher's nature. At one moment she's in a dangerous predicament (i.e., being held prisoner at gun point) and the next she is joyfully attending a party (i.e., the surprise birthday bash for Dr. Seth Hazlitt).

Trivia: Wayne Rogers's Charlie Garrett had last appeared in 1993's "Dead Eye" (#187). In the 12th and final *Murder, She Wrote* weekly season, he would appear twice again as the unsuccessful gumshoe. Matt Mulhern played the well-meaning 2nd Lieutenant Gene Holowachuk on the sitcom *Major Dad* (1989–1993). Rebecca Cross had supported Jaclyn Smith in TV's *Christine Cromwell* (1989–1990). On *Stephen King's Golden Years* (1991), R.D. Call appeared as ruthless Jude Andrews.

211. "Murder on the Thirtieth Floor"

(2/6/94) 60 mins.

Director: Walter Grauman **Teleplay:** Robert Van Scoyk

Regular: Angela Lansbury (Jessica Fletcher)

Guest Law Enforcer: Jay Acavone (Lieutenant Nick Acosta)

Guest Cast: Dennis Boutsikaris (Dr. Jerry Santana); Wren Brown (The Attorney); June Christopher (Donna Kendricks); Robert Curtis-Brown (Steve DiNapoli); Lisa Darr (Carrie Benton); Robert Desiderio (Edward Graham, the Book Editor); Bruce Gray (Ted Hartley); Kenneth Magee (Mel, the Painter); Ray Reinhardt (Henry Filbert); Stewart Rose (Security Guard); Lisa Wilcox (Lori Graham); Michael Zelniker (Leonard Ambler)

The Setting: New York City

The Case: At a major Manhattan-based publishing firm, Ted Hartley is the publisher. One of his associates, book editor Edward Graham—who had worked with Mrs. Fletcher's manuscripts at her previous publisher—is editing Jessica Fletcher's latest novel. She is deeply disturbed when, one day, Edward praises her writing and on the next he explodes that her work is unpublishable!

Jessica is shocked when Graham, who had been suffering from nightmares since his wife's death, jumps to his death. She is amazed to discover that she has been named executor of his estate. In trying to fathom his strange demise, she visits the late man's psychiatrist, Dr. Jerry Santana, who had been providing his patient with unorthodox treatment and medication.

It develops that another publishing company employee, Steve DiNapoli, had initially referred the disturbed Graham to Santana. Then there is Carrie Benton, recently promoted to children's book editor at the firm. She had been dating the widowed Graham, and he had bequeathed to her his book library. As for his niece, Lori, who used to live in Oregon, she inherits the deceased's Connecticut home as well as being the beneficiary of a huge life insurance policy that his firm had taken out on Edward. Finally, there is the publishing house's accounting chief, Leonard Ambler, who has his hands in too many pies.

Highlights: As so often happens to Jessica Fletcher, there are as many deadly intrigues in the publishing business as in her novels. Pitted against a sinister therapist, her snooping must be more ingenious than usual to circumvent the roadblock of patient confidentiality. In the process, she is caught short at a spooky country house on a stormy night, with danger afoot.

It is a revealing footnote to observe how sensitive Jessica can be to criticism about her writing. Since she is constantly being praised for her novels, the negative judgment shocks her, even knowing it comes from a deeply disturbed individual.

Trivia: Since 1991's "Bite the Big Apple" (#153), police detective Acosta has risen from sergeant to lieutenant in the homicide division of New York's finest. Series credits for Dennis Boutsikaris range from *Nurse* (1981–1982) to *The Jackie Thomas Show* (1992). On the 1991 sitcom *Flesh 'N' Blood,* Lisa Darr played a Baltimore district attorney.

212. "Time to Die"

(3/6/94) 60 mins.

Director: Anthony Shaw **Teleplay:** Laurence Heath

Regular: Angela Lansbury (Jessica Fletcher)

Guest Law Enforcers: Richard Dano (Detective Vic Boyd); Stan Shaw (Detective Sergeant Laughton)

Guest Cast: Robert Beltran (Frank Garcia); Brigid Coulter (Tammy Fisher); Marta Dubois (Maria Garcia); William Gallo (Chris Garcia); Gladys Jimenez (Alida Alvarez); Ronald G. Joseph (Joe Mancuso); Marco Lopez (Man); Janet MacLachlan (Barbara Fisher); Rudy Ramos (Mario Fernandez); Greg Thomsen (Manny Castillo)

The Setting: New York City

The Case: Chris Garcia is a student in Jessica Fletcher's creative writing class. His other activities include raising pigeons and being a compulsive street graffiti artist. Chris's girlfriend, Alida Alvarez, is in a rock band called Full Moon. (Manny Castillo is the group's leader and is romantically interested in Alida). Full Moon performs at an antigraffiti rally that Jessica attends at the local Koffee Cafe.

Also present at the benefit is Sergeant Laughton, whose late partner was Alida's dad. Another guest is Barbara Fisher, once Mrs. Fletcher's college classmate. Barbara is currently the principal of Columbus High and in charge of an antigraffiti squad. Her daughter Tammy is also at the get-together.

When Barbara is injured in a car mishap, Jessica identifies the car as belonging to Frank Garcia, Chris's stepfather. Later, Frank, a tough loan shark, is found shot to death on the roof of an apartment building. Jessica sets out to pinpoint his killer.

Rooting out the culprit depends on her understanding the procedures of the Montauk Pigeon Racing Club, where both the deceased and Mario Fernandez were members. To accomplish her task Jessica quizzes another member of the Garcia family, Maria, as well as using a new gadget for her, an infrared video camera.

Highlights: Graffiti artists and pigeon racing would not seem likely teammates for a *Murder, She Wrote* episode. However, the scripters successfully mesh the two subjects. Here, pigeon racing proves to be not only an intricate sport, but also its protocol leads to solving the homicide. Again demonstrating that she is always ready to break routine, Jessica steps out on the dance floor at the antigraffiti rally, keeping time with hulking Sergeant Laughton.

Trivia: Janet MacLachlan and Stan Shaw were veterans of the Hollywood black exploitation film cycle. She had been in *Uptight* (1968), *Halls of Anger* (1970) and *Maurie* (1973). He had performed in *Truck Turner* (1974), *Darktown Strutters* (1975) and *TNT Jackson* (1975). Ronald G. Joseph was Sheriff Sanchez on *Falcon Crest* (1988–1989).

213. "The Dying Game"

(3/13/94) 60 mins.

Director: Jerry Jameson **Teleplay:** Bruce Lansbury

Regular: Angela Lansbury (Jessica Fletcher)

Recurring Character: Michael Tolan (Lieutenant Allan Terwilliger)

Guest Law Enforcers: Matthew Sullivan (Plainclothes Officer)

Guest Cast: Peter Donat (Floyd Larkin); Joel Fabiani (Thornton Brewer); Wendell Grayson (Security Guard); Mimi Kuzyk (Tina Poulos); Felicia Lansbury (Gloria); Andrew Lauer (Ernie Fishman); Martin Milner (Bill Maguire); Kate Mulgrew (Maude Gillis); Charles Parks (Henry Wilson); Fred D. Scott (Fritz); Musetta Vander (Shirin Hourani); Harley Venton (Clint Hollowell)

The Setting: New York City

The Case: Jessica Fletcher is a board member of the Manhattan-based Museum of Cultural History. The institution is having financial difficulties, a reflection of its involvement with Larkin's Department Store. Going through its own rough times, the latter is being bought out by the Amalgamated combine. Meanwhile, when accountant Henry Wilson is murdered (with a bow and arrow) after he discovers that someone is ripping off the store's pension fund account, Jessica is engulfed in the case.

According to Lieutenant Allan Terwilliger, Larkin employee Bill Maguire—in charge of the sporting goods department—is the chief suspect in Wilson's death. On the other hand, inquiring Jessica Fletcher finds more likely parties. There is Tina Poulos, a trustee of the Larkin pension plan, as well as the manipulative Maude Gillis in charge of the personnel department. The latter is blackmailing store fashion designer Shirin Hourani. Additionally, to be considered are Thornton Brewer, who is dating Maude, store window dresser Ernie Fishman, as well as the emporium's upper class owner, Floyd Larkin.

Highlights: One of the most repeatedly surprising elements of *Murder, She Wrote* is the ability to make the most mundane setting take on a sinister and frightening personality of its own. Such is the case with the department store here, where death can loom behind any counter or mannequin.

Trivia: Michael Tolan's big screen credits encompass *Hiawatha* (1952) and *All That Jazz* (1979). He had previously appeared as Lieutenant Allan Terwilliger in 1993's "The Sound of Murder" (#184). In one of her few theatrical film releases, *A Stranger Is Watching* (1982), Kate Mulgrew was the TV newscaster held hostage in a cavern beneath Grand Central Station. Peter Donat was among the cast of *The Godfather, Part II* (1974), *F.I.S.T.* (1978) and *The China Syndrome* (1979). Long-established performer Martin Milner began his screen career with such entries as *Life with Father* (1947), *Sands of Iwo Jima* (1949) and *Halls of Montezuma* (1951).

214. "The Trouble with Seth"

(3/27/94) 60 mins.

Director: Anthony Shaw **Teleplay:** Tom Sawyer

Regulars: Angela Lansbury (Jessica Fletcher); Ron Masak (Sheriff Mort Metzger); William Windom (Dr. Seth Hazlitt)

Recurring Character: Louis Herthum (Deputy Andy Broom)

Guest Cast: Katherine Cannon (Marion Taylor); Anthony Fasce (Dan Castino); Ann Hearn (Connie Anderson); Paul Mantee (Ronald Olson/Jack Landers [Leo David Fender]); Ben Masters (Evan Rafferty [Stanley Barton]); Tim McLaughlin (Dave Archer); Steve Nevil (Neal Kraus); Ethan Randall (Jimmy Taylor); Kim Johnston Ulrich (Julia Harris); Jay Underwood (Will Rafferty)

The Settings: Boston, Massachusetts; Cabot Cove, Maine

The Case: Widower Evan Rafferty is the owner of Digital Computer Sales in Cabot Cove, where Connie Anderson is his faithful employee. Evan's son, Will, has no interest in the family business, preferring to buy into the local boat repair business operated by Dan Castino. Meanwhile, Evan is slated to marry single parent Marion Taylor. She, in turn, views this union as a stabilizing force in raising her son, Jimmy, who works at a Cabot Cove coffee shop.

Things go wrong when strangers start flooding into town. There is Julia Harris, who works for Back Bay Development Company and claims she wants to purchase property owned by Evan. She has a working relationship with underhanded Leo David Fender who is also visiting Cabot Cove. Then there is Neal Kraus, an ex-convict who participated in an armed robbery heist in Boston back in 1974. Events snowball into a crescendo when Fender is stabbed to death in Dr. Seth Hazlitt's office and his transported corpse is found later in the woods.

Highlights: Much more so than usual, this segment has a very complicated plot line. It bridges events between two decades and ties together both the participants in and the surviving family of a murderous Boston robbery of years ago. Because Jessica Fletcher has such close ties to Dr. Hazlitt, she is deeply agitated when this creature of habit mysteriously disappears. It not only adds tension to the plot, but it reveals the depth of feeling between these two independent souls.

Of special note is how computer literate most everyone in Cabot Cove has become. By the end of the installment, even old-fashioned Seth is tempted to become a computer hacker!

Trivia: Born Paul Marianetti, Paul Mantee had a leading role in *Robinson Crusoe on Mars* (1964) and lesser parts in *They Shoot Horses, Don't They?* (1969), *W.C. Fields and Me* (1976) and *The Great Santini* (1980). Ann Hearn worked as Margaret Fouch on *Evening Shade* (1990–1993).

215. "Roadkill"

(5/1/94) 60 mins.

Director: Walter Grauman **Teleplay:** Mark A. Burley

Regular: Angela Lansbury (Jessica Fletcher)

Guest Law Enforcers: Dirk Blocker (Sheriff Jim Monday); Heath Kizzier (Deputy Sutton)

Guest Cast: Joanna Cassidy (Willie Greenwood); Patrick Cassidy (Rob Platte); Beth Grant (Meg Thomas); Melora Hardin (Cindy Warrick); Earl Holliman (Wayne Platte); Whip Hubley (Randy Jinks); Ron Leath (Doctor); Gary Lockwood (Sam Mercer); Robert O'Reilly (Lance Taggart); Bret Porter (TV Repair Shop Worker); Reni Santoni (Juan Ramez)

The Settings: Houston, Texas; San Dimas, Texas

The Case: Jessica Fletcher is in Texas researching a new book project at the Lyndon B. Johnson Space Center. She is assisted in her background work by NASA employee Juan Ramez. Before long, Mrs. Fletcher's studies run far afield from spacecraft.

Wayne Platte, a former rodeo rider, owns a trucking company which hauls computer hardware to the Space Center. (Jessica is a longtime friend of Platte as well as his now dead wife, Lynn.) One of Wayne's recent shipments to NASA has been hijacked, leaving the manufacturer, Sam Mercer, no alternative but to replace the lost merchandise. As far as Sheriff Jim Monday is concerned, Platte may be guilty of dummying up a robbery to collect on the insurance money as well as to profit from selling the "stolen" goods.

Meanwhile, Wayne is feuding with his very independent son, Rob, a singer at Willie's country western bar. Rob is in love with Cindy Warrick, a waitress there. (Cindy has a daughter, Tammy, by her ex-husband Randy Jinks). The bar is owned by tough-as-nails Willie Greenwood, who agrees to help Randy unload the computer equipment stolen from Platte's eighteen-wheeler. Further on, Lance Taggart, an ex-con and former lover of Willie's, arrives, forcing her to take him back. Before long, he's pointing out that Randy is cheating her on their deal.

When Jinks is run down during a hijack operation, Jessica pursues the killer to prove to the sheriff that his suspect, Rob, is an innocent party. In the process, Mrs. Fletcher uncovers the strange hold Willie has over Meg Thomas, Wayne's longtime employee.

Highlights: As part of her sleuthing strategy, Jessica Fletcher traces stolen goods to a TV repair shop where, to gain needed information, she pretends to be a suspect's maiden aunt from Maine. During the course of the story line, Patrick Cassidy's Rob Platte performs a song number at the country western bar.

Trivia: Patrick Cassidy is the son of actors Shirley Jones and Jack Cassidy, the brother of Shaun Cassidy and the half brother of David Cassidy. Patrick was featured in *Bay City Blues* (1983), a baseball drama series. Ten years before his film career began with *Pony Soldier* (1952), Earl Holliman had hitchhiked to Hollywood at age fourteen hoping to break into movies. When that failed, he enlisted in the navy, but was dismissed when he was found to be underage. Among Joanna Cassidy's several TV series are *240-Robert, The Family Tree,* and *Codename: Foxfire.* Born John Gary Yusolfksy in Van Nuys, California, Gary Lockwood's TV movie credits include *Earth II* (1971), *The Incredible Journey of Doctor Meg Laurel* (1979) and *The Return of the Six Million Dollar Man and the Bionic Woman* (1987).

216. "A Murderous Muse"

(5/15/94) 60 mins.

Director: Anthony Shaw **Teleplay:** Bruce Lansbury

Regular: Angela Lansbury (Jessica Fletcher)

Recurring Characters: Eddie Barth (Richie Kanpinski, the Doorman); Jon Polito (Lieutenant Peter DiMartini)

Guest Cast: Pamela Bellwood (Vanessa Cross); Wayne C. Dvorak (Martin Tribly, the Critic); Ronald Guttman (Byron Toscarti); Joseph Kell (Steven Hoyt); Robert Knepper (Owen McLaglen); Jenny Lewis (Leslie Walden); Kay Tong Lim (Bok, the Valet); Matthew Ryan (Solly Prinze); Craig Wasson (Hank Walden); Michael White (TV Newscaster)

The Setting: New York City

The Case: Among the many tenants in Jessica Fletcher's Manhattan apartment building are charismatic but arrogant concert maestro Byron Toscarti, who lives in the penthouse; Leslie Walden, his concert pianist protégée and ward; Vanessa Cross, Byron's longtime assistant and lover; and a newcomer, Solly Prinze, a talented if rebellious young musician who finds Ms. Walden very appealing.

As a board member at a city museum, Jessica pursues the arrogant Byron to honor a commitment he once made for Leslie to perform at a charity fund-raiser. In the process, Mrs. Fletcher is caught up in a new murder. The victim is Toscarti, who is shot to death in his living room. According to investigating lieutenant Peter DiMartini, the killer stood on a nearby rooftop and used a rifle to shoot his victim through an open window.

Jessica cannot agree with that theory. Nor does she accept the police officer's conclusion that Leslie's estranged father, one-time promising musician Hank Walden, is the guilty party. After all, the victim had just fired hard-working Owen McLaglen as Leslie's manager, and CD label owner Steven Hoyt has a great deal to lose if the maestro moved his prize artist to another recording company.

Highlights: With her widespread philanthropic and cultural interests, Jessica Fletcher appears never to have a free moment, let alone spare time to create her ongoing series of mystery novels. Nevertheless, as here, she is amazingly available to play matchmaker for young lovers, and to right the wrongs between generations. If she gains as much information from the talkative doorman, Richie, as from lovelorn Vanessa Cross, credit that to her communication skills. Although he hardly seems her type, Jessica is most cordial to the romantic overtures of courtly Lieutenant DiMartini.

For the record, the killer's modus operandi here is one of the series' most far-fetched, further discrediting an already shaky story line.

Trivia: Jon Polito's burly Lieutenant Peter DiMartini resurfaced from 1992's "The Dead File" (#179). Polito was a veteran of TV's *Crime Story* (1986–1987) and *Ohara* (1987). Craig Wasson, playing another of his very downbeat roles here, had appeared in such movies as *The Boys in Company C* (1977), *Ghost Story* (1981) and *A Nightmare on Elm Street 3: Dream Warriors* (1987). Jenny Lewis, of the high-pitched Sandra Dee-type voice, had been Lucille Ball's granddaughter in *Life with Lucy* (1986). New York City-born Pamela Bellwood had acted in such TV movies as *The Wild Women of Chastity Gulch* (1982) and *Deep Dark Secrets* (1987).

217. "Wheel of Death"

(5/22/94) 60 mins.

Director: Walter Grauman **Teleplay:** Robert Van Scoyk

Regulars: Angela Lansbury (Jessica Fletcher); Ron Masak (Sheriff Mort Metzger); William Windom (Dr. Seth Hazlitt)

Recurring Characters: Louis Herthum (Deputy Andy Broom); Madlyn Rhue (Jean O'Neill, the Librarian)

Guest Cast: Thom Bierdz (Richard Binyon); Marie Canals (Carmen); Jimi Defilippis (Nicodemus "Nicky" Newton); Bradford Dillman (Carl Dormer); Lisa Lawrence (Lisa Farrel); Jennifer Manasseri (Gwen); Judson Mills

(Toby Grant); Richardson Morse (Sherman Hastings, of the IRS); Cindy Pickett (Joanna Sims); Charles Siebert (Don Sims)

The Setting: Cabot Cove, Maine

The Case: Since both Jessica Fletcher and Dr. Seth Hazlitt are on the fund-raising committee for local charities, they coordinate donations to be made by the carnival currently in town. Meanwhile, several Cabot Cove residents, including Jessica upon her return from New York City, discover that their homes have been burgled. According to Sheriff Mort Metzger, the thieves have not taken expensive electronic items, just mostly jewelry and antiques.

One night after the carnival closes, the enterprise's shifty co-owner, Carl Dormer, is found dead on the whirlywind ride. Lisa Farrel, a young carnival volunteer from town, had returned that evening to meet roustabout Toby Grant for a date. When she spied a shadowy figure killing Dormer, she had fled. Now she fears for her life and wonders whether Toby was the murderer.

Among the other suspects are Joanna Sims, the carnival's co-owner, and Don, her alcoholic husband, who loathes his declining life-style. In addition, there is Nicky Newton, the knife-throwing juggler; Carmen, Nicky's jaded partner; and a mysterious man in a gray suit who has been spying on Dormer to see if he has been doctoring his financial statements. Finally, there's Richard Binyon, an ambitious local grocery store owner who has made a nice profit from the carnival purchasing food supplies from his store.

Highlights: It was to be hoped that there would have been a more creative use of the carnival atmosphere than here. A brief highlight is Bradford Dillman's oversized performance as the adept midway magician and con artist. Much attention is focused on the bittersweet reunion of college sweethearts Joanna Sims and Mort Metzger. Twenty years ago she had ditched Mort to marry Don. The latter's promising football career soon ended, leading him into substance abuse and Joanna into years of unhappiness. In contrast, much is made of Metzger's devotion to his beloved wife, Adele, who is currently visiting her sister in Brooklyn.

Trivia: Cindy Pickett had been a cast member of *Call to Glory* (1984–1985) and *St. Elsewhere* (1986–1988). Before enrolling as Dr. Stanley Riverside II on *Trapper John, M.D.* (1979–1986), Charles Siebert had been on such daytime soaps as *Another World* and *Search for Tomorrow*. Proficient actor Bradford Dillman had won an Emmy Award as Best Actor in a Daytime Drama Special for *The Last Bride of Salem* (1975).

SEASON ELEVEN

1994–1995

218. "A Nest of Vipers"

(9/25/94) 60 mins.

Director: Anthony Shaw **Teleplay:** Rick Mittleman

Regular: Angela Lansbury (Jessica Fletcher)

Recurring Character: Gregory Sierra (Lieutenant Gabriel Caceras)

Guest Law Enforcer: Billy Mayo (Sergeant Nutley)

Guest Cast: Dion Anderson (Joe Gondolph); David Beecroft (Mark Atwater); Susan Blakely (Joyce Hacker); Corinne Bohrer (Bea Huffington); Lisa Darr (Kelly Michaels); John Dye (Dr. Ray Stinson); Jerry Hardin (Norman Gilford); Taylor Nichols (Ted Fraley); Glenn Taranto (Jimmy Russell); Meadow Williams (Docent)

The Setting: Los Angeles, California

The Case: As her next novel focuses on murder at an exotic zoo, Jessica Fletcher flies to Los Angeles to soak up atmosphere at the regional wild animal park. She couldn't have picked a worse time: 1) Southern California—including the animal facility—is recovering from a major earthquake; 2) the quake-damaged zoo is in a precarious financial state; 3) rumors insist that corruption is rampant at the institution and that the park's head, Norman Gilford, will be replaced; 4) EarthSpeak environmentalists are demanding the zoo be closed and the caged animals returned to their natural habitats.

Mrs. Fletcher tours the trouble-plagued facility with its publicity person, Kelly Michaels. Jessica encounters *Los Angeles Chronicle* reporter Jimmy Russell, who is being supplied confidential data on zoo mismanagement by a mysterious female informant. Jessica also meets Mark Atwater, EarthSpeak's local leader. When Mark is later found dead in the reptile house, police lieutenant Gabriel Caceras assumes he was poisoned by a deadly black snake which had somehow gotten loose. Perceptive Mrs. Fletcher, however, disagrees, proving that the victim was actually injected with a deadly venom.

The police in due time arrest nerdy zoo official Ted Fraley, claiming his motive was to prevent the deceased from blackmailing him. (Atwater knew that Ted had once purchased illegally acquired animals.) Mrs. Fletcher again dissents from the police's deductions. She uncovers that Atwater had also demanded a huge fee from the zoo's chief, Gilford, not to expose the latter's shady activities. Moreover, wealthy Joyce Hacker had been having a clandestine romance with Atwater, although the latter was engaged to Kelly Michaels. And there is Dr. Ray Stinson, the zoo veterinarian, who had been lovers with Kelly before she turned to Atwater.

Before solving the case, Jessica must assess the complicity of Councilman Joe Gondolph, who agreed to a $150,000 payoff from Gilford not to take the latter down with the zoo, if the facility was closed. Also to be weighed is the relevance of a valuable 172-acre land parcel adjacent to the animal park. And what of Bea Huffington, Gilford's executive assistant, who is tied romantically to Stinson and has her own ax to grind?

Highlights: With its intriguing behind-the-scenes look at a zoo, there is sufficient creepy atmosphere as hazards lurk around every corner from potentially dangerous animals. Then, too, it's reassuring—and satisfying—to see that Jessica Fletcher has lost none of her edge in staying several steps ahead of the police. Observing Mrs. Fletcher so at ease with her laptop computer shows again how adept she is at keeping current with cutting-edge technology.

Trivia: Jessica Fletcher had last matched skills with the not-always-tolerant Lieutenant Caceras in 1993's "The Petrified Florist" (#189). By now, he is resigned to the fact that whenever a homicide occurs, there are good odds that "meddlesome" Mrs. Fletcher will somehow be part of the crime scene. As he acknowledges, "Corpses seem to just be part of our job description."

David Beecroft is familiar to viewers from his TV series work: *Falcon Crest* (from 1988–1989 he played Nick Agretti), *Hearts Are Wild* (1992) and *Class of '96* (1993). Corinne Bohrer is an alumnus of the sitcom *E/R* (1984) and *Man of the People* (1991). John Dye's TV series encompassed *Tour of Duty* (1989–1990), *Jack's Place* (1992–1993) and *Hotel Malibu* (1994). This was Susan Blakely's fourth guest appearance on *Murder, She Wrote*, while it was the second for Lisa Darr—both performers playing new characters each time.

219. "Amsterdam Kill"

(10/2/94) 60 mins.

Director: Jerry Jameson **Teleplay:** Jerry Ludwig

Regular: Angela Lansbury (Jessica Fletcher)

Guest Law Enforcer: Theodore Bikel (Inspector Van Horn)

Guest Cast: Nicole Eva-Maria Brand (Chambermaid); Lilyan Chavin (Dispatcher); Cliff Emmich (Harry Tigner); Marcus Gilbert (Colin Biddle); Leann Hunley (Lydia De Kooning); Cornelia Kiss (Panel Chairwoman); Richard Lynch (Philip De Kooning); Joseph Maher (Nigel Allison); Andreas Renell (Hendrik Kuyper); Alex Rodine (Herr Kronin); Albie Selznick (Walter Burger); Camilla Soeberg (Monika Vidal); Erick Weiss (Muller); Richard Young (Nick Halsey)

The Setting: Amsterdam, Netherlands

The Case: Soon after telephoning information to police inspector Van Horn, Hendrik Kuyper is a hit-and-run victim on the streets of Amsterdam. Meanwhile, Jessica Fletcher has arrived in the Dutch city as a panel member of the International Copyright Conference. She is pleased to reencounter fellow author Nigel Allison, who writes thrillers. Through Nigel, Jessica is introduced to two other hotel guests, South African diamond industrialist Philip De Kooning and his younger wife, Lydia.

When Allison vanishes from his room (#1420), perplexed Jessica is given little cooperation by the hotel's manager, Walter Burger, or from Inspector Van Horn. On the other hand, another hotel guest, Colin Biddle, a British publisher's representative, insists that Allison has returned to London on business. Jessica doesn't believe this because Nigel departed without his passport. Later, De Kooning is murdered in his suite, and Mrs. Fletcher, who had a scheduled meeting with the entrepreneur, is considered a prime suspect.

To clear herself, she begins to investigate. She learns that illegal arms sales and not diamonds were the victim's primary business; that Lydia De Kooning had been having an affair with gigolo Nick Halsey, who pilots De Kooning's private jet; and that a persistent reporter, Monika Vidal, is not what she seems to be. Others implicated in the intrigue are sinister Harry Tigner and gem dealer Herr Kronin.

Highlights: This exercise in daring international terrorists, double-crossing criminals and secret lovers recalls Alfred Hitchcock's *Foreign Correspondent* (1940) and Roman Polanski's *Frantic* (1988). Here Jessica Fletcher remains unbowed by the many forces who label her a busybody with an overactive imagination who is causing more harm than good. On one occasion, as she snoops about a suspect's hotel suite, she is surprised by another intruder. In a flash of creativity, she pulls out her purse-size hair spray, an impromptu substitute for Mace.

Trivia: While there is little genuine rapport between Mrs. Fletcher and Inspector Van Horn—due to inadequate scripting—this is perhaps the first time Jessica has found herself the subject of a portrait painted by a police detective, who finds art work relaxing.

Viennese actor, singer and guitarist Theodore Bikel made his screen debut in *The African Queen (1951).* Wings Hauser, as often a villain as hero on screen, had participated in the TV series *The Last Precinct* (1986) and *Lightning Force* (1991). In 1979–1980, Leann Hunley was on *Lobo;* from 1986 to 1988 she was Dana Waring Carrington on *Dynasty* and, in 1994, was on *Models, Inc.* Joseph Maher had played the heavenly St. Peter in *Second Chance* (1987–1988), and he was a British TV critic on *Anything But Love* (1989–1990). Richard Lynch has done sinister roles on-camera for decades, including Al Pacino's *Scarecrow* (1973) and *Little Nikita* (1988).

220. "To Kill a Legend"

(10/9/94) 60 mins.

Director: Anthony Shaw **Teleplay:** David Bennett Carren, J. Larry Carroll

Regulars: Angela Lansbury (Jessica Fletcher); Ron Masak (Sheriff Mort Metzger); William Windom (Dr. Seth Hazlitt)

Recurring Character: Louis Herthum (Deputy Andy Broom)

Guest Cast: Todd Eric Andrews (Scott Patterson); Greg Cruttwell (Paul Taverner [Jeffrey Caldwell]); Alan Fudge (Thomas Godfrey); Pierrette Grace (Louise Peabody); Molly Hagan (Amelia Farnum); Anthony Heald (Bob Kendall); Judith Hoag (Nancy Godfrey); Tiiu Leek (Newsperson); Jeffrey Nordling (Richard Hawkes); Whitney Rydbeck (Dr. Roy Blakely); Gail Strickland (Edith Peabody); Jacob Witkin (Alexander Sandsby)

The Settings: London, England; Cabot Cove, Maine

The Case: Cabot Cove is preparing for its annual salute to Joshua Peabody, Maine's finest clock maker in Colonial times and a Revolutionary War hero. This year's reenactment of the colonists' fight against the British is special because Boston's WRTW-TV is filming the "spectacle" for a documentary to be narrated by Jessica Fletcher. In the midst of the shooting, local antique dealer Thomas Godfrey is asked to repair a prop—a valued music box that once belonged to the heroic Peabody. Godfrey finds a letter secreted in the box which, if authentic, proves that Major Peabody was not only *not* a war hero, but that he may have been a traitor!

The turn of events upsets the locals, who fear this could ruin their yearly festival and the associated tourist trade. The situation is compounded by the murder of Amelia Farnum, the documentary's cinematographer-turned-director, admist a fire in the movie production office.

Sheriff Metzger once again turns to Jessica Fletcher for much-needed guidance. The gallery of potential murderers includes Cabot Cove's own Edith Peabody, in shock that she may have wasted decades preserving her forebears' homestead as a museum when her ancestor-in-law may have been a scoundrel; arrogant documentary director Richard Hawkes, a past Emmy Award winner fallen on hard times who was replaced on the shoot by Amy and then reinstated after her demise; manipulative producer Bob Kendall, who thinks the twisted situation could improve the program's audience ratings. There is also Britisher Paul Taverner who holds a secret, and Edith Peabody's daughter, Louise, who was jealous that Hawkes paid more attention to the deceased than to her. Not to be overlooked is Godfrey's disgruntled wife, Nancy, who had romantic ties to a production crew member. Then, too, there was the murder of a London-based con artist, Alexander Sandsby.

Highlights: Usually Jessica Fletcher is firmly supportive to her neighbors and friends. However, here, she puts the cause of American history—i.e., the full account of Joshua Peabody's place in history—above Cabot Coveers who are blinded by greed and pride. A running gag involves huffing and puffing Dr. Hazlitt's ever-expanding waistline.

Trivia: Back in 1985's "Joshua Peabody Died Here—Possibly" (#29), the local Revolutionary War hero had been the story line focus as an unearthed skeleton was conjectured to be his. To be noted here is that high tech equipment is now a real part of Cabot Cove's police force—Sheriff Metzger frequently uses a cellular phone in this episode.

In both *Eisched* (1979–1980) and *Bodies of Evidence* (1992–1993), Alan Fudge's TV series role was that of a police official. Alabama-born Gail Strickland had made such TV movies as *Ellery Queen* (1975), *The Gathering, Part II* (1979) and *Life of the Party: The Story of Beatrice* (1982). Jeffrey Nordling had appeared in such feature films as *Dangerous Heart* (1993) and *Holy Matrimony* (1994).

221. "Death in Hawaii"

(10/16/94) 60 mins.

Director: Don Mischer **Teleplay:** Laurence Heath

Regular: Angela Lansbury (Jessica Fletcher)

Guest Law Enforcers: Tom Hallick (District Attorney Randall Thompson); Robert Duncan McNeill (Danny Kinkaid); Steve Park (Joe Yoshanaga); Steve Ruge (Matt, a Honolulu Police Department Detective); Tamlyn Tomita (Detective Sharon Matsumoto).

Guest Cast: Nina Foch (Rebecca Kinkaid); Gretchen German (Liz Dougherty); Ted W. Henning (Jeff Kinkaid); Ken Howard (Matt Kinkaid); James F. Kelly (Brett Reynolds); Karen Lew (Registration Clerk); Marty Rackham (Boone Aldrich); Ata Scanlan (Ben Kamaka); David Tress (Martin Osborn)

The Setting: Honolulu, Hawaii

The Case: Returning from a whirlwind book tour in Japan and other neighboring countries, Jessica Fletcher stops over in Honolulu at the Kinkaid Oahu for a vacation. She is the guest of hotel tycoon Matt Kinkaid. Jessica has a reunion with Matt's elegant if demanding mother, Rebecca. From this matriarch, Mrs. Fletcher learns that Matt's two sons are feuding: Jeff is running for a U.S. Senate seat and everyone, including Liz Dougherty, Jeff's campaign manager, is unhappy that younger brother Danny is a law-enforcement assistant to Jeff's rival for office, Honolulu District Attorney Randall Thompson. On the other hand, deeply honest Danny is angry that his brother is accepting dirty money for his campaign from Island International Bank head Brett Reynolds. (Danny's associate, Joe Yoshanaga, is working undercover in Reynolds' banks.)

When Danny disappears while swimming in the ocean, it's feared he was killed by sharks. Later, Ben Kamaka, Rebecca's faithful houseman and Danny's good friend, is murdered. Assigned to investigate is Detective Sharon Matsumoto, Danny's girlfriend. Among the possible wrongdoers are Randall Thompson, who has been hiding his relationship to a young woman who is associated with his long-ago military tour of duty in Vietnam; Brett Reynolds, who is being pressured by underworld figure Martin Osborn to keep Jeff under tabs at all costs; and Boone Aldrich, who is helping an associate spy on a third party.

Highlights: As usual, when *Murder, She Wrote* features an exotic paradise setting, the episode boasts many minisequences devoted to capturing the lush scenery, unique local customs and the special temperament of the locale. If Jessica Fletcher is too youthful in action and person to be a grand dame, she is, nevertheless, a gracious match to queen bee Rebecca Kinkaid in good breeding, determination and respect from those around her. Thanks to a substantial performance by Nina Foch, the several interactions between the two women are charming and credible.

Trivia: Dutch-born Nina Foch had been a studio contract player in the 1940s *(My Name Is Julia Ross, The Dark Past,* etc.) and 1950s *(An American in Paris, Executive Suite,* etc.). Still later, she became a respected Los Angeles acting coach. Tom Hallick had been a regular on *Search* (1973) and a host on *Entertainment Tonight* (1981). Steve Park was a troupe member of *In Living Color* (1991–1992). Tamlyn Tomita's movie credits include *The Karate Kid: Part 2* (1986), *Come See the Paradise* (1990) and *The Joy Luck Club* (1993).

222. "Dear Deadly"

(10/23/94) 60 mins.

Director: Anthony Shaw **Teleplay:** Donald Ross

Regular: Angela Lansbury (Jessica Fletcher)

Guest Law Enforcer: Seth Jaffe (Lieutenant Evans)

Guest Cast: Daphne Ashbrook (Alexis Hill); Mike Barger (Lab Man); Casey Biggs (Max Charles); Eileen Brennan (Loretta Lee [Claire Hogan]); Kristen Cloke (Emma Kemp); Charles Gunning (T.D.); Rosanna Huffman (Nell Carson); Laurence Luckinbill (John Galloway); John Rhys-Davies (Harry Mordecai); Jerry Taft (Guard); Eric Woodall (Troy Higgins)

The Setting: San Francisco, California

The Case: Jessica Fletcher is in San Francisco to supervise the serialization of her new novel, *The Launch Pad Murders,* in the *Daily Union.* She is disheartened to learn that since signing the contract, the newspaper has been bought by ruthless media tycoon Harry Mordecai, who rules by unrelenting intimidation. Bridling under the new regime, Jessica's friend John Galloway, the paper's managing editor, quits, but is then persuaded to stay on briefly. Galloway's leaving distresses Loretta Lee, the longtime lonely hearts columnist, who also threatens to resign. In contrast, reporter Alexis Hill insists she can adapt to Mordecai's tyrannical ways.

Loretta, who has been receiving anonymous death threats, is wounded by gunfire in the lobby of the newspaper building. Thereafter, Galloway has her "hide out" at a bay city hotel. However, the precautions don't save Ms. Lee from being murdered, smashed over the head with a water pitcher.

Mrs. Fletcher conducts her own investigation—sometimes in tandem with police lieutenant Evans, a man plagued by cat allergies. What perplexes Jessica is how to explain the incriminating message scratched in the murder room's mirror with Loretta's diamond ring. The death note implicates Galloway. Other points of concern are why Troy Higgins, the paper's gofer, lied about his whereabouts on the afternoon of the killing, or why Max Charles, the *Daily Union's* financial reporter, needed to visit Loretta's hotel room around the time she died. In addition, there's bag lady Nell Carson, one of Ms. Lee's sources, who recently confided a surprising truth to the late columnist. Not to be ignored is the fact that the deceased was lost without her hearing aid.

Highlights: If there is anything Jessica Fletcher won't abide, it's a tyrannical bully. As such, she does battle—and holds her own—with the blustery communications magnate Mordecai. These are moments to relish, far outweighing the weak "flavor" offered by the newspaper setting.

Trivia: San Francisco police lieutenant Evans would return in 1996's "Death by Demographics" (#261), again played by Seth Jaffe, but with a slightly changed surname (i.e., Everett).

John Rhys-Davies, a veteran of 1982's *The Quest* TV series, was active in 1990s TV shows: *Under Cover, The Untouchables, Sliders.* Laurence Luckinbill, wed to Lucie Arnaz, had been part of such features films as *Messenger of Death* (1988) and *Star Trek V: The Final Frontier* (1989).

Eileen Brennan had been featured in the original Broadway cast of *Hello, Dolly!* (1964). She made her movie debut in *Divorce American Style* (1967) and was starring in the TV sitcom *Private Benjamin* (1981–1982) when she was almost fatally injured in a car accident. Two of Daphne Ashbrook's teleseries were *Fortune Dane* (1986) and *Our Family Honor* (1985–1986). Rosanna Huffman had been featured in the 1973–1974 detective drama *Tenafly.*

223. "The Murder Channel"

(11/6/94) 60 mins.

Director: Walter Grauman **Teleplay:** Jerry Ludwig

Regular: Angela Lansbury (Jessica Fletcher)

Guest Law Enforcers: John Capodice (Lieutenant Giordano); James Kiriyama-Lem (Medical Examiner)

Guest Cast: Katherine Cressida (Darlene Farber); Dan Ferro (Roy Phipps); Betty Freeman (1st Committee Woman); Charles Hallahan (Barry Noble);

Gary Harshberger (Rob MacKenzie); Vincent Howard (College Professor); Heidi Kling (Kitty Colfax); Aaron Lustig (Augie Blumbacher); Stephen Quadros (Alex Dorsey); Perrey Reeves (Susan Constable); Doris Roberts (Mrs. Leah Colfax); Jessica Walter (Gwen Noble); Don Yesso (Leo Kositchek)

The Setting: New York City

The Case: At Midtown Precinct South, Lieutenant Giordano, still convinced that Roy Phipps participated in a bank robbery five years earlier with Leo Kositchek who went to jail, has Roy take a new lie detector test. The man passes the quizzing. As he leaves the station house, Giordano tells him Kositchek has been paroled recently. Meanwhile, back at her apartment building, Jessica Fletcher is doing battle with Gwen Noble over nominees for the Museum of Cultural History's board of directors.

One of the neighbors in Jessica's building, Kitty Colfax, a student nurse, receives an unusual birthday gift from her boyfriend, Rob MacKenzie. He's a TV cable installer and illegally hooks her system to the pay cable legitimately installed in apartment 3C beneath her. What Rob doesn't know is that he has patched Kitty's television into a sophisticated surveillance system geared to spy on the activities in 3C. Before long, the unsuspecting Kitty—and sometimes Mrs. Fletcher when she visits the young woman—finds herself unknowingly eavesdropping on events happening one floor below. They assume they are watching bizarre cable TV movies.

Chaos spirals when Gwen Noble is murdered on-camera in 3C. Later, Kitty is kidnapped because she has seen too much via her TV set. As Mrs. Fletcher strives to find Kitty, she crosses paths with Lieutenant Giordano, who has been tracking the activities of both Phelps and Kositchek and their thieving pals. The trail leads to the jewelry store owned by Gwen's husband, Barry. Others involved in the mayhem are Augie Blumbacher, Barry's chief diamond cutter; Darlene Farber, Barry's staff worker with whom Noble is having an affair; Leah Colfax, operator of a nearby fruit/vegetable stand; and Kitty Leah's daughter who has a penchant for drink, drugs and dangerous companions.

Highlights: The gimmick of the high technology surveillance system providing a clear view of a murder (if not the murderer) is the most creative aspect of this often bland outing. Another bright moment is provided by Kitty Colfax, who performs a musical number at the diamond store, all contrived so she can photograph Barry Noble's safe with the miniature camera secreted in her cane. Sadly, actor Doris Roberts, who usually shines on-camera, was given very little footage.

Trivia: Dan Ferro had been Tommy Ortega on *Falcon Crest* (1988–1989). Vincent Howard was on *Mr. Novak* (1963–1965), *Barnaby Jones* (1973) and *Emergency* (1976–1977). Don Yesso is noted for the sitcoms *Frank's Place* (1987–1988) and *My Two Dads* (1989–1990).

224. "Fatal Paradise"

(11/13/94) 60 mins.

Director: Jerry Jameson **Teleplay:** Tom Sawyer

Regular: Angela Lansbury (Jessica Fletcher)

Recurring Character: Wayne Rogers (Charlie Garrett)

Guest Law Enforcers: Marc Andrew Gomes (Sergeant Courbet); Maurice Roeves (Police Captain)

Guest Cast: Christopher Allport (Maurice Delagre); Patricia Barry (Melanie Venable); Michael Callan (Phillip Sparling); Rodney Eastman (Jeff Delagre); Cynthia Harris (Lauren Delagre); Anne Lockhart (Norma Villens [Mary Beth Carlson]); Stephen Meadows (Graham Farrow); Andrew Hill Newman (Hilton Venable); Marie-Alise Recasner (Collette, the Hotel Clerk); Cassie Yates (Dorie Sparling)

The Settings: Martinique, West Indies; Washington, D.C.

The Case: In Martinique, Lauren and Maurice Delagre, formerly of Cabot Cove, operate a small resort hotel. Lauren is distressed by her husband's constant gambling, while Maurice, a former military attaché, is bothered that he has let his family down. Their young adult son, Jeff, who is romancing the hotel clerk, Collette, dreams of leaving the island.

Jessica Fletcher arrives at the Delagres' on holiday. She is surprised to encounter bungling detective Charlie Garrett from Chicago. Since they last met in Cabot Cove under peculiar circumstances, Garrett has undergone a redeeming change of heart. He admits he is in love with Dorie Sparling, the woman his client, Phillip Sparling, hired him to locate and escort back to the Windy City. He also tells Mrs. Fletcher that Dorie has been involved with Graham Farrow, who used to be Phillip Sparling's partner and whose yacht is berthed nearby. Also on the scene is Norma Villens, a vacationing schoolteacher.

In the process of Dorie leaving Farrow, she is shot by an unknown assailant. Jessica feels guilty about the killing, because she was part of Garrett's plan to distract Farrow as Dorie and Charlie made their getaway. Thus Jessica is very intent on entrapping the murderer, even if she competes with police sergeant Courbet. She eventually realizes that the key to the crime lies in (1) a missing $6 million, (2) Interpol identifying a contract killer and (3) a cigarette lighter.

Highlights: Several elements buoy this diverting segment. One is Jeff Sturges's music score which creates a proper *film noir* atmosphere. Another is the relaxed mood inspired by intrepid Mrs. Fletcher being on holiday. As she admits, "I didn't even bring my laptop." Another positive element is the marvelous rapport between level-headed, honest and enterprising Jessica Fletcher versus rascally, self-serving and bumbling Charlie Garrett. While everyone marvels at their growing affinity, Mrs. Fletcher appreciates the underlying appeal of this seedy gumshoe. As she observes; "You're a romantic. There aren't enough people like you in the world today!"

Trivia: Struggling private investigator Charlie Garrett last turned up on *Murder, She Wrote* in 1994's "Deadly Assets" (#210). This was his third series appearance.

Primarily a TV actor, Wayne Rogers appeared in several movies: *Once in Paris* (1978), *The Gig* (1985), *The Killing Time* (1987), etc. In the 1960s, former teen heartthrob Michael Callan played in such screen fare as *The Interns* (1963) and *Cat Ballou* (1965). Cassie Yates was featured on *Nobody's Perfect* (1980) and *Detective in the House* (1985). This was Anne Lockhart's fourth *Murder, She Wrote* performance. Cynthia Harris's TV credits date back to *Sirota's Court* (1976–1977) and more recently to the sitcom *Ann Jillian* (1989–1990). Among Christopher Allport's movies are *Savage Weekend* (1980) and *News at Eleven* (1986).

225. "Crimson Harvest"

(11/20/94) 60 mins.

Director: Anthony Shaw **Teleplay:** Bruce Lansbury

Regular: Angela Lansbury (Jessica Fletcher)

Guest Law Enforcer: Ismael East Carlo (Sheriff Serafio Zuniga)

Guest Cast: Joseph Cali (Philipe); Diane Dilascio (Alicia Grimaldi); Elizabeth Gracen (Michelle Scarlotti Grimaldi); Gregg Henry (Lars Anderson); Lainie Kazan (Anna Grimaldi); David Newsom (Henry Wilson); Robert Pine (Edgar Warner); Leon Singer (Felipe Paez); Eddie Velez (Pete Grimaldi)

The Settings: San Francisco, California; Sonoma Valley, California

The Case: When Paul Grimaldi, the elder son of a Sonoma Valley winery clan, is shot dead in San Francisco, Jessica Fletcher rushes to the Grimaldis' homestead near San Severo to console the grieving family. Jessica has known Anna Grimaldi for years, long before she had wed wine grower Silvio. A recent widow, Anna confides that the winery is suffering financial reverses and that the family is at odds over selling the estate to neighboring vintner Lars Anderson. The latter, who once dated Anna's daughter, Alicia, is threatening to foreclose on the valuable property by purchasing the second mortgage. Lars tries unsuccessfully to gain the support of Pete, the Grimaldis' adopted son, who inherited no share of the estate. Meanwhile, financial advisor Edgar Warner is a steadying force for Anna and would like to marry her.

One late evening, Anderson is murdered in the vat room of the Grimaldi winery. Sheriff Serafio Zuniga, whom Pete berates for discriminating against his own people, concludes that Felipe Paez, an aged estate worker, is the likely felon. Mrs. Fletcher disagrees wholeheartedly.

Before the criminal is singled out, Jessica must fathom the latest arrival at the winery. It's Michelle Scarlotti, who insists that she married Paul shortly before he was killed. If her claim is legitimate—and there is doubt about her past life in Seattle, Washington, and her prior relationship with Lars in Modesta, California—this widow is entitled to one-third of the Grimaldi assets. Other factors are Felipe's nearly telepathic dog, Bolivar, and the part that Henry Wilson, the egghead winery manager who loves Alicia, played in the tragic turn of events.

Highlights: There's something about dealing with mature women of similar strength and humanity that brings out the best in Jessica Fletcher. She and longtime friend Anna—whom she knew from Cabot Cove—interact on equal terms, even if Mrs. Grimaldi is no match for Mrs. Fletcher's deductive powers and her ability to understand high finance. Their joint scenes are warm, incisive, and rise above the shtick of Lainie Kazan's usual ethnic-embellished performance. In contrast, Jessica has little patience with the remote Sheriff Zuniga, who frequently fails to follow Mrs. Fletcher's advice. In a moment of pique, she threatens the law enforcer that she will use her San Francisco police connections if he doesn't speed up the investigation.

Trivia: In 1988's "A Very Good Year for Murder" (#82), the setting had also been a Sonoma Valley winery, and that case had involved a similar Italian dynasty also embroiled in internal spats and business survival.

New York-born singer Lainie Kazan, once considered a Barbra Streisand rival, had long made an on-camera specialty of portraying colorful Jewish and Italian mothers: *My Favorite Year* (1982), *Beaches* (1988), *The Cemetery Club* (1993), etc. Gregg Henry, a frequent *Murder, She Wrote* performer, had been in several movies: *Mean Dog Blues* (1978), *Body Double* (1984), *Kiss of a Killer* (1993), etc. Joseph Cali was a regular on *Flatbush* (1979) and *Today's F.B.I.* (1981–1982). Eddie Velez boasted major roles in such teleseries as *Trial and Error* (1988–1989) and *True Blue*

(1988–1990). Robert Pine's movie work dates back to *Empire of the Ants* (1977) and *Mysterious Two* (1982).

226. "Murder By Twos"

(11/27/94) 60 mins.

Director: Anthony Shaw **Teleplay:** Bruce Lansbury

Regulars: Angela Lansbury (Jessica Fletcher); Ron Masak (Sheriff Mort Metzger); William Windom (Dr. Seth Hazlitt)

Recurring Character: Louis Herthum (Deputy Andy Broom)

Guest Cast: Bibi Besch (Imogene Shaughnessy); Ben Browder (Ollie Rudman); Claire Malis Callaway (Emily Bryce); Thomas Callaway (Sam Bryce); Lise Cutter (Terry Deauville); Troy Evans (Harvey Hoffman); Kelly Flynn (Biddeford Bomber); Chris Mulkey (Al Wallace); Douglas Roberts (Ron Friendley); Vinessa Shaw (Gloria Bryce); Zane Shaw (Waitress); Jennifer Warren (Medora Finney)

The Setting: Cabot Cove, Maine

The Case: After a decade of New York life, Imogene Shaughnessy returns to Cabot Cove. She intends to purchase the home Terry Deauville, who teaches math and domestic science at the local high school, inherited from her mother.

Meanwhile, tragedy stalks the Maine town. First, Sam Bryce, the town bully who, along with his wife Gloria, owns a beauty salon/barbershop, is electrocuted in his home workroom. Then, Terry Deauville is found hung in her mother's house. At first blush, Sheriff Mort Metzger assumes both deaths are suicides and are each isolated events. Disagreeing, Jessica Fletcher demonstrates that they were murders and that they *are* connected.

Before long, Mrs. Fletcher ponders the involvement of Bible-quoting Medora Finney, Terry's gossipy next-door neighbor; as well as Harvey Hoffman, the hardware store owner; Ron Friendley, who operates the Marine Supply Company; and Ollie Rudman, who had long wanted to marry the Bryces' daughter, Emily, against Sam's opposition. The clues click into place when Jessica realizes that Terry was having an affair with Sam and that Sam's ungrieving widow, Gloria, knew about his adultery. And there's Al Wallace, whose pharmacy burned down three weeks earlier, and who was a secret partner in a condo development with one of the victims. Everything becomes very clear when Jessica realizes the killer "placed the cart before the horse."

Highlights: Not since *Peyton Place* (1957) has a New England town been depicted as so full of scandal, murder and hidden secrets. One of the series' recurring points—emphasized here—is that because Cabot Cove is so compact a village, many of its citizens share long histories of intermixed relationships. On the other hand, even with gossip a favored local preoccupation, the townspeople still maintain many secrets. As usual, the production values and character portrayals present a thorough view of small city life.

Trivia: As viewers came to expect on *Murder, She Wrote,* at the oddest moments of happenstance, Jessica Fletcher focuses on a particular item or picks up on a thread of conversation. This, in turn, clarifies the who and why of an open murder case. This segment is an excellent illustration of that useful conceit.

Veteran performer Bibi Besch (1940–1996) was a graduate of two nighttime soap operas. *Secrets of Midland Heights* (1980–1981) and *The Hamptons* (1983). In the Western TV series, *The Boys of Twilight* (1992), Ben Browder performed as a deputy sheriff. Lise Cutter's movies number *Havana* (1990) and *Fleshtone* (1994). Chris Mulkey played police officers on the series *Arresting Behavior* (1992) and *Bakersfield P.D.* (1993–1994). Frequent TV actor Jennifer Warren had been active in 1970s movies: *Night Moves, Slap Shot, Ice Castles,* etc. Troy Evans portrayed Sergeant Pepper on *China Beach* (1989–1991) and construction worker Artie MacDonald on *Life Goes On* (1991–1993).

227. "Murder of the Month Club"

(12/4/94) 60 mins.

Director: Walter Grauman **Teleplay:** Donald Ross

Regular: Angela Lansbury (Jessica Fletcher)

Recurring Characters: George DiCenzo (Lieutenant Harry Fogel); Leonard Lightfoot (Detective Henderson)

Guest Cast: W. Earl Brown (Ernie, the Security Guard); Dena Burton (Fran); Jeff Conaway (Tom Powell); David E. Elliott (Stewart Murphy); Patrick Fabian (Larry Shields); Kerri Green (Sara); Gale Hansen (Arnold Wynn [a.k.a. Jason Bayer Saxon]); Ian Ogilvy (Wade Foster); Cec Verrell (Joellen Waller); Gwynyth Walsh (Gina Powell); Anthony Zerbe (Matt Matthews)

The Setting: New York City

The Case: Mrs. Fletcher is one of the popular mystery writers being featured by the Murder of the Month Book Club. To promote the project,

Jessica films an infomercial. Other writers on the studio shoot are alcoholic Matt Matthews, famous for his Nick Hanna detective book series but now suffering through a bleak nonproductive period, and Joellen Waller, whose first whodunit novel suggests a promising writing career.

Trouble brews on the Telesales sound stage as established Hollywood actor Wade Foster, hosting the infomercial, proves temperamental due to his pending divorce and coping with the soused Matthews, who makes a near-farce of the taping. Then, too, the commercial's producers, Tom and Gina Powell, are battling over control of their company as well as Tom's involvement with staff worker Sara. Matters are further complicated by Arnold Wynn, a pestering fan who sneaks on the set and joins the audience of paid extras.

Later, Ernie, the studio security guard, finds Arnold's body. According to police lieutenant Harry Fogel, it's a case of accidental death. This is countered by Jessica Fletcher, who notes the victim is no longer wearing a distinctive identification bracelet that he had on earlier that day. After it is discovered that the victim had once taken a creative writing class with Matthews in upstate New York and that the two had violently argued a year previously, Matt is booked on suspicion of murder. Jessica knows better and must now unmask the real villain. Once realizing the relevance of (1) an earlier murder in Buffalo, New York, (2) an enigmatic note from Jason Bayer Saxon and (3) a medical alert symbol, catching the killer is inevitable.

Highlights: Usually (see episodes #104a, 104b, 196) Jessica Fletcher's escapades find her tangling with rival women mystery writers. Here her friend/the suspect is a burned-out member of the Dashiell Hammett school of detective fiction. Never patronizing and always supportive, Mrs. Fletcher goads and encourages her colleague Matt Matthews to rediscover his confidence. The empathy she displays for a fellow writer in need is wonderfully handled.

Trivia: This episode was intended initially as another reunion of Jessica Fletcher with the team of New York police lieutenant Artie Gelber and Detective Henderson, last heard from in 1995's "Twice Dead" (#232). However, when actor Herbert Edelman (1930–1996), suffering from emphysema, was unavailable, the script was doctored to have Gelber be on holiday. Therefore, Henderson is on temporary assignment with Lieutenant Fogel. Unfortunately, the give-and-take between these two cops or between Fogel and Mrs. Fletcher does *not* pay dividends. The running gag of Henderson being an infomercial product buyer junkie also is flat.

For the record, it's Mrs. Fletcher's first novel, *The Corpse Danced at Midnight*, that Arnold Wynn asks her to autograph.

This was George DiCenzo's fifth *Murder, She Wrote* appearance. On the James Arness police drama, *McCain's Law* (1981–1982), DiCenzo was cast as Lieutenant Edward DeNisco. Anthony Zerbe was a TV series veteran of *Harry O* (1974–1976) and *The Young Riders* (1989–1992). Cec Verrell was Lieutenant Commander Ruth "Beebee" Rutkowski on *Supercarrier* (1988). Early in his career, British actor Ian Ogilvy appeared in such horror quickies as *The She-Beast* (1965) and *The Conqueror Worm* (1968).

228. "An Egg to Die For"

(12/11/94) 60 mins.

Director: Robert M. Williams, Jr. **Teleplay:** Maryanne Kasica, Michael Scheff

Regular: Angela Lansbury (Jessica Fletcher)

Guest Law Enforcers: Efrain Figueroa (Lieutenant Perez); Steve Odill (Officer Long); David Ogden Stiers (Detective Sergeant Sergei Nemiroff)

Guest Cast: Kaitlin Hopkins (Marcie Stone Devon); Lazarus Jackson (Security Guard); Peter Lucas (Russian Thief); Sara Melson (Valerie Harris); Allan Miller (Victor Roscoe); Cyril O'Reilly (Leo Stone); Andrew Robinson (James Harris); Paul Scherrer (Ben Peterson); James Stephens (Charles Devon); Christopher Thomas (Connors)

The Settings: St. Petersburg, Russia; Miami Beach, Florida

The Case: In Miami Beach for the annual World Book Fair, Jessica meets with her friends, Marcie and Charles Devon, bookstore owners. They are having problems with wealthy James Harris, a fine arts book publisher who had reneged on his promise to loan them money for a business expansion. Meanwhile, Marcie's brother, Leo Stone, involved with countless scams, pressures his former backer, Victor Roscoe, for additional loans to pay debts owed to the sinister Mr. Connors. Roscoe refuses. Later, Marcie and Charles give Leo a small sum, hoping to get him out of their lives.

When Harris is found dead in his secret home indoor flower pool, everything gets terribly complicated. For example, Sergei Nemiroff, who claimed to be a Russian publisher, is really a Soviet police officer. He has been tracking the thief of a priceless Faberge blue egg stolen from the Hermitage Museum in Russia a year ago. Nemiroff's brother, Gregorian, a Museum employee, had been falsely accused and sentenced for the crime, including the murder of the heist accomplice. As a consequence, he is scheduled to be executed in forty-eight hours *unless* Sergei catches the actual perpetrator. Harris could have provided the link to save Gregorian.

Facing a deadly deadline, Jessica and Sergei try to keep one step ahead of Miami Beach police lieutenant Perez as they follow the clues. Also involved is young Ben Peterson, who works for the Devons and loves Harris's daughter, Valerie, a relationship Harris had forbidden. Mrs. Fletcher also learns that Marcie once had considered marrying the deceased and that seemingly well-heeled Victor Roscoe has his own agenda.

Highlights: Typically, Jessica Fletcher works in tandem with the local police on a given case. Here the situation is muddied by her joining forces with the desperate Russian law enforcer who has *no* jurisdiction in Miami Beach. It places Jessica outside the law with the Florida police.

Trivia: Mrs. Fletcher, a master at detection, proves that she is extremely cosmopolitan as well. She demonstrates her basic grasp of Russian as she eavesdrops on Sergei's private conversations.

A recurring *Murder, She Wrote* character—not often seen but, nevertheless, a strong part of Mrs. Fletcher's activities—is her publisher Ted Hartley. (He appeared in 1993's "Murder at a Discount" [#205] played by Bruce Gray.) Ted is always arranging Jessica's book tours, asking her to do favors while on treks, providing introductions to interesting people, and the like. It often sets the stage for a logical plot device so the intrepid New Englander can be plunked into her latest adventure.

Most of TV actor James Stephens' movie work was in the 1980s: *First Monday in October, Pancho Barnes,* etc. Typecast as a villain, Andrew Robinson made such low-budget 1990s movies as *Trancers 3: Death Lives* (1992) and *Pumpkinhead 2: Blood Wings* (1994) and would, later, have a recurring role on TV's *Star Trek: Deep Space Nine.* Allan Miller played Dr. Allan Posner on *Soap* (1980–1981) and Scooter Warren on *Knots Landing* (1981–1982). Paul Scherrer's resume lists *The [Dick] Van Dyke Show* (1988), *Free Spirit* (1989–1990) and *Sons & Daughters* (1991).

229. "The Scent of Murder"

(1/8/95) 60 mins.

Director: Anthony Shaw **Teleplay:** Laurence Heath

Regulars: Angela Lansbury (Jessica Fletcher); William Windom (Dr. Seth Hazlitt)

Guest Law Enforcers: Tom Mason (Sergeant John Lindley); C. Eric Miles (Deputy Tom Ardmore)

Guest Cast: Walter Bevis (Dr. Travis); David Byron (Dan Wilkes, Esq.); Greg Callahan (Edward Delaney); Ann Cusack (Margaret Barkley); Robert Hooks (Kendall Ames); Sally Kirkland (Evelyn Colby); Patrick Y. Malone

(Billy Ames); Dakin Matthews (Buford Hazlitt); Craig Richard Nelson (Rob Hazlitt); Melanie Smith (Nina Larson); James Staskel (Cory Davis)

The Setting: Riverton, South Carolina

The Case: Obliging Dr. Seth Hazlitt drives Jessica Fletcher to Orlando, Florida, for her business meeting. En route, they stop in Riverton, South Carolina, so Seth can pay a duty visit to his least-liked cousin, Buford. The latter, a botanist, is a grumpy older man who owns a sizable estate. He is partnered with Kendall Ames in developing a new natural perfume scent that could be worth millions. Nina Larson, who represents a perfumery, has an agreement to market the scent and wants to acquire Buford's formula. She doesn't care if she gets it legally from the blender—who disapproves of her company's synthetic scents—or illegally by uncovering the hidden magnolia tree from which Hazlitt distills the special mint essence.

One night Buford is smothered in his sleep. According to Sergeant John Lindley, the most likely suspect is Evelyn Colby, the deceased's live-in romance. Sensing that the law is off-base in their assumptions, Mrs. Fletcher, with Seth in tow, burrows into the facts. She remembers that she saw Kendall Ames's trouble-prone son, Billy, leaving the Hazlitt house about the time of the homicide. Kendall himself is also a jittery suspect, since it's found he badly needs money to send his son to college. Not to be overlooked is perfume promoter Nina Larson who, through her redneck flunky, Cory Davis, had tried to bribe Kendall and Billy to betray the deceased. In addition, the dead man's cousin, Rob, a former alcoholic, would financially benefit from Buford's death. This also holds true for the victim's stepdaughter, Margaret Barkley. She, a fledgling off-Broadway playwright, had come home to beg Buford for a big loan, but had been refused.

Highlights: Irascible, inflexible Dr. Seth Hazlitt is delightfully cranky under the best of circumstances. Here, prodded by Jessica to mend his longstanding differences with his greedy cousin, he comports himself like an overgrown, sulky child. And even in death, Buford causes the good doctor further problems. For example, nosy Seth is called to task for interfering with the official autopsy process—all due to his and Jessica's attempt to solve the crime. Thereafter, when the deceased man's will is read, Hazlitt finds himself an unwilling beneficiary of part of the estate.

Trivia: Reflecting just how much twentieth century morals had changed in America, on TV and on *Murder, She Wrote,* there is no effort made here to disguise the fact that socialite Evelyn Colby, who once dated Sergeant Lindley, is now cohabiting—without benefit of marriage—with Buford.

Sally Kirkland, known for her sexually daring stage roles, had been Oscar-nominated for *Anna* (1987). Her earlier film roles included *Coming Apart* (1969) and *Cinderella Liberty* (1973). Robert Hooks had costarred on *NYPD* (1967–1969) and *Supercarrier* (1988). Since 1989, Dakin Matthews had been on five teleseries, including *Drexell's Class* (1991–1992) and Valerie Harper's *The Office* (1995). Tom Mason's resume lists such series as *Two Marriages* (1983–1984) and *D.E.A.* (1990–1991). Craig Richard Nelson had been on *Paul Sand in Friends and Lovers* (1974–1975) and a troupe member of *The Carol Burnett Show* (1979). Ann Cusack was seen on Tom Arnold's sitcom, *The Jackie Thomas Show* (1992–1993) and, later, on the revamped *Jeff Foxworthy Show* (1996–).

230. "Death 'N Denial"

(1/22/95) 60 mins.

Director: Jerry Jameson **Teleplay:** Mark A. Burley

Regular: Angela Lansbury (Jessica Fletcher)

Guest Law Enforcer: Chaim Jeraffi (Inspector Omar Halim)

Guest Cast: Mike Akrawi (Waiter); Turhan Bey (Sherif Faris); Finn Carter (Sally Otterburn); Michael Paul Chan (Loan Shark); Steve Inwood (Rudy Grimes); Lee Meriwether (Vanessa Thorpe); Eric Pierpoint (Bradford Thorpe); Jim Pirri (Nasar, the Cabby); James Read (Boyd Venton); Jeri Lynn Ryan (Maura); Michael A. Saad (Minister of Interior)

The Setting: Cairo, Egypt

The Case: As a board member of Manhattan's Museum of Cultural History, Mrs. Fletcher accompanies MCH employee Sally Otterburn to Egypt. Their mission is to arrange a cultural exchange program with a Cairo art museum administered by Sherif Faris. At the airport, Jessica's carry-on bag is stolen.

At their hotel, Jessica learns that its owner, Boyd Venton, once dated Sally when she worked at the Cairo Museum. Later, Sally confesses that the real purpose of her trip was to sneak back into the country a 4,000-year-old statuette from the reign of Queen Nefartari. It had been stolen two years ago by unknown parties and had found its way eventually to the MCH where Sally recognized its origin. Cairo curator Sherif Faris, desperate to retrieve the artifact, has offered Sally, a former employee, an administrative post if she brings the statue to him. Before she can do so, the object is stolen from her room. Jessica, Boyd and Sherif Faris—for Sally's sake—agree not to summon the police.

Still later, the unscrupulous Rudy Grimes, a former CIA agent, who had grabbed the precious antique from Sally's room, is shot to death in the hotel elevator. His finish is welcome news for several people, including socialite Vanessa Thorpe, who had hired Grimes to trap her parasitic spouse, Brad, into remaining with her by gathering blackmail intelligence about his affair with boutique worker Maura and other matters. Brad had had his own deal with Grimes, but had been double-crossed by him, leaving Brad in a dangerous position with a demanding loan shark. Then, too, Boyd had known the dead man in a past career and had unsuccessfully begged him not to reveal his secret.

Highlights: One of Jessica Fletcher's most endearing traits is a willingness to befriend (near) strangers, relying often on her ingenuity and celebrity connections to solve their problems. Here, she assists cabby Nasar in gaining legal emigration to the United States. In another creative vein, the stouthearted New Englander pretends to be the deceased's mother to gain access to his mail. This leads to a marvelous situation in which Jessica is forced—out of politeness to her Egyptian hosts—to consume an entire bowl of *highly* spicy green stew. Her ill-disguised grimaces are wonderful to behold!

Not to be overlooked is Inspector Omar Halim, who proves to be one of the most cultured and astute law enforcers with whom Jessica has ever been associated.

Trivia: Debonair Turkish leading man Turhan Bey had been a Hollywood success in the 1940s with *Dragon Seed* (1944), *A Night in Paradise* (1946) and *Song of India* (1949). He had retired from movies in 1953. Now in his mid-seventies, he made this rare appearance on the American entertainment scene, returning to film the episode at Universal Studios, where he had been under contract fifty years prior. James Read had been Stephanie Zimbalist's original private eye partner, Murphy Michaels, on *Remington Steele* (1982–1983). Steve Inwood's screen assignments ranged from *Hurry Up or I'll Be Thirty* (1973) to *The Human Shield* (1992).

231. "Murder in High 'C'"

(2/5/95) 60 mins.

Director: Anthony Shaw **Teleplay:** Jerry Ludwig

Regular: Angela Lansbury (Jessica Fletcher)

Recurring Character: Lorenzo Caccianza (Inspector Piero Amato)

Guest Law Enforcer: Sam Ingraffia (Policeman)

Guest Cast: Bruce Abbott (Drew Granger); Charles Cioffi (Paul Corelli); Robert Costanzo (Rudolfo Petrocelli); John Getz (Jonas Cole); Khrystyne

Haje (Andrea Beaumont); Carol Lawrence (Stella Knight); Anthony Marciona (Stage Manager); Pierrino Mascarino (Carlo Rossi); Ely Pouget (Vicki Lawson); Benito Prezia (Doctor)

The Setting: Genoa, Italy

The Case: The show must go on, but at the Genoa Opera Festival there is great doubt. Gifted but temperamental Andrea Beaumont, who has replaced jealous Stella Knight as the company's leading diva, is receiving anonymous death threats. The hysterical soprano, who had been stalked last year in New York by the now imprisoned Albert Garmes, threatens *not* to proceed with the scheduled performances. Meanwhile, Jessica Fletcher, a longtime acquaintance of Andrea's husband, wealthy Jonas Cole, has flown to Italy for the premiere and is quickly drawn into the fracas.

Among the opera company personnel affected by Andrea's plight is handsome maestro Drew Granger, who hopes to break his contract and return to America. Stella sees Andrea's problems as a means for returning to her former glory as the prima donna. The cast changes challenge company publicity person Vicki Lawson, who loves arrogant Granger and is angered when he refuses to bolster her career back in America. Lead singer Paul Corelli is too self-directed to admit his true reactions to the turn of events. As for opera manager Rudolfo Petrocelli, whose troupe faces bankruptcy (a fact known by crooked company accountant Carlo Rossi), he'll collect a healthy insurance reimbursement if Andrea does not appear at the festival.

When Petrocelli is shot at the theater, Jonas is branded the chief suspect. Therefore, Jessica intervenes. As such, she matches her skills with Inspector Piero Amato, who had earlier scoffed at Andrea's death threats, suggesting they were merely a publicity gimmick. Next, it's learned that back in the U.S., Garmes has been paroled from prison, but that his present whereabouts are unknown. Solving the case hinges on Mrs. Fletcher understanding why the theater's air-conditioning system has been jammed.

Highlights: Whatever part of the world of arts and letters that Jessica Fletcher inhabits, she is always a sophisticated participant. (This contrasts with the early seasons of *Murder, She Wrote* in which she is depicted as being in awe of famous people, smart settings, etc.) Here the widow is quite at ease in the realm of grand opera, instinctively able to pierce through any inflated ego in her path.

One of the more delightful law enforcers within *Murder, She Wrote* is Inspector Piero Amato. He is handsome, charming and an expert at his job. After Jessica mocks his pretense of being a simple policeman used to small village ways, he reverts to his intelligent, cosmopolitan self. Working together proves a satisfying experience for both the writer and the police official.

Trivia: For aficionados of movie history, the plot has a similarity to the often-filmed *Phantom of the Opera* and Doris Day's *Midnight Lace* (1960). Back in 1989, a similar backstage-at-the-opera caper—set in San Francisco—had provided the basis for "When the Fat Lady Sings" (#189) which also featured Carol Lawrence.

Although a seasoned stage and TV performer, including three previous *Murder, She Wrote* episodes, Carol Lawrence has made few feature films: *New Faces* (1954) and *Shattered Image* (1993), etc. Lorenzo Caccianza played Nick Schillace/Dimitri Pappas from 1990 to 1993 on TV's *Knots Landing.* Bruce Abbott was Judge Nicholas Marshall on *Dark Justice* (1992–1993). Khrystyne Haje was a graduate of the TV sitcom *Head of the Class* (1986–1991). Ely Pouget was Maggie Evans on the revival of the gothic soap opera *Dark Shadows* (1991). In the TV series *Get Christie Love* (1974–1975) and *Kojak* (1989–1990), Charles Cioffi played police officials.

232. "Twice Dead"

(2/12/95) 60 mins.

Director: Walter Grauman **Teleplay:** Paul Schiffer

Regular: Angela Lansbury (Jessica Fletcher)

Recurring Characters: Herbert Edelman (Lieutenant Artie Gelber); Lisa Long (Officer Rizzoli)

Guest Cast: Sam Anderson (Stuart Himes); James Brockelman (Mailroom Person); Wren T. Brown (Desk Clerk); Annie Corley (Liz White); Robert Curtis-Brown (David Randall); Bradford Dillman (Richard Ellston); Mario Machado (Reporter); Richard Portnow (Walter Pell); W. Morgan Sheppard (Dr. Frederick Grundberg); Kathleen Sullivan (TV Reporter); Shannon Tweed (Pamela Lake); Bruce Weitz (Daniel Weldon [Dr. Max Franklin])

The Settings: Long Island, New York; New York City

The Case: A plane crash on Long Island Sound claims the life of Nobel Prize-winning biophysicist Dr. Max Franklin. He had been working for BioMed Technologies, Inc, on project L214, a breakthrough cancer cure. The next day, Jessica Fletcher keeps an appointment at BioMed's Long Island lab with department worker Liz White, whom she is helping to organize a scientific book project. BioMed is in an uproar. Dr. Frederick Grundberg, head of the facility, still has high hopes for Franklin's research saving the company financially. As such, he has slimy private investigator Walter Pell break into the dead man's home to locate essential research data. Meanwhile, Richard Ellston, whose firm is underwriting the BioMed stock offering, fears that Franklin's death will sink the stock's value. Meanwhile, he is conspiring with Pamela Lake, a BioMed executive, to oust Grundberg.

Back in Manhattan, Mrs. Fletcher can't believe her eyes when she spots Dr. Franklin in a passing cab. Tracking down the "deceased," Jessica learns that he had faked his death to circumvent Grundberg's pressure to rush the untested cancer vaccine onto the market. Later, Franklin's town house is torched, and still further on, the doctor is bludgeoned at the hotel where he has registered under an alias. This time he is truly dead!

Lieutenant Artie Gelber is in charge of the homicide case and with his unofficial partner, Jessica, focuses on the BioMed staff as likely suspects. They discover that Liz White had once had an affair with Franklin; grumpy Stuart Himes had been doctoring Franklin's data; and dedicated David Randall, the technician, loves coworker Liz. Of equal importance is stalking Pell, who tries to double-cross his client, Grundberg, and the financially ruined Ellston.

Highlights: Rubbing elbows in the world of advanced medical research, Jessica Fletcher demonstrates how far she has come in today's high tech world by her familiarity and ease with computer paraphernalia. As always, matching Jessica with salt-of-the-earth Lieutenant Gelber provides diverting moments. Here, the unsophisticated police detective repeatedly asks Mrs. Fletcher's advice about which (touched-up) photo portrait of himself he should submit to his Brooklyn high school's Alumni Wall of Fame.

Trivia: This was the seventh and final appearance of police lieutenant Artie Gelber on *Murder, She Wrote.* (Actor Herb Edelman, who played Gelber, died at age sixty-six in July 1996.) This time Gelber is without his trusty partner, Detective Henderson.

Shapely Shannon Tweed had paid her cinema dues in such low-budget features as *Hot Dog . . . The Movie!* (1983), *Cannibal Women in the Avocado Jungle of Death* (1989), *Night Eyes 2* (1991) and *Night Eyes 3* (1993). Bruce Weitz, who won an Emmy (1984) for his continuing role on *Hill Street Blues* (1981–1987), had also been a regular on *Mama's Boy* (1989) and *Anything But Love* (1991–1992). Richard Portnow's movie credits ranged from *Kindergarten Cop* (1990) to *Sister Act* (1992) and *Trial by Jury* (1994). W(illiam) Morgan Sheppard had been a cast member of the fiction TV entry *Max Headroom* (1987). Noted television journalist Kathleen Sullivan appeared as herself.

233. "Film Flam"

(2/19/95) 60 mins.

Director: Anthony Shaw **Teleplay:** Donald Ross

Regular: Angela Lansbury (Jessica Fletcher)

Recurring Characters: Mike Connors (Boyce Brown); Gregory Sierra (Lieutenant Gabriel Caceras)

Guest Law Enforcer: Cali Timmins (Barbie Lippin [Sergeant Barbara Warshaw])

Guest Cast: Paulo Andres (Delivery Boy); John Astin (Fritz Randall); James Caviezel (Darryl Harding); Richard Dano (Scotty, the Security Guard); Kim Darby ("Wee" Joan Kemp); Stacy Edwards (Elaine Brown); Howard French (Manheim); Kerrie Keane (Audrey Young); Richard Libertini (Carson Robbins); Justin Lord (Lloyd Nader); William O'Leary (Hank Duncan)

The Setting: Los Angeles, California

The Case: Jessica Fletcher is on the Monolith Pictures lot negotiating with studio head Boyce Brown to produce one of her novels. However, he is preoccupied with the release of *Cry of Destiny*, a picture left uncompleted since the 1960 untimely death of wunderkind director Austin Young. Now, under the aegis of Boyce's producer daughter, Elaine, who shot additional footage, the project has been finished at a $40 million cost.

Jessica attends a well-received screening of the landmark film. However, the next day she discovers the corpse of Fritz Randall, who had been Young's assistant years ago and was now finishing a book on the life and death of the great director. Jessica finds it's more than coincidental that Fritz's death from an overdose of barbiturates and alcohol is similar to how his mentor died decades earlier.

Now on friendly terms with Los Angeles police lieutenant Gabriel Caceras from past cases they solved "together," Jessica has near carte blanche to question a colorful array of too interested parties to Fritz's death. There is middle-aged, former child star "Wee" Joan Kemp, who hopes *Cry of Destiny* will signal her comeback. Audrey Young is on the lot claiming that Austin adopted her a year before he died. If true, she legally controls all picture rights. Producer Elaine Brown had been feuding with Randall over artistic control of the revamped movie. Also under suspicion are Hank Duncan, Carson Robbins and Manheim, three Monolith Studio employees involved in pirating studio movie negatives—especially *Cry of Destiny*—for black market video duplication. Additionally, there's the mysterious Darryl Harding, who is attracted to Elaine and claims to be an actor, and who lives secretly on a deserted sound stage. Another ambiguous participant is movie-struck Barbie Lippin, whom lusting Duncan promises to help get a screen test in exchange for sexual favors.

Highlights: There is guaranteed audience fascination with a behind-the-cameras peek at the workings of a movie studio. The gimmick had been used in several past *Murder, She Wrote* episodes. Here the focus is *not* on the glamorous aspects of the business, but on day-to-day survival tactics (i.e., profit-and-loss statements, out-of-control budgets, the sinister New York home office, illegal duping of major features, right of final cut, etc.) Of all the Hollywood business characters presented, has-been"Wee" Joan Kemp is the most bizarre and pitiful.

Trivia: Universal Studios, the berth of *Murder, She Wrote*, was used as the Monolith lot.

With parts stretching from *Bus Riley's Back in Town* (1965) to *Teen Wolf Too* (1987), Kim Darby remains best known for John Wayne's *True Grit* (1969). Stacy Edwards was part of the TV drama *Sons & Daughters* (1991). Richard Libertini's series work includes *Soap* (1977–1978) and *The Fanelli Boys* (1990–1991). Before she was Suzanne Steele on *Beverly Hills 90210* (1993–1994), Kerrie Keane appeared on *Hot Pursuit* (1984) and *Studio 5-B* (1989). Cali Timmins played Maggie Davenport on *Rin Tin Tin K-9 Cop* (1988–1989). William O'Leary was Ben on the sitcom *Dear John* (1991–1992) and later appeared as Tim Allen's brother on *Home Improvement.*

234. "Murder a la Mode"

(2/26/95) 60 mins.

Director: Jerry Jameson **Teleplay:** Laurence Heath

Regular: Angela Lansbury (Jessica Fletcher)

Guest Law Enforcers: Frank Bruynbroek (Detective); Francois Eric Gendron (Inspector Marc Gautier)

Guest Cast: Clifford David (Claude Faragere); David Garrison (Dan Morgan); Francois Guetary (Edmond Faragere); Daniel Markel (Rick Evans); Maureen Mueller (Thea Vaughn); Natalija Nogulich (Denise Naveau); Yuji Okumoto (Kim Huan); Bettina Spier (Invitation Checker); James Sutorius (Paul Vaughn); Ellia Thompson (Carrie Quinn)

The Setting: Paris, France

The Case: Jessica Fletcher is in Paris to supervise publication of the French edition of her latest novel. Since *Runway to Murder* deals with the fashion world, her literary agent, Dan Morgan, has Jessica attend Vaughn Fashions' showing of their new ready-to-wear dress collection. Once settled at the Hotel Inter-Continental, Mrs. Fletcher contacts her friend, super model Carrie Quinn, who confides that she has lost interest in fashion photographer Rick Evans and now loves Edmond Faragere. Jessica learns that the roguish Edmond is the estranged stepson of legendary designer Claude Faragere and that Edmond is scheming to build his own fashion empire.

After Edmond is shot down outside his home and Inspector Marc Gautier names Carrie the chief suspect, the novelist feels obliges to redeem her friend. Her detection disrobes several more likely suspects. There is vengeful Cambodian Kim Huan whose wife died in a fire at the sweatshop owned by the deceased. Fashion promoter Paul Vaughn knew that his designer wife, Thea, had been having an affair with Edmond and that she planned to join him in business. Rick Evans was none too pleased to lose Carrie to Faragere. Meanwhile, it develops that Carrie had found out that Edmond was still romancing Thea. As for Claude Faragere, he may have forgiven the deceased for embezzling company funds, but now that he planned to launch a new fashion firm, he was humiliated that his stepson should have tried to steal away key employees. Finally, there's Denise Naveau, once a leading fashion model and now a seamstress for the Vaughns, who had never gotten over her attraction to Edmond. Added to the mix is an international gem-smuggling operation.

Highlights: Discerning Jessica, increasingly stylishly dressed herself, never allows the world of haute couture to distract her from her crime-solving mission. Almost equally at home in sophisticated Paris as in unpretentious Cabot Cove, she arouses a protective feeling in Inspector Gautier. On the other hand, he fears that if she is harmed, it would dishonor the name of France.

This episode's runway fashion show (courtesy of Saks Fifth Avenue) lends a chic ambiance to the proceedings, even if the event is constructed in a haphazard miniformat.

Trivia: The chic world of French high fashion was not a new topic for *Murder, She Wrote.* It had been used in 1987's "A Fashionable Way to Die" (#66). Once again, as in many past installments, it's Mrs. Fletcher's knack for spotting a seemingly unimportant item dropped at the murder site that leads her to solving the homicide case.

David Garrison was employed on such TV series as *It's Your Move* (1984–1985) and had played Steve Rhoades on *Married . . . with Children* (1987–1990). Francois Guetary played a suave native of Martinique on *Fly By Night* (1991). Maureen Mueller was Dr. Dierdre Bennett on the sitcom *Doctor, Doctor* (1989–1991), while Natalija Nogulich was Aunt Miriam on

Brooklyn Bridge (1991–1992) and Francois Eric Gendron was seen on the detective series *Dangerous Curves*, playing a member of a global law enforcing agency.

235. "The Dream Team"

(3/19/95) 60 mins.

Director: Anthony Shaw **Teleplay:** Tom Sawyer

Regulars: Angela Lansbury (Jessica Fletcher); Ron Masak (Sheriff Mort Metzger); William Windom (Dr. Seth Hazlitt)

Recurring Characters: Louis Herthum (Deputy Andy Broom); Michael Horton (Grady Fletcher)

Guest Cast: Katherine Cannon (Lorna Buffum); Frank Converse (Everett Buffum); John D'Aquino (J. Peter Carmody); Richardson Morse (Travis Lawder); Mary Gordon Murray (Pauline Higgins); Charles Napier (Denver Martin); Yvette Nipar (Toni Simpson); Jay Patterson (Nosh Farmer); Pat Stewart (Onlooker)

The Setting: Cabot Cove, Maine

The Case: The Cabot Cove gossip mill buzzes about a new commercial venture coming to town, and they've heard that Jessica Fletcher's accountant nephew, Grady, is part of the team behind the project.

When Grady arrives—having left wife Donna and their child back in New York—he informs Aunt Jess that he is now working for Columbia Ventures. This firm plans to construct a residential/business/marina/golf course super complex between Cabot Cove and Craggy Neck. Grady also mentions that his employers—president J. Peter Carmody, backer Everett Buffum and company executive Toni Simpson—have engineered similar sites in Florida and Oregon.

Before long, many townsfolk eagerly invest in the project while others, like Travis Lawder, organize Cabot Cove-ers Against the Marina. Everything turns sour one rainy night when Everett Buffum's wife, Lorna, a guest at the local Hill House Motel, dies when her car runs off a cliff and plunges into the waters below. The facts suggest that she was a victim of her own drunk driving. Meanwhile, a new rumor circulates that the marina project might be a scam.

Jessica's digging—to extricate Grady from the Columbia Ventures mess—reveals that Lorna was a victim of foul play. Mrs. Fletcher finds that Everett had planned to quit the venture and that he and the demanding victim had argued about divorcing. (The jealous Lorna had discovered

Everett's extracurricular relationship with Toni.) Also to be considered is Denver Martin, another stranger in town, who has a great interest in the building scheme. And what of Nosh Farmer of Hill House, who, like so many others, had been caught up in the investment fever, or Carmody, who had a lot to lose if Lorna had divulged damaging information she had overheard about Columbia Ventures. Then, too, there's Grady, who was humiliated at being duped by his latest employers.

Highlights: No longer a full-time Cabot Cove resident, Jessica is more hyperactive than usual in pinpointing the killer. As Dr. Seth Hazlitt observes, "Now that you're living in New York, you're becoming as impatient as the rest of the people down there." But when her trouble-prone nephew is concerned, Mrs. Fletcher's maternal instincts lead her to push harder in her crime-solving.

Trivia: Grady Fletcher, now looking much older and still unlucky in securing permanent work, had last been on *Murder, She Wrote* in 1990's "The Szechuan Dragon" (#129). This would be Grady's final weekly series appearance.

Katherine Cannon played Mae Woodward Murphy on *Father Murphy* (1981–1982). Veteran actor Frank Converse's TV series spanned from *Coronet Blue* (1967) to *Dolphin Cove* (1989). In the science fiction entry *seaQuest* DSV (1993–1994), John D'Aquino was Lieutenant Benjamin Krieg. Charles Napier, a graduate of *The Oregon Trail* (1977) Western series, was later the voice of Duke Phillips on the TV cartoon program *The Critic* (1994–). On *Robocop—The Series* (1993–1994), Yvette Nipar was Detective Lisa Madigan.

236. "School for Murder"

(4/30/95) 60 mins.

Director: Vincent McEveety **Story:** Robert Brennan **Teleplay:** Robert Brennan, Jerry Ludwig

Regulars: Angela Lansbury (Jessica Fletcher); Ron Masak (Sheriff Mort Metzger)

Recurring Character: Louis Herthum (Deputy Andy Broom)

Guest Cast: Dana Barron (Sarah Tyler); Leslie Bevis (Barbara Desmond); Roy Dotrice (Dr. Myles Purcell); Robert Foxworth (Professor Harry Matthews); Scott Marlowe (Avery Nugent); Richard Minchenberg (Irv Tripler [Joey Marlowe]); Maryann Plunkett (Claire Vickers); Ethan Randall (Mike Seresino); Trevor St. John (Colin Forbes); Nicolas Surovy (James Ryerson)

The Setting: Cabot Cove, Maine

The Case: Under the aegis of Professor Harry Matthews, Jessica Fletcher gives her annual lecture on detective literature at St. Crispin's Academy, an exclusive prep school situated on the outskirts of Cabot Cove.

Mrs. Fletcher discovers hotbeds of unrest at the academy. There is intrigue afoot to find the replacement for headmaster Dr. Myles Purcell. Since teacher Avery Nugent has withdrawn from the race, the two most likely candidates are Matthews and history instructor James Ryerson. Students and faculty alike are torn in support of the rival factions. Then there is the Society of Prometheus, a secret student group that not only discriminates against outsiders but conducts a great deal of unorthodox activities, including a rash of thefts on campus.

Much to everyone's surprise, Ryerson, who stole, plagiarized and presented Matthews' reorganization plan for the academy, is, nevertheless, selected as the new headmaster. However, after his celebration party he is murdered in his office. Because Matthews seemingly had the most to gain from his rival's demise and has only a vague alibi, he becomes Sheriff Mort Metzger's prime suspect. However, Jessica disagrees, after learning, for example, that someone had been hiding at the death site when students Mike Seresino and Sarah Tyler found the corpse.

Further investigation reveals that teacher Claire Vickers had once dated the victim, a romance that ended when she discovered his dishonest ways. More recently, he had offered to drop out of the headmaster race if she would sleep with him. It also surfaces that Dr. Purcell was being blackmailed for a tragedy in his past and that music teacher Irv Tripler knows far more than he is willing to tell. It is a song, "Life Is Like This"—a favorite tune of Jessica and her late husband Frank—that triggers the caper's resolution.

Highlights: This is a particularly well scripted segment in which the action and characterizations are logically intertwined. It is revealing of her talents as both teacher and mentor to observe Jessica Fletcher's interaction with the students. There are fine nostalgic moments as Jessica reminisce about her late husband and "their" song. The murderer's last-minute confession, a fixed element of each *Murder, She Wrote* episode, is extremely well showcased here.

Trivia: The "crowd" scenes at the academy reveal that—by now—Cabot Cove has a more diverse ethnic mix than ever before. Apparently, from last-minute editing, the roles of Barbara Desmond and Avery Nugent—two of the St. Crispin's faculty—were severely truncated. A rarity for the series was to have a character (Trevor St. John) bare his chest as he changes clothes on-camera. And for all who might have wondered, this segment reveals that 03041 is Cabot Cove's zip code.

Dana Barron had been Nikki Witt on *Beverly Hills 90210* (1992). Well-established actor Roy Dotrice had appeared in such 1990s features as *Suburban Commando* (1991) and *The Cutting Edge* (1992). Robert Foxworth's acting credentials include being Chase Gioberti on the nighttime soap opera *Falcon Crest* (1981–1987). Scott Marlowe had been a juvenile performer when he made such pictures as *Men in War* (1957) and *A Cold Wind in August* (1961). Nicolas Surovy costarred with Suzanne Pleshette in the TV drama series *Bridges to Cross* (1986) and supported Jack Scalia in the detective entry *Wolf* (1989–1991).

237. "Another Killing in Cork"

(5/7/95) 60 mins.

Director: Anthony Shaw **Teleplay:** Bruce Lansbury

Regular: Angela Lansbury (Jessica Fletcher)

Recurring Character: Mark Rolston (Sergeant Terence Boyle)

Guest Law Enforcer: Francis Guinan (Edward Pryce [Mr. Bond])

Guest Cast: Eleanor Comegys (Brigid Ahearn); Bairbre Dowling (Kate Dempsey); Gerry Gibson (Shamus Riley); Martin Jarvis (Cyril Ruddy [Edward Montgomery]); Ross Kettle (Dennis McSorley); James Lancaster (Councilman Harold Early); Felicia Lansbury (Shauna); Carolyn Seymour (Nellie Ruddy); Rod Taylor (Tom Dempsey); Lyman Ward (Walter Ickes); Kent Williams (Freddie Layton); Amanda Wyss (Laura Maples)

The Setting: Kilcleer, Ireland

The Case: On holiday in Kilcleer, Ireland, where her great-grandfather once lived, Jessica Fletcher is a guest of Tom and Kate Dempsey at their quaint fishing lodge. Meanwhile, Walter Ickes (head of Miranda Mining which had undertaken a similar project in the Colorado Rockies) and Harold Early (on the Kilcleer council) are pressuring Dempsey to support strip mining in the valley. However Tom, a staunch environmentalist, is strongly opposed. Later, Ickes and Early try to bribe farmer/councilman Dennis McSorley (who dates Brigid Ahearn, an inn employee) to persuade Dempsey to go along with the scheme.

One evening, guest Edward Pryce, an English teacher who is at the lodge to study the flora and fauna, fails to return from a day of salmon fishing. Later, his body is found stuffed in a well. Sergeant Terence Boyle, along with Jessica who worked with the police on a previous holiday in Kilcleer, interviews the lodge staff and guests, hoping to unmask the killer who had discovered Pryce's real reason for coming to Kilcleer. There is posturing Cyril Ruddy and his sexually frustrated, flirtatious wife, Nellie, as well as pretty Laura Maples, an avid photographer. The latter is coupled with accountant Freddie Layton, whose New York-based troubles are catching up with him. Shamus Riley is the lodge's opinionated fishing guide who is not fond of the too demanding guests. And what of the craggy man in black who keeps appearing along the roadside?

Highlights: Boasting strong production values and appealing background photography of County Cork, Ireland, this excursion is a balanced mix of reality (e.g., Brigid's pregnancy, Dempsey's battle against the capitalists, the graphically shown corpse being lifted out of the well) and folk tale fancy (e.g., curses, sprites).

Trivia: Jessica Fletcher's last visit to Kilcleer in 1993's "A Killing in Cork" (#203) was her first occasion to test her deductive skills with Sergeant Boyle of the local constabulary. Angela Lansbury's niece, Felicia, has a small acting assignment here as Shauna, a lodge worker. In an unusual sequence—by *Murder, She Wrote* standards—the Nellie Ruddy character is given saucy dialogue referring to her sexually anemic marriage.

Australian-born Rod Taylor hit his Hollywood peak in the 1960s with movie leads in *The Time Machine, The VIPs* and *Hotel.* Kent Williams had appeared as the assistant district attorney on TV's *Mickey Spillane's Mike Hammer* (1984–1986) and Amanda Wyss had been Randi McFarland on the syndicated series *Highlander* (1992–1993).

238. "Game, Set, Murder"

(5/14/95) 60 mins.

Director: Walter Grauman **Teleplay:** Philip John Taylor

Regular: Angela Lansbury (Jessica Fletcher)

Guest Law Enforcer: Iona Morris (Lieutenant Estelle Garr)

Guest Cast: J.C. Brandy (Louise Henderson); Bobby Hosea (John McCarver); Joyce Hyser (Portia Dekker, Esq.); Marta Martin (Francesca Garcia); Barry Newman (Andrew Bascombe); Alyson Reed (Wendy Maitlin); Leon Russom (Lane Henderson); Jonathan Scarfe (Jamie Carlson)

The Setting: New York City

The Case: Jessica Fletcher agrees to her publisher's request that she organize a charity tennis tournament in conjunction with the publishing house staff lawyer, young Portia Dekker. Jessica is an asset to the project because she has long known rising court star Louise Henderson who is needed for the fund-raiser. Years before, as a youngster, Louise witnessed her mother's murder, but details of the crime were blocked out by her amnesia. Back then, Louise recuperated in Cabot Cove with her grandmother.

Jessica is distressed at how disturbed seventeen-year-old Louise is now and that her psychiatric therapy hasn't resolved her childhood trauma. Mrs. Fletcher finds Louise's father, Lane Henderson, an overbearing control freak who plans to move Louise—as well as her sports rival Francesca Garcia—away from their joint career manager, Andrew Bascombe. (Bascombe has been having an affair with the much younger Ms. Garcia.)

When Louise's therapist is murdered and the tape recording of Louise's last session with him is missing, police lieutenant Estelle Garr is put in charge. The investigation takes a new twist when Lane Henderson is shot dead at Bascombe's hotel where he had come for a business dinner. However, the autopsy presents surprising findings which seem to clear Bascombe of the crime. But several others also wished Henderson dead. At the top of the list is the victim's daughter, who had discovered that he would have willingly sacrificed her career if he could make more money turning Francesca into *the* court champ. Another suspect is Wendy Maitlin, Louise's tennis coach and confidant whom Henderson had recently fired, and then rehired. There's also John McCarver of Plaza Sports Merchandising, whom Lane had been blackmailing for past kickbacks, as well as Louise's boyfriend, Jamie Carlson, also a tennis pro. He has past unresolved drug charges and confesses that Lane threatened to reveal them to the authorities unless he broke off with Louise.

Highlights: Using a favorite device of the classic *The Thin Man* movies, Jessica Fletcher gathers together all the suspects and, by elimination, exposes the actual killer(s). There are several notable differences to the police investigator seen in this caper. For one, she is a woman; for another she is much classier than most of the American law people Jessica encounters. Additionally Garr has a sly sense of humor.

Trivia: Massachusetts-born Barry Newman gained prominence as the star of the *Petrocelli* TV series (1974–1976) playing an attorney. J.C. Brandy was a cast member of the detective series *Wolf* (1989–1991). In *The O.J. Simpson Story* (1994), Bobby Hosea portrayed the famed gridiron star involved in a sensational murder case. Earlier, Hosea was on the sitcom *Singer & Sons* (1990). Leon Russom was principal Edward Steadman on the drama series *TV 101* (1988–1989).

SEASON TWELVE

1995—1996

239. "Nailed"

(9/21/95) 60 mins.

Director: Anthony Shaw **Teleplay:** Donald Ross

Regular: Angela Lansbury (Jessica Fletcher)

Guest Law Enforcer: Vic Politzos (Lieutenant Sam Kriley)

Guest Cast: Daphne Ashbrook (Kathy Stafford); Rosalind Chao (Phoebe Campbell); Leslie Easterbrook (Antoinette Fishman); Denise Gentile (Nancy Rayburn); Carol Kiernan (Madelyn Sweetzer); Sean O'Bryan (Steve Burke); John O'Hurley (Ralph Stafford); Wayne Pere (Jimmy Neiman); Kathy Trageser (Diane); Michael Woods (Billy Blake); Eddie Zammit (Allie Simpson)

The Setting: New York City

The Case: At her Manhattan apartment, Jessica Fletcher hosts the new board members of the Museum of Cultural History. One of her guests, Agnes Frasier, leaves early due to a bad headache. Later, at her upper East Side apartment, Agnes surprises a cat burglar. Although she is knifed in the skirmish, she survives. The next day, Lieutenant Sam Kriley interviews Jessica, and the two discuss how this is the seventh such robbery in seven weeks.

It later occurs to the mystery writer that several of the robbery victims were customers at Antoinette of Fifth Avenue's chic hair salon—where Jessica is also a client. It leads Jessica to wonder about the staff there. Besides owner Antoinette Fishman, there is star hair stylist Jimmy Neiman, who recently became engaged to manicurist Diane. The salon is managed by Phoebe Campbell, who grew up in the city's tough neighborhoods along with Jimmy and who was once the hair stylist's lover. There is also Steve Burke, a fledgling whodunit novelist whom Jessica has taken under her wing. She introduced him to her publisher, who bought his first novel on condition he do rewrites to make the story's backdrop (murder at a plush beauty shop) more credible. As such, Mrs. Fletcher helped Steve get a gofer's job at Antoinette's.

Meanwhile, Ralph Stafford, who relies on his supermarket heiress wife, Kathy, for financial support and social position, pressures Jimmy to head a new salon that Stafford will launch. Knowing of Stafford's unsavory business associates, Neiman is reluctant to sign the contract. To insure the deal, Ralph uses damaging information he possesses to force both Phoebe and Diane to convince Jimmy to make the deal. Later, Stafford visits TV talk program host Nancy Rayburn. Although she is one of his wife's best friends, she is having an affair with Ralph. She gives Stafford a $400,000 loan for the salon project. As security he loans her a rare 1804 silver dollar that he has borrowed from his trusting wife to make the deal with "unnamed" investors. Nancy is unaware that the coin is a counterfeit, a replica created by Stafford's underworld cohort, Allie Simpson.

Jimmy quits Antoinette's as planned, and Stafford hosts a celebration cocktail party. The next morning, Ralph is found dead at Antoinette's. He has been stabbed with Jimmy's special cutting shears, and the police find a note in which Jimmy instructed the victim to meet him at the salon after the party.

The suspects also include Billy Blake, the maitre d' at the Café Metropole who knows Allie Simpson, as well as Antoinette Fishman, who gave Jimmy his start years ago and who was once the deceased's lover. In addition, there's Madelyn Sweetzer, Nancy Rayburn's TV show assistant. Finally, such clues as duplicate coin boxes and a 1985 group photo of four young women bonded together as The Hellraisers provide Mrs. Fletcher with the needed insight to wrap up the case.

Highlights: The story line offers an interesting twist in providing Mrs. Fletcher with a mystery writing protégé, a young man with talent not only for a good plot but with a keen sense of observation—truly a person Jessica enjoys mentoring.

If several of the episode's lesser characters are cliched and/or skimpily conceived, Leslie Easterbrook brings full dimension to her role as the aging salon owner fearful of losing out to a trendier competitor. She is an ambitious yet vulnerable soul with whom Jessica can easily relate and wish to help.

Trivia: *Murder, She Wrote* devotees will have spotted that the cast list of featured players for this segment is out of the usual alpha order in the opening title credits: actor John O'Hurley is listed before Sean O'Bryan.

Michael Woods appeared on *Our Family Honor* (1985–1986), as well as *Capital News* (1990) and starred in the violent *Private Eye* (1987–1988). A graduate of several teleseries, including *Diff'rent Strokes* (1982–1983), Rosalind Chao made her mark as Keiko O'Brien aboard both *Star Trek: The Next Generation* (1991–1993) and *Star Trek: Deep Space Nine* (1992–1994). Leslie Easterbrook was sharp-tongued model/dancer Rhonda Lee on *Laverne & Shirley* (1980–1983). Sean O'Bryan was part of the grunge sitcom *Pig Sty* (1995). John O'Hurley's resume includes such sitcoms as *Scorch* (1992) and *A Whole New Ballgame* (1995). On the adventure series *Pointman* (1995), Kathy Trageser had the occasional role of Jennifer Ellis who worked at Jack Scalia's health club.

240. "A Quaking in Aspen"

(9/28/95) 60 mins.

Director: Vincent McEveety **Teleplay:** Tom Sawyer

Regular: Angela Lansbury (Jessica Fletcher)

Recurring Character: Wayne Rogers (Howard Dietrich [Charlie Garrett])

Guest Law Enforcer: Kurt Fuller (Sheriff Milo Pike)

Guest Cast: Wendy Benson (Gina Sherman); Victor Bevine (Anthony Pembroke [Anthony O'Brien]); Thom Bierdz (Phil Carmichael); Tom Everett (Mr. Vernon [Grant Boswell]); Elizabeth Gracen (Sydney Pembroke); Leslie Horan (Nancy Boswell); Deborah Lacey (Olivia Archer); Gerald McRaney (Terry Folger, Esq.); Leigh Taylor-Young (Laney Sherman Boswell); Scott Valentine (Darman H. Keene)

The Settings: Aspen, Colorado; Chicago, Illinois; Denver, Colorado

The Case: Jessica Fletcher flies to Colorado to do a TV interview with former network newscaster Laney Sherman Boswell, who now works at a small Aspen station. Recently, Laney has experienced several traumatic situations. A month ago, she was planning to divorce Grant Boswell, her third husband. Just as her attorney, Terry Folger, was to file divorce papers, Grant died in a fiery auto crash in Denver. As his insurance policy beneficiary, she now stands to gain several million dollars as does Grant's niece, Nancy.

Meanwhile, Olivia Archer at Chicago-based Majority Insurance hires luckless private investigator Charlie Garrett to fly to Aspen to determine if there is any good reason (e.g., suicide, murder) why the claim should not be paid. Garrett poses as Howard Dietrich, a stock broker from Palm Beach, Florida. Before long, Jessica encounters Dietrich/Garrett and, out of past friendship, reluctantly agrees not to tell Laney the truth about his objective—at least for a few days. Later, Sheriff Milo Pike determines that Grant's death vehicle had been triggered to crash and explode, and singles out Laney as the killer, claiming an eye witness saw her purchase the incendiary materials that led to her husband's death. For a hefty fee, Laney hires Folger to represent her in the criminal proceedings while Mrs. Fletcher hastens to prove her friend's innocence.

Later, broke con artist Anthony Pembroke, who, with his society wife, Nancy, has recently returned from Morocco, is murdered in an alleyway of downtown Aspen. Mrs. Fletcher has a hunch that there's a link between the two months-apart murders.

Jessica and Charlie—along with Sheriff Pike—eventually have a full complement of suspects, many of them with overlapping relationships. Laney's daughter, Gina, had no love for her late stepfather. Another player is Grant's niece from Denver who is in Aspen to collect her portion of the insurance proceeds. Even Laney's attorney/beau, Folger, has ulterior motives. Not to be overlooked is Mr. Vernon, a visitor in Aspen who says he has friends who know (the actual) Howard Dietrich of Palm Beach. Before the murderer is revealed, Mrs. Fletcher realizes that many of the interested parties are not at all whom or what they claim to be.

Highlights: As always, the teaming of successful, altruistic Jessica Fletcher and ineffectual, self-concerned gumshoe Charlie Garrett presents a delightful contrast. This duo is especially entertaining when he is at his most exasperating (lying, breaking promises, ignoring police procedures) and an embarrassed Jessica must double talk to save him and herself from further disaster with the law and the deadly unidentified murderer.

Superior special effects are an infrequent ingredient on *Murder, She Wrote.* However, as a bonus there's a spectacular car crash here in which a vehicle careens over the mountainous roadside and explodes into flames.

Trivia: Gerald McRaney's teleseries have encompassed *The Law* (1975), *Simon & Simon* (1981–1988), *Major Dad* (1989–1993) and the 1996 drama *CPW.* Leigh Taylor-Young, once married to actor Ryan O'Neal, costarred with O'Neal on *Peyton Place* (1966–1967) and in *The Big Bounce* (1969). An alumnus of *Family Ties* (1985–1989), Scott Valentine's 1990s movies included *Write to Kill, To Sleep with a Vampire* and *Object of Obsession.* Victor Bevine had been a 1991 cast member of Sharon Gless's TV series *The Trials of Rosie O'Neill.* Elizabeth Gracen was aboard James Brolin's adventure series *Extreme* (1995).

241. "The Secret of Gila Junction"

(10/5/95) 60 mins.

Director: Anthony Shaw **Teleplay:** Jerry Ludwig

Regular: Angela Lansbury (Jessica Fletcher)

Guest Law Enforcers: Robert Seals (Highway Patrolman); Jay Underwood (Sheriff Spencer Gates)

Guest Cast: Lawrence Bayne (George Creech); Guy Boyd (Whitey Deaver); Paul Ivy (Lawson Parks); Dorothy Lyman (Norma Shey); Maya McLaughlin (Dena Harding); Bruce E. Morrow (Corley Thompson); Douglas Roberts (Tiny Kerns); Robert Rusler (Pete Menteer); Bo Svenson (Cal Harding); Dale Swann (Bus Driver); Kari Whitman (Marge Deaver); Biff Yeager (Todd Hawkins)

The Setting: Gila Junction, Arizona

The Case: After leaving Las Vegas, Jessica Fletcher visits Norma Shey in the small desert community of Gila Junction, Arizona. In the past, Norma was a high-powered Associated Press reporter, who had covered the Vietnam War. Now semiretired, she devotes her energies to pottery making, and to fending off Cal Harding, owner of the local Grand Hotel, who wants her to "settle down." However, she has other priorities. For example, she has sniffed out a possible cover-up from twenty-five years ago of spilled toxic chemicals at Camp Roslyn, a now-deserted army base near Gila Junction. Norma intends to look into the story.

When Norma injures her ankle following a car accident caused by someone shooting at her vehicle, she is house-bound. She asks Jessica to be her surrogate investigator. Mrs. Fletcher agrees reluctantly, and seeks the help of Spencer Gates, the part-time sheriff who also operates a car repair business. He is involved in investigating a rash of "truck stop" robberies plaguing the area.

Later on, Whitey Deaver, who runs a liquor/convenience store and who, decades ago, was stationed at Camp Rosyln, is stabbed to death in the desert. He is found by George Creech, a Native American (Navajo) who says that he is in Gila Junction to complete a survey for the Department of Transportation's Highway Department. Deaver's much-younger widow, Marge, is unshaken by Whitey's death, but regrets all the debts he left her. (Later, it is suspected that Whitey was the "truck stop" bandit and that his killer vanished with the $100,000 horde.)

Kari continues her affair with Pete Menteer, who works at the hotel for Cal, Marge's financially strapped father. When Pete suddenly decides to leave town with money he claims he won in a crap game, Marge concludes he just might have killed her dad and taken the stolen money. As for Pete, he still lusts for Cal's other daughter, Dena, who works for the Department of Interior's Fish, Game and Wildlife Division. She's accepted a new position with the department on the Oregon peninsula, a fact which upsets her actual boyfriend, Gates. Then there is retarded Tiny Kerns, with his lifelong dream to find rumored buried treasure in the desert. He claims that a few years back he actually stumbled upon it, but lost his bearings and was never able to retrace his steps to the bonanza. Another involved in the case is Todd Hawkins, a vengeful victim of the "truck stop" bandit.

After many false leads, the old and new inquiries—including the identity of the "truck stop" bandit and Whitey's killer—are tied into a logical package by the indomitable Jessica.

Highlights: Usually the only amateur sleuth on a *Murder, She Wrote* adventure is Jessica Fletcher. Here resourceful reporter Norma Shey is present, and, despite her injury, this feisty woman is constantly jumping back into the fray. She and Jessica share many similar traits: ingenuity, determination, creativity and self-reliance. In contrast, the local sheriff is not even a full-time worker and seems far more competent tinkering over car parts.

As part of the 1990s emphasis on political correctness, many *Murder, She Wrote* segments feature ethnic minorities, who prove, despite their bigoted detractors, that they are bright, good-hearted and worthy. Such is the case with the character of George Creech who is disparaged frequently by intolerant Pete Menteer.

Trivia: Again, as in episode #239, the cast list of featured players for this segment is out of alpha order in the opening title credits, with actor Robert Rusler's name appearing *before* that of Douglas Roberts.

Dorothy Lyman won two Emmys playing Opal Gardner on the daytime soap opera *All My Children* (1981–1983). As Naomi Oates Harper, Lyman was seen as Ken Berry's tacky wife on the sitcom *Mama's Family* (1983–1985; 1986–1990). In the mid-1990s, she became the director of Fran Drescher's weekly sitcom, *The Nanny.* Bo Svenson's movie credits stretch from *The Great Waldo Pepper* (1975) to *Heartbreak Ridge* (1986) and to such later low-budget action features as *Steel Frontier* (1994). Guy Boyd played Dick Lochner on *Knots Landing* (1991–1992) and was Loren Bray in the pilot episode of *Dr. Quinn, Medicine Woman* (1993). (However, he was replaced in the actual series by Orson Bean.)

242. "Big Easy Murder"

(10/12/95) 60 mins.

Director: Vincent McEveety **Teleplay:** Cynthia Deming, William Royce

Regular: Angela Lansbury (Jessica Fletcher)

Guest Law Enforcer: G.W. Bailey (Lieutenant Alex Tibideaux)

Guest Cast: Ayo Adeyami (High Priest); Lisa Akey (Cynthia Broussard); Elizabeth Ashley (Emily Broussard Renwyck); Olivia Cole (Yvette Dauphin); Steve Curtis (Jim Nash); Robert Forster (Frank Roussel); Juliette Jeffers (Vera Welles); Anne-Marie Johnson (Priscilla Dauphin); Nick LaTour (Charlie); Brian McNamara (Tom McCray); Clifton Powell (Ralph Danton); Mitchell Ryan (Senator Brent Renwyck); George Sharperson (Waiter); Devino Tricoche (Fire Eater); Lewis Van Bergen (Mal Carter)

The Setting: New Orleans, Louisiana

The Case: Jessica Fletcher has come to Louisiana to research voodoo, jazz, illegal gambling and the like for her new book. However, her "tour" guide, Jimmy Nash, a young reporter on the *New Orleans Daily News*, has been murdered in the bayous. His is the fourth such machete killing in three months, in which a rooster foot talisman was placed next to each corpse. According to Tom McCray, a newspaper pal of Nash's, Jimmy thought these trademark homicides were a cover for the escalating turf wars among local supper clubs.

Jessica visits with longtime friend, wealthy Emily Broussard whose daughter, Cynthia, is an intern at the *Daily News*. Emily has recently married former Senator Brent Renwyck. The latter is opening a new night spot in New Orleans and, unknown to his wife, has been siphoning off money from her bank accounts and borrowing from underworld figures—such as Frank Roussell and his associate Mal Carter—to launch the enterprise. Working at the club is singer Priscilla Dauphin, whose mother, Yvette, has been the Broussards' housekeeper for thirty-five years. Another club worker is musician/helper Charlie, who once was the Broussards' chauffeur.

In pursuing her background study of voodoo, Jessica is assisted by curio shop employee Vera Welles. The latter takes her to a secret voodoo ceremony near the Goula Ruins where Nash was killed. Vera apparently had dated Nash and knows a great deal about his investigations into the turf war murders. She also is under the thumb of sadistic Ralph Danton, a thug employed by Roussel and Carter.

Later, Renwyck is found dead at home, an apparent heart attack victim. However, stubborn Lieutenant Alex Tibideaux—goaded by Mrs. Fletcher—determines that the hex doll found by the body and a pinprick puncture mark on the victim's right hand indicate it was murder. Everything becomes more complex when Priscilla admits to having been at Renwyck's home that night. There is also the question of the anonymous note Priscilla received involving the identity of Yvette's long-ago lover who is Priscilla's father.

Highlights: Curiosity about local atmosphere and her friend's murder lead Jessica Fletcher into the heart of voodoo country—the dank bayous—where she witnesses a frenzied ritual ceremony (shown in extended detail). More engaging, however, is Mrs. Fletcher's rapport with magnolia-sweet Emily Broussard Renwyck and sometimes feisty, sometimes fearful, Vera. Also, there is a richly entertaining sequence in which ever-inventive Jessica quickly adopts a syrupy Southern accent at an outdoor café to create a diversion so Tom McCray can escape the clutches of hulking Mr. Danton.

Trivia: This wasn't Jessica Fletcher's first visit to the atmospheric, dangerous Big Easy—the metropolis reputed to have the highest crime rate in the U.S. She had been there before for 1985's "Murder to a Jazz Beat" (#13), 1986's "The Perfect Foil" (#43) and 1991's "Judge Not" (#158).

Best-remembered as the foil of the misfits in the *Police Academy* movie series, G.W. Bailey had been Luther Rizzo on *M*A*S*H* (1979–1983) and Dr. Hugh Beale on *St. Elsewhere* (1982–1983). Mitchell Ryan's roster of TV shows include *Executive Suite* (1976–1977) *The Chisholms* (1980) and *2000 Malibu Road* (1992). Lisa Akey was in *Models, Inc.* (1995).

Robert Forster, who had been in an earlier New Orleans-set *Murder, She Wrote* escapade (#43), had starred in the private eye series *Banyon* (1972–1973). A member (1993–1994) of the *In Living Color* comedy troupe, Anne-Marie Johnson was featured as Virgil Tibbs's wife on the TV adaptation of *In the Heat of the Night* (1988–1993). Clifton Powell was a veteran of the TV sitcoms *Roc* (1993–1994) and *South Central* (1994). Brian McNamara's credits encompass *Homefront* (1992–1993) and *Pig Sty* (1995). Lewis Van Bergen had the lead in the adventure teleseries *Sable* (1987–1988).

243. "Home Care"

(10/19/95) 60 mins.

Director: Anthony Shaw **Teleplay:** Robert Van Scoyk

Regulars: Angela Lansbury (Jessica Fletcher); Ron Masak (Sheriff Mort Metzger); William Windom (Dr. Seth Hazlitt)

Recurring Characters: Louis Herthum (Deputy Andy Broom); Madlyn Rhue (Jean O'Neill)

Guest Cast: Mark Arnott (Dr. Kyle Adderly); Frances Bay (Sarah McCoy); William Converse-Roberts (Justin Haynes); John R. Crown (Reporter); Megan Porter Follows (Lila Nolan); James E. Hurd, Jr. (George, the Security Guard); Ivanek Zeljko (Eddie Saunders); Audra Lindley (Maggie Saunders); Kathryn Masak (Reporter); Ed Nelson (Henry Post); Stephanie Niznik (Dori Saunders); Tom O'Brien (Jason Giles); Robert Rothwell (Lucas McCoy); Elizabeth Wilson (Serena Haynes)

The Settings: Boston, Massachusetts; Cabot Cove, Maine

The Case: Jessica Fletcher rushes back to Maine to comfort her chum, Maggie Saunders, who, although released from the hospital, is still gravely ill. Dr. Seth Hazlitt felt his patient would fare more happily at home even if her live-in help is cranky Sarah McCoy and Sarah's alcoholic husband, Lucas. To insure Maggie's proper medical attention, Seth puts private nurse Lila Nolan, in charge of Ms. Saunders' round-the-clock needs. (Lila had recently returned to Maine after ending a bad relationship with possessive Dr. Kyle Adderly.)

Things do not run smoothly for well-to-do Maggie. Her grasping nephew, Eddie Saunders, wants her to support him and his pregnant wife. Equally avaricious Dori, who like her brother Eddie was raised by Maggie after their parents died, is goaded by her boyfriend, Jason Giles, to get her aunt to finance the Cabot Cove boutique Dori wants to open. However, testy Maggie has never forgiven Dori for moving out of the house to live with Jason. Then, there's banker Justin Haynes, who handles Maggie's finances. He has long had a crush on Dori but gains no points with her for refusing Jason a bank loan for Dori's boutique. On the plus side, there's portly Henry Post, an ex-marine who has known Maggie for years.

Early one morning Lila finds Maggie dead in bed. This causes a tumult in Cabot Cove, especially from Serena Haynes, whose elderly father had been tended by Lila. When he died, Serena had insisted that Lila had something to do with his sudden death and the deceased's missing jewelry. At the time, Dr. Seth Hazlitt had dismissed this as hogwash, as had Serena's son, Justin. However, Sheriff Mort Metzger is now pressured into investigating both deaths. Soon—with Jessica pointing the way—it evolves that Maggie died of strychnine poisoning. Further scrutiny uncovers that Lila, back in Boston, had had a string of aged patients who died under questionable circumstances.

Highlights: Many things have changed over the years in Cabot Cove, especially with Dr. Seth Hazlitt. Although he is still an old-fashioned doctor who believes in house calls, he now uses modern technology (e.g., a beeper). Moreover, never has the autocratic, aging soul appeared so vulnerable as when he wonders whether he has been an unwilling instrument of death by bringing Lila into Maggie's household.

Trivia: To be noted is the appearance of Kathryn Masak, the daughter of cast regular Ron Masak. She has the brief role of a reporter.

Audra Lindley is fondly recalled as acid-tongued, sex-hungry Helen Roper from the classic sitcom *Three's Company* (1977–1979) and its spin-off, *The Ropers* (1979–1980). Stage and film actress Elizabeth Wilson had been a cast member of TV's *East Side/West Side* (1963–1964) and *Morningstar/Eveningstar* (1986). Megan Porter Follows' credentials include being the ten-year-old offspring on *The Baxters* (1980–1981). Ivanek Zeljko had been the young priest in *Mass Appeal* (1984) and Ann-Margret's Aids-infected offspring in the TV movie *Our Sons* (1991). In his heyday, Ed Nelson was Dr. Michael Rossi on *Peyton Place* (1964–1969). William Converse-Roberts was Blair Brown's ex-husband on *The Days and Nights of Molly Dodd* (1987–1989; 1989–1991). Stephanie Niznik was government agent Judith Phillips on the syndicated series *Vanishing Son* (1995). Tom O'Brien was featured on the short-lived TV series *Men* (1989).

244a. "Nan's Ghost: Part One"

(11/2/95) 60 mins.

244b. "Nan's Ghost: Part Two"

(11/9/95) 60 mins.

Director: Anthony Shaw **Teleplay:** Bruce Lansbury

Regular: Angela Lansbury (Jessica Fletcher)

Guest Law Enforcers: Mark Lindsay Chapman (Policeman Matthew Ryan); John Karlen (Superintendent Arthur Joyce); Rod Taylor (Inspector Rory Lanahan)

Guest Cast: James Bartz (Jonathan Fisk); Leslie Bevis (Andrea Nader); Edita Brychta (Deidre O'Bannon); Leslie Davis (Walter Berkley); Fionnula Flanagan (Eileen O'Bannon); Peter Jason (Vincent Nader); Ross Kettle (Ian O'Bannon); Thomas Kopache (Leonard); Felicia Lansbury (Moira); Christopher Neame (Dr. John Sullivan); John St. Ryan (Jack Conroy); Raphael Sbarge (Peter Franklin); Wendy Schaal (Zuleika Brown); James Warwick (Paul Lafferty)

The Setting: County Cork, Ireland

The Case: Jessica Fletcher is in Ireland to visit good friend Rory Lanahan, who has just been promoted to police inspector. He is on holiday and is accompanying Jessica to Ballynook Castle, which Eileen O'Bannon, widowed for two years, has turned into a bed and breakfast operation. Thirty years ago, Rory had almost married Eileen and wants now to repropose to her. Belatedly, Mrs. Fletcher learns that Lanahan is using his vacation to go undercover and ferret out a gang of antique smugglers who are operating near Ballynook.

When Jessica and Rory arrive at the estate, everyone is still recoiling from the tragic death of eighteen-year-old Nan Conroy, a domestic at the castle whom everyone had assumed had left town suddenly. In reality, months ago, she had been accidentally locked in a dank basement room in the old section of the castle. Unable to summon help, she had died eventually. Her remains had only recently been discovered—by her father Jack, a town shopkeeper. Now, many folks, including Eileen, insist Nan's spirit "haunts" Ballynook, adding to the legends of the castle where supposedly a Celtic treasure trove has long remained hidden.

Meanwhile, grasping American tycoon Vincent Nader offers to purchase the castle and convert it into a modern hotel. Eileen's daughter Deidre, studying to be a doctor in Dublin, thinks her mother should sell, while Eileen's son, Ian, who supervises the estate farm, believes she must keep the property in the family.

Jessica has barely settled in at Ballynook when she hears strange noises and sees fleeting figures in the upstairs corridors. By the next day, Mrs. Fletcher has met the rest of the household. There's domestic Moira, Nan's best friend, and Leonard, the houseman/cook who has a hidden past. A frequent visitor is Dr. John Sullivan, owner of a Dublin antique shop, who has been courting Eileen in vain. He has also offered to lease the estate, leave the castle and lands as is, but close the farm. Among the paying guests is American book writer Zuleika Brown, an alcoholic divorcee, whom Jessica thinks she may have met before. Local police superintendent Arthur Joyce takes a fancy to Zuleika, and they are dating secretly. Another police enforcer with ties to the castle is young Matthew Ryan who loves Deidre.

One evening, Eileen hosts a party at the castle. Nader is shot to death on the lawn outside. The array of suspects includes Peter Franklin, a young hitchhiker who showed up at the castle ostensibly to return Mrs. Fletcher's wallet that she had lost en route to the castle. Also involved is Paul Lafferty, the dead man's solicitor. Later, there are two additional murders, as well as eccentric guests who hastily depart town and law-abiding people with hidden agendas.

Highlights: This two-part episode again shares with *Murder, She Wrote* viewers Jessica Fletcher's love of her ancestral country, full of quaint and dramatic history and boasting lush scenery. More so than ever before, Jessica's physical peril when "accidentally" locked in the rat-infested cellar is translated into a suspenseful physical soliloquy as she maneuvers to attract help to her plight. The camaraderie between the American novelist and the Irish police inspector, Rory Lanahan, is well-textured and warm-hearted. And as a bonus, there are the interludes where Jessica bristles from her encounters with the drunken, posturing American writer, the exotic Zuleika Brown.

Trivia: A previous *Murder, She Wrote* excursion set in the Emerald Isle (1995's "Another Killing in Cork" #203) had featured Rod Taylor in a different characterization. In his leading man days, he had starred in such teleseries as *Hong Kong* (1960–1961) and *Masquerade* (1983–1984). On *Falcon Crest* (1988–1990) he was Frank Agretti who weds Jane Wyman's character. Dublin-born Fionnula Flanagan was considered essential when it came to this series' Irish-set episodes (see #73, 203). She had won an Emmy as Best Supporting Actress in a Single Appearance for playing Clothilde in the miniseries *Rich Man, Poor Man* (1976).

Long before his Emmy Award-winning role on *Cagney & Lacey* (1982–1988), John Karlen made episode appearances on such series as *Look Up and Live* (1961), *The Gallant Men* (1962) and *East Side/West Side* (1964). Ross Kettle was also in the 1995 *Murder, She Wrote* installment "Another Killing in Cork." Wendy Schaal, daughter of comic actor Richard Schaal (once wed to Valerie Harper), had several ongoing roles on TV series: *AfterMASH* (1983–1984), *Nearly Departed* (1989), etc. Raphael Sbarge had the lead in the quickly canceled sitcom *Better Days* (1986). Angela Lansbury's niece Felicia has a larger role here than in past series assignments.

245. "Shooting in Rome"

(11/16/95) 60 mins.

Director: Vincent McEveety **Teleplay:** Jerry Ludwig

Regular: Angela Lansbury (Jessica Fletcher)

Recurring Characters: Lorenzo Caccialanza (Inspector Amati); Mike Connors (Boyce Brown)

Guest Cast: Bruce Abbott (Monte Hayes); Victor Alfieri (Italian Assistant Director); Lisa Banes (Lucy Hendrix); Allen Cutler (Gary Hayes); Louis Giambalvo (Raimondo Bonelli); Sam Hennings (Webb Prentiss); Allan Miller (Jake Farber); Antony Ponzini (Tomaso Curillo); Ben Reed (Rex Toland); Lisa Vultaggio (Adrianna Bonelli); Shawn Weatherly (Kate Danbury)

The Setting: Rome, Italy

The Case: Jessica Fletcher is in the picturesque Eternal City, but under a great deal of pressure at Cinecitta Studios. Producer Boyce Brown is filming one of her novels, but director Monte Hayes is demanding constant rewrites on the sets. Matters are not helped by flare-ups between Monte and his ex-wife, Kate Danbury, who is starring in the picture. Monte and Kate's son, Gary, who is a gofer on the production, is constantly smoothing over the conflicts between his parents. Meanwhile, this young man with a rebellious past has a crush on production assistant Adrianna Bonelli. The latter is the daughter of Raimondo Bonelli, who has trouble financing this production. He has turned to underworld figure Tomaso Curillo for "interim financing." This loan shark has been using his connection with Bonelli to have his thugs sneak on the sound stages at night and steal valuable equipment.

While hunky Rex Toland is the film's leading man, it's Webb Prentiss who handles the more dangerous stunt work. One key sequence involves a careening car chase which demands split-second accuracy. Prentiss claims the scene has been so carefully choreographed and the equipment so carefully inspected that even eighteen-year-old Gary could handle it, to which the latter agrees. At the last minute, Webb steps in and, while driving the stunt car, dies in a fatal smash-up. It's almost the last straw for harassed Boyce Brown, whose career depends on this picture being a hit.

Police inspector Amati, who has already been investigating the sound stage burglaries, supervises the homicide case. Others implicated in the fatality are script coordinator Lucy Hendrix, whose late father was a famous stuntman, and aggressive talent agent Jake Farber.

Highlights: *Murder, She Wrote* had employed filmmaking and TV production backdrops in several past episodes (e.g., #25, 233), but this offering provides the most sharply tuned depiction of the filmmaking process. (One character notes the irony of a movie about Texas being shot in Rome.) The day-to-day complexities, confusions and clashing egos of sound stage life are well represented.

Yet again, Jessica Fletcher displays her theatrical bent while gathering intelligence from slimy Curillo. She pretends to be Dominique, the efficient Italian executive assistant of Bonelli. It's a joyful conceit. On another level, in deciphering this mystery, Mrs. Fletcher demonstrates that her knowledge of math and calculators is very useful.

Trivia: In 1995's Hollywood-set "Film Flam" (#233), Jessica Fletcher had been pitching one of her novels to producer Boyce Brown. Also in 1995, in "Murder in High 'C'" (#231), Mrs. Fletcher had dealt with Inspector Piero Amato when a homicide occurred in Genoa, Italy. Now, he returns to the fore in this installment, recalling on-camera his year-ago encounter with Jessica during the Opera Festival murder case. (For no explained reason, Amato's surname has undergone a slight spelling change. He is now Inspector Amati.)

Lisa Banes was a veteran of *The Trials of Rosie O'Neill* (1990–1992).

Sam Hennings was a cast member of TV's *Trade Winds* (1993). Anthony Ponzini of *Flatbush* (1979), turned up in another teleseries, the failed night-time soap opera *Rituals* (1985). Allan Miller had assorted TV stints: *Battlestar Galactica* (1980—as Colonel Sydell), *Knots Landing* (1981–1982—as Scooter Warren), *The Human Factor* (1992), etc. After *J. J. Starbuck* (1987–1989), Shawn Weatherly was Jill Riley on *Baywatch* (1989–1990).

246. "Deadly Bidding"

(11/23/95) 60 mins.

Director: Anthony Shaw **Teleplay:** Tom Sawyer

Regular: Angela Lansbury (Jessica Fletcher)

Recurring Character: Wayne Rogers (Charlie Garrett)

Guest Law Enforcers: Tyrees Allen (Sergeant Unger); Charles Hoyes (Detective McKenna)

Guest Cast: Edd Byrnes (Kenneth Rundle); Kathleen Garrett (Mrs. Serena Rundle); Doug Hutchison (Angus Neville); Arahron Ipale (Lawrence Mezznou); Martin Jarvis (Giles Havelock); Renee Jones (Reggie Evans); Paul Lieber (Milt Solomon, Esq.); Dana Taylor Matthews (Waiter); Craig Richard Nelson (Felix Wesker); Melanie Smith (Diana Barrow); Jeff Williams (Pete Dunning)

The Setting: New York City

The Case: Two years previous, swindler Kenneth Rundle, in possession of a stolen Edward Degas painting, hires young forger Angus Neville to paint over the rare canvas. Neville assures Rundle his new oil work will not affect the masterpiece beneath that is worth $15 to $20 million.

Just before the start of this episode, Lawrence Mezznou and another thug assaulted Rundle at knife point on the streets of Manhattan. They demanded the missing Degas art work. The frightened Kenneth had a heart attack and died on the spot.

Today, Jessica Fletcher, on behalf of the Museum of Cultural History, is negotiating for a rare Sir Arthur Conan Doyle journal that has surfaced. However, she won't approve the purchase from fine arts dealer Felix Wesker until he provides documentation of authenticity. (In a past transaction, the effete merchant sold the Museum a forged etching.) Because she has delayed so long in making a decision, Wesker has consigned the Doyle manuscript for sale at the Greylight Auction Gallery run by Giles Havelock. Meanwhile, Angus Neville wants another loan from Wesker, who has already advanced him $50,000 in exchange for his output of paintings. Angus intends to buy back "Arrangement in Gray and Red" (the painting covering the Degas original) which has been put up for auction by Kenneth Rundle's widow, Serena. Felix refuses to advance Neville further funds.

Along comes unsuspecting private investigator Charlie Garrett. He has been hired by attorney Milt Solomon to attend the auction and bid up to $100,000 to acquire the "Arrangement." A lowbrow on the best of occasions, Garrett is totally out of his element at the auction, even after he encounters a very surprised Jessica and she vainly coaches him on proper auction etiquette. A perplexed Charlie outbids himself (!) as well as Mezznou and Wesker and becomes the owner of "Arrangement" for $400,000. Until he pays the amount, Garrett's purchase remains locked at the auction gallery. Later that night, Neville breaks into the auction warehouse and retrieves the precious painting. However, back at home, he is stabbed to death.

The police not only have to decipher the crime scene, but must cope with Jessica and Charlie, who (un)intentionally work at cross-purposes with one another. Helping with needed information is Reggie Evans, a Cultural History Museum employee whose boyfriend, Pete Dunning, is an assistant at the Greylight Gallery. Then there is Diana Barrows, who is in league with her double-dealing boyfriend, the married Milt Solomon.

Highlights: Foolhardy Charlie Garrett is perhaps the least likely soul one would imagine invading the world of fine art. However, he remains unfazed. In fact, the situation makes him more cocky. Nevertheless, he tags after Mrs. Fletcher knowing that she will wrap up the case long before he can. The fly in the ointment is that Jessica has been lied to one time too often by Charlie and—almost—doesn't help the befuddled man this time around.

There's a gem of a scene at a fancy Manhattan restaurant. To extricate herself and inept Garrett from Mezznou and his henchman, Jessica pretends there's a bug in her soup. Jumping up, she screams and grimaces as she ladles the imaginary bug onto the floor. In the ensuing confusion, she and the impressed Charlie beat a hasty retreat.

Trivia: This is the fifth *Murder, She Wrote* appearance of downtrodden private investigator Charlie Garrett.

Kathleen Garrett was Dana Burns on *WKRP in Cincinnati* (1991–1992). On *L.A. Law* (1989–1990), Renee Jones played Diane Moses. Craig Richard Nelson made such films as *The Paper Chase* (1973) and *My Bodyguard* (1980). Jeff Williams was Dr. Lewis Niles on the TV medical drama *Birdland* (1994).

247. "Frozen Stiff"

(11/30/95) 60 mins.

Director: Paul Lazarus **Teleplay:** Mark A. Burley

Regular: Angela Lansbury (Jessica Fletcher)

Guest Law Enforcers: Christopher Curry (Sheriff Mike Chubb); Red Sanders (Coroner)

Guest Cast: Dirk Benedict (Gary Herling); Don Bovinglow (Kyle McGregor); Kristen Dalton (Carol Herling); Ann Hearn (Peggy Evans); Gregory Itzin (Ralph Brewer); Sarah Koskoff (Victoria); Christina Pickles (Susan McGregor); Bill Smitrovich (Larry Armstrong [Leonard Atkins]); Bryan Travis Smith (Woodstock "Woody" Seabrook); Charles C. Stevenson, Jr. (Priest); George Wyner (Jim Kenton)

The Setting: Wisconsin

The Case: One evening, Kyle McGregor, accountant for the rural Wisconsin-based Gary and Larry's Frozen Stuff ice cream company, is shot in the executive offices. His death is partially witnessed by Woody Seabrook, a young mailroom employee who, from his place of concealment, cannot see the murderer. (Woody had been there searching for confidential data he wanted.)

Sheriff Mike Chubb and the coroner conclude it's most likely a case of suicide. Kyle's widow, Susan, is shocked. But worse news comes later. It's revealed that twenty years ago in California, the deceased had been involved in an embezzlement swindle and only escaped a prison sentence by testifying against his cohorts: his then wife and her boyfriend. As it turns out, McGregor was a bigamist when he later wed Susan in Wisconsin.

That same evening, Jessica Fletcher is a house guest of Larry Armstrong, co-owner of the ice cream company. She has known him since 1974 when he returned from college in France. Now, as a member of the Literary Foundation board, she is here to collect the sizable funds raised by G & L for her charity and to discuss further fund-raising efforts.

Visiting the plant, Mrs. Fletcher observes the growing dissension between altruistic Larry and his grasping partner, Gary Herling. Things take a sour turn when the $750,000 earmarked for the Literary Foundation is missing. There is also the problem of appeasing Ralph Brewer of the Verity consumer group. He insists he will announce to the world that the plant is using impure ingredients unless the irregularities are remedied at once.

As tensions mount at G & L, another death occurs: Herling is found frozen stiff in the warehouse freezer. It's determined he was first shot dead. Later, Gary's avaricious widow, Carol, announces that she intends to become the company's new CEO. (Her unsavory ways are no surprise to Brewer, who knew her years ago in New York. Recently, he has renewed their affair.) Meanwhile, the other key employees are in turmoil: security head Peggy Evans; Victoria, McGregor's assistant who is now in charge of the accounting department; and Jim Kenton, the corporation's public relations man who used to be a scandal tabloid reporter. The latter is a specialist at digging up dirt on others and has used this skill at G & L for personal financial gain.

Highlights: With *so many* of this episode's participants not whom they seem to be and so many individuals bursting with anger and regret, the installment benefits from balancing levity. One such instance is the running gag of Larry Armstrong betting Jessica that she can't analyze the ingredients of G & L's Tropical Secret ice cream. Thanks to the state police lab at Racine, Mrs. Fletcher wins the $1.00 wager!

Trivia: Bill Smitrovich played police detective Danny Krychek on *Crime Story* (1988) and, more impressively, was Drew Thatcher, the head of the household in the teledrama *Life Goes On* (1989–1993). British-born Christina Pickles's series ranged from *The Guiding Light* (1970–1971) to *The People Next Door* (1989), but she made her mark as Nurse Helen Rosenthal on *St. Elsewhere* (1982–1988). An alumnus of *Chopper One* (1974) and *Battlestar Galactica* (1978–1979), Dirk Benedict was cast as hunky Templeton "Faceman" Peck on *The A-Team* (1983–1987). Ann Hearn has been in such 1990s features as *My Father, The Hero* (1993). Gregory Itzin was part of Gene Wilder's *Something Wilder* (1994–1995). Sarah Koskoff was on the sitcom *Great Scott!* (1992). George Wyner was a TV series staple: *Delvecchio, Nero Wolfe, Good Advice* and, most importantly, *Hill Street Blues* (1982–1987—as Assistant District Attorney Irwin Bernstein).

248. "Unwilling Witness"

(12/14/95) 60 mins.

Director: Anthony Shaw **Teleplay:** Robert Van Scoyk

Regular: Angela Lansbury (Jessica Fletcher)

Guest Law Enforcers: Randall Carver (U.S. Marshall Morgan); Lisa Eichhorn (Special Prosecutor Annette Rayburn [Carla Annette Holland]); Stan Ivar (Lieutenant Shawn Riley); Paul Ivy (U.S. Attorney John Wicks); Dree Lange (Police Sergeant)

Guest Cast: Joel Brooks (Ted Duffy); Vicki Browder (TV Newsperson); Ron Dean (Lou the Lawyer); J. Downing (Nicholas Logan); Shea Farrell

(Reed Harding); Larry Linville (Paige Corbin); Janel Moloney (Maria Corbin); Sydney Walsh (Tiffany Beckman); Peter White (Mason Logan)

The Setting: New York City

The Case: It's no surprise to Mason Logan, the ailing board chairman of Logan Investment Services, that federal authorities are about to raid his Wall Street firm for Security Exchange Commission irregularities. Already, the firm's executive vice-president, Douglas Freemont, has fled New York, and now Logan departs before Special Prosecutor Annette Rayburn and her team arrive. CEO Paige Corbin, numbed by the turn of events, risks arrest by refusing to cooperate with Rayburn. Later, Logan advises Corbin, his longtime buddy, to (1) stay off the bottle and (2) not say a word about Hong Kong (where the firm has unorthodox stock holdings).

Soon thereafter, while signing copies of her latest book, *The Venomous Valentine*, at a Manhattan shop, Jessica Fletcher is subpoenaed to appear before the grand jury in the Logan fraud case. At the courtroom hearing, baffled Jessica claims her only association with the firm is having bought a few mutual fund shares for her grand-niece. Rayburn counters that according to phone records, Corbin had called Mrs. Fletcher the night he vanished. Jessica denies this violently, but later recalls that she did have a strange hang-up call that evening. When Jessica cannot supply Rayburn with more details, the writer is held in contempt of the grand jury. Thanks to her attorney Lou, who had once dated Annette, Jessica is freed on a technicality.

Helped by accommodating police lieutenant Shawn Riley, Jessica "breaks" into Corbin's apartment, and the trail leads them to the Soho Storage Company. There Corbin is found stabbed to death. As the case gets more complex, Jessica must circumvent the federal marshal who has a new summons for her. Meanwhile, she analyzes the roles played by the others engulfed in this mounting disaster. They include Logan's son, Nicholas, who spirited Corbin to the deadly hideout; Corbin's schoolteacher daughter, Maria, who was at polar odds with her dad; Logan firm executive Reed Harding, who conspired with company vice-president Tiffany Beckman to turn the bad situation to their advantage; and unscrupulous newspaper photographer Ted Duffy, who has been blackmailing certain parties to the case.

Highlights: As many have learned, Jessica Fletcher is *not* one to be trifled with, especially when she is in the right! Her courtroom confrontations with the badgering Annette Rayburn prompt the exasperated writer to be at her most vitriolic. Throughout the episode, there's the running joke of Jessica keeping—barely—a few steps ahead of U.S. Marshal Morgan, who is determined to hand her the latest subpoena.

Trivia: For the record, Jessica Fletcher's New York City apartment phone number is (212) 124–7199.

Joel Brooks of the droopy mustache was a member of TV's *Private Benjamin* and *Hail to the Chief*, and was seen as J.D. Lucas, the photography agent on *My Sister Sam* (1986–1988). Peter White was in the off-Broadway (1968) and film (1970) versions of *Boys in the Band.* More recently, on *Sisters* (1991–1996), in flashbacks and fantasy sequences, White appeared as WASPish Dr. Halsey, the deceased father of the siblings. Shea Farrell, remembered as Mark Danning, the public-relations director of *Hotel* (1983–1986), turned up as Agent Sean Quinlan on *The Untouchables* (1994). Randall Carver played John Burns on TV's *Taxi* (1978–1979). Stan Ivar was John Carter on *Little House on the Prairie* (1982–1983). Ron Dean played Chief Kramer on *Crime Story* (1986–1987) and Sydney Walsh appeared in *Melrose Place* (1992–1994) as Kay Beacon.

249. "Kendo Kill"

(1/4/96) 60 mins.

Director: Walter Grauman **Teleplay:** Laurence Heath

Regular: Angela Lansbury (Jessica Fletcher)

Guest Law Enforcer: James Ishida (Inspector Ota)

Guest Cast: Jesse Borja (Chauffeur); Maggie Han (Nobu Hitaki); George Kee Cheung (Ikuma Nakata); Bruce Locke (Koji Hitaki); Byron Mann (Yosuke Ishida); Pat Morita (Akira Hitaki); David Stratton (Rick Walsh); James Wong (Waiter); Tom Wopat (Bill Dawson); Vivian Wu (Miko Ishida)

The Setting: Osaka, Japan

The Case: Jessica Fletcher is now in Osaka, Japan, to lecture at the university. At her hotel she is the victim of a burglary, but the thief does not get a computer diskette which Mrs. Fletcher later delivers to motorcycle racer Rick Walsh on behalf of his mother. Mrs. Walsh had found it in the father's possessions after his death. To Miko Ishida, Jessica presents an advance copy of *From the Heart,* a translation of poetry that Jessica helped Miko get published.

Jessica quickly finds herself caught up in the romantic and business rivalries of her friends. Miko loves Rick, but her traditionalist brother, Yosuke, demands that she wed Koji Hitaki, to whom she was pledged as a child. (Yosuke knows that he cannot win an upcoming political campaign if his sister is still dating a Caucasian.) However, Miko regards Koji as a brother. She knows that his only interest is racing motorcycles, not wedding her or taking an assertive role in the Hitaki Motors conglomerate founded by his father, Akira. On the other hand, Koji's ambitious sister Nobu hungers to succeed her father as CEO, a role not usually available for Japanese women. Also, Mrs. Fletcher is reintroduced to Bill Dawson, a former cyclist who is competing with Rick to sell Hitaki Motors a new fuel injection system. If Dawson is successful, he will become head of the company's U.S. plant division in Dallas, Texas.

During trial runs of Motorcycle Team Hitaki, coached by Ikuma Nakata, Rick's bike explodes, but Walsh escapes injury. It becomes apparent that someone tampered with the fuel mixture. Later, at the Kendo Hall, where Koji and Rick are scheduled to practice fencing, Koji is killed by a masked duelist. The news leads to Akira's near fatal heart attack, but allows Nobu her dream—to run the company. When Rick is arrested for the murder, Jessica must prove her friend's innocence, working in tandem with Inspector Ota.

Highlights: Two qualities that keep Jessica Fletcher vibrant—and her adventures fresh—are her ability to keep up with the times technologically and her capacity to adapt easily to alien environments. She does both in this caper, demonstrating her growing resourcefulness with the computer, her ease at using chopsticks, and her ability to cope diplomatically with a foreign food delicacy (spoiled beans) that she orders by error.

Trivia: Although she had been to Hong Kong in past episodes, this was Jessica Fletcher's first real on-camera trek to Japan.

Japanese-American character actor Pat Morita was Academy Award-nominated for *The Karate Kid* (1984), a film hit which led to sequels. His TV series ranged from *Sanford and Sons* (1974–1975) to *Happy Days* (1975–1976; 1982–1983). Tom Wopat, a real-life country singer, gained fame as hunky Luke Duke on TV's *The Dukes of Hazzard* (1979–1985) and enjoyed a career resurgence with the sitcom *Cybill* (1995-), as well as a Nashville-based television talk show. David Stratton was part of the syndicated adventure teleseries *Lightning Force* (1991–1992). Maggie Han of *Teech* (1991) and *Black Tie Affair* (1993) costarred with George Segal in the detective drama *Murphy's Law* (1988–1989).

250. "Death Goes Double Platinum"

(1/7/96) 60 mins.

Director: Anthony Shaw **Teleplay:** Philip John Taylor

Regular: Angela Lansbury (Jessica Fletcher)

Guest Law Enforcer: Maria O'Brien (Lieutenant Abbe Esposito)

Guest Cast: Jason Bernard (Wilson Sloane); Robert Clohessy (Max Daniels); Nick Corri (Alex Lebron); Rosana DeSoto (Iza Decalde); Ramon Franco (Sam Desoto); David Labiosa (Tomas Aguilar); Dee McCafferty (Updike, the Hitman); Jacqueline Obradors (Patricia Decalde); Tony Plana (Desi Ortega); Marco Sanchez (Luiz Decalde); Amy Stock-Poynton (Amy Ortega); Ray Young (Culligan)

The Setting: New York City

The Case: Once more teaching at Manhattan University, Jessica Fletcher arranges for blind musician Desi Ortega and his group of fellow Latin instrumentalists to use the school's sound lab. Her faith in their exciting new sound (bolstered by the group's engineer, Sam Desoto) is proven when they turn out a hit single.

This is good news for Desi and his pregnant wife. However, Max Daniels, a punk from the old Brooklyn neighborhood, who now operates illegal enterprises, suddenly reacquaints himself with Desi. Daniels demands that Ortega fire Alex Lebron, the group's young manager who owns a small CD label, and make Max their manager. If Desi refuses, Daniels threatens to cut off his local record distribution and/or hurt Amy. To improve the odds, Max has henchman Tomas Aguilar persuade former pal Luiz Decalde, the band's bass guitarist, to make Ortega comply. Making matters more complicated, Luiz's sister, Patricia, dates Alex Lebron, and Aguilar still lusts for her.

Next, Jessica arranges for her pal, Wilson Sloane, owner of Paragram Records, to be at a showcasing of Desi's group at the Casino Decalde run by Luiz's widowed mother, Iza. It develops that years before, Sloane had gotten Daniels arrested on a payola charge. (Jessica asks police lieutenant Abbe Esposito, currently lecturing to Mrs. Fletcher's class, to verify this data.) Before the Friday night playdate, Desi and Amy are almost run down in a garage, and Alex, unknowingly, comes close to being killed by Daniels' hit man. He is saved only when Patricia agrees to go to bed with Aguilar. Learning of Tomas's independent actions, Max tells him he is "dead."

At the crucial Friday performance, while the lights dim for special effects, Aguilar is murdered. A puncture wound in the victim's neck sets the stage for trapping the killer. The climax revolves on Desi's unusually sharp hearing, employed by Jessica to recall particular sounds during crucial moments of the group's performance that murderous evening.

Highlights: Much energy is devoted to capturing the Latin beat and the ethnic ambiance, all to give *Murder, She Wrote* a more "with it" contemporary flavor. As was typical in this series, few of the female law enforcers are sympathetic or memorable characters. Here, Lieutenant Abbe Esposito of the Anne Meara school of acting is especially abrasive, making quite a contrast to the more genteel and astute Mrs. Fletcher.

Trivia: Jason Bernard was Deputy Inspector Marquette on *Cagney & Lacey* (1982–1983) and Robert Clohessy was Officer Patrick Flaherty on *Hill Street Blues* (1986–1987). Rosana DeSoto was part of the sitcom *The Redd Foxx Show* (1986). Ramon Franco enacted Private Alberto Ruiz on *Tour of Duty* (1987–1990). Tony Plana's work includes the detective TV show *Veronica Clare* (1991) and the police sitcom *Bakersfield P.D.* (1993–1994). Marco Sanchez was aboard *seaQuest DSV* (1993–1996).

251. "Murder in Tempo"

(1/11/96) 60 mins.

Director: Kevin Corcoran **Story:** David Thoreau **Teleplay:** Laurence Heath

Regulars: Angela Lansbury (Jessica Fletcher); Ron Masak (Sheriff Mort Metzger); William Windom (Dr. Seth Hazlitt)

Recurring Characters: Louis Herthum (Deputy Andy Broom); Madlyn Rhue (Jean O'Neill)

Guest Cast: Sam Anderson (Dan, the Electrician); Keith Coulouris (Tommy Vaughn); John D'Aquino (Wylie Trey); Megan Gallivan (Rachel Weldon); Amy Hathaway (Udella Vaughn); Whip Hubley (Musician); Lawrence Noel Larsen (Abner, the Banker); Ernie Lively (Hal Palmer); John Livingston (Blue Maddox); Josh Taylor (Jim Maddox)

The Setting: Cabot Cove, Maine

The Case: Dr. Seth Hazlitt heads a local committee to Save the Maine Woods. As such, he is in charge of a benefit concert to feature nationally popular Tommy Vaughn and his band, In Tempo. Jessica Fletcher has even flown in from New York City to deliver a fund-raising address.

Despite Seth's reassurances, Jessica senses trouble brewing. For starters, construction company owner Jim Maddox demands the overdue payment for equipment rentals. Meanwhile, Jim has little to say to his son, Blue, a member of Vaughn's band. Next, at the concert rehearsal, the sound system proves faulty, which Dan, the electrician, is ordered to repair. Then, an unknown assailant shoots at Tommy. Vaughn is unharmed, but as everyone drops to take cover, Seth sustains injuries. Later, Mrs. Fletcher recalls that a stalker had pursued Vaughn in Denver, Colorado, last year.

Dissension escalates as Tommy, the Bad Boy of Music, has trouble hitting the high notes. Then he and his wife, Udella, the group's lead singer, argue about divorcing. Although it will mean losing the pending Comet Records deal, Udella is tired of coping with her husband's drinking problem and his flirtatious habits. (Currently, he is romancing Rachel Weldon, employed at Hal Palmer's local emporium. The latter, a widower, has a romantic interest in Rachel as does Blue.) Meanwhile, Maddox offers Wylie Trey, the band's agent, a huge payoff to have the concert canceled. Double–dealing Wylie shares Maddox's proposal with Tommy, but lies about the true amount offered.

To Wylie's disgust—since he had already taken Maddox's money—Tommy decides to give the concert. At the final rehearsal, with the stage wet from a rain shower, Vaughn is electrocuted by an equipment short circuit. Sheriff Mort Metzger arrests Dan, the electrician, when it's learned Maddox had paid him to sabotage the gig. However, Jessica is not so easily convinced. After all, there was a miniature guitar left at the murder site, similar to the trademark symbol used by the Denver stalker. And what of the fact that the deceased, unlike the other band members, had been wearing leather-soled shoes?

Highlights: Episodes set in Cabot Cove have a special coziness not found in other *Murder, She Wrote* segments. It's a special bonus when the focus is on crusty Dr. Seth Hazlitt, whose waistline is expanding as fast as his civic conscience. Also the great rapport between Seth and Jessica has grown more complex over the years as irascible Hazlitt relies increasingly on Mrs. Fletcher's companionship and her problem-solving skills. (And to please young viewers here, there are the contemporary sounds of the band rehearsals.)

Trivia: Josh Taylor played Valerie Harper's husband on *Valerie* (1986–1987), which became *The Hogan Family* (1987–1991) when she quit the TV sitcom. He was Luke Perry's father on *Beverly Hills 90210* (1991–1993). Megan Gallivan was seen on *Married People* (1990–1991) and *Sweet Justice* (1994–1995). Amy Hathaway was part of TV's *My Two Dads* (1989–1990) and *Arresting Behavior* (1992). This was character actor Sam Anderson's fourth *Murder, She Wrote* appearance and the fifth for Ernie Lively. In every instance, each character actor played a different role.

252. "The Dark Side of the Door"

(2/1/96) 60 mins.

Director: Anthony Shaw **Teleplay:** James L. Novack

Regular: Angela Lansbury (Jessica Fletcher)

Guest Law Enforcers: Rodney Frazier (Detective Rogers); Richard Libertini (Lieutenant Phil Corelli)

Guest Cast: Richard Beymer (Dirk Matheson); Dennis Creaghan (Charles, the Literary Agent); Meg Foster (Laura Kerwin); Mary-Pat Green (Nora Delano); Tracy Middendorf (Erin Garman); Taylor Nichols (Drew Finley); John Oliver (Mike Holbert); Marcia Strassman (Terry Garman Holbert); Brittny Trouville (Little Erin); Michael Tylo (Sonny, the Physical Fitness Trainer)

The Setting: New York City

The Case: Author Dirk Matheson hasn't had a new novel published in over a year. He is currently writing *Blindfold,* a thriller dealing with a kidnapping, which is to be published by Hartley House, the firm that releases Jessica Fletcher's whodunits. Matheson's editor at Hartley House is Laura Kerwin, with whom he is having a romance. A copy of the manuscript lands on the desk of junior editor Erin Garman, who is fact checking Jessica's latest work.

When Erin reads *Blindfold,* she is greatly upset because it's so factually similar to her own kidnapping years ago. Then, her mother, Terry Garman, had ransomed her for $3 million. Distraught Erin phones police lieutenant Phil Corelli, who had handled the old unsolved kidnapping and whom Erin has contacted several times since—always with a new case lead that never bore fruit. Cynical Corelli reminds her that the statue of limitation on the kidnapping has run out. Besides, he is busy now with a homicide, that of Nora Delano found shot to death on the docks.

Hysterical Erin, still under a therapist's care, receives only token sympathy from her preoccupied mother, Terry, who in recent years has wed Mike Holbert. The Holberts operate a chic health club, Nirvana, and plan to open a larger facility on Long Island. Their current staff physical trainer is Sonny, who hopes to become manager of the new club. On the other hand, Erin's boyfriend, Drew Finley, who works for the city, is sympathetic to the anxiety caused Erin by Matheson's "fiction."

Clues in the Delano murder lead Corelli to Matheson's hotel suite. Dirk admits he met Nora Delano two years ago in a Tucson, Arizona, bar and that he paid her for her kidnapping "story" which became the basis for *Blindford.* He claims he had not seen her again until a few days ago when she attempted to blackmail him at the docks. He insists he did not kill Delano, who the police have deduced was involved in Erin's childhood kidnapping. Later, Matheson is found dead, an apparent suicide. He left a typed confession that he was the other kidnapper and that he had murdered Nora. Jessica notes that several tapes containing his background interviews with Nora are now missing from Dirk's desk and suspects Dirk was murdered as well.

Highlights: Overburdened with plot "coincidences" and extended flashbacks, this episode relies on fast pacing to distract the viewer from storyline flaws. A running gag has doting father, Lieutenant Corelli, insisting that his five-year-old son has genius-level talents. Each time he projects a new adulthood career for his offspring, he asks the amused but indulgent Mrs. Fletcher to use her contacts to pave the way—*now*—for Bobby's future.

Trivia: Richard Libertini previously played a lawman on *Murder, She Wrote.* On 1993's "Dead to Rights (#192), he was Portland, Maine's, Lieutenant Gabriel Rodino.

Among Meg Foster's recent movies are *Blind Fury* (1990), *Hidden Fears* (1993) and *Shrunken Heads* (1994). Marcia Strassman, whose series work encompassed *M*A*S*H* and *Booker,* played Gabe Kaplan's wife on *Welcome Back, Kotter* (1975–1979). Tracy Middendorf was Laura Kingman on *Beverly Hills 90210* (1993–1994). Taylor Nichols was a veteran of the James Garner sitcom *Man of the People* (1991), while Michael Tylo had been Luis Ramone, the Alcalde, on TV's *Zorro* (1990–1991).

253. "Murder Among Friends"

(2/8/96) 60 mins.

Director: Vincent McEveety **Teleplay:** Jerry Ludwig

Regular: Angela Lansbury (Jessica Fletcher)

Guest Law Enforcers: Frederick Coffin (Lieutenant Roy Flint); Kirk Thornton (Policeman)

Guest Cast: Jim Bochelman (Featured Cast Member of the TV Sitcom *Buds*); Bill Brocktrup (Gene Gains); Robin Curtis (Rosemary Tynan); Cameron Dye (Alex Bower); Terri Hanauer (Joy); Garrison Hershberger (Timothy Flint); Cindy Katz (Ricki Vardian); Allison Smith (Carly McAllister); Nicolas Surovy (Leo Vardian); John Terlesky (Vince Denisco); Barbara Alyn Woods (Dyan Emery)

The Setting: Los Angeles, California

The Case: Jessica Fletcher is in Hollywood taping her hosting chores for *Education on the Air: The Mystery.* This TV documentary is focusing on classic screen mysteries, especially those of Alfred Hitchcock.

Jessica's harried producer is Leo Vardian, who is preoccupied with his more commercial venture, the hit TV series *Buds.* Leo is having domestic and professional problems with his adulterous wife, Ricki, the show's executive producer and head writer. Moreover, the new network management demands that the Vardians cut costs by eliminating at least one of the six *Buds'* stars. Ricki diplomatically agrees, while Leo would prefer to trim behind-the-camera dead weight.

Jessica becomes enmeshed in the behind-the-scenes turmoil at *Buds* because Gene Gains, one of her former Manhattan University students, is now a staff writer on the series. Gene tells Jessica that he is doing most of the scripting, but that Ricki takes the credit. It's also evident that Gains has a unrequited crush on Carly McAllister, one of the *Buds.*

Word spreads on *Buds* that a cast regular is to be fired. This is good news for blond Dyan Emery, who is up for a movie lead. In contrast, Vince Denisco, who is dating costar Carly, fears that he may be the one discharged, especially since Ricki has ended their affair. As for cast member Timothy Flint—whom Jessica also knew from Manhattan University—he wonders if his lack of promoting the series will ruin his career. (It also doesn't help that Timothy's controlling father, police lieutenant Roy Flint, acting as his son's unofficial agent, has been making a big nuisance of himself with the Vardians.)

Ricki plans to write out one of the *Buds* that night and then lock the script in her wall safe until it's time to shoot that key episode. Meanwhile, Leo, aware of Ricki's relationship with Vince, pays Alex Bower, a former L.A. vice squad officer, to have Roy Flint pull Denisco's police record. The file was sealed long ago because Vince, at the time, was a youthful offender.

That evening, Jessica comes to Ricki's office where she finds the woman sprawled dead on the floor, and the wall safe is wide open.

Highlights: It was no secret that series star Angela Lansbury was miffed when *Murder, She Wrote,* going into its 12th season, was switched from its Sunday night berth to the fatal time slot opposite a rival network's hit comedy, *Friends* (1994-). The similarities between *Buds* and *Friends* are overt (e.g., the similar theme music, the parallel physical looks of the two casts and the comparable plot lines in which six twentysomething individuals hang about a trendy coffee shop discussing life and love.)

Beyond the satirical barbs aimed at *Friends,* this script is a superior insiders' look at how a sitcom operates, including the hassles on the sound stages and elsewhere. The gimmick of Jessica gaining sudden insight to the current crime by watching a sequence from Alfred Hitchcock's *Strangers on a Train* (1951) is clever plotting. Additionally, there are the down-to-earth moments as Jessica dispenses career and relationship advice to several characters.

Trivia: Once again, as in 1995's "Film Flam" (#233), the action is set at Monolith Studios. This was the first *Murder, She Wrote* episode to feature a police investigator who is also an obsessive stage father. Although he eventually repents of this sin, manipulative Lieutenant Flint could benefit from a refresher course in police ethics.

Frederick Coffin's acting resume includes movies like *Hard to Kill* (1989) and *There Goes My Baby* (1992). The son of opera star Rise Stevens, Nicolas Surovy's recent films are *Forever Young* (1992) and *12:01* (1993). Gary Hershberger was Mike Nelson on *Twin Peaks* (1990–1991). William Bochtrup had a recurring role as the gay civilian assistant on *NYPD Blue* (1995-). Allison Smith played Jane Curtin's daughter on the sitcom *Kate & Allie* (1984–1989). John Terlesky's series work includes *Paradise* (1991), *Sirens* (1993) and *Last Frontier* (1996).

254. "Something Foul in Flappieville"

(2/15/96) 60 mins.

Director: Anthony Shaw **Story:** Dan Wilcox **Teleplay:** Robert Van Scoyk

Regular: Angela Lansbury (Jessica Fletcher)

Guest Law Enforcer: Brian Cousins (Lieutenant Spevak)

Guest Cast: Corinne Bohrer (Helena McKenna); Maryedith Burrell (Nattie Holt); Bryan Cranston (Parker Foreman); Richard Dano (Terry Fusco); Thom Fountain (Puppeteer); Alan Fudge (Gus Hayward); Wendy Hoffman (Carol); Kimberley Kates (Kim Swatner); Stephen T. Kay (Darren Crosley); Robert Knepper (Robbie Dorow); Steven Martini (Jason Cardino); Richardson Morse (Arvin Buckwell); Rene (Puppeteer); Douglas Seymore (Puppeteer); Ian Shaw (Stevie); Dey Young (Mary Dorow)

The Setting: Los Angeles, California

The Case: No one is more surprised than Jessica Fletcher when one of her children's stories—written initially for her grand-nephews and grand-nieces—comes to the attention of TV producers. In particular, it's her delightful character, Inspector Le Chat. Involved in the Saturday morning TV program on which Le Chat will be tested is arrogant master puppeteer/producer Darren Crosley. He insists that there's no finer character than his own creation—Pound Dog, the chief hound in the fantasy town of Flappieville. However, smarmy network executive Parker Foreman disagrees, claiming that Pound Dog is dying in the audience ratings. According to double-dealing Foreman, Le Chat might become a lead character on its own show—without Crosley's input.

Meanwhile, toy manufacturer Robbie Dorow is distracted from making preproduction decisions regarding Le Chat products due to network intrigues and problems with his wife, Mary. Others involved are Jason

Cardino, a new creative force on the children's show, as well as Helena McKenna, his department coworker. There is also the show's stressed-out director Gus Hayward and his ex-wife, Nattie Holt, the queen of voices for puppet programming.

Le Chat is tested in front of a focus group of children. Young Stevie, a foster child, and the other kiddie audience members agree that the inspector is a wonderful personality (even if the voice—presently supplied by Crosley—sounds too much like Pound Dog). It's initially decided that Le Chat should be given his own show and that Stevie should be a "consultant" on the new project. Fearful that his program will be canceled, Crosley offers Mrs. Fletcher a higher percentage of royalties if she will insure that Le Chat remains part of the Pound Dog entry. Meanwhile, other avaricious behind-the-camera talents angle to take advantage of the bounty that Le Chat is sure to create.

Later, Arvin Buckwell, a studio security guard, is found dead at the TV facility, a victim of a massive blow to the head. Near the corpse is the Inspector Le Chat puppet with a flatiron in his fuzzy hand.

One thing of which Mrs. Fletcher is certain, Inspector Le Chat could not have been the murderer. As she and Lieutenant Spevak assemble the clues, they realize the importance of an audio cassette recording made of a confidential outdoors meeting between two of the program's staff and how blackmail figures into the homicide. Also to be unraveled is how Terry Fusco fits into the life of Mary Dorow.

Highlights: It was a novel approach to have a children's TV show be the backdrop for a murder, even if the villains were all adults. Jessica Fletcher's great love for children is apparent in her interaction with the kiddie focus group.

Trivia: This chapter boasted three generations of the Lansbury clan: Angela, her director son Anthony, and six-year-old Ian, Ms. Lansbury's grandchild.

Corinne Bohrer was a pretty young witch in TV's *Free Spirit* (1989–1990) and later was on *Double Rush* (1995). Maryedith Burrell appeared on such sitcoms as *Throb* (1986–1988) and *Parenthood* (1990). This was the fourth *Murder, She Wrote* assignment for character actor Alan Fudge. Kimberley Kates was one of the cast of the teleseries *On Our Own* (1994). Dey Young participated on James Brolin's adventure series, *Extreme* (1995).

255. "Track of a Soldier"

(2/25/96) 60 mins.

Director: Vincent McEveety **Teleplay:** Bruce Lansbury

Regular: Angela Lansbury (Jessica Fletcher)

Guest Law Enforcer: Ben Lemon (Sheriff Jed Bullock)

Guest Cast: Vaitiare Bandera (Luisa); Brandon Douglas (Pete Levering); Wings Hauser (Howard Levering); Linda Kelsey (Ellen Levering); Audrey Landers (Greta Bayer); Fredric Lane (Lloyd Nichols); Stephen Macht (Arthur Wainwright); Katherine Olsen (Marla Hastings); James Victor (Juan); Michael Zelniker (Harley Foote)

The Setting: Grand Tetons, Wyoming

The Case: Much in need of a holiday, Jessica Fletcher flies to the Starcrest Lodge in the Grand Tetons area of Wyoming. The resort is owned by Howard and Ellen Levering. Ellen tells Jessica of Howard's recent decision to run for the state senate. However, she is worried because, even now, he doesn't take time to bond with his teenage son Pete (a product of his first marriage), let alone pay attention to her. Ellen also confides that Howard, an ex-Green Beret of the Vietnam War and thereafter, still has horrific nightmares from his combat years.

Among the lodge guests are businessman Arthur Wainwright and his financial assistant, Harley Foote. Others include Greta Bayer, who upon check-in calls her home answering machine and leaves a message for boyfriend Lloyd Nichols to immediately move out of her apartment. The next thing Greta does is hide a large diamond in the ice cube tray of her room's refrigerator. There's also new arrival Marla Hastings, here for a rendezvous with her financial provider, the married Wainwright. The staff includes maid Luisa as well as Juan, the latter having served under Colonel Levering in Vietnam.

New developments occur rapidly. Harley receives a call from his doctor stating that his lab tests confirm that he has a fatal disease and not long to live. As such, the nerdish Foote reassesses his humdrum life. He quits working for the demanding Wainwright and begins romancing the very attractive Greta.

Before long, Nichols appears at the lodge, which is no surprise to Marla (with whom he has been having an affair), but it is to the angry Greta. Later, Jessica has a run-in with the nasty Lloyd, when she attempts to dissuade him from further bothering Greta. Thereafter, an explosive Nichols confronts Howard, insisting that Levering was responsible for the death of Lloyd's brother when the latter was under Levering's command in Vietnam years ago. Howard is so shaken by this showdown that he decides to withdraw from the senatorial race.

During the night, Nichols is knifed, and Pete is found with the weapon in his hands. He is arrested by Sheriff Jed Bullock. Shortly after, Greta realizes that her $2 million diamond has vanished. Before the true culprit can be identified, Jessica, along with Sheriff Bullock, must find out what other people were at the murder site that night.

Highlights: Increasingly in recent episodes, Jessica Fletcher displays a fondness for animals. Here she has warm-hearted scenes with Soldier, a dog she appreciates even more after he unwittingly provides the clue needed to solve the homicide. It is also refreshing to observe that here, Jessica admits to being a very typical writer—one who suffers from bouts of noncreativity and a desire to be far away from her (laptop) computer. The subtheme of the workaholic Harley, who thinks he is dying, reevaluating his life and finding romance with a beautiful woman, is very reminiscent of the Lionel Barrymore-Joan Crawford segment of the classic movie *Grand Hotel* (1932).

Trivia: Linda Kelsey played Billie Newman on TV's *Lou Grant* (1977–1982) and opposite Douglas Sheehan in the sitcom *Day By Day* (1988–1989). Audrey Landers, older sister of actress Judy Landers, was a regular on *Somerset* (1970–1972), *Dallas* (1981–1984), and in the 1990s, *One Life to Live.* Veteran performer Stephen Macht was featured in several of the Trancers film series: *III* (1992), *IV* (1993) and *V* (1994). Besides TV's *Ferris Bueller* (1990) and *Class of '96* (1993), Brandon Douglas was Ben Agretti on *Falcon Crest* (1988–1989). James Victor was Sergeant Hymen Mendoza on the TV Western *Zorro* (1989–1993).

256. "Evidence of Malice"

(3/28/96) 60 mins.

Director: Anthony Shaw **Teleplay:** Tom Sawyer

Regulars: Angela Lansbury (Jessica Fletcher); Ron Masak (Sheriff Mort Metzger); William Windom (Dr. Seth Hazlitt)

Recurring Character: Louis Herthum (Deputy Andy Broom)

Guest Law Enforcers: Tyler Robert Owen (Deputy Kenneth); Jack T. Wright (Deputy Caleb)

Guest Cast: Colleen Coffey (Wendy Arnold [Wendy Arnett]); Stephanie Dunnam (Meg Berrigan); Rick Lenz (Isaac); Lawrence Monoson (Craig Haber); Monica Parker (Hannah Parkins); Jennifer Parsons (Patty); Tim Ransom (George Parkins); Vyto Ruginis (Fred Berrigan); Anne Shaw (Customer); Peter Stader (Leverett Boggs); Mark Voland (Dean Sorenson)

The Setting: Cabot Cove, Maine

The Case: Since grade school, blue collar Deputy Andy Broom and blue blood Fred Berrigan, owner of Down East Footwear, have been rivals. One night, Sheriff Mort Metzger and Andy stop Fred for drunken driving.

Broom asks Mort to forget the charge. However, the ungrateful Fred accuses Andy of having planted the evidence and reminds Broom that despite the favor, the down payment on the house he is buying from Fred is still due tomorrow. (Broom plans to wed Patty, a bookkeeper, and thus wants a real home.)

Soon thereafter, Mort discovers the corpse of Leverett Boggs. He has been strangled at home and his pockets are empty. Jessica, who happens to be with Metzger, notices a piece of nylon cord not far from the body.

At Down East Footwear, Fred assigns Wendy Arnold to replace Boggs in the accounting department. She quickly proves to be a manipulating individual when she dates leather salesman Craig Haber with whom Berrigan refuses to do business and, later, agrees to dig up dirt on her employer if Craig pays her $1,000. When George Parkins, her work supervisor who is romantically interested in her, asks Wendy who she thinks is causing the factory workflow problem, she lies and says Isaac, in charge of supplies and materials, is guilty. As a result, Fred fires this worker who has been with the company thirty years. Later, Wendy plays up to the married Berrigan (who is feuding with his wife), and sabotages Parkins with the owner. Further on, in Boggs's office effects, she finds reference to a mysterious computer file called "nordcom." Curious at its value, she devotes hours to locating it on his computer.

Further investigation of Boggs's murder leads to Berrigan's arrest. Again Fred insists that Andy, who has been feuding with Berrigan over hidden repair costs needed for the purchased house, planted the incriminating evidence. Later, the city prosecutor announces he is dropping the case, in case Andy may have tainted the evidence. Mort places Broom on "sick leave." While following up clues on his own, Andy trails Fred to his plant office. When Broom goes inside shortly thereafter, Berrigan is dead. Metzger has no choice but to arrest Andy on a homicide charge.

These events are all the impetus Jessica needs to get to the bottom of the misadventure. The climax hinges on a swinging gate on which Mrs. Fletcher snags her sweater and who is actually embezzling funds from Down East Footwear.

Highlights: One typically associates back-stabbing office politics with urban high-level business. However, Cabot Cove proves to be just as vulnerable to such workplace war games. Seldom has this New England town harbored a character as deceitful and double-dealing as Wendy Arnold.

Trivia: This is the first *Murder, She Wrote* episode in which Louis Herthum's Andy Broom has a sizable role in the story line. It is also the first occasion to explore the personal side of the deputy's life. In contrast, the Cabot Cove coffee shop run by bustling Hannah Parkins is filled with flavorful ambiance, including Dr. Seth Hazlitt's annoyance that Hannah's menu has gone fat-free, cholesterol-free and taste-free.

This episode's running gag again revolves around Jessica Fletcher's creative frustration with completing her latest novel. The payoff suggests that real-life sleuthing is a great inspiration for one's writing career.

Stephanie Dunnam had been on *Emerald Point N.A.S.* (1983–1984) and then was Karen Atkinson on *Dynasty* (1987–1988). Veteran actor Rick Lenz had had a far different role earlier on *Murder, She Wrote:* in 1987's "If It's Thursday, It Must Be Beverly Hills" (#72), he was the flirtatious deputy sheriff working under Sheriff Mort Metzger. Vyto Ruginis has been featured in such movies as *Descending Angel* (1990) and *Clean Slate* (1994).

257. "Southern Double-Cross"

(4/4/96) 60 mins.

Director: Walter Grauman **Teleplay:** Mark A. Burley

Regular: Angela Lansbury (Jessica Fletcher)

Guest Law Enforcer: Alaistair Duncan (Sergeant Colin Baxter)

Guest Cast: Briony Behets (Melba Drummond); Donald Burton (John Marlin); Lisa Darr (Ronda Brock); Sofia Formica (Linda Marlin); Spencer Garrett (Tim Darby); John Garwood (Bartender); Trevor Goddard (Boyd Hendrix); Kendrick Hughes (Donald Jarvis); Peter Lavin (Roo Drummond); Nick Tate (Tim Jarvis); Adam Wylie (Boy)

The Setting: Kookaburra Downs, Queensland, Australia

The Case: What could possibly bring Jessica Fletcher to the outlands of Australia? It all started when Eamonn Magill, the brother of Jessica's grandmother, left Ireland in 1890. Three years later he arrived in Queensland, and somehow bought 130,000 acres of valley land at sixpence an acre. When he died, he left the property in trust to Jessica's grandmother. The trust was for one hundred years, which expires momentarily. Australian lawyer Simon Cathcart had been hired to trace the Magill family tree and, only recently, located Mrs. Fletcher in the United States. Exhausted by her trip to Kookaburra Downs, Jessica learns two startling facts: Mr. Cathcart is missing and old Eamonn was hung for bankruptcy. (Despite that fact, the town has an annual Eamonn Magill Day to celebrate his passing.)

There is great interest in how the American will handle her bequest, known as Magill Valley. The town's mayor, Tim Jarvis, who also owns the local inn, has already accepted a big money advance (which he can't now pay back) from Ronda Brock and Tim Darby, representatives of a U.S.-based mining company. This firm, which has a bad track record regarding toxic waste, wants to strip mine for bauxite in the valley. The opposing force, led by Melba Drummond, the town's treasurer, and her son Roo, are sheepherders who hope Jessica will insure that the valley will remain grazing land. Each side pressures Mrs. Fletcher to favor their proposition.

With Roo as her guide, Jessica becomes acquainted with the locals. There is librarian John Marlin, whose library is broken into and valuable town records stolen. His daughter, Linda, a barmaid at Jarvis's inn, would like to become a veterinarian, much to the approval of her beau, Roo. Others in town include Donald Jarvis, Nick's no-good son from Brisbane, who used to date Linda (he is back to borrow money from his financially strapped dad to pay off $40,000 in debts) and loan shark Boyd Hendrix (who has followed Donald to Kookaburra Downs to insure payment).

Soon there are two murders with which to contend: Cathcart's body is located in the outback and, later, Donald, who was to meet Jessica to confess his wrongdoings, is found hung from a rafter in the stable. What adds to the difficulty for Jessica in solving the double homicides is coping with aloof Sergeant Colin Baxter, who would rather have her leave town.

Highlights: With its down under setting and a boisterous cast of characters, this episode is reminiscent of the high quality segments of earlier *Murder, She Wrote* seasons. Usually a match for any person—male or female—Jessica Fletcher definitely is awed by rough-and-tumble, cigar-smoking Melba Drummond. In contrast, Mrs. Fletcher eventually relates to Sergeant Colin Baxter, a Britisher who feels out of place in Australia and a man still grieving for his wife and child who died in a car accident. In a touching moment, he confides how he permitted his job to take over the man.

A comic highlight occurs at the story's finale, as the townsfolk of Kookaburra Downs honor a very surprised Jessica Fletcher!

Trivia: For some reason, Jessica Fletcher's family name of "Macgill" is spelled "Magill" in this episode.

Nick Tate was a veteran of such TV fare as *Space: 1999* (1975–1976), *Dolphin Cove* (1989) and *Open House* (1989–1990). Adam Wylie played young Zack Brock on *Picket Fences* (1992–1996).

258. "Race to Death"

(4/28/96) 60 mins.

Director: Vincent McEveety **Teleplay:** Laurence Heath

Regulars: Angela Lansbury (Jessica Fletcher); Ron Masak (Sheriff Mort Metzger); William Windom (Dr. Seth Hazlitt)

Recurring Character: Louis Herthum (Deputy Andy Broom)

Guest Cast: Curtis Blanck (Tommy Larkin); Dwier Brown (Bill Richards); Christopher Buchholz (Jon Vandervelt); Steve Forrest (Ned Larkin); John Getz (Kyle Kimball); Kate Hodge (Alana Kimball); Vincent McEveety (Security Guard); Martin Milner (Admiral Len Spalding); Andrea Parker (Anne Larkin); Cathy Susan Pyles (Safe Technician); Rick Rossovich (Steve Gantry); Matthew Saks (Crew Member); Ronnie Troup (Process Server)

The Setting: Cabot Cove, Maine

The Case: Ned Larkin's racing yacht, *Free Spirit*, is berthed at the Cabot Cove Marina, being prepped for a World Cup qualification event. The millionaire skipper has old-fashioned ideas about sailing, contrary to his young assistant, Bill Richards, who has convinced Larkin to try the newly installed winglets for speed stability. Leaving the yacht that night, Ned scuffles with a masked intruder—who had been taking photos of the winglets. In the melee, Larkin injures his ankle and is ordered by Dr. Seth Hazlitt not to skipper *Free Spirit* in the upcoming competition.

Named honorary Commodore of this year's World Cup Trials at Cabot Cove, Jessica Fletcher calls Ned's daughter, Anne, in Rhode Island with the latest news about her father. Anne, a teacher and a master sailor, has been feuding with her dad since she had a relationship with Larkin's longtime racing competitor, Kyle Kimball. Anne had a child from that affair, but Larkin has never wanted Tommy to be part of his life. As for marina owner Kimball who is Larkin's racing equal, he has made life difficult for Anne because she left him after discovering he was married. She has always refused to let Kimball see Tommy.

Jessica brings Anne and Ned together, and he agrees that if his daughter has the crew's support, she can skipper the *Free Spirit*. This is good news for Bill who loves Anne, but another crewman, Steve Gantry—who had hoped to take over for Ned—is secretly antagonistic.

Once Kyle learns that Anne will skipper the competition, he threatens to fight her in court and win Tommy back. Meanwhile, Kimball has wrongfully patented an innovative boat design by his employee, Jon Vandervelt, a Dutchman. As for Kimball's wife, she despises her philandering, wealthy husband who refuses to support her own business plans.

Kimball is found dead in his office, apparently bludgeoned with a trophy. Before the Cup race can go on—with Vandervelt filling in for Kyle—several individuals' alibis must be examined. Meanwhile, Jessica smokes out the actual killer, using a crucial video tape to trap the felon.

Highlights: Beyond the intricately structured murder plot, there is a pleasant diversion provided by the ongoing skirmishing between Seth Hazlitt and Mort Metzger. This time their battleground is Hollywood trivia. Mort's wife Adele (still an off-camera figure) is home nursing a cold and Metzger rents movie musicals to amuse her. The two men constantly argue over who really costarred with whom in the classic features Mort picks up at the video store.

A scene-stealing cameo is provided by the female safe technician, Cathy Susan Pyles. Her pantomime while determining the combination to Kimball's office wall safe is a great attention-grabber.

Trivia: It is revealed that Jessica and her late husband, Frank, loved to sail; hence her agreeing to be honorary Commodore at this year's racing gala in Cabot Cove.

This was the fifth time in which Steve Forrest costarred on *Murder, She Wrote* as it was for Martin Milner. Rick Rossovich's series work included *MacGruder & Loud* (1985), *ER* (1994–1995—as Julianna Margulies's physician fiancé) and as the commander of the police bicycle squad in *Pacific Blues* (1995-). Christopher Buchholz was on-screen in *No Fear, No Die* (1990) and *Covert Assassin* (1994). John Getz was also on the police series *MacGruder & Loud*, in the costarring role of Detective Malcolm MacGruder. In the quickly aborted sitcom *The George Wendt Show* (1995), Kate Hodge played an auto mechanic. On *ER*, (1994-), Andrea Parker took the role of Linda Farrell.

Once again, frequent *Murder, She Wrote* director Vincent McEveety chose to play a bit role in one of his own episodes, this time as a security guard.

259. "What You Don't Know Can Kill You"

(5/5/96) 60 mins.

Director: Kevin Corcoran **Teleplay:** Robert Van Scoyk

Regulars: Angela Lansbury (Jessica Fletcher); Ron Masak (Sheriff Mort Metzger); William Windom (Dr. Seth Hazlitt)

Recurring Character: Louis Herthum (Deputy Andy Broom)

Guest Law Enforcer: Kathryn Masak (Deputy Olsen)

Guest Cast: Michele Abrams (Mickey); Anthony Michael Hall (Les Franklin); Jerry Hardin (Tom Sampson); Laurie Holden (Sherri Sampson); William Keane (Johnny Carter); Bruce Kirby (Jeremy Woods, Esq.); Geoffrey Lewis (Roger Yates); Judson Mills (Tom Sampson); Kathryn Morris (Doreen, the Waitress); Cari Shayne (Amy Walters); Will Foster Stewart (Stu Yates)

The Setting: Cabot Cove, Maine

The Case: Sherri Sampson, a single mother with a baby, lives with her dad, Tom, who runs a Cabot Cove towing service. According to Sherri, the father is her former boyfriend, Johnny Carter, a landscape gardener whom she rarely sees nowadays. Another past friend, the reckless Les Franklin, blames Carter for Sherri turning from him. One night, Les scuffles with Johnny as he leaves the Sampson home.

Meanwhile, Amy Walters, Dr. Seth Hazlett's grown-up niece, a college dropout, has returned to town. She and Johnny have begun dating and now plan to marry. Amy has no knowledge of Carter's double life, although vengeful Les threatens to tell everyone. Meanwhile, Roger Yates, an extremely unhappy client of Carter's has hired attorney Jeremy Woods to sue Tom regarding disputed gardening work.

Tragedy strikes when Johnny dies in a motorcycle accident at Rocky Point on Route 9. Amy insists it must be murder because her boyfriend was an excellent driver. Prodded by this information, Jessica Fletcher investigates the situation as does Sheriff Mort Metzger. One of Mrs. Fletcher's hunches revolves around a recently replaced telephone pole at the accident site. The novelist has Attorney Woods contact a phone company friend for further information. Soon thereafter, Woods's car breaks down. While waiting for it to be towed, he stops at a Cabot Cove coffee shop. He is the only customer, and while waitress Doreen is in the kitchen, Woods is stabbed to death.

As the clues pile up, the loyalties of former friends shift. Mickey, one of Les's "gang," tells Amy about Johnny and Sherri's past relationship. After Franklin lets the police think Roger Yates was responsible for tearing up Jessica's garden and bizarre Roger is hospitalized for psychiatric observation, Yates's son Stu, another of Les's pals, turns against him. Stu informs the police that the knife that killed Sampson belonged to Les. However, as Mrs. Fletcher and Sheriff Metzger soon discover, this is not the whole story. What follows, including a crazed individual holding others hostage, leads Jessica to the identity of the true killer.

Highlights: New England small-town life used to be synonymous with above-board living. (One character says proudly, "This ain't Hollywood. Cabot Cove folks get married and have babies [in that order]." However, this episode demonstrates there are juvenile delinquents and unwed mothers in this picturesque village. Yet some things remain the same, such as gossipy neighbors. At the end of this segment, Jessica Fletcher notes that keeping secrets caused the recent double tragedies. On a lighter note, she adds, that doesn't happen too often in Cabot Cove—not with gossipy Dr. Seth Hazlitt around. Once again, *Murder, She Wrote* ends a somber murder mystery on a light note!

Trivia: As in episode #243, Kathryn Masak, daughter of series regular Ron Masak, has a small role. This time she is cast as a deputy sheriff. As an in joke, when Deputy Andy Broom warns her that Sheriff Metzger is a stickler for details, she replies, "So I noticed. Reminds me of my father."

Anthony Michael Hall, a one-time child actor on TV and stage, has made several features: *Sixteen Candles* (1984), *The Breakfast Club* (1985), *Edward Scissorhands* (1990), *Six Degrees of Separation* (1993), etc. Jerry Hardin was Deep Throat on *The X-Files* (1993–1994). Bruce Kirby performed in many teleseries: *Car 54, Where Are You* (1961–1963), *Shannon* (1981), *Anything But Love* (1989), etc. Geoffrey Lewis was on *Flo* (1980–1981), the spin-off of *Alice* and *The Smothers Brothers Comedy Hour* (1989), as well as a player in various Clint Eastwood films. Cari Shayne an aluminous from the daytime soap *General Hospital*, where she was paired with future Calvin Klein model Antonio Sabato, Jr., had the occasional role of Nina on *Party of Five* (1994-).

260. "Mrs. Parker's Revenge"

(5/12/96) 60 mins.

Director: Anthony Shaw **Teleplay:** Anne C. Collins

Regular: Angela Lansbury (Jessica Fletcher)

Guest Law Enforcers: Dena Acosta (Police Lieutenant); William O'Leary (FBI Agent Ed Crider); Tony Todd (National Security Agent Nathan Mitchell); Peter Van Norden (CIA Agent Dennis Quinlan); Greg Allan Williams (Lieutenant Paul Bragg)

Guest Cast: Erick Avari (Raul Jaffa); Frederick Dawson (Hotel Clerk); Karen Hensel (Techie); Gregg Henry (Mark Reisner); Mary Elizabeth McGlynn (Karen Reisner); Gustav Vintas (Carl Van Ness); Time Winters (Dr. James Lamont)

The Setting: Atlanta, Georgia

The Case: As this year's keynote speaker for the Georgia Amateur Mystery Writers Conference, Jessica Fletcher checks into Atlanta's Gambler Hotel. Instead of her preregistered room (#1209) which by error has been given to Raul Jaffa, Mrs. Fletcher is assigned another suite (#1220). Her conclave contact is Karen Reisner, the wife of Mark Reisner. The latter, whom Jessica knew from his past employment at Manhattan University, is now the director of security at the Atlanta Biological Research Institute, which conducts top secret chemical and drug experiments.

Meanwhile, Dr. James Lamont, a top ABRI researcher, meets with the sinister Jaffa. They have made a deal in which Lamont is to provide a vial of a deadly Project 14 virus now stored in the institute's maximum containment area. In exchange, Lamont is to receive $2 million. This conversation at the Gambler Hotel is secretly monitored by Carl Van Ness, an international arms dealers and assassin. Later, Lamont confers with FBI Agent Ed Crider, as Lamont is a paid decoy.

When Jessica accidentally receives a packet of photos that Van Ness addressed to Jaffa, she attempts to return them to Jaffa. However, by now Van Ness, who wants a Project 14 vial to sell on the international black market, has murdered Jaffa. Mrs. Fletcher discovers the body and is ensnared in the cat-and-mouse game between Van Ness and the U.S. security/spy agents (Ed Crider, Nathan Mitchell, Dennis Quinlan, *et al.)*, who have set up a command post at the hotel. Soon thereafter another murder occurs.

Highlights: Not even in the movie heyday of James Bond international espionage have so many different U.S. government agencies been embroiled in a single case. And, as could be anticipated, Jessica Fletcher remains undaunted by the quantity of rival investigators. As for their quality, she proves to be far more resourceful than the entire group, even with their high tech listening devices and other gadgets.

A haunting moment in this well-choreographed segment occurs when Mark Reisner is murdered in the hotel lobby. Jessica's impassioned and tremulous "Oh, Mark. Oh, Mark" is filled with such highly charged emotion that it remains lodged indelibly in the viewer's memory.

Trivia: This was one of the few scripts in the entire *Murder, She Wrote* canon to be written by a woman, Anne C. Collins.

Tony Todd, featured in the 1990 remake of *Night of the Living Dead*, is best known for playing the serial killer in *Candyman* (1992) and *Candyman II: Farewell to the Flesh* (1994). Erick Avari was in such movies as *The Beast* (1988) and *Stargate* (1994).

261. "Death by Demographics"

(5/19/96) 60 mins.

Director: Anthony Shaw **Teleplay:** Donald Ross

Regular: Angela Lansbury (Jessica Fletcher)

Recurring Character: Seth Jaffe (Lieutenant Everett)

Guest Cast: James Acheson (Russell Connell); Christian Bocher (T.T. Baines); Diana Canova (Annie Lawson); Robert Curtis-Brown ("Bud" Forbes); Paul Linke (Eddie Mapes); Robert Pine (Graham Forbes); Robin

Riker (Colleen Sellers); David Ogden Stiers (Howard Deems); Kenneth Tigar (Dave Pittman); Lucinda Weist (Lauren Hayward)

The Setting: San Francisco, California

The Case: Promoting her new novel, *A Case and a Half of Murder*, in San Francisco, Jessica is to be a guest on KLOY-FM's *A Look at Books*, hosted by Howard Deems. She arrives at the station where chaos has erupted. Faced with low ratings, owner Graham Forbes is switching 114.3 on the dial from a cultural and classic format to one of talk/contemporary music.

This decision staggers Graham's son, Bud Forbes, just returned from a holiday abroad. Bud is upset to learn he must now share his Director of Programming title with glib Russell Connell. The latter has joined KLOY as part of a package with no-holds-barred talk show host T.T. Baines. Bud becomes suspicious of the format switch when he meets his father's new, and younger girlfriend, Lauren Hayward.

Others at KLOY affected by the new direction are veteran ad sales executive Dave Pittman, who immediately loses established accounts to younger, more hip Colleen Sellers, an aggressive newcomer at the station. Annie Lawson of finance/accounting is torn between the old and new regime, especially when Connell demands $2,000 weekly to remain quiet about her questionable bookkeeping practices. As for erudite, portly Howard Deems, he despises the low-brow program changes being instituted.

When Deems tries to quit KLOY, Connell reminds him that his contract has fourteen months to go. As such, he forces Deems to co-anchor a morning talk/music program with obnoxious Baines, hoping their conflicting personalities and the generation gap between them will enhance listener ratings.

Meanwhile, local police lieutenant Everett investigates a shooting incident in which T.T. Baines barely escaped serious injury. Howard is the chief suspect because of his known antipathy to the victim and since he is an expert marksman. Unknown to most, Lauren is actually a shill in league with Connell and Baines. However, she has fallen in love with Graham and hopes to marry him. Russell vetoes this idea because he plans for the team to next conquer Los Angeles. He threatens to expose her seamy background to Forbes.

Later, Russell is run through with a fireplace poker in his hotel room. Again, the police label Howard the chief suspect since a hotel maid saw him leave the building at about the time of the homicide. To prove Deems' innocence, Jessica joins forces with Lieutenant Everett. The pivotal clues to solve the whodunit are a telltale soot mark and a high school class ring (which link several suspects more closely than most realized).

Highlights: Beyond the behind-the-microphone look at radio station operations, there is the amusing if predictable antagonism between highbrow Deems and Neanderthal Baines. On a finer level is the on-the-air verbal skirmish between Jessica Fletcher and T.T. She proves a worthy opponent of the schlock jock radio host.

As a coda to this landmark episode which ended the long-running series, Jessica Fletcher is seen seated at her computer. As she busily works at the keyboard, there are montage shots of Cabot Cove, Maine, on the TV screen, while her voice-over says:

> Dear Friends,
>
> Tonight on *Murder, She Wrote,* you have watched our last and final *weekly* episode. My gratitude and appreciation to all of you, our great family of viewers . . . over twelve great years.
>
> With Love, Jessica Fletcher.

This gracious finale to twelve seasons of high-class whodunit adventures prompts a nostalgic, lump-in-the-throat response from viewers. It's a moment to be long savored and cherished.

Trivia: The much-publicized irony of the season/series finale episode to *Murder, She Wrote* was not only its title, "Death by Demographics," but the focus of its story line. Just as radio station KLOY found itself slipping in the ratings because younger viewers wanted more contemporary programming, so did *Murder, She Wrote* fall victim to TV audience ratings when CBS-TV switched it from its Sunday night berth to one on Thursday, scheduled opposite a trendy twentysomething sitcom. Not to be overlooked in this episode is the final plot line barb which has an obvious inference. At the story's conclusion, KLOY management, having had its fill of hip personalities, joyfully returns to its former cultural format. Enough said!

EPISODE CHECKLIST

[Numbers After the Dates Refer to Episode Entry]

INDEX

OF GUEST PLAYERS, DIRECTORS, AND SCRIPTERS